PARAMILITARY IMPRISONMENT
IN NORTHERN IRELAND

CLARENDON STUDIES IN CRIMINOLOGY
Published under the auspices of the Institute of Criminology,
University of Cambridge, the Mannheim Centre, London School of
Economics, and the Centre for Criminology Research, University
of Oxford.

Recent titles in this series:

Prisons and the Problem of Order
Sparks, Bottoms, and Hay

The Local Governance of Crime
Crawford

Policing the Risk Society
Ericson and Haggerty

Law in Policing: Legal Regulation and Police Practices
Dixon

Sexed Work: Gender, Race and Resistance in a Brooklyn Drug Market
Maher

Procedural Fairness at the Police Station
Choongh

Crime in Ireland 1945–95: 'Here be Dragons'
Brewer, Lockhart, and Rodgers

Private Security and Public Policing
Newburn and Jones

Violent Racism: Victimization, Policing, and Social Context
Bowling

Crime and Markets: Essays in Anti-Criminology
Ruggiero

Paramilitary Imprisonment In Northern Ireland

Resistance, Management, and Release

Kieran McEvoy

OXFORD
UNIVERSITY PRESS

OXFORD

UNIVERSITY PRESS

Great Clarendon Street, Oxford OX2 6DP

Oxford University Press is a department of the University of Oxford.
It furthers the University's objective of excellence in research, scholarship,
and education by publishing worldwide in

Oxford New York

Athens Auckland Bangkok Bogotá Buenos Aires
Cape Town Chennai Dar es Salaam Delhi Florence Hong Kong Istanbul
Karachi Kolkata Kuala Lumpur Madrid Melbourne Mexico City Mumbai
Nairobi Paris São Paulo Shanghai Singapore Taipei Tokyo Toronto Warsaw

with associated companies in Berlin Ibadan

Oxford is a registered trade mark of Oxford University Press
in the UK and in certain other countries

Published in the United States
by Oxford University Press Inc., New York

British Library Cataloguing in Publication Data

Data available

Library of Congress Cataloging in Publication Data
McEvoy, Kieran.
Paramilitary imprisonment in Northern Ireland:
resistance, management, and release/
Kieran McEvoy.
p. cm.—(Clarendon studies in criminology)
Includes bibliographical references and index.
1. Political prisoners—Northern Ireland. 2. Imprisonment—
Northern Ireland. 3. Government, Resistance to—Northern Ireland.
4. Prison administration—Northern Ireland. I. Title. II. Series.
HV9649.N674 M34 2001   365'.45'09416—dc21   2001036395

ISBN 0-19-829907-9

1 3 5 7 9 10 8 6 4 2

Typeset in Sabon
by J&L Composition Ltd, Filey, North Yorkshire
Printed in Great Britain on acid-free paper by
Biddles Ltd, Guildford and King's Lynn

For Lesley, Therese, and Paddy

General Editors' Introduction

The *Clarendon Studies in Criminology,* the successor to *Cambridge Studies in Criminology,* aims to provide a forum for outstanding work in criminology, criminal justice, penology, and the wider field of deviant behaviour. It is edited under the auspices of three criminological centres: the Cambridge Institute of Criminology, the Mannheim Centre for Criminology and Criminal Justice at the London School of Economics, and the Oxford Centre for Criminological Research.

Kieran McEvoy's *Paramilitary Imprisonment in Northern Ireland* pursues a theme developed in other works, and particularly in Sparks, Bottoms, and Hay's *Prisons and the Problem of Order,* an earlier study in this series. It is a history of the prison as a site of contested legitimacy set within an evolving political economy of penal policy, but nowhere can that theme have been seen more starkly or to such effect as in Northern Ireland. The book is at once a detailed chronicle of the relations between the governments of Britain and Northern Ireland, prison managers and groups strenuously claiming the status of political prisoner, on the one hand, and, on the other, an acute sociological analysis of shifting, problems of politics, policy-making, authority, control, definition, and identity between 1969 and 2000. Ministers, governors, officers, and prisoners moved together through a complicated succession of interlocking political regimes, managerial strategies, and tactics of resistance and accommodation. They experimented with different public accounts of motive, meaning, and relationship, those administering prisons asserting at times that paramilitaries were no more than criminals, the prisoners themselves laying claim to the very different role of freedom fighter or defender of a beleaguered community. They resorted to physical violence: prisoners killing officers and governors, one another, and themselves; and officers sometimes initiating violence, sometimes retaliating, and sometimes virtually ceding control, and all within a shifting and sometimes capricious context of structural coercion. They played out their politics in all the forums that prison life afforded: participation in trials raised questions about whether defendants should appear tacitly to accept the authority of the courts and the State; escape and recapture became opportunities for prisoners to ridicule a seemingly ineffectual authority and the State to present itself as in ultimate command; the body and cell could be used as instruments of protest; hunger strikes became 'committed theatre'; and decisions about segregation and classification became crucial signifiers of political standing.

Paramilitary Imprisonment in Northern Ireland relies on extensive interviewing with members of almost all the major groups in contention. It is based on external comparison with the histories of other penal regimes—in South Africa, the United States and elsewhere—where some have identified themselves as political prisoners. It is based on internal comparison over time and *within* the prisons of Northern Ireland—between, for example, the emerging identities of Republican and Loyalist prisoners, the one organised around a strain towards the politics of refusal and the other around an ambivalence towards a State that is both defended and criticised, the one group organised and collectivist, the other loosely-co-ordinated and individualistic. Although McEvoy is modest in representing this book as but one of the stories that could be told about the politics of paramilitary imprisonment, it is difficult to imagine that any other account could succeed in being quite so nuanced, informed, and disinterested.

David Downes and Paul Rock

Acknowledgements

In completing this book I owe a huge debt of thanks to a large number of people. To John Morison and Stephen Livingstone who supervised the original thesis upon which it is based, I am extremely grateful for their patience and encouragement. Brian Gormally has been a constant source of intellectual support and friendship over the period and has been a seminal influence on the way my thoughts developed on this and much else. To all of my colleagues at NIACRO, CAJ, and Queen's who helped me and whom I have bored rigid with this topic over the years, in particular Fergus Cooper, Mike Ritchie, Martin O'Brien, Maggie Beirne, Dave O'Mahony, Graham Ellison, Rachel Murray, Heather Conway, and Colin Harvey—I am sorry and I promise it will not come up again. To Chris Moore, former producer on *Counterpoint* at Ulster Television, thank you for the box of transcripts from the UTV documentary *Unlocking the Maze*. Thanks also to the staff at all of the libraries I visited, in particular the political collection at the Linen Hall Library in Belfast, who make every researcher feel that the work they are doing is of vital importance. To Fran Buntman who considerably improved my thinking on resistance and to Steve Martin who did the same on prisoners and the law, thanks. Nancy Loucks, Aogan Mulcahy, and Gordon Anthony all kept me on the path of righteousness at various times when I needed it. Tony Bottoms, Duncan McLaughlan, Stan Cohen, John Jackson, Harry Mika, and Richard Sparks all read the entire thesis. Any improvements in the subsequent transformation to a book are doubtlessly down to their suggestions and guidance and I thank them and assure them that remaining errors are my responsibility alone.

I am hugely grateful to all of the former Republican and Loyalist prisoners I interviewed, the prison governors, prison staff, lawyers, civil servants, victims of violence, and others who gave me their time. Many of these people have lived through the most harrowing of historical events and carry their loads with commendable dignity and grace.

To my family and friends, Paddy, Therese, Eileen and Charlotte, TC, Tom, Paul, Neill, Barbara, Stevie, Paula, and all the rest, your warmth and encouragement have sustained me through a lot of late nights, both here at the computer and out when I should have been here at the computer.

Finally sincere thanks to my wife and friend, Lesley, who inherited this project with me as a going concern and who put up with it as guest in our home for far too long.

K. McE.
May 2001

Contents

Epilogue: Political Prisons and the Construction of Memory   354

List of Figures

List of Tables

1

Background and Definitions

> In the animal kingdom the rule is eat or be eaten; in the human
> kingdom, define or be defined.
>
> **Thomas Szasz (1971)**

Introduction

Since the beginning of the most recent phase of conflict in Northern
Ireland, the treatment of paramilitary prisoners, and in particular the
question as to whether and to what extent their political motivation
has been recognized by the prison authorities, has been a defining issue
for all of the protagonists. Prisoners have asserted their political status
through a variety of resistance strategies over the course of the conflict.
Ministers, prison managers and staff have acquiesced, denied, and
reframed the prisoners' assertion of political status in their attempts to
manage paramilitary prisoners. Under the terms of the Good Friday
Agreement in 1998, the British and Irish governments, together with
the range of pro-agreement parties, agreed to release most of the prisoners by the year 2000. This book examines that history of resistance,
management, and release.

Definitional Issues and the Recognition of Political Motivation

Much of this book focuses on the struggle between the prisoners'
assertion of their status as *political* prisoners and attempts by the
prison authorities to deny, undermine, and manage that assertion.
Such a struggle regarding the distinction between what constitutes
political and what constitutes *criminal* acts is not, however, unique to
Northern Ireland. The difficulties are well rehearsed within the literature across a range of disciplines from which I wish to draw a number
of points.

For some criminologists, the starting point for unpacking such definitional difficulties is an acknowledgement that all acts deemed criminal arise as a result of a political process of definition (Quinney 1970, Chambliss 1976). As Tunnell (1993: p. xi) has argued 'crime as an act, and the social reactions to it, are political constructs. After all, crime is a violation of legal norms legislated by a political body as criminal deviance'.[1] While such broad definitions are arguably true, at least at the conceptual level, they do not necessarily elucidate the relationship between crime and politics. Attempts by criminologists to rescue criminality from positivistic notions concerning determinism and pathology in the 1960s and 1970s led to some reductionist accounts in which crime was seen as 'either the expression, symbol or equivalent of political resistance or the product of the political order of capitalism' (Cohen 1996: 3). As Cohen argues, the excesses of such discourses, in which virtually all crime became *political*, gave the whole enterprise a bad name. That said, the notion of state as a constitutive actor in the *political* process of defining crime is of direct relevance for current purposes.

Other criminologists have defined *political* crime by reference to the ideology or beliefs of the particular offender. For example, Cesaro Lombroso devoted separate chapters to both the causes of political crime and to its prevention (Lombroso 1968). He argued that political crime was a version of a 'crime of passion . . . especially frequent amongst the young and in the most intelligent and cultivated of nations' (Lombroso 1968: 227). Schafer (1974: 145) too has described political criminals as 'convictional criminals', those who are convinced of the truth and justification of their own beliefs and who will carry out 'ordinary crimes' (e.g. murder, kidnapping, robbery, etc.) as a means to a higher political or ideological end. Similarly Hagan (1997: 2) defines political crime as 'criminal activity committed for ideological purposes' such as sociopolitical reasons, moral ethical motivations, religious beliefs, scientific theories or political causes. Hagan goes on to argue that such crimes may be either committed against a

---

[1] This definition mirrors closely that of Schafer who suggested 'In the broadest sense, it may be argued that all crimes are political crimes in as much as all prohibitions with penal sanctions represent the defence of a given value system, or morality, in which the prevailing social power believes. Taking this to the very extreme, even a bank robbery, a shoplifting or a rape is a political crime. After all, making such acts criminal offences is a protection of the interests, values and beliefs of the law making power, actually the political-social system, which regards certain things as right and worthy of safeguarding with the threat of penal consequences' (Schafer 1974: 19).

government or by a government. For such commentators the focus is on the motive rather than the act of the 'criminal'.

In other disciplines, however, greater emphasis has been placed on the nature of the acts carried out rather than the motivation of the protagonists. For example, when Amnesty International began to campaign for the release of political detainees they originally limited their mandate to 'prisoners of conscience', those imprisoned for their political beliefs who had never used or advocated violence. These were distinguished from others who had used or advocated violence for whom Amnesty's focus was on the protection of human rights such as fair trial, the prohibition on torture, and so forth (Desmond 1983). Neir (1995: 393) has used a similar definition of political prisoner to include only those incarcerated for his/her beliefs or for peaceful expression or association, excluding those who have employed or 'imminently incited' violence. While such a comparatively narrow definition of political crime may be understandable for the pragmatic campaigning purposes of an organization such as Amnesty, it is of little epistemological use in a context where large-scale violence has been committed for ostensibly political ends.

Other disciplines including international relations, political science, terrorism studies, and international law have also struggled with providing adequate definitions of terms such as 'crime', 'political violence', and 'terrorism'.[2] These too have variously focused on the nature of the violent acts (Van Den Wijngaert 1980, Greenwood 1989, Teichman 1996), instrumentalist views such as those discussed below which rely primarily upon domestic and international legislative definitions of certain acts (Wilkinson 1986, Schmid, Jongman, and Stohl 1990), attempts to define such acts by reference to the status of the victim/s as a combatant or civilian (Primoratz 1990), and other principles of either international humanitarian (Greenwood 1989) or extradition law (Campbell 1989, Keightley 1993). The common feature of all such attempts at definition have been shaped by the means chosen for either distinguishing or indeed disregarding the 'political' or 'politically motivated' element of the offenders' *actions*.

Another method with which scholars have attempted to distinguish ordinary from political offenders is to examine the manner in which individuals are tried by the state. Such logic would suggest that if an individual can be determined to have received a 'political trial', then

---

[2] See Gearty (1996) for a useful overview.

his/her status as a 'political prisoner' if convicted would seem assured. Unfortunately of course the definition of what constitutes a 'political trial' is itself problematic.[3] Whether individuals are tried by military courts such as the post-Second World War trials in Nuremberg and Tokyo (Lane 1979), trials of former Eastern bloc officials, or government and military personnel in deposed Latin American regimes (Huntington 1991, Borneman 1997), trials of Western European 'terrorist' groupings in the 1970s (Becker 1989, Moss 1989), or even the show trials of the Soviet regime (Szász 1972), there is, inevitably, what Osiel refers to as 'a game being played on two levels, legal and political, doctrinal and histiographical' (Osiel 1997: 223). Even in such trials, there remains the potential for a narrow interpretation of the process which holds that 'whatever the political background of the individual case, . . . the trial court will sift the evidence and apply the law; the difference in the subject matter, the stature of the individuals or groups involved, the degree of public interest, or the widespread implications of the verdict will not matter' (Kirchheimer 1961: 49).[4]

In a similar vein with regard to the Northern Ireland conflict, the British state and the British courts have had relatively few problems in defining and understanding what is meant by 'terrorism' in a straightforwardly technical or instrumentalist fashion.[5] From 1972 until the present day 'terrorism' has been defined in successive pieces of Emergency Legislation as 'the use of violence for political ends and includes any use of violence for the purpose of putting the public or any

---

[3] Hain cites an illustrative quote from Judge Alan King-Hamilton in the 1979 case of four young anarchists charged with firearms and explosives offences. 'Some counsel have described this trial as a political trial. I direct it is not a political trial. We do not put people on trial for their political views in this country. . . . Merely being an anarchist is not a crime.' However Hain suggests that Judge King-Hamilton's denial is so compulsory a statement by a presiding judge at a political trial that 'one can formulate a handy layman's rule—it's a political trial if the judge (or the prosecutor) specifically denies that it is' (Hain 1984: 12). Henry Cockburn, a 19th-century Scottish lawyer who handled political trials suggested a similar 'common sense' approach, 'to see no difference between political and other offences is the sure mark of an excited or stupid head' (Cockburn 1888: 68).

[4] Kirchheimer goes on to suggest that the key determinant in a political trial is that the action of the court is designed to exert influence on the distribution of political power (Kirchheimer 1961: 47). Hain has argued similarly that the purpose of political trials, particularly when directed against critical or radical groups, should be understood by analysing the exercise of power by the dominant. He argues that the advantages of such trials are that they may intimidate, discredit, exhaust, and divert the defendants from their real goal as well as symbolize the application of power by making a public example of them (Hain 1984: 282–3).

[5] See *McKee v Chief Constable for Northern Ireland* (1984) 1 WLR 1358 (HL).

section of the public in fear.' A terrorist is defined as 'a person who is or has been concerned in the commission or attempted commission of any act of terrorism or in directing, organising or training persons for the purpose of terrorism'.[6] Since 1973 in Northern Ireland, any person who has been charged with a suspected terrorist offence (a 'scheduled offence') has had their case heard before a single judge in special juryless courts with amended rules of evidence (Jackson and Doran 1995).[7] In practice the political characteristics of such trials have contributed comparatively little to the prisoners' assertion of their status as political.

An instrumentalist view of terrorism has enabled successive British governments and Northern Irish judges to acknowledge that while people may be engaged in acts of violence 'for political ends', these acts remain criminal in nature and should be treated as such, albeit by using a necessarily amended criminal justice process.[8] Unlike many European jurisdictions,[9] the British tradition has been to resist strongly any suggestion of 'special' treatment for politically motivated offenders. Indeed, for some of the most influential commentators on terrorism in Britain, to acknowledge the political nature of terrorist crimes appears to suggest that such acts are in fact more heinous than 'ordinary decent' criminality because they represent an attack on the value system of society.[10] Such a view does not, for example, permit any distinction which

---

[6] The original definitions, replicated in later versions of the Emergency Provisions Act and the Prevention of Terrorism Act, are taken from the legislation to enact internment (discussed below), the Detention of Terrorists (NI) Order 1972, Art. 2(2).

[7] Scheduled offences are those normally associated with the commission of terrorist acts (e.g. murder, manslaughter, explosions, serious offences against the person, riot, collecting information likely to be of use to terrorists, etc.) and are listed as an appendix to the Emergency legislation. The Act also empowers the Attorney General to decree that certain acts of murder, manslaughter, etc. should not be treated as 'scheduled' offences and should therefore be tried by jury, normally in a case where there is no suspected paramilitary involvement.

[8] 'Political trials' in Northern Ireland are considered in some detail in Chapter 6.

[9] 'Political crime was a version of crime passionel. The "bon delinquent politique" justified a "regime de faveur", and the concept found its place in several contemporary penal codes. To those on the Continent it seemed strange that this attitude was so utterly alien to England, the home of liberalism. The English denied that political motive or objective as such and in itself, should secure for the offender a different mode of punishment or a different penal regime. They were emphatic that there was no provision for it in Criminal Law or Statutory Law' (Radzinowicz and Hood 1979: 1422).

[10] 'If we attach any meaning and value to our Western Judaeo-Christian, liberal and humanist values and the ethical and legal systems that have been shaped by this tradition, we must logically recognise the criminal nature of terrorism . . . It is a moral crime, a crime against humanity, an attack not only on our security, our rule of law and the safety of the state, but on civilised society itself' (Wilkinson 1986: 66).

might be seen to lend the slightest degree of legitimacy to 'terrorism' such as distinguishing between attacks on civilian non-combatants and military or security force personnel.[11] Rather, its sees the state, whether in the form of its armed personnel or its civilian citizens, as the *victim* of terrorism. Within such a paradigm, any political rationale which underpins criminal acts is proof positive of greater wickedness.

Despite the fact that the definition of terrorism enshrined in Emergency legislation has explicitly recognized 'political ends' as the rationale for terrorist activity, this has had little ideological impact on the state. As discussed below, the denial or *de facto* recognition of the political motivation of the prisoners has waxed and waned at different stages of the conflict. A technocratic approach to defining who exactly were the politically motivated prisoners in the system has, however, been of considerable benefit to the process of releasing prisoners under the terms of the Good Friday Agreement and this is discussed in the final chapter of this book.

In sum therefore it is sufficient for current purposes to make two related points with regard to defining the 'political' nature of the prisoners who form the subject-matter of this book. First, as with all crime and deviant behaviour, it is important to remain aware of the significance of the state and criminal justice system as constitutive influences upon what is or is not deemed 'political'. A 'political' trial does not necessarily result in recognition of a political prisoner. The legislative acknowledgement of the 'political' character of 'terrorist' violence did not represent a practical or ideological acceptance of prisoners' political motivation once imprisoned. Second, and related to this point, the actions, targets, motivation, and ideology of the prisoners themselves are all at least equally as important (as the degree of recognition by the state) in assessing the claim to 'political status'. The struggle between the state and the prisoners concerning that status is the essence of the book to follow.

---

[11] One of the fundamental principles of humanitarian law (the laws of war) is that attacks on civilian non-combatants are outlawed. For example, Common Article 3 (1a) of the 1949 Geneva Conventions regarding conflicts 'not of an international character' outlaws violence to life and person, in particular murder of all kinds, mutilation, cruel treatment, and torture to persons taking no active part in the hostilities. While there is a considerable debate as to its applicability to Northern Ireland (Hogan and Walker 1989, Boyle and Campbell 1992), in line with a broader international trend (Petrasek 2000), a number of human rights groups such as Amnesty International and Human Rights Watch have used international humanitarian law principles to criticize the actions of paramilitaries in Northern Ireland.

Background to Prison Research in Northern Ireland

John Whyte (1991) has asserted that, in relation to its size, Northern Ireland is the most heavily researched area in the world. Despite the centrality of prisons to the conflict, however, they have generated comparatively little scholarly work over the past thirty years.

A number of book chapters have been written from critical sociological and human rights perspectives highlighting the hypocrisy of the state's attempts at criminalising politically motivated prisoners and the impact upon their families (e.g. Hillyard 1978, Rolston and Tomlinson 1986, 1988, Tomlinson 1995). More recently an M.Sc. dissertation completed by a former Probation Officer at the Maze, based largely on interviews with Loyalist prisoners in the early 1970s, has been expanded and published as a book (Crawford 1979, 1999). Two psychological articles were also published in the 1980s (Lyons and Harbinson 1986, Curran 1988) which included some analysis of paramilitary prisoners. Within the field of anthropology, there has been one book and one academic article written on the 'dirty protest' and hunger strike era (Feldman 1991, Aretxaga 1995). There has also been one history written of the hunger strikes era (O'Malley 1990) and two sociological articles, one on the media coverage of the hunger strikes (Mulcahy 1995) and one which analysed their political consequences (Smyth 1987).

The primary output on prison-related matters has been produced by journalists and biographical accounts by serving and former prisoners. Journalistic accounts of the dirty protest, hunger strikes, and their aftermath (Coogan 1980, Feehan 1983, Collins 1986, Clarke 1987, Beresford 1987) have varied from the excellent and well researched to the poorly written and partial. There have also been two journalistic texts on prison escapes in Ireland which included details of some of the escapes of the most recent period of conflict (Dunne 1988, MacUileagoid 1996). A number of other journalistic accounts have been written, which, while primarily concerned with the broader political and historical context of the conflict, have offered useful insights into the prison history (Coogan 1995, Stevenson 1996, Taylor 1997, 1999). Biographical accounts from serving and former Republican prisoners have offered a rich and detailed insiders' view of key prison events (Adams 1990, Campbell, McKeown, and O'Hagan 1994, Sands 1998, Morrison 1999). In addition a number of former prisoners have undertaken research degrees since their release (McKeown 1998), and two 'prison service histories' have been completed, one by a serving prison officer and the other by a local journalist (Challis 1999, Ryder 2000). There are also numerous political pamphlets, leaflets, poems, artefacts, some musical tapes, and other primary sources which contain accounts of the prison experience, many of them produced by former and serving prisoners.

While informed by the above accounts, this book seeks to explore some of the issues of broader theoretical and ideological significance through developments in Northern Ireland prisons since 1969. It is a period which is rich in detail and it is not my intention to submit an exhaustive narrative of each and every event which occurred over that period.[12] Rather the analysis is divided into three overlapping themes—prisoner resistance, prison management, and prisoner release—in an attempt to draw out some of the more salient features which that history reflects. Such an analysis cannot lay claim to being the definitive or 'true' story of paramilitary imprisonment in Northern Ireland. Rather, it represents one attempt to understand and explain a complex series of interacting events, dynamics, and relationships which I believe have significantly characterized the history of male paramilitary imprisonment over the past three decades.

It is important at this juncture to enter the caveat that this book is predominantly focused on male paramilitary imprisonment. Some of the key histories of punishment and imprisonment have been rightly criticized for ignoring the experience and insight provided by considering female imprisonment (Howe 1994). My focus on male imprisonment in this book should not be interpreted as a lack of awareness of the significance of female political imprisonment.[13] Instead it is based on the fact that while conducting the research which led to this book I only had access to male prisoners. Aware that a number of other scholars had

---

[12] A chronology of key prison events is provided in Appendix I of this book.

[13] Female prisoners have constituted between 2–5% of the politically motivated population throughout the conflict (NIPS 1970–1999). Amongst the most obvious issues of interest with regard to politically motivated female prisoners are the intersections between both gender and resistance and gender and management; the relationship between the low numbers of female prisoners and the apparent ability of the prison authorities to engage in arguably more repressive actions such as mass strip searching; the qualitatively different relations between ordinary and politically motivated prisoners which have evolved in the female prisons; the tensions within Republicanism in particular between sexist and revolutionary discourses; and finally the ability of female prisoners to build broader alliances within the women's movements and with other constituencies which were beyond the reach of male prisoners. For a journalistic account of the experiences of female paramilitary prisoners in the 1970s see McCafferty (1981).

begun doctoral theses and research projects looking specifically at female imprisonment in Northern Ireland, I took the decision at an early juncture that I would leave those stories for others to tell.

With that caveat in mind, it may be useful at this juncture to offer a very brief synopsis of the background and principal protagonists to the Northern Ireland conflict for those readers less familiar with its contours. Such a synopsis is, by definition, oversimplified.

Background to the Conflict in Northern Ireland

Since 1969 over 3,600 people have been killed and over 40,000 people have been injured in a conflict which has cost the British and Northern Irish economy several billion pounds (Fay, Morrissey, and Smyth 1999, McKittrick *et al.* 1999). With a relatively small population of just over 1.5 million people, the scale of the Northern Ireland conflict is appropriately compared to those in Sri Lanka, Cyprus, or Lebanon (McGarry and O'Leary 1993). As was noted above, the conflict has produced a plethora of literature in political science, history, the social sciences, law, and a range of other disciplines, the breadth of which it would be impossible to do justice to in a book such as this.[14]

For current purposes, the Northern Ireland conflict is best described as involving three sets of protagonists: Nationalists/Republicans, Unionist/Loyalists, and the British state. Each set of protagonists has more moderate exclusively 'political' expressions of their ideology as well as more militant armed groupings. In addition, each of the protagonists has been guilty of acts of extreme violence, and in the case of Republicans, Loyalists, and a very small number of state combatants, have been imprisoned as a result of those actions.

Nationalism/Republicanism

Moderate Nationalism is politically represented by the Social Democratic and Labour Party (SDLP) (Routledge 1997*b*, Murray 1998).

---

[14] By way of a flavour of this literature, see Whyte (1991) for an excellent introduction to the Northern Ireland conflict. For detailed analysis from a political science perspective see McGarry and O'Leary (1990, 1993, 1995) and Ruane and Todd (1996). For a range of historical accounts see Farrell (1976), Bowyer Bell (1993), Coogan (1995), Bew, Gibbon, and Patterson (1996). For an exceptional overview of policy formulation see Cunningham (1991), and for a range of legal accounts see Boyle, Hadden, and Hillyard (1980), Hogan and Walker (1989), and Morison and Livingstone (1995). For a good account of the peace process see Mallie and McKittrick (1996). The literature on paramilitarism in Northern Ireland is referred to extensively in the ensuing chapters.

Republicanism, the less moderate expression of Irish Nationalism, is represented by Sinn Fein. Both parties draw their support primarily from the Catholic community. The SDLP is the largest Nationalist party in Northern Ireland with approximately 45 per cent of the Nationalist vote. Sinn Fein, which did not contest elections until the 1980s, has, however become the fastest growing political party in Ireland. They received 18 per cent of the overall vote in Northern Ireland (42 per cent of the Nationalist vote) in the elections held in June 1998 to the new Northern Ireland Assembly (NI election website 1998). Sinn Fein is the political wing of the largest and best known Republican paramilitary grouping, the Provisional Irish Republican Army (IRA).

While there have been a number of Republican groupings engaged in political violence over the course of the Northern Ireland conflict, the largest and most active is the IRA.[15] Interrupted by three major cease-fires (the most recent called in July 1997 and still in place) the IRA has

[15] As with many revolutionary groupings, Republicanism has been marked by numerous 'splits' and schisms. Other violent Republican groupings have included (a) the Official IRA, (b) the Irish National Liberation Army (INLA) and Irish People's Liberation Organisation (IPLO), and (c) a number of groupings which have come to prominence in the wake of the IRA ceasefires, the Continuity IRA and the Real IRA. For the sake of reference for the discussions to come, below is a very generalized thumbnail sketch of these various groupings.

(a)   The Official IRA, which formally declared a ceasefire in the early 1970s, was formed from the largely Marxist wing of the Republican movement which saw political and sectarian violence as a distraction from broader class-based struggle. They split from the Provisional wing (the latter included the modern Republican leaders such as Gerry Adams and Martin McGuinness) and after a number of violent feuds, formed the Workers Party (which in turn became Democratic Left) and ultimately went on to form a coalition government in the Irish Republic in the 1990s. In common parlance in Northern Ireland, they became known as the 'stickies' because they used an adhesive rather than pins to attach their Easter lilies during the annual Republican Easter commemoration of the 1916 Rising. As will be seen in some of the interviews in this book, the Provisional IRA, the largest Republican armed grouping, are still referred to in some quarters as the 'Provos' (Coogan 1987, Bishop and Mallie 1987).

(b)   The INLA (Irish National Liberation Army) were formed as a splinter group from the Official IRA after the latter had declared a ceasefire. Regarding themselves as more left wing than the mainstream IRA, they too have been involved in a range of armed actions over the conflict. While they have attacked members of the security forces and other traditional Republican targets, their actions have been characterized by violent internal feuding, criminality, and sectarian attacks on Protestant civilians. The IPLO (Irish People's Liberation Organisation) emerged as a result of one such internal feud although they subsequently disbanded under pressure from the IRA (Holland and McDonald 1994).

been engaged in political violence since 1969 including bombings and shootings in Northern Ireland, Britain, and Europe (Bowyer Bell 1979, Bishop and Mallie 1987, Ryan 1994). That campaign has included attacks on the security forces (primarily members of the British Army and the local police the Royal Ulster Constabulary), political and judicial figures, Loyalist paramilitaries, and civilians. The IRA has also carried out a campaign of bombings on economic and commercial targets designed to damage the British and Northern Irish economy, in their terms to 'make the occupation of Ireland costly for the British'.

Civilians killed by the IRA have included those who have been targeted deliberately, those who have been adjudged guilty (by the IRA) of 'informing', those considered guilty of antisocial activity such as drug dealing or car theft, and numerous 'mistakes' wherein civilians have been erroneously or negligently killed in botched attacks on economic targets, the security forces, or Loyalist paramilitaries. In the late 1980s deliberate attacks on civilians increased after the IRA extended their range of 'legitimate targets' to include those involved in construction for, or service provision to, the security forces (O'Doherty 1998).

The IRA and other Republican groupings regard themselves as the inheritors of a Republican tradition in Ireland, stretching back at least to the United Irishmen Rebellion of 1798, which has seen a number of major campaigns seeking to remove the British presence from Ireland through armed struggle (Toolis 1995, Taylor 1997). Republicans point to the partition of the island designed to gerrymander a Unionist majority, the endemic discrimination against Catholics in the Northern state under Unionist domination, and the activities of the Royal Ulster Constabulary as in effect the armed wing of Unionism as amongst the causes of conflict (Adams 1986). Their stated objective throughout the conflict has been a removal of British jurisdiction and a reunification of the island of Ireland partitioned in 1921.

The IRA is a very centralized and relatively disciplined paramilitary grouping. After reorganizing in the mid-1970s into a cellular

(c)   The Continuity IRA emerged in the wake of the 1994 IRA ceasefire. They are a small group of irredentist Republicans whose political wing, Republican Sinn Fein, split from Sinn Fein in 1986 after the Adams/McGuinness leadership persuaded the party to abandon its policy of abstentionism with regard to taking up seats in the Dáil (Dublin Parliament). The Real IRA also emerged in the wake of the 1994 ceasefires after a senior member of IRA Army Council led a breakaway group in protest over Sinn Fein's acceptance of the principles of non-violence contained in the Mitchell Report designed to pave the way to all-party political negotiations.

structure, they have proved to be a ruthless and persistent organization throughout the conflict. Well-armed and apparently highly motivated, they have been consistently recognized in British and international military and intelligence circles as amongst the most effective 'terrorist' organizations in the world (Wilkinson 1986). While there has been some leakage of IRA personnel and weapons to dissident Republican groupings during the period of the ceasefires (including the 'Real IRA' who killed twenty-nine civilians in a bomb attack in Omagh in 1998), they appear at the time of writing to remain as a cohesive and organized group.

Unionism/Loyalism

The two principal voices of constitutional Unionism are the Official Unionist Party (Cochrane 1997) and the Democratic Unionist Party founded by Ian Paisley (Moloney and Pollak 1986). In the 1998 elections the Official Unionist Party secured 21 per cent of the vote and twenty-eight seats in the Northern Ireland Assembly and the Democratic Unionist Party 18 per cent of the vote and twenty seats (NI Election website 1998). There is also a smaller more moderate Unionist party known as the Alliance Party who have attempted to straddle the sectarian divide by attracting votes from both Protestants and Catholics. They secured 6 per cent of the vote and six seats in the Assembly in the 1998 elections (NI Election website 1998). All Unionist parties favour the retention of the Union with Britain. Unionism has always been somewhat fragmented. The emergence (and sometimes disappearance) of a plethora of smaller Unionist parties has been a constant feature of the political landscape over the past thirty years. Of particular significance for current purposes has been the emergence of the Progressive Unionist Party and the Ulster Democratic Party as the political wings of the two main Loyalist paramilitary groups, the UVF and the UDA respectively. While collectively achieving less than 3.5 per cent of the vote (two Assembly seats both of which went to the PUP), these parties have none the less been justifiably praised for helping to achieve and trying to maintain the 1994 Loyalist ceasefires.

Loyalist paramilitaries have also carried out a violent campaign in support of the maintenance of the Union with Britain and the perceived failure of the government to deal effectively with Republican terrorism (Bruce 1992). The three main Loyalist paramilitary groupings are the Ulster Defence Association (also sometimes referred to as the Ulster Freedom Fighters), the Ulster Volunteer Force, and the Red Hand Commando—with a number of splinter groups having been established during the peace process period including the Loyalist Volunteer Force.[16]

Their targets were traditionally uninvolved Catholic civilians, economic or civilian targets in the Irish Republic, or Republican activists (Cusack and McDonald 1997). Regarding themselves as primarily defensive in nature, they consider that they have been driven to the use of political violence because of the IRA, defending not only the link with the United Kingdom, but their community from Republican violence (McAuley 1994, 1995).

Loyalists argue that, with few clear Republican targets other than identified IRA members or elected representatives of Sinn Fein, they have been forced to attack the Catholic community as a whole. Although Loyalists have periodically sought to justify their attacks by claiming that they had information relating to the secret IRA activities

---

[16] (a) The Ulster Defence Association is the largest of the Loyalist paramilitary groupings. They emerged from working-class Protestant vigilante groups in the late 1960s and early 1970s set up to defend Protestant areas from IRA attacks. At one stage their membership was estimated to be in excess of 30,000 when they played a leading role in the Loyalist general strike in protest at the 'power-sharing' government and links with the Irish Republic proposed under the Sunningdale Agreement in 1974. While their numbers declined sharply in the 1970s, they were not officially 'banned' as an organization until 1992, when Northern Ireland Secretary of State Sir Patrick Mayhew determined that they had been killing Catholic civilians under the guise of the Ulster Freedom Fighters (Bruce 1992, McAuley 1994, Taylor 1999).

(b) The Ulster Volunteer Force emerged in the 1960s as a small paramilitary group under the leadership of Gusty Spence which was opposed to some of the liberalizing policies of the then Stormont government under Terence O'Neill. The UVF took their name from the mass movement of Protestants which had organized against the Home Rule Bill of 1912. Although smaller than the UDA, the UVF has been involved in political violence and sectarian killings throughout the conflict and is generally considered to be the better organized of the Loyalist groupings (Cusack and McDonald 1997).

(c) The Red Hand Commando are a small group established by William 'Plum' Smith and others after the arrest of Gusty Spence had thrown the UVF into some disarray. They have retained very close links with the UVF (Stevenson 1996, Taylor 1999).

(d) The Loyalist Volunteer Force emerged in the wake of the Loyalist ceasefire in 1994. Centred predominantly around Portadown, this organization was formed by a split from the UVF mid-Ulster brigade led by Billy Wright. Wright was opposed to the peace process and the left-wing direction in which he perceived the political leaders of the PUP and UDP to be taking Loyalist politics (Cusack and McDonald 1997).

of their victims, much of their violence has been described as sectarian and indiscriminate (Bruce 1995).

In the 1970s and 1980s various attempts were made by the British intelligence agencies and security forces to infiltrate Loyalist organizations. One of the apparent objectives of that infiltration has been to improve the quality of the Loyalists' intelligence by passing on security information on Republican suspects. This was in turn designed to encourage the Loyalists to carry out more directed attacks against Republican activists rather than Catholic civilians (Dillon 1990, Urban 1992, British & Irish Rights Watch 2000). Despite these efforts, from the late 1980s onwards Loyalist groupings have been increasingly forthright about their policy of indiscriminate attacks on Catholics in bars, bookmaker shops, and other public areas.[17]

Loyalists, as members of a pro-state paramilitary group, have by definition had an ambivalent relationship with that state (Nelson 1984). They were arrested and imprisoned by the state for which they were fighting and by and large did not contest its legitimacy. They have appeared more ready to accept that they have broken the law and must pay for their crimes, but felt that their loyalty was not sufficiently recognized (Clayton 1996). 'Their only crime is Loyalty' has long been the graffiti slogan on walls in Loyalist areas. Loyalist command structures are considerably looser than their Republican counterparts. While some of the most capable political and community leaders during the period of the ceasefires have come from the ranks of former Loyalist prisoners, in general Loyalist paramilitary organizations are widely viewed by academics, journalists, security, and prison staff as less organized and less disciplined than their Republican counterparts (Dillon 1990, Bruce 1992, Stevenson 1996, Taylor 1999).[18]

The British State as an Armed Protagonist

The final armed protagonist in the Northern Ireland conflict has been the security forces of the British state. These have included the Royal Ulster Constabulary, the British Army (including special forces such as

---

[17] 'The IRA gets its support from the Catholic community. That community must pay a heavy price for the IRA's murderous campaign against the Protestant community. Keeping the pressure on the Catholic community to get the IRA to stop their killing spree is the only way that we can defend our communities from being driven into a united Ireland' (*New Ulster Defender* 1992: 2).

[18] e.g. Differences between Loyalist and Republican prisoners with regard to their attitude to prison escape are discussed below in further detail in Chapter 3.

the Special Air Service (SAS) and the locally recruited Ulster Defence Regiment), and the various intelligence agencies (Dillon 1990, Ryder 1991, Urban 1992, Weitzer 1995). Other than direct armed actions against paramilitaries and civilians (McCann, Shiels, and Hannigan 1992, Ní Aoláin 2000) the range of other political and security policies and practices which the state has directed against the terrorists are discussed in detail throughout the ensuing chapters.

While state practices have obviously varied considerably over the period of the conflict, there is a heated debate in the literature as to whether or not a coherent state strategy on managing Northern Ireland can be traced (Cunningham 1991). There are those who argue, largely from an anti-imperialist framework, that tactical shifts have been underpinned by a 'strategic continuity' in the maintenance of sectarian division, capitalist hegemony, and the integrity of the United Kingdom (Martin 1982, O'Dowd, Rolston, and Tomlinson 1980, Rolston 1986). Other commentators argue that British policy has been characterized by inconsistency, constructions of 'common sense intuition', and crisis management (O'Malley 1983, Bew and Patterson 1985, Bew, Gibbon, and Patterson 1996, Bowyer Bell 1993). Still others argue that while there have been changes and inconsistencies, there are salient features in security policy, political initiatives, and other aspects of state policy which remain consistent (Boyle and Hadden 1985, McGarry and O'Leary 1995).

One central tenet (of direct relevance to a book on paramilitary imprisonment) which has pervaded British policy in Northern Ireland has been the disavowal of the notion of the state as a combatant in the Northern Ireland conflict. At least up until the latter stage of the peace process in the late 1990s, there has been a tendency to view the conflict largely as a sectarian one fought between two warring traditions, with the state's responsibility being to 'hold the ring' between the two oppositional sects (Tomlinson 1998). Such a view has fundamentally coloured government policy and practice regarding recognition of the political character of the conflict and the vexed question of recognition of the political motivation of the terrorist protagonists.

Background to the Prisons in Northern Ireland

Until 1997, there were five main institutions for male prisoners in the Northern Ireland prison system, each with a fairly distinct and unique role. The system was designed to imprison politically motivated prisoners, from different and implacably opposed paramilitary organizations (between 50 per cent and 66 per cent of the overall population at various junctures in the conflict) as well as 'ordinary' criminals, or 'o.d.c.'s—ordinary decent criminals' as they are colloquially referred to in Northern Ireland. Given the seriousness of the offences committed by many paramilitary prisoners, long-term prisoners have always made up a considerably large proportion of the overall prison population. By way of example, in 1993/4 (the last year before changes in remission in wake of the IRA and Loyalist ceasefires affected the population) 57 per cent of the average daily population were serving long-term sentences (longer than five years) and 19 per cent of those were life sentenced prisoners (NIPS 1994: 7, 35).

As can be seen from Fig. 1.1, the prison population rose dramatically in the wake of the outbreak of violence in 1969, from approximately 600 to almost 3,000 prisoners by 1979. It stabilized from the 1980s to the late 1990s between 1,600–1,900 prisoners and has reduced dramatically since 1998. The changes in population numbers (discussed in greater detail below when looking at the operation of different prison management strategies) was due to factors such as the sustained release of life sentence prisoners, the gradual stabilization of levels of violence at lower levels from the 1980s onwards and, of course, the release of paramilitary prisoners under the Good Friday Agreement.

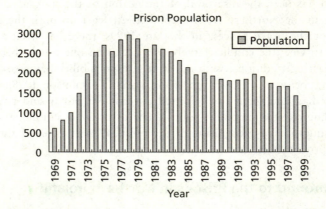

Fig. 1.1. Average daily Northern Ireland prison population, 1969–1999

Below is a brief description of each of the five male prisons. More detailed histories are developed throughout the text.

Crumlin Road (also known as HMP Belfast, closed in April 1996)

This prison was the main male remand prison in Northern Ireland until it closed in 1996. It was an old Victorian prison with perhaps the worst physical conditions in the system. Crumlin Road was a high security prison which housed conforming (i.e. those who had left the paramilitary ranks and who by and large conformed to the prison regime and integrated with other prisoners from oppositional paramilitary groups) and non-conforming politically motivated prisoners (those who maintained their paramilitary allegiance). It also contained ordinary remanded prisoners, and an assessment unit where recently sentenced prisoners were assessed in order to decide to which of the other prisons they should be sent.

Maze Prison (closed August 2000)

Originally an old RAF base known as Long Kesh, this site held prisoners who were interned without trial, special category prisoners in compound conditions segregated by paramilitary faction, and, after the construction of the H Blocks on the same site (known as Maze cellular), a mixture of segregated and integrated paramilitary prisoners at different times over the conflict. The Maze was the high security male prison which housed sentenced non-conforming politically motivated prisoners and, from 1994, most remand non-conforming prisoners. In the Maze paramilitary prisoners were at various junctures segregated according to their paramilitary allegiances, they elected their own Officers Commanding (OCs) and other ranks of responsibility. Maze was the main prison under focus throughout the conflict. It closed following the completion of the early release scheme under the terms of the Good Friday Agreement in August 2000 and remains mothballed while consideration is given to the future of the site.

Maghaberry Prison

Maghaberry is actually two separate prisons: one a maximum security, custom-built prison housing conforming sentenced male politically motivated prisoners (opened November 1987) and long-term ordinary prisoners, and the other a small female prison housing all remand and sentenced female prisoners, conforming, non-conforming politicals as well as ordinaries (opened March 1986). The conditions in both prisons compare quite favourably with the majority of prisons in Britain. The male prison has served, in part, as an institution designed to give the authorities the flexibility to offer a location for former paramilitary prisoners who no longer wish to retain their allegiance to their organization. The female prison was built to replace the womens' prison at Armagh, which, like Crumlin Road, was an old establishment in very poor condition. It now houses male remand prisoners (mostly although not all ordinaries) since the closure of Crumlin Road.

Magilligan Prison

Magilligan is a medium security male prison which currently houses mainly ordinary sentenced prisoners who have either been given short-term sentences or are approaching the end of longer fixed sentences. In the past, however, in particular before the opening of Maghaberry, it too held substantial numbers of paramilitary prisoners, most of whom were serving shorter sentences. Magilligan is also a former internment camp and before that an RAF base.

Young Offenders Centre

The Young Offenders Centre is a male prison which houses mostly male ordinary remand and sentenced prisoners between the age of 18–21, serving sentences of up to four years.

Outline of Book Structure

The book is divided into four substantive sections. Following the introduction and background in Chapter 1 these offer an analysis of resistance, management, and release. Chapters 2–6 focus on prisoner resistance, Chapters 7–10 on prison management, Chapter 11 on prisoner release, and the Epilogue discusses prisons and the construction of memory.

Chapter 2 begins with an overview of the sociological and psychological literature on coping with imprisonment. It explores a number of elements of that literature which are of relevance in the context of paramilitary prisoners in Northern Ireland. After examining that literature the chapter goes on to locate the analysis that follows within a resistance framework. It is argued that such a framework is more suited to understanding the collective resistance of paramilitary prisoners to criminalisation. It is contended that resistance had a number of key features which included resistance as political struggle, resistance as a challenge to the power relations within the prisons, resistance as a collective enterprise, and resistance as a struggle to control space within the prisons.

Chapter 3 considers escapes and escape attempts as an example of resistance as ridicule and a direct assertion by the prisoners of their status as prisoners of war. It is argued that escapes required disproportionate resources on the part of the paramilitaries, and that the business of capturing successful escapees a correspondingly disproportionate effort on the part of the state. This suggests that they represented a considerable political, ideological, and symbolic battle between the protagonists regarding the power of the state to contain the political struggle.

Chapter 4 considers the use of hunger strikes and dirty protest as a mechanism for transforming the body and its waste products into symbolic sites of struggle. It is argued that such tactics may be understood within a framework of resistance as self-sacrifice and endurance. They are examined as an attempt to abrogate power from the prison authorities, to make human bodies an object of the disproportionate application of power and a site through which power could be redirected and reversed. Dirty protest and hunger strikes were presented for Republicans as a historical template of struggle from which to draw inspiration and legitimacy as resistance was achieved through endurance and self-sacrifice.

Chapter 5 considers the use of violence and related activities such as destruction or intimidation as a mechanism for resistance, a continuation of the violence outside the prison gates. It is argued that prison-related violence became another arena of the armed struggle. The state's monopoly on the use of force was challenged in a place which should have been the zenith of the state's capacity for power and control. Violence, it is argued, constitutes resistance through infliction.

Chapter 6 examines prisoners' attitudes towards law and its usage in pursuing prison-based struggles and the relationship between such activities and political struggle outside the prison. Changing attitudes towards law from non-recognition of the courts through to the use of judicial review by prisoners, international human rights fora, and other legal avenues of challenge are explored as pragmatic adaption in resistance strategies, showing willingness to utilize and transform the discourses of the dominant to a form of resistance. The increased awareness by prisoners of the potential for law as praxis and law as an extension of political and military struggle represented resistance as tactical innovation and flexibility, appropriating the tool of the dominant.

Chapter 7 begins the analysis of prison management by examining the relevance of the academic literature on prison management and prison staff to the Northern Ireland context. Three key themes are identified from the literature which are of assistance in the elucidation of the proposed models of prison management for Northern Ireland which are considered below. These themes are the response of prison management to organized groupings of prisoners, the significance of power relations to the process of prison management, and the relationship between prison management and prison staff. With regard to relations with prison staff, a number of further issues are identified from the literature which are of particular relevance to the current study. These include the nature of the staff/prisoner relationship and the attitudes of staff towards prisoners, the particular difficulties with regard to staff morale in the Northern Ireland Prison Service, and a brief discussion on the political and ideological influences of the different prison management models and their effects on staff.

Chapter 8 proposes a model referred to as reactive containment which it is argued characterized the management of prisons until 1976 in Northern Ireland. Reactive containment is described as a relatively crude military model for the management of paramilitary prisoners and, to an extent, the broader conflict in Northern Ireland. The British authorities *reacted* to the loss of control by the Unionist government, dispatched troops to regain control, and sought to *contain* levels of violence and violent perpetrators while a political solution was sought. Internment, Special Category Status, and the Diplock Courts are all examined as ways of detaining and processing large numbers of terrorists and terrorist suspects. It is argued that this style of prison management was characterized by a recognition of the political character of the inmates; the facilitation of negotiations between the prison authorities and paramilitary commanders; and no real efforts being made to deny the prisoners' assertion of their political status.

Chapter 9 considers a model of prison management referred to as criminalisation which it is contended operated in Northern Ireland between 1976 and 1981. It is argued that this strategy was linked to a broader political and security strategy (Ulsterisation) designed to reduce the role of the British army, give security primacy to the RUC, and reframe terrorist violence as a 'law and order' problem rather than a political one. It is contended that in the prisons this required the denial of political status to the prisoners, the removal of tangible symbols of political rather than ordinary imprisonment, and forcing prisoners to conform to the same regime as ordinary criminal prisoners in any other prison in the United Kingdom. It is argued that the model was characterized by a number of features including rule enforcement and the assertion of power; the internalization of propagandist positions; brutality, violence, and dehumanization; and hothouse management and political interference from ministers. It is further argued that this strategy failed in its stated objective.

Chapter 10 develops a model referred to as managerialism which it is argued characterized the management of prisons in Northern Ireland from the period after the 1980/1 hunger strikes until the present day. The distinct features of this model included an increased acceptance that the prison system could not defeat political violence and a tendency to view the management of paramilitary prisoners as a technical rather than ideological endeavour. It is also argued that the Prison Service was increasingly affected by changes elsewhere in the British public sector designed to transform such bureaucracies into more efficient, effective, and value for money endeavours. While such changes did not directly impact on prison management until the late 1980s, it is argued that they provided a legitimating framework or organizational language of scientific and instrumentalist discourses for a set of practices which had emerged in any case in the prisons after the hunger strike era. This chapter also argues that managerialism was characterized by attempts to demarcate and limit the power of paramilitary prisoners as well as the emergence of greater autonomy and self-confidence amongst prison managers in the formulation of policy with less ministerial interference. After offering a detailed account of the material consequences of these managerialist characteristics in the prisons, it is argued that the increasing instrumentalist view of prison management served to obscure the reality of political motivation which directly impeded progress on prisoner issues in the wake of the IRA ceasefires. This argument is developed in the final chapter.

Chapter 11 examines the period from 1994 to 2000 which saw the evolution of the peace process and the early release of paramilitary prisoners. This chapter groups together the role of both prisoners and prison managers in analysing their contribution to that period. It firstly explores the historical context of prisoner release in Ireland North and South. Secondly, the role of prisoners in the process of conflict resolution in the 1990s is examined including the period before and after the breakdown of the first IRA ceasefire. The provisions within the Good Friday Agreement and subsequent legislation are then analysed under four themes. These include prisoner release as an incentive for peace amongst organizations outside the peace process; the relationship between prisoner releases and the decommissioning of paramilitary weapons; the impact of prisoner releases on the victims of violence; and the issue of prisoner reintegration. The author argues that the issue of prisoner release represents a crucial acknowledgement by the British government of the political character of the conflict, and suggests that such a view will be required to spread to all of the protagonists in the Northern Ireland body politic to ensure the continuance of the conflict resolution process.

The book concludes with some final remarks on the notion of prisons as important *spaces* in the construction of collective memory.

2

Coping, Resistance, and Political Imprisonment

Introduction

The next five chapters of this book concern the ways in which paramilitary prisoners have 'resisted'[1] during their incarceration in Northern Ireland over the past thirty years. The section begins with an overview of the traditional literature of how prisoners cope with their imprisonment. It then considers what is meant by the notion of resistance and seeks to apply that theoretical construct to four key components of prisoner resistance in Northern Ireland. The four strategies of resistance considered in detail are (a) escape, (b) dirty protest/hunger strike,[2] (c) violence, (d) attitudes towards and usage of law.[3]

---

[1] It is difficult to find a brief yet satisfactory definition to describe the complexities of what is meant by resistance. The rich anthropological use of the term (e.g. Scott 1985, 1990, Sluka 1995) tends to offer definitions which become so broad as to encompass almost any action. Within that framework, resistance is normally understood as being characterized by purpose, either implicit or explicit, manifesting itself in *opposition* to the application of power (Foucault 1983). It is described as the giving of (resistant) meaning to things and the finding of tactics for avoiding, taunting, attacking, undermining, enduring, hindering, and mocking the everyday exercise of power (Pile 1997: 14). The use of the term within the Northern Ireland prison context is developed throughout this chapter.

[2] Hunger strike and dirty protest are considered in one chapter given the fact that the former explicitly emerged as a technique of resistance as a result of the perceived failings of the latter.

[3] In a similar vein, Cohen and Taylor identified five types of resistance amongst long-term prisoners in the E wing of Durham prison. *Self-Protection* was defined as the ways in which prisoners attempt to make life more bearable by active or passive individual refusal to co-operate with the staff and deliberate challenging of staff rules. *Campaigning* was referred to as the formalizing of such responses as moaning, niggling, complaining, and making a nuisance of oneself. While self-protection and to a lesser extent campaigning were essentially individualistic in nature, *Escapes* were viewed as requiring some form of collaboration and as important in defining the relationship with

Coping with Imprisonment

Before considering in some detail what is meant by resistance amongst politically motivated prisoners in Northern Ireland, it is necessary first to examine the relevance of the more familiar coping or adaptation literature in the Northern Irish context. Although this literature does overlap with notions of resistance (e.g. Sykes 1958, Mathiesen 1965, Cohen and Taylor 1972, 1976, Scraton, Sim, and Skidmore 1991, Sparks, Bottoms, and Hay 1996, Matthews 1999), and indeed I will argue that resistance can be an effective *coping* strategy, it is more traditionally understood within the framework of the sociological or psychological literature as the mechanism employed by prisoners to adjust or adapt to the implications of their imprisonment.

The Sociology of Prison Coping

The sociological literature on prison coping is dominated by accounts of prisoners' adapting subcultural norms, forms of behaviour, or argot roles.[4] Such studies detailed the emergence of an informal world within prisons with its own rules, jargon, prescribed behavioural categories, informal economy, and value system which governed the behaviour of the majority of inmates.

One significant element of much of this literature is taken up with exploring and explaining the forms of behaviour which are adapted by inmates in the process known as prisonization. Clemmer (1940: 299) defined prisonization as the 'taking on the greater or less degree of the folk ways, mores, customs and general culture of the penitentiary'. Goffman (1961*b*) described a process referred to as the mortification of the

authority, whose sole role was often seen as the prevention of escapes. *Striking*, the tactic of hunger strike, was viewed as likely to provoke some humanitarian response. Finally *Confronting* was described by Cohen and Taylor as the ways in which prison protest was forced into the popular consciousness, confirming the importance of prison as a metaphor for the understanding of race and class conflict (Cohen and Taylor 1972: 134–46). As in this book, the types of resistance noted amongst these prisoners were neither mutually exclusive nor linked to particular periods in the prisoner's sentence. Neither could they be explained by simple reference to an inmate subculture. Rather their resistance *styles* were linked to contrasting relationships to authority outside the prison and ideologies which informed such styles, which gave meaning to the life inside and outside the prison (Cohen and Taylor 1972: 166).

[4] Argot roles were defined by Sykes as the language developed by prisoners, words which 'carry a penumbra of admiration and disapproval, of attitude and belief, which channels and controls the behaviour of the individual who uses them or to whom they are applied' (Sykes 1958: 86).

self, in which an inmate's self-respect, dignity, and other elements of the 'former self' are stripped away through exposure to a total institution's (e.g. psychiatric hospital, prison, monastery) dehumanizing and routinized procedures. He argues that inmates often adopt a 'story or a line' to explain their predicament and develop a new value system in seeking support from others in this 'egalitarian community of fate' as a means of 'making out' while incarcerated. Morris and Morris (1963: 469) wrote of prisonization as the continuous and systematic destruction of the psyche and the adoption of new attitudes and ways of behaving which are not only unsuited for life in the outside world, but which may frequently make it impossible for the individual to act successfully in any normal social role. Similarly Toch codified a 'transactional' process (wherein prisoner adaptations shape and are shaped by the prison environment) involving seven dimensions of prisoners' needs in the process of coping with their imprisonment. These included the need for activity, privacy, safety, emotional feedback, support, structure, and the maximization of autonomy (Toch 1977: 16–17).

Many of these writers were fascinated by the social organization of prisoners within a prison which they viewed as a 'total institution', meaning an 'isolated, artificially created, social enclave in which people are subject to a depersonalised and totalitarian regimen' (Adams 1992: 278). In these total institutions, prisoners learned an inmate code of solidarity, distinguished between acceptable and unacceptable forms of behaviour amongst inmates, and were characterized by hostility towards prison guards, a functional response to imprisonment which allowed inmates the chance to 'reject their rejecters' (McCorkle and Korn 1954).

Sykes (1958), and later with Messinger (1960), explored the 'inmate social system' and unearthed various elements of the inmate code which evolved in response to the pains of imprisonment. The pains of imprisonment included the deprivation of liberty, goods, and services, heterosexual relations, the loss of autonomy, and deprivation of security (Sykes 1958: 65–78). The argot roles which emerged as a result of these deprivations such as 'never ratting on a con', not 'losing one's head', being able to 'take it' without whining, loyalty to other inmates, and despising of prison officers (Sykes and Messinger 1960: 6–9) and the distinctions between rats, wolves, punks, fags, ball busters, real men, toughs, and hipsters (Sykes 1958: 87–105) were all offered as varying 'generalized behavioural tendencies', with prisoners playing different roles at different times (Sykes 1958: 106). Some were 'alienative', in which prisoners try to make their prison life easier at the expense of fellow prisoners, and some were 'cohesive' where behaviour was governed by admired values such as loyalty, generosity, and sexual restraint which appear to take the prisoners in the direction of greater inmate solidarity.

A key feature of Sykes's work which is directly relevant to the Northern Ireland context is the extent to which coping with the deprivations of imprisonment could be achieved on a *collective* basis. He argued that more 'cohesive' or collectivist strategies generate greater inmate solidarity and therefore had a greater potential for alleviating the deprivations of imprisonment (Sykes 1958: 107). Solidarity amongst prisoners, he argued, left prisoners feeling less isolated, less vulnerable, and less open to staff repression.

While Sykes's focus was primarily upon prisons as closed institutions, another significant genre of the prison sociological literature focuses more upon what prisoners 'import' with them from the outside (Adams 1992). The importation school challenged the closed-system emphasis on prison-specific influences, and focused more upon pre-prison socialization and experience. These studies analysed factors such as the prior criminal history of prisoners measured by previous convictions or prison sentences (Alpert 1979, Zingraff 1980), their gender, socio-economic status, educational levels, race, and employment histories (Jensen and Jones 1976, Thomas 1977, Alpert 1979), or the perceived self-worth of the individual (Hepburn and Stratton 1977).

Whilst 'prisonization' and 'importation' models of understanding prison coping were originally postulated as competing paradigms, they have increasingly merged with the acknowledgement that prison setting, the previous characteristics of an inmate, and the outside social and political context were all relevant in understanding the ways in which prisoners adapted to their imprisonment (Thomas 1977, Matthews 1999). In attempting to delineate more precisely the importance of competing factors, only 'weak and inconsistent relationships'(Zamble and Porporino 1988: 8) have been established between either pre-prison or intra-institutional factors and the way people behave once imprisoned. One review of the literature in 1980 concludes, with evident exasperation, that 'each inmate who experiences prolonged confinement reacts to this situation in an idiosyncratic manner: Some individuals show deterioration in response to confinement, others show improved functioning whereas others show no appreciable change' (Bukstel and Kilman 1980: 487).

Some of these 'prisonization' studies have also been criticized on methodological grounds. For example, Zamble and Porporino (1988: 9) have suggested that often such studies used different indicators of questionable reliability or measurability such as conformity or non-conformity with staff expectations, or commitment to the inmate code. Little longitudinal analysis was carried out and the complexities and range of individual responses to imprisonment were simply not adequately reflected.

However, perhaps a more significant failing by some of the prisonization studies in particular can be attributed to their functionalist, deterministic, and rehabilitative roots. Levels of solidarity and homogeneity within the prison setting tended to be exaggerated,[5] at times presenting an image of a rather static or stable equilibrium which struggled to explain riots and disturbances which broke out throughout the 1970s (Matthews 1999). The tendency towards viewing certain behaviours as the *inevitable* (my emphasis) response to 'the pains of imprisonment' within closed institutions at times obscured important institutional dynamics such as the way in which power was administered in prisons as well as external political, sociological, and ideological forces, all of which interact directly with the nature of the imprisonment experience.

By way of remedy, the work of Jacobs (1977, 1983) in particular has been crucial in critiquing the implicit assumptions of the prison as a closed institution largely divorced from the influences beyond the walls. He skilfully depicts the changes in Illinois's Stateville maximum security prison from its authoritarian isolationism in the pre-war era to its increased permeability to the influences of black militancy, civil rights campaigns, and greater legal challenge in the 1960s as well as intra-prison influences such as the organization of Muslim prisoners (Jacobs 1977). His approach was to view prison as 'an organization in action, in dynamic relationship with its political, moral and institutional environments' (Jacobs 1977: 11). Such a view allowed not only a more fluid understanding of the operation of prisons themselves, but

---

[5] By way of example, in outlining their range of adaptation typologies to Albany prison, King and Elliot (1977: 260) argue convincingly that the nature of the prisoners and the type of prison are crucial in understanding the ways in which prisoners adapt to their imprisonment. They contend that the typologies developed by Cohen and Taylor's study in the maximum security wing at Durham with long-term prisoners was of limited analytical use in examining a sample of mostly thieves (rated category C prisoners) doing shorter sentences.

also the chance to use prisons to provide insights into 'society's values, its distribution of power, and its system of legal rights and obligations' (Jacobs 1983a: 17). Taken together with Sykes's work on the institutional dynamics of running a prison, his work is of particular significance in trying to understand the relations between political imprisonment in Northern Ireland and the broader contours of the political conflict.

The Psychology of Prison Coping

Much of the psychological literature on coping with imprisonment attempts to quantify the range of psychological effects on performance, personality, and attitudinal implications of imprisonment (Bukstel and Kilman 1980). It appears to be based largely on the truism that imprisonment must be in some way psychologically damaging. Although less numerous than their sociological counterparts, such studies tend to have been completed more recently. Early psychological studies attempted to explore whether various symptoms such as defects in cognitive functioning (e.g. loss of memory or inability to think clearly and rationally), or emotional problems or problems relating to others or indeed the appearance of various psychotic tendencies could be related to imprisonment (Shorer 1965, Heather 1977).

Attempts to use standard measures of psychological deterioration such as the Minnesota Multiphasic Personality Inventory (MMPI) have met with inconclusive results (Gearing 1979). Similarly efforts to measure self-esteem have had a range of results from an increase after a period of imprisonment (Bennett 1974), to remaining unchanged (Culbertson 1975) to decreasing (Hepburn and Stratton 1977). Cross-sectional studies in England (Bolton et al. 1976), Germany (Rasch 1977), and Canada (Wormith 1984) which looked at the length of time served found little evidence of steady deterioration of cognitive functioning skills and in fact Mackenzie and Golstein (1985) found that in comparing prisoners who had served ten years and those who had served between one and two years, the prisoners who had served the longer sentences reported less anxiety, less fear of inmates, less depression, and higher self-esteem.

In more recent times two overlapping paradigms have come to dominate research on inmate adjustment which, it could be argued, incorporate aspects of both sociological and psychological literature. The stress coping paradigm (Lazarus and Folkman 1983, Porporino and Zamble 1984, Zamble and Porporino 1988) incorporates a trans-actional relationship between people and environment. Utilizing a framework derived from environmental psychology, such a view advo-cates an interactionist approach to the study of human behaviour. Individuals are seen to identify stressors (e.g. threats to their emotional or psychological well-being), appraise, and act upon them. Within this framework, unsuccessful coping can result from overwhelming levels of stress, skewed or counterproductive appraisals of situations, or imma-ture or poor coping skills (Adams 1992: 281).

Using this framework, Zamble and Poporino (1988: 93) found that the most common coping strategy adopted by prisoners was what they termed a reactive approach to problem solving. Their research acknowledges the deterministic tendency of much psychological liter-ature on prison coping towards universalizing prisoners' experiences (Porporino and Zamble 1984: 409). None the less over the course of a series of three interviews with the same group of prisoners, they found that prisoners' methods of coping with problems while in prison were by and large similar to likely responses from the same individuals on the outside, with the most significant difference being the apparent limited availability of alcohol or drugs in jail. Zamble and Porporino characterize the coping strategies as reactive, non-anticipatory, unplanned, or escapist (e.g. pretending to be somewhere else) (Zamble and Porporino 1988: 93–5). They concluded that the conditions of imprisonment ultimately limited coping ability because they made it difficult for inmates to acquire superior sorts of responses and strat-egies for dealing with problems (Zamble and Porporino 1988: 100).

Thus the stress coping paradigm focuses on a number of external features which act as stressors, the individual's perceptions of the situ-ation and the influence of various developmental factors such as cul-ture and education, and lastly the range of coping skills developed by the individual over time. The overlapping interactionist paradigm looks at individual and environmental factors such as the types of peo-ple with whom one must associate and argues that the probability of adjustment problems is greatest where there is a mismatch between the individual (with his/her particular coping skills and indeed self-image) and the demands of their environment (Wright and Goldstein 1989, Sappington 1996).

Like its sociological counterpart, psychological literature on prison-ers' coping abilities has been criticized on a number of grounds. Zamble and Porporino (1988: 11) suggest that samples were often unrepresentative, for example having been selected systematically by the attitudes of parole boards; that researchers were overly reliant upon cross-sectional design, and tended by their nature to veer either towards mono-causality or become so multi-factoral as to be of limited analytical use. They have also, like their sociological counterparts, tended to generalize about prisoner coping mechanisms and correspondingly underemphasize the variances and differences amongst prisoners (Gibbs 1991).

A broader criticism of this literature relates to the applied nature of some psychological studies of prisoners' coping mechanisms. Such studies may offer a largely depoliticized analysis. For example, they may fail to take sufficient account of notions of legitimacy within the prison system or the prison system's compliance with its own legal norms and values which are explored by more critical commentators (Mathiesen 1965, Sparks and Bottoms 1995). Similarly, attempts at acknowledging the significance of political or ideological factors as impacting upon a prisoner's coping abilities in psychological research have often resulted in mechanistic and unwieldy typologies which obscure rather than illuminate the complex interaction between individual and social setting.[6]

The Relevance of Sociological and Psychological Literature on Prison Coping to Northern Ireland[7]

Paramilitary prisoners in Northern Ireland were not immune from the traditional pains of imprisonment. They had to cope with the intrinsic

---

[6] Similar limitations have appeared in some of the psychological literature on the Northern Ireland conflict. Some psychologists have by and large rejected the notion of terrorists as psychopaths or sociopaths (Heskin 1984), suggesting in fact that paramilitary murderers were more 'stable' than non-paramilitary murderers (Lyons and Harbinson 1986). Such studies have produced some interesting findings on the process of distancing human reactions from destructive acts through political justification, euphemistic language, displacement, and dehumanization (Bandura 1990) and more tightly knit mentally 'healthy' communities as a result of 'terrorist' violence (Curran 1988). However, better known is analysis dominated by the notion of the IRA campaign as a 'super-ego trip' (Heskin 1994), Authoritarian Personality Theory—linking conservative individuals to prejudice and sectarianism (Cairns 1994), and Social Identity Theory (Trew 1992), linking the conflict to self-esteem and membership of differing groups. Such analyses share common failings of locating the causes of conflict largely in the tensions between the Catholic and Protestant communities and minimal, if any, critical reflection on the role and responsibility of the British state as a protagonist.

[7] The limited sociological literature which has focused upon political imprisonment in Northern Ireland has focused explicitly on its relationship to the politics and ideology of the conflict (e.g. Rolston and Tomlinson 1986, 1988, Tomlinson 1995).

personal and familial problems familiar to any long-term prisoners (McEvoy *et al.* 1999). Fears of deterioration, family breakdowns, concerns regarding release, these have all been features of their prison experience. Indeed, a number of prisoners interviewed for this book have suggested that such problems have been amplified in a context where the prisoners were reluctant to avail themselves of professional services available, lest this be interpreted by the authorities as weakness on their part.[8] Within such a paradigm, it might be possible to argue that the activities of paramilitary prisoners over the past thirty years have been a particular style of adaptation to their imprisonment in the classic Clemmer fashion.

I would argue, however, that there are important differences between prisoners who do what they can to *get by* during their incarceration and those who *resist*. Such a distinction has been referred to by Cohen and Taylor (1972: 131) as the difference between 'making out' and 'fighting back'. They argue that the 'adaptive accounts of the 1960s and 1970s were of limited value to the context of American prisons of an era where general adjustment had long since given way to "active co-ordinated resistance"'. Of course resistance and coping are located somewhere along the same spectrum. As suggested above, 'active co-ordinated resistance' is indeed an excellent coping strategy to deal with incarceration. In the Northern Ireland context it is also centrally linked to the assertion of political status and the political character of the conflict. It is this link which places the activities of politically motivated prisoners in Northern Ireland firmly at the *resistance* end of the spectrum.

A number of key themes run through the four principal resistance strategies discussed in the chapters below. These are the notion of resistance as political struggle, the notion of resistance as a struggle to curtail the power of the prison authorities within the prisons, the collective character of prisoner resistance in Northern Ireland prisons, and the key relationship between resistance and control over space within prisons. These themes form the theoretical backdrop to much of the subsequent discussion.

Resistance as Political Struggle

The ability of prisoners to resist in captivity has been underpinned by their focus upon their captivity as an assertion of their status as

[8] e.g. interview with former IRA prisoner and Sinn Fein councillor (16 Jan. 1995).

political prisoners who are part of an overall political struggle. Small acts of resistance may be given political meaning by factors such as the status of the prisoner, the reason for his/her imprisonment, and the context within which resistance takes place.

As Gramsci (1971) has emphasized, obtaining consent is a key element in the hegemonic project.[9] One way in which those who seek to resist can appropriate power is to refuse to consent to hegemonic definitions of, for example, the purpose or rationality of their imprisonment. Prisoners may interpret and act upon their material circumstances by refusing to accept the legitimacy of their imprisonment, the symbols of criminal rather than political imprisonment, the trial which convicted them, or even the state itself. As Comaroff (1985: 195) has noted, 'resistance is typically neither an all or nothing phenomenon nor an act in and of itself, it is frequently part and parcel of subjective and collective reconstruction'.[10]

For example, by locating an analysis of their imprisonment within the context of an 800-year struggle against British imperialism in Ireland in which prison resistance has played a crucial role, Republican prisoners could appropriate power at both a symbolic and material level. Their traditional ability to mobilize a powerful political power base in the community was given added impetus and strategic direction by the growth of Sinn Fein since the 1980–1 hunger strikes (Clarke 1987). They were sustained by a view of imprisonment as a continuance of the struggle, the epicentre of which was resistance to the criminalisation of the political roots of the conflict.

For Loyalists, on the other hand, with a more ambivalent relationship to the state and no history of political imprisonment outside the most recent conflict, such clear oppositional resistance was more problematic. In promulgating that 'their only crime is loyalty', they were forced to conceptualize and acknowledge a prison system (and by extension a state) which was legitimate but one which has punished them either erroneously or over-zealously for acting for the best of

[9] Gramsci described hegemony as the processes by which a dominant group, in his case one of the 'fundamental' social classes (either bourgeoisie or proletariat), achieves and maintains 'cultural, moral and ideological leadership' over allied and subordinate groups. Hegemony is achieved by consent rather than coercion, direction rather than domination, by building alliances with, and appealing to the self-interest of, such subordinate groupings (Forgacs 1988 esp. 189–222, 422–4).

[10] Buntman (1996: 17) describes this process well on Robben Island as 'resignification', interpreting the prison world in ways that empower and encourage rather than ways which reinforce weakness or vulnerability.

motives in defence of the state. Their capacity for resistance was correspondingly muted (reliant primarily on the potential for violence), with a considerably smaller political constituency in the community, and less clearly linked to macro-political struggle.

In her analysis of the activities of politically motivated prisoners on Robben Island, Buntman suggests a number of components to the prisoners' resistance. These include resistance as survival, resistance as dignity and self-consciousness, resistance as open challenge, resistance as reducing state power or defeating the ends of the oppressor or dominator, and resistance as the appropriation of power (Buntman 1996: 10). Some of the activities which she explores in relation to Robben Island were what Scott (1985) referred to as the hidden transcripts of resistance (through mocking of jailers behind backs, addressing warders using the word Meneer (Mister or Sir) rather than the more offensive Baas (Master) or adding the word 'tard' silently after Baas) as well as more open challenges such as hunger strikes, letter writing, and work go-slows.

Other prisoners, admittedly imprisoned in the most extreme of circumstances, have spoken of resistance as the very act of survival itself, the act of maintaining one's humanity where dehumanization is the project of the jailers. Solzhenitsyn (1963) notes the importance of extracting and focusing upon any positive element of the micro prison experience, an act of kindness from a guard, a change in the daily routine, or a minor improvement in the prison food, all can be 'stored' and utilized in a clandestine fashion to resist the brutality of the regime (Solzhenitsyn 1963).[11]

In the Northern Ireland context resistance has been largely defined by what Scott (1990: 202–3) referred to as 'public refusals'. The actual techniques employed by prisoners (explored below) may to some extent reflect material differences in the nature of the detention of paramilitary groupings in Northern Ireland compared to Apartheid South Africa. Hidden or less overt forms of resistance such as the education of prisoners, political and military classes, the learning of Irish, the decoration of prison wings in paramilitary and political

---

[11] 'Shukov took off his hat and laid it on his knee. He tasted one bowl, he tasted the other. Not bad there was some fish in it . . . He dug in. First he only drank the broth, drank and drank. As it went down, filling his whole body with warmth, all of his guts began to flutter inside him at their meeting with the stew. Gooo-oood ! And now Shukhov complained about nothing; neither about the length of his stretch, nor about the length of the day, nor about their swiping another Sunday. This was all he thought about now: we'll survive. We'll stick it out, God willing, till its over.' (Solzhenitsyn 1963: 136).

iconography have also formed part of the armoury of paramilitary prisoners in Northern Ireland over the period of the conflict. However, these have always been in conjunction with, rather than as an alternative to, more expressive forms of resistance. The central tenet of both expressive and hidden forms of resistance has been the prisoners' assertion of their status as political prisoners.

Resistance and Power[12]

Central to any notion of resistance in a prison context is the interplay between resistance and power relations within the prison. Many of the most influential commentators on resistance have viewed the interplay between resistance and power as the key to understanding the former (e.g. Scott 1985, 1990). For example, Scott (1990: p. xii) reasoned that the task of conceptualizing resistance was to study 'power relations' (Scott 1990: p. xii). Similarly Foucault has argued 'where there is power, there is resistance and yet, or rather consequently, this resistance is never in a position of exteriority in relation to power' (1978: 95), i.e. there has to be some exercise of power for someone to resist to it. The reverse is also possible. 'Power is never in a position of exteriority to resistance' (Scott 1990: 111); they are intertwined.

In the prison context, while the material conditions within the prisons cannot completely determine resistance, they do influence, shape, and even contort both the operation of power and resistance. For example, the hardline approach taken by prison management during the hunger strike era (discussed below) clearly influenced the techniques of resistance employed by the prisoners. Similarly a more pragmatic political and managerial approach during the 1980s was mirrored, at least in some areas, by prisoners' exploration of less confrontational avenues of struggle. As Scott (1985: 299) has suggested, the parameters of resistance are also set, in part, by the institutions of resistance. It is not just that 'where there is power, there is resistance'. Rather, resistance and the exercise of power are mutually shaping, defining, and changing in an ongoing dialectic.

The intensity of that dialectic, either inside or outside prison walls, is increased in the context of a political struggle. Attempts by the state

---

[12] The theme of power relations between staff and inmates in the Northern Ireland prisons runs throughout this book but is addressed most directly in Chapter 5 and Chapter 8.

to criminalise political struggle and by the opponents of the state to resist such a process are the key ingredients which intensify that interaction.[13] In the context of such political struggles, the techniques discussed below (such as hunger strikes) are designed to underline the political motivation of the resistant actors and to expose the realities of the state's explicitly political application of power, the latter usually being framed in terms of law and order discourses and the determination not to surrender to terror.

Foucault also argued that resistance, like power itself, is diffused throughout the social body, that 'points of resistance are present everywhere in the power network. Hence there is no locus of great refusal, no soul of revolt, source of all rebellions, or pure law of the revolutionary' (Foucault 1980: 96) He views resistance as counter-power, broad enough to include 'agitations, revolts, spontaneous organisations, coalitions' (Foucault 1986: 219) anything which can horizontally or vertically challenge power.

There is a tendency in this and other literature on power and resistance to focus on the two as though they were binary opposites, power as something that is practised over and resistance as something that is practised against (Ortner 1995: 174). Buntman (1996: 20) argues that rather than see resistance as the opposite to power, we should view it as aspiring to power, it is the process of the less powerful seeking to approximate or appropriate power. Such a view of power/resistance, it is argued, offers the potential for a much more fluid dialectic. It is not a teleology in which power is the promised land at the end of a linear process which begins with resistance to survive, developing through resistance as gradual appropriation to an end point where the once vanquished becomes victor, and must in turn face the threat of resistance from the newly subordinated.

Clearly Foucault's work is of seminal importance in understanding the nature of power in prisons (Foucault 1979) and informs this project.[14] His interest in the 'micro-physics' of the operations of power in prisons is based upon the premiss that the process of discipline, surveillance, education, control, timetables, and so forth—together

---

[13] For example, Alison Young has suggested that with regard to the struggle between the suffragettes and the state in the early part of the century, 'the political motivation and signification of the suffragettes' militancy were sucked out and transformed into the predefined concepts of criminality, public disorder and illegal activity' (Young 1990: 150).

[14] For a more detailed analysis of Foucault's work on power see Dreyfus and Rabinow (1982), McNay (1992, 1994).

with the architecture and organization of the institution—provide an excellent model for understanding broader modes of control and disciplinary techniques throughout the social body (Garland 1990, esp. chs. 6 and 7). While the nature of the altered power relations in the Northern Ireland prison system is considered below, it is important to acknowledge a number of caveats with regard to the Foucauldian analysis of power from the perspective of the prisoners.

Sparks, Bottoms, and Hay (1996), have offered three critiques of applying a Foucauldian analysis to power relations in the prison context, all of which are relevant for current purposes.

Firstly they argue that Foucault's work, in particular *Discipline and Punish*, was much more concerned with the diffusion of disciplinary mechanisms throughout the social body than the concrete ways in which prisons are managed or ordered. Secondly, as Garland (1990: 160) also has argued, in Foucault's emphasis on the Panopticon in order to explain the micro application of power, and in particular in his work on prisons, he appears to hold out the possibility of near complete domination, whatever his later qualifications. Thirdly, drawing upon Giddens (1984: 154, 1991: 57), they contend that while Foucault does talk of power as always being 'a way of acting upon an acting subject', in practice he tends towards a depersonalized and machine-like view of people not as human agents but rather as the objects of power. They contend that Foucault's analysis is skewed towards the official representations of institution rather than the voices and bodies of those being controlled and that little theoretical reason is provided to anticipate resistance, subversion, or innovation (Sparks, Bottoms, and Hay 1996: 67).

Such criticisms are equally valid in understanding the power/resistance nexus in the Northern Ireland prison context. While this book is clearly informed by the intersection between the prisons and the political and ideological context in which they operate, it is primarily a book about relations between prisoners and prison authorities. Secondly, as the chapters below will demonstrate, the resistant capacity of the prisoners' fundamentally altered power relations in Northern Ireland certainly resulted in a prison system which was a world away from the kind of complete domination by the authorities hinted at by Foucault. Thirdly, and linked to the latter point, the resistant abilities of the prisoners ensured that the prisoners 'had faces',[15] they were throughout

---

[15] In his critique of the passivity of the objects of power in Foucault's work, Giddens suggests that 'Foucault's bodies do not have faces' (Giddens 1984: 157).

the conflict key players in determining the nature of power relations in the prisons rather than passive objects to whom power was applied.

It is worth making one final point with regard to the relationship between resistance and power in prisons. While this book considers four particular techniques of resistance in the Northern Ireland context, all of which reflect to a varying degree particular configurations of power relations at different junctures, there are dangers in allowing one's analysis to become overly determined by the state of such relations (e.g. see Hecht and Simone 1994). Power relations, while crucial, are not the only determining influence on the styles of resistance adopted.

Resistance as Collective Action

A cohesive inmate society provides the prisoner with a meaningful social group with which he can identify himself and which will support him in his battles against his condemners—and thus the prisoner can at least in part escape the fearful isolation of the convicted offender. (Sykes 1958: 107)

In asserting their status as political prisoners, a further defining characteristic of paramilitary prisoners in Northern Ireland has been their determination to be treated as collective factions rather than individuals. The often repeated Prison Service commitment to 'treat prisoners as individuals' (e.g. NIPS 1996/7) was viewed by many prisoners as a direct challenge to their assertion of political status. As Buntman (1996: 15) has argued with regard to politically motivated prisoners in South Africa, the forging and maintenance of a notion of community was both a product of basic struggles against a malevolent regime and a bulwark against the state's onslaught.

The symbolic and material significance of treating such prisoners in a collective fashion has often been underpinned by the determination of the state to resist such attempts at all costs. For Red Army Faction prisoners in West Germany, the state's refusal to recognize the collective identity of the prisoners became the key battleground of the late 1970s (Becker 1989, Wright 1991). In Spain, the dispersal of ETA prisoners since 1989 to a large number of prisons as far away as the Canary Islands has been explicitly framed as an attempt to 'break the back' of the Basque separatist movement.[16] Similarly in Northern Ireland, the refusal at times to recognize prison leaders or the insistence by prison authorities at

---

[16] Interview with Deputy Director Spanish Prison Service, 9 Mar. 1995.

various stages of the conflict that they were discussing issues with prisoners' spokespersons rather than Officers Commanding offered instructive insights into the significance of prisoners' collective identity.

In Northern Ireland, since 1969, prisoners have organized themselves into paramilitary grouping with hierarchical command structures.[17] While there have been variances over time and between different paramilitary factions, the prison experience for non-conforming paramilitary prisoners in Northern Ireland has been largely a collective one. Paramilitary prisoner groupings have had their hierarchies, functional responsibilities, norms and values, support structures, and policing mechanisms. While the latter have occasionally included extreme violence against individuals from the same organization, particularly amongst Loyalist prisoner groupings,[18] such activities have rarely reached the levels of violence and intimidation suggested in the literature on gangs in American prisons (e.g. Jacobs 1977, Pollock 1997).

The collective nature of politically motivated imprisonment in Northern Ireland and the difficulties associated with maintaining institutional surveillance and control obviously holds the potential for intra-prisoner domination and violence. As Scott (1990: 26) has argued, amongst prison inmates who are all subject to a common domination from the institution and its officers, there frequently develops a tyranny as brutal and exploitative as anything that the guards can devise.[19]

Collective imprisonment in Northern Ireland was obviously not without its tensions. Such tensions resulted in some prisoners leaving the paramilitary wings, for a range of interpersonal and ideological reasons.[20] However, almost without exception,[21] prisoners interviewed

[17] Much of the analysis in this book is focused upon those prisoners who remained part of the paramilitary command structures. A similar and potentially enlightening study could be carried out upon those paramilitary prisoners who chose to leave the paramilitary wings, disassociate from their former comrades, and from the mid-1980s onwards move to the integrated wings of HMP Maghaberry.

[18] One such example was the murder and torture of LVF inmate David Keyes in 1997 after he was suspected of being a police informer by his fellow prisoners.

[19] Cressey and Krassowski (1958) have also suggested that in the context of some prison settings such as concentration camps or prisoner of war settings, organized groupings may do little to protect inmates from (and in some instances may actually make prisoners more vulnerable to) theft, assault, informing, and other normal vicissitudes of imprisonment leading to a state of anomie in some such settings (Cressey and Krassowski 1958: 217–30).

[20] For an excellent discussion of the tensions amongst Republican prisoners see McKeown (1998).

[21] On the Republican side (also discussed in McKeown 1998), the exceptions referred to were a number of prisoners who referred to the ideological and interpersonal tensions

for this book spoke of the positive elements of their collective detention including friendship, support, 'craic', and a clear self-image of
greater power as a result of their numbers and organization. Even prisoners who had left the collective wings of the Maze for integrated
wings at Maghaberry acknowledged that the collective nature of the
prison experience was a key strength. While such descriptions may
be somewhat self-serving, they also reflect the reality that for collective
resistance to function properly it must be based upon more than intra-
prisoner domination and tyranny.[22] As is discussed below, it is no accident that the resistance of Republican prisoners has been more evident
and effective over the period of the conflict, and their sense of collec-
tivity correspondingly more developed, than the more individualized
culture of Loyalist prisoners.

As Cohen and Taylor (1972: 122) have argued, cohesion and solidarity in long-term prisons are normally dependent upon prolonged
interaction between individuals. Forging a sense of 'prison community'
(Clemmer 1940) is clearly easier in a context where prisoners have
already been members of illegal and clandestine organizations with
clear command structures and share a political or an ideological base.

in the IRA compounds in the 1970s when Gerry Adams and others became highly critical of the Republican Movement's direction on the outside. Similar tensions arose in the
mid-1980s when Tommy McKearney and a number of other close associates split from
the IRA prisoners in the Maze to pursue a more stringent Marxist/Leninist line and
moved to Maghaberry. On the Loyalist side, a number of UVF prisoners who were held
in Special Category Status during the 1970s and 1980s criticized the strict military discipline which was imposed in some compounds which included lengthy route marches and
constant drilling, activities which these prisoners viewed as of limited relevance in the
circumstances of their detention. One other Loyalist prisoner who left the nonconforming wings of the Maze for the conforming wings of Maghaberry also noted a degree of
fear on his wing because of the particularly fearsome temper and propensity to violence
of the Officer Commanding on his wing (interviews with former IRA prisoner, 15 Dec.
1994, former IRA prisoner, 9 Oct. 1998, former UVF prisoner, 27 July 1998, former UDA
prisoner, 24 July 1998).

[22] One instructive example of this was provided in an interview with a leading criminal lawyer who defended large numbers of Republicans over the period of the conflict.
The interviewee was asked what sanctions he thought would be applied to sentenced
prisoners where it became apparent that they had made damaging statements in interrogation or at the trial stage: 'To be honest I think that the sanctions would be minimal.
Once a prisoner moves from the Crum [Crumlin Rd remand prison] to the Kesh [Maze]
the key thing is to get him onto the wings, make him feel that he is still part of the struggle, included, still part of the collective movement. If you start beating people up, or
worse, it will be bad for morale on the wings generally. Such prisoners might be a long
time in before they are given a staff position [prison leadership] but that would probably be the only sanction' (interview with solicitor, 16 Jan. 1996).

In the case of Republicans, they can also conceptualize the state as a powerful enemy, the struggle against which requires a disciplined and organized community. Even when the actual organization of that community is materially difficult, such as during the dirty protest era (discussed below) when prisoners spent large amounts of time confined to their cells, the conceptualization of themselves as belonging to an organization or prison community was itself an act of resistance.[23]

Crucial to the establishment and functioning of such communities has been the prisoners' insistence that they should be distinguished from both rival factions and non-politically motivated prisoners. While the various campaigns for segregation by paramilitary faction are discussed in detail below (see especially Chapter 10), this may serve as a useful juncture to examine the relationship between the *collective* nature of the resistance of politically motivated prisoners and their relations with ordinaries.

Central to their collective resistance project was the determination amongst politically motivated prisoners that they should be seen as distinct, other, and apart from ordinaries as well as their opposing political factions. Such a view was demonstrated at the practical and symbolic level, particularly for Republicans, in their refusal to wear a prison uniform or to carry out prison work. At an organizational level, it was also highlighted by a determination that politically motivated prisoners should avoid behaviour, such as assaults on sex offenders, which would offer the authorities the opportunity to portray them as ordinary criminals.[24] Of course the driving dynamic in relations with

[23] In his work on the construction of 'imagined communities', Benedict Anderson (1991: 6–7) has suggested that notional communities require at least four components. He suggests that the community be imagined in so far as not all of its members actually know each other, that the community be limited by clear parameters as to who is and is not a member, that the community be explicitly conceptualized or imagined as a community, and that the community imagines itself as sovereign. While the sovereignty of prisoners' organizations was clearly encroached upon by the paramilitary leadership on the outside and prison authorities on the inside, none the less the conceptualization of the 'prison community' is a useful one. Within the security of that community, prisoners have been able to arrange niches within which they can adapt in their own terms as leaders, foot soldiers, extroverts, introverts, and so on. Seymour (1977: 180) has described such spaces well as 'a functional subsetting, containing objects, space, resources, people and relationships between people'. The collective resistance of politically motivated prisoners has permitted and encouraged the development of such niches.

[24] 'It wasn't that views of Republican prisoners were very sympathetic regarding sex offenders. Most of the time in the Crum (Crumlin Road) you would have been separated from them. However, there would have been a general line from the staff (prison leader-

such prisoners, as with much else in the prisons, was the assertion of political status. However, the relationship was also shaped by a number of additional features.

One such feature was that for some politically motivated prisoners—particularly those who enjoyed *de facto* segregation according to paramilitary faction at various junctures—they had only rare contact with ordinary prisoners (O'Malley 1990). Minimal contact with ordinary prisoners who, for example, worked as orderlies or trustees in the prisons, allied to the potential security threat that such prisoners might have represented in passing on information to the authorities, to some extent mitigated against the development of close relations with such prisoners.

The placement of ordinary prisoners on the same wings, or in close proximity to paramilitaries, was usually viewed (correctly) by the politicals as part of the prison authorities' broader strategy of criminalisation, treating all prisoners as equal regardless of motivation. Within such a framework, ordinary prisoners were often viewed as pawns, being used to undermine the collective identity of the paramilitary factions.[25] At various times when prolonged interaction with ordinaries was inevitable, unlike in similar prison settings such as South Africa, the USA, or Palestine (Cummins 1994, Buntman 1996, Addameer 2000), little systematic efforts were made to *politicize* or convert such prisoners in Northern Ireland.[26] With large numbers of their own factions continuously being arrested and imprisoned, many

ship) that they should not be beaten up or anything because that is what ordinaries would've done and the NIO could have used it as propaganda against us . . .' (interview former IRA prisoner, 1 Dec. 1994).

[25] This phrase was used a number of times in interviews with former paramilitary prisoners, e.g. interviews with former IRA Officer Commanding Maze, 12 Sept. 1994, interview with former UDA prisoner, 12 Jan. 1996.

[26] In conducting the fieldwork for this book I have come across a number of examples where ordinary offenders were permitted by the respective factions to be held on the segregated Loyalist and Republican wings despite the fact that they were not convicted for terrorist-type offences. The reasons offered for such placements included that the offenders would be 'better protected' on paramilitary wings, that such wings offered a greater sense of solidarity or even, in the case of one parent, that associating with politically motivated prisoners might prove a good influence on their son in deterring him from future offending. It may also be true, however, that some prisoners who were convicted of ordinary offences but permitted on to the wings of the paramilitary groupings were in reality paramilitary members who had been convicted of ordinary offences. It is also possible, particularly with regard to the smaller paramilitary factions (e.g. INLA, LVF) that ordinaries were encouraged to apply to join their wings in order to boost their numbers.

of whom were potentially as much in need of politicization having just come from the respective military campaigns, there was little impetus for a concerted attempt at politicizing non-paramilitary prisoners in the Northern Ireland context.[27]

The collective resistance process, and the sense of community formed, was, to an extent, a version of the paramilitary structures within which prisoners had operated while on the outside. While power relationships, opportunities for debate and discussion, and other particularities of the nature of communal resistance varied greatly over time and between factions, its *collective* character was a perennial feature of the Northern Ireland prisons.

Resistance and Control of Space

A further feature of the assertion of political status by paramilitary prisoners was a determination to maximize control over their living space within the prisons. In the compounds from 1971 to 1976 and in the H Blocks from the early 1980s onwards, prisoners physically removed themselves from one of the key components of power and discipline within a prison, the constant surveillance of the authorities. Alternative loci of power were established in the huts, or H Blocks, where prison guards could often only patrol with prior discussion and consultation with the prisoners' Officers Commanding. Resistance happens in places, it takes place in a geographical location. Control over locations offers practical opportunities for techniques of resistance such as escapes but also suggests a symbolic critique of one of the defining characteristics of imprisonment, the control of space. As Pile has argued: 'resistance does not just act on topographies imposed through the spatial technologies of domination, it moves across them under the nose of the enemy, seeking to create new meaning out of the imposed meanings, to rework and divert space to other ends' (Pile 1997: 16).

In order to effect forms of resistance, resistors must establish (however temporarily) social spaces and socio-spatial networks which are insulated from control and surveillance (Routledge 1997: 71). Hooks (1991) has referred to such spaces as 'homeplaces' which act as sources of self-dignity, agency, and solidarity in which resistance is

---

[27] The relationship between the treatment of paramilitary and ordinary prisoners is discussed further in Chapter 10.

both organized and conceptualized. In the prison context of a maximum security wing in Durham prison Cohen and Taylor described such a process as demonstrating identity, clearing 'some subjective spaces which were relatively uncontaminated by the institutional reality—that they had sites upon which identity work might be mounted. They could display their specialness within the very style of disassociation from the regime' (Cohen and Taylor 1976: 20).

In the context of prisons in Northern Ireland, such spaces may be the prison wings controlled by paramilitaries, or (in the most rigid era of the hunger strikes where prisoners were largely confined to their cells) the mouths and body cavities of prisoners smuggling 'comms' between the hunger strikers and the IRA Army Council. Such places of resistance are never completely fixed unfractured practices but rather they may be viewed as 'third spaces' (Bhabba 1994) intersecting with practices of domination such as attempts at marginalization or segregation (Hooks 1991).

In sum therefore the various techniques of resistance outlined below are informed by these key notions of the relationship between resistance and political struggle, resistance and power, the collective character of prisoner resistance, and the relationship between resistance and control over space within prisons.

Techniques of Resistance Employed by Paramilitary Prisoners in Northern Ireland

As discussed above, there is a tradition within critical criminological and prison literature referred to by Cohen and Taylor (1976: 11–12) as the desire to attribute implicit political motivation to the actions of prisoners which appear, on the surface at least, more directly related to the satisfaction of personal needs. The focus of this book is not constricted by the difficulties of implying or seeking out an inchoate political motivation. The prisoners' profession of their status as political was explicit, clearly articulated, understood, and acted upon.

I have chosen to use the word 'resistance' to characterize the actions of politically motivated prisoners in Northern Ireland, because I believe that it best captures the collective assertion of their status. Paramilitary prisoners in Northern Ireland arrived into a ready-made collective organization. These were organizations characterized by a shared political ideology and range of political objectives, the paramilitary capacity to carry out extreme violence, varying degrees of a supportive constituency outside the prison, and an organization determined to resist not only material deprivations but (particularly in the case of Republicans) to assert their status as *political* prisoners.

The resistance strategies detailed in the chapter below are not presented as a comprehensive account of resistance techniques employed by politically motivated prisoners in Northern Ireland. Such an account would have included the use of education, religiosity, political and military training, the political sectarian iconography on the prison wings, and a range of other aspects which could have formed the subject for an entire book. However, this book seeks also to examine the managerial context of paramilitary imprisonment in Northern Ireland and therefore only an illustrative sample of resistance techniques could be explored in sufficient detail. The areas chosen are presented as heuristic narratives, designed to draw out key features of resistance by paramilitary prisoners. Resistance is presented and understood as the collective assertion of the political status of the prisoners, and by extension, the political character of the conflict. It is argued that (a) escape, (b) dirty protest and hunger strikes, (c) violence, and (d) the use of law have been key elements of that assertion.

Escapes are examined first as a feature of resistance which were a constant in Northern Ireland prisons throughout the conflict. Escapes are ostensibly a less expressive form of resistance. They are, at least in the planning stages, a 'hidden transcript' (Scott 1990) of resistance. In such circumstances, the prisoners' apparent acquiescence to domination are often crucial for success. Escapes from prison are both metaphorically (and in the case of tunnels, literally) resistance practices happening beneath what De Certeau called 'the monotheistic apparatuses of the panopticon' (De Certeau 1984: 48).[28] However, they do challenge the very *raison d'être* of imprisonment (Sparks, Bottoms, and Hay 1996: 58). They are a direct challenge to the power of the institution and the state once either successfully executed or indeed if a near miss becomes public (Learmont 1995). For paramilitary prisoners, escape offered a ready-made template for assertion of their status as prisoners of war. Representing the opportunity to demonstrate

---

[28] In this context the panopticon is used as a model to describe the disciplining and normalizing discourses of the prison and by extension society in general. For a fuller exposition of the usefulness of the panopticon as a conceptual device see Mathiesen (1997).

stealth, courage, daring, and good public relations, escapes constituted resistance through ridicule.

The use of hunger strike and dirty protest represented the transformation of the body and its waste products into symbolic sites of struggle. It is a classic weapon of the weak (Mathiesen 1965), an attempted abrogation of power using the most basic and essential of human tools. It is 'committed theatre' (Obafemi 1990), an act of violence against the self which in effect offers a powerful critique of the assumed rationality of punishment and the axiomatic legitimacy of the punisher. It is a method of 'giving voice to one's protest' (Orbach 1986), of making one's body an object of the disproportionate application of power when there is a clash between two unequal clashing forces (Deleuze 1977: 80–1). For paramilitary prisoners, it offered the potential for a redirection and reversal of power. Dirty protest and hunger strike (for Republicans in particular) offered a historical template from which to draw inspiration and legitimacy, they represented resistance through endurance and self-sacrifice.

Violence within prisons is usually seen as either a response to prison conditions or as a result of values imported into the prison upon incarceration (Harer and Steffenmeier 1996). For paramilitary prisoners, it was arguably a case of both. They entered prisons as members of secret groupings who had already been engaged in violent acts, and their reaction to incarceration often depended on the prevailing conditions within the prison. When the contest with the authorities was intense, the use of violence was an assertion that the war or struggle went on, that the prisons represented one battleground of that war and that prisoners were willing to continue engaging in organized acts of extreme violence in pursuance of their own objectives. Violence against prison staff or other inmates (normally from opposing factions) is a direct challenge to the prison authorities, it is a direct appropriation of power. The state's monopoly on the use of force is challenged in a place which should be the zenith of the state's capacity for power and control. Prisoners who use violence, particularly against prison staff, demonstrate 'a refusal to be ground down into social submission' (Abbott 1981: p. xii). Violence is resistance through infliction.

Finally prisoners' attitudes towards law and its usage reflected the need for pragmatism in resistance, of ultimately showing willingness to utilize and transform the discourses of the dominant to a form of

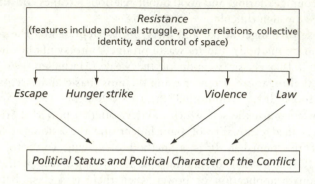

Fig. 2.1. Outline of strategies of resistance

resistance. As Fanon (1959) has argued, the necessities of violent political conflict can have radicalizing effects on the 'resisters', encouraging them to remain tactically flexible as the contours of conflict change.[29] In the context of Northern Ireland, such flexibility was underlined by the changing attitudes of politically motivated prisoners from non-recognition of the courts in the 1970s to a heightened awareness of the potential for law as praxis, law as dialogue both inside and outside the political movement, and law as a challenge to legitimacy with prisons. Changing attitudes towards law represented resistance as dialogue, tactical innovation, and appropriation of the tool of the dominant.

These four resistance techniques are utilized, as suggested in Fig. 2.1, to highlight the most important features in the Northern Ireland context. To recap, resistance for politically motivated prisoners has been characterized by a number of interrelated features. The central characteristics have been the notion of resistance as political struggle; the constant challenge to the power of the prison authorities; the collective nature of the resistance process; and a persistent struggle

[29] Fanon demonstrates how the Algerian revolutionaries used and adapted the discourses of the dominant in their struggle for independence. The French encouraged Algerian women to discard their traditional veil, thus wearing the veil became an act of defiance. However, as the movement of men became restricted, women were needed to carry arms, munitions, and messages. Consequently many Algerian women went unveiled, and moved around with minimal molestation from French soldiers given their apparent assimilation into Europeanness (Fanon 1959: 51–9).

concerning control over space within the prisons. There have been variation over time, between individuals and between factions, ambiguities, acquiescences, co-options, and defeats. None the less, these features have remained the essence of the resistance process.

3

Escape: Resistance as Ridicule

Introduction

In this chapter I want to explore in some detail the role played by the planning and attempting of escapes as a strategy of resistance for politically motivated prisoners in Northern Ireland. I will examine the notion of escape as ideological conflict, the historical antecedents of escapes by Republicans and the different phases and types of escape during the current conflict, and finally the differences in attitudes to escape between Loyalists and Republicans.

For those imprisoned as a result of a political conflict and who consequently regard themselves as prisoners of war, the duty to escape has often been identified as one of the defining characteristics which sets them apart from other prisoners (Prungh 1955), part of the broader campaign of thwarting the enemy (Walzer 1969). For prisoners who fall within the terms of the additional Protocols to the Geneva Conventions or the definitions established in extradition law (Keightley 1993) and whose political status is clear, the duty to escape may be viewed as a logical by-product of incarceration. For those whose assertion of political motivation is rigorously contested by the state, escapes and escape attempts give added impetus to the ideological and practical 'claims making' (Best 1989) of that status.

The reasons for a prisoner's desire to escape may be varied and complex. At a basic level, it is the natural desire of anyone incarcerated to desire their freedom. As Mathiesen (1965: 75) suggests, prisoners may seek to escape because they see themselves in the prison context as 'deplorably deprived as compared with the (often exaggerated) pleasures of the outside'. Amongst politically motivated inmates, as Cohen and Taylor argue (1972: 129), such a prisoner is expected to 'try to escape, join with his fellows in making life as difficult as possible for the authorities'. For prisoners held in captivity in concentration camps or prisoner of war camps the organization of underground networks and planning and execution of escapes have been described as crucial to the inmates' survival (Swedberg 1997, Dear 1997). Such prisoners explained their desire to escape because they were bored, seeking adventure, wanting to see loved ones, annoy their captors, contribute to the war effort as well as because they saw it as their duty as POWs (Vance 1993: 675–6).

In the context of Northern Ireland, Republican prisoners in particular were keen to stress their perceived duty to escape. As one former IRA Officer Commanding told the author:

It is the duty of every Republican POW to escape if possible and to resist any attempts at criminalising them or undermining their status as political prisoners while incarcerated . . . Escapes demonstrate to the British that they cannot imprison our struggle, that it continues behind the prison walls and that despite the might of their war machine, their supposedly escape proof prisons, with determination, skill and patience, our Volunteers can defeat them.[1]

Whilst there are some similarities in the attitudes to escape experienced by interstate combatants such as allied prisoners of the Second World War, it is important to acknowledge a number of caveats. Firstly, of course the political nature of the detention of terrorist prisoners in Northern Ireland was a highly contentious issue throughout the conflict. Secondly, as is discussed below, there were variances in the attitudes to escape amongst Northern Ireland's paramilitary prisoners, in particular between Loyalist and Republican prisoners. Thirdly, successful escapers from a Northern Ireland prison have faced a very different experience from a Second World War prisoner. While they may well have been treated as a hero in their own community, in practice a successful escape meant a life spent on the run, normally away from home and family, perhaps living under an assumed name in another jurisdiction fearful of capture and extradition (Dillon 1992) or returning full time to the military campaign, without having a home base.

However, despite these obvious differences, I believe that the POW analogy is a useful one in that it does offer an insight into the remarkable persistence and success rate of IRA jailbreaks during the current conflict. Whatever the debate over the political nature of their detention, they have regarded themselves as political prisoners, they have viewed themselves as continuing their struggle while in prison, and they have seen their duty to escape as a clear assertion of their status.

---

[1] Interview with former IRA Officer Commanding, HMP Maze, 12 Sept. 1994.

Escape as Ideological Conflict

The escape from prison of politically motivated prisoners goes to the very heart of the ideological struggle between the combatants and the state. The combatant organization which is organizing an escape, which in the case of Northern Ireland was mostly the IRA (Coogan 1987, Bishop and Mallie 1987), is willing to commit disproportionately large numbers of volunteers and resources than would normally be the case for an ordinary military operation.

The state for its part sees escape as an affront to its ideological and political position in the conflict. If, other than killings by the security forces, imprisonment becomes the ultimate sanction which the state can impose on its enemies then escape undermines any claim to coercive omnipotence by the state. It represents an actual and symbolic loss of power. While the state will inevitably stress the ruthless and dangerous nature of the threat arising from the escapees, a well organized, planned, and executed escape, more than any other action by the insurgent group, has the potential to instil a sneaking admiration in the most unlikely of places.[2] Like the insurgent organization, the state is willing to spend disproportionate amounts of time and resources in seeking the return of escaped prisoners, even if it means that they will in effect serve very little time in prison once returned.

I suppose it is a bit crazy when you think of the amount of money and staff time which we have devoted to trying to extradite escapers. None the less it is important for a number of reasons. It sends a message to those still inside that if you escape we will never stop trying to hunt you down. It is also important on an international level that you are seen to be taking a stand because let's face it escapes like the Maze are highly bloody embarrassing.[3]

From the 1970s to the 1990s the British government devoted considerable resources to securing the extradition of escaped Republican politically motivated prisoners from the Irish Republic, Europe, and

---

[2] In a remarkably candid interview on an Ulster Television documentary on the Maze escape of 1983, Sir James Hennessey who conducted the inquiry into the escape remarked 'I would refer to the Maze prison at that time as rather like Colditz during the War, an impregnable fortress . . . for these prisoners to have got control of their block, the H 7 block from which 38 escaped, in a matter of 20 minutes was absolutely staggering. For anyone to have achieved that, it must be regarded as a matter for congratulation.' Interview with Sir James Hennessey, *Unlocking the Maze*, *Counterpoint*, Ulster Television. Broadcast 22 Sept. 1993. Transcripts made available to the author by producer Chris Moore.   [3] Interview with prison governor, 12 Feb. 1996.

the United States (Farrell 1985, McElrath 1997, 2000). As is discussed below in the chapter on law and resistance, part of the reason for the tenacity of the British government's pursuance of such cases was the international platform which such hearings afforded to Republicans asserting that they could not be extradited because of the politically motivated nature of their defence (Broderick *et al*. 1995). In addition, however, as one senior prison official who gave evidence on behalf of the British government at a number of hearings told the author, 'there was a determination to show escapers that there was nowhere to hide'.[4] The extradition of escaped IRA prisoners from overseas was considered of such political importance during the conflict that, for example, it often appeared on the agenda for discussion between former British Prime Minister Margaret Thatcher and former US President Ronald Reagan (Kelly 1992). As McElrath (2000) argues, the struggles to extradite Irish Republicans have been a problematic issue for Anglo-Irish relations in particular for well over a century. The tradition of escapes by Irish politically motivated offenders from British prisons is considerably longer.

The Attitudes of Republican Prisoners Towards Escape

The tradition of Republican escapes is sometimes traced back as far as the Irish clan leaders Hugh Ruadh O'Donnell and Art O'Neil who escaped from their English gaolers in 1591 (Foster 1988: 10). Similar events were associated with the various armed uprisings of the nineteenth century such as escape by seven Fenian prisoners from their penal exile in Western Australia in 1868 (Bolton 1991: 300). In the twentieth century there were more than twenty separate escapes by Republican prisoners during the Anglo-Irish war between 1918–21 (O'Donoghue 1971) and over twenty IRA prisoners from Crumlin Road and Derry prisons in 1943 during the IRA's campaign of the Second World War (Coogan 1987: 238–40). Such endeavours are an intrinsic feature of Irish Republican ideology, celebrated in songs, poetry, and Republican historical texts.[5]

Sir James Hennessey, in his report which followed the mass escape of the thirty-eight IRA prisoners from the Maze prison in 1983, clearly

---

[4] Author's conversation with NIO official, 18 Dec. 1997.

[5] O'Donoghue's views are fairly typical of this tradition. 'The escapes of Irish political prisoners from British jails in this country and abroad are part of the thrilling story of the nation's long struggle for freedom' (O'Donoghue 1971: 34).

grasped the significance of escape to the Republican prisoners. His analysis is worth repeating.

The prison population [in HMP Maze] is totally dissimilar to the usual criminal recidivist population to be found in the nearest equivalent establishment in England & Wales. It consists almost entirely of prisoners convicted of offences connected with terrorist activities, united in their determination to be treated as political prisoners, resisting prison discipline, even if it means starving themselves to death, and retaining their paramilitary structure and allegiances even when inside. Bent on escape and ready to murder to achieve their ends, they are able to call upon the help of their associates and supporters in the local community and—though increasingly less frequently—to arouse the sympathy of the international community: they are able to manipulate staff and enlist the support of the paramilitary organisations in the process of intimidation. (Hennessey 1984: 59)

As Hennessey suggests, escape had a number of useful functions from the perspective of the prisoners and their organizations. It provided an opportunity to continue the struggle while in prison, giving the prisoners involved a focal point around which to plan and mobilize. Successful attempts, or even daring attempts which failed,[6] offered a wonderful opportunity for scoring a propaganda coup.[7] They also allowed valuable volunteers, often with considerable operational experience, to return to the military campaign.[8] Escapes may have involved considerable drains on the paramilitary organization on the outside. Such arrangements included providing the immediate logistical support for the escape, organizing transport and safe houses, and, more long term, in providing escape routes out of the jurisdiction. In a number of incidents, it also required the mobilization of larger numbers of armed volunteers than the IRA would

[6] 'Operation Tollan: In This Article Five of our Comrades tell the Story of An Tollan (the Tunnel) in Their own Words', *An Glor Gafa* (*The Captive Voice*) (Summer 1997).

[7] 'The propaganda value for us of the 1983 escape was enormous. We showed that the end of the hunger strikes had not beaten us. We had regrouped, we had waited and we had planned and pulled off the biggest prison breakout seen in Europe since World War Two from *the* [interviewee's emphasis] maximum security prison. It was brilliant for the morale of prisoners, volunteers on the outside, and the international supporters of the struggle and highly embarrassing for the Brits.' Interview with former IRA Officer Commanding, 12 Sept. 1994.

[8] Generally only those who had agreed to rejoin the military campaign have been permitted to escape. This rule was apparently waived with regard to the 1983 escape (because of the propaganda value of having larger numbers of prisoners escaping), however, three of the escapers were later killed and several others captured while 'on active service' (*Sunday Tribune*, 26 Sept. 1993).

normally have been permitted.[9] However, such considerations have consistently been outweighed by the opportunities presented by escape.

In the following section I offer brief narrative details on some of the most significant escapes and attempted escapes by Republican prisoners since 1969. Considerable efforts have been made to crosscheck the narratives of the escapes and attempted escapes by use of the limited academic, historical, and official texts, contemporaneous newspaper accounts, and, where possible, interviews with some of the protagonists, their legal representatives, and prison staff and management. The escapes detailed below are by no means a comprehensive account. Rather they represent an attempt to offer sufficient detail regarding some of the escapes and attempts which occurred over the past thirty years in order to inform some of the broader discussions concerning the role of escapes as a form of resistance.

Escapes in the Early 1970s: Opportunism and Adventure

The escapes and attempts of the early 1970s were characterized by prisoners taking advantage of the opportunities presented and what one former Official IRA prisoner described as 'the sense of adventure' which characterized the attitude of many of the young protagonists in the early days of the conflict.[10] In a prison system which was struggling with an inmate population rise from 600 to over 3,000 in three to four years, considerable lapses of security were inevitable.

In September 1971, five IRA prisoners attempted to escape from Crumlin Road prison by using ropes fashioned from bedsheets. They climbed to the top of the outside wall but were intercepted by a British army patrol. The escape had been designed to coincide with an IRA bomb planted at the outside wall but the timing went awry when the inmates heard an unconnected nail bomb go off on the nearby Antrim Road and mistook this for the signal (McGuffin 1973: 101). One month later, nine prisoners escaped from the same prison after rope ladders were thrown over the perimeter wall. Dressed in football gear, they climbed over the wall, through the already cut perimeter wire, and into awaiting cars. Two of the prisoners were captured in Omagh but the

---

[9] Interview with former IRA prisoner, 14 June 1996.
[10] Interview with former Official IRA prisoner, 15 July 1996.

other seven appeared the following week at a press conference in Dublin.

In January 1972 seven detainees escaped from the *Maidstone* prison ship moored in Belfast harbour. The ship, described by one former inmate as 'a stinking, cramped, unhealthy, brutal, and oppressive floating sardine tin' (Adams 1990: 12), had been used to house internees after the introduction of internment. Having observed the movements of seals through the barbed wire in the water, the prisoners greased themselves in butter and oil to protect them from the cold, sawed through the porthole bars into Belfast Lough, and swam the 400 yards to shore. Having been delayed in setting off, they missed their rendezvous, entered a bus station, and, dressed in their underwear, stole a bus and drove to the nearby Markets area. Abandoning the bus, the prisoners were given clothes and transport by the local people and drove off to West Belfast.[11] Their exploits were quickly recorded in a Republican ballad.[12] They appeared two weeks later at a Dublin press conference and were lauded by Republicans as IRA heroes. As one of the escapees told the author:

Well the purpose of the press conference was to show we had done it, thank the people of the markets for their help and give a boost to Republican morale and of course, a boot up the arse to the Brits.[13]

In 1976 several IRA prisoners were arrested and charged with attempted escape having dressed as British soldiers, and begun to head for the main gate from Cage 16 in the Compounds at Long Kesh. Having been taken to Newry Courthouse awaiting trial for the offence, the prisoners noticed that the grille was loose and ten of them escaped by prising it open (MacUileagoid 1996: 162).

However, not all of the successful Republican escapes were executed by IRA members. In 1976, nine special category INLA prisoners tunnelled out of Long Kesh, for a distance of 40 feet from under a prison

---

[11] Interview with former IRA prisoner and one of the *Maidstone* escapees, 9 Oct. 1998.

[12] 'It was on a Monday Evening when just to cause a lark
They said "lets go and have a swim while its nice and dark"
They swam across the water right to the other side
And the Belfast Corporation gave them a bus to ride.
They drove down the Markets which isn't very far.
And there the local people, well you know what they are.
They dressed them up in fine clothes, the colours they were gay
And before the army could get there, the boys were far away.'
Extracts from 'The Magnificent Seven' by 'Wolfhound' (reprinted in MacUileagoid 1996: 27).

[13] Interview with former IRA prisoner and *Maidstone* escapee, 9 Oct. 1998.

hut. Once they reached the prison fence they cut through the wire using tools stolen from the prison workshop, and climbed over the wall (Holland and McDonald 1994: 102). One was recaptured a short time later in a field eight miles from the prison and a second while trying to hitch-hike on the nearby M1. Two were never recaptured and appeared on a BBC *Panorama* programme in 1982 filmed in Dublin.

The early 1970s also saw a number of significant escapes and escape attempts in the Irish Republic. In October 1973, an IRA unit hired a helicopter and forced the pilot to fly to Mountjoy prison, landing in the exercise yard of the jail (Bishop and Mallie 1987: 245–6). Three senior Republicans including Seamus Twomey (who had been Chief of Staff of the Provisional IRA before his arrest and resumed the position after his escape) climbed on board. Twomey later gave the obligatory interview in *Der Spiegel* (Bowyer Bell 1979: 401). Similarly in Portlaoise prison in August 1974, following the discovery of a tunnel into the prison the previous June, nineteen IRA prisoners blew their way out of the prison using tiny amounts of smuggled gelignite. In the ensuing confusion, which included the prison guards and the prisoners' contacts on the outside, the prisoners escaped on foot and in commandeered cars.[14]

The Risks Involved in Escapes and Escape Attempts

The risks and stresses involved in attempting to escape were obvious to prisoners who embarked on any attempt. As one former prisoner involved in a tunnel attempt in 1978/9 from the IRA compounds told the author:

I was working on this tunnel, I was working at the face of it, we weren't shoring it up because wood was very scarce. It was very claustrophobic, there was no air in it, it was like breathing moisture. It was about 30 feet long. We had a lighting system in it, and if any screws came along we turned the lights off. You see when you turned those lights off, it was the nearest thing to being buried alive you will ever get. It is below you, and you can feel it above your head. I was lying at the face of it, I don't know it felt like forever like but it was probably about two minutes. You see when the lights came on, I backed the whole way up. OOOOh! I said that's fuckin' me. I am not going back into that tunnel. Fucking Charles Bronson effort it was.[15]

---

[14] Interview with former IRA prisoner, 15 June 1994.
[15] Interview with former IRA prisoner, 5 Aug. 1998. The reference to Charles Bronson here refers to the claustrophobic character 'Danny the Tunnel King' played by Bronson in *The Great Escape* film set in a Second World War prisoner of war camp.

Quite apart from the natural hazards and difficulties, escapers have also faced the risk of being shot by passing security forces or the army who have traditionally been given the responsibility of guarding the perimeters of Northern Ireland prisons. In November 1974, IRA prisoner Hugh Torney was shot dead in disputed circumstances by British soldiers as he and thirty-two others emerged from a 65-yard tunnel from the compounds at Long Kesh.[16] In June 1981 as eight escaping IRA prisoners (some disguised as prison officers) passed the final gate of Crumlin Road prison, the alarm was sounded and a gun battle between the prisoners and a number of police patrols ensued.[17] No one was injured and the prisoners escaped in a waiting car and on foot after one prisoner dressed in a prison officer uniform stood up and ordered the police to stop firing (Dillon 1992: 124–9).[18]

In the same prison in 1991, IRA prisoners abandoned a major escape attempt after the expected logistical support from outside the prison wall did not materialize. According to court papers examined by the author,[19] the plan had been that an IRA unit would drive a large digger, with a bomb in the front bucket, through the exterior wall of the prison. Simultaneously prisoners on the inside, armed with small firearms would blow the inner walls with small quantities of Semtex high explosives which had been smuggled into the prison and escape in cars which were waiting outside the prison. The security forces around Belfast were to have been previously stretched by an elaborate series of hoax and real bomb threats at strategic locations throughout the city. The armed prisoners were waiting in the exercise yard, with the inner charges set, when the plan was abandoned because the digger failed to appear. In reading the papers from the subsequent trial, it is apparent

[16] *Republican News* (16 Nov. 1974), 'The Long Kesh Escape—As Told In Exclusive Statements By Some Of The Republican Prisoners Who Were Involved'.

[17] Sixteen IRA prisoners, including the eight preselected for escape, had requested visits from their legal representatives. Consultations were taking place in adjoining rooms when the prisoners produced small firearms and herded solicitors and staff into one room. The prison officers were stripped of their uniforms which the prisoners put on. They also removed the briefcases from the solicitors. Thus disguised, the prisoners passed through a series of gates, overpowering the guards as they went. Interview with former IRA prisoner, 15 June 1994.

[18] A number of the prisoners were later recaptured in the Irish Republic. In Dec. 2000 Secretary of State for Northern Ireland Peter Mandelson used the royal prerogative of mercy to ensure that these prisoners could return to Northern Ireland without fear of prosecution following the early release provisions of the Good Friday Agreement. *Belfast Community Telegraph* (29 Dec. 2000), 'Queen Lets Jail Break IRA Men Go Home'.

[19] Court papers made available to the author by Belfast solicitor firm.

that the authorities had become aware of the plan, sabotaged the digger, and had deployed specialist units outside the prison to intercept the prisoners as they left the prison. A number of prisoners who took part in the planning of the escape, the prisoners' legal representative, and a prison officer interviewed by the author have all alleged that a 'shoot to kill' operation was planned in order to ambush the senior IRA figures who had been chosen to lead the escape,[20] regardless of the danger in which it placed prison staff.[21]

Prison Escapes in England

Given the logistical difficulties of providing organizational support other than occasional weapons, escapes and attempted escapes in Britain appear to have relied heavily upon the prisoners themselves rather than the organization on the outside. As one prisoner who served over twenty years in British prisons told the author, 'I suppose there was a feeling that we were more on our own, we certainly didn't want to be a drain on resources on the outside.'[22] Given such difficulties, the considerably fewer numbers in English prisons, and the suggestion that Irish politically motivated prisoners were subject to the most stringent of security measures (Borland, King, and McDermott 1995), it is perhaps unsurprising that there have been few successful escape attempts.

In 1981 IRA prisoner Gerard Tuite escaped from Brixton prison, together with an ordinary English prisoner by drilling through three cells with a crowbar fashioned in the prison and throwing a home-made ladder over the perimeter wall (Bean 1994: 197).[23] Successful escapes such as Tuite's clearly boosted the morale of prisoners beyond the ranks of the Republicans. A former Italian politically motivated

---

[20] Interview with former IRA prisoner, 1 June 1997, interview with prisoners' solicitor, 16 Jan. 1996.

[21] 'I have no doubt that they knew all about the escape plans but didn't bother to fill the prison officers on the ground in on it. Our people were expendable so long as they could get the Provos [IRA] they were after. Of course they were setting up a shoot to kill.' Interview with Prison Officers Association 17 Sept. 1996.

[22] Interview with former IRA prisoner who served life sentence in English prisons, 17 Jan. 1996.

[23] Tuite had in fact been arrested along with Bobby Storey (later to command the 1983 Maze escape) for coming to London to organize the helicopter escape of yet another IRA prisoner, the senior Republican Brian Keenan who had been convicted of co-ordinating the bombing campaign in Britain (Bowyer Bell 1993: 559).

prisoner, held in the same wing as Tuite, told the author of his memory of Tuite's escape thus.

The night before he escaped he went around the wing giving his things away. He gave me a load of newspapers and told me he wouldn't be needing them, he was leaving the next day. I thought he meant being transferred so it was quite a shock when I heard he had escaped. I was very happy of course, and not just because of the newspapers . . .[24]

Ten years later two other IRA prisoners escaped from the same prison. Using a small calibre weapon which had been smuggled in a training shoe, the prisoners forced prison officers to hand over their keys, placed a wheelbarrow on a dog kennel and climbed over the perimeter fence. They then hijacked a passing car, shooting the motorist in the thigh, and escaped (Bowyer Bell 1993).

The Maze Escape

The most notorious escape of Republicans occurred on 25 September 1983 when thirty-eight IRA prisoners broke out of HMP Maze in the largest mass escape of serious offenders in British prison history. The plan was the culmination of over a year of planning which had seen an orchestrated campaign within the prison by the IRA leadership to appear to co-operate with the prison authorities.[25] The prisoners gradually encouraged the staff into a more lax attitude to security, particularly in H7 where the escape was to originate. This included permitting the IRA leadership to become orderlies which allowed them access to all parts of the prisons (thus gathering greater information on the layout of the prison), and enabled them to smuggle in a range of small weapons (Hennessey 1984: 7).

On a signal from MacFarlane, the prisoners overpowered the officers, shooting and injuring one of them in the face after he attempted to raise the alarm. The prison officers were forced to remove their

[24] Interview with former Primea Linea prisoner, 15 Jan. 1995.
[25] 'I would have helped screws with their crosswords, talked to them about football, etc., etc. . . . some people were maybe a bit taken aback that so soon [after the 1981 hunger strikes], we were moving into this new regime, that we were being a bit too "palsy walsy" with the screws . . . but obviously you can't tell people that the only reason we're doing this is that there is a lot of equipment coming in here, that there is an escape coming up.' Interview with Brendan 'Bik' MacFarlane, IRA Officer Commanding in the Maze during the 1981 hunger strikes and one of the leaders of the escape in *Unlocking the Maze* (1983). For a more in-depth look at the conditioning of prison officers see Chapter 5 on violence and intimidation of prison officers.

uniforms and hand over their keys and the prisoners took control of H Block 7. Many of the prisoners not involved in the escape did not actually realize what was happening.[26] Their plan was to await a delivery truck, and squeeze as many prisoners as possible into the truck. The driver would then have a gun trained on him and be forced to drive the van out the main gate. However, the truck was late so having passed through the inner gates unmolested the truck stopped at the main gate just before a new shift of prison officers arrived for work. The original plan was to take over the post at the gate lodge, open the gates, and allow the prisoners to leave in the truck or the prison officers' cars for which they had acquired keys (Dunne 1988: 162–5).

After they had overpowered the guards at the main gate, the prisoners had difficulty in opening the gate and were faced with the added problem of 'arresting' fresh officers as they arrived for work, tying them up, and guarding them. Eventually one prison officer broke from the lodge to raise the alarm; he was stabbed by a prisoner and later died of coronary arrest. Other officers were then stabbed, and, with the alarm raised, the prisoners piled out of the truck and the gate lodge and attempted to escape in hijacked cars and on foot.[27]

Thirty-eight prisoners escaped, twenty-one of them avoiding immediate recapture in the environs of the prison. Three were killed years later on 'active service', three were later arrested and charged with further IRA offences, three are awaiting extradition hearings in the USA, two were extradited from Holland (one since released), three successfully contested extradition hearings and are living in the Irish Republic, one was arrested 48 hours after the escape, one was successfully extradited from the Republic, and four have never been arrested and remain at large.[28]

One prison officer died, four others were stabbed, and two wounded by shooting. No prisoner was convicted of the murder of the prison officer. Lord Chief Justice Lowry, noting that the escape had been 'ingeniously planned and cleverly executed', concluded that the cause of James Ferris's death was not proven because of unreliable identification evidence from staff, and medical evidence that Mr Ferris had a serious coronary problem and had previous heart attacks and that his

---

[26] *Irish News* (23 Sept. 1993), 'The Key to Freedom'.
[27] *Sunday Tribune* (26 Sept. 1993), 'Escape from H Block Seven'.
[28] *Irish News* (25 Mar. 1997), 'Escape Attempt is Latest in History of Break-outs'.

wounds would not have caused serious incapacity or death in an otherwise healthy individual.[29]

The implications of the escape were considerable for the morale of the prisoners and equally damaging for the prison service and the politicians responsible for the prison service. One IRA prisoner who did not take part in the escape described the impact on morale within the prison and amongst Republicans generally as 'excellent—a poke in the eye for them and a real coup for us'.[30] Nicholas Scott, then minister in charge of prisons who subsequently resisted calls for his resignation, acknowledged that the escape constituted 'a major boost to the morale and propaganda of the IRA and their supporters'. In the subsequent report by Sir James Hennessey he described the prison as having poor security procedures, inadequately followed by staff, and recommended a radical overhaul of the prison security system (Hennessey 1984: 60–71).

As noted above, the escape had been facilitated by the understandable relaxing of the regime at the Maze, in contrast to protests which had gone before during the dirty protest and hunger strike era. In the wake of those protests, the prisoners had deliberately sought to improve relations with the prison staff, minimizing confrontation, maximizing co-operation. This was clearly misinterpreted by the authorities as evidence that the prisoners' desire for resistance had dissipated. As Bobby Storey, one of the leaders of the escape has argued:

Strategically and tactically we needed to break out of the wings, into the central mechanisms of the jail i.e. their workshops, their circle, areas where in an escape situation we would need access to . . . the NIO were determined in their criminalisation policy . . . they thought that Brendan MacFarlane [OC during the second hunger strike] offering himself as a kitchen orderly was too good an opportunity to miss, . . . there's Brendan MacFarlane, a broken Republican, they fell for it and they paid for it.[31]

[29] Court papers relating to the murder of prison officer James Ferris, and other charges relating to the escape from HMP Maze Sept. 1993, made available to the author by Belfast solicitors and Chris Moore, Producer UTV *Counterpoint*.

[30] Interview with former IRA prisoner, 11 Dec. 1996.

[31] Interview with Bobby Storey, IRA OC during the escape—unbroadcast extract from UTV *Counterpoint*, *Unlocking the Maze*, 1993, transcripts made available to the author by producer Chris Moore.

Post-Ceasefire Escapes and Escape Attempts

It became apparent after the first IRA cessation of violence in 1994 that the perceived duty to escape from prison when an opportunity presented itself appeared unfettered by the declaration. Nine days after the IRA declared their complete cessation of 'military' operations on 31 August 1994, five IRA prisoners and one British 'ordinary' cut through the wire fencing in the exercise yard, scaled an inner wall, cut through a further fence, and scaled the outer wire of the recently built Whitemoor prison in Cambridgeshire. The prisoners had been held in the prison's Special Secure Unit, in effect a prison within a prison. They had with them 30 feet of home-made rope ladder, a home-made metal clamping device to clamp to the top of the wall, and two small loaded pistols. One prison officer was shot by a prisoner sitting on top of the wall as he attempted to tackle the last two prisoners ascending the rope ladder.

As the prisoners ran from the perimeter wall they were chased by prison officers with dogs and attempted to fire on them but the gun jammed whereupon the prisoners threw pepper at the dogs. They were all captured within 90 minutes, with the help of a thermal imager. In a subsequent search of the prison, prison staff found a quantity of Semtex explosives which had not been used in the escape (Woodcock 1994). The attitude of Republicans to this escape (in which firearms were discharged) in light of the 31 August 1994 ceasefire is instructive. While the use of firearms arguably constituted a breach of a ceasefire (to which Republicans and Loyalists adhered to a remarkable degree compared to the previous years of violence until the IRA ended the first ceasefire on 9 February 1996), none of the senior Republicans interviewed by the author was willing to criticize the actions of the prisoners. The views of one former prisoner who served over twenty years in England were typical.

I suppose it could have happened that there were communication difficulties with the prisoners in England, or that they didn't think escapes came within the definition of 'military operations' specified in the August cessation or that the lads had been planning it for some time and they just thought they would go for it . . . while the shooting may have been a bit politically embarrassing for a short time, there is no way that I would criticize or condemn Republican prisoners for trying to escape under any circumstances.[32]

---

[32] Interview with former IRA prisoner, 17 Jan. 1996.

In March 1997, three months before the IRA reinstated their ceasefire, a tunnel was discovered running from H 7 in the Maze to within 30 metres of the perimeter fence.[33] The prisoners had managed to tunnel 40 metres from the block, had shored the tunnel with wood, and installed an electric lighting system using computer cables. They had also deposited between 30–40 tonnes of soil in a number of cells, a fact which served to underline the absence of effective cell searches on the wings.[34] Having embarked on the enterprise with 'the backing of the Army [IRA] at the highest level' the tunnel was uncovered when the prisoners raised the level of tunnelling to compensate for water seepage, and an irreparable collapse resulted in discovery by prison staff.[35] Gerry Kelly, speaking on behalf of Sinn Fein, reiterated to the press that 'it is the duty of every Republican prisoner to escape'.[36]

In December 1997, four months after the renewal of the IRA ceasefire, IRA prisoner Liam Averill escaped from the Maze by dressing up as a woman visitor. From 1994 the prison authorities had permitted Christmas parties in the Maze where prisoners' children came and spent the day in the prison and from 1996 the children were accompanied by their mothers.[37] The subsequent report which examined the

[33] *Irish Times* (25 Mar. 1997*a*), 'Maze Governor's Resignation Sought After Tunnel Found'.
[34] *Irish Times* (25 Mar. 1997*b*), 'Rubble Noticed in Maze Cells After Tunnel Find' *Guardian* (25 Mar. 1997), 'Who Runs the Maze?'
[35] *An Glor Gafa* (Summer 1997), 'Operation Tollan: In This Article Five of our Comrades tell the Story of An Tollan (the Tunnel) in Their own Words'.
[36] *Irish Times* (25 Mar 1997*c*) 'Republican Prisoners See Escape as Their Duty'. Kelly's biography as a leading Republican is worth offering in brief, not least because it underlines the significance of escape and status within the Republican movement. He joined the Fianna (junior wing of the IRA) in 1971, was arrested and given a two-year sentence, escaping from St Patrick's Detention Centre in Dublin, joined the IRA, and became active again. He was arrested in 1973 for the bombing of the Old Bailey and New Scotland Yard and attempted to bluff his way past Special Branch, who were waiting at the airport, disguised as a businessman. He was caught trying to escape from Wormwood Scrubs as he clambered over the final wall in 1973, again in Lagan Valley Hospital (after his transfer to Northern Ireland) in 1977, and again in the Maze prison. In Musgrave Park Hospital in 1982 he was spotted using a bolt cutter and screwdriver to cut though the perimeter fence by a nurse who informed the authorities. In 1983 he was one of the leaders of the successful Maze escape and remained at large until his capture by the Dutch authorities in 1986. He, along with senior Republican and Sinn Fein Vice-President Martin McGuinness, represented the Republican movement in secret negotiations with the British government between 1990 and 1993. In June 1996 he was arrested at an anti-Orange march demonstration and escaped from custody, making his way to a local house where his handcuffs were removed with a grinder. In 1998 he was elected as a Sinn Fein Assembly member for North Belfast and was one of their key negotiators of the Good Friday Agreement.
[37] *Irish Times* (12 Dec. 1997), 'IRA Man's Escape from the Maze is a Hiccup, says Hume'.

circumstances of the escape concluded that 'the laxity in procedures may, in part, have resulted in a perception amongst staff that there was a tacit agreement with all the factions in the jail that the privilege of parties would not be abused' (Narey 1998: 12) Narey concluded, however, that such a view was mistaken. The accusations that his escape constituted a breach of the ceasefire, or at the very least a breach of trust regarding the family visit, were dismissed by Sinn Fein.[38] When questioned about this escape, the day before his historic first meeting with British Prime Minister Tony Blair, Gerry Adams declared: 'While there are prisoners, there will be prisoners who try to escape. I tried it myself. Liam Averill succeeded where I didn't. Good luck to him.'[39] Averill's escape was followed by the customary exclusive interview with *An Phoblacht*, the Republican newspaper.[40]

It is clear from these instances, two of which occurred while the IRA was on ceasefire (and the other which might not have been completed until after the July 1997 cessation), that the perceived duty to escape supersedes decisions to halt 'armed struggle'. At one level, as was argued by Unionist politicians and commentators, this could be interpreted as an indicator of Republicans' lack of sincerity in halting violence.[41] At another level, it could be argued that the perceived duty is so ideologically ingrained amongst the prisoners, so key to their survival and resistance within the prisons, that it may go beyond the particular political or paramilitary configuration of a given era, even when a peace process appeared to be emerging.[42]

---

[38] A Republican spokesperson interviewed regarding this point was noticeably careful to draw distinctions between the Christmas Home Leave Scheme, for which an agreement had been reached between the prisoners and the authorities that all prisoners would return, and this scheme for which they claimed no such agreement had been reached. Interview with Mitchel McLaughlin, Sinn Fein Chairperson, BBC Radio Ulster, 12 Dec. 1997.

[39] *Irish News* (12 Dec. 1997), 'Mother Defends her Maze Escaper Son'.

[40] *An Phoblacht* (8 Jan. 1998), 'How the Audacious Escape was Done: First Interview with Liam Averill'.

[41] *Irish Times* (12 Dec. 1997), 'IRA Man's Escape from the Maze is a Hiccup, says Hume'.

[42] The author attended a large gathering in Mar. 1996 where a number of professional agencies, human rights groups, interested individuals, and Republican prisoners' families met to discuss various tactics to increase pressure on the British government to transfer Irish prisoners from Britain. At that meeting a senior figure from the Northern Ireland Probation Service suggested that since some of the government's objections to transfer were based on security grounds, perhaps the Republican prisoners seeking transfer should give an undertaking not to attempt to escape. The suggestion was met with a mixture of derision and anger from the families with one elderly lady concluding (to rapturous applause from the families) that 'her son would cease to be a Republican if he was to give an undertaking not to escape'.

Loyalist Prisoners' Attitude Towards Escape

Loyalist prisoners have, by and large, not engaged in escapes or escape attempts with anything like the same commitment or regularity as their Republican counterparts. The only successful Loyalist escape attempt of which I have been able to find evidence was the escape from Crumlin Road Magistrates Court by a member of the Ulster Defence Regiment (locally recruited regiment of the British army) charged with loyalist paramilitary offences. Sammy Tweed, later dubbed 'Super Tweed' by East Belfast graffiti artists, escaped from the court after a crowd of Loyalist sympathizers invaded the court and he was able to slip away in the ensuing confusion. He was never recaptured. An attempted escape from Compound 16 by UDA prisoners was thwarted in 1973 when the tunnel was discovered (Challis 1999: 64) and a further UDA attempted escape by two prisoners in 1984 ended in tragedy when one of them was accidentally killed (NIPS 1985: 9).[43]

As has been noted elsewhere, there are a number of explanations for the behaviour of Loyalist prisoners once incarcerated by the state for which they were fighting. These can be grouped under three headings, the nature of the recruits to Loyalist paramilitaries, the ambivalence of their ideological attitudes to escape, and a combination of logistical aptitude and philosophical attitudes.

Firstly, as has been previously noted, some of the literature on Loyalist paramilitaries suggests a lower calibre of recruits amongst the Loyalist paramilitaries in comparison to their Republican counterparts (Boulton 1973, Nelson 1984, Dillon 1989). Bruce, in the most thorough analysis of Loyalist paramilitarism, has suggested that the Loyalist paramilitaries generally recruited those who were not acceptable to the 'legitimate' security forces.[44] Escapes from high security prisons require high levels of planning and sophistication, arguably qualities which are not required for the majority of Loyalist military

[43] They had attempted to escape by concealing themselves in a refuse bin, hoping to be brought to freedom by the refuse truck. However, when one of them, Benny Redfern, was tipped into the back of the truck he was crushed to death by the machinery in the bin lorry and his screams alerted the prison staff who captured his colleague (MacUileagoid 1996: 169).

[44] 'The state and the pro-state terror group recruit from the same population. The Crown forces have the advantage of being legal, respectable and paying well . . . An East Antrim Protestant who feels moved to "do something about the IRA" can join the UDR [local regiment of the British army, now called the RIR] or RUC; A West Belfast Catholic who wishes to drive out the colonial oppressor has only Republican terrorism' (Bruce 1992: 272–3).

actions.[45] It is perhaps not surprising that there have been so few successful or unsuccessful escape attempts by Loyalist prisoners over the past twenty-seven years.

Perhaps of equal significance is the ideological attitude to escape amongst Loyalist prisoners. As has been previously stated, Loyalist prisoners as members of a pro-state paramilitary group had a complex relationship with the prison authorities which represented the state for which they perceived themselves as having fought. As such, while they paid lip-service to the concept of being prisoners of war, they did not appear to feel the duty of escape so sharply as Republicans.

Loyalist prisoners were imprisoned by the state for which they were fighting. They perceived themselves as having been *driven* to use political violence because of the inadequacies of the state's response to the threat from Republicans. They appeared more ready to accept the fact that they had broken the law and must pay for their crimes, at least while the conflict was ongoing. They appeared to feel that their loyalty was not sufficiently recognized.[46] As is noted above, escape is the most direct challenge to the authority of the state which can be mounted by prisoners. It is part of a struggle of contested legitimacy and authority. Loyalist prisoners by and large did not contest the authority of the state.[47] Their opposition to criminalisation was, at least until the

---

[45] Bruce (1992: 276) also argues that 'In contrast to most IRA actions, which show a great deal of planning, many Loyalist "moves", especially in the early days, were haphazard and spontaneous, involved little more organisation than a few people drinking in a pub and deciding to go and do something. In contrast to IRA actions, a very high proportion of Loyalist killings were committed by people who had been drinking.' It should be acknowledged, however, that in the 1990s when Loyalist paramilitaries began 'outkilling' Republicans for the first time in the conflict, many of these attacks on Catholic bookmakers and pubs were characterized by more careful planning than similar Loyalist 'operations' in the 1970s and 1980s (see Cusack and McDonald 1997, Taylor 1999).

[46] 'Republican prisoners who are presently outwardly conforming are non-conforming rebels at heart yet they receive full privileges whereas Loyalist prisoners who are the real conforming prisoners, are classified as being non-conforming and subject to loss of more privileges.' Letter from a Loyalist prisoner to the *Ballymena Observer* (Feb. 1983), reproduced in Clayton (1996).

[47] One former Official IRA prisoner, who served a life sentence in the Irish Republic, compared the attitude of Loyalists to that of the Official IRA in the Irish Republic. 'I suppose you could say that some of the ambivalences in our relationship with the Free State government were analogous to the Loyalists in the North. We did not dispute the legitimacy of the 26 County government from the early 1970s onwards . . . and while we would have had campaigns around issues within the prisons, conditions and so on, and our status as political prisoners was not in question, escapes would have been frowned upon, partially because of the drain it would have presented on the movement,

1990s, much more sporadic and haphazard than that of Republicans, circumscribed by their ambivalent relationship to the state. As one former Loyalist prisoner put it:

When I went to prison I had to question a lot of things. I had fought to maintain my British identity and to protect my community from the IRA and yet everywhere I looked, the people who were imprisoning me, and abusing me, they were all wearing crown insignias . . . I was a political prisoner but I suppose it is more difficult for Loyalist prisoners than for Republicans since we are supposed to be on the same side as the state.[48]

The third explanation combines philosophical and logistical aspects of imprisoned Loyalist prisoners. One of the least developed features of prisoners' cultural attitudes in the sparse literature on Loyalism is the prisoners' view of themselves as coming from a highly individualistic culture, anti-collectivist, tolerant of a lack of centrally driven uniformity of actions and views.[49] This is often contrasted with Loyalist prisoners' view of Republican inmates as automatons who toe the party line, have rigid command structures, and leave little room for individuality amongst their prisoners. Allied to this view of self-reliance and individuality is a view that the logistics of escaping would place unnecessary and unrealistic demands on the organizations on the outside.[50]

In sum, therefore, due to the personnel of the prisoners recruited by

partially because our political wing was striving for respectability at the time but also, what was the point?' Interview with former Official IRA life sentenced prisoner, 15 July 1996.

[48] Interview with former UVF life sentenced prisoner, 14 Mar. 1994.

[49] In the formal interviews which I carried out for this book, and in my frequent professional contact with serving and former Loyalist prisoners, this was a view repeated on a number of occasions. At its crudest it was expressed in religious terms, comparing what some prisoners characterized as the centralized and authoritarian nature of the Catholic Church with the more diverse and tolerant attitudes of the Protestant Churches, and then linking this to the religion of the various factions of politically motivated prisoners.

[50] 'Every week I would have someone presenting me with an escape plan but I always knocked them back. My view was that most of them wouldn't work and that even if they did it would only cause an unnecessary drain on the organization on the outside. We weren't like the Provos, being able to slip people across a nearby border or out to the States . . . my view was that people should do their time and stay where they were.' Interview with former Officer Commanding Ulster Volunteer Force, HMP Maze, 14 Mar. 1994. A UDA prisoner, who had himself hatched a plan to escape which was rejected by the UDA leadership told the author: 'You look at the Maze escape, how successful it was, the Prods [Loyalists] could have done a better escape if they had wanted but they didn't want to. They didn't have anywhere to go, you could go to Millisle, Donaghadee [Loyalist areas on the Ards Peninsula in N. Ireland] or wherever, the Republicans could

Loyalist organizations and their ideological and logistical objections to escape, there have been very few successful or unsuccessful escapes by Loyalist prisoners.

Conclusion

Once imprisoned, physically removing oneself from domination is a direct challenge to the power of the prison authorities and the state. Escapes cause disarray amongst the enemy, they lead to official inquiries and calls for resignations (Barker 1998). They are a source of grudging admiration for daring and organization,[51] they drain resources and offer the potential for propaganda coups. In short, for politically motivated prisoners, they are a rich source of both material and symbolic resistance ridiculing the supposed omnipotence of the state.

While escapes by paramilitary prisoners cannot be broken down into distinct phases, it is possible to determine certain patterns over the period of the conflict.

Firstly, as previously discussed, the earlier escapes tend to be more opportunistic, relying upon the inevitable weaknesses in the physical security of a prison system which had increased its population from around 600 to 3,000 in three to four years, using untrained military staff in inadequately designed prisons. In Northern Ireland, from the opening of the H Blocks in 1976, built to be escape proof, the escape plans from both there and Crumlin Road tend to become less frequent, much more involved and organized, generally requiring substantial logistical support from the organization on the outside.[52]

go across the border. The Prods can't go across the border, you can't go to Britain. The only other alternative is probably South Africa which is a long way away.' Interview with former UDA prisoner, 24 July 1998.

[51] In her work on the fictionalized portrayal of criminality and imprisonment, Martha Duncan (1996) suggests a distinction between rationalized admiration and repressed admiration. In the former we may acknowledge admiration of deviants' behaviour because of the pureness of their motives or the unjustness of the law being broken, the weakness of the state being exposed or because it allows us to give vent to innate anti-authoritarianism by focusing upon elements of criminal acts which we may interpret as attractive (Duncan 1996: 72–82). In the latter, Duncan suggests, our repressed admiration may manifest itself in punitive zeal, our desire to 'bring criminals to justice' masking our own anti-social impulses (Duncan 1996: 112).

[52] It has been argued by some commentators that the period of the mid- to late 1970s saw the beginning of a similar spiral upwards in the sophistication of the security battle between Republican 'terrorists' in particular and the security forces. Such commentators argue that the 'terrorists' moved away from open pitched battles on the streets, produced

Secondly, for an organization which refined and honed guerrilla tactics over nearly thirty years, the IRA in particular has shown itself willing to take very large, even disproportionate risks in attempting to assist escapes. It could be argued that prison escapes provide an interesting illustration of where ideology leads a combatant organization to take greater risks than they would normally for a purely military operation. For example, Mallie and McKittrick (1996: 48–9) argue that in 1986, with their stockpiles of weapons considerably increased by new supplies from Libya, the IRA Army Council seriously considered what Republicans described as a 'Tet Offensive,' i.e. a switch from guerrilla tactics to committing large numbers of volunteers to standing and fighting pitched battles. The tactic was discussed but the idea abandoned because they considered it would not work militarily and because of the traditional reluctance of an organization used to guerrilla tactics to commit such large-scale numbers to the field. Despite such reservations, the IRA committed over 100 armed volunteers to manning the back-up logistics to the Maze escape,[53] more than any other single operation since the open battles with the security forces in the early 1970s (Dunne 1988).[54] In a mirror image of the state's determination to expend apparently disproportionate amounts of time and resources in the tracking and attempted extradition of escaped prisoners, clearly escapes, for Republicans, carried considerably greater ideological significance than their normal paramilitary activities.

Thirdly, while the organization has shown willingness to extend logistical support to organize escapes in Britain (and even to risk valued operatives dependent on the seniority of the prisoner, for example those arrested planning for the Brian Keenan escape), IRA jail breaks in Britain have generally been achieved or attempted in co-operation

---

more sophisticated bombs and imported better quality arms and explosives. In turn the authorities openly acknowledged the deployment of specialist units such as the SAS, attempted better co-ordination between the military, RUC, and MI5 and greatly improved their technical surveillance equipment. See Dillon (1990), Murray (1990, 1998), Urban (1992).   [53] Interview with former IRA prisoner, 14 June 1996.

[54] Gerry Kelly has suggested an additional reason for the level of support for the 1983 escape from the IRA was that 'a number of senior and very experienced and committed volunteers had recently been imprisoned. The leadership on the outside knew them well, valued their judgement on military matters, and trusted them to be circumspect in the handling of weapons. If they believed the escape was possible then the leadership on the outside was prepared to play its role in assisting its implementation' (cited in McKeown 1998: 216).

with ordinary British prisoners, with minimal external organizational support other than the smuggling of escape equipment and weapons.

Fourthly, as in the conflict generally, Republicans have shown willingness to use extreme violence in their determination to escape.[55] Prison officers have been shot, beaten, and one has been killed during escapes. Escaping prisoners have also shown willingness to hijack cars from members of the public, and to steal equipment and supplies.

Fifthly, for a range of practical and ideological reasons, Loyalist prisoners have been less willing to engage in escape and escape attempts.

Finally, in the numerous accounts of prison escapes read and listened to in researching this book, clear frameworks or templates have emerged regarding discourses on prison escapes in Northern Ireland. If we regard claims-making as a rhetorical process through which claims-makers make contentions to advance their position, status, or objectives (Best 1987, Ibarra and Kitsuse 1993), then escapes have clearly been a key terrain during the Northern Ireland conflict. Republican and Nationalist discourses[56] place much emphasis on prisoners' ingenuity, daring, courage, and triumph over overwhelming odds. These tend to be juxtaposed with the prison system's lethargy, repression, and administrative incompetence.[57]

Considerable efforts were expended to gain maximum propaganda advantage. Escaping Republicans appeared much more conscious than Republicans engaged on normal operations that their actions will be

---

[55] 'When we allocated weapons on the Maze escape, that was done on the basis that the volunteers who received them would be willing to do whatever was necessary in order to achieve the success of the operation, whatever was necessary.' Unbroadcast extracts from interview with Bobby Storey in UTV *Counterpoint* documentary, transcripts made available to the author by Chris Moore, producer.

[56] The *Irish News* is the main Nationalist daily newspaper in Northern Ireland which has consistently been highly critical of Republican violence and more supportive of the constitutional nationalist position articulated by the SDLP. None the less they have run large features on prison escapes over the years including a week-long series of major articles including photographs and interviews with the main protagonists in Sept. 1993 commemorating the tenth anniversary of the Maze escape (e.g. *Irish News,* 23 Sept. 1993).

[57] Such discourses are a familiar part of British popular culture with regard to the conflicts between Second World War prisoners of war and their captors. As Cohen and Taylor suggest 'the noble nature of such battles is enshrined in those innumerable British prisoner of war films where the heroes—everyone British—seem to spend all their time planning escapes, digging tunnels, making fun of their loutish captors and generally being a nuisance' (1972: 129).

subject to close scrutiny by the media.[58] Escapes and escapers are celebrated and eulogized in Republican popular culture. Escapers have
been variously nicknamed the Magnificent Seven (Maidstone), the
Crumlin Road Kangaroos (1972 Crumlin Road escapers), the Whirly
Birdies (Mountjoy helicopter escape), and the Great Escapers (a title
apparently shared by both the Crumlin Road 1981 escapers and the
1983 Maze escapers). Press conferences, folk songs and poems, secret
interviews with successful escapees, these all became familiar aspects
of the escape as icon of prison resistance and struggle.

On the other hand Unionist discourses concerning prison escapes
have tended to follow patterns of attributing blame, demanding ministerial resignations, and using the escape or escape attempt as illustrative of the laxness of regimes, the holiday camp nature of
imprisonment in Northern Ireland, and justification for crackdowns
on paramilitary prisons. Excluded from political power since the imposition of Direct Rule, and always predisposed to a security rather than
a political response to Republicanism (arguably until 1998 at least),
Unionist politicians have in effect adopted the mantle of a permanently
critical opposition (English and Walker 1996, Cochrane 1997). In such
criticism they are inevitably joined by prison officer representatives
complaining that 'warders' hands are tied by the NIO and its rules'.[59]

British government discourses on escapes, as evidenced in the various ministerial statements and escape-related official inquiries in
Northern Ireland, largely focus upon the managerial difficulties of
keeping such large numbers of organized and disciplined paramilitary
prisoners locked up and the danger they represented to the public
either in prison or at large. Paramilitary prisoners were considered
much more likely to escape than ordinary top security prisoners in
Britain (Hennessey 1984), and indeed more of a threat to prison staff
in British prisons (King and McDermott 1995: 134). While the British

---

[58] Perhaps one of the most deftly handled escape-related actions, in public relations
terms, was that of Brendan (Bik) MacFarlane after the Maze escape in 1983. MacFarlane
and a group of IRA men took over the home of a family in the process of their escape.
Having divined that the family were devout Christians, he made them all swear on the
Bible that they would not contact the RUC for 72 hours rather than tie them up. Having
taken a range of food, clothing, and camping equipment, MacFarlane wrote out and
signed an inventory of the items taken, gave it to the family and told them that they
would be recompensed if they presented the receipt containing his signature to the
Republican movement in Belfast (*Unlocking the Maze*, 1993).

[59] 'Another Great Escape: Greg Harkin on how IRA prisoner Liam Averill Walked Out
the Maze "Holiday Camp" ', *Ireland on Sunday* (14 Dec. 1997).

government's approach to managing paramilitary prisoners in Northern Ireland has changed over the period of the conflict (as discussed below), these concerns have remained the constant themes in response to escapes by such prisoners (Hennessey 1984, Narey 1998).

These competing discourses on escapes (as daring assertions of political motivation, underlining the need for a security crackdown and reflective of managerial difficulties) neatly encapsulate the positions of the key political protagonists in Northern Ireland.

As a strategy of resistance, escape encapsulates the key dynamics identified in Chapter 2. The conceptualization of escape as a duty is at its core, an assertion of the political status of the inmates. The planning and execution of escapes is the quintessential assertion of the political nature of the prison struggle. Escape represents a direct critique of the assumed power of the prison authorities. To be successful, escapes require considerable collective planning and endeavour. And finally with regard to space within prisons, while escapes may require control or at least access to areas within the prison (e.g. in the digging of tunnels, distribution of soil, or taking over key areas), by removing oneself from that environment, prisoners have been able to highlight the limitations of managerial strategies designed around the control of given physical space. Escape is in essence, resistance through ridicule.

4

Hunger Strike and Dirty Protest: Resistance as Self-Sacrifice

> There is a custom,
> An old and foolish custom, that if a man
> Be wronged, or think that he is wronged and starve
> Upon another's threshold till he die,
> The common people for all time to come,
> Will raise a heavy cry against the threshold,
> Even though it be the King's.
>
> **William Butler Yeats, *The King's Threshold***[1]

Introduction

The use of hunger strike as a strategy of resistance or protest in political, ethnic, and social conflicts is well documented. It has been used by suffragettes (Holton 1996, Cullen Owens 1984), pacifists (Erickson 1969) as well as human rights and student activists (Niming 1990). While hunger strikes have been employed by ordinary prisoners (Scraton, Sim, and Skidmore 1991: 17), organized protests to the death are more associated with politically motivated prisoners in particular. In South Africa (Alexander 1992, Buntman 1996), Palestine (Healy 1984), the former Soviet Union (Amnesty 1980), West Germany (Schubert 1986), and many other jurisdictions, politically motivated prisoners have long resorted to hunger strike as a way of pressurizing prison authorities.[2]

---

[1] This one-act play tells the story of Seanchan, poet in the court of King Guaire of Gort, who went on hunger strike to seek reversal of a decision to remove the traditional right of poets to sit in the King's Council. In 1922 Yeats noted 'When I wrote this play neither suffragette nor patriot had adopted the hunger strike, nor had the hunger strike been used anywhere as a political weapon' (quoted in Alspach 1979: 315–16).

[2] In his review of hunger strikes around the world Healy offers details of 52 countries which experienced hunger strikes between 1972–81, involving a total of 196 different hunger strikes, resulting in 23 deaths, 12 of them related to the Northern Ireland conflict (Healy 1984: 84–6).

Hunger strikes may be viewed as what Obafemi (1990) has referred to as 'committed theatre'. The violence against the self entailed in abstaining from food to the point of death offers a powerful critique of the assumed rationality of punishment and the axiomatic legitimacy of the punisher.

This chapter examines the significance of the tactic of hunger strike for politically motivated prisoners during the most recent phase of conflict in Northern Ireland. Given the historical and political importance of the 1980/1 hunger strikes in which ten Republican prisoners starved themselves to death, it will obviously focus considerably upon that period. However, background material is also provided on the historical significance of hunger strike for Republicans in particular. I will suggest that for prisoners who had been through the harrowing ordeal of the blanket and dirty protest between 1976 and 1980 following the removal of Special Category Status, and who were well cognizant of their prison history, recourse to the tactic of hunger strike was a logical and pragmatic step in resistance to the policy of criminalisation.

In addition, this chapter provides some analysis on the little reported phenomena of Loyalist hunger strikes during the years in question. While it is true that generally Loyalist prisoners have appeared less willing to use the tactic of hunger strike until death, none the less a number of significant developments have arisen from Loyalist hunger strikes and threats to hunger strike.

The structure of this chapter is as follows. A brief discussion on the notion of hunger strike as a means of protest; the historical context of hunger striking for Republicans; the dirty protest 1976–80, the 1980–1 hunger strikes and their social and political consequences; and an analysis of the protests of Loyalists and some discussion as to why these tend to be compared unfavourably to those of Republicans.

Hunger Strike: The Political–Historical Context

The act of self-starvation, whether expressly political or not, is in essence a clear protest at an existing set of conditions (Orbach 1986).[3] In Ireland, hunger striking as a form of protest against alleged

---

[3] Orbach argues, for example, that with regard to women suffering from anorexia nervosa: 'Like the hunger striker she [the anorectic] is in protest against her conditions. Like the hunger striker, she has taken as her weapon a refusal to eat. Like the suffragettes at the turn of the century in the United Kingdom or the political prisoners of the contemporary world, she is giving voice to her protest' (Orbach 1986: 1).

injustice or ill treatment can be linked to the indigenous Brehon Law which predates Christianity and the Norman invasion (Ginnell 1894). One legitimate form of redress under the Brehon Code was for the aggrieved individual to take up a place close to the dwelling of the alleged wrongdoer and begin to fast, thus drawing the attention and the potential for opprobrium from the remainder of the tuath or clann (Patterson 1989). Sweeney (1993: 422–3) argues that the fusion of that tradition, with Catholic notions of self-sacrifice, may be linked to the revival of Gaelic traditions which accompanied the rise in nationalism in the late nineteenth and early twentieth centuries and which pervaded the 1916 Rising. Similarly O'Malley (1990: 25) has argued:

Hunger striking fuses elements of the legal code of ancient Ireland, of the self denial that is the central characteristic of Irish Catholicism and of the propensity for endurance and sacrifice that is the hall mark of militant Irish nationalism.

While there are obvious merits in placing the phenomenon within its appropriate historical context, such accounts may become reductionist or deterministic unless they are accompanied by a real understanding of the social and political context in which they occur. For example, as O'Malley himself points out, the 1980/1 IRA hunger strikes were preceded by a lengthy and harrowing series of protests (the blanket, no wash, and dirty protest discussed below) and occurred in a context of demoralization and reduced options (O'Malley 1990: 28). In a situation where actions within the prison are laden with political significance to the conflict on the outside, and options narrowed, hunger striking may appear a rational, pragmatic, and strategic tactic to employ. Thus any exploration of hunger striking by paramilitary prisoners in the Northern Ireland conflict must be informed primarily by the political and military significance for prisoners of attempts at the criminalisation of their political motivation.

The analysis offered in this book will therefore focus more on the historical tradition within Republicanism of hunger striking and the pragmatism of embracing hunger strike as a tactic rather than upon the fact that the prisoners came from a Catholic background.[4] The

---

[4] Such an analysis does not denigrate or undervalue the significance of the Catholic faith in which a number (although not all) of the former Republicans interviewed professed to believe with varying degrees of commitment. However, in none of those interviews, or indeed in the literature written by prisoners themselves (e.g. Campbell, McKeown, and O'Hagan 1994, Sands 1998, McKeown 1998), did I come across

prisoners began the blanket, no wash, and dirty protests as a result of a series of reactive collective responses, without any clear strategic goal other than to resist criminalisation. The hunger strikes represented a rational and focused attempt by the prisoners to regain the momentum in the battle with the authorities and bring to an end a clearly ineffective and self-damaging form of protest.

Historical Background to Republican Hunger Strikes

As in other aspects of resistance within prisons, the tactic of hunger strike used by Bobby Sands and his colleagues in 1980/1 was a familiar one within Republican history. The modern use of the tactic by Irish Republican prisoners is normally traced to the period after the 1916 Rising (O'Malley 1990: 26).[5] Following the Rising, Republican prisoners were imprisoned in Dartmoor, Frongoch, and other British prisons. Eamon De Valera, one of the surviving leaders of the Rising, went on hunger strike in protest at the overly rigid application of prison rules (Coogan 1993: 81). He maintained his fast for four days until the governor conceded. Similarly, at Lewes where De Valera and other prisoners had been moved to a more relaxed regime, a further hunger strike was organized in May 1917 and a campaign of destruction of the cell fixtures and fittings which led to the prisoners being dispersed to a number of other prisons (Longford and O'Neill 1974: 52–60).

In September 1917 a Republican prisoner Thomas Ashe, one of forty Republican prisoners on hunger strike for political status, died from force feeding at the hands of the prison authorities in Mountjoy jail (Coogan 1993: 100). His funeral was attended by over 3,000 uniformed members of the Irish Volunteers walking openly through the streets of Dublin and an oration by Michael Collins was preceded by a volley of shots. The dramatic increase in support for Republicans following the executions of the 1916 leaders and the reaction to the death of Ashe made the authorities wary of creating further Republican martyrs.

convincing evidence that the prisoners were influenced to any great extent by Catholic notions of self-denial. I have therefore directed my analysis elsewhere. For an alternate view on the significance of the prisoners' Catholicism see O'Malley (1990).

[5] In fact James Connolly, later to become the socialist chief of the Irish Citizens Army and a key leader in the Rising, had previously employed the tactic in Sept. 1913. Connolly began a hunger strike when sentenced to three months for addressing a banned demonstration. His hunger strike lasted eight days until he was released from prison when the British Viceroy ordered his release following the pleadings of Connolly's wife Lillie (Morgan 1988).

Following Ashe's death, his fellow prisoners were transferred to Dundalk prison and the decision was taken to release them after a second hunger strike had begun. In 1919 eight Republican hunger strikes occurred, the most significant of which involved fifty prisoners in Mountjoy demanding political status. Once again, with the political authorities reluctant to create more martyrs and unsure of the time it took prisoners to die, the prisoners were released, much to the delight of Sinn Fein and the IRA (Sweeney 1993: 427).

By 1920 the government's resolve in dealing with hunger strikes had stiffened considerably. Previous concessions to prisoners were considered to have been mistakes which merely served to encourage the 'Sinn Feiners' (Hart 1998). The government had introduced martial law, the Defence of the Realm Act, and were determined to have a tougher policy in dealing with the Republicans generally (Campbell 1994). As a result, Terence MacSwiney, Lord Mayor of Cork city[6] and leader of the IRA in Cork, died in Brixton prison after 75 days on hunger strike (Hart 1998). His hunger strike had commanded significant press coverage around the world and elicited widespread sympathy from the most unlikely of quarters.[7]

Between August 1918 and October 1923 there were over thirty prison hunger strikes by Irish Republicans (Healy 1981, 1982). Despite the apparent failures of hunger striking in the latter part of the Anglo-Irish War, it remained an avenue of recourse for the anti-treaty faction of the IRA in the wake of the ensuing Irish Civil War. In 1923, six months after the formal cessation of hostilities, a hunger strike began in Mountjoy jail in Dublin amongst such prisoners (many of whom had been interned) aimed at securing their release and, potentially, providing a rallying cry for the Republican cause outside the prison (O'Donnell 1966, MacEoin 1980). In the spring of that year the pro-treaty government had secured a majority in the Dáil (Irish Parliament)

---

[6] MacSwiney's inaugural address as Lord Mayor of Cork has become one of the most cited in Republican history and was repeated often during the hunger strikes of the 1980s. 'This contest on our side is not one of rivalry or vengeance but of endurance. It is not those who can inflict the most, but those who can suffer the most, who will conquer' (cited in Metress 1983: 1).

[7] Sweeney (1993: 427–8) reproduces an account from the London *Times* from a correspondent whom he describes as 'almost certainly a Unionist sympathiser'.: 'Despite the government, the Lord Mayor of Cork has stirred imagination and pity . . . Alderman MacSwiney, a man whose name was unknown outside his own city, will, if he dies, take rank with Fitzgerald, with Emmet, and with Tone in the martyrology of Ireland—his memory infinitely more eloquent and infinitely more subversive of peace than he himself ever could be.'

for a bill permitting hunger strikers to die (Philips 1923). At one point the strike included about 8,000 prisoners, had spread to ten prisons and internment camps, and lasted a total of 41 days (Healy 1982). While most prisoners ceased within a month, over 200 continued and two died around the fortieth day. The rest of the prisoners ceased by 23 November.

The strike was widely viewed by contemporaneous and subsequent commentators and participants as having been a failure (MacManus 1933, O'Faolain 1939, Andrews 1979). Many Republicans were embittered at its collapse (Bowyer Bell 1979: 45). None the less most of the hunger strikers were released within a month as the government feared an outbreak of influenza amongst the prisoners (Cardozo 1979). With a supportive Dáil and a large apathetic public, it appears that the Free State government were prepared to allow prisoners to die. As McGuffin (1973: 137) has argued, 'from 1922 onwards hunger strikes were of value only when a government was likely to be embarrassed sufficiently by the death of a prisoner'. Such embarrassment was unlikely in the North after partition.

In 1940, this time under a Fianna Fail government,[8] IRA prisoners again began a hunger strike in Mountjoy prison in order to put pressure on the government that they be treated as political prisoners or released. That hunger strike had been preceded by a number of others where individual prisoners including a disabled veteran from the Anglo-Irish War had indeed been released as a result of hunger strikes (Coogan 1987: 185). De Valera, now Taoiseach (Prime Minister), was regularly taunted by the opposition.[9] De Valera's arguments were to a large extent replicated by Mrs Thatcher in the North some forty years later. He argued that while the government did not want the hunger strikers to die, 'prisoners would not be allowed to dictate the conditions under which they would be kept in detention'.[10] By 1946, three

[8] Fianna Fail was a party led by Eamon De Valera which was formed largely from the ranks of the anti-treaty IRA and went on to take their seats in the Dáil in 1927 and to head the government of 1932. A residue of militants remained who refused to recognize the 'partitionist' Dáil, vowed to continue the 'armed struggle' until the Republic was properly constituted, and retained the title of the IRA. Fianna Fail remains the largest political party in Ireland.

[9] The comments by William Norton, leader of the Irish Labour Party are typical: 'am I to now understand that hunger strikes or thirst strikes of this nature which were right in 1922 and 1923 are wrong in 1939?' Dáil Debate No. 77, 19 Nov. 1939, 831.

[10] Letter from Eamon De Valera to Mrs Dillon, mother of one of the hunger strikers, 2 Apr. 1940 (extract reprinted in Lee 1989: 223).

prisoners were to die on hunger strike in jails in the South (two in 1940 and one in 1946), and none was released or had the conditions of detention significantly altered as a result of the hunger strikes (Farrell 1976: 183, Lee 1989: 224).

In sum, the historical rationale for Irish Republican hunger strikes has generally evolved around either campaigns for release or recognition of the political status of prisoners. The normal variables in the hunger strike equation have been the determination or otherwise of the prisoners to see their protest through to the finish, British and Irish governments' oscillating between firmness and leniency (with firmness being the predominant trend from 1922 onwards), and the potential for residual sympathies for prisoners amongst large sections of Nationalist opinion who might not otherwise have supported the activities of militant Republicanism. The interaction of these variables were to set the scene for the hunger strikes of the modern campaign.

Hunger Strikes and Special Category Status in the Early 1970s

During the most recent period of political violence in Northern Ireland, the tactic of hunger strike was first used in the wake of internment introduced in August 1971. The poor planning and execution of the initiative (discussed in Chapter 8 below) led to large numbers of innocent civilians and civil rights activists being arrested and imprisoned without trial, as well as Republican activists (Spujt 1986). In 1972, as the Stormont Parliament was being prorogued, a solid food hunger strike by internees in protest at the deplorable conditions aboard the *Maidstone* prison ship moored in Belfast Lough was viewed by Republicans as having led to the ship being closed (Adams 1990: 12).

In May 1972 Billy McKee, leader of the IRA in Belfast and another senior Republican, Proinsas MacArt, led a number of Republican prisoners on hunger strike in Crumlin Road prison seeking political status (McGuffin 1973: 147). One week later five other male prisoners joined them on the strike, six Republican women in Armagh and forty internees at Long Kesh (Farrell 1976). When a false rumour spread that McKee had died, it set off a wave of hijackings and rioting in Nationalist areas of Belfast. On 14 June 1972 the IRA leadership, including Martin McGuinness, gave a press conference in Derry inviting the Conservative Secretary of State William Whitelaw to Free Derry,[11] and offering a suspension of hostilities during the discussions. While Whitelaw rejected the offer of a public meeting, he did offer a private meeting (Bishop and Mallie 1987). The IRA agreed to this on the condition that political status be granted to IRA prisoners and that Gerry Adams be released to take part in the negotiations. With McKee near death, the British government agreed to the IRA terms and the truce was established.

As Coogan (1980: 51) has argued, Special Category Status was conceded not least because British political thinking hoped that it would encourage the truce on the ground outside the prison. In the context of simultaneous negotiations with the IRA, serious overcrowding in Crumlin Road, the impossibility of building a new prison in time (Crawford 1979), and the potential destabilizing effect of prisoners dying on hunger strike, concessions may have appeared the most expedient course of action. Although Republicans have subsequently acknowledged the importance of this range of favourable political circumstances (e.g. Adams 1990), none the less the idea that political status had been 'won' as a result of the McKee-led hunger strikes was to remain as a significant residual memory for those prisoners who had that status 'removed' after 1976.

Paradoxically in the Republic, a firmer line was taken by the authorities in the early 1970s than in the North. In May 1972, after the establishment of special courts (similar to the Diplock courts introduced in the North a year later), IRA prisoners Joe Cahill and the O'Bradaigh brothers (Ruairi and Sean) went on hunger strike for 8, 13, and 19 days respectively (Coogan 1987: 513). Although they were subsequently released for lack of evidence, the authorities had shown little inclination to waver (Farrell 1976: 295).

In November 1972 IRA Chief of Staff Sean Mac Stiofain, who had been arrested and charged with IRA membership in the Irish Republic after doing a television interview, went on hunger and thirst strike in November 1972 demanding political status. After transfer to the military hospital at the Curragh, he remained on hunger strike but began accepting water and glucose. Following 57 days on hunger strike, he came off in January 1974 following an IRA Army Council statement which requested him to do so (Mac Stiofain 1975). His standing within

---

[11] At that time various areas of Derry were no-go areas for the security forces and effectively controlled by the Provisional IRA.

the IRA never recovered, however, and he never regained his position of power after it was alleged that he had put pressure on the Army Council to release the statement in order to save face (Coogan 1987: 518, Bishop and Mallie 1987: 244–5). A further mass hunger strike at Portlaoise prison, led by Daithi O'Conaill, ended in April 1977 after 47 days with no concessions won by the striking prisoners.

Republicans were not the only prisoners who resorted to the tactic of hunger strike in the early 1970s. On 7 July 1973, Michael Farrell, a civil rights campaigner and leader of the socialist People's Democracy along with Tony Canavan (another PD activist) embarked on a hunger strike in Crumlin Road prison (Coogan 1995: 165) They had been arrested and sentenced to eight and six months respectively for participating in a banned procession and were demanding political status. They were released on 8 August having been on hunger strike for 31 days along with almost 100 other non-terrorist prisoners and internees (Farrell 1976: 309, Bowyer Bell 1993: 382).[12] The apparent 'success' of such hunger strikes in the early 1970s was, however, mitigated by the experiences of Republican prisoners held in British prisons.

Political Status and the Transfer of Prisoners from England

For Republicans imprisoned in England (since the middle of the nineteenth century), the key issues around which they have resisted have been the recognition of political status and transfer back to Ireland (NIACRO 1994). The first such prisoners to resort to hunger strike during the most recent period of conflict were those convicted of the Old Bailey bombing in 1973. On 12 November 1973, seven of the eight Old Bailey bombers began refusing food, demanding to be treated as political prisoners, and to be transferred to Northern Ireland. After three weeks three dropped out leaving the campaign centred on Marion and Dolours Price, Hugh Feeney, and Gerry Kelly (Bowyer Bell 1979: 404).

---

[12] Given the longevity of their strike, the prisoners had been moved to hospital in the days preceding their release as their condition deteriorated considerably. While the PDs understandably claimed the releases as a victory for the clearly determined prisoners, the decision to release them on 8 Aug. may well have been influenced by the fact that the Emergency Provisions Act became law at midnight on 8 Aug. This legislation ended mandatory sentences under the old legislation such as the Public Order Act, under which they had been sentenced.

The prisoners on hunger strike were force-fed over a lengthy period.[13] In a letter to the *Irish News* on 14 March 1974, Hugh Feeney described the process thus.

Forced feeding meant being held down and a clamp being shoved into the mouth. Refusing as I do to wear prison clothing, I am naked except for a towel. On being force fed I became violently sick. After being sick I was naturally enough covered in vomit. When I requested a towel to clean this from my body I was refused.

Public demonstrations of the process of force-feeding were held in Nationalist areas of Belfast, and led not only to the volunteers vomiting and retching but also some of the onlookers as well.[14] A sizeable publicity campaign emerged, focused in particular on the plight of the two Price sisters, demanding that they be transferred back to Northern Ireland. William Whitelaw, then Secretary of State for Northern Ireland argued:

The return of a terrorist to a prison system where he might be regarded as a hero by a substantial proportion of his fellow inmates might well diminish, and be seen to do so, the deterrent value of the punishment imposed for the offences. (cited in Kelly 1982: 224)

On 3 June 1974, Michael Gaughan died on hunger strike having been force fed for a month and a half (Bowyer Bell 1979: 410). With intense public pressure, and Kelly and Feeney very ill, the then Home Secretary announced that the prisoners would be transferred, denying that his decision had been influenced by the hunger strikes. The prisoners came off their hunger strike in June 1974, but were not transferred until the

---

[13] Political, legal, and medical discussions on the ethics of force-feeding have flourished in Britain since the suffragette era. In the early 1970s there appears to have been confusion with some of the political discussions regarding the prisoners referring to the dictum of Lord Alverston in 1909 who had directed a jury that it was the duty of persons in charge of prisoners to force-feed them if necessary to prolong their lives. In their Tokyo declaration of 1975 the World Medical Association declared 'where a prisoner refused nourishment and is . . . rational . . . he or she shall not be fed artificially'. In more recent times the law has been considerably clarified in *Airedale NHS Trust v Bland* [1993] AC 789 when Lord Keith stated that the principle of the sanctity of life is not an absolute one so that doctors are not liable for failure to force-feed, but that they are not authorized to undertake that treatment. Thus, as the law does not compel the temporary keeping alive of a terminally ill patient, so too it does not compel the keeping alive of one who, as a sane person, goes on hunger strike (Case Note, *R. v Home Secretary ex p Robb* (1995), 275–6).

[14] *Irish News* (30 Mar. 1974), 'Letter from IRA Prisoner Hugh Feeney Re Force-feeding in An English Prison'.

following year because of the continued IRA bombing campaign in Britain. In fact the transfers were ultimately carried out in 1975 to support the ailing IRA ceasefire of that year (Coogan 1987: 515). Another IRA prisoner, Frank Stagg, who had been on the first fatal strike with Gaughan and had come off, died in February 1976 in Wakefield prison after 61 days of his second hunger strike.[15]

While the question of the transfer of Irish politically motivated prisoners remained an extremely significant prison issue during the ensuing twenty-two years, and in particular in light of the 1994 ceasefires, Republican prisoners did not again engage in an organized hunger strike to the death in support of their right to be held near their families.[16]

The Body, Dirty Protest, and the Origins of the 1980–1981 Hunger Strikes

The hunger strikes of 1980–1 were preceded by a lengthy and protracted struggle between those prisoners sentenced after 1976 and the prison authorities. Increasingly during this period Republican prisoners began to use their bodies as the practical and symbolic subjects of their resistance to criminalisation. Initially these protests took the form of nakedness as prisoners refused to wear a prison uniform and

---

[15] Stagg's funeral and the unseemly wrangling which occurred over his body between Republicans, elements of his family, and the authorities in the Republic offer instructive insights into the political and symbolic importance of those who have died on hunger strike. The Irish government were determined to ensure that Stagg's dying request of an IRA military funeral procession from Dublin airport to Ballina in County Mayo would not take place. As the media waited at Dublin airport for the expected clash between Republicans and the authorities, the plane was deliberately diverted to Shannon, the body removed and buried in a grave in Ballina dug by the police (rather than in the Republican plot as Stagg had requested) which was covered with eighteen inches of concrete. The following day IRA Army Council Representative Joe Cahill gave the funeral oration over the grave promising that one day Stagg would be reburied in the Republican plot. The grave was guarded around the clock for six months by the Garda. Shortly after the guard detail was withdrawn, on 6 Nov. 1976, a group of Republicans accompanied by a priest dug a tunnel into the grave under the concrete and removed the coffin, reinterring it in the Republican plot 100 yards away (Bowyer Bell 1979: 425, Coogan 1987: 521).

[16] Interview with former IRA prisoner who served the majority of his 22-year life sentence in English prisons (17 Jan. 1996). This prisoner suggested that while there were sporadic hunger strikes by Irish Republicans in English prisons, by and large prisoners recognized that the lack of a political constituency which was capable of being mobilized in Britain, and the distance from Northern Ireland, meant that the tactic had little chance of success.

wore only blankets. They then began a 'no wash' protest, refusing to leave their cells, which escalated into a dirty protest as the prisoners smeared their cells with excrement and urine. Finally they resorted to the tactic of hunger strike. Former blanketmen and hunger strikers interviewed by the author were explicit about their conceptualization of their bodies and their waste products as political weapons. In the reduced environment of captivity where the weapons of the weak (Mathiesen 1965) are few, the residual control over one's own body becomes a crucial locus of resistance.

The idea of the body as the instrument of resistance and as a part of a complex dialectic in the exercise of power has been explored by a number of scholars. For example, Frank (1991: 49–50) has suggested that the human body can be understood as an equilateral triangle, at the points of which are institutions, discourses, and corporeality.[17] The idea that the body can become an instrument of resistance in such an intersection has also been developed by Nietzsche. Referring similarly to the body as a 'political structure' (1968: 492) rather than as a material or biological given, he suggests that the body becomes a site for agency when there is a clash between two unequal clashing forces (Deleuze 1977: 80–1). Similarly Foucault (1979) offers an analysis of the body as the object of the exercise of power and refers specifically to any 'prison revolt' beginning with the body. As Feldman argues, for prisoners, the body as the place to which power is directed also defines the place for a redirection and reversal of power.[18] For Feldman, in revolt the prisoner 'objectifies the body as an instrument of violence'

---

[17] The example Frank uses to illustrate his point is that of fasting amongst medieval holy women. In that example the institution is the medieval church; the discourses include those doctrines of the church which eulogize the virtues of fasting but also include discourses on medieval marriage, the role of women, the corporeality of the body which poses the practical questions of how much self-starvation, the limits of endurance, and so forth (Frank 1991).

[18] Bettelheim also offers an instructive example of how the limits of endurance of the human body may become an instrument for the reversal of power, particularly when that power is applied disproportionately. He recounts how after an attempted escape from the camp prisoners were forced to stand for several hours in the cold without coats after an exhausting day of forced labour with little food. 'After about twenty prisoners had died from exposure, the discipline broke down. The threats of the guards became ineffective . . . Open resistance was impossible, as impossible as it was to do anything to safeguard oneself. A feeling of utter indifference swept the prisoners. They did not care whether the SS shot them; they were indifferent to acts of torture committed by the guards. The SS no longer had any authority, the spell of fear and death was broken . . . Unfortunate though the situation was, the prisoners felt free from fear and therefore were actually happier than at most times during their camp experiences' (Bettelheim 1986: 77–8).

(Feldman 1991: 178). In the context of a prison where other forms of resistance are narrowed and may become obfuscated by the isolation of setting (Scott 1990), the body may move to 'the centre of a political struggle' (Turner 1984: 39).

The initial steps in the political struggle concerning criminalisation occurred with the imprisonment of Ciaran Nugent, the first Republican prisoner charged with an offence committed after 1 March 1976 (the cut-off date for the ending of Special Category Status).[19] He told prison officers 'if you want me to wear prison gear you will have to nail it to my back' (Clarke 1987: 50). As more prisoners were processed by the Diplock Courts (leading to a total of 450 prisoners on the blanket by 1980) the distinctions in the level and type of resistance required between those prisoners *with* and those *without* Special Category Status became increasingly apparent. It became clear that a separate command structure for IRA prisoners within the H Blocks was required.[20] Prisoners were experiencing great difficulties in communicating with those prisoners who retained Special Category Status and remained in the compounds at the opposite end of the prison complex. In effect the prison at the Maze became divided into three separate prisons, those Special Category prisoners held in the Compounds, those convicted (Republican and Loyalist) after 1976 who opted to conform, and those (predominantly Republican) who refused to become conforming prisoners and went 'on the blanket'.

Protesting prisoners were subject to a punishment regime of loss of remission (thus doubling their sentence), removal of the three privileged visits per month, and were denied access to radios, TV, writing materials, and all published material other than the Bible. Any prisoner who refused to wear a prison uniform on the once monthly statutory visit had this removed also. Eventually the prisoners realized that the lack of communication with the outside world brought about as a result of not taking the statutory visits was damaging their overall campaign and undermining morale on the outside.[21] Visits also allowed

[19] The cut-off date was to be tightened subsequently to include all offences charged after 1 April 1976, regardless of when the offence was committed.

[20] Interview with former IRA Officer Commanding Maze, 12 Sept. 1994.

[21] 'After a lengthy debate, we decided to take a visit with our loved ones . . . In my first visit in almost 18 months my family were very shocked when they saw the state I was in. They nearly didn't recognise me when they came into the visit boxes. To them I looked like someone from an asylum. My eyes were staring and glazed over, with dark rings under them, and my face was deadly pale. I had lost a lot of weight by then and the

for regular communication with the IRA on the outside and the smuggling in of materials useful to the prisoners.[22]

In November 1976 the prison administration attempted to enforce a single towel rule at the showers. The blanketmen, refusing to wash naked under the eyes of the guards, decided to wash in their cells.[23] The administration relented and a second towel was permitted. In late 1977 the single towel rule was reintroduced. In the beginning of 1978 mirror searches were initiated where prisoners were forced to squat over a mirror while their anus was searched, before and after visits and wingshifts (O'Malley 1990: 22). The physical harassment of prisoners intensified with strip searching becoming routinized. On 17 March 1978 the blanketmen began to refuse to leave their cells and on 18 March the dirty protest began.[24] Urine and excreta were thrown out the windows and under the door. The prison officers retaliated by sweeping it back under the door and hosing prisoners' cells.[25] By April 1978 the prisoners were smearing the walls and ceilings and by December the guards had initiated the policy of forced washing.[26] At this stage there were 360–400 prisoners involved in the protest (Feldman 1991).

beard I had been growing for almost a year didn't help matters at all . . . We found out that people outside didn't understand the situation inside. Because of our stance of refusing to take the monthly visit, we had in effect isolated ourselves. The people were only hearing the British government lies and propaganda. After this we realised it was in our interests to continue with the visits.' Interview with Kevin Campbell, former blanketman (cited in Campbell, McKeown and O'Hagan 1994: 38).

[22] Prisoners smuggled communications or 'comms' in a variety of body cavities including rectums, foreskins, navels, mouths, and noses. Things smuggled included cigarette papers (used for smoking and writing), tobacco, pens, and a number of quartz crystal radios especially designed for the blanketmen by a Swedish technician (Feldman 1991: 199).

[23] Interview with former IRA prisoner who took part in the blanket protest, 5 Sept. 1997.

[24] Interview with former IRA prisoner who took part in the blanket protest, 5 Sept. 1997.

[25] Another former IRA blanket protester described the deteriorating situation thus: 'Things just went downhill fast. We put the shit and piss out the window and under the door and the screws threw it back in at us. Sometimes we would try to hit them with it or make them slip in it as they went past . . . at one stage they were going around with a big bucket in which they had gathered up the contents of a load of pots and they would jut pick a cell and throw the lot in.' Interview with former IRA prisoner, 15 Dec. 1996.

[26] 'Forced washing meant being grabbed by four or five screws, dragged from your cell and beaten and kicked as you were hauled down the landing—usually by the hair—to the punishment block. Once you got there you were dropped into a bath of freezing cold water and scrubbed all over by screws with deck scrubbing brushes, including your genitalia. It was excruciatingly painful . . . I used to dread it, I hoped that somebody else would be picked to tell you the truth and then felt ashamed if they were.' Interview with former IRA prisoner, 1 Dec. 1997.

Deprived of reading materials, prisoners passed their time in the cells by learning and communicating in Irish. Blank spaces were left on the cell walls where Irish words, phrases, and grammar were written down and learnt using adapted empty toothpaste tubes.[27] The prisoners clearly viewed this activity also as a tactic of resistance.

All the news and business was given out the doors in Gaeilge [Irish]; it was not only a means of communication but became a weapon in our hands to use against the screws. They hadn't a clue what we were saying and this really got to them. It helped to isolate them. (cited in Campbell, McKeown, and O'Hagan 1994: 48)

Similarly all the prisoners interviewed for this book who took part in the protest stressed the importance of the solidarity of their fellow prisoners and the significance of humour as a weapon in such circumstances.[28]

In January 1979 the prison authorities took the decision to remove thirty-two of the leaders of the protesting IRA prisoners and to place them in isolation in H 6. This decision was taken on the assumption that with the leadership removed, the will of the remaining prisoners would be weakened.[29] The prisoners, having heard that such a move was being planned, had actually appointed new Officers Commanding, Adjutants (second in command), etc. before the shifts began. None the less there was a growing consensus amongst the prisoners that the protest was going nowhere. As Leo Green, later to become IRA OC of the entire prison argued: 'Our protest as it stood showed little sign of bringing about the conclusion we sought. We were in a corner and

[27] Interview with former IRA blanketman, 5 Sept. 1997.

[28] See Campbell, McKeown, and O'Hagan 1994, esp. ch. 5. Feldman reproduces an illustrative interview of the kind of humour which developed in the H Blocks during the dirty protest: 'At one stage they were moving us very quickly from one cell to another so that cells didn't get in too bad a state. I found myself in a cell of my own and I am saying to myself "how am I going to get these walls covered." There was only one of me and they would be moving me soon. So I shat in the pot and put some water into it diluting it. I started to bang it around the walls and I was looking up at the ceiling. The shite was slashing all over me from the ceiling. At that moment the door opened and in came a priest, prison officer, and the governor of the jail. And here I was standing with the pot covered in shit . . . I looked down at the pot of watered down shite and all I said was "more miles to the gallon".'(cited in Feldman 1991: 184).

[29] 'I suppose we thought at the time that there were quite a number of prisoners on the protest at the time falling under the influence of particularly strong personalities and that if we could take them out of the equation, the prisoners might see sense . . . It was a bit naive in retrospect.' Interview with prison officer, in service HMP Maze 1978–82, 12 June 1997.

becoming increasingly aware of it' (cited in Campbell, McKeown and O'Hagan 1994: 90).

Bringing the leadership together into one block did, however, have the effect of allowing such prisoners to think strategically about the way forward in the protest. An inner core of three to four of the leadership discussed the possibility of undertaking a hunger strike, the critical stages of which would coincide with the planned visit of the Pope to Ireland in September 1979.[30] The Republican leadership on the outside had made clear their repeated opposition to employing the tactic of hunger strike. The IRA Army Council's view at the time appeared to be that having gone through a painful process of reorganizing the entire paramilitary organization into a cellular structure, and mindful of the difficulties in raising public support around the issue, they were extremely reluctant to accede to the prisoners' demands to employ the hunger strike tactic (Taylor 1997: 231). Sinn Fein President Gerry Adams summed up the view of Republicans on the outside when he wrote to the prisoners 'We are tactically, strategically, physically and morally opposed to a hunger strike' (White 1984: 219).

After an intervention by Cardinal Thomas O'Fiaich, Archbishop of Armagh and Primate of Ireland, the prisoners were persuaded to shelve their planned hunger strike around the Pope's visit (Campbell, McKeown, and O'Hagan 1994: 95). After visiting the prisons in July 1978, O'Fiaich had held a highly critical press conference which in turn provoked an apoplectic response from the British government, described by one *Guardian* correspondent as 'like a wounded bull' (Coogan 1980: 161).[31] O'Fiaich subsequently formed an alliance with the chairmen of the prison Boards of Visitors at the Maze and Armagh and in the autumn of 1980 submitted proposals to the British government suggesting concessions on prison clothes and prison work (Collins 1986: 324). In order to maximize the potential from the

---

[30] Interview with former IRA prisoner who took part in the blanket and dirty protest, 5 Sept. 1997.

[31] 'One would hardly allow an animal to remain in such conditions, let alone a human being. The nearest approach to it I have seen was the spectacle of hundreds of people living in sewer pipes in the slums of Calcutta. The stench and the filth in some of the cells, with the remains of rotten food and human excreta scattered around the walls was almost unbearable. In two of them I was unable to speak for fear of vomiting . . . From talking to them [the prisoners] it is evident that they seem intent to continue their protest indefinitely and it seems they would prefer to face death rather than submit to being classed as criminals. Anyone with the least knowledge of Irish history knows how deeply rooted this attitude is in our country's past' (cited in Coogan 1987: 158–9).

Cardinal's efforts the IRA had suspended attacks on prison officers in the community. The Northern Ireland Secretary of State replied that they would not discuss or negotiate the principle of political status and released a statement saying 'murder is murder wherever it is committed' (Collins 1986: 327). The strident tone of the British rejection of the Cardinal's intervention brought a predictable response, the IRA declared that it was again 'open season on prison officers'.[32]

The tactic of removing the leadership from the Blocks into one location having apparently failed to make any real impression on the prisoners' determination, the leadership were returned to the Blocks in broad agreement that neither the blanket nor the dirty protest had worked and determined to bring the latter to a close.[33]

As the prisoners themselves have subsequently acknowledged, while it would be all too easy to present the blanket era as a carefully planned and 'worked out' strategy, in reality prisoners responded to the circumstances of the criminalisation era as they evolved.[34] Nugent's example of 'going on the blanket' was reminiscent of the Fenians who, one hundred years previously, had similarly opted to wear their blankets rather than wear a prison uniform (Kee 1976). The decision to embark on the dirty protest arose out of the deterioration in relations between the prison staff and the prisoners rather than as a considered strategy of resistance. The prisoners' view at the beginning of the dirty protest was that once the world became aware of the circumstances of their detention the British government would be embarrassed into concessions.

Looking back on it we were very naïve on the dirty protest. We thought if we got a letter into the *Irish News* [main Northern Ireland Nationalist daily newspaper] or a bit of coverage of a rally we could bring the Brits to their knees. In reality of course they could argue that it was all self-inflicted, say it was being directed by the Godfathers of the IRA or that we were the sort of animals who liked living in our own excrement and so on. With nobody other than Republicans appearing to care about the beatings and so on, it was self-defeating I suppose.[35]

---

[32] Interview with former IRA prisoner who took part in the blanket and dirty protest, 5 Sept. 1997.

[33] Interview with former IRA prisoner who took part in the blanket and dirty protest, 5 Sept. 1997.

[34] *An Phoblacht* (18 May 1998), 'Reflections on the H Block/Armagh Prison Struggle'.

[35] Interview with former IRA prisoner, 1 Dec. 1997.

Aretxaga has described the dirty protest as 'primordial symbols' designed to achieve 'existential recognition' in a battle wherein 'prison discipline, with their uniformity, the substitution of names for numbers and extreme forms of humiliation, constituted the ultimate form of erasure' (Aretxaga 1995: 133). The prisoners also sought to counter the government's campaign which claimed that the move to cellular accommodation at the Maze was motivated by a desire to offer better and more civilized physical living conditions than in the Special Category compounds.[36] Excrement was used as a direct critique of the state's pretensions of a 'civilizing process' happening within the prisons.[37] As Elias (1998) has argued, there is a link between the development of manners and etiquette regarding the removal of bodily functions from public space and the evolution of the modern state.[38] As in other closed institutions, in a context of reduced options, prisoners fell back on using their own waste products as symbolic weapons against the assumed civilization of the prison authorities.

The smearing of cells also represented an attempt to take greater control over space and territory, albeit within the limited confines of the cell, by prisoners experiencing extreme vulnerability to staff assaults. Prison officers were understandably reluctant to enter cells, unless wearing protective clothing.[39] As one commentator has suggested, 'Although their world was reduced to four cramped walls, within that tiny compass self was everywhere' (Ellman 1993: 99).

---

[36] As is discussed in some detail in the chapter below on criminalisation much of the official discourse concerning the Maze from 1976 onwards emphasized that these were amongst the best prison conditions in Europe.

[37] Such usage of excrement as a symbolic critique of the state has a considerable antecedence in Irish political writing. For example, in Part Four of *Gulliver's Travels* in 'A Voyage to the Country of the Houyhnhnms' Gulliver encounters the Yahoos who use excrement as an instrument of self-expression and aggression, shooting excreta at Gulliver after he arrives. In the subsequent narrative, however, Swift makes it clear that the civilized humans are actually nastier than the savage Yahoos. The excreta flung at Gulliver represented a direct challenge to the self-image of imperialism as civilized and benign (see Brown 1959, Swift 1967).

[38] Simplifying for the sake of brevity, Elias (1998) argues that the evolution of the modern state has required an incremental monopolization of the use of legitimate violence by the state. Parallel with that evolution has been the proliferation of complex systems of manners and etiquette which increasingly govern human behaviour (including bodily functions) while simultaneously narrowing the potential of the individual subject legitimately to exercise violence.

[39] One former protestor described the outfits worn by prison officers to clean the cells as 'like bad extras from a Dr Who episode'. Interview with former IRA prisoner, 15 Dec. 1995.

Prisoners had quite literally spread themselves around their cells, implicating the prison guards in the cyclical squalor as they periodically removed prisoners to clean the cells with high power hoses.

However, the prisoners' notion that their endurance of such conditions within the prison would eventually gain public sympathy beyond the Republican constituency would appear to have been misplaced. Notions of dirtiness have been a metaphor for a lack of civilization in anti-Irish racism for centuries (McVeigh 1995). Images of the dirty Irish, applied frequently in Protestant anti-Catholicism in Ireland itself, have appeared to proliferate in times of political conflict (Darby 1993). As Aretxaga (1995: 135) suggests, the image of the prisoners living amongst their own excrement created an image *par excellence* of the uncivilized, uncouth, and barbarous. Peter Robinson, deputy leader to Ian Paisley's Democratic Unionist Party, wrote in a pamphlet published at the time 'if cleanliness is next to Godliness, then to whom are these men close?' (Robinson 1980a: 9).[40]

The prisoners lived in an unreal scatological environment, some of them for three and four years, and this obviously took a psychological and physical toll.[41] Spending much of their time naked, they had been exposed to prolonged periods of extreme fear and vulnerability during the worst excesses of prison officer assaults and intimidation.[42] The tried and tested tactic of hunger strike which had brought Special Category Status in 1972 offered the prisoners a pragmatic and logical step to end ultimately a protest which had become widely acknowledged as both 'self-damaging and ineffective'.[43]

---

[40] Robinson goes on to reproduce a poem from an anonymous woman, whom he states has been personally affected by Republican violence: 'Like animals they live, | But that's their way, | . . . existing in their filthy degradation day by day. | And those who protest the loudest, | shout aloud . . . | the world can weep for the H Blocks, | I will weep for you.'

[41] 'In the early days of the dirty protest we tried to find out what would be the medical consequences of living and eating in such an environment. We heard we might get lice, scurvy, dysentery, all sorts of stuff, I have to say I never actually got physically ill, but it was still very unpleasant. We all looked and felt physically terrible.' Interview with former IRA prisoner, 15 Dec. 1994.

[42] 'It is inconceivable to try to imagine what an eighteen-year-old naked lad goes through when a dozen or so screws slaughter him with batons, boots and punches, while dragging him by the hair along a corridor, or when they squeeze his privates until he collapses, or throw scalding water around his naked body. It is also inconceivable for me to describe, let alone for you imagine, our state of mind just sitting waiting for this to happen. I can say that this physical and psychological torture in the H Blocks has brought many men to the verge of insanity' (Sands 1998: 152).

[43] Interview with former IRA prisoner, 1 Dec. 1997

The 1980–1981 Hunger Strikes

The pressure from within the prison for a hunger strike had grown to such an extent that had the IRA Army Council not acceded, a strike may have begun in any case causing a damaging split in the movement.[44] The potential for such unauthorized strikes had been highlighted by veteran Republican Martin Meehan who had gone on hunger strike in the autumn of 1980 in protest at his conviction on the basis of dubious witness evidence. Meehan was only persuaded to come off his hunger strike after 66 days by an intervention from the IRA Army Council and the concerns of his fellow prisoners that he was ceding valuable tactical ground by allowing the authorities to monitor a hunger strike and its political impact closely so soon before the main event began (Campbell, McKeown, and O'Hagan 1994: 111). Finally, on 10 October 1980, the IRA Army Council having given their consent, Sinn Fein announced that a hunger strike would begin in ten days (Beresford 1987: 360).

On 27 October an initial seven prisoners at the Maze went on hunger strike. The six IRA prisoners and one INLA prisoner were chosen from those who had put their names forward on the basis of achieving a geographical spread across Northern Ireland (Taylor 1997: 231). The prisoners' announcement referred to the traditional demand for political status,[45] and not the five demands to which political status had been refined in 1979.[46] The seven prisoners went on hunger strike at the same time, a tactical error which was not repeated in the second hunger strike.[47] On 1 December the hunger strike was joined by three

[44] Interview with former IRA hunger striker Lawrence McKeown cited in Taylor (1997: 231).

[45] 'We the Republican Prisoners of War in the H Blocks, Long Kesh, demand as a right, political recognition and that we be accorded the status of political prisoners. We claim this right as captured combatants in the continued struggle for national liberation and self determination . . . We declare that political status is ours of right and we declare that from Monday 27th October 1980, a hunger strike by a number of men representing H Blocks 3, 4 and 5 will commence. Our widely recognised resistance has carried us through four years of immense suffering and it shall carry us through to the bitter climax if necessary' (reprinted in Campbell, McKeown, and O'Hagan 1994: 115).

[46] The five demands were (i) the right to wear their own clothes, (ii) to be exempt from prison work, (iii) to have freedom of association with fellow Republican prisoners, (iv) the right to organize educational and recreational facilities, (v) the restoration of remission lost as a result of the protest.

[47] 'Yes it was a mistake for us all to go on hunger strike at the same time. The second hunger strike, where we staggered the going on points so that people reached the critical stages at different times better maximized the political impact . . . I suppose it sounds a bit cold looking back on it like that, but it was a very serious business you know.' Interview with former IRA Officer Commanding, HMP Maze, 14 Sept. 1994.

Republican women prisoners (Bowyer Bell 1993: 601).[48] Brendan Hughes, former OC and one of the hunger strikers, received word from John Hume that, with all party support in the Dáil, he would arrange a meeting with Humphrey Atkins (Northern Ireland Secretary of State) where he would press for reforms in the areas of uniforms and association. That meeting was followed on 4 December by a statement from Atkins which, while spelling out the government's core opposition to the five demands, added that they were willing to 'discuss the humanitarian aspects of prison administration in Northern Ireland with anyone who shares our concern with it', Methods of communication opened up with the prisoners via the clergy and the civil servants in charge of the prisons (Clarke 1987: 126).

As one of the initial prisoners, Sean McKenna, neared death, a further twenty-seven prisoners went on strike on 15 December and a further seven on 16 December 1980. The hunger strike ended when Humphrey Atkins, then Secretary of State, gave a 34-page document to the prisoners via a mediator which appeared to contain the basis of a settlement. The document, the text of a speech which Atkins proposed to read out in Westminster the following day, addressed the prisoners as 'Republicans' (rather than criminals), and offered concessions on 'civilian style clothing', letters, food parcels, visits, and association. The British had dispatched a senior civil servant from London to explain the details of the proposals. With medical advice that McKenna might not last 24 hours, and encouraged by the fact that another line of communication had been opened up (to the traditionally more sympathetic Foreign Office), Hughes took a gamble and called off the strike (Beresford 1987: 43, O'Malley 1990: 33).

The official Republican history of this deal is that 'all the phrases contained in the document about the situation not being static, work not being interpreted narrowly and the prison regime being progressive, humane and flexible were soon shown to be empty platitudes. On January 9th Atkins reneged by reversing the order by which POWs received their own clothes' (Republican Fact File: 1991).

It is often difficult in hindsight to ascertain exactly why the details of one deal are acceptable and another is not. Certainly it would

---

[48] In Feb. 1980 thirty-two IRA women had gone on dirty protest in Armagh smearing excreta, urine, and menstrual fluids on their cell wall in support of the men at the Maze. As Aretxaga (1995: 129) argues, the actions of the women provoked strong negative reactions, even amongst the ranks of Republican men.

now appear that the IRA had badly overcalculated the degree of flexibility the government would permit in order to enable a peaceful settlement. The concessions given, such as the staged issue of civilian-style clothing simultaneous with prisoners being allowed their own clothes, and the experimental movement of prisoners into clean cells with furniture, were subject to delays, demands, and brinkmanship by both sides. As Bowyer Bell (1993: 605) has argued, the authorities sought to pursue the tactical victory on to a demonstrable crushing of prisoner resistance. The prisoners felt that they had called off the hunger strike too early, without a firm enough commitment in either form or will from the authorities. The public perception, and the perception amongst many Republicans, was that without concessions of substance the hunger strikers had lost (Bowyer Bell 1993: 604). Perhaps, as O'Malley has suggested, the view of the authorities may well have been that 'the prisoners had backed down when they saw McKenna's life was on the line' (O'Malley 1990: 32)

Bobby Sands, who had taken over as the prison OC once Hughes had gone on the first strike, was particularly incensed and felt that they had been outwitted and taken in by false promises (Feehan 1983). While Adams and the Republican leadership on the outside advocated caution, patience, and vigilance, he was faced with increasing pressure from the INLA OC Patsy O'Hara (who was threatening an independent second hunger strike from the smaller organization), depleted morale, and prisoners drifting back into conforming wings (Clarke 1987: 132). Sands met with the prison managers over the following months to seek implementation of the agreement but concluded that they had not the will to implement it.[49] The prisoners responded to the perceived obduracy by smashing their cells and plans for the second hunger strike began in earnest.[50]

---

[49] 'I honestly believe that they thought they had us beaten and wanted to rub our noses in it. Had they instead of shutting all the doors, given us a face saver, there would have been no [2nd] hunger strike . . . I think Bobby went to great lengths to get that face saver and that possibly the NIO/prison administration perceived this as weakness on our behalf and decided to put the boot in when—as they perceived it—we were down.' Interview with former IRA prisoner Jaz McCann, reproduced in Campbell, McKeown, and O'Hagan 1994: 137.

[50] Interview with former IRA hunger striker, 15 Dec. 1994.

The Second Hunger Strike and Political Mobilization

The second hunger strike began on 1 March 1981, the fifth anniversary of the end of political status with the issuing of the statement reproduced below.[51] Bobby Sands was to lead the second hunger strike himself and was replaced as OC by Brendan 'Bik' MacFarlane. The day after his hunger strike began MacFarlane called an end to the no-wash protest, having concluded that it had run its course, would yield no further propaganda value, and would provide for an easier transition into a new regime after the hunger strikes if clean and furnished conditions were already in place.[52] Sands and his fellow hunger strikers had concluded that some would certainly die, with some of the prison leadership estimating that perhaps up to seven deaths would occur before the British conceded (Clarke 1987: 138).

In the second hunger strike prisoners were to join the strike in stages. One week after Sands went on hunger strike he was joined by IRA man Francis Hughes and one week later by Patsy O'Hara (INLA OC) and Raymond McCreesh (IRA). The initial tactics of the prison authorities in dealing with the hunger strikers lacked sophistication.[53] None the less, as the prisoners themselves subsequently acknowledged, on the outside it was initially difficult to garner much public support, even amongst Republican supporters who were still suffering the aftereffects of disappointment and disillusion at the inconclusive end to the first hunger strike (Campbell, McKeown and O'Hagan 1994: 146). On the Sunday before Sands began his hunger strike 3,500 people had marched at an H Block demonstration in West Belfast, four months earlier there had been over 10,000 at a similar event (Taylor 1997: 239).

---

[51] 'We are still able to declare that the criminalisation policy which we have resisted and suffered, has failed . . . If a British government experienced such a long and persistent resistance to a domestic policy in England, then that policy would almost certainly be changed . . . We have asserted that we are political prisoners and everything about our country, our arrests, interrogations, trials and prison conditions, show that we are politically motivated.' (Iris 1991: 17).

[52] One former prisoner described the end of the protest thus. 'Other than a couple of forced washes, which just hurt but didn't actually clean you, this was my first time actually washing myself in nearly three years. It was incredible. I cut my beard and washed the grime off me with the prison issue soap, . . . it felt like pure luxury, like bloody Cleopatra, who used to wash in ass's milk. I still love showering.' Interview with former IRA prisoner 5 Sept. 1997.

[53] On Friday, 6 Mar. 1981, the sixth day of his hunger strike, Sands wrote: 'They [the screws] are unembarrassed by the enormous amount of food they are putting into the cell and I know they have every bean and every chip counted or weighed . . . Regardless, I have no intention of sampling their tempting morsels.' (Sands 1997: 324).

The event which lifted that inertia and focused world attention on this hunger strike was the death of Frank Maguire, independent Nationalist MP for Fermanagh South Tyrone on 5 March, and the decision that Sands should run as a candidate.[54]

While there was a natural Nationalist majority in the constituency, Republicans were unsure as to whether 'Constitutional Nationalists' would vote for a serving IRA man. Sands's chances improved considerably when the other Nationalist party, the SDLP, decided not to field a candidate and Noel Maguire, the locally popular brother of the deceased MP, decided not to run after interventions from Gerry Adams and other senior Sinn Fein figures (Adams 1996: 292). Running on a platform of support for the prisoners' five demands (rather than support for the armed struggle), Sands topped the poll with 30,092 votes, beating the Unionist candidate by 1,446 votes (Bishop and Mallie 1987: 368) with an 86.9 per cent turnout.[55] He was on the fortieth day of his hunger strike and had lost two stones.

Mrs Thatcher announced that the result changed nothing, 'A crime is a crime is a crime . . . It is not political, it is a crime' (O'Malley 1990: 60) and swiftly introduced legislation forbidding serving prisoners from standing for parliament. Four days after the election the Northern Ireland Office announced that Sands was in a critical condition and on 5 May, the sixty-sixth day of his hunger strike, he died, producing a world-wide response.[56] His funeral was attended by over 100,000 people and a huge contingent of international media watched his burial with full paramilitary honours (Taylor 1997: 243).[57] Sands was

[54] 'In the blocks we had discussed the possibility of fielding a prisoner as a candidate if the opportunity came up. While the movement was reluctant on the outside, in the Kesh I think we felt strongly that it was an opportunity not to be missed.' (Interview with former IRA hunger striker, 15 Dec. 1994).

[55] The prisoners' reaction within the H Blocks was predictably euphoric (interview with former IRA dirty protester, hunger striker and later Officer Commanding, 15 Dec. 1994).

[56] 'The *Hindustani Times* said Mrs Thatcher had allowed a fellow member of Parliament to die of starvation, an incident which has never before occurred in a civilised country. Tehran announced it would be sending its ambassador in Sweden to represent the government at the funeral . . . In India, Opposition members of the Upper house stood for a minute's silence in tribute . . . In Spain the Catholic YA newspaper described Sand's hunger strike as "subjectively an act of heroism", . . . In Russia *Pravda* described it as another tragic page in the grim chronicle of oppression, discrimination, terror and violence, in Ireland. In Poland Lech Walesa paid tribute' (Beresford 1987: 132).

[57] Owen Carron, Sands's election agent and later to take the seat himself, gave the oration at Bobby Sands's funeral. He concluded 'Finally I salute you Bobby Sands. Yours has been a tough lonely battle but you have been victorious. Your courage and bravery have been an inspiration to us all and today we take strength from your example. Your Sacrifice will not be in vain' (Feehan 1983: 20).

replaced on the hunger strike by Joe McDonnell the day after his death and within two weeks the three other initial hunger strikers died.[58] At the end of that month, in which four hunger strikers had died, Mrs Thatcher visited Northern Ireland and suggested to a packed press conference that defeat of the hunger strikers might lead to the demise of the IRA.[59]

The prisoners had been boosted by the political impact of the hunger strikes in the Republic. In May 1981 a 250,000 signature petition was presented to Irish Taoiseach Charles Haughey in support of the prisoners. In the Dáil elections of June 1981 H Block candidates gained over 40,000 first preference votes and two hunger strikers were elected (Smyth 1987: 186). This was despite lack of any significant electoral machine in the Republic, nor indeed any developed political platform other than support for the five demands of the prisoners (Adams 1996: 299). However, as the hunger strikers died and were replaced, and the British position appeared to 'vary only between extremely and very intransigent',[60] the original tensions between the prisoners and the organization on the outside remained.[61]

Despite the numerous interventions by a variety of civic and religious mediators (Collins 1986), and direct channels of communication open to the British government through the Foreign Office, ten hunger strikers were ultimately to die before the hunger strike was called off on Saturday, 3 October, 217 days after it had begun. With the situation in an apparent impasse, prisoners' families began to make medical interventions once prisoners had slipped into a coma. Having been galvanized by prison chaplain Father Denis Faul who had been deeply opposed to the hunger strike (Beresford 1987: 419), and under intense

---

[58] Once embarked upon, a collective hunger strike encourages further sacrifice, not simply to achieve the original objective but in order not to let down the efforts of those who have gone before. As Peadar O'Donnell (1966: 85), himself a former hunger striker in the 1920s, noted, 'once a group of prisoners go on hunger strike there is a sort of moral conscription which sweeps the others into it.'

[59] 'Faced with the failure of their discredited cause, the men of violence have chosen in recent months to play what may well be their last card' (Bew and Gillespie 1993: 149).

[60] Interview with former IRA dirty protester, hunger striker, and later IRA Officer Commanding, 15 Dec. 1994.

[61] One of the hunger strikers, Lawrence McKeown, who joined the hunger strike towards the end of June 1981, recounted the following: 'I remember when it came to the time to actually join the hunger strike a "comm" came from the Army Council . . . It said "Comrade, you have put your name forward to embark upon the hunger strike. Do you realise the full implication? What it means comrade, is that in a short time you will be dead. Rethink your decision"' (cited in Taylor 1997: 245).

emotional, psychological, and theological pressure regarding the religious consequences of standing by while their sons and husbands effectively committed suicide,[62] the families' interventions spelled the end of the hunger strikes. While some commentators have suggested that Father Faul in particular (e.g. Taylor 1997: 249) had found the Achilles heel of the prisoners, as Adams (1996: 314) has acknowledged, even without the clerical intervention it was inevitable that some prisoners would eventually pull back at the brink and that some families would feel duty-bound to intervene.[63]

The arguably more skilled Jim Prior had taken over from Humphrey Atkins as Secretary of State for Northern Ireland in the final weeks of the hunger strike, refusing to speak of victory or defeat (Beresford 1987: 420). On 6 October the British government announced that all prisoners would be allowed to wear their own clothes, there would be 50 per cent remission of time lost through the protests, greater freedom of association between adjacent wings in the H Blocks, more visits, and the definition of prison work reviewed (O'Malley 1990: 211). While it would be several years before the rest of the five demands were granted in full, and the strikes were perceived contemporaneously by the prisoners as a failure, both the prisons and the political landscape had been irrevocably altered by the hunger strikes.

The Implications of the 1980–1981 Hunger Strikes

The hunger strikes had a profound impact both within the prisons, upon the Republican movement and to the Northern Ireland body politic.[64] Within the Maze, the Republican leadership resolved never again to employ a strategy of resistance where prisoners attempted to damage themselves and move the authorities by the strength of their endurance. As one subsequent IRA Officer Commanding (himself a former hunger striker) told the author: 'a new strategy which avoided harming ourselves had to be evolved which built upon the gains made

---

[62] A complex and at times heated theological debate has been waged within Irish Catholic ecclesiastical circles for much of the last century regarding the ethics of hunger striking and whether or not such activities should be considered suicide and therefore sinful (see O'Gorman 1993 for an overview of the debate).

[63] For a more sympathetic account of Faul's role in the ending of the hunger strikes see Clarke (1987: 201).

[64] The implications of the hunger strikes for prison management are discussed more fully in the management chapters below.

by the hunger strikers' sacrifice.'[65] No further organizationally sanctioned hunger strike has occurred amongst Republican prisoners in Northern Ireland since 1981.

For the Republican movement the election of Bobby Sands, Owen Carron, and two hunger strikers to the Dáil considerably dissipated the traditional Republican antipathy towards electoral politics.[66] Shortly before the first hunger strike the Sinn Fein Ard Fheis (annual conference) had voted overwhelmingly against participation in elections as a distraction from armed struggle and had, in 1979, refused to support Bernadette McAliskey as an H Block candidate in the European Parliament Elections (Bowyer Bell 1993: 630). One month after the hunger strikes ended, leading Republican Danny Morrison told the delegates, 'Will anyone here object if, with a ballot paper in one hand and the Armalite in the other, we take power in Ireland?' (Taylor 1997: 282). The origins of Sinn Fein's political machine and subsequent electoral successes can be traced directly to the hunger strikes. As Brendan 'Bik' MacFarlane, IRA Officer Commanding during the second hunger strike, argued in an article in 1998:

The reluctance of Republicans to engage in electoral politics in the 1970s left the field open for the SDLP to exploit. Since then we have constantly had to deal with the potential of the SDLP being co-opted into a British agenda. The election of Bobby Sands opened the door for building a political movement which played the Brits at their own game. By standing candidates in the Assembly elections [1998] Sinn Fein is undercutting any attempt by our opponents to retreat and retrench, Republicans have the ability and the confidence to pursue their objectives in all arenas. The struggle continues.[67]

The twin strategies of violence and electoral politics were to form the basis of Republican tactics until at least the first IRA ceasefire of September 1994.

At a micro level the experience of the hunger strike campaigns offered insights into the way in which the political wing of the Republican

---

[65] Interview with former IRA Officer Commanding, 12 Sept. 1994.

[66] The significance of the electoral successes of the hunger strike era were not appreciated by all commentators at the time. Writing in 1982, the 'terrorism' expert Paul Wilkinson (who acted as an adviser to the British government on Northern Ireland up until the 1990s) argued: 'If there were voices arguing for a more political line in the North they seem to have been largely overruled since the collapse of the 1981 hunger strike' (Wilkinson 1982: 148).

[67] An Phoblacht (18 May 1998), 'Reflections on the H Block/Armagh Prison Struggle'.

movement should in future do its business. The value of building broader coalitions around particular issues beyond the immediate Republican constituency (Smyth 1987), thus adding legitimacy to their claims (Mulcahy 1995), had become clear during the latter stages of the campaign. The IRA had always derived considerable support from elements of the British Left (Curtis 1981) but much of this was from sources who offered largely uncritical support for the armed struggle (Berry 1980). In Ireland, the early development of the Relatives Action Committees and H Block Committees in support of the prisoners (the latter of which ultimately spanned a broader constituency of leftist organizations including the PDs, the Communist Party, civil rights activists, trade unionists, and others) had been hampered by doctrinaire Republicans, insisting upon support for the armed campaign as a prerequisite for involvement (Clarke 1987: 90).[68] As Adams and his associates took increasing control over the Republican movement, however, greater effort was made to listen to others, to seek consensus, to co-operate and co-ordinate, and avoid the imposition of the party line (Bowyer Bell 1993: 598). Such an approach was to characterize the painstaking developments in the 1990s when, despite their obvious differences, the Sinn Fein leadership forged an alliance with first the SDLP and then the Irish government which brought about the IRA ceasefire in 1994 (Mallie and McKittrick 1996).

As one former prisoner, now a senior member of Sinn Fein, told the author:

I suppose the whole hunger strike experience saw us come of age as a movement. It certainly sowed the seeds, which admittedly grew slow at first, but it still sowed the seeds that there were additional strategies to the armed struggle. It took a long time however for us to conclude that armed struggle should not be the predominant strategy.[69]

[68] In his autobiography Adams recounts his reaction to one such broad meeting in 1979 and the attempts by Sinn Fein leadership to involve those not involved in the party: 'Then we took our eyes off the ball very badly. A conference was called in Coalisland, at which one of our people insisted that anyone involved in campaigning for the prisoners should accept the legitimacy of the armed struggle. It was perhaps an instinctive response—certainly the traditional response—in the context of the British criminalisation policy, but I knew it was a mistake the moment I heard about it' (Adams 1996: 283).   [69] Interview with former IRA prisoner, 15 Sept. 1997.

Loyalist Dirty Protest and Hunger Strikes

Question. What is the difference between a wine gum and a Loyalist hunger striker?

Answer. A wine gum, it lasts longer.[70]

The above joke is typical of the disparaging attitude towards Loyalist prisoners shared almost universally by the Republicans, prison staff, and prison managers interviewed for this book. That disparagement is often highlighted by a juxtaposition of the endurance of the Republican prisoners during the era of the dirty protest and hunger strike and the perceived lack of significant resistance to criminalisation amongst Loyalist prisoners.[71] While Republicans' resistance to criminalisation is better known,[72] it should be acknowledged that Loyalist prisoners too can point to some history of using the tactics of dirty protest and hunger strike in resisting criminalisation initiatives.

In 1972, the then UVF Brigadier (Officer Commanding) Gusty Spence, went on a hunger strike simultaneously with Billy McKee and other IRA prisoners in the demand for political status (Stevenson 1996: 131).[73] UVF prisoners received a standing order from at least 1974 that they were to refuse to wear a prison uniform.[74] Similarly, when large numbers of Republicans were participating in the dirty protest in the 1970s, there were a few Loyalists taking part in a 'clean' protest—refusing to do work or wear a prison uniform but keeping their cells clean and using the toilet facilities normally (NIPS 1979: 16). That protest ended after five months when the UDA leadership on the

---

[70] Old Northern Ireland joke, retold to the author in interview with former IRA prisoner, 1 Dec. 1997.

[71] As one serving prison officer recounted, 'You can say what you like about the Provies [IRA], they were willing to die for their principles. Loyalists on the other hand, their principles never lasted beyond dinner time.' Interview with former prison officer, 12 Sept. 1996.

[72] For a discussion on the Loyalist 'success' in achieving the segregation of remand prisoners in the early 1990s see Chapter 5 below.

[73] According to one former prisoner, Spence continued to have health problems related to the 35 days which he had spent on hunger strike in 1972. Interview with a former UVF Officer Commanding in the Maze (Compound) 2 Dec. 1994.

[74] 'The wearing of civilian clothes by UVF personnel is an essential pre-requisite to the maintenance of self respect and individualism. When compelled to dress up in prison garb the prisoner feels anonymous and indeed he is treated anonymously by the authorities, he becomes a number rather than a name, a thing rather than a human being.' Extract from Internal UVF document, reproduced in Crawford 1979: 34.

outside issued three separate orders for the prisoners to stop emulating the Republicans (Clarke 1987: 65).

During the first Republican hunger strike of 1980, as Sean McKenna entered the critical phase, six UDA prisoners began to refuse food on 10 December 1980 and demanded segregation from Republican prisoners (Bowyer Bell 1993: 603–4). Cardinal O'Fiaich, then mediating between the British government and the Republican hunger strikers, argued to the British that the UDA hunger strike gave the British additional room for manoeuvre as the concessions would now be seen as even-handed (Clarke 1987: 127). The Loyalist prisoners ended their strike six days later once the Republicans had done the same.

In the 1980s Loyalist prisoners continued various forms of protest, including a no-wash protest and the smearing of their walls with excreta, again primarily designed to achieve segregation from Republicans. By 1983, through protest and refusal to conform to prison rules, Loyalist prisoners had in fact achieved *de facto* segregation and formally ended their two-year protest a few months after the escape by Republicans in that year.

With *de facto* segregation achieved at the Maze from 1983 onwards, attention shifted to Magilligan where Loyalists again claimed to be under threat from Republicans and pressed for segregation. In 1985 from 17 June eight Loyalist prisoners at Magilligan went on hunger strike for periods varying from 4 to 25 days with no inmate suffering any long-term medical damage as a result (NIPS 1986/7: 14, Colville 1992: 8). Subsequently another brief hunger strike occurred, new visiting arrangements were boycotted, and further riots and disturbances continued. However, while Loyalists may have taken the lead in the pressure for segregation, as Rolston and Tomlinson argue (1988: 178), the only substantial presentation of the detail of the problem was outlined at a two-day public inquiry organized by Republicans.

In 1997, Billy Wright, leader of the breakaway Loyalist Volunteer Force (opposed to the peace process), was initially held in Maghaberry on the grounds that he was under a death threat from both the UDA and UVF and therefore his safety could not be guaranteed. Wright threatened to go on hunger strike to coincide with the annual stand-off between Orangemen and Nationalist residents at Drumcree unless he was moved to a separate wing at the Maze. Having played a significant role at Drumcree the previous year, and with a significant power base in that volatile mid-Ulster area (Cusack and McDonald 1997: 346), the authorities concluded it was too potentially destructive to let such a hunger strike go ahead and transferred Wright and a number of his followers to separate accommodation at the Maze.[75] As one prison governor told the author:

In reality we had little choice. Wright was clearly the kind of character who would have gone the distance on hunger strike. When you think of the potential political consequences of him in critical condition around the time of Drumcree, not to mention the destabilizing effect on the regime at Maghaberry, we really were between a rock and a hard place.[76]

In sum, while there have been collective and individual attempts by Loyalists to use the tactics of dirty protest and hunger strike to achieve the aim of segregation in particular, these have been on the whole less well organized, less determined, and, with some notable exceptions, apparently less willing to take such protests to the death. While it is reassuring to Republicans to point to this as evidence of less purely *politically* motivated recruits,[77] adhering to a less coherent political ideology, more substantial analysis is required. As can be seen from the better accounts of the Republican dirty protest and hunger strikes of the late 1970s/early 1980s (Beresford 1987, O'Malley 1990, Campbell, McKeown, and O'Hagan 1994), mass protests of this nature require considerable planning, organization, and public relations skills as well as commitment. Such skills were clearly lacking amongst Loyalists at various key junctures during the era of criminalisation. As Duncan McLaughlin, one of the most experienced governors in the Northern Ireland prison service has opined:

The Republican side has always been much better organised, well disciplined: it has really thought out what it is about. Republicans, generally speaking, are working from an ideological base. The Loyalists are a reactive group—they have reacted to the actions of the Republicans, so they don't have an ideological base. So they have never been well organised. It takes a pretty severe mistake by us, if you like, to get them to work as a group (quoted in Stevenson 1996: 141).

---

[75] Given the small numbers of LVF inmates at the Maze, Wright and his followers were forced to share alternate arms of one of the H Blocks with INLA prisoners. Wright was subsequently murdered by prisoners from the INLA faction (discussed in Chapter 4 below). [76] Interview with prison governor, 13 Sept. 1997.

[77] As is discussed elsewhere, there is some data to support this thesis, at least with regard to recruits during the 1970s. Bruce (1992: 293) cites data which suggest that a considerably higher number of Loyalists than of Republicans were convicted of ordinary criminal offences before they were arrested for paramilitary offences.

Another key feature in pursuing a determined protest is the nature of the Loyalist leadership. The command structure and decision-making processes of the IRA within the prisons tend to be based upon extensive consultation followed by directed action within a paramilitary hierarchical structure. In contrast, Loyalist groupings are often described as having 'too many chiefs and not enough Indians' with prison staff unsure who to talk to in order to get things done.[78] As discussed previously, in some instances the maintenance of authority amongst Loyalist prisoners appears to have been based more upon influence on the outside, fear, and violence rather than leadership abilities.[79]

The calibre of their prison leadership has been questioned by a number of former Loyalist prisoners. For example, one former UDA prisoner who took part in the Loyalist protests in the Maze in the early 1980s suggested that their protest lacked a clear strategy and was poorly directed by the Loyalist prison commanders. In that instance the protest continued for one and a half years after the objective had been secured.

Interviewer. You are being critical of the leadership within the prison, why, why does it take 18 months to realize that you have actually achieved *de facto* segregation?

Respondent. I think it probably was a lack of communication, a lack of thinking. You need to sit down and assess the situation. I personally don't believe that they [Loyalist prison leadership] were good at that.[80]

The same prisoner also suggested that in effect Loyalists had been able to sit back during the Republican protests of the 1970s, and garner the rewards without having to mount effective protests themselves. However, in the early 1980s with the Republicans having internalized the lessons of the hunger strike and dirty protest, they reversed the tables, placing the Loyalists in a position where they were protesting, paying the price, and Republicans reaped the benefits.

---

[78] Interview with former prison officer HMP Maze, 16 July 1997.
[79] Bruce refers to an insightful discussion between David Morley (IRA OC in the compounds), Gusty Spence (UVF OC), and James Craig (UDA OC) on how they maintained discipline in their respective camps. Craig is reputed to have said 'I've got this big fucking hammer and I've told them that if anybody gives me trouble I'll break their fucking fingers' (Bruce 1992: 245).   [80] Interview with former UDA prisoner, 24 July 1998.

I think the first and foremost thing is that we didn't have as much to fight for in reality because the provies [IRA] had won everything we had got. To be honest about it, because everything they fought for we got it off their backs . . . I admire a couple of the Republican leadership . . . what they done was they got other Republicans off the protest and forced the Loyalists onto one. I think it was a very shrewd move and I think it was well thought out.[81]

In his book, which is clearly unsympathetic to Republicanism[82], Jonathan Stevenson none the less points to what he refers to as a 'superior prison culture' amongst Republicans. He juxtaposes their taste for political documentaries, team sports, and training of personnel for campaigns on the outside with the Loyalist taste for pornographic films, pumping iron, and drug problems on the wings (Stevenson 1996: 143). He argues that in grappling with criminalisation, Loyalists were impeded by the political difficulties of aligning themselves with Republicans to achieve progress on the same issue. Having been cushioned to some extent in the compounds where they were treated better than Republicans by the prison staff, he further argues that criminalisation removed that psychological advantage, galvanizing Republicans and demoralizing Loyalists (Stevenson 1996: 144).

Loyalist protests have traditionally focused almost exclusively upon segregation, separation from the enemy. While Republicans too have protested in support of segregation, the five demands which became the focal point of the dirty protest and hunger strikes came about in 1979 as the result of a conscious effort by the prisoners to break down into practical components the traditional demand of political status, a package which might be capable of garnering more widespread support (Clarke 1987: 101). The Loyalists lacked the organizational capacity on the outside to mount the kind of campaigns of mass protest which had accompanied the hunger strikes and dirty protest as well as the public relations skills to present their case effectively.[83] With an ambivalent ideological relationship with the state which was imprisoning them, little comparable prison history to fall back upon, less

---

[81] Interview with former UDA prisoner, 24 July 1998.

[82] Stevenson describes Republicans as totalitarian and fascistic and the hunger strikers as 'fanatical, perhaps outright brain washed' (Stevenson 1996: 144).

[83] As is noted above, despite the fact that Loyalists led the protests at Magilligan for segregation, it was a Republican support group which actually provided the only significant articulation of issues surrounding the question of segregation (Concerned Relatives/Ex-prisoners Committee 1987).

obvious leadership talents within the prisons, and a much smaller and less organized constituency outside the prisons, it is perhaps unsurprising that Loyalist prisoners' efforts at resistance through hunger strike and dirty protest have gone largely unnoticed in the limited literature.

Conclusion: Hunger Strike and Dirty Protest as Resistance

Hunger strikes by Republican prisoners have been widely used as forms of protest and resistance throughout the twentieth century. No doubt influenced by what Seamus Heaney has referred to as the 'afterlife of former protests' (Ellman 1993: 14), they have played a key role in the prison conflict during the most recent decades of violence and were of considerable significance in the 1980/1 period and beyond. The 1980/1 hunger strikes went some way to achieving their objectives within the prisons after Prior's concessions and provided the basis for the political platform subsequently developed by Sinn Fein. However, those successes were achieved at a high cost, to the prisoners who died, their families, the prisoners who survived the strike but were permanently damaged, and the prison staff who were traumatized by the experience of the dirty protest and hunger strikes (discussed below). The abandonment of the strategy of hunger strike after 1981, and the determination of the Republican leadership within the prisons and on the outside that it should not be employed again,[84] is testament to that high price.

Although criticized by some former politically motivated prisoners as an 'altogether too passive' strategy (Mandela 1994: 502–3), hunger striking does offer the potential to critique the authorities' taken-for-granted legitimacy and expose hitherto untapped pockets of sympathy and support. Hunger strike shares with dirty protest the Foucauldian notion of the 'body' becoming 'instrumentalized' against the technologies of domination, an instrument subject to political technologies managed now by both prisoners and prison staff (Feldman 1991). In both instances prisoners assumed ownership and control over their bodies, found 'spaces' to organize self-dignity and solidarity (Hooks 1991), and fractured the apparent dominance of a 'total institution' (Goffman 1961a). Prisoners who were willing to starve themselves to

---

[84] Interview with former IRA Officer Commanding, HMP Maze, 12 Sept. 1994.

death were clearly able to expropriate power, denigrate legitimacy, and politically contest the position of an intransigent British government.

The dirty protest as a form of resistance has been rightly criticized as ultimately self-defeating. The refusal to wash and the fouling of cells did not emerge as considered strategies designed to defeat criminalisation. Rather, the resort to dirty protest was an amalgam of reactive and immediate responses to crude management and staff brutality which gathered momentum and shape by the collective nature of the protest, the ideological determination of the prisoners in particular not to wear prison clothing, and the difficulty for the prisoners of extricating themselves from the course of action once embarked upon without an alternative strategy which would prevent the government from claiming victory. However, in allowing themselves to be portrayed as 'dirty', 'animalistic', and 'living in their own filth' (Robinson 1980a), the prisoners were leaving themselves exposed to a series of racist and sectarian discourses which did little to further their claims for political status.

The key difference between the dirty protest and hunger strikes as forms of resistance lay in the ability of the prisoners and their supporters to diffuse resistance beyond the apex of the operation of power during the hunger strike period. While both sets of practices demonstrated a willingness to 'endure pain for longer than the enemy could inflict it' (Lynch 1997: 16), the ability of Republicans to present the self-sacrifice of the hunger strikes in particular within a framework of British imperialism and intransigence offered a considerably clearer critique to assumptions about the legitimacy of the British government's actions in Northern Ireland.[85] Resistance was not simply a question of endurance but also a question of ensuring that the reason for resistance was understood within the appropriate analytical framework.

As Govan Mbeki, a former South African political prisoner told the author:

Prison resistance works best when its link to the political struggle is clearly understood. That was something we continuously reminded our people on the Island, the world must understand the reasons for our defiance, our motives and our actions, these must be clear.[86]

---

[85] For views on the efficacy of Republican propaganda during the hunger strike era see Von Tangen Page 1996, Curtis 1984.

[86] Interview with Govan Mbeki, 2 Feb. 1995.

The spectacle of prisoners willing to starve themselves to death in their assertion of political rather than criminal status was considerably more communicable than prisoners living in their own excrement and urine. The hunger strikers gave Republicanism a considerable cultural capital, which readily translated into images in popular culture of resistance and struggle (Rolston 1991, Mulcahy 1995), many of which transcended the traditional Republican constituency. They remain to this day the defining symbol of the Republican assertion of the political character of the conflict in the North of Ireland.

5

Resistance and Violence: Power, Intimidation, and Control of Space

Introduction

This chapter explores the use of violence, destruction, and intimidation as a strategy of resistance for paramilitary prisoners in Northern Ireland. The occurrence of such activities within the prisons, and of prison-related incidents on the outside, is predictable given the centrality of the prisons to the overall political conflict. Since 1969, Northern Ireland prisons have always held a uniquely large proportion of long-term prisoners, many of them convicted of the most serious offences of paramilitary violence. Given such an inmate population and their proven commitment and capacity to carry out acts of violence and destruction, it is perhaps surprising that there has not been considerably more prison-related death and destruction. Levels of such activities have, however, ebbed and flowed over the period, linked inextricably to changing contours of the conflict.

The use of violence, destruction, and intimidation by prisoners and their paramilitary colleagues on the outside is perhaps best understood within at least three interconnecting frameworks: (*a*) the achievement of particular strategic and political objectives within the prisons, normally related to the assertion of the political character of the inmates; (*b*) the carrying out of such activities by paramilitary outside the prisons, in support of the demands of their imprisoned colleagues; (*c*) events which have arisen, not because of broader strategic or political concerns related to the overall struggle of the various paramilitary groupings, but rather because of issues, events, or personalities within the prisons.[1]

---

[1] For example, these have included spontaneous eruptions linked to conditions, individual personalities of prisoners, variations amongst prisoner faction leadership, the conduct of prison staff and management, misunderstandings and a range of other matters associated with outbreaks of prison violence or destruction elsewhere.

It is important to stress that it is not being argued that all violence which has been either carried out by, or on behalf of, politically motivated prisoners can be explained by neat all-encompassing strategies. Rather, by analysing particular incidents in the history of prison violence, certain key themes can be drawn out which are related to the interaction between the prisoners, the prison staff, and the political conflict.

Before offering an analysis of prison violence it is important to acknowledge at least two limitations in the methodology employed. First, the sources for analysis include the numbers of charges brought for assaults and damage within the prison, Prison Officers Association and NIO figures on violence, threats, and intimidation against officers and their families in the community, and, most importantly, interviews with both the perpetrators and victims of prison-related violence. With regard to the recorded disciplinary charges, their limited reliability has been previously identified within British prison settings (King and McDermott 1995: 98, Sparks, Bottoms, and Hay 1996: 237). Such difficulties have undoubtedly been exacerbated at various times in the prisons in Northern Ireland where paramilitary prisoners have gained increasing control over their own living space, judicially challenged loosely prepared disciplinary charges, and generally made the effective identification and prosecution of rule breakers increasingly difficult. Second, the figures for violence and intimidation made available by the Prison Officers Association and the Northern Ireland Office were not in the ideal level of detail and the mechanisms for recording them altered over the period being studied.

With these caveats in mind, however, setting this data alongside interviews with prisoners and prison staff and published secondary sources does allow for a fairly reliable analysis of the role which violence, intimidation, and so forth has played in the resistance process in Northern Ireland prisons.

Prison Violence and Resistance

The broad relationship between violence and notions of resistance is well established in the literature of war, political science, terrorism, revolution, and psychology (Glad 1990, Braithwaite 1992, Burton 1996). While violent resistance is widely acknowledged and understood, views on its morality and efficacy vary widely across a range of settings. In the context of political conflicts such as Northern Ireland, views on violence range across a wide spectrum including violence as indicative of the pathological and criminal nature of terrorists (Wilkinson 1986), violence as armed propaganda (Schmid 1982), violence as an instrument of social change (Lenin 1962), or violence as a response to injustice and repression (Carmichael 1968, Mbeki 1991). While there is some discussion within the psychology of political conflict as to whether humans are intrinsically violent (e.g. Berkowitz 1990, 1993), more often the decision to use violence is ultimately (at least where it is planned) understood as 'a matter of judgement in the philosophical sense' (Keane 1996: 92).[2] This chapter explores some of the judgements which have informed prison-related violence in Northern Ireland over the past thirty years.

Studies of prison violence usually entail an analysis of the individual and/or structural reasons why prisoners resort to violence while incarcerated (e.g. Cohen, Cole, and Bailey 1976, Davies 1982, Ellis 1984, Brasswell, Montgomery, and Lombardo 1985, Cooke 1989, 1991, Stevens 1994, Harer and Steffenmeire 1996, Edgar and O'Donnell 1998). These may include a psychological approach to an individual's propensity to prison violence (Toch 1976, Gibbs 1981), links to previous offending behaviour, or policy-focused studies designed to improve the prisoner's coping or anger management skills (Porporino and Zamble 1984). Some scholars have emphasized the structural or environmental factors within the prison which may lead to prison violence (Bidna 1975, Atlas 1984, Eckland Olson 1986, Cooke 1991) including the effective impunity from successful prosecution of many of the most dangerous and predatory inmates (Eichental and Jacobs 1991). Stevens (1994: 142) argues that even prisoners with a non-violent past will 'accept the values and lifestyle of their round the clock environment which is centred on violent orientations'. Others have looked at factors related to the prison staff and management including the provisions of educational and self-improvement facilities (McCorckle, Miethe, and Drass 1995), staff communication skills with inmates (Cooke 1991),

---

[2] Keane defines judgement as the publicly learned capacity to choose courses of action in public contexts riddled with complexity. 'Judgement avoids categorical imperatives which instruct those who act to always act in the same way so that the criteria for their acts becomes a general law. Judgement tacks between the unique and the general. Judgement relies on the recognition that the practical choice of how to act in any context must be guided by the recognition of the particularity of that situation . . . In matters of violence, we can say, the most plausible working maxim is that the decision to use or not to use violence for power-political ends is always risky, and plagued by ongoing confusion and unintended consequences' (Keane 1996: 92–3).

the training of prison officers (Davies and Burgess 1988), and the willingness of the prison guards themselves to use violence as an instrument of power or in response to their own fear of attack (Ben-David, Silfen, and Cohen 1996).

There have been a number of attempts at classification of the different types of prison violence, in particular violence against staff. For example, Bowker (1980) argues that violence against officers may be characterized as either (a) spontaneous but predictable attacks (where staff are attacked conducting routine tasks in risk-prone environments such as interventions between inmates or in dealing with a prisoner with a history of violence) or (b) unexpected attacks which occur in an apparently random and unpredictable fashion which cannot be avoided unless officers shun all contacts with prisoners. Light (1991) has attempted to develop a much more comprehensive classification system. In his study, which looked in some detail at the circumstances of 694 assaults based upon the reports of staff in thirty-one New York State prisons, he devised fourteen themes to characterize assaults. These included altercations resulting from prisoners refusing to obey a command, attempted searches, inmates fighting, the discovery of contraband, applying or removing some form of restraint, prisoners with a history of emotional instability or mental illness, sexual harassment of officers and prisoners under the influence of drugs or alcohol. By far the largest category of explanations offered, over 25 per cent of the total sample, were characterized as unexplained where the officer had frequently entered 'for no apparent reason' in their report.

Such analysis, however, tends to overconcentrate on the particular characteristics of the prisoner involved—usually in an understandable attempt to identify and manage particularly dangerous prisoners—and to ignore the broader interaction between the prisoner, the power relations between individual or groups of prisoners, and the institution at a particular juncture in time and space (Toch 1992). For example, some commentators have traced the roots of organized prison violence, in either prison disturbances or riots, to prisoners protesting their treatment or the conditions of their detention within prison (King and Elliot 1977, Fitzgerald 1977, Cooke 1989, Scraton, Sim, and Skidmore 1991). The consideration of broader structural issues has also included the availability of effective redress mechanisms for aggrieved prisoners (Woolf 1991) and the extent to which power is legitimately exercised. As Light (1991: 258) has argued:

prisoners constantly evaluate the legitimacy of the command in relation to powerful unofficial norms. Conduct which is perceived as arbitrary, capricious, spiteful, unnecessary or petty may be viewed as an occasion for resistance.

As noted above, prisoners who are themselves subject to acts of violence by staff or fellow inmates may also resort to violence or destruction. For example, some serving and former prisoners have sought to show prison violence as an individualized response to coping with the 'pain of imprisonment', where prisoners are brutalized to such an extent by their fellow inmates and/or the prison authorities that violence becomes a natural response (Boyle 1977, 1984, Abbot 1981). Such commentators have pointed to the importance of fear as a factor in prison violence (Abbott 1981: 121–2), the desire to 'retaliate first' in a perennial cycle of inmate/inmate and staff/inmate violence.

Clearly the nature of the prison regimes may have an impact on the nature and levels of violence within a prison. For example, in the United States in recent years, much of the literature on prison violence in America has looked at the increasing collectivization of prisoners, particularly amongst gangs, and explored its relationship with increased levels of violence within prisons (Silberman 1995). Similarly Harer and Steffenmeier (1996) argue that prisons have become increasingly violent and fragmented in part as a result of large numbers of black and Latino gangs importing habits of street violence into the prison setting. In the prison literature generally, such gangs are viewed as a threat to the institutional order and security (e.g. Hunt *et al.* 1993, Tachiki 1995, Pollock 1997). As is discussed in the chapters below concerning prison management, the presence of organized groupings can have beneficial outcomes for prison managers and staff. None the less the segregation of paramilitary prisoners in Northern Ireland by faction, and their increased control over public spaces within the prisons, has undoubtedly facilitated the planning and execution of *collective* violence, destruction, and intimidation as a strategy of resistance within the prisons.

In sum, therefore, this analysis of prison violence in Northern Ireland is informed by a number of factors. Firstly a recognition that prison-related violence, both inside and outside the prison, should be understood as an intrinsic element of the broader conflict between the paramilitaries and the British state. Secondly while some such acts of violence were clearly strategic, carefully planned judgements designed to achieve particular objectives, others were not, arising instead as a result of the range of institutional, personality, and other variables which would be found in any prison setting. Lastly, the character and extent of prison violence has been directly related to the collective nature of the detention and support infrastructure of paramilitary prisoners in Northern Ireland.

Assassinations and Intimidation of Prison Staff and their Families

Any screw that was killed deserved it. I am sorry but that is how I feel about it after what they put us through.[3]

As can be seen from Table 5.1 twenty-nine prison officers have lost their lives over the course of the past thirty years with the majority of them having been killed by Republican paramilitaries. Of those killed, only one officer has been killed in the prisons over the course of the conflict, the officer who died of a heart attack after having been stabbed in the IRA escape from the Maze in 1983. The rest have been killed either at home, in transit to or from work, or elsewhere in the community. Clearly Northern Ireland's paramilitary prisoners have been able to rely upon their comrades still at large to carry out political assassinations of prison staff related to events within the prisons.

In analysing the death statistics, it is clear that some violence against prison officers was linked to particular events in the conflict such as the removal of special category status or the hunger strikes.[4] In one year, 1979, at the height of the dirty protest within the Maze leading up to the first hunger strike, nine prison officers were murdered. This figure constitutes almost one-third of the total number of prison officer casualties over the entire period of the conflict. It would appear that such murders were based upon both the strategic aim of pressuring the authorities who were seen to be implementing the policy of criminalisation and individual targeting of officers alleged to have committed particular acts of brutality against Republican prisoners.[5]

[3] Interview with former IRA prisoner, 15 June 1994.

[4] 'In the 1970s, after the removal of Special Category Status, there was a broad sweeping thing, the screws are the ones that are going to implement this [criminalisation] so they should pay the price.' Interview with former IRA prisoner, 5 Sept. 1997.

[5] For example, in Mar. 1984 Assistant Governor William McConnell was killed by the IRA in his home in East Belfast. One of the witnesses at the subsequent murder trial testified that McConnell was killed because 'he was giving prisoners in Long Kesh a hard time.' *Belfast Telegraph* (21 Oct. 1986). Similarly McKeown argues that another prison officer killed by the IRA in the 1980s was targeted because he was 'viewed by prisoners as the instigator of most of the brutality in H4' during the blanket protests (McKeown 1998: 286).

TABLE 5.1 *Prison staff murdered during current period of political violence*

Date	Name	Prison where worked	Method and faction
September 1974	Mr W. McCully	Retired	Shot (Republican)
April 1976	Mr P. C. Dillon	Magilligan	Shot (Republican)
April 1976	Mr J. D. Cummings	Belfast	Shot(Republican)
October 1976	Mr R. J. Hamilton	Magilligan	Shot (Republican)
June 1977	Mr J. W. Milliken	Belfast	Shot (Republican)
July 1977	Mr T. G. Fenton	Magilligan	Shot (Republican)
October 1977	Mr D. E. Irvine	Maze	Shot (Republican)
November 1978	Mr A. Miles	Maze	Shot (Republican)
December 1978	Mr J. McTair	Belfast	Shot (Republican)
February 1979	Mr P. Mackin (and wife)	Retired	Shot (Republican)
16 April 1979	Mr M. C. Cassidy	Belfast	Shot (Republican)
19 April 1979	Mrs A. J. Walker	Armagh	Shot and grenade (Republican)
14 September 1979	Mr G. Foster	Belfast	Shot (Republican)
19 September 1979	Mr E. D. Jones	Belfast	Shot (Republican)
5 November 1979	Mr T. Gilhooley	Belfast	Shot (Republican)
7 November 1979	Mr D. W. Teeney	Belfast	Shot (Republican)
23 November 1979	Mr G. F. Melville	Maze	Shot (Republican)
3 December 1979	Mr W. Wright	Belfast	Shot (Republican)
17 Decembrer 1979	Mr W. Wilson	Belfast	Shot (Republican)
18 January 1980	Mr C. F. Cox	Magilligan	Shot (Republican)
30 December 1980	Mr W. C. Burns	Belfast	Shot (Loyalist)
December 1982	Ms E. Chambliss	Armagh	Shot (Republican)
September 1983	Mr J. A. Ferris	Maze	Stabbed during escape (Republican)
March 1984	Mr W. McConnell	Maze	Shot (Republican)
February 1985	Mr P. J. Kerr	Maze	Shot (Republican)
March 1987	Mr L. Jarvis	Magilligan	Shot (Republican)
October 1988	Mr B. Armour	Maze	Car bomb (Republican)
May 1989	Mr J. Griffiths	Maze	Car bomb (Republican)
September 1993	Mr J. Peacock	Belfast	Shot (Loyalist)

Note: Table compiled by the author from Prison Officers Association Roll of Honour and contemporaneous newspaper accounts.

Interviewer. Do you think that during that period [hunger strike era] that the violence employed by Republicans against staff in terms of assassinations and assassination attempts were directed against specific officers, or do you think that it was any officer will do?

Respondent. A combination of both. It is interesting that while the protest was really on in the Maze at that time, many of the officers shot were from Belfast. You have to say they were more easily targeted and opportune. A lot of them were clerical grades and so on, people who don't really have any contact with prisoners . . . After the hunger strikes I would say that there were three or four on our roll of honour who were specifically targeted for what they inflicted on Republican prisoners during that period. That is what I have heard from others. I mean yes that is what Republicans would say.[6]

Another prison officer acknowledged that there were abuses of prisoners, but argued that this could only be understood within the context of the ongoing IRA campaign of violence.

Look, I am not going to try and tell you our people were angels during the period of the hunger strike and dirty protest. Of course they weren't. People overreacted and violence was used . . . but you have to put that in the context of conditions inside the prison and the Provos' campaign. The Provos were killing us at the time—and we were being fingered from inside the prison—what would you expect.[7]

In some instances, Republican violence against prison staff appeared to be directed against random prison officers. Peter Taylor (1997: 218–19), a respected journalist and commentator on Northern Ireland affairs, recounts a tale of an interview in his documentary *Life behind the Wire* in the autumn of 1977 with a prison officer. The officer spoke honestly and in direct contravention of government policy about the reality of the Republican prisoners as a disciplined and highly motivated army, describing their drill, military training, and command structures. He also described his respect for them in refusing to wear prison uniforms. He was told after the programme by the IRA spokesperson that 'they respected his frank answers and would act in a reciprocal manner' giving him hope of a new phase of co-operation between staff and prisoners. Two weeks later the IRA shot the officer dead, later claiming to Taylor that he had been killed because he was

---

[6] Interview with prison governor, 9 April 1998.
[7] Interview with prison officer, 13 Aug. 1997.

Secretary to the Prison Officers Association, and not because he had appeared on television.

In other instances, attacks were carried out which were quite clearly personal. One former Republican Officer Commanding suggested that IRA targeting policy became more refined in the wake of the hunger strikes.

By and large assassinations stopped after the hunger strikes, apart from one or two selected targets after the escape [1983] . . . and I would say that as the years went by there would have been a recognition, that while at the time it was understandable, it possibly wasn't the way to tackle it.[8]

According to a number of Republican prisoners therefore, the use of violence became more targeted and more selective in the 1980s, a back-up tactic to other forms of prison struggle. Undoubtedly prisoners took some pleasure in the deaths of particular prison officers. IRA Officer Commanding in the Maze Brendan 'Bik' MacFarlane (Campbell, McKeown, and O'Hagan 1994: 70) recorded that he took comfort from a number of developments in 1978 including 'the response to the barbarity of the screws by our comrades outside . . . particularly with the execution of the second in command of Long Kesh Governor Miles, who was the chief perpetrator of the regimes in the Blanket Blocks.'[9] Similarly another former IRA prisoner recounted his suffering at the hands of one officer who was subsequently killed by the IRA:

Respondent. There was one man in particular, RIP, he's dead. He was the most thoroughly evil person I ever met, [name] you called him. This man was at you twelve hours a day seven days a week . . . His particular forte was during mirror searches he would literally poke his finger up your anus, turn you around and say 'right what's that you have in your mouth there, and put the same finger in your mouth. You would never get a full cup of tea when he was on the wing, sometimes with urine in it, sometimes with disinfectant. He was nakedly sectarian and he had an outlet for it. I used to wonder what his family circumstances were, could he go home and switch off.

---

[8] Interview with former IRA Officer Commanding, HMP Maze, 12 Sept. 1994.

[9] Seamus Finucane, a former prisoner and senior Republican, gives a similar account in an interview with Kevin Toolis (1995: 138). 'The IRA executed numerous screws; in some cases they were killed as symbols of the uniform but some of them deserved it like the Red Rat (Brian Armour) . . . he was a Reinhard Heydrich sort of character or Doctor Mengele, an animal. I am sure a lot of people were glad to see him get his just desserts.'

Interviewer. How did you feel when you heard the IRA had blown him up?

Respondent. I felt it would have been a crime against humanity if that man had died of old age.[10]

Taylor (1997: 226) also recounts an interesting example of the depth of hatred generated against prison officers during that period, even amongst the leadership of the modern Republican movement.[11] Some prisoners interviewed for this book appeared to recognize that their brutalization during the dirty protest and hunger strike era had impacted upon their ability to think strategically about the use of prison-related violence. As one former IRA prison leader, then a Sinn Fein councillor, indicated:

Of course the beatings and humiliations of that era made us angry and made us think about revenge. We were only human after all. I am not trying to tell you that we never let it cloud our judgement but if we [the prison leadership] had tried to get the IRA to get every individual screw who tortured a Republican prisoner, the IRA would have done little else other than shoot screws.[12]

The bitterness and violence generated by the hunger strike era did not end with the concessions granted after the hunger strikes were over. In November 1981 Robert Bradford, an Official Unionist MP, who had spoken out strongly against the hunger strikers, describing them as 'sub-human vermin', was shot dead by the IRA. Although he was 'a strident loyalist, friend of Paisley and a symbolic sectarian bigot' (Bowyer Bell 1993: 635), this was clearly a sectarian 'operation' against a political opponent. The IRA had canvassed local units throughout Northern Ireland for suitable targets to carry out a symbolic act of punishment against the Unionists for their triumphalist attitude during the hunger strikes, and Bradford was chosen for 'his outlandish

[10] Interview with former IRA prisoner, 9 Oct. 1998.

[11] 'The hatred prisoners and prison officers felt for each other was mutual and lasting. Nothing brought it home to me more forcefully than a production of the Bobby Sands epic "the Crime of Castlereagh" which I watched in a parochial hall in West Belfast. It was staged by former prisoners and prisoners out on parole and home leave. One scene depicted a prisoner being turned upside down and whilst a prison officer with rubber gloves gloating searched his anus. As the officer walked off the stage a shot rang out and he fell down dead. It was a dramatic piece of theatre. The packed audience, among whom were many of the Republican Movement's most prominent figures, including members of the leadership, broke out in spontaneous applause and cheering. It was a chilling moment' (Taylor 1997: 226).

[12] Interview with former dirty protester, IRA hunger striker, and later Officer Commanding, 15 Dec. 1994.

sectarian remarks' (Bishop and Mallie 1987: 388). A caretaker who was in the MP's surgery by chance when the IRA unit arrived was also killed.

As can be seen in Table 5.1, murders of prison officers by Republicans continued throughout the 1980s, albeit at a reduced rate. It is clear, however, that some changes occurred in the targeting policy of Republicans over that period, whereby prison officers were no longer considered axiomatically legitimate targets. For example, in 1990 the South Armagh Brigade of the IRA stopped a policeman and four prison officers who were returning from a fishing trip in the Irish Republic. Two of the prison officers managed to escape just after the car was stopped by the IRA checkpoint. The policeman was executed but the prison officers were released unharmed. The prison officers were told that since they were serving at the Maze, their lives would be spared as the IRA 'had no grudge against screws at the Maze' but that their fate might have been different had they been working at Crumlin Road (Harnden 1999: 165–7).

The two murders of prison staff by Loyalist organizations both occurred during periods of Loyalist protest. It is important to note that, despite the fact that Republicans carried out the vast majority of deadly attacks on prison officers, Loyalist threats against prison staff have been a constant feature of prisons in Northern Ireland, and of considerable concern to prison staff given that the vast majority of the staff live in Protestant areas where they are more vulnerable to attack from Loyalists.[13] In 1980, when William Burns was killed, Loyalist prisoners were protesting against the policy of forced integration on wings with non-protesting Republicans at HMP Maze. His murder was claimed by a previously unheard-of group but the death was widely attributed to the UVF (Cusack and McDonald 1997: 188). The other murder was that of Jim Peacock, a prison officer at HMP Belfast who was also shot dead by the UVF in 1993.[14] This murder also occurred during the violence and protests concerning compassionate home leave at HMP Maze.[15]

[13] Interview with Prison Officers Association spokesperson, 17 Sept. 1996.
[14] *Newsletter* (2 Sept. 1993), 'Terror Gang Kills Warder'.
[15] The murder of prison officer Jim Peacock is an instructive example of how micro issues of prison management can lead to violence in the absence of restraint by paramilitary organizations either inside or outside the prisons. While the murder did follow a summer of tension and disruption amongst Loyalist inmates at the prison, even within the lexicon of Northern Ireland, there would certainly appear to be a question as to the 'proportionality' of the UVF response to events in the Maze. On 1 Sept. 1993, the

One former UVF Officer Commanding in the Maze told the author:

Respondent. There was always pressure on the organization on the outside coming from prisoners wanting to take out this screw or that screw. I was always against such actions and tried to dissuade people from acting in this manner.

Interviewer. Why, because it would have been perceived as killing fellow Protestants?

Respondent. No, definitely not. You have to understand that there is often a great deal of anger amongst Loyalist prisoners towards prison officers, their own kind locking them up . . . I was opposed to it because it could have been the thin end of the wedge . . . one could be unsure where such targeting would stop . . . In terms of the Peacock killing, that came about because of a lack of discipline on the inside [by prisoners' leaders], poor management by the prison authorities and it is possible that the UVF had been attempting to frighten him but that the operation had been bungled.[16]

Violence and the threats of violence against prison officers by Loyalists remained a persistent feature in the 1990s,[17] with only sporadic threats emanating from the Republican side from splinter factions such as the INLA. The granting of a separate wing to the extremely volatile and unpredictable Loyalist Volunteer Force faction considerably exacerbated that tendency. Threats of direct action, serious consequences,

---

UVF broke into the home of prison officer Jim Peacock, an officer off on sick leave who had been based at Crumlin Road prison, and shot him several times in front of his family. The attack was linked to a dispute about the availability of compassionate home leave for a UVF prisoner *Newsletter* (2 Sept. 1993), 'Terror Gang Kills Warder', *Belfast Telegraph* (2 Sept. 1993), 'UVF Murder Fuels Fears of Warders'. The UVF statement released after the murder stated that 'we were left with no option but to take appropriate action' following the failure of the authorities to hold discussions about their failure to grant home leave to the prisoner in question *Irish Times* (3 Sept. 1993), 'Loyalist Threat to Kill More Warders: UVF Demand Talks on Prison Conditions'. They warned of more violence unless 'UVF inmates were allowed to serve their sentences with dignity and safety' *Newsletter* (3 Sept. 1993), 'New Threat to Prison Staff'. The prison service countered with a statement claiming that the prisoner who was refused compassionate release to visit a sick relative had previously been allowed three such visits in three weeks. On hearing the request for the fourth, he was refused on the grounds that the relative had died which entitled the prisoner to 24 hours compassionate leave but only when the funeral arrangements had been made *Belfast Telegraph* (4 Sept. 1993), 'Bereaved Loyalist: Prison Service Clarifies'. One senior manager within the prison service complained to the author at the time that 'the essential problem was the poor quality of the UVF prison leadership' (confidential source).

[16] Interview with former UVF Officer Commanding, 2 Dec. 1994.
[17] *Irish Times* (3 Sept. 1993), 'Loyalist Threat to Kill More Warders'.

etc. emanating from this and other Loyalist factions continued to be issued with predictable regularity up to the final releases of the factions on ceasefire.[18]

Paramilitary groups' capacity for lethal prison-related attacks in the community is clearly an additional dynamic in understanding violence as resistance in this context.[19] In a conflict characterized by the willingness of all the protagonists to use lethal force in the pursuance of political objectives, it is unsurprising that prison-related armed struggle played a significant role. Violence was not, however, an inevitable product of political imprisonment in Northern Ireland as was demonstrated in the 1980s and 1990s when Republican prisoners declared the Maze prison as 'removed from the war zone'. It became a tactic which could be turned on and off, depending upon the state of relations between the prisoners and the authorities in the prison. The relevance of the prisoners' capacity for organized violence and the power relations with the prison authorities are discussed in the final part of this chapter.

Organized Destruction within the Prisons

I suppose it is a tactic which is always there . . . I mean if you are a prisoner and you are pissed off at the conditions, or protesting about Special Cat Status or whatever there is only so much you can do. It is an easy thing to give the order and say lets wreck the jail . . . It is a tactic which we used less frequently in the prison struggle, however, you are still going to have to live in the conditions after its over . . . I think it is something which you should keep in reserve but make it clear that there are a lot of steps before things get to that stage.[20]

As with prisons in Britain (Woolf 1991, Scraton, Sim, and Skidmore 1991), politically motivated prisoners in Northern Ireland have persistently resorted to the destruction of the prison fabric and attacks on prison staff within the prison as a mechanism of protest. Sometimes these protests have been planned and organized and directed at achiev-

[18] *Irish News* (3 Mar. 1998), 'LVF Threatens Maze Guards: Direct Action will Follow if Loyalists are Mistreated'. This typical threat was issued against prison staff in light of a series of searches and regime restrictions in the Maze following the LVF torture and murder of one of their own remand prisoners after he was suspected of becoming an informer.

[19] For example, a number of the prison officers interviewed for this research have recounted incidents of prisoners relaying prison officers the correct details of their names and addresses in order to underline their vulnerability.

[20] Interview with former IRA prisoner, 1 Sept. 1995.

ing a clear objective such as segregation from rival factions, resistance to the symbols of criminal rather than political imprisonment, or more micro issues such as improvements in conditions within the prisons. Other such protests have arisen spontaneously and apparently with less clear objectives. Sometimes they have been led by Republicans, sometimes by Loyalists, and sometimes there has clearly been a degree of interfactional co-operation to achieve mutually desirable goals. I do not intend to offer details on every such event which has occurred over the period. Rather I have chosen to focus upon two key events, one carried out by Republicans and the other by Loyalists, in order to draw out some salient points about how such activities may be understood within a resistance paradigm.

The Burning of Long Kesh and Related Destruction (October 1974): A Conditions-Based Protest

The destruction of Long Kesh is a useful example of a prison-based riot which while not explicitly linked by prisoners to the question of political status, quickly spilled over into violence and destruction at other prisons and public disorder in Nationalist areas. Those who took part in the protest were all either Special Category prisoners or internees, and were to all intents and purposes already recognized as prisoners of war. Their burning of the camp had been preceded by an ongoing protest over conditions within the prison.

The compound system encouraged a degree of co-ordination between the factions.[21] The collective camp council consisting of all the Officers Commanding (i.e. Provisional IRA, Official IRA, Ulster Defence Association, Ulster Volunteer Force, and Irish Republican Socialist Party) had organized a boycott of all visiting facilities from April 1974. That protest was only called off when the camp OCs were assured of improvements and were invited to inspect the visiting facilities (Crawford 1979: 55). In the summer and autumn of 1974 the focus

[21] Crawford (1979: 57–8) describes one example of interfactional co-operation regarding what became known as the 'Ho Chi Minn Trail'. Interned prisoners were held in separate compounds from the sentenced Special Category compounds. When the latter were on protest and therefore denied privileges, the prisoners fashioned makeshift ropes from wires, cords, clothing, etc., strung these from various high vantage points from around the camp and devised a pulley system where fresh provisions of food, meat, vegetables, and cigarettes were supplied to the Special Category compounds. This system required and was afforded co-operation between factions as goods were passed across opposition compounds to reach their goal.

of protests had been redirected to the quality of the food and heavy-handed treatment by prison staff (Bowyer Bell 1993: 427).

Provisional IRA prisoners had protested regarding these concerns by draping their blankets over the wire of the compounds, obscuring the guards' view as to what was happening inside the compound, and throwing their food over the perimeter fences. Their camp OC having previously threatened to burn down the camp after a series of beatings by the British army, senior members of the IRA were debating the possibility of combining a mass escape with the burning when trouble broke out in compound 13.[22] The trouble had arisen when the compound commander for compound 13 had asked to have a prison officer removed from his compound because he was deemed unacceptable by inmates. When the officer refused, he was assaulted by inmates. The camp OC asked to see the compound to defuse the situation and when he was refused permission, he ordered that the entire camp be burned (Adams 1996: 237–8).[23]

Prisoners armed with a variety of implements attacked staff and a large area of the prison including much of the living, dining, recreational, and visiting accommodation was destroyed by fire. The army responded with CS Gas and rubber bullets and a total of twenty-three soldiers, and fourteen prison officers were injured and thirty-one prisoners required hospital treatment (NIPS 1976: 11). The Provisional IRA prisoners were subsequently joined in the protest by Official IRA prisoners while the Loyalists did not respond, but rather congregated in two compounds for safety of numbers (Ryder 2000: 141).

One prisoner who took part in the burning described his feelings thus:

To be honest I was shitting myself. There were flames everywhere, rubber bullets whinging everywhere, dogs, CS Gas and all I had was a lump of plank. . . I suppose at the back of your mind you knew that we hadn't a chance and that we would probably get a good digging when it was over . . . [24]

Predictably the authorities' reaction led to demonstrations and rioting in Nationalist communities and sympathy protests by Republican prisoners held at Magilligan, Belfast, and the women's prison at Armagh (Bew and Gillespie 1993). Republican women prisoners at Armagh

---

[22] Interview with former IRA prisoner, 5 Aug. 1998.
[23] For an alternative view of the origins of this dispute from the prison officers' perspective see Challis (1999: 60–63).
[24] Interview with former IRA prisoner, 5 Aug. 1998.

took the governor and three senior officers hostage, after the governor had gone down to the wing to persuade them not to start a fire, demanding assurances that the men injured in the riots at the Maze were 'safe and not being ill-treated'. The governor and staff were released unhurt some twelve hours later after interventions by clergymen. Republican prisoners at Magilligan burnt a number of huts, the kitchen, and the hospital and 131 prisoners rioting at Belfast prison were injured. The total cost of the destruction was put at £2 million (NIPS 1976: 11).

The ability to destroy the instrument of one's detention, to alter radically the environment in which one is imprisoned is a direct and powerful form of resistance. As King and McDermott argue, whilst riots and destruction are nearly always quickly characterized by anarchy, they can also bring a real, if fleeting, sense of liberation (King and McDermott 1995: 114). Resistance is a process rather than simply the achievement of an objective. In a dispute related to food and visits Republicans had wrecked the prison, engaged the British army (albeit for a limited period in hopeless circumstances), and delivered upon their previous threat to burn the prison unless conditions improved. While prisoners are unsentimental about the results of their efforts, the act of 'having a go', particularly in circumstances where no victory such as escape is possible, is clearly an act of resistance itself.[25]

Destruction by Loyalist Prisoners: The Campaign for Segregation

Loyalist protests have, since the 1970s, been characterized as less organized and less disciplined than their Republican counterparts. They are normally described as spontaneous, violent, or lacking in any clear sense of purpose. For example, during the dirty protest at the Maze by Republican prisoners 1976–9, the Northern Ireland prison service *Annual Report* (1979: 16) notes that 'at Belfast there were occasional outbreaks of indiscipline by Loyalist untried prisoners in pursuit of their claim for segregation, and a more co-ordinated protest by those with Republican affiliations'. Loyalist prisoners had taken hostages and gone on to the roof at Crumlin Road prison in December

[25] 'Well I wouldn't say it was the greatest victory of all time. We got a few digs in like but they kicked the shite out of us. We were left lying for a couple of weeks in what was left of the canteen, you know just the timbers, like the shell. We were lying on mattresses the Brits gave us that must have been left over from the Crimean War . . . still, it was worth it though.' Interview with former IRA prisoner, 5 Aug. 1998.

1980, damaged a number of cells in Crumlin Road in 1981, and 300 in the Maze in October 1982. Both of these were linked to their campaign (being matched by the Republicans) for interfactional segregation.

In 1994, following prolonged disturbances by Loyalist prisoners, a group of Loyalists succeeded in reaching the roof of Belfast prison.[26] The prisoners' protest began when UDA prisoners refused to return to their cells after exercise. Claiming subsequently that fellow Loyalist prisoners in the Maze were being harassed by staff, and pointing to the poor physical conditions and overcrowding in Crumlin Road prison, the prisoners began wrecking their cells and made their way on to the roofs. These actions were followed two weeks later when Loyalist prisoners in A and B wing rioted, destroying over 100 cells in one night and ultimately doing so much damage to the fabric of the prison that the authorities decided that the prison was uninhabitable.[27] What had begun as a protest in sympathy with fellow Loyalists at the Maze and over the poor physical conditions at Crumlin Road, resulted in all paramilitary prisoners (including Republicans) being moved to *segregated* accommodation at the Maze.[28] As one prison governor told the author:

Once the decision was made to move the remand paramilitaries to the Maze, there was no question that we could impose an integrated regime on them up there. We were stuck for space, it would have been a managerial nightmare and the protests would have spilled over to the sentenced prisoners. Having lost Crumlin Road, which I think we could have avoided, there was no way we could lose another prison.[29]

The campaign to achieve segregation of remand prisoners had been at the forefront of the prison struggle since the beginning of the conflict. Arguably it marked the final symbolic recognition of the political status of paramilitary prisoners (short of their early release in light of the ceasefires) and it was achieved by Loyalists. As is discussed below, the campaign for this objective over the preceding decades had included serious violence between Loyalists and Republicans, attacks on prison staff, and considerable political pressure to accede to the wishes of the

[26] *Newsletter* (8 July 1994), 'Inmates on the Rampage'.

[27] 'Following the second incident [riots of 16 July 1994] the damage was such that high risk remand prisoners could no longer be held securely and it was decided to transfer these prisoners to HMP Maze.' *Annual Report* of the NIPS (1994/5: 8).

[28] *Belfast Telegraph* (19 July 1994), 'NIO Denies Surrender Over Rioting Loyalists: Cells Uninhabitable as Inmates are switched to the H Blocks'.

[29] Interview with prison governor, 12 Feb. 1996.

prisoners, all of which had been steadfastly resisted by the authorities (Colville 1992). The move occurred in a political context in which Loyalist paramilitaries had killed more people over the preceding three years than Republicans (McAuley 1995). As one former Loyalist prisoner described it:

It was excellent for our morale. We achieved segregation [of remand prisoners] when the Provos had been pushing for it for years. With the military campaign on the outside hurting the IRA more than it had ever done, it meant that everybody had to take us seriously.[30]

One prison officer, having requested that the tape recorder be switched off, argued that the movement of prisoners to the Maze, following the riots of 1994, represented a lack of resolve on the part of the prison management because the rioting prisoners were Loyalists.

If Crumlin Road had been wrecked by Republicans, we would have been ordered to go in and kick the fuck out of them, handcuffed them to the radiators and rebuilt the prison around them as they lay in their own shite—we weren't because they were Loyalists—it was the same with those Loyalists on the roof of the Maze in 1995, if those had been provies [IRA] we would have been ordered to hose them off the fucking roof. I told that to the NIO.[31]

Whatever the merit of such assertions, it is unarguable that the destruction and subsequent closure of Crumlin Road and the securing of segregation for the remand paramilitary prisoners represented the most significant and successful act of resistance on the part of Loyalist prisoners throughout the conflict. What was also of interest was the decision by the Republican prisoners to stand back while 'the Loyalists made the running',[32] much as the Loyalists had done during the dirty protest and hunger strike era.

I suppose we felt we had nothing to prove. We didn't think the Loyalists' tactics would work but we thought well they might as well get on with it and providing our people were not being harmed, we could just wait and see what would happen.[33]

---

[30] Interview with former Loyalist prisoner, 12 Jan. 1996.

[31] Interview with prison officer, 17 Sept. 1996.

[32] Interview with former IRA remand prisoners held at Crumlin Road during the Loyalist protests, 1 Mar. 1996.

[33] Interview with former IRA remand prisoners held at Crumlin Road during the Loyalist protests, 1 Mar. 1996.

Inmate on Inmate Violence

Violence amongst inmates has been a predictable feature of prisons in Northern Ireland over the past three decades. As in the USA, where the rise in violence in many prisons has been directly linked to feuds between rival gangs (Irwin 1980), many of them divided on ethnic grounds (Harer and Steffenmeier 1996), the dangers of holding such large numbers of paramilitary enemies in close proximity has led to predictable outbreaks of violence between the rival factions. Such outbreaks have been both organized in pursuit of strategic objectives (such as segregated accommodation) and spontaneous eruptions as adversaries have come into contact. In addition, given the considerable control which paramilitary offenders have been able to exercise over their living space, there have been limited but significant incidents of prisoners carrying out acts of violence against members of their own paramilitary factions. Again such incidents may be divided into strategic or organized violence related to matters such as ensuring organization security and assertions of control as well as sporadic disputes arising between individuals and groups of prisoners. Once again, only a small number of the most significant attacks are drawn upon.

Throughout the 1970s and 1980s violence was commonplace as the prison authorities attempted to integrate Loyalist and Republican inmates (Relatives Action Committee n.d. approx 1993). The *Annual Reports* of the Northern Ireland Prison Service report actions such as assaults, scaldings, and interfactional riots with a resigned monotony (NIPS 1971–97), often arguing that the paramilitary factions colluded in their acts of violence to achieve mutually desirable objectives such as segregation.[34] A number of prisoners interviewed for this book have confirmed collusion in certain circumstances, although as circumstances changed so too did the rules governing inmate violence. As one former UDA life sentenced prisoner suggested.

Interviewer. Did you regard it as your duty to attack Republicans if you got an opportunity, at the dentists, or wherever?

[34] For example the 1990 prison service *Annual Report* notes 'a number of interfactional assaults in A and C wings of Crumlin Road were recorded, the result of collusion between Republicans and Loyalists. A number of staff were injured in intervening. For the remainder of the year, apart from a small number of opportunist attacks by both factions, the segregation issue passed into one of its recurring latent phases' (NIPS 1990: 10).

Respondent. There was always neutral areas, at the visits and hospitals. There was a scenario at one stage during the 1980s where it was forced upon us, there was fire bombs going off in cells, and a lot of that stuff, but there was a lot of collusion too . . . After the Loyalists came off their protest [*c.*1984], the danger time came. The government said 'right, the protest is over' so they got ten Republicans together and ten Loyalists and put them in the wing together. The orders were to open the door and get stuck into them [Republicans], it didn't matter what size they were, big or small. They tried that for one week and that was it, they never tried to mix us again.[35]

In the wake of the hunger strikes and the gradual granting of the demands of paramilitary prisoners at the Maze, the continued policy of integrating remand prisoners, ostensible at least,[36] became a key focus of Loyalist and Republican prisoners in the 1980s. The related campaign of violence culminated in November 1991 when the IRA detonated a small Semtex-based bomb in the dining room of C Wing at Crumlin Road prison, apparently by use of a timer, killing two Loyalist inmates. The Republicans had been able to plant the bomb in a dining area knowing that it would be occupied by Loyalists after their departure (Colville 1992).[37] Loyalist paramilitaries retaliated to the bomb in the dining area by launching a rocket-propelled grenade attack at the dining area of the prison although the grenade missed its intended target and no one was injured (Bew and Gillespie 1993: 282).

Both of these violent attacks are illustrative of an interplay between the broader objectives of the paramilitaries regarding their desire to achieve segregation, the reality of their ongoing military campaign against each other, and more immediate incidents such as the attack on the minibus or the bomb in 1991 which led respective factions to devote resources to prison-based attacks.

[35] Interview with former UDA prisoner, 24 July 1998.

[36] In effect the prisoners had a policy of self-segregation wherein a 'good day/bad day system' operated wherein Loyalists and Republicans would use the dining facilities, exercise yards, etc. at alternative times or days of the week.

[37] It has been suggested that the decision to plant the bomb may have come about as a result of a Loyalist attack on a Republican minibus carrying prisoners' families to a visit in Crumlin Road in Aug. 1991. That attack, which breached an apparent hitherto unwritten rule that prisoners' families were off-limits from attack by either faction, led to frantic efforts to reinstate that moratorium by go-betweens operating between the factions (confidential source). In admitting the attack, the IRA stated that it was carried out 'in direct response to outside attacks upon Republican prisoners and their families by Loyalists which have occurred over a considerable period, often with the collusion of wardens'. In his report on the bomb, Lord Colville speculates that the Loyalist attack on families may have been 'one step too far' (Colville 1992: 14).

The other most noteworthy interfactional attack actually occurred during the peace process of the mid-1990s when the Republican splinter group the INLA (Irish National Liberation Army) murdered Billy Wright, leader of the Loyalist splinter group the LVF (Loyalist Volunteer Force), in the Maze prison. Wright, the former leader of the larger UVF (Ulster Volunteer Force) in mid-Ulster, was expelled from that organization and formed his own band of dissidents in explicit opposition to the UVF ceasefire and the involvement of their political wing (the Progressive Unionist Party) in the peace negotiations (Cusack and McDonald 1997: 346–9). Wright was also one of the most well-known Loyalist paramilitaries in Northern Ireland, operating under the name of 'King Rat' and was widely linked in the media to the killings of a large number of Catholics in the mid-Ulster area (McPhilemy 1998).

As noted previously, Wright had originally been held at Maghaberry. However, after a series of protests and a threatened hunger strike, the authorities had granted him and his small band of LVF prisoners a wing in the Maze prison. The status which accompanied the granting of a separate wing in the Maze had in turn been a major boost for pro-Wright dissidents both in the prison (where some Loyalist prisoners left other factions to go on to the LVF wing) and as a recruiting point for activists on the outside.

Wright's murder was also of considerable political significance to his killers and to the broader community.[38] The block in which Wright was held (Block 8) in the Maze also held INLA prisoners who had repeatedly warned of the dangers of keeping their sworn enemies in such close proximity. The INLA, which was also opposed to the peace process at that time, had been riven with deadly internal schisms and feuds, and linked to criminal activities including drug dealing, all of which had seriously damaged their credibility with potential supporters in the Republican community (Holland and McDonald 1994). The opportunity to kill such a hated figure as Wright and his proximity in the same prison block was described excitedly to the author by one former INLA activist as 'an absolute Godsend, the best thing we have done since the hunger strikes or Airey Neave'.[39] In addition, the man who assassinated Wright, Christopher 'Crip' McWilliams, himself a

[38] *Irish News* (29 Dec. 1997a), 'King Rat was a Thorn in the Side of the UVF Leadership'.
[39] Airey Neave was the political adviser to Margaret Thatcher who had helped steer her to the leadership of the Conservative Party. He was blown up in Mar. 1979 by the INLA in the underground car park of the House of Commons (conversation with the author, 12 Jan. 1998).

life sentenced prisoner, had been convicted of the non-politically motivated murder of a doorman who had thrown him out of a bar, an act
which had caused widespread revulsion and ostracization of
McWilliams by fellow Republicans.[40] Wright's killing was laden with
political symbolism both within the prison and in the world of paramilitarism on the outside.

The other principal form of organized inmate on inmate violence
has been associated with the maintenance of control, discipline, and
security within paramilitary factions. A number of examples offer
illustrative insights. In 1972 Lennie Murphy, leader of the UVF's
'Shankill Butchers', poisoned another Loyalist prisoner who had
agreed to turn Queen's evidence against him. After forcing him to sign
a letter of retraction, he forced a tube of cyanide down the victim's
throat (Dillon 1989). In 1982, during the 'Supergrass era' (Greer 1995),
UVF prisoners managed to smuggle cyanide into the prison kitchens
and poured some into custard which was destined for the segregation
unit (Bew and Gillespie 1993). However, the cyanide discoloured the
custard and the plot was uncovered. Similarly, in March 1998, LVF prisoners tortured a fellow LVF remand prisoner, and then murdered him
by hanging him with a bed sheet and slashing his wrists,[41] after they
suspected him of becoming an RUC informer. All LVF prisoners on the
wing then smeared themselves with the blood of the victim in order to
subvert the possibilities of forensic detection.[42] Examples of extreme
intrafactional violence are rare on the Republican side, particularly
amongst the mainstream IRA.[43] As one prison governor suggested:

I am not suggesting they don't run a fairly disciplinarian regime but they do
tend to *think through* [interviewee's emphasis] their use of violence. They
want to keep the whole group solidarity thing going and you can't do that
through fear and intimidation. You are more likely to get thrown off the wings

[40] *Irish News* (29 Dec. 1997b), 'No Stranger to Violent Death'.

[41] *Irish News* (17 Mar. 1998), 'Dead LVF Man Was Tortured', *Irish Times* (17 Mar.
1998), 'Authorities Must Have Known Keys was at Risk'.

[42] *Observer* (25 Mar. 1998),'Loyalist Smeared Blood on Maze Inmates to Shield
Killer'.

[43] There have been a number of incidents wherein the INLA planned or attempted to
kill their own members while in prison. These included the plans to poison or shoot
INLA supergrass Harry Kirkpatrick when he was held in Annex A of Crumlin Road
prison (Holland and McDonald 1994: 207). IRA tactics with regard to dealing with
imprisoned informers or supergrasses, assuming that they could not be successfully
killed while in prison, appears to have been to use intimidation and leverage against the
informer's family, and a promise of safety in exile, in return for a retraction of evidence
(Greer 1995).

as a serious sanction if you cross the Provo leadership. Even if someone does get a hiding down the wing, we are the last ones who will hear about it.[44]

Intimidation, Conditioning, and the Struggle for Control of Space within the Prisons

Institutional control over, and restriction of, the movement of prisoners within prisons has traditionally been viewed as a key component for the maintenance of security (King 1987, Bottoms, Hay and Sparks 1990). Prisoners and staff often have different notions of space within a prison. Prisoners often view it in relation to their ability to engage in personal or group activities while prison officers conceptualize it in relation to particular goals such as moving prisoners easily, monitoring their behaviour, and provision of certain facilities (Canter and Ambrose 1980, cited in Sparks, Bottoms, and Hay 1996: 229).

Unsurprisingly in the context of Northern Irish prisons, staff notions of space within the prisons are associated with the concerns of any high security prison regarding the prevention of escapes and the security of staff and other inmates. For the prisoners, quite apart from the desire to effect escapes, issues of access to, and control of, space within the prison are of direct relevance to the political and ideological questions of their 'political' status. For example, in the period when internees and Special Category prisoners were held, they effectively controlled the space within their compounds at Long Kesh. They were able to drill, to hold military and political lectures, and effectively to exclude prison officers and soldiers for large parts of the prison day. Such places allowed prisoners to 'rework and divert space to other' ends' (Pile 1997: 16), to create 'sites of resistance'. Similarly, as argued previously, the period of the dirty protests and hunger strikes saw prisoners reduced to asserting their resistance on their own bodies or in the confined spaces of their cells while the authorities controlled the public spaces of the prison.

The significance of the relationship between the contraction of personal space and the capacity to resist was not lost on those prisoners who lived through that period:

After the hunger strikes, we needed the space to move, to try to break it [criminalisation] we said we need to be able to meet up with the other prisoners, let's take control of the space, of the wings . . . When you control the living space

---

[44] Interview with prison governor, 13 Sept. 1997.

move it out, gradually, let them get comfortable with it. We said from here on there would be no more hurting ourselves, we had to find ways of breaking down control without stepping over the limit.[45]

In the wake of the hunger strikes era the prison authorities in the early 1980s viewed the increased willingness of IRA prisoners to leave their cells, engage in discussion and negotiation (rather than violence and threats), and even undertake some prison work as a welcome development. As was discussed previously, some of the rationale for this behaviour became all too obvious after the mass IRA escape in 1983. The prisoners' change of tactics throughout the 1980s was of course noted by the prison authorities. As one *Annual Report* notes regarding the low figures for violent assaults upon staff and general disruption:

The absence of serious incidents did not however reflect a change in objectives on the part of the paramilitary type prisoners, but rather a shift in strategy. The nature of their challenge to the authorities has changed from direct confrontation of the 1970s and early 1980s, exemplified by the blanket and dirty protests and culminating in the hungerstrikes, to a more subtle campaign characterised by attempts to secure concessions by pressurising staff and by exploiting the legitimate grievance procedures.[46]

The exploitation of 'legitimate grievance procedures' is explored in some detail in the next chapter. However, the pressurizing of staff was intimately linked to gaining increasing access to the public areas of the prison. Having secured free access to their own wings in the early 1980s, they continued to press for, and were ultimately successful in achieving, interwing association between 1986 and 1989. One prison officer who worked in the Maze throughout this period described it thus:

They were always wanting more territory, they had the cell, then they had the landing, then they had the dining hall. They wanted to have control over the areas that we thought we controlled.[47]

The mechanisms for achieving the prisoners' objective of 'breaking down control without stepping over the limit' had, by definition, to seek to avoid physical confrontation with prison staff on the wings.

---

[45] Interview with former IRA Officer Commanding, HMP Maze, 12 Sept. 1994.
[46] *Annual Report* of the NIPS (1985: 7).
[47] Interview with former prison officer, 12 Sept. 1996.

Any over-resort to violence on the wings would inevitably lead to a response from the riot squad, prisoners potentially forced back into their cells, and the loss of whatever gains had been made. Rather than simply attacking prison officers, or threatening them that they would be killed on the outside, prisoners instead sought to achieve their objectives by conditioning prison officers.

The dangers presented by such conditioning is neither new nor indeed unique to Northern Ireland. For example, in 1987 the Home Office research report on special secure units argued that the 'relaxed atmosphere and easy relations between staff and inmates can condition staff into being less vigilant about security matters' (Home Office 1987). That report concluded that such conditioning had contributed to two serious escape attempts at Leicester in 1968 and Parkhurst in 1976. In the Woodcock Report (1994: 72), one governor suggested that conditioning of staff had been so successful by prisoners that prison officers were shocked and surprised that escaping IRA prisoners would actually shoot at one of them in the attempted escape at Whitemoor. Similarly the Learmont Report (1995) discussed the conditioning of prison staff amongst the 'litany of errors at every level' which led to the Parkhurst breakout. It is arguable that, in Northern Ireland, the combination of paramilitary power, patience, and organization exercised by paramilitary prisoners has taken conditioning to an entirely new level in prison management.

In 1984, in his report on the Maze escape of 1983 Sir James Hennessey equated conditioning with:

lowering the level of tension in the Block and avoiding, where ever possible, confrontation with staff . . . So successful was this policy in diverting the attention of the prison authorities away from H7, that an atmosphere was soon created in which abuses of normal security procedure came to be regarded by the majority of staff in H7 as almost routine—certainly as practices which did no harm. (Hennessey 1984: 14)

The techniques employed, particularly by Republican prisoners, developed considerably throughout the 1980s. The tactics identified by prison officers (and acknowledged by some of the prisoners who employed them) included friendliness to officers, reasonableness of demands and willingness to compromise, physical isolation of prison staff, changeability, good prisoner/bad prisoner routines, creating and exploiting divergences both between management levels and at different locations within the prison, and a range of other tactics universally acknowledged by all prison staff interviewed for this book as 'well thought out and executed'.[48]

The account of one governor (with over ten years' experience of dealing with the IRA prisoners on the wings at the Maze during the 1980s) is worth reproducing in some detail.

Respondent. With the Republicans, they will not use violence unless as a weapon of last resort but you are always aware that they have the power of life and death over you . . . They are generally very polite, don't use bad language, everything is stage managed, everything is role played. Their conditioning process, the psychology books those boys read twenty years ago we are only reading today . . . And then from time to time officers would go down the wings, and they would be over the top nice to you, offering you cups of tea and coffee, no harassment and then on a particular day that same officer would become a major problem, and he would spend his day being harassed off the face of the earth with the threat of violence and the threat of violence outside to his family.

Interviewer. Do you think it was strategic, do you think they sat down and worked that stuff out?

Respondent. Very much so—you used to go down one wing and it was what about you [name], how are you doing, what have you got for us today, nothing as usual the same old story, laughing and joking, happy days. You go into the next wing and you knew something was wrong because there were no prisoners on the wings and you think they have all escaped, they hadn't but you couldn't see them and the eerie thing was that all the cell doors are open. You get to the bottom of the wing, and you and the governor are confronted by three inmates. You can see the space on the wing being filled in behind them by prisoners doing innocuous things. And the three invade your body space, talking, making you edge backwards, back, back until you were in the corner. And you can see that up the wing your principal officer, your only means of support is also surrounded by three prisoners . . . it was scary, and it was clever and it was well thought out all right, totally stage managed.[49]

Republican prisoners in the 1980s have acknowledged to the author role playing interactions with governors and prison staff concerning discussions on conditions.[50] Prisoners deliberately used to arrange

[48] Interview with prison officer, 12 Oct. 1995.
[49] Interview with prison governor, 13 Sept. 1997.
[50] Interview with former IRA prisoner, 10 Oct. 1995.

discussions with different governors, minute those discussions highlighting any divergences, and 'play staff off' against one another. Often prisoners would stand beside officers on the wings as the officers made telephone calls to senior managers (to demonstrate their bona fides) passing on the requests of prisoners. As the governor above recounted:

I have seen times in the Maze when an officer would phone me up and he was under so much pressure to deliver that I thought this is actually a prisoner I am talking to.[51]

Conclusion: Power, Space, and Violence as Part of the Furniture

Much of the commentary by the media and other visitors to the Maze prison in the 1980s and 1990s, particularly those more familiar with British prison settings, has questioned how the prisoners achieved such a degree of unsupervised autonomy in the prison.[52] While some of the answer is obviously related to the style of prison management adopted in the 1980s, from the prisoners' perspective, much of the increased control of the space within the prison was achieved by a painstakingly incremental extension of their collective presence.

Prisoners recognized that they could better exercise their collective power and influence in the public spaces of the prison rather than within the confined spaces of their cells. They recognized that they could better influence and co-opt the prison staff by more subtle tactics than direct confrontation. Republican prisoners in particular recognized that while violence had a role to play in resistance within the prisons, it was perhaps ultimately more effective as an implied threat or back-up to other strategies, rather than as the immediate response to difficulties or impediments within the prison. In the Maze, at least, and in parallel with developments generally within Republicanism from the mid-1980s on the outside, resistance became more multifaceted and arguably more sophisticated than simple reliance upon armed struggle. However, the threat of violence remained as a backdrop, an often implicit but ever present element of relationship between prisoners and staff. One prison governor described it thus:

[51] Interview with prison governor, 13 Sept. 1997.

[52] As the Narey Report (set up to investigate the escape of IRA prisoner Liam Averill and the killing of LVF leader Billy Wright) suggested: 'Not infrequently the Maze is characterised as a holiday camp. It is nothing of the sort. It is a prison which, while tolerating high levels of prisoner freedom on the wings had, until Dec. 1997 [when the escape and murder happened], and for 14 years, an enviable security record' (Narey 1998: p. i).

The problem with the Loyalists is that they have no sense. If they have a problem, their immediate response is to put out a death threat against prison staff. Regardless of the issue, if it's compassionate parole, cell searches, or the fucking tuck shop, their response is 'we're going to shoot a screw'. The Provies [IRA] on the other hand play a much cleverer game, . . . they are eminently reasonable, they will negotiate, they will put in twenty demands, and let you haggle them down to ten so you think you have a result. But those are the ten they wanted in the first place . . . the threat is so far at the back of it all that it becomes part of the furniture. It is very effective.[53]

Violence, intimidation, destruction, and conditioning of staff have all served as techniques of resistance employed by paramilitary prisoners over the past thirty years in Northern Ireland. Of course not all such activities were linked to strategic and symbolic power struggles between the authorities and the prisoners. Such were the inevitable consequence of a prison system charged with managing large numbers of serious long-term offenders. However, I would contend that the collective and organized nature of paramilitary groupings in Northern Ireland, and their willingness to use these tactics, has given prisoners considerably greater power in their relations with the authorities.

The prisoners' capacity to carry out organized violence on prison staff (both inside and outside prisons) presented a unique dynamic. For example, Sykes (1958) and Mathiesen (1965 and esp. 1974) have argued that while the authorities' application of power in prison is never absolute, in the final analysis the authorities are always likely to win through because of factors such as coercive force (e.g. literally surrounding and invading a prison with overwhelming force as in the case of the Attica riots of 1971—see Melville 1972). As one prisoner interviewed by Sykes suggested, 'they have the guns, we don't' (1958: 41). Similarly ordinary prisoners in a non-conflict scenario may be hampered by an inability to organize properly or a lack of capacity for building broad political alliances which can critique the illegitimate exercise of power.

Such factors were less true in the Northern Ireland context. Prisoners (particularly Republicans) had a supportive constituency on the outside. They had an organized and collective identity inside the prisons and, for most parts of the conflict, enjoyed considerable control over their own living space. The British state of course retained a considerably greater capacity for coercive power. However, the

---

[53] Interview with prison governor, 12 Feb. 1996.

prisoners' capacity for organized violence meant that, both symboli-
cally and literally, the state was not the only protagonist with guns.

The potential for violence, referred to by the prison officer above 'as
part of the furniture' became an embedded discourse in the interaction
between prisoners and prison staff. It was arguably all the more effective when only applied selectively, more implied than explicit, and only
carried through in a targeted and thought-out fashion. This unspoken
capacity for violence, allied to a continuous contest regarding space
within a prison and what might be accurately described as the tyranny
of relentlessly reasoned argument, was a potent combination.

Prison staff were forced to operate in a context where their personal
safety, details about their families, their control and ownership of areas
of the prison, and their capacity to defend the organizational line were
constantly being probed, tested, and undermined by the relentless challenge of potentially ruthless prisoners. Such conditioning and intimidation of staff significantly altered power relations and had a crucial
impact in moulding the shape of paramilitary imprisonment in
Northern Ireland.

As one governor in the Maze summed it up well:

You have to understand what it is like walking down an IRA wing in the Maze.
You go in there, maybe you have a meeting set up with the OC and they are
expecting you. So the gate is locked behind you, you walk down the wings.
Suddenly after you have passed the first couple of cells, prisoners will start to
mill about in the wing—not menacing but just to let you know that they are
between you and the gate. Maybe along the way some people are looking a bit
unhappy and then when you get to the OC, you are relieved to see he is happy
and he presents you with his list of demands and they are eminently reasonable . . . You debate, discuss, and sometimes you feel you are holding to a
completely unreasonable and irrational line which has been arrived at by the
NIO. You give way because it would be stupid not to. And you know you are
down the wing, and you know that if they really want to they can get you here
or on the outside. It is all brilliantly worked out psychological intimidation but
no matter that you know that, it works.[54]

---

[54] Interview with prison governor, 13 Aug. 1997.

6

Resistance and the Law: Prisons and Political Struggle

Introduction

The notion of law providing useful insights into the ideology, strategy, and practices of a state during violent political or civil unrest is well established.[1] States wherein the legal system and its legitimacy are contested have long been used as case studies to draw out broader theoretical issues. Hart (1983) and Fuller's (1958) dispute regarding Nazi Germany and legal positivism, Dyzenaus (1991) and Abel's (1995) discussion on law in Apartheid South Africa, Cover (1975) and Sebok's (1999) consideration of American slavery are all examples of scholars seeking to understand better the operation of law more generally through the elucidation of particularly extreme case studies.

In such instances, many understandably focus on the capacity of 'wicked legal systems' (Dyzenhaus 1991) to legitimate repression and thwart progressive social and political movements. For example, Balbus (1977: 12) has argued that legal repression by formal rationality served to depoliticize collective violence and to undermine the solidarity of the participants in the struggle for racial equality in the USA. Similarly while the Apartheid government paid particular attention to the legitimating potential of legal formalism[2] (Van Zyl Smit 1987), such legality was often backed up by the states' capacity for violence, harassment, and intimidation.

There is a similar wealth of legal literature on the British state and Northern Ireland, much of it written from a human rights perspective critical of state activities during the conflict. Such activities have

---

[1] Parts of this chapter were first published in the *Journal of Law and Society* (McEvoy 2000). I am grateful to the journal and its editor Phil Thomas for their kind permission to reproduce some of those arguments here.

[2] For a discussion on the merits of legal formalism see Weinrib 1993, Sumners 1997.

included torture, internment without trial (discussed in detail below), the shooting of unarmed suspects in disputed circumstances, and discriminatory policing (e.g. Amnesty International 1988, 1994, Spujt 1986, Lawyers Committee 1996, O'Rawe and Moore 1997). As Hillyard (1987) has argued, the repressive capacity of law is well illustrated in the Northern Ireland context in the range of British state responses to the conflict.

While there has been considerable focus on the repressive character of law in Northern Ireland as an instrument of state counter-insurgency, other than tangentially, little systematic analysis has been carried out of the attitudes of the non-state protagonist towards law during the conflict. This is surprising as, perhaps paradoxically, the potential of law as an instrument of political struggle or resistance is also demonstrated in the setting of a political conflict (Abel 1995). If law is galvanized and utilized by those engaged in resistance (particularly in politically charged settings such as political trials, prisons, or in the assertion of political standing by political parties who have the stated intention of overthrowing the state) then it can provide equally instructive insights into the ideology of non-state actors as it can with regard to the state.

This chapter focuses primarily on the views of Republican prisoners and former prisoners,[3] in particular towards law as a resistance strategy. While there is some focus on the activities of Loyalists, as is discussed below, their *attitudes* towards law, and *their usage* of legal challenge have been much less explicitly linked to their overall struggle. It begins with an examination of the attitudes of paramilitary defendants towards law at their trials and in seeking to draw international legitimacy to their cause in extradition and international human rights fora. It then considers litigation as a strategy of resistance in the prisons themselves. Finally it analyses the relationship between law and the prison struggle and the use of law in the political arena as Republicans (many of whom were ex-prisoners) began in the 1980s to contest seats in local, Westminster, and Republic of Ireland elections.

By charting the varying attitudes towards law in these settings, I hope to explore the interrelated themes of (*a*) law and struggle as

[3] This chapter includes analysis of paramilitary defendants' attitudes towards law during their trials as well as after sentencing. Of course such defendants were almost invariably remanded in prison since few such defendants were granted bail (Walsh 1983: 82).

processes of dialogue or communication, (*b*) law as instrumental struggle, and (*c*) the impact of such legal struggle in prison and related settings in shaping broader political and military strategy.

Paramilitary Defendants, the Legitimacy of the Courts, and Law as Dialogue

Legal hearings concerning politically motivated prisoners are of course sites of material state repression and violence (Balbus 1977). Indeed, the actions of the state or judiciary can serve to crystallize the *real* political nature of a trial (Bankowski and Mungham 1976: 139, Mandela 1994: 432–8). The repressive character of such hearings in Northern Ireland has been well documented elsewhere (Walsh 1983, Amnesty International 1992). Less well covered, however, is the way in which such settings have served as material and symbolic sites of resistance. As Kirchheimer has argued, while political trials may authenticate political repression, none the less the courtroom also offers the potential for 'new images and myths' to be pressed forward by enemies of the regime to undermine the established authority (Kirchheimer 1961: 49). Claims are made, and denied, concerning not only the material issues of the case but their relationship to the broader conflict and the legitimacy of the state.[4]

Legal hearings concerning paramilitaries also provide important venues in which some form of dialogue or exchange actually takes place between the state, the judiciary, and the paramilitary movement. Habermas has defined such dialogue as requiring that the protagonists develop positions which are capable of being universalized, tested, or 'communicatively shared' with a broader constituency (Habermas 1975: 108, cited in White 1988: 71). Such a relational view of the legal process, what Harvey has referred to as 'a continuing conversation of argumentation and justification' (Harvey 1999: 566), required not only forms of engagement between the paramilitaries and the state but also an ongoing critical appraisal of attitudes towards law amongst the prisoners themselves.

---

[4] For an overview of relevant literature on claims-making see Best (1987, 1989), Bockman (1991), Crelinsten (1998).

Non-Recognition of the Court, Historical Legacy, and Law as Internal Dialogue

Trials of those accused of politically motivated offences are always played out against a potent historical and political background. Lane has suggested that trials either during or after a conflict are always framed within their own particular set of political circumstances, looking to history as a sort of 'supreme court for the future' (Lane 1979: 280). As Albertyn and Davis (1990: 104) argue, such trials are 'always retrospective in some sense, freezing and reflecting past political struggles, and seeking to reflect and reconstruct historical images'. For Republican prisoners in particular who began to appear before the courts from 1969 onwards, there was a considerable historical reserve to draw upon in the shaping of their attitudes to the law as a site of struggle and resistance. The dialogical aspects of Republicans' attitudes and conduct at their trial were drawn from the movement's historical traditions and aimed primarily at their own internal constituency.

For Irish Republicans, a refusal to recognize the jurisdiction of British courts in Ireland has been an integral part of their political and military strategy for at least 150 years. It has provided an opportunity for staged defiance, political speeches from the dock (where permitted by the court), and a denial of legitimacy to the authorities. In order to understand the significance of the tactic of non-recognition in the most recent phase of conflict in Northern Ireland (and in particular the changes which occurred during the 1970s and 1980s), it will be necessary to provide some detail on its historical antecedence. For the sake of brevity, it is possible broadly to characterize non-recognition as an *ad hoc* tactic used by prisoners in the various Irish insurrections of the nineteenth century, which became more formalized and strategic in the early part of the twentieth century. The principal characteristics of the more strategic approach were (i) the attempts by Republicans to establish their own alternative state system with a separate parliament, criminal justice system, and police force, and (ii) consistent efforts either to ignore or seek to delegitimize the British legal system as the most tangible symbol of the British presence in Ireland.

The United Irishmen, widely regarded as the founding fathers of Irish Republicanism (e.g. Connolly 1987: 88, Adams 1986) have been characterized as being quite 'respectful' of those presiding in their military trials (Dunne 1982, Elliot 1989) following their abortive 1798

Rising. However, in the subsequent revolt of 1848, a number of the 'Young Irelanders' refused to recognize the courts. John Mitchel, one of the leaders who was convicted of high treason and sentenced to transportation, regarded any such move as 'a grovelling acknowledgement of criminal conduct' (Mitchel 1918). This tactic was subsequently adopted by a number of the Republican prisoners who took part in the Fenian uprising, a generation later in 1865.[5]

After the 1916 Easter Rising, Patrick Pearse (leader of the Rising) used his court martial to make a political speech while in effect recognizing the military court in pleading guilty in an attempt to gain amnesty for his followers (Dudley-Edwards 1977: 317). In the aftermath of the 1916 Rising, however, IRA activists increasingly combined non-recognition with using their trials as a political stage during the ensuing War of Independence (Hart 1998: 57). The authorities began to exclude newspaper reporters from the trials and to enter pleas of not guilty on behalf of defendants who refused to recognize the court (Campbell 1994: 72, 76).

As in the modern era, the symbolic importance of Republicans' attitudes to the law was deeply interwoven with the political struggle for legitimacy. In 1917, in deliberate contravention of British law, Sinn Fein had established Dáil Eireann as a new National Assembly in Ireland in an attempt to supplant British rule in Ireland, in essence 'to act as if the British weren't there'. In the 1918 general election, Sinn Fein (running on a platform of abstentionism from the British Parliament) won 73 of the 105 seats, giving them a majority in all but four counties and electorally devastating the traditional constitutional Nationalist Party (Foster 1988). They then established ministries, indicated that the IRA were to serve as the 'legitimate' police force, and began to offer greater structure to the Sinn Fein Arbitration Courts which had recently developed in rural areas (Kotsonournis 1994). While the British government continued to offer strong military and political opposition to independence, both the political and the military wing of Irish Republicanism saw attitudes to law and its administration as a key ideological battleground for the *de facto* and *de jure* governance of Ireland.

That struggle continued after 1921 when the signing of a treaty with

---

[5] 'I have employed no lawyer in this case, because, in making a defence of any kind, I should be recognising British Law in Ireland. Now I deliberately and conscientiously repudiate British law in Ireland—its right or even its existence, in Ireland: and I defy any punishment, and despise any punishment, it can inflict on me' (cited in Piggot 1883: 169).

the British and the Unionists in the North partitioned the island, and led to a civil war between pro- and anti-treaty factions of the IRA. Once again many on the Republican side (anti-treaty) refused to recognize the courts of the newly established Irish Free State (Hopkinson 1988, Campbell 1994: 205). Such actions were viewed as a combination of political ideology and practical resistance. The non-recognition tradition continued in the next serious outbreak of IRA violence in the 1940s (Behan 1958: 144),[6] and in the IRA Border campaign of the late 1950s and early 1960s.[7]

Following that disastrous campaign, the IRA had become largely a moribund organization, led by a left-wing Dublin-based leadership increasingly interested in mainstream politics (Bowyer Bell 1979). The outbreak of political violence in 1970, the reluctance of the Dublin leadership to engage fully in armed struggle, and their continued dalliance with constitutional politics led to a split within the movement with the more militant Northerners establishing the Provisional IRA. In such a context, in which two elements of the IRA were disputing the mantle of the *true* inheritance of the Republican tradition, the appeal to historical Republican fundamentals such as non-recognition of the court became all the more significant.

As violence escalated and Republicans were arrested and tried in both the North and the South, large numbers of IRA prisoners began again to use their trials to deny legitimacy to either administration. As Toolis (1995: 118) notes, 'IRA volunteers on trial were expected to maintain this tradition [non-recognition] and deny the legitimacy of the courts despite the personal cost to themselves'. Prisoners either refused to speak during their trials, refused to hire a lawyer, attempted to make political speeches or speeches asserting their non-recognition of the court, or made clear by their demeanour that the courts held no legitimacy for them. Similar to political defendants in other trial settings (Epstein 1970), prisoners were at pains to highlight their disinterest and lack of respect for the proceedings.[8]

---

[6] For a discussion of the differences, albeit slight, between Behan's account and the contemporaneous records of the proceedings see O'Connor (1970: 53).

[7] Interview with former IRA volunteer, imprisoned during the 1956–62 campaign, 2 Feb. 1994.

[8] In his autobiographical account of the practicalities of non-recognition, Gerry Adams, former IRA internee and now President of Sinn Fein, sewed his jeans during his hearing, refused to stand when addressed, and chatted with other prisoners and read newspapers. He was on trial for attempting to escape and taking part in the burning of Long Kesh where he had been interned (Adams 1996: 240).

Although prisoners' non-recognition was often characterized by a disrespectful demeanour, their actions constituted more than the indifference or insolence associated with some non-political defendants during their criminal trials. Such actions by ordinary criminal defendants may be viewed as 'hidden transcripts of resistance' (Scott 1990: 8), one of the ways in which resistant meaning is given to the everyday exercise of power by the relatively powerless against the powerful (Pile 1997: 14). Such actions by politically motivated prisoners, on the other hand, in particular for Republicans given their historical, political, and ideological struggle with the state, are better understood as what Scott (1990) refers to as a 'public refusal' to recognize the legitimacy of the exercise of power in the first place. As Scott argues:

Any public refusal, in the teeth of power, to produce the words, gestures, and other signs of normative compliance is typically construed—and typically intended—as an act of defiance. . . . When a practical failure to comply is joined with a pointed, public refusal it constitutes a throwing down of the gauntlet, a symbolic declaration of war. (Scott 1990: 203)

On the political and ideological front, non-recognition fitted within the assertion that the IRA was the sole legitimate government of Ireland and that special juryless courts established, both north and south of the border, had no authority in trying its members for politically motivated offences.[9] At a more individual level, a number of former prisoners have also stressed to the author that non-recognition was also designed to have practical consequences for prisoners. It was designed to inculcate in volunteers a sense that their prison resistance had begun, and that they had a responsibility to continue to struggle, now that they were subjected to the power, formalism, and ritual of the criminal justice process. Finally, at the organizational level of the IRA, the refusal by volunteers to recognize the court, and therefore to give evidence, meant that the risks

---

[9] The logic of this claim was essentially that the 1918 general election, in which Sinn Fein received the majority of the vote, was the last legitimate assertion of the Irish people's right to self-determination. The first Dáil, created in 1917, was the sole legitimate authority in Ireland. Partition having been imposed against the will of the majority of Irish people, the partitionist assemblies North and South were not legitimate and therefore the IRA (wearing the mantle of the first Dáil) was the legitimate government of Ireland. This remained as a central tenet of Republican philosophy until the decision by Sinn Fein to take up seats in the Dáil in 1986, and in the new Northern Assembly which arose from the multi-party peace talks in 1998.

of significant military or internal security information coming out during the trial were reduced.[10]

Similar organizational dynamics may have been a partial motivator for those 'few Loyalists' (Boyle, Hadden, and Hillyard 1980: 76) who refused to recognize the courts in the early to mid-1970s. The dialogical aspects of their actions were also largely internal. The author has interviewed a number of these former prisoners. These were mostly UVF and RHC (Red Hand Commando) prisoners under the influence of UVF leader Gusty Spence. Spence was a former British soldier, who expended considerable energies in seeking to mould imprisoned UVF prisoners into a disciplined and organized paramilitary organization. Although Loyalists had no comparable prison history to Republicans, an original UVF document obtained by the author offers guidance upon when UVF prisoners (in consultation with their Officer Commanding) were expected not to recognize the court.[11] Volunteers charged with murder who had 'some glimmer of hope' could enter a defence, people who did not have a reasonable chance, or whose chances were slim were told not to plead guilty and that they should instead refuse to recognize the court. Such volunteers were encouraged to read from a prepared statement.

As a volunteer of the Ulster Volunteer Force (or Red Hand Commando) I refuse to recognise this court because it denies British citizens the right to trial by jury. I reserve the right to cross-examine and wish to be given the opportunity to make a closing address.[12]

For Loyalists whose allegiance to the Northern Ireland state was taken for granted, their refusal to recognize the courts was not directed as a challenge to the state's legitimacy. Non-recognition was in essence a

---

[10] 'I suppose we would have ideally wanted our volunteers to view their trial as one stage in the process from arrest to jail and to treat it in the same way. Once people were lifted they were told to say nothing, sign nothing. Similarly at the trial volunteers were encouraged to be confident in their identity as Republicans, remember their history and give nothing away.' Interview with former IRA Officer Commanding, 12 Sept. 1994 (interviewee had himself refused to recognize the court).

[11] It should be noted that all politically motivated prisoners in Northern Ireland were expected by their organization to report to their respective Officer Commanding once remanded in prison. Normally he/she was given the papers relating to the trial by the defendant and these were then reviewed by the OC in order to assess if any information damaging to the security of the organization had been passed to the authorities during interrogation. The OC may also have proffered advice with regard to the conduct of the trial.

[12] UVF/RHC Instructions Regarding Behaviour in Court (undated, probably 1971–2).

reformist measure for Loyalists, a protest over the introduction of the juryless Diplock Courts and a broader protest of the notion that they were being unfairly punished for crimes in defence of *their* state and their community. The lack of a prisoner tradition of non-recognition, the ambivalent position regarding the legitimacy of the legal system, and the arguably less disciplined nature of the Loyalist prisoners discussed in previous chapters ensured that the number of Loyalists not recognizing the courts was always low and disappeared completely by 1976.

The Dissipation of the Non-Recognition Strategy

If the origins of the practice of non-recognition can be seen as an amalgam of historical, ideological, and practical forms of protest, then the gradual dissipation of the practice should be seen as a similar interaction of forces from below and above. The practice declined sharply after 1976, being continued only by experienced IRA operatives against whom there was ample evidence and little chance of success.

The practice had never been an entirely uncontested one. For the prisoners themselves, in the context of low acquittal rates for Diplock trials generally (Hogan and Walker 1989: 104), the conviction rates for prisoners who refused to recognize the courts were understandably high (Boyle, Hadden, and Hillyard 1980: 61). As the military reality became clearer that a short victory would not be forthcoming and the IRA radically restructured into small cellular units in preparation for 'long term armed struggle' (Taylor 1997: 211), other historical givens such as non-recognition became increasingly perceived by some IRA prisoners as a 'purist but impractical' stance.[13]

The practical consequences of losing experienced volunteers, some of whom might have fought successful cases and therefore rejoined the paramilitary campaign, was not lost on the IRA leadership.[14] With pressure from below as well as organizational imperatives, the tactics amongst Republican remand prisoners gradually changed from the mid-1970s onwards. While the *de facto* change in the attitude of Republicans was acknowledged by the movement as a whole, the IRA

---

[13] Interview with former IRA prisoner, 1 Sept. 1995.

[14] One former IRA prisoner has suggested to the author that the relaxation in policy may have come about after an IRA leader, Daithill O'Connell, had decided to recognize the special criminal court in the Republic on strong legal advice that he would be successful in defending the charge (interview, 12 Mar. 1994).

continued to assert that the behaviour of their prisoners towards the courts remained a leadership decision.[15] Prisoners were strongly discouraged from plea-bargaining to achieve a reduced sentence, as such a move was considered 'too much like co-operation'.[16] With that proviso, by the late 1970s/early 1980s Republicans were fighting almost all cases, even when there appeared little opportunity for success. In Walsh's survey of 170 Diplock cases between January and March 1981, only one Republican and no Loyalists refused to recognize the courts (Walsh 1983: 81).

I was caught red handed on a job. The Brits stopped us at a checkpoint, we tried to make a run for it but were nabbed . . . There was a couple of rifles and a handgun in the car. When it came to the trial we went through all the motions even though we knew it was hopeless . . . I suppose we wanted to cost them as much as possible with the lawyers, cops' time and so on . . . [17]

Another former prisoner, also convicted in the 1980s, told the author:

To be honest I was intending not to recognize the court. I had been in before and had refused to recognize that time in the 1970s. My second time around was in 1986 but the line had changed, so we fought the case . . . I suppose I could have pushed it [non-recognition] if I had wanted to but, well, there was always a chance of getting off . . . [18]

As with other revolutionary movements, when the orthodoxy had been demonstrated as no longer appropriate to the circumstances (Suchliki, Jorge, and Fernandez 1985, Livingston 1997), a new orthodoxy emerged which located a pragmatic change of tactics within a familiar political and ideological framework. The IRA had, from 1970, engaged in what it termed the 'economic war' wherein bombings of civilian and economic targets in Northern Ireland and England were justified by the cost of compensation and rebuilding borne by the British state (Bowyer Bell 1979). Similarly bomb-scares, riots, public disorder, and other tactics were utilized throughout the conflict in order to tie down or stretch the state's resources. The change in

[15] 'A Volunteer's attitude in court shall be at the discretion of the Army Authority' Part 4, Oglaigh na hEireann (Irish Republican Army) General Headquarters, General Army Orders (as revised 1987) taken from the *Green Book*—the IRA Constitution.

[16] Interview with former IRA prisoner, 1 Mar. 1996.

[17] Interview with former IRA prisoner convicted in the 1980s, 14 June 1996. Some of the details of the arrest have been omitted so as to prevent identification.

[18] Interview with former IRA prisoner, 1 Dec. 1994.

attitudes towards Republican recognition of courts fitted well within both of those frameworks, binding up court and security forces time, making the state work harder for convictions, costing the British Exchequer (who funded the costs of the trial, prosecution, defence, etc.), and generally viewing the courtroom as a practical, rather than solely a symbolic, site of struggle.[19]

In the era of non-recognition, attitudes towards law may be legitimately described as a process of internal dialogue within Republicanism. It was essentially a reactive strategy drawn from the rich historical template of Republicanism but which paid little attention to the potential of legal challenge as a source of external or objective validation. The dialogue was largely focused inwards, directed primarily at the Republican constituency itself, and focused almost exclusively on promulgating a sense of historical continuity amongst its own members and supporters. The desire to portray Republican activities post-1970 as a continuation of previous struggles against British imperialism shaped the movement's attitude to law and took precedence over any view of the potential of law to underpin any external support or legitimation. When attitudes towards law changed, they did so due to pressure from the defendants themselves and because of the pragmatic organizational requirements for personnel to return to acts of political violence. Trial contests were then transmogrified into a discourse of consuming the enemy's resources, and fermenting a sense of resistance amongst the prisoners for the prison struggle to come.

Law, Dialogue with Legal Professionals, and 'Adopting the Evidence'

Changes in attitudes amongst IRA personnel from the mid-1970s regarding trials did not occur in the context of a static judicial system and legal profession. Lawyers too played a role in that transition. While cause-lawyering has had a considerable influence internationally in other political and social struggles (Sarat and Scheingold 1988), Northern Ireland has not seen the evolution of struggle lawyers publicly aligning themselves with one or other of the various protagonists.[20] Of the 1,700 hundred solicitors in Northern Ireland in 1998, only 20–30 have been regularly involved in defending paramilitary

---

[19] Interview with former IRA prisoner, 1 Sept. 1995.
[20] Interview with Belfast solicitor, 12 Jan. 1996.

clients (Cumaraswamy 1998: 2). Such lawyers have been the object of persistent threats and intimidation from the police and two (Pat Finucane and Rosemary Nelson) have been murdered by Loyalist paramilitaries amidst widespread allegations of security force collusion (Lawyers Committee for Human Rights 1993, Cumaraswamy 1998).

Anxious to represent their clients properly, lawyers in the early 1970s were hugely frustrated at defendants' unwillingness to contest sometimes winnable and ill-prepared prosecution cases. In such a context, however, their views could only be marginal. However, once the Republican line changed, the role of solicitors and barrister of course became more relevant. While lawyers' 'professional dominance' (Parker 1994) over decisions on the conduct of trials was mitigated by the organizational and political imperatives of their paramilitary clients, their influence became increasingly significant as defendants began to fight every case.[21] This policy, of fighting the majority of cases (including clearly unwinnable ones) and refusing to plead guilty in order to get reduced sentences, continued up until the 1990s.[22] While occasionally in the 1980s and 1990s prisoners refused to recognize the court, such instances became increasingly rare.[23] In the early 1990s, a new tactic developed which served further to highlight the significance of lawyers and judiciary as actors in the relationship between the state and paramilitaries.

In the early 1990s, a new tactic developed wherein, despite the ostensible prohibition on plea-bargaining in Northern Ireland, a number of defence lawyers began a process known as 'adopting the evidence'. This entailed the defendant pleading not guilty, not mounting a defence, and accepting the evidence presented in the papers, and thus

[21] 'I would have to say my relationship with my solicitor was very good. He had represented me before and had a good reputations amongst our ones [members of the same paramilitary group] as straight, very thorough and professional about all the angles to be explored in your defence . . . Obviously my attitude at the trial was dependent on the movement's line at the time, but of course I listened to the advice of the solicitor and barrister too . . . ' Interview with former IRA prisoner, 1 Dec. 1994.

[22] In some instances prisoners' fighting of their cases included run throughs in which prisoners pleaded not guilty but entered no defence thus forcing the prosecution to run through their entire case but forbidding the defence lawyers actively to engage in the trial, much to the frustration of their lawyers (interview with solicitor, 12 June 1996).

[23] A refusal to recognize the court was still considered a potential source of status on the Republican wings in the 1990s. Those who behaved impeccably from a Republican perspective (e.g. not speaking during interrogation or not recognizing the court), may have had an enhanced reputation once transferred to the Maze with other sentenced IRA prisoners (interviews with former IRA prisoners, 12 Jan. 1995, 1 Mar. 1996).

saving the time-consuming process of a lengthy case. It is important to remember that this occurred in a jurisdiction wherein any suggestion that plea-bargaining occurs is strongly contested by the judiciary. One of the leading criminal solicitors in Belfast described the origins of the process thus:

There is a provision within one of the Criminal Justice Acts of the 1960s[24] which allows for the adoption of the evidence. [Lawyer's name] had the bright idea of using one of these provisions in such a way to get around the difficulty of prisoners' refusal to plead. Not guilty, no defence, adopt the evidence. The prisoners loved it, they weren't pleading which was frowned upon . . . we all latched on to it then.[25]

Of course the strategy of 'adopting the evidence' was not simply a result of productive dialogue between resourceful lawyers and their clients. It also required the acquiescence (at least) of senior figures in the Northern Ireland judiciary. Such increased pragmatism in the conduct of paramilitary trials did not occur in the context of an increasingly progressive or liberalizing judicial process. On the contrary, the two most noteworthy features of such trials since the 1970s had been the normalization of the juryless Diplock trials for terrorist suspects with a heavy reliance upon confessional evidence (Dickson 1992, Jackson and Doran 1995) and the supergrass mass trials of terrorist suspects upon the word of informer evidence (Greer 1995), also heard in juryless Diplock Courts. While the supergrass system ultimately collapsed in response to 'strong and cogent criticism' (Greer 1995: 174), the Diplock Courts have remained an integral part of the Northern Ireland legal system. That said, some of the most illiberal judges presiding in the Diplock Courts were supportive of the process of 'adopting the evidence'.

As the lawyer above told the author:

Ironically enough it was Justice [name—a reputed right-wing member of the bench] who pioneered adopting the evidence, he has a very practical head on him you know. Judge [name] also liked it. On the other hand the then Lord Chief Justice refused to give discount on this process, you would get the odd judge like the LCJ who said I am not going to give you anything for that . . .[26]

Thus the system of 'adopting the evidence' emerged because of a dialogical process between paramilitaries, their lawyers, and the

[24] Criminal Justice Act (Northern Ireland) 1968, s2(1).
[25] Interview with solicitor, 16 Mar. 1996.
[26] Interview with solicitor, 16 Mar. 1996.

judiciary. The prisoners were attracted by lighter sentences, without apparent ideological compromise, and a more tangible result than the rather diffuse benefit of using up state resources. The lawyers succeeded in better representing the interests of their clients. While arguably not adopting the explicitly political stances of other divided jurisdictions (Rojas 1988: 204), they engaged in what McBarnet referred to as 'legal creativity', using the 'law's substantive, institutional and ideological contradictions to produce routes through the maze of regulation which minimise its undesirable effects for clients' (McBarnet 1994: 83–4). The judges, perhaps motivated by an efficient and less costly trial process (rather than any formal cognizance of the political and ideological motivation of the defendants), none the less went along with a process which accommodated exactly that political and ideological position. The dialogical nature of the interaction between the various actors resulted in a legal process with which all could live.

Law as External Dialogue: The Strategy of Internationalization

As with other revolutionary groupings in South Africa and Latin America, one of the key strategies of Republicans in Northern Ireland has been to encourage and develop support and resources for their campaign internationally.[27] Republicans have focused their attentions in particular upon the Irish community in America, left-leaning governments in Europe and the Middle East, and of course the Irish Republic. Their aim has been to garner material assistance in the form of arms and finance as well as to apply political and occasional economic pressure on the British government (Holland 1989). Legal challenges in such settings were aimed primarily at an external international audience. International courtrooms were viewed as crucial venues in highlighting state abuses, countering the British position that the conflict was in fact a law and order problem and asserting the political character of their struggle. While there are other instructive examples, I have chosen to concentrate in particular on legal settings which involved prisoners' use of law as a form of dialogue designed to internationalize

---

[27] Other than some support from British and European fascist groupings and sporadic assistance from Libya, Loyalist paramilitaries have had comparatively little success in garnering an international constituency (Bruce 1992).

their struggle, i.e. extradition hearings and recourse to international human rights bodies.

Even during periods when Republicans were refusing to recognize the courts in Northern Ireland, prisoners arrested in the Irish Republic or abroad apparently had few ideological misgivings in mounting the most spirited of defences in resisting extradition back to Northern Ireland (Campbell 1989). In a series of unreported cases in the early 1970s Republican prisoners successfully challenged extradition warrants in the Irish Republic (Farrell 1985: 57–63). Given that the key feature of most extradition hearings centres around the question of the political nature of the offence (Keightley 1993), the prisoners' willingness to use the courts to make that assertion is perhaps unsurprising. Judicial affirmation of politically motivated offending went to the very core of the struggle between paramilitary prisoners and the state. Thus comments by the Irish Lord Chief Justice O'Dalaigh that 'there could be little doubt that an IRA raid on a military barracks constituted a political offence',[28] or the comment by New York District Judge John E. Sprizzo that the IRA killing of a British SAS officer was 'the political offence exception in its most classic form' for extradition purposes,[29] was hugely significant for Republican morale and propaganda.

The political and ideological significance attributed by the Republican movement to such hearings was reciprocated by the British state. The refusal by successive American and French governments (until the 1980s) to extradite Irish political offenders became a source of serious diplomatic tensions with Britain (Carbonneau 1983, McElrath 2000). The passage of the US–UK Supplementary Extradition Treaty by the US Congress in 1986 was explicitly linked by President Ronald Reagan to the need to extradite IRA terrorists in recognition of the special relationship with Britain and in particular Prime Minister Margaret Thatcher's support for the US bombing of Libya (Scharf 1988).

Similarly with regard to the Irish Republic, the view in the 1970s and early 1980s of successive Irish governments and the Irish courts that they were constitutionally barred from extraditing political offenders became a source of much solace for Republicans and a key area of dissent in Anglo-Irish relations.[30] Movement on the question of

[28] *The State [Magee] v O'Rourke* [1971] IR 205.
[29] *Matter of Doherty*, 599 F.Supp. 270 (SDNY) 1984.
[30] Section 29.3 of the Irish Constitution provides 'Ireland accepts the generally recognised principles of international law as its rules in relation to its conduct with other states'. Until 1976 the Irish government interpreted international law as precluding

extradition became a key bargaining counter by the government of the Irish Republic in political negotiations in the 1970s and 1980s designed to secure a greater influence in the governance of the North (Campbell 1989: 595). While tensions did ease somewhat with the increasingly narrow interpretation of the meaning 'political' by the Irish courts,[31] and the Irish government's signing of the European Convention on the Suppression of Terrorism, Republicans continued to use extradition battles to assert the political nature of their struggle even beyond the 1994 ceasefires.

The second important platform upon which prisoners have sought to use law to internationalize the conflict was through usage of international human rights instruments to which Britain was a signatory. The notion of recourse to supra-state standards has been one of the fundamental concepts in the development of international human rights and humanitarian law over the past fifty years (Steiner and Alston 1996, Durham and McCormack 1999). In both instances the internationalization of alleged human rights abuses or disputes holds out the promise of providing a more objective framework, a moral base beyond the rules of the nation state where judgments can be made removed from the exigencies of a particular jurisdiction (Shelton 1999). Whatever the ability of human rights or humanitarian law instruments to deliver upon such potential, their capacity to place the political nature of the conflict on an international stage was at least partially attempted by paramilitary prisoners, although with less obvious success than in extradition hearings of the 1970s and early 1980s.

Given the importance of their assertion as political prisoners, the potential for Republicans to use the provisions of international humanitarian law (the laws of war) in support of that claim are

---

extradition of political offenders. In 1976, after heated negotiations with the British, the Criminal Law Jurisdiction Act was introduced. This meant that offences committed in the North could be tried before courts in the Irish Republic. This provision, however, was very infrequently used. In 1977, largely in response to Palestinian-related terrorism, the Council of Europe passed the Convention on the Suppression of Terrorism excluding various offences (e.g. bombings) from being designated political. The Irish Republic refused to sign. Following a number of Supreme Court cases in the 1980s which considerably narrowed the political offence category (one of which involved a Maze escapee), the Irish government were able to pledge to sign the Convention as they signed the Anglo-Irish agreement. The Convention was duly ratified in 1987 and challenges to extradition became extremely technical, focusing, for example, on the proper execution of warrants and the nature of the arrest and detention (Connolly 1982, Farrell 1985, Campbell 1989).

[31] See e.g. *McGlinchey v Wren* [1982] IR 154; *Quinn v Wren* [1985] IR 323.

obvious. Under the two Additional Protocols of the Geneva Convention signed in 1977, prisoner of war status was extended to include guerrillas fighting in both international and non-international conflicts. However, humanitarian law scholars appear broadly to agree (see Boyle, Hadden, and Hillyard 1980: 94, Walker 1984: 201, Ní Aoláin 2000, esp. ch. 5) that the failure to control territory (notwithstanding the no-go areas controlled by the IRA for brief periods in the early 1970s) appeared to rule out an assertion by Republicans or Loyalists that they came under the terms of the Additional Protocols. Accordingly the author has found no evidence of any organized attempt to utilize international humanitarian provisions by Republicans or Loyalists in support of their claim to political motivation.

Paramilitary prisoners have, however, attempted to use the provisions of international human rights law such as the European Convention of Human Rights, although these too have been largely ineffectual.[32] For example, in 1978 a number of Republican prisoners engaged in the dirty protest decided to take a case to the European Court of Human Rights. As discussed previously, the prisoners had for some time been engaged in smearing the walls of the cells with their own excreta and urine in protest at the government's attempts to impose the criminalisation strategy in the prisons. The basis of the prisoners' case was that the actions of the authorities constituted inhuman and degrading treatment under Article 3 of the ECHR. They also claimed interference with their right to privacy, correspondence, and association and of discrimination in comparison with those who had been granted *de facto* political status before 1976. Most interestingly, perhaps, they also argued that their view of

---

[32] The one notable prison-related success in actions taken to Strasbourg, was an inter-state case taken by the Irish government against the United Kingdom (Series A No. 25 EHRR 2 (1978)). The case concerned the use of the five techniques of sensory deprivation by the security forces against terrorist suspects in the early 1970s including standing spreadeagled for prolonged periods, white noise, sleep and food deprivation, and having hoods placed over their heads. It resulted in the highly controversial finding of 'torture, inhuman and degrading treatment' under Article 3 by the Commission and 'inhuman and degrading treatment' by the European Court of Human Rights. For a general review of Northern Ireland cases before the European Court and Commission of Human Rights see Livingstone (1995b). It should be noted, however, that human rights scholars are critical of the record of the European Commission and Court of Human Rights in the area of prisoners' rights in general, much less assertions of political status in Northern Ireland (e.g. Douglas and Jones 1983). As Wilson (1993: 247) argues, 'the ECHR has provided a less than totally effective avenue for safeguarding or extending the rights of prisoners.'

themselves as political prisoners was protected under Article 9 (1) of the Convention which guarantees the right to 'freedom of thought, conscience and religion'. This attempt by the prisoners to invoke the European Convention of Human Rights went to the core of their assertion of political status.[33]

The European Commission came to a majority decision in 1980 that the case was manifestly ill founded. The Commission's discomfiture with the notion of political status being underpinned by the Convention is obvious in the judgment. It rejected the assertion that 'the right to preferential status for a certain category of prisoner' was covered under Article 9. It also held that while conditions were clearly inhuman and degrading they were 'self imposed by the applicants as part of their protest for special category status, and, were they motivated to improve them, could be eliminated almost immediately'. The Commission did, however, criticize the authorities for failing to find an acceptable solution out of the impasse.[34] A subsequent case, lodged by the sister of hunger strike leader Bobby Sands, was abandoned when Sands refused to meet Commission representatives unless Sinn Fein leaders and the IRA prison Officer Commanding were present, a condition refused by the prison authorities (O'Malley 1990: 62, Livingstone 1995*b*: 21).

Loyalist prisoners experienced a similarly unsuccessful attempt at using the European Convention of Human Rights to assert their political status. In the case of *McQuiston and others v UK* (1986 46 DR 162), a group of Loyalist prisoners held in integrated conditions followed up an abortive hunger strike in 1984 by lodging a case with the European Commission. They argued that the policy of forced integration constituted inhuman and degrading treatment under Article 3 because of attacks from Republicans and the fear of such attacks which meant prisoners were *de facto* confined to their cells for 23 hours per day. The Commission confirmed again that the Convention did not

[33] 'The applicants state they were subjected to requirements of wearing prison uniform and engaging in prison work contrary to their beliefs and consciences. They similarly regard the prison uniform and compulsory prison work as the badge of ordinary convicted criminal status whereas they have deeply held beliefs that they are not criminals in the ordinary sense in that their offences were politically motivated and treated in law as such . . . In the context of imprisonment, their "beliefs" include the perception of themselves as prisoners of war or political prisoners.' *McFeely, Nugent, Hunter, and Campbell v United Kingdom* (Application No. 317/78), Partial Decision of the European Commission on Human Rights (adopted 15 May 1980).

[34] ibid, 86.

guarantee a right for prisoners of opposing political factions to be held separately. Since no such right existed under the Convention, the prisoners' contention that they were being subjected to discrimination 'on the grounds of political opinion' under Article 14 was also rejected by the Commission.[35]

These cases underline the limited potential for using the mechanisms of the European Convention of Human Rights in what might be called frontal assaults on the issue of political status. Similarly attempts to use the provisions of the Convention in local courts in, for example, judicial review actions, have been firmly resisted by the Northern Ireland judiciary.[36] Even in cases where the focus of the arguments has avoided the claim to political status, but has focused rather on the conditions of imprisonment of politically motivated prisoners, there has been little success via the ECHR mechanisms.

In cases where arguments have avoided an explicit assertion of political status but rather focused upon the arrest and detention of paramilitary suspects there have been more mixed results under the ECHR. For Republican defendants, the European Court has found in favour of a number who argued that the power to detain suspects for up to seven days under Emergency legislation was in breach of Article 5(3),[37] and the denial of access to a solicitor (in conjunction with adverse inference drawn from remaining silent) constituted a breach of Article 6(1) and 6(3).[38] For paramilitary prisoners and their families, however, the European Convention provided little by way of comfort during the

---

[35] In a somewhat ironic twist, the question of discrimination on the grounds of political opinion under Article 14 was raised again in 1998, this time by the British government who put it forward late in the Stormont negotiations on prisoner release as a potential impediment to the early release of politically motivated prisoners. The argument was essentially that release of those factions in observance of a ceasefire, and the continued detention of those not on ceasefire, might leave the government open to legal challenge under this provision. After a somewhat heated swapping of position papers on the matter, the government abandoned their position (confidential source).

[36] As recently as 1992, the then Lord Chief Justice McDermott indicated that at most the Convention might be consulted in cases of statutory or common law ambiguity. The Human Rights Act 1998, reinforced by the Good Friday Agreement concluded in April of 1998, allows for the first time breaches of the Convention to become actionable in the local courts.

[37] See *Brogan v United Kingdom* Series A, No. 245-B, (1988) 11 EHRR 117; *Brannigan and McBride v United Kingdom* Series A No. 258-B, (1994) 17 EHRR 539.

[38] *John Murray v United Kingdom* Application No. 18731/91, Decision of the Commission, 27 June, 1994.

conflict.[39] Some high profile cases aside, as Livingstone has argued (1995b: 27), the government has prevailed in the vast majority of cases brought in Northern Ireland.[40]

That said, the fact that neither extradition hearings (at least since the mid to late 1970s) nor international human rights mechanisms provided large numbers of successful cases for prisoners did little to erode their significance. The contests provided by legal challenge in an international setting were of considerable symbolic as well as material significance. Extradition hearings provided opportunities for political mobilization, perhaps most notably in the extradition/deportation case of Joseph Doherty from the USA.[41] Human rights challenges offered the opportunity to embarrass British governments and to expose state abuses. It was the international setting, the *site* of the contest as well as the practical benefits accrued, which made them important. The British government's reactions, in expending disproportionate resources on extradition hearings or expressing howls of outrage at ECHR challenges on Northern Ireland-related cases further raised the political stakes. These contests became what Scott has referred to as 'ideological struggles, . . . a struggle over facts and their

[39] For example, in 1978 the Commission heard the case of the wife of an IRA prisoner held in a British prison. She alleged a breach of her right to family life under Article 8 of the European Convention arising out of the conditions in which visits were allowed (*X v UK*, Application No. 8065/77, DR 14). These included a partition between the prisoner and visitor and the presence of a prison officer who noted down all the conversation which took place. While the Commission accepted that these amounted to a breach of the right to family life under Article 8 (1), they were satisfied that the interference was 'in accordance with the law and necessary in a democratic society' on the grounds that 'exceptional security risks may clearly be involved in the detention of persons connected with such terrorist organisations' (*X v UK* at 246). Similar grounds were used to reject more recent cases seeking to challenge the British government's reluctance (until the post-1994 ceasefire period) to transfer Irish prisoners back to Northern Ireland or the Republic. Such a policy caused considerable hardship to prisoners' partners, children, or elderly parents forced to travel long distances to inaccessible English prisons (Coulter 1991). These cases met with little success. The 1992 decision in *Kavanagh v UK*, Application No. 1908/91, was typical. The European Commission noted the high risk category of the prisoner and the danger of escape, and found that the policy did not constitute a breach of the right to family life under Article 8 of the Convention.

[40] e.g. see *Margaret Murray v United Kingdom* Series A No. 300-A, (1994) 19 EHRR 193.

[41] In his lengthy and ultimately unsuccessful cases against firstly extradition and then deportation from the USA to Northern Ireland Doherty's supporters included a broad cross section of the American body politic including New York Mayor David Dinkins and other senior figures in the Democratic Party, well beyond the traditional support base of Irish Republicanism in the USA (Dillon 1992).

meaning, over what has happened and who is to blame, over how the present situation is to be defined and interpreted' (Scott 1985: 178). The legal process in such settings offered Republican prisoners in particular an opportunity to undermine the hegemonic understanding of the conflict offered by the British state overseas and a chance to put over *their own* competing interpretation.

Law and Struggle in the Prisons

While legal challenges abroad (and in the Irish Republic) offered the opportunity for struggle on the international stage, the use of law in the prison context became a key domestic tactic from the 1980s onwards. In particular, the increasing use of judicial review of the actions of prison administrators became a major source of irritation to prison managers and a corresponding source of solace for the prisoners. Before examining the detail of those developments, however, it is important to place them within the broader context of US, British, and European literature on prison litigation.

For the purposes of clarity, some of that literature is grouped below under the overlapping themes of (*a*) the relationship between prisoners' cases and the broader social and political conditions in which they occurred and (*b*) the ways in which the courts have in effect come to the prisoners in establishing and maintaining jurisdiction over elements of prison management. Having then considered some of the Northern Irish cases, this section concludes by considering the ways in which the Northern Ireland context throws an interesting light on some of the broader issues identified.

Prison Litigation in its SocioPolitical Context

Any understanding of prison litigation must be located within an understanding of imprisonment both as it is experienced by the individual prisoner and within its broader social and political context. A number of competing views have emerged in the prison literature which place increased legal activism by prisoners within such a setting.

In their well-known article examining the huge increase in numbers of prison-related cases coming before the courts in the 1970s and 1980s in the USA, Milovanovic and Thomas (1989) have argued that an understanding of this phenomenon normally falls into three categories. These categories are the 'importation model', the 'deprivation model' and the 'revolutionary consciousness model' and all are characterized by Milovanovic and Thomas (1989: 50–1) as either unsatisfactory or inadequate.

They argue that importation is a limited model because they can find little relationship between those who become legal activists in prisons (what they refer to as jailhouse lawyers) and the previous experiences of these prisoners. With regard to the deprivation model, similarly they find that the decision to litigate as opposed to pursuing other activities such as fighting, body building, drug use, gang activity, and so forth is not sufficiently explained by a view of litigation as a response to the deprivations inherent in the prison setting. Finally, while they acknowledge a degree of inchoate revolutionary consciousness (see also Jackson 1970, Fitzgerald 1977) in their sample, they argue that such radical prisoners were a minority and that it was unclear the degree of support which they actually enjoyed amongst the other prisoners. They instead base their analysis upon a number of existential themes where law is used to mitigate the absurdity of prisons and prisoner litigants may be viewed as what Hobsbawm (1969) referred to as 'primitive rebels', holding at bay their own and other prisoners' complete oppression (Milovanovic and Thomas 1989: 48).[42]

It could be argued, however, that Milovanovic and Thomas's clear distinctions between the various models is somewhat overly schematic and fails to take account of some blurring between the boundaries. For example, Jacobs (1983a) locates the prisoners' rights movement in the USA with the context of other social and political struggles of the 1960s and 1970s including the civil rights movement, the student movement, the anti-Vietnam war mobilization, and radical black activists. He argues that in the prisons of America in 1960s it was the Black Muslims who 'carried the torch of Black protest' (Jacobs 1983a: 36), notching up a total of sixty-six reported federal cases between 1961 and 1978. Such a view would appear to fit within the importation model of broader socio-political struggles seeping into the prisons. However, as Jacobs goes on to argue, once US federal courts had

---

[42] In earlier work, Thomas (writing with Keeler, and Harris) had suggested a number of additional reasons why prisoners sue including litigation as a psychological coping mechanism, notions of a permissive judiciary, demographic explanations linked to a growing prison population and litigation linked to the particularly objectionable conditions in US prisons' (Thomas, Harris, and Keeler 1986). Milovanovic's concerns with regard to prisoners' legal activism (particularly amongst jailhouse lawyers) undermining the radical project is discussed later in this chapter.

reached into prisons on issues of clear constitutional significance,[43] the deplorable conditions in American prisons ensured that they stayed there (Jacobs 1983a: 37).

Similarly with regard to notions of revolutionary consciousness amongst prisoners, Jacobs suggests that the prisoners' rights movement in the USA also contained a more complex interaction between the politicized Black Muslim prisoners, their supporters and sympathizers on the outside, and issues of prisoners' rights. In most accounts of the USA prisoners rights movement, the activities of Muslim prisoners are chronologically placed as the catalyst for an increasingly litigious general population.[44] Jacobs argues (1976, 1983b), that the Muslims were highly disciplined, and organized a new morality—'group time', demonstrating how through legal activism prisoner groups could achieve solidarity and some tangible successes.[45]

The potential of the prisoners' rights actions was viewed in radical circles as of considerably broader political significance (Scheingold 1974).[46] The legal activism of such prisoners, and their links with groups of dedicated lawyers on the outside, many of whom have been involved in civil rights actions (Bershad 1977, Bronstein 1977), led to the creation of several specialist prisoners' rights groupings in the 1970s. Groupings such as the NAACP Legal Defense Fund and Education Fund (Martin and Ekland-Olson 1987, Schlanger 1999), the American Civil Liberties Union Prison Project (Hickey 1996), and the legal resource centre of the American Bar Association's Commission

[43] The first modern prisoners' rights case concerned an appeal from a lower court to the Supreme Court which challenged the discretion of prison officials to withhold Muslim prisoners access to their Korans, constituting religious discrimination under Section 1983 of the 1871 Civil Rights Act (*Cooper v Pate* 1963 US 546).

[44] In an interesting parallel in Northern Ireland, a number of the lawyers interviewed for this book argued that a similar spillover effect had occurred in Northern Ireland amongst ordinary prisoners following on the heels of a more litigious paramilitary population from the 1980s onwards (e.g. interview with criminal lawyer, 16 Jan. 1996).

[45] Jacobs goes on to argue that paradoxically once the Muslim prisoners had been afforded the basic rights pertaining to their freedom to worship, etc., they became a quiescent and stabilizing force in most prisons, which began to be disturbed by new cohorts of violent and disorganized ghetto youth (Jacobs 1983b: 67).

[46] 'Regardless of problems of implementation, rights can be useful political tools. It is possible to capitalise on the perceptions of entitlements associated with rights to initiate and mobilise political mobilisation—a dual process of activating a quiescent citizenry and mobilising groups into effective political units—Since rights carry with them connotations of entitlement, a declaration of rights tends to politicise needs by changing the way people think about their discontent' (Scheingold 1974: 131 cited in Jacobs 1983a: 43).

on Correctional Facilities and Services (Jacobs 1983a: 40) offered some strategic focus to the prisoners' cases which were lodged.

In sum, a context where prison conditions or managerial decisions are vulnerable to judicial challenge, and where prisoners are both organized within the prison and have developed relationships with outside lawyers and social/political movements is a scenario where legal activism within the gaols is likely.

The Courts come to the Prisoners

Of course the process by which prisoners seek to use the courts to further their objectives requires a parallel willingness on the part of courts to hear such grievances. Until relatively recently, the management of prisons in many jurisdictions operated with minimal interference from the courts (Jacobs 1983a, Van Zyl Smit 1987, Gearty 1991a), what Feeley and Rubin (1998) refer to as the 'hands-off era'. In Britain, as Livingstone and Owen (1999: 448–9) have argued, the effect of imprisonment, in terms of its ability to lock people up and regulate their daily lives, is to make prisons 'entirely the creation of law'. None the less as late as 1972, Lord Denning MR was observing that the courts would not entertain claims from 'disgruntled prisoners'.[47]

However, in the 1970s and early 1980s the courts became increasingly interventionist in both Britain and the USA (Jacobs 1983a, Wood 1990, Loughlin 1993, Richardson 1993, Feeley and Rubin 1998).[48] As Martin and Eckland-Olson (1987) detail in their meticulous account of the landmark *Ruiz v Estell* case, litigation exposed the dark underside of the 'surface efficiency' of the Texas Department of Corrections and the tenacious pursuit of the implementation of the court's findings dramatically altered the way the prisons were run there. In the USA as a whole, the courts were described at one stage as 'one of the principal agents of change in the nation's prisons and jails' (Feeley and Hanson 1990: 12). In the British context, the landmark decision of *St Germain* came in 1979 when the English Court of Appeal accepted that the High Court had jurisdiction to review the disciplinary adjudications of the prison Board of Visitors.[49] The Court of Appeal rejected the notion that judicial intervention would render the

[47] *Becker v Home Office* [1972] 2 QB 407.
[48] For a revisionist critique of the traditional hands-off account of the judicial attitude to prisons in the 19th and early 20th centuries see Wallace (1997).
[49] *R. v Board of Visitors ex p St Germain, No. 1*, 1 AU ER 1979, 701.

prisons unmanageable. While the majority in that decision based their views on the quasi-judicial powers of Boards of Visitors, the judicial door had clearly been wedged open and judicial interventions were gradually extended beyond disciplinary hearings to include transfer of prisoners, separation of mothers from babies, and prison conditions.[50]

Such an interventionist trend has been at least partially reversed (in the USA at least) in the late 1980s and 1990s (Yackle 1989, Livingstone 1995a), with the conservative revolution considerably restricting prisoners' ability to utilize the courts to effect change (Collins 1995, Freeman 1999). A conservative US Supreme Court, in tune with those changes, has led the way in the retrenchment of judicial reform in prisons and admonished lower courts 'wading in' to the complex area of prison management (Feeley and Rubin 1998: 47). In the United Kingdom, judicial intervention has been partial and procedural, focused more on extending the authority of the courts over prison administrators than extending prisoners' rights (Livingstone and Owen 1999: 456).

That said, the second requirement for sustained and organized prison litigation remains the intersection of judicial interest of whatever form in the area with favourable sociopolitical circumstances which encouraged the lodgement of such cases in the first place.

Litigation as Prison Struggle in Northern Ireland

As noted previously, the period after the 1980/1 hunger strikes saw Republican prisoners begin what they refer to as a new phase of the prison struggle. Many of the prisoners who came through those experiences were resolved to develop new and less 'self-hurting' forms of struggle (Campbell, McKeown, and O'Hagan 1994). In a context of less directly confrontational interactions with staff, individual prisoners (with the support and encouragement of their lawyers) became increasingly amenable to the idea of using the courts to press their claims. Remand prisoners began to challenge their rights to association with other prisoners,[51] and reductions in the number of visits on the grounds of staff shortages.[52] Amongst the sentenced paramilitaries, recourse to the courts was even more closely linked to aspects of the

---

[50] See e.g. R. v Secretary of State ex p McAvoy [1984] 1 WLR 1408, R. v Secretary of State ex p Hickling [1986] 1 FLR 543; R. v Home Secretary, ex p Herbage (No. 2) [1987] QB 872.   [51] McKernan v Governor HMP Belfast [1982] 17 NIJB.
[52] Mulvenna v Governor of HMP Belfast, unreported 23 Dec. 1985.

prison and political struggle, including attempts at rectifying the consequences of the protests of the late 1970s and establishing the right to visits from representatives of Sinn Fein.

In 1986 Brendan Hughes, who had been (as noted earlier) the IRA's Officer Commanding during the dirty protest and a former hunger striker, instigated a judicial review of governors' adjudications held between 21 January 1978 and October 1981.[53] The prisoners' actions during the protests regarding the refusal to wear prison uniforms, damage to cells, etc. all constituted breaches of prison disciplinary rules. Given the large numbers of protesting prisoners, the authorities had instigated a cyclical system of reports being written, charges laid, and adjudications heard every 14–28 days which resulted in the prisoners losing large amounts of remission. Hughes claimed that the hearings had not been fair. Such hearings were conducted in filthy cells and were constantly interrupted by the deliberate noise-making tactics of the prisoners. Hughes claimed that charges were improperly communicated to prisoners and that the lack of opportunity to respond failed to meet the test of 'fair in all the circumstances' as outlined in the *St Germain* case. Carswell LJ at 73 dismissed the case at first instance, finding that the defects in procedure did not impede Hughes from making an effective defence, and that Hughes' own conduct had contributed to the poor quality of the hearings. Carswell's decision was upheld by the Northern Ireland Court of Appeal.[54]

In 1987 Raymond McCartney, who assumed the leadership of the IRA prisoners in the Maze in the 1980s, lodged a judicial review challenging his right to receive visits from a Sinn Fein Councillor.[55] The Sinn Fein councillor in question had been a personal friend of McCartney and had visited him since 1977, but in 1985 he was forbidden to visit (after being elected as a Councillor) on the grounds *of* 'Sinn Fein's support for political violence'. McCartney argued *inter alia* that such actions discriminated against individuals on the grounds of their political opinion, as prohibited under the Northern Ireland Constitution Act 1973. Rejecting his application, the Northern Ireland Court of Appeal held (at 102) that 'the decision to prohibit visits by elected members was taken not because of the political opinions which such

---

[53] *Re Hughes' Application* [1986] No. 9, 55.
[54] *R. v Hughes' Application* [1986] No. 13, 2.
[55] *Re McCartney's Application* [1987] NIJB, No. 11, 94.

elected members might hold but because of their support for violence as a method of achieving political objectives'.

While both of these cases were taken by IRA leaders within the prisons, it would be wrong to suggest that prison litigation emerged as a top-down strategy. Rather it appears that a combination of individual prisoners lodging applications in Northern Ireland, and the willingness of IRA prisoners in English prisons to take high profile challenges,[56] alerted the IRA leadership to the potential of such legal actions in the struggle. As Brendan Hughes acknowledged in his application by way of explanation for the long delay in challenging adjudications held in the 1970s (an argument accepted by Carswell LJ at 64), he had only 'recently heard' of cases challenging governors' decisions on loss of remission.[57] Similarly, another leading IRA prisoner told the author:

I suppose the potential of it sort of dawned on us, it wasn't any great thought out strategy. We were getting legal aid, it was a pain in the arse for management in the prisons, it tied up judges and cost them money and sometimes you might get a result in the areas we were pushing in the prison like visits, or home leave or whatever.[58]

In terms of judicial reviews lodged, it was in the area of prison disciplinary adjudications that the prisoners appeared to apply themselves most strategically. As one prisoner told the author, 'if you make it hard to impose prison discipline, you make it very hard to run the prison.'[59] Prisoners continuously challenged issues such as refusal to grant legal representation at disciplinary hearings,[60] the make-up of Board of Visitor disciplinary hearings,[61] the failure to give prisoners prior

---

[56] It would appear that the usefulness of legal challenges to the struggle had already been recognized by IRA prisoners held in England. One former IRA prisoner, the instigator of almost twenty legal challenges, who served most of his life sentence in English prisons, has told the author that he and his colleagues in England began using legal challenges earlier than their counterparts in Northern Ireland. His rationale for this was that prisoners in England were fewer in number (and therefore less powerful), often subject to harsher treatment, and largely left to their own devices in developing their resistance techniques including, for example, building alliances with ordinary prisoners in British prisons. Interview, 12 Feb. 1995. See e.g. *R. v Gov. of HMP Brixton ex p McComb* 29 Mar. 1983 (unreported); *R. v Governor of Brixton ex p Walsh* [1984] 2 AU ER 609 [185] AC 54.

[57] See also *R. v McKieran's Application* [1985], NIJB, 6.

[58] Interview with former IRA prisoner, 15 Sept. 1997.

[59] Interview with former IRA prisoner, 9 Oct. 1998.

[60] *Re Lillis' Application* [1984], No. 15, 1; *Re Carroll's Application* [1987], NI 6; *Re Hones' Application* [1987], NI 160.

[61] *R v McNally's Application* [1985], 3 NIJB 1.

copies of witness statements,[62] failure to adjourn hearings,[63] and a range of other procedural matters regarding discipline. In reading through the transcripts of disciplinary hearings it is clear that prisoners had properly prepared themselves with an eye on future judicial reviews, for example citing the precise legal criteria as to why they should be permitted legal representation before a Board of Visitor hearing as well as co-operating with one another in preparing cases.[64]

While many of these cases were dismissed, as Livingstone and Owen (1999) argue, over a period of time a significant jurisprudence evolved in Northern Ireland regarding the procedural requirements of disciplinary hearings, in some instances differing from that in Britain.[65] Even where challenges were rejected, as Cripe (1990) has argued in the American context, judicial interference in prison management is often viewed by prison administrators as bad for staff morale. A number of the prison staff interviewed in the course of research for this book noted their irritation with the persistence of judicial reviews, and indicated their reluctance to take part in adjudications. Staff also claimed to have allowed prison rule infractions to go unpunished because of court weariness. As one prison governor with ten years' experience at the Maze prison told the author:

I think their [Republican prisoners] use of judicial review had an immediate impact on the Maze and on every other institution, because when you were making a management decision the first thing you thought about was, 'what I propose to do, will it stand the light of judicial review?' now the mere threat is enough and staff will say, ahem, well maybe we will go back and think about this one.[66]

Hadfield and Weaver (1994: 117) note that, between 1987 and 1991, 42 per cent of all judicial reviews in Northern Ireland were prison related. Many of those judicial reviews were taken by paramilitary prisoners.[67]

---

[62] *Re Crockards Application* [1985] 13 NIJB, 1.
[63] *Re Holland's Application* [1988], 2, NIJB, 85.
[64] See e.g. *Re O'Hare & Others' Application*, [1988] No. 2. at 56. A letter to a disciplinary hearing, again specifying precise criteria for a legal challenge, led one judge to comment sarcastically that 'on the view it might seem that the reasons were written by a different hand from the signature, but further than that I cannot say'. Gibson LJ in *Re Hones' Application*, [1985] 9 NIJB, 96 at 99–100.
[65] See *R. v McEvoy & Others* [1991] 8 NIJB 89.
[66] Interview with former prison governor at HMP Maze, 13 Aug. 1997.
[67] Hadfield and Weaver do not specify whether or not prisoner judicial review applicants were lodged by paramilitary or ordinary prisoners. However, by examining the prisons from which the judicial reviews emanated, interviews with solicitors, prisoners,

Over 70 per cent of prison cases were challenges to the decisions of prison governors at adjudication on charges brought against prisoners for breach of prison rules. The remainder included conditions-related challenges (20.8 per cent), release and temporary release, access to the courts, and other issues such as visits, home leave, and correspondence. Numbers reduced substantially by the mid-1990s (Dickson 1998) perhaps suggesting, as one former prison officer told the author, 'either we have gotten a lot better, which we have or they [the prisoners] have decided that they have extracted all that they can out of that particular strategy'.[68]

As to the reasons for such a dramatic rise in prison litigation over that ten-year period, Hadfield and Weaver suggest that relationships with lawyers,[69] the availability of legal aid, the granting of interim relief (which requires prorogation of sentences in governors' adjudications until the hearing), and the fact that prisoners' cases are speedily processed account for the large number of prison-related judicial reviews (Hadfield and Weaver 1995: 120–1). While I agree that all of these factors were relevant, I would suggest that a number of further issues are worthy of consideration.

Firstly, judicial reviews permitted Republican prisoners to challenge the legitimacy of the exercise of power in the prisons. Concepts of legitimacy permeate much of the recent British scholarship regarding 'order' within prisons, linking disorder to a perceived 'lack of justice' in British jails (Woolf 1991, para. 9.24, Sparks and Bottoms 1995, Sparks, Bottoms, and Hay 1996). However, the lack of effective remedy (before *St Germain* in 1979) and unwillingness by prisoners to seek legal redress meant that the illegitimate exercise of authority in Northern Irish prisons during the protest era had been the norm (Campbell, McKeown, and O'Hagan 1994, Taylor 1997). Legal challenges offered

and prison officials tasked to respond to the reviews, and by analysing the cases lodged (case notes kindly provided by the Northern Ireland Office), I have been able to make reasonably informed assessments as to the proportion of cases taken by paramilitary prisoners.

[68] Interview with former governor at HMP Maze, 9 Apr. 1998.

[69] Hadfield and Weaver (1995: 121) note that in a large proportion of the cases they surveyed judicial review actions were brought by the same solicitor who represented the prisoner at their original trial. Given the relatively small number of criminal law firms who specialize in terrorist trials, a relationship and expertise developed in Northern Ireland between criminal specialists and judicial review specialists amongst both solicitors and barristers. In their sample one firm brought 18% of the total judicial reviews in Northern Ireland, over four times that of their nearest rivals. This firm also handled a sizeable proportion of terrorist-related criminal trials (Hadfield and Weaver 1995: 131).

some check on some of the worst excesses which had become integral to prison officer culture during that period.

A second and related point is that legal challenges contributed to a realignment of the power relations within the prisons. In winning cases on issues such as prison discipline, or encouraging a mindset amongst staff which saw rule infraction go unpunished to avoid the hassle of reviews, law contributed significantly to changing the way in which the prisons were run. Prisoners had a clear organizational infrastructure and a strong resultant power base *within* the prison and mobilized an influential political *and* paramilitary constituency on the outside. Unlike other prisoners rights movements (see Cummins 1994, Schlanger 1999), Republican prisoners did not depend solely on litigation as the engine of change. Rather, legal challenge became one facet of struggle and legal victories (or the threat of legal action) one further expression of radically altered power relations.

Thirdly, as was noted above, the decision to rely upon legal challenges against the prison authorities occurred within a context where the prisoners were seeking to minimize violence and conflict within the prisons. As discussed previously, violence had been a prime prisoner strategy during the protest era of the 1970s when communication with prison staff was minimal, a strategy which came to be viewed as counterproductive in the 1980s and 1990s. While the capacity for violence or threats remained, prisoners employed much greater energies in campaigning, lobbying, and negotiation with their jailers. Legal hearings as dialogical contests between prisoners and the authorities may be seen as the logical extension of that changed relationship.

The final point concerns the relationship between prison and political struggle. As is noted above, the recognition of the prisoners rights movement in the USA as part of what Jacobs (1983b: 35) referred to as 'a larger mosaic of social change' is sometimes marred by an overstating of the 'revolutionary' or 'political' nature of the prisoners involved (Milovanovic and Thomas 1989: 86). This was not the case in Northern Ireland. As with Republicans' attitudes towards the courts at their trials or in international settings, prison-related challenges became part of their broader political struggle. Law in the prisons, the setting rightly defined by Mrs Thatcher during the hunger strikes as key to the defeat of the IRA, continued as an integral part of the overall Republican political struggle.

The Prisons, Sinn Fein, and Law as Political Struggle

The section below considers the relationship between law as an instrument of prison struggle and law as political struggle. In particular it seeks to identify the extent to which increased reliance upon legal challenge in both settings and a focus upon notions of rights has impacted upon the conduct of the overall Republican struggle.

Arising out of developments within the prisons, Republicans began to adopt more obvious forms of political struggle. As was noted above, the era after the hunger strikes saw a formalization of the strategy of 'the armalite and the ballot box' (Clarke 1987). Sinn Fein emerged as a political party geared to contest elections while the IRA's armed struggle remained as the cutting edge of the Republican movement (Taylor 1997: 285). In May 1985 Sinn Fein contested local council elections for the first time, and took fifty-nine seats with Sinn Fein members becoming Chairman and Deputy Chairman of Fermanagh and Magherafelt Councils respectively (Bew and Gillespie 1993: 184–5). With the IRA's campaign of violence ongoing, the appearance of Sinn Fein members (many of whom were former IRA prisoners) on local councils in Northern Ireland caused considerable consternation amongst Unionist councillors.

A number of Unionist-controlled local councils in Northern Ireland attempted a range of tactics in protest over the presence of the Sinn Fein councillors. Tactics included adjourning meetings before any business could be transacted,[70] shouting, walking out, and blowing whistles when Sinn Fein members attempted to speak, and, later, delegating all the lawful business of the council to a committee from which Sinn Fein councillors were excluded (Maguire 1995).

Sinn Fein adopted a strategy of challenging the legality of these actions. In 1985, in the first of the cases taken by Sinn Fein councillors against Craigavon Council,[71] the *de facto* delegation of all council business was held to be unlawful. Despite finding in favour of Sinn Fein, judicial unease at the Sinn Fein strategy is palpable in the relevant judgment. Lord Justice Carswell opined (at 24–5):

---

[70] These tactics were later extended to include permanent adjournments by Unionist-controlled councils in protest over the signing of the Anglo-Irish agreement in Nov. 1985. The latter policy was ultimately judged unlawful following a legal challenge by a member of the moderate Unionist Alliance Party. See *Re Cook and Others' Application* [1986] NI, 243.   [71] *Re Curran & McCann's Application* [1985] 7 NIJB 22.

I take judicial note of the facts that the policy and aims of Sinn Fein are to take power in Northern Ireland with a ballot box in one hand and an armalite in the other, that Sinn Fein gives unambivalent support to the armed struggle . . . and that when elected representatives of Sinn Fein take part in the normal work of an elected council that is but one plank of their policy; the other being the unambivalent support of murder and other acts of terrorist violence committed to overthrow democratic government in Northern Ireland. Notwithstanding these facts . . . Sinn Fein has been permitted to operate as a political party without being proscribed and that being so, it has to be regarded by the law as a legitimate party whose members are legally entitled to stand for election and take their seats as councillors.

A similar case taken against a different council where all business had been delegated to subcommittees resulted in identical findings.[72] In that instance, the Court of Appeal disagreed with Lord Justice Carswell arguing (at 36):

I do not subscribe to the view that Sinn Fein has to be regarded as a lawful organisation or by necessary implication a legitimate political party . . . that is a different thing from saying that individual members of Sinn Fein cannot legally stand for elections and take their seats as councillors, but they are entitled to do so despite their membership of Sinn Fein and not because of it.

Unionist arguments that it 'ill-behoves Sinn Fein supporters who support a terrorist campaign to ask a court to force councils to resume normal meetings and procedures' were rejected by the courts.[73]

While prominent Unionist councillors were occasionally overly frank to the courts regarding their rationale for unusual council practices,[74] those who continued to refuse to resume normal council business were occasionally personally levied with fines. While not all cases lodged by Sinn Fein with regard to local government have met with judicial success,[75] Unionist councillors had abandoned the strategy by

[72] *Re Neeson's Application* [1986] NI 92.
[73] *Re Hogan's Application* [1986] NIJB, No. 5, 81.
[74] 'The purpose of the sub-committees is to (a) keep the gunmen off them (b) to guarantee a system of Unionist/Loyalist domination (c) to deny Sinn Fein its say in Council business.' Sworn statement by former Unionist Lord Mayor of Belfast in *Re McCann's decision* [1992] NIJB, No. 9, 22.
[75] In *Re French and Others' Application* [1985] NI 310, Justice Carswell held that a council was not acting unreasonably in excluding Sinn Fein councillors. He argued that to do so could be justified under Art. 17 of the European Convention of Human Rights which permits the abrogation of some of the rights of the Convention in certain circumstances where an individual or group is seeking to destroy the other rights of the Convention. Carswell J argued that Sinn Fein's relationship with the IRA permitted such an abrogation.

the late 1980s. The use of such legal challenges is now accepted amongst Republicans as a crucial factor in asserting the Sinn Fein mandate on the political stage.[76] As one former Sinn Fein councillor has acknowledged:

Some traditional Republicans had harboured deep reservations about using the British courts to bring the Unionists to boot but I had no such qualms. As for the judges they seemed quite nonchalant about the prospect of ruling on matters brought before them by Republican politicians who wished to make them redundant. In fact, if anything, they frequently exhibited more sympathy to Sinn Fein than to the boorish and loutish Unionists who they saw as letting down the pro-British cause . . . One wonders just how comfortable Lord Justice Nicholson, Lord Justice Campbell and Lord Justice Murray might feel at seeing themselves listed in the Pantheon of Republican heroes—beside many of those they sentenced to lengthy prison sentences. (O'Muilleoir 1999: 102)

Sinn Fein and their supporters' use of the courts as an arena of political struggle continued into the 1990s and broadened beyond the assertion of the rights of local councillors. Recourse to the courts became an almost automatic Republican response across a spectrum of political issues. By way of example, in 1991 Sinn Fein supporter Mrs Josie Quigley successfully overturned a decision by the Unionist-dominated Belfast City Council not to put swings and other play equipment in a West Belfast playground in the predominantly Republican Whiterock area.[77] In 1993 a legal challenge was mounted by another Republican supporter to the Westminster election result in which Gerry Adams had lost his seat to the SDLP's Dr Joe Hendron on the grounds that Dr Hendron had overspent in his election campaign.[78]

---

[76] Interview with former IRA prisoner and Sinn Fein councillor, 16 Jan. 1995.

[77] The presiding judge, Lord Justice Nicholson opined, 'I am satisfied that the Unionists' hostility to Sinn Fein spilt over and led to the decision not to spend money on the playground . . . because parents of children at Whiterock who would make use of the facilities there were seen by the Unionist councillors as supporters of Sinn Fein in view of the fact that they had voted in four Sinn Fein councillors out of five' (quoted in O'Muilleoir 1999: 86).

[78] The Republican constituent argued that Dr Hendron had overspent the legal limit specified under the Representation of the People Act. The court decided that while the illegal overspend had occurred this was largely due to the decision of the poor skills of Dr Hendron's election agent and the result was upheld (*McCrory v Hendron and Another* [1993] no. 1 JIJNI). When the Republicans lost that case, despite the clear breach, the author was in earshot of a conversation between a senior Sinn Fein and a senior IRA figure as they exited the court. After the Sinn Fein member had finished a long tirade about the unfairness of the decision his IRA colleague turned to him and said sarcastically 'Well fuck goes your faith in British justice'.

In 1994 Sinn Fein Councillor Bobby Lavery successfully challenged a decision by the government not to provide him with financial assistance towards installing special security measures after his home had been attacked twice by Loyalists and his son killed.[79] In 1997 Sinn Fein MP Martin McGuinness sought leave for a judicial review challenging the ruling by House of Commons Speaker Betty Boothroyd that he and Gerry Adams should swear an oath of allegiance to the Queen before accessing full House of Commons facilities.[80] Similarly in 1998 Sinn Fein again used the courts to appeal their expulsion from the all-party peace talks in 1998 after the IRA had been accused of a number of ceasefire breaches.[81] Finally in 2001 Sinn Fein ministers Martin McGuinness and Bairbre De Brun successfully challenged a move by Unionist First Minister David Trimble to ban them from attendance at all-Ireland ministerial meetings.[82]

The key point for current purposes is the interaction between prison struggle, political mobilization, and the use of litigation in both arenas. As noted above, many of the Republican litigants on political matters were former IRA prisoners who had seen law put to good use in the prisons. However, the relationship between legal challenges in both settings over the same timeframe was clearly a fluid and unschematic one. In early attempts to discern a clear chronology as to which had come first, the author was continuously told by lawyers,[83] former prisoners, and Sinn Fein representatives that such a focus was essentially to miss the point. As one Sinn Fein councillor and former prisoner told the author:

I don't think it really matters. Obviously once Sinn Fein decided to fight elections it was only logical that we would legally challenge the Unionists' attempts to gerrymander us out of representing the interests of our constituents. Similarly within the prisons, as it became obvious that we could pursue the prison struggle through the courts, it was the sensible thing to do—the two strategies sort of evolved from the circumstances.[84]

---

[79] *Lavery* [1994] NI 209.

[80] *Re McGuinness*, judgment delivered 3 Oct. 1997.

[81] See *Irish Times* (17 Feb. 1998), 'McGuinness Says Sinn Fein Not Accountable for the IRA', *Irish Times* (20 Feb. 1998), 'Law May Feel "Political Question" Marks No-Go Area'.

[82] *Irish Times* (31 Jan. 2001), 'Trimble Acted Unlawfully in Sinn Fein Ban'.

[83] A number of the legal firms most prominent in pursuing the prisoners' judicial reviews were also responsible for taking cases on behalf of Sinn Fein councillors.

[84] Interview with former IRA prisoner and Sinn Fein councillor, 16 Jan. 1995.

The extension of legal struggle into the political arena by Republicans was a logical and organic development of the movement's attitude towards law. In the early 1970s Republicans' attitudes towards law had been seen as a vehicle for a largely symbolic assertion of the continuity of their struggle. Later, in international hearings and the prisons, that resistant symbolism was accompanied by a greater awareness of the possibility of law as a source of political mobilization and an occasional source of material victory over the British state. The challenges in the political arena, particularly the council cases, were the first direct legal engagements against the Unionists. In each of these settings (particularly after the courts began to be recognized), legal challenges became fiercely contested dialogical exchanges underpinned by radically different political and ideological views of the world. Whatever the heat of those exchanges, they did at least represent an exchange other than violent confrontation.

Law as Absorption or Reconfiguration of Struggle?

The final issue to consider is the impact which the use of law as a strategy of prison and political resistance has had on Republicanism in particular.[85] There is considerable literature on the impact of political or social movements adopting legal challenges or rights discourses as a form of struggle. Some critical commentators have discussed 'the myth of rights' (Scheingold 1974: 5), wherein revolutionary potential and real social change are sidetracked into a liberal, reformist, and ultimately hegemonic agenda (Handler 1978, Tushnet 1984, Ray 1993). Such a process entails the state acting as what Melucci (1996: 235) has described as 'a reform filter', reshaping a movement's demands by filtering out those elements that pose the most fundamental challenges to powerful constituents and co-opting those elements that can be made consistent with prevailing interests. Milovanovic (1988: 469) has captured this dilemma well for radical activists in the USA prison setting when he argued that legal activism amongst prisoners may actually have helped to underpin the rule of law ideology of Western capitalism, channelling energies away from outright upheaval and undermining their true political potential.[86]

---

[85] There have been insufficient cases lodged by Loyalist prisoners and politicians to carry out a similar analysis on the impact upon their ideology and practices.

[86] Bankowski and Mungham (1976: 138) make a similar point when they claim that the starting point for those who seek to resist is to attack the reification of the law, legal institutions, legal processes, and the role of the lawyer in our society.

The work of Thomas Mathiesen is perhaps most relevant to the current analysis, given its focus on the analysis of both prison and social movement struggles (Mathiesen 1965, 1974, 1980). He suggests that, in order to be alive, a living political movement must 'stand in a relationship of contradiction to the prevailing system'. By this he means that 'basic premises of the prevailing system are opposed' (Mathiesen 1980: 227). Any political movement which does not stand in such opposition, 'dies' in the sense that the possibilities of movement are narrowed or halted by the boundaries established by the prevailing system. Mathiesen goes on to argue that contradiction must be accompanied by *competition* with the existing system. By competition he appears to suggest an alternative vision or epistemology which sets apart the oppositional movement (Mathiesen 1980: 229–30). The absorbent character of prevailing political systems, or indeed subsystems such as the operation of prisons, makes the maintenance of contradiction and competition all the more important for the survival of a political or social movement.

The absorption of the Republican movement is the exact criticism levelled against the current Republican leadership by dissidents opposed to the peace process (MacIntyre 1995). They regard the Good Friday Agreement as a sell-out and the willingness of mainstream Republicans to hold seats in a Northern Irish government as an acceptance of partition and a betrayal of the struggle for which many including the hunger strikers died. They argue that the current leadership have been bought off from the objective of a United Ireland by human rights guarantees within a partitionist statelet (O'Bradaigh 1998). In effect, the apparent faith of the mainstream Republican movement in the ability of law to deliver is, for many dissidents, proof positive of the latter's abandonment of the movement's traditional objectives. For them, Republicans' new-found faith in law has become the instrument of betrayal.

It is indisputable that an apparent confidence in the ability of law to deliver in certain key areas has been one of the cornerstones in the process which led to abandonment of armed struggle. Following the 1994 and 1997 ceasefires (McEvoy and Gormally 1997) and a lengthy negotiation process involving most of the political parties and the British and Irish governments, the Good Friday Peace Accord was signed in April 1998 (discussed in Chapter 11). That agreement included provisions for the incorporation of the European Convention of Human Rights; a Bill of Rights for Northern Ireland; a Human

Rights Commission; a new Equality Commission; as well as major reviews of the police and criminal justice systems (CAJ 1998, Morison 1999, Harvey and Livingstone 1999). While all political parties in Northern Ireland also supported the rights agenda, Sinn Fein were amongst its strongest advocates (Mageean and O'Brien 1999).

Mainstream Republicans would, however, strongly dispute the view that their focus upon the rights and equality agenda represents an abandonment of traditional objectives. They argue that the desire for rights and justice has always been a key objective of the Republican campaign.[87] In support of that assertion, they point to the involvement of Republicans in the 1960s civil rights campaign and argue that it was the Unionist government's violent reaction to peaceful protest for civil and political liberties which led to Republicans being 'forced' to engage in armed struggle (Adams 1996). While in private, at least, some Republicans would concede that abuses carried out by the IRA such as brutal punishment attacks and shootings of alleged anti-social criminals undermined their credibility in pressing a human rights agenda, their public position remains that it has always been an integral part of their struggle.

Such assertions are only partially true. It is a fact that Republicans were one part of a broad progressive alliance campaigning for reform before the outbreak of violence in 1969 (Purdie 1990). However, during the conflict the primacy of armed struggle meant that (at least until the 1980s) those advocating a rights-based analysis of the conflict were liable to be treated with suspicion as 'partitionist'. As was discussed above, Adams himself has admitted that 'broad front' political alliances were hampered on issues such as supporting the hunger striking prisoners by the early insistence by Republican fundamentalists that support for the armed struggle was a prerequisite for involvement in any such campaign (Clarke 1987). The increased emphasis on the use of law in the prisons and in the political arena from the 1980s clearly had an impact on Republican thinking but changes came arguably slowly from below and as a result of other actors rather than simply because of the movement's intrinsic commitment to such notions.

That said, the increased resort to legal forms of struggle has clearly impacted upon the overall philosophy of the Republican movement rather than simply becoming another weapon in their armoury. As

---

[87] Interview with Republican spokesperson, 1 July 1999.

Hunt has argued, engagement in rights-based struggle plays a part 'in constituting the social actors, whether individual or collective, whose identity is changed by and through the mobilisation of some particular rights discourse' (Hunt 1993: 247). Material and symbolic legal victories in the prisons or elsewhere underlined that the state was not the omnipotent monolith which had refused the demands of the civil rights movement (Ellison and Martyn 2000). This transformation reflected not just a series of tactical changes incorporating law as another tool of struggle but also a different style of engagement with the state and an appeal to external, objective sources of validation and justification.

Such an appeal returns us to the notion of dialogue discussed in the first part of this chapter. Recourse to law and indeed political struggle is a dialogical process and dialogue requires the participation of at least two parties. As Habermas has argued, dialogue should allow participants at least the possibility of reaching 'more truthful interpretations of their own particular needs as well as especially of those which are common and capable of consensus'. Such dialogue or discourse requires a test of reciprocity. Any normative claim must be one that can be universalized or 'communicatively shared' if the claim is to be acceptable to a broader constituency (Habermas 1975: 108 cited in White 1988: 71). Communicative actions are thus actions or assertions which can be communicated and assessed as rational or irrational, legitimate or illegitimate, within a framework where objective judgements can be made (Habermas 1981: 8, 9, 15). An increased reliance upon, and appeal to, legality by Republican prisoners and councillors represented exactly such a process of dialogue. Republicanism could not engage in such dialogue with actors outside the movement and remain totally unaffected.

It would be wrong, however, to give the impression that engagement in legal forms of struggle led inexorably to unarmed struggle. It did not. The range of complex factors which led to the IRA cessation is beyond the scope of this chapter, but, suffice to say, it was not driven by the attitudes of prisoners and politicians towards law.[88] That said, it

---

[88] Such an analysis should be located in the literature on organizational strategy within armed movements. That literature may be divided into broad traditions, the *instrumental* and the *behavioural*. The former tends to see change as the result of a process of rational cost/benefit analysis usually in response to external factors such as shifts in government strategy. The behavioural tradition tends to focus upon internal discourses and relationships within the group and to suggest that strategy is both shaped and constrained by internal cultural and organizational symbols and mythologies. Some

is possible to argue that gradual engagement in legal and other forms of struggle, whether in the prison or the political arena, represented at the very least an acknowledgement of the limitations of armed struggle.

If as Weber has suggested the defining characteristic of a state is its monopoly on the use of coercion (Weber 1966), then primary reliance upon violence represents an absolute denial of the legitimacy of the state, at least to the supporters of an armed organization. However, the realities of armed struggle mean that the price for such absolute denial is that it is difficult to communicate the political philosophy which underpins the violence, at least to an audience beyond the immediate support base. Engagement in legal and other non-violent forms of struggle does not afford the same absolute denial. Such forms of struggle do imply some form of legitimacy to the existing order, some expectation of 'regime responsiveness' to grievances (Kitschelt 1986). On the other hand, in the absence of serious violence, legal struggle does hold out the possibility of rational communication of a particular position to a much broader audience.

This does not mean that one must accept the inevitability of what Mathiesen (1980) referred to as the 'absorbent' capacity of the state. All political movements need to be critically reflective about their strategies and tactics, particularly when political violence is one of those strategies. The adoption of the legal forms of resistance, both inside and outside the prisons, clearly contributed to a critical appraisal of the efficacy of armed struggle. For IRA prisoners and other Republican activists (coming as they did from such a traditionally militaristic movement) to appraise critically the use of political violence was arguably a sign that the movement was alive in the Mathiesen sense rather than that it had either stagnated or sold out.

Conclusion

This chapter has sought to go beyond the traditional critique of the repressive potential of law and legal formalism associated with Northern Ireland (Hillyard 1987) to highlight the insights provided by attitudes towards law and the potential for legal praxis amongst

commentators, drawing upon both traditions, have also suggested a life cycle approach to such organizations in which external sociopolitical, organizational, and finally individual activists, are key to understanding an organization's attitude to violence. For an overview see Crenshaw (1990), Della Porta (1995), Irvin (1999).

politically motivated prisoners and their colleagues. There are a number of points of potentially broader applicability.

Firstly, the experience of paramilitary prisoners and their political comrades' attitudes to law underline the usefulness of an analysis of law which is sensitive to the dialogical and processual nature of the legal endeavour. The early attitude of paramilitary defendants to their trials may be viewed as a process of internal dialogue whereupon Republicans sought to emphasize the continuity and legitimacy of their struggle, by resorting to a practice with a long history within the Republican tradition. That practice was modified not only because of its practical consequences but also because of a dialogical process which saw pragmatic accommodations between competing ideologies of paramilitaries, their lawyers, and the judiciary. The attitudes of Republican prisoners towards extradition hearings and hearings before international human rights fora was shaped by the opportunity for external dialogue on an international stage.

Secondly, the prison litigation experience in Northern Ireland demonstrates the capacity of law to be used by social and political movements both to resist and to contribute towards the transformation of powerful social institutions. As in the USA in the 1960s and 1970s (Feeley and Rubin 1998), it is clear that the use of litigation in the prisons in Northern Ireland contributed significantly to changing the ways in which prisons were administered. The intersection between favourable sociopolitical conditions, judicial expansion of administrative law, and organized prison litigators has considerably curtailed the potential for the repressive application of power in the prisons.

Thirdly, the Northern Ireland experience offers support to the thesis that political mobilization around rights issues inevitably shapes or reconfigures to some extent the nature of overall struggle. Engagement in legal struggle has both circumscribed and enriched Republicanism in Ireland. Isolated from political dialogue with other actors because of the ongoing violence and their policy of abstention from political institutions until the 1980s, Republicans were not forced to engage substantively with the fact that the Unionist majority in Northern Ireland could not be militarily coerced into a united Ireland. Dialogical engagement, in legal and other arenas, has necessitated a gradual acceptance that Unionists have a *right* to a British identity, and to a link with Britain while they constitute a majority in Northern Ireland.

On the other hand, the requirement to reflect critically more deeply on axioms of Republican tactics and philosophy has arguably unearthed a more grounded analysis of the appropriate focus of the Republican struggle. Republicans have always been dedicated to the destruction of the Northern state. However, as in the campaign for political status in the prisons during the late 1970s, they have been forced to articulate the meaning of such a project beyond the slogan of 'the removal of the British presence'.

From their perspective, it is arguable that the state was built on the three key pillars of Unionist hegemony in the political arena, systemic discrimination against Catholics in most areas of public and private life, and a Unionist-controlled police force with exceptional powers as coercive back-up. Other than Emergency law, all of this has changed considerably and law, it is envisaged, will continue to play a crucial part in that transformation.

Law became a key resource for those predisposed to ending armed conflict and pressing for their political objectives through other strategies. Many such individuals, particularly former Republican and Loyalist prisoners, have experienced at first hand the repressive potential of law. Whether such a complex, inexact, and unpredictable tool as law can live up to the high expectations of a society emerging from three decades of violence remains to be seen. Law's ability to eliminate the social and political conditions which led to conflict is neither a simplistic nor mechanistic process.[89]

What can be said with greater certainty, however, is that, within the prisons, law delivered for politically motivated prisoners. Law gave prisoners a platform to engage in dialogue outside their political constituency, contributed to internal dialogue within the Republican movement, and, from the mid-1980s onwards (despite the high numbers of unsuccessful cases), had a direct impact on prison management in key areas such as prison discipline. Whatever the reality, many prison managers and staff considered that the courts were 'invariably on the side of the prisoners'.[90] In effect, paramilitary prisoners successfully adapted a tool of repression into one of resistance.

[89] Morison has well described the capacity of law to effect change as a 'Heath Robinson contraption, a ramshackle device where creaking pulleys operate to overbalance buckets of water that trigger off other forces which in turn activate other processes with the final result that (possibly) an egg is boiled or a banana skinned' (Morison 1990: 11).

[90] Interview with former prison governor at HMP Maze, 13 Aug. 1997.

7

Prison Management and Prison Staff

Introduction

This chapter draws upon those elements of the academic literature on prison management which are of direct relevance to the management of paramilitary prisoners in Northern Ireland. While there is some discussion of prison staff as an element of that endeavour, the emphasis is primarily upon the *management* element of the process. This does not entail an exclusive focus upon the activities of prison headquarters-based staff or prison governors in the individual prison settings. Rather it suggests an understanding of prison management as the description of a *process* by which matters such as planning; the nature of regimes; relations with prisoners, politicians, and the community; managerial structures and culture; and a range of other key variables coalesce to determine the *shape* or *style* of a given prison system (Barak Glanz 1981, Brydensholt *et al.* 1983).

As has been underlined in the previous discussions, the Northern Ireland Prison Service between 1970 and 2000 was not a normal prison system. Prison management in such a context provided a unique and challenging set of circumstances. In the ensuing chapters three heuristic models are proposed to detail the particularities of the Northern Ireland experience.[1] These models are used to describe different styles of managing paramilitary offenders over the past thirty years. However, despite the specific exigencies of the Northern Ireland context, there are clearly generic issues concerning the management of prisons and the role of prison staff which are of direct relevance and these are examined below.

---

[1] Two of the models discussed below were first mooted in a co-authored article in *Crime & Justice* in 1993 (Gormally, McEvoy, and Wall 1993). While my views have changed considerably since that publication, I am grateful for permission from *Crime & Justice* and its editor Micheal Tonry to re-examine some of those ideas here.

Models of Prison Management

While there has been a proliferation in management literature in general, this has not been matched until the last two decades or so with regard to literature on prison management (Livingstone and Owen 1999). Jim Jacobs's (1977) account of changes at Stateville, Barak Glanz's (1981) article, and the report commissioned by the Council of Europe on prison management (Brydensholt *et al.* 1983) are amongst the most noteworthy of early attempts to conceptualize changes in the ways in which prisons are managed. More recent writings have extended the analysis of prison management, either under the rubric of the maintenance of control or order (e.g. DiIulio 1987, Ditchfield 1990, Sparks, Bottoms, and Hay 1996), accountability (Vagg 1994), or increasingly in the context of 'correctional science' in the USA through which better prison management and leadership is encouraged (Houston 1995, Freeman 1999). To varying degrees, these and most other studies on the topic share a view of prison management as something more complex than the internal technical exercise of *running* a prison. Rather prison management is viewed as an endeavour in which organizations and human actors must carry out their responsibilities while responding to an array of external political, social, legal, and ideological factors all of which render it a highly complex business.

Barak Glanz (1981) suggests that there are four basic models of prison management. The first, the authoritarian model, began in the nineteenth century and lasted well into the twentieth century. This model was characterized by an autocratic management style, with much power concentrated in the personage of the prison warden, a considerable degree of patronage guiding the lives of the guards, and a prison inmate system maintained by 'a combination of terror, often brutal corporal punishment, some rudimentary incentives and favouritism'.

The second model to emerge, after the Second World War, was what he referred to as the bureaucratic-lawful model, where prison life was bureaucratized and codified. Both wardens and guards had their powers curtailed by rules. Prison wardens became just another link in the chain (Vagg 1994: 111). Prison manager–inmate relations were determined by the extent to which decisions relating to the prisoners are free from arbitrariness and determined by a framework of general rules and principles (Ditchfield 1990: 10).

Barak Glanz's third model, shared power, emerged in the 1950s and 1960s as one where the inmates also have an input to the running of the

prison. The rehabilitative and democratic goals of this model emphasized additional help and support from therapeutic and caring profes-
sions. Such an approach has also been referred to as 'participative
management' (Irwin 1980, DiIulio 1987).The results of this, Barak
Glanz argues, is that tensions were created amongst prison warders
between these therapeutic objectives and their traditional correctional
role and that the democratization process created a power vacuum to
which inmates in particular responded by setting up well-organized
pressure groups which were much more difficult to deal with than previous troublesome individuals.

The fourth model, inmate control, is, according to Barak Glanz, the
logical extension of the shared power model. The major difference
between the two is in the nature of the organization of prisoners. In the
shared power model these are organized around ideological and religious principles (e.g. the Black Muslim Group), however in the inmate
control model they are simply organized around competing gangs,
usually based on ethnicity and mirroring their street counterparts on
the outside. Much of the institutional balance is maintained through
inter-gang negotiations, conflict, or dispute resolution and management and staff have little influence on matters.

DiIulio (1987) offers a slightly different set of models in his analysis
of prison management in Texas, California, and Michigan and is quite
forthcoming about his preferences between the styles of management.
Referring to the styles of management practised in these three states,
he argues that they represent respectively control, responsibility, and
consensual models of prison management. The control model places
most emphasis on inmate obedience, tight monitoring on inmate activities and movement and swift and rigorous rule enforcement. The
responsibility model places less emphasis on the regimentation of prisoners, and emphasizes prisoners' grievance procedures, counselling,
and delegated decision-making to staff close to the prisoners on the
ground. It is based on the premiss that, subject to security, prisoners
can be given some responsibility for their lives through consultation
rather than orders. The consensual model is a combination of both
control and responsibility, where a hierarchical staff deal with inmates
in a firm but fair way.[2]

---

[2] As Vagg (1994: 111) has argued, it is probably fair to view DiIulio's model as a
bureaucratic and hierarchical system under the control of an authoritarian leader, the
responsibility model, as something approximate to Barak Glanz's 'shared powers' model,
and the consensual model as somewhere between the two.

DiIulio is sceptical about what he regards as the accepted sociological wisdom regarding prison management as an attempt to build upon the positive aspects of inmate mores, values, and social systems. Within such a paradigm, he argues, 'inmates must be coaxed, not coerced' (DiIulio 1987: 19). He argues that the three ends of good prison management are 'order, amenity and service' and that Texas (the control model) had the most 'orderly' prisons with the fewest homicides, assaults, suicides, riots, and breaches of prison discipline (DiIulio 1987: 53). He argues that this model not only improves order within prisons with regard to inmates' behaviour but also inspires greater staff morale, less staff turnover, and greater 'attachment' to the organization.[3]

His advocacy of the control model has been criticized by a number of scholars writing on prison management. For example, Martin and Ekland-Olson (1987) and Crouch and Marquart (1990) question the contention that the Texas state prison system was in fact safe for inmates in the 1960s and 1970s under the control model. As Crouch and Marquart argue, while in the old days before courts ordered reforms powerful prison service directors may have been able to limit official violence and maintain apparently orderly prisons, many of the prisoners did not share DiIulio's belief that the prisons were either safe or orderly (Crouch and Marquart 1990: 121). Similarly, in their comparison of five prisons designed to test DiIulio's contention regarding the control model and staff morale, Stohr et al. (1994: 495) found that the control model did not have the positive benefit claimed and that continued adherence to this style of staff management would be 'imprudent'.

In the British context, some commentators have characterized prison management as having become somewhat directionless in the last few decades as overarching penal philosophies have fallen into disrepute. For example, Ditchfield (1990: 24) argues that no generally accepted penal ideology has yet succeeded the treatment model of

---

[3] Dilulio also argues that a number of additional factors are key to the success of the control model. These include a formal bureaucratic organizational structure which includes specialized labour, published rules and regulations, merit-based promotions, and impersonal relations; a willingness for managers to be involved in hands-on leadership, in which they involve themselves in the daily running of the prison such as visiting the wings at least once per day as well as being able to deal with the political chicanery which the job entails outside the prison; and a need for consensus amongst prison staff, judges, politicians, and the media on the conditions required for the proper working of the prisons (DiIulio 1987: 237).

imprisonment. Similarly, Vagg (1994: 113) characterizes British and European prisons as experiencing an interregnum in prison management philosophy, in which disappointment with the empirical results of rehabilitation has led to some disillusionment with the bureaucratic lawful and shared power models. He argues that competing dynamics such as increased concerns with justice and inmates, and the political drift rightwards and corresponding focus on retribution, has created 'a situation in which the aim of many governors has been simply to keep the institution operating, without any official sanctioned and long term goals in mind' (Vagg 1994: 113).

Sparks, Bottoms, and Hay (1996: 151–2), however, have suggested that all British long-term prisons at least may be formally described as fitting within Barak Glanz's bureaucratic-lawful model, although with some variation between institutions based upon the individual histories of the prisons and the occupational culture of the staff. As they point out, even taking into account such variations, differences between individual British prisons and American prisons in different jurisdictions may be less pronounced as all prisons in England and Wales are bound by the same rules and regulations.

It may also be possible to argue that the increased managerialism of the British prison system (Newburn 1995, Cavadino and Dignan 1997), in which an underpinning penal philosophy has been largely replaced by a series of technical, managerial, and scientific discourses (discussed in detail in Chapter 10), has led to even greater levels of bureacratization. Key Performance Indicators, corporate and business plans, increased emphasis on value for money, financial accountability, and so forth are now the dominant influences in managing British prison systems. In a context where such managerial dynamics are combined with the increased willingness of the courts to review the operation of prison management decisions, it may be fair to suggest that the bureaucratic-lawful model probably comes closest to describing most British prison establishments.

Models of Prison Management in the Northern Ireland Context

As noted above, and in similar fashion to Barak Glanz and DiIulio, this book seeks to develop particular models which reflect the different styles of prison management which have arguably occurred in this jurisdiction. As with those authors and others (e.g. Jacobs 1977), such developments are examined as a dialectic between material conditions within the prisons (e.g. the prisoners' strategies of resistance) and a range of social, political, and ideological influences outside the prisons.

In the chapters below I argue that prison management may be characterized over the period by reference to three Weberian ideal type models of management termed reactive containment (1969–76), criminalisation (1976–81), and managerialism (1981–2000). While neither necessarily evolutionary nor indeed mutually exclusive, these models are sufficiently different in character to highlight distinct changes and developments in the philosophy and practice of prison management in Northern Ireland over the period.

As is detailed in Chapter 8, reactive containment (1969–76) is described as a largely military-driven model for the management of paramilitary prisoners. Informed by colonial experiences in Cyprus, Kenya, Malaysia, and other locations, this model was born from the need of the British authorities to *react* to the loss of control by the local Unionist government. Troops were dispatched to regain control and support the security forces and assist prison staff in guarding the prisons. To *contain* the violence, terrorist suspects were interned without trial, the criminal justice system amended to process large numbers of terrorist cases through the non jury Diplock Courts, and convicted prisoners were granted *de facto* prisoner of war status while the government sought to negotiate with the paramilitary leaders to seek a political solution.

Chapter 9 examines criminalisation (1976–81) as part of a broader political and military strategy designed to deny any implicit or explicit acknowledgement of the political character of the conflict, defining terrorist violence as a law and order problem rather than a political one. In the prisons this entailed an end to internment and the refusal of *de facto* political status to paramilitary prisoners. It required forcing prisoners to conform to the same regime as ordinary criminal prisoners and accept the tangible symbols of ordinary imprisonment such as the wearing of prison uniforms and the carrying out of prison work. Prisons were seen as key battlegrounds in the project designed to defeat terrorism.

Chapter 10 is an exposition of the third proposed model, termed managerialism to characterize the management of paramilitary prisoners in Northern Ireland from 1981 until the final early releases in 2000. This model sees an acceptance that the prison system cannot defeat political violence. Instead prison management is increasingly understood as a technical question rather than an ideological one. While not primarily influenced by the managerial changes to the British public sector that occurred before the 1980s, it is argued that the scientific and instrumentalist discourses which characterize managerialism generally provided a useful legitimating framework to justify practices which had emerged in the Northern Ireland prison system in any case after the hunger strikes. This period was also characterized by greater pragmatism in relations with paramilitary prisoners, simultaneous attempts to limit their power and influence, greater autonomy and self-confidence amongst prison managers and less ministerial interference, and a number of additional features.

It is possible to see traces of the prison models identified elsewhere in each of the Northern Ireland prison management models. Reactive containment contains a number of elements of Barak Glanz's shared power model. Criminalisation could be viewed as an attempt to impose a fairly crude version of DiIulio's control model, albeit with a political and ideological agenda which went far beyond the maintenance of order in the prisons here. Managerialism may be seen as containing elements of the bureaucratic-lawful model as well as describing a process in which prison management was arguably transformed to something between Barak Glanz's shared power and inmate control models.

While it is descriptively useful to locate my attempts at characterizing prison management in Northern Ireland within existing typologies, there are a number of specific issues within the prison management literature relevant to the Northern Ireland context. While there may be more, I have chosen to focus in particular upon three key areas which I believe to be of direct theoretical and material relevance to the Northern Ireland context. These are (i) the ways in which prison management responds to organized groups of prisoners; (ii) the significance of power relations in the application of prison management strategies; and (iii) the relationship between models of prison management and prison staff.

Prison Management and Relations with Organized Groups of Prisoners

It is possible to detect at least two traditions in the literature regarding the management of organized prisoners groupings. These approaches were summed up over forty years ago by Cressey in his preface to Clemmer's *Prison Community*. He identified two choices: 'One is to keep inmate society as unorganised as possible, to prevent individuals from joining forces, the other is to enlist, unofficially, the aid of the inmates themselves in running the prison' (Clemmer 1958: p.ix). Those two positions remain the essential options when considering the appropriate response to organized prisoners.

Some commentators have appeared quite quiescent regarding the question of inmates' organization and have viewed it as an inevitable feature of prison life which could be harnessed towards management goals through patronage and affording limited privileges to inmate leaders (Sykes 1958). Similarly, others have suggested that the increased politicization of prisoners in the 1960s and 1970s enabled greater participation by the prisoners in management of the institution (Irwin 1980). Jacobs, for example, describes some of the Stateville gangs as providing their members with psychological support and 'rudimentary solidarity' as well as having contributed to the 'politicisation' of the prison (Jacobs 1977: 152–4).

Others, however, have expressed considerable unease at inmate organization. De Beaumont and De Tocqueville, writing in the 1830s, argued that where inmates were permitted to associate freely, they are bound to think and act in ways that make them less manageable and 'still more corrupted' (De Beaumont and De Tocqueville 1997: 49). Clemmer (1940) was also inclined to see the inner worlds of prisons as places where the weak could be preyed upon by organized groups unless regulated by more formal controls on behaviour. Similarly DiIulio (1987: 18) has referred to a 'Hobbesian state of the inmate predators' which is facilitated by recognition of prison gangs and hierarchies. While some have suggested an overemphasis on the role of race gangs in changing prisons from 'a repressive but comparatively safe "Big House" to an unstable and violent social jungle' (Johnson 1996: 133), many American commentators do appear to bemoan the perfidious influence of modern gangs as organized criminal enterprises motivated by profit and competing for power and influence in the prisons (e.g. Paige 1997). Such analysis tends to be focused on ways in which the effectiveness and cohesiveness of gangs can be broken up through strategies such as the identification and separation of suspected gang members (Hunt *et al.* 1993), longer prison sentences for such prisoners (Tachiki 1995), and cognitive retraining (Toller and Tsagaris 1996).

In British prisons, while there is some evidence of gang-related prison violence (e.g. King and McDermott 1995: 134–6), prison managers have not had to deal with the issue of organized criminal gangs on anything like the same scale as in the USA. The attempts at political organizing amongst groups of prisoners in the early 1970s (Ryan 1978) appear to have by and large faded away by the late 1970s. In fact, perhaps the most problematic prisoner groupings which British prison managers have been forced to deal with have been terrorist prisoners, most of them Irish Republicans convicted of offences in Britain.

After a number of high profile escapes in the 1960s, a considerable debate emerged concerning the prison service in England and Wales as to whether it was better to concentrate together high risk prisoners in one setting or to disperse such prisoners throughout the system (Home Office 1966, Advisory Council on the Penal System 1968, Home Office 1979, King and Morgan 1980).[4] For example, the May Committee specifically acknowledged the difficulties of concentrating Category A terrorist prisoners in the one establishment in that it would allow such prisoners to organize themselves and 'pose unprecedented security problems' (Home Office 1979: para. 6.72). While the arguments in favour of dispersal prevailed, King and Morgan (1980: 93), who had been in favour of concentration, also conceded that terrorist prisoners created particular problems and suggested that they should be dispersed and accommodated in some variant of special security wings.

The strategies for dealing with such prisoners in England and Wales have therefore included their dispersal to various Category A prisons in Britain, sudden and unannounced movements of prisoners between prisons (also known as 'ghosting'), and tighter security procedures for such prisoners (Coulter 1991, Borland, King, and McDermott 1995). All Republican paramilitary prisoners in British prisons normally appointed their own Officers Commanding and paramilitary command structure as in Northern Ireland. However, the relatively small numbers and the constant potential for the movement of such prisoners largely prevented a similar formalizing of organizational relations between prisoners and staff in Britain. As was noted above, it also

---

[4] Owing to its smaller size, and the relatively small numbers of maximum security prisoners, the Scottish prison service has not historically had to choose between concentration and dispersal (Coyle 1987). Instead it opted for the development of small specialist units to separate these prisoners from the main population and experimented with some highly innovative regimes. Features of these units included more relaxed relations between staff and inmates, a less rigidly structured environment, and greater opportunity for the personal development of such prisoners (Boyle 1984, Cooke 1989, Bottomley, Liebling, and Sparks 1994).

required the prisoners to build relations with the ordinaries who considerably outnumber them in all prisons.[5] While prison staff in some prisons in Britain have indicated fear of terrorist prisoners (King and McDermott 1995: 134), this cannot be compared in scale and intensity to the Northern Ireland context.

None the less a number of lessons can legitimately be drawn from the British prison service's experience of dealing with politically motivated prisoners. With a big enough prison system, dealing with smaller numbers of prisoners who are incarcerated away from their influential political and community base, more control-orientated strategies such as dispersal, ghosting, and restricted regimes have been available to the authorities. However, in the Northern Ireland context, with a small prison system, much larger numbers of paramilitary prisoners to manage, and a highly organized paramilitary, political and community support base, such strategies have only been possible at considerable human and political cost. The key difference perhaps has been the very different set of power relations with which prison managers in Northern Ireland were forced to contend.

Prison Management and Power Relationships with Prisoners

As was suggested throughout the discussions on the prisoners' resistance strategies, the concept of power is of considerable significance in understanding the management of prisoners. As closed institutions, the prison setting may be viewed as a setting in which custodians appear to hold an unparalleled 'almost infinite' power (Sykes 1958: 41). Of course such an illusion of power differs from the reality in all but the most extreme of circumstances (Sparks, Bottoms, and Hay 1996: 309). The systems of power in prisons are, as Sykes suggested, a 'cracked monolith', undermined, diverted, and defective because those who are ruled do not feel the need to obey and because those who are supposed to rule fail to do so (Sykes 1958: 53). In the real world of prisoners outnumbering guards, incompetence amongst staff, increased external judicial and political scrutiny of the prisons, and so forth, the application of power in any prison becomes, at best, an uneven process (Jacobs 1977, Stojkovic 1984).

---

[5] Interview with former IRA life sentenced prisoner who served most of his life sentence in a variety of English prisons before being transferred to Maghaberry, 17 Jan. 1996.

If we accept that the application of total power is inevitably defective in prison management, one method of examining such defects is to look at the different sources of power for prison managers and staff and their impact on the way that power is expressed. French and Raven (1968) have argued that there are at least five bases from which power can be utilized in order to gain the compliance of others and, as Stojkovic (1984) argues, these bases may be reasonably applied to the prison context. The five bases of power are reward power, coercive power, expert power, referent power, and legitimate power.

Reward power is a perceived understanding between those in authority and their subordinates that compliance with direction or rules will result in material benefits. Stojkovic (1984) has argued that there is a strong reliance upon reward power amongst prison staff and managers. Rewards for prisoners such as particular jobs or housing assignments, furloughs, parole, visiting, and so forth may, in some prison settings, become the dominant expression of power relations between prison managers, staff, and the inmates. Such a view has recently come to the fore in Britain with a particular interest having developed in the potential for incentive-based prison regimes (Liebling and Bosworth 1995). However, the actual discretion available to prison managers and staff in the distribution of significant rewards may be becoming increasingly limited (Livingstone and Owen 1999).

Coercive power, through formal punishment for alleged rule violations or informal punishment such as beatings or psychological abuse, is regarded by some as the defining characteristic of 'the violent institution' of imprisonment (Scraton, Sim, and Skidmore 1991, esp. ch. 3). The ability of prison managers legitimately to use force in their relationships with prisoners in certain settings underlines their superior power base. That said, organized and sustained violence against inmates by staff is perhaps more commonly associated with the era in prison management before the courts and other sources of scrutiny took a greater interest in the events behind prison walls (Martin and Ekland-Olson 1987). Coercive power is now more regulated, and arguably more symbolic in the shape of activities such as strip searching, cell searches, handcuffing, and other control and restraint techniques, all of which may be used to underline the power differential between inmates and staff and humiliate the prisoners.

Expert power is a power base in which the perception of special skills, knowledge, or experience of prison managers or staff may be of benefit or use to prisoners. As Cressey (1961, 1965) argued with regard to a treatment-based prison regime, if prisoners see that staff have particular technical competencies in areas such as education, work, rehabilitation, or other areas which impact directly on their daily lives, the status of such staff is likely to be raised in the eyes of the inmates. However, in cases where the tasks of prison staff or managers require little apparent skill or expertise, or where they can do little positively to enhance the quality of prisoners' existence (such as in highly incapacitative supermax prisons—see Tachiki 1995), staff have little potential for access to expert power.

Referrant power is a type of power which is based on an earned respect of staff and managers amongst the prisoners. Prison managers or staff who treat prisoners with dignity and respect, are impartial and fair, and who keep their promises to inmates may be described as having referrant power (Hepburn 1985: 149). Hepburn argues that respect for such a member of prison staff by prisoners may be translated into a greater willingness to comply with regulations, orders, and so forth and therefore contribute to a more stable prison regime. In the British context, this kind of referrant power may perhaps be held by those prison officers described by Sparks, Bottoms, and Hay (1996: 194) 'who would do what they could to help prisoners, not lock them up unnecessarily, display a sense of humour, not promise what they could not deliver, were prepared to be slagged off, did not play "mind games" and did not "wind prisoners up" '.

Finally, as the title suggests, legitimate power suggests that the power which is exercised in a legitimate fashion creates a base by which inmates may be persuaded or directed to adhere to regulations and maintain order within prisons. A few scholars have seen the exercise of legitimate power in prisons as relatively uncomplicated. For example, Freeman argues that all correctional officers possess legitimate power, 'it comes with the position' (Freeman 1999: 202). Others, both critical and conservative, appear to base their analysis on the assumption that prisons are institutions which are somehow outside the loop in terms of any legitimate exercise of power (Scraton, Sim, and Skidmore 1991, DiIulio 1987).

More convincing, however, is the analysis by Sparks, Bottoms, and Hay (1996) which views legitimacy in prisons as a much more fluid dynamic in prison management. Their argument is essentially that any claim to the legitimate exercise of authority in prisons will be affected by material conditions in the prison, the formal and procedural aspects of administration as well as its cultural or relational features, and the way in which authority or power is represented to prisoners by prison administrators and staff.

What is striking about these various bases of power in relation to the management of paramilitary prisoners is that each would appear significantly weakened by the particular demands of the Northern Ireland context.

Reward power was undermined by the limited discretion available to managers and staff dealing with litigious groups of *organized* prisoners wherein sweeteners could not be given to one prisoner but had to be given to the whole group. While applied at various junctures over the past thirty years, as I have argued above, coercive power too was limited by the organized nature of the prisoners, their support base, and their capacity for violence. Expert power has little apparent relevance when the staff have no real opportunity to engage with individual prisoners and where many prisoners consider themselves superior to their gaolers.[6] In the Northern Ireland context, staff were either effectively excluded from the wings or compounds or engaged in nakedly repressive interactions (e.g. during the era of criminalisation), neither of which provided a base for staff skills or abilities as a source of power. Referrant power, winning the acquiesence of prisoners by treating them with decency and respect, was arguably liable to be overridden by the more pressing organizational and ideological concerns of the prisoners such as the duty to escape.[7] Finally the exercise of legitimate power was complicated by the fact that a sizeable proportion of

[6] 'Big screws, wee screws, strong screws, weak screws, Screws of all shapes and sizes: smart clean regimental screws: washed out, bogging, scruffy screws, Security screws, visit screws, sports screws, friendly screws and nasty screws. Screws performing all kinds of functions, every role programmed to suit their abilities. Every role programmed to subvert our attitudes . . . I really don't hate them. I'm not so much against anything or anybody, its just that I am for a lot of things. None of them include screws' (Adams 1990: 27). A similar sense of condescension regarding staff was clear in the interviews conducted for this research, particularly although not exclusively amongst former Republican prisoners. This was not an expression of frustration at individuals from a similar social and economic background separated by a uniform and social circumstances (e.g. Morris and Morris 1963, Kauffman 1988, Fleisher 1989). Rather it was indicative of an attitude amongst many paramilitary prisoners that they were more intellectually capable, better organized, and had a more coherent ideological and political philosophy than the majority of the prison service personnel who imprisoned them.

[7] As was noted above, one telling example of the overestimation of referrant power in relations with paramilitary prisoners appears in the Woodcock Report on the attempted escape by IRA prisoners from Whitemoor Special Secure Unit. Some staff appeared genuinely shocked that prisoners with whom they had developed good relationships and whom they had treated with considerable humanity and decency, were none the less willing to shoot them in order to effect an escape (Woodcock 1994: 72).

prisoners contended that the prison system was representative of a state and a political order that could never be legitimate regardless of the elements of procedural fairness which it introduced.

In sum, therefore, while the application of power in any prison setting is inevitably a honeycombed affair, it was all the more uneven in a context such as Northern Ireland where it was met by organized resistance from groups of prisoners with a considerable power base of their own. That disjunction was perhaps most acutely felt by the prison staff who were forced to deal with its consequences in the prison setting.

Prison Management and Prison Staff

The job of prison or correctional officer is one of the most maligned in the literature of social sciences. They have been variously described as 'sadists' (Davidson 1974), possessing the IQ of an imbecile (Toch 1978), and repressors of the capitalist system (Quinney 1977). Some critical researchers have even tried to introduce complex research instruments designed to demonstrate how certain individuals were drawn to the career of prison officer by the desire to exercise authority over inmates and inflict punishment upon them (Melvin, Gramling, and Gardner 1985). Prison officers are usually either omitted from prison analysis 'the invisible ghosts of penality' or the 'ghastly alter ego' of liberal enlightened senior management (Liebling 2000: 337).

Much of the literature on the occupational culture of prison officers has been based on the development of typologies which characterize the nature of their interaction with prisoners. These typologies normally locate officers somewhere along a spectrum between those most interested in the control and punishment aspects of their job and those more interested in treatment or rehabilitation. For example, Klofas and Toch (1982) argue that there are three types of subcultures amongst correctional staff, the 'subculture custodians', the 'supported majority', and the 'lonely bravehearts', all of whom are more or less defined by their attitudes towards the rehabilitation of prisoners.[8] However, perhaps the best known of these typologies are those developed by

---

[8] The subculture custodians, who are the smallest prison officer group, are opposed to the treatment of inmates and place a high value on security and control. The supported majority, the largest group, express attitudes which are supportive of inmates, treatment programmes, and the increasing professionalization of prison officers. The lonely braves are overwhelmed by the subculture custodians and are unable to speak up in favour of treatment programmes (Klofas and Toch 1982: 247).

Kauffman (1988, ch.10). She contested that prison officers could be broken down into five types, based upon positive, negative, or ambivalent responses to questions posed about prisoners although her attitudinal work is expanded to include the views of fellow officers as well. Kauffman's five officer types are 'pollyannas', 'white hats', 'hard asses', 'burn-outs', and 'functionaries'.

Pollyannas were identified as officers who liked both officers and inmates and who derived considerable satisfaction from helping inmates with institutional adjustment and providing services to them.[9] White hats, while they too liked prisoners and derived satisfaction from their job, had more negative feelings towards fellow officers and hoped to improve the prison through their positive attitude to prisoners. Hard asses, also referred to by Owen (1988) as 'John Wayne/Clint Eastwood Types', intensely disliked inmates, focused instead upon the controlling functions of their jobs and the requirement of loyalty above all else from their colleagues. Theirs was an uncomplicated view of prisons in which officers were pitted against inmates in contest of good against evil (Kauffman 1988: 253). Burn-outs were officers characterized by negative attitudes to both officers and inmates, paranoid relations with inmates, relationship and other difficulties outside the prison because of the job, and who were only remaining in the job for the money. Finally functionaries were described as officers who were ambivalent or indifferent to inmates and other officers, with no desire to rehabilitate or punish, rather who simply carried out the job because they needed employment and viewed it as 'maintaining a human warehouse' (Kauffman 1988: 257). Such prison officers were described as insulating themselves by going through the motions or functions of the job.

Such a custody–therapy conflict has been rightly described as outmoded (Steadman, Morrissey, and Robbins 1985), offering only limited insights into the possible direction or emphasis which prison officers can adopt in their work (Ben-David 1992). For example, the stage of an officer's career may have an important bearing on his or her attitude to prisoners. Kauffmann (1988) viewed her types as almost evolutionary with younger officers progressing from the positive attitudes of the Pollyannas to the more cynical hard asses or functionaries as their career developed. In contrast Klofas and Toch (1982)

[9] In fact Kauffman only found one such officer amongst a sample of thirty at one of the prisons she studied (Kauffman 1988: 250).

argued that younger officers initially had the more negative attitudes towards inmates but mellowed as they matured. Owen (1988) found something of a halfway house largely dependent upon the individual officers, and their ability to adjust to the authority of the job of prison officer.

Sparks, Bottoms, and Hay (1996: 156–7) offer an alternative, more subtle matrix to these typologies or ideal types of prison officers (see Fig. 7.1 below). They argue for a hypothetical matrix of two orthogonal scales to describe the interactional style of prison officers. On the vertical axis prison officers move between two spectrums of close to prisoners and distant from prisoners and on the horizontal between flexible and consistent.[10] While they argue that individual staff members may vary on these scales in different social situations in the prison, they too acknowledge that 'it may be possible that there are systematic variations in the positions which members of different institutions take up, resulting from the consolidation of policies or occupational cultures over time' (Sparks, Bottoms, and Hay 1996: 157). In their analysis, regressive 'canteen cultures' may arise when staff feel in a defensive or unsupported position—alienated from, and afraid of, prisoners on the one hand, distanced from, and mistrustful of, management on the other. They may also arise when the power of certain staff is excessive or when the unopposed exercise of power becomes a matter of casual habit (Hay and Sparks 1992, cited in Sparks Bottoms, and Hay 1996).

While these and other more recent studies (e.g. King and McDermott (1995) offer a more subtle account of the attitudes of prison officers towards prisoners), the overall image of the job remains bleak. In general the impression in much of the literature is, as Philliber (1987: 9) suggests, of prison officers as 'alienated, cynical, burnt out, stressed but unable to admit it, suffering from role conflict of every kind and stressed beyond imagining'.

---

[10] Lombardo (1989) takes a not dissimilar approach, arguing that prison officers can be divided into two typologies 'people workers' and 'bureaucrats' but adding that both concepts are important and officers must at times be flexible enough to move between the two. Lombardo's notion of a people worker is an adaptation of Goffman's similar term (Goffman 1961a: 74–83). An officer in people worker mode develops human feelings towards prisoners, and deals well with the different challenges presented by the varying personalities of prisoners as he or she develops relationships with them. People workers are flexible and personable and they adapt the rules of their institution to develop better working relationships with prisoners and to secure the co-operation of prisoners. Bureaucrats are officers who are most concerned with the job as part of a large bureaucracy wherein relationships and problem solving with prisoners is carried out in a mechanistic fashion and by adhering strictly to formal procedures.

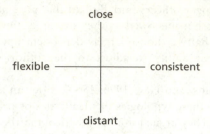

Source: Sparks, Hay, and Bottoms 1996: 157.

FIG. 7.1. Dimensions of interactional style used by prison staff

The notions of low morale and high levels of stress associated with working as a prison officer are indeed a common feature of the literature. For example, Lindquist and Whitehead (1986: 12), in a survey of 241 correctional officers, found that 38 per cent viewed their jobs as very stressful, 29 per cent reported moderate stress, and the remaining 32 per cent were in the slightly or more than slightly stressful category. Similarly Cheek (1984) reported that correctional officers had an average life expectancy of 59 (compared to the US national average of 75), twice the national divorce rate average, and experience high rates of suicide, alcoholism, heart attacks, ulcers, and high blood pressure. The sources of stress in the job include the fear or perceived danger from prisoners (Cullen *et al.* 1985, Ben-David, Silfen, and Cohen 1996), the poor physical conditions in which officers are sometimes forced to work (Cavadino and Dignan 1997), and the perceived low social status of the job (Freeman 1999). As Scraton, Sim, and Skidmore (1991: 56) conclude, 'the nature of the job, the anti-social hours, and the social isolation experienced by prison officers outside their workplaces reinforce the strengthened camaraderie of the occupational culture and encourage a reliance upon the regime and its routines'.

It is important to note, however, that prison managers too must share some responsibility for high levels of stress and low morale amongst prison staff. The perceived failure of managers to support their staff (Brodsky 1982, Lombardo 1989), the undermining of the professional status of officers by managers and other professionals (Carter 1995), and a view that managers are more concerned with adverse publicity or litigation rather than the concerns of staff (Stojkovic 1995) have all been cited as sources of staff tension and poor self-esteem. Staff's view of themselves is often shaped by pointing to the failings of management. As Sparks Bottoms, and Hay suggest, staff views on the virtues of 'a good officer' such as 'common sense', 'maturity', and fairness are often explicitly defined in stark contrast to managers, 'the jargon of intellectuals and the scheming of mandarins' (1996: 143). The them and us view of prison managers is both a source of stress and a defining characteristic of the profession for many prison staff.

The final relevant characteristic of literature on prison staff is a concern with the nature and purpose of punishment and the impact of such notions on the way in which the job becomes defined. A key assumption in both the literature on prison officer typologies and the more fluid schema charting staff relations with prisoners is that the function and self-image of prison officers is intimately concerned with the perceived purpose of imprisonment in a given era. 'Being a prison officer' is a very different process in a prison that is informed by retributive, rehabilitative, or incapacitative thinking on punishment. Whether prison officers are tasked with overseeing the infliction of physical punishment or supervision of hard labour, sidelined by professionals in the treatment of deviants, or trained in advanced control and restraint techniques assisted by new technologies, *who they are* and *what they do* is inevitably shaped by broader political and ideological views of the purpose of imprisonment.

Prison Officers in Northern Ireland

At a structural level, the staff of the Northern Ireland prison service might appear little different from their colleagues in England and Wales. As can be seen in Fig. 7.2, while there are no local area management boards, the hierarchical management structure from headquarters, to governors, principal officers, senior officers, and main grade prison officers is quite similar. Governor grade staff are members of the British Prison Governors Association and the main grade staff are members of the Prison Officers Association, an affiliate to the British Prison Officers Associations.

However, while the structure is similar to that in Britain, the nature of the task required of those prison staff involved in the incarceration of paramilitary prisoners in Northern Ireland was considerably different. The number of prison officers increased dramatically in the wake of the outbreak of violence and the upsurge in the prison population

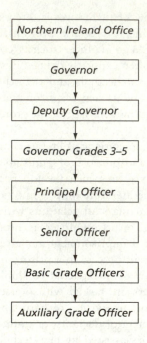

FIG. 7.2. Structure of Northern Ireland prison service

in the early 1970s. In 1969 there were 292 staff in the prison service, by 1976 this had risen to 2,184 (NIPS 1977: 8) and throughout the 1980s and early 1990s numbers stabilized at over 3,000 (NI Affairs Committee 1998: p.vi). The huge increase in staff was achieved by a massive recruitment campaign and trawling of the British prison system for those interested in secondments to Northern Ireland.[11]

---

[11] One NIACRO senior manager interviewed for this book recalls an advertising campaign in the 1970s which consisted of a uniformed prison officer waving a bunch of £10 notes as he stood in front of a set of prison gates. Interview with NIACRO senior manager, 15 Apr. 1996. A similar account is produced in a Republican document produced by prisoners in the Maze in 1977: 'We were sitting watching TV the other night when that advert came on about joining the Prison Service. Yes that's right, the one where your woman says "Oh Joe" at the end of it, as if he had just won a million pounds on the pools. This never fails to get a good laugh from the lads. I must say though it does sound very tempting when you hear the job and its benefits or read about it in the paper. Steady career promotion opportunities, generous rent allowance, travel expenses, good pay, over-time, pension scheme, and last, but surely not least, a free uniform with a wee badge on a cap' (Republican Press Centre 1977: 24–5).

Attitudes to Paramilitary Prisoners

No one in the current prison service disputes that some staff recruited in the early 1970s were of a fairly low calibre. Many recruits were drawn from the ranks of former British army personnel and consequently the self-image of staff was often explicitly militaristic. In the early 1970s prison officers at Long Kesh and Magilligan wore macabre motifs such as a portcullis and a twist of barbed wire on their uniforms (Loftus 1980: 79) as well as keeping their peaked caps at an angle in order to shade their eyes.[12] Since the late 1970s, particularly in light of the IRA's campaign of assassinations of prison staff, prison officers and their officers have understandably sought to present themselves as a civilian service, implementing rather than devising policy, and explicitly distinct from other elements of the security forces such as the RUC and British army.

As with the RUC and the locally recruited regiment of the British army the Royal Irish Regiment[13] (Ryder 1991, McGarry and O'Leary 1999), the staff of the Northern Ireland prison service is largely male and drawn predominantly from the Protestant/Unionist community. In 1998 the prison service reported 9 per cent of its staff were female, that 78 per cent of its staff were Protestant, 7 per cent Catholic, and 15.5 per cent were undetermined (Northern Ireland Affairs Committee 1998: 14i).[14] As with many areas of Northern Ireland life, sectarianism has been identified as a problem in the prison service. There was an Orange Order lodge organized by staff and made up of prison officers.[15] Prison officers have been reprimanded for decorating an officers' hut with Loyalist iconography including a picture of King Billy and a poster of Michael Stone which read 'Michael Stone is our hero'.[16] As was discussed previously, it is clear that sectarian attitudes

[12] This latter practice was forbidden in the Code of Conduct drawn up for prison staff in 1990 (NIPS 1990).

[13] This regiment was an amalgam of the Ulster Defence Regiment and Royal Irish Rangers.

[14] Under Fair Employment Legislation in Northern Ireland employers are required to monitor the religion of their employees. Those born outside Northern Ireland are regarded as 'other' under the terms of the legislation. The phrase 'undetermined' therefore most probably refers to staff who were born in England, Scotland, or Wales and recruited to the Northern Ireland prison service.

[15] Interview with prison governor, 20 Apr. 1999.

[16] Interview with voluntary sector senior manager, 15 Apr. 1996. Michael Stone is a Loyalist paramilitary who attacked an IRA funeral in Milltown cemetery in 1988 killing three mourners and injuring several others (Dillon 1992). He later became one of the leaders of the UDA prisoners in the Maze prison.

underpinned some of the most abusive practices by staff during the dirty protest and hunger strikes. Prison officers live and socialize in mostly Protestant/Unionist communities. Indeed, like a substantial section of the Unionist community, many prison staff view the Good Friday Agreement with 'considerable ambivalence' and the prospects of their own unemployment as 'scant reward for 20 or 30 years of loyal and faithful service to the crown'.[17]

While sectarianism and pro-British/Unionist views may be a feature of the outlook of some prison staff, it would be erroneous to assume that such attitudes determined relations with Republican and Loyalist prisoners. While there were exceptions, prison staff were not necessarily more sympathetic to Loyalist prisoners simply because they came from the same community background. Studies elsewhere have shown that such social or ethnic origins is an unpredictable variable in staff–prisoner relations.[18]

One clear reason for a lack of empathy for Loyalist prisoners was undoubtedly because the familiarity of the Loyalist paramilitaries with the areas and communities in which the prison staff lived left them more open to threats, violence, and intimidation from that quarter.[19] One instructive example of such a dynamic was recounted to the author by a former UVF prisoner who discussed how Loyalist prisoners would make sure they had their associates present when the prison service Orange lodge marched on 12 July 'to remind them not to be giving the lads in the Kesh a hard time'.[20] While Republicans have been responsible for the vast majority of killings of prison staff during the conflict, these are murders which have generally required a degree of logistical organization and planning. Republican paramilitaries have generally had to travel from their own areas, carry out attacks, and then return to their

[17] Evidence of Northern Ireland prison service chief executive Alan Shannon to the Northern Ireland Affairs Committee, 29 Apr. 1998, at 20.

[18] For example, increased numbers of black and Hispanic correctional officers recruited from the 1970s onwards in US prisons (Kinsell and Shelden 1981) did not result in automatic improvement of relations with prisoners. While some commentators did note some improvements (Jurik 1985), others found either no difference (Crouch and Alpert 1982), or indeed that black and Hispanic officers were more punitive in their attitudes towards prisoners in order to demonstrate their toughness and dependability to white fellow officers (Jacobs and Kraft 1978).

[19] 'With regard to the Loyalists, obviously the majority of our men live in Loyalist areas. It is so easy for them to get to us. I have had the hooded men in my house. I knew right away they weren't Provos because I wasn't dead when I saw them. It was bloody terrifying though . . .' Interview with prison governor, 13 Sept. 1997.

[20] Interview with former UVF prisoner, 22 Sept. 1994.

own communities. Loyalist paramilitaries often live in or near the same communities as prison staff. Thus the staff were arguably more vulnerable to routine harassment in their homes, their pubs, the schools which their children attend, and so forth by the Loyalist paramilitaries.

More interestingly perhaps, it is not just vulnerability to intimidation and attack that framed the attitudes of prison staff to Republican and Loyalist prisoners. In the interviews I carried out for this book amongst prison officers and prison managers, clear distinctions emerged regarding their perceptions of the respective sets of paramilitaries. Republican prisoners were variously described as 'ruthless', 'well organised', 'smart', 'dedicated', 'ingenious', 'disciplined' 'committed' 'able to deliver what they promise' and so forth. Loyalists on the other had tended to be described as 'rabble', 'poorly organized', 'not very bright', 'hot headed', 'unpredictable', 'having too many chiefs and not enough Indians', 'like ordinary criminals but more dangerous', and generally regarded as being of a lower calibre than their Republican counterparts.

This in no way suggests a straightforward admiration for Republican activists and a distaste for Loyalists. Both had killed and injured their colleagues in the community and had demonstrated a willingness to use violence and intimidation inside the prisons. Rather it is suggestive of a fairly cold-eyed and pragmatic assessment of the different protagonists with whom they were required to work.[21] In order to function in an environment of substantially altered power relations with paramilitary prisoners, staff had to develop effective ways of predicting the behaviour of the prisoners. Such an analysis required, at least in the material relations with such prisoners, making professional, rational, and reasoned judgements about prisoners which increasingly overrode considerations such as views upon their political philosophy or chosen means of achieving it.

The Morale Morass: Perfidious Management and Professionalism

The key thing I have learned about trying to assess staff morale in the Northern Ireland prison service is never to ask a question which has the word morale in it if you wish to find out how people are actually feeling.[22]

---

[21] It is fair to say that a similarly phlegmatic view regarding the respective paramilitary factions pervades a number of the key official reports on Northern Ireland prisons (e.g. Hennessey 1984, Colville 1992, Ramsbotham 1998).

[22] Conversation with senior Northern Ireland Office official, Northern Ireland Board of Visitors Conference, June 1999.

Staff morale amongst Northern Ireland prison staff has been identified as problematic almost since the inception of the troubles. Resentment against the advertisement campaigns which had attracted them to the posts were expressed in parodying cartoons on lockers and high drop-out rates in the early 1970s.[23] In 1975 one in five recruits left after a number of months, in 1976 one in three (Loftus 1980). Morale was undermined further in the late 1970s and early 1980s as prison officers were forced to work in the deplorable conditions of the protesting wings at the Maze and the IRA campaign of violence against prison staff was intensified.

Understandable concerns regarding personal security have been linked in other contexts with other morale sapping fears and insecurities. For example, the continued encroachment of outsiders, imposing legal and bureaucratic standards and thus limiting officer power and discretion, has been identified as a source of insecurity for prison officers (Hepburn 1985, Poole and Pogrebin 1987). Similarly, professional insecurity, or lack of peer managerial, or administrative support or even understanding of the difficulties of the job, have been suggested as further sources of fear and concern (Willet 1983, Ben-David, Silfen, and Cohen 1996). In addition staff misgivings regarding the leadership qualities of senior correctional managers have been described as sources of anxiety for prison staff down the line (Cohn 1998), which only serve to exacerbate the real worries about personal safety.

As the Northern Ireland Prison Officers Association Chairman told the Northern Ireland Affairs Committee:

the quality of morale depends upon the quality of leadership, unfortunately in the Northern Ireland Prison Service, quite a number of years ago, the message was sent out to paramilitaries 'Shoot a prison officer and you'll get what you want.' That is what happened. Every time they shot a prison officer they got what they wanted. . . . So our officers in the Maze see all this happening. They see all the appeasement which goes on. What better way to push the morale of prison officers. Prison officers say what is the point in me troubling? What is the point in me doing my job because people above will not support me doing the job.[24]

Such a view of management as the primary source of stress and poor morale amongst staff is typical of the non-management ranks of the

---

[23] *Irish Times* (7 Dec. 1977), 'Hard Times for Her Majesty's Prison Service'.
[24] Evidence of NI POA Chairman Finlay Spratt to the Northern Ireland Affairs Committee, 13 May 1998, at 32.

prison service. Such a cynical view of management, and the power of the prison officers' trade union—the Prison Officers Association—resulted in a long history of poor industrial relations (discussed further in Chapter 10). Prison officers rightly point out that the civil servants who make up the senior management of the service have often never been inside a prison before taking up such a position. As one prison officer described it, 'getting moved across from the Department of Agriculture or Health and Social Services, and then running a prison system when the closest you have been to one is watching old episodes of Prisoner Cell Block H'.[25] Prison managers were often accused of making promises to prisoners which they could not or would not keep, which inevitably resulted in the front line staff bearing the brunt of the prisoners' disgruntlement.[26]

Linked to the perceived failings of management in eroding staff morale in the Northern Ireland prison service, has been a perception of the job as lacking in appropriate professional status. For example, prison officers have traditionally received little specific training on the handling of paramilitary prisoners other than cursory discussions on the dangers of conditioning.[27] Indeed training in the Northern Ireland prison service has, until very recently, been somewhat rudimentary.[28] While the standard has improved, officers remain highly critical.[29]

In addition, staff argue that they have been deskilled by the nature of the interaction with paramilitary prisoners. The refusal of paramilitary prisoners to conform to a normal prison regime means that those

[25] Interview with prison officer, 12 Sept. 1996.

[26] 'We had one official here who was from England—thought he knew everything about how to deal with paramilitary offenders—would go down the wings and promise the earth, things which were not deliverable. Then of course when it doesn't happen it is the officer on the wing who is the bastard who won't let this happen. Oh but "... [name deleted] was down here last week and he said it would happen and now it must be you who is blocking it" ... he is the shining knight and you are the worst in the world. It is very stressful.' Interview with prison officer, 13 Aug. 1997.

[27] Interview with prison governor, 13 Sept. 1997.

[28] As the 1971–6 Annual Report acknowledges, 'In the early days of the rapid expansion there was little opportunity for formal training but in May 1973 a 2 week training course was introduced for recruits' (NIPS 1977: 8). By 1977 this had increased to a two week familiarization course at Crumlin Road prison followed by a four week course at the prison officer training college at Milisle.

[29] 'In the old days the quality of training was awful—you came in and did two weeks training and then you were working in a prison. Even today the quality of training is abysmal. You get about thirteen weeks of the basics, control and restraint, prison rules, standing orders and all that ... it is a well known fact that when you go to your establishment, the first thing you learn is to forget what you learned down at Milisle.' Interview with POA spokesperson, 17 Sept. 1996.

officers with a genuine interest in the rehabilitation of prisoners are inevitably frustrated. In addition, the security concern regarding the vulnerability of prison officers to threats and intimidation means that apparent levels of trust in the Northern Ireland prison service are lower than elsewhere. For example, no prison officer working with paramilitaries has a pass key which gives him or her access to all of the prison. As Carter (1995) has argued, the possession of keys is of particular symbolic importance in prisons and thus such an omission is symptomatic to some officers of their demeaned status.[30]

The result of these various factors has been a prison service plagued with a chronic staff morale problem. High levels of staff absenteeism have become endemic from the mid-1990s onwards and increased dramatically after the ending of overtime meant that in effect staff were paid the same when they were off sick as when they were on duty.[31] It is difficult to conclude other than that when, faced with little monetary incentive to go to work rather than stay at home, many staff have increasingly opted for the latter option.

Prison Staff and the Broader Political and Ideological Setting

The final dynamic of note with regard to prison staff in Northern Ireland has been the influence of the broader political and ideological framework within which staff have been required to operate. As a former prison service chief executive acknowledged above, many staff may have had serious misgivings about the dramatic events which saw the release of paramilitary prisoners under the Good Friday Agreement. However, such a direct impact from the political arena has not been a unique experience for prison staff in determining the nature and self-image of their profession. As with the prisoners and prison managers, the key variable for staff has been the nature and extent of the political recognition of the paramilitary inmates.

The model of prison management described below as reactive containment saw prison officers acting as *de facto* prisoner of war camp

---

[30] Interview with former prison officer, 12 Sept. 1996. However, other prison officers have argued that the presence of keys could make a prison officer more likely to be the target of an escape-related attack in the Northern Ireland context.

[31] In 1994/5 52,420 operational days were lost due to staff sickness, an increase of approximately 700 on the previous year. However, in the following year, after overtime was completely abolished, this increased to 70,497 (Northern Ireland Affairs Committee 1998: 7). I am grateful to Tony Bottoms for bringing this to my attention and pointing out its significance in comments on an earlier draft.

guards. As is detailed below, with little real training, many former security force members were recruited as gaolers and asked to do little other than contain prisoners whose political motivation was recognized. Under the criminalisation model, prison officers were placed at the apex of a state strategy designed to defeat terrorism in the prisons. Their status was arguably raised by the high political stakes and the clear price paid by officers being murdered as a result of the strategy. Finally, during what is discussed below as managerialism, staff were required to operate in a context wherein political motivation became increasingly recognized but where it could not be publicly acknowledged until comparatively recently. It is clear that many prison officers saw what they regarded as an essentially weak and duplicitous Northern Ireland Office engaged in a process of continuously making concessions to paramilitary prisoners without publicly acknowledging it.[32] For some such officers, the increased *de facto* recognition of the paramilitaries and the gradual ceding of control of the prisoners became a source of considerable disquiet and corroded staff morale.

[32] Interview with former prison officer, 12 Sept. 1996.

8

Reactive Containment, 1969–1975

Introduction

The reactive containment model described here as a strategy for the management of paramilitary prisoners and the broader conflict was a relatively crude military-led response to political violence. The outbreak of violence in Northern Ireland was perceived in political and security circles in Britain as a quasi-colonial insurrection similar to that which had been faced in Kenya, Malaysia, Cyprus, Aden, and Oman (Dewar 1985, Kitson 1991). The essential similarity was that the British government had to react because the locally based Unionist authorities had lost control (Faulkner 1978). The government were willing to send in the troops as a temporary measure to regain control and support the security forces and prison staff (Callaghan 1973). The view was essentially that with a fairly tough security policy directed primarily from London, levels of violence and violent perpetrators should be contained while a political solution was sought.

In the 1960s, influenced at least in part by similar agitations in the USA and other places in Europe, Catholic frustration and disenchantment at the way the Northern Irish state had functioned (Cameron 1969, Devlin 1969) began to express itself in a form other than the traditional Republican response of armed insurrection.[1] The repeal of the special powers legislation, an end to discrimination in housing and jobs, and the cessation of gerrymandering formed the central demands

---

[1] That disenchantment was partially vindicated by the Cameron Commission which was established by the Northern Ireland government in 1969 to look into the origins of the disturbances. It produced some explicit criticisms of the way the Northern Ireland state had operated between 1921 and 1969. This Commission, which consisted of a Northern Ireland Protestant, a Northern Ireland Catholic, and a Scottish judge as chairman concluded that there was widespread resentment amongst Catholics at inequities in housing allocation, discrimination in local government employment, gerrymandering of local government boundaries, and a partisan law enforcement system (para. 229).

of the Northern Ireland Civil Rights Association who were chiefly responsible for the mobilization of Catholic grievances (Purdey 1990).

The campaign largely took the form of civil rights marches. The campaigners included a broad cross-section of reform-minded activists including trade unionists, Communists, and other left-wing groups, Nationalists, Republicans, and student activists. Predictably the demonstrations provoked a hostile reaction from elements of the police (the Royal Ulster Constabulary and B Special Reservists) and sections of the Protestant population.[2] Some in the Unionist government saw the civil rights campaign as little more than an IRA front which needed to be faced down by stern security measures. Those Unionists more minded to offer progressive reforms on issues such as housing and discrimination were constantly being harassed by supporters of Ian Paisley as traitors and sell outs (O'Neill 1972).[3] As Moloney and Pollak suggest:

> To Unionists the State itself was under threat from civil rights demands; to Nationalists, the attempt to achieve equality of citizenship by peaceful non-sectarian means was being resisted by the whole Unionist apparatus dancing to the Paisley tune. (Moloney and Pollak 1986: 157)

The Unionist government response to these competing demands was to clamp down severely on the marches and using the police and B Specials to break them up by force. These measures, along with their failure to protect Catholic communities from sectarian attack, ensured that the usually precarious relationship between the Catholic population and the government, and in particular the RUC, was to deteriorate still further (Ryder 1989). As the violence and rioting escalated in both volume and frequency, the RUC, having lost the confidence of the Catholic community, found itself unable to cope and ultimately the British army was called in to play a peace-keeping role. Within months,

---

[2] As one key left-wing civil rights activist has subsequently acknowledged, such a reaction had been envisaged. 'By this time [1969] our conscious if unspoken strategy was to provoke the police into over-reaction and thus spark off mass reaction against the authorities. We assumed that we would be in control of that reaction and that we were strong enough to channel it' (McCann 1974: 35).

[3] As noted in Chapter 1, Ian Paisley is leader of the Democratic Unionist Party and Free Presbyterian Church in Northern Ireland. Since he came to prominence in the 1960s he has been an arch critic of Nationalism, Republicanism, Catholicism, and those strains of Unionism which have sought an accommodation with Nationalists in the North of Ireland. (For a range of views on, and insights into, the Reverend Paisley's contribution to Northern Irish political and religious life see Moloney and Pollak 1986, Paisley 1986, Smyth 1987, Paisley 1988, Bruce 1994.)

that role had changed as the attitudes of Republicans and the colonial training of the British army combined to ensure that the army's role became seen as an exercise in counter-insurgency (Hamill 1985, Arthur 1987).

It is unnecessary for current purposes to go into extensive detail on the violent events which unfolded from 1969 onwards as the different factions of the IRA, Loyalist paramilitaries, and security forces became embroiled in the most vicious period of the conflict. Over half of all the 3,600 deaths in the conflict occurred between 1971 and 1976 (Fay, Morrissey, and Smith 1999: 137). The security measures introduced were harsh and included the use of internment, severe interrogation techniques,[4] and the imposition of a temporary military curfew on the predominantly Catholic Falls Road in Belfast.

Within the prisons during this period there were three classes of prisoners in the Northern Ireland system. The first class were the ordinary criminals convicted of ordinary decent crimes. The second were the internees who were held subject to administrative detention in segregated accommodation. The third were those convicted of offences related to the troubles, after 1972 referred to as Special Category prisoners. What is important to stress during this period was that the political character of the violence was explicitly accepted by the authorities. Guarded and in some cases administered by British soldiers, interned without trial and granted *de facto* prisoner of war status, the prisoners were the most obvious expression of the political understanding of the conflict.

The Deployment of British Troops and the Ownership of Security Policy

The British army's leading expert on counter-insurgency, who arrived in Northern Ireland in September 1970, described the strategy governing troop deployment thus:

The British Army was struggling to adapt ideas gained in the colonies to the circumstances prevailing in part of the United Kingdom i.e., Northern Ireland, and it was doing so in partnership with a number of London based politicians

---

[4] As noted above, these techniques included hooding prisoners, beatings, constant humming noises, standing with arms outstretched, and other sensory deprivation techniques. They were found to be in breach of Article 3 of the European Convention of Human Rights by the European Court of Human Rights, constituting 'inhuman and degrading treatment'. See *Ireland v UK* (S310/71) Judgment (18 Jan. 1978) 23.I.

and civil servants who had thought very little about the problems of insurgency, and a number of Northern Ireland politicians and civil servants whose whole political system had been devised with this very problem in mind, but in a context that had become out of date from a political point of view. Progress was only made after an extended period of trial and error. (Kitson 1991: p.x)

The British army was deployed by the Westminster government in Belfast and Derry in August 1969 initially to safeguard besieged Catholic enclaves. The army were welcomed at first by the Catholic communities who saw them as offering protection from Protestant mobs which the RUC and B Specials either could or would not (O'Dochartaigh 1997). Some leading political figures in Britain rightly predicted that the British army's honeymoon period with the Catholic community would be short lived.[5] Elements within the IRA, which had been remobilized reluctantly to act as defenders of such communities, saw the symbolism of British troops on Irish soil as a means to regalvanize their ranks, until then depleted and disorganized because of the failure of the Border campaign of a decade before (Ryan 1994). Within weeks of their deployment, both the Provisional and the Official IRA took up the orthodox Republican mantle of attacking Crown forces.

For their part, the British army also played a significant role in underlining their unsuitability for the policing functions which they were given in the early 1970s. During the Falls curfew in 1970, British soldiers shot dead four civilians and injured sixty as 3,000 troops, supported by armoured vehicles and helicopters, fought skirmishes as they wrecked houses searching through exclusively Catholic areas of Belfast (Bishop and Mallie 1987: 119). Similarly the events of Bloody Sunday on 30 January 1972, when members of the Parachute Regiment shot thirteen unarmed demonstrators dead in Derry, ensured that the relationship between the Catholic community and the soldiers was one of open hostility (McCann *et al.* 1992, Mullan and Scally 1997). As former soldiers have acknowledged, their colonial experience and reluctance to fight a war on two sides ensured that they inevitably came to see the IRA and by extension the Catholic community as the enemy and the Loyalists and Protestant community as being 'vaguely on our side' (Coogan 1995).

The British army were given a prominent role in the administration of the prison system during this period. The army's role was firstly to

[5] 'Once the Catholics and Protestants get used to our presence, they will hate us more than they hate each other' (Crossman 1977: 620).

convert and construct old army camps to house the large influx of prisoners and then to provide back-up security and searching functions to the civilian authorities in running the prison. Their functions served to underline the military nature of the detention during the era of reactive containment. As one former governor at Long Kesh told the author:

The army had a very significant role in the very early stages, they built the damn thing [Long Kesh]. Once it was built the army role was perimeter security, stopping the outside world getting in or stopping the inside world getting out. Their secondary role was to come if you had a riot or an escape. . . . Their third role was in terms of doing searches. Because the one thing about the army is they are well organised, they know how to assemble, they know how to marshall, they are good at that. The prison service would search the bodies, they would search the buildings, the huts and the Army engineer would track down the tunnels because they had the expertise. It was a sensible division of labour.[6]

Sending in the troops also led to considerable confusion regarding the ownership of security policy in Northern Ireland at a political level. In deploying the army, the British government had insisted that control over their activities would not be ceded to the local government at Stormont. The political control of security policy by Stormont had been previously recognized as politically sensitive.[7] In effect increased use of the army left an uncomfortable halfway house where the army GOC retained operational control over his troops but took advice from the Unionist government who retained effective control over the RUC and B Specials (Bowyer Bell 1993: 116).[8]

In March 1971 Chichester-Clarke expressed his frustration at Britain's

---

[6] Interview with former prison governor, Long Kesh, 20 Apr. 1999.

[7] As the then Home Secretary Jim Callaghan subsequently indicated: 'It was always in my mind that, by British standards, the Northern Ireland cabinet and parliament was little more than an enlarged county council . . . with an unhealthy political control over the police' (Callaghan 1973: 77).

[8] 'The British government provided the troops who were employed in an increasingly prominent role as the terrorist situation worsened. The Northern Ireland government had devolved responsibility for law and order, but they had no constitutional authority to direct the policy to be followed by the British army, which was playing, at times, the dominant part in dealing with violence. Inevitably, as the security situation deteriorated, the actions of the security forces became even more entangled in the basic controversy of the Northern Ireland situation. . . . As a result, the British government found itself increasingly condemned for troop actions when the basic responsibility had been delegated to the Northern Ireland government. Really neither the British government nor the Westminster Parliament could be expected to tolerate such a state of affairs for long' (Whitelaw 1989: 80–1).

failure to agree to implementing sufficiently harsh security measures (especially internment) and resigned because he could see no other way 'of bringing home to all concerned the realities of the present constitutional, political and security situation' (Kelly 1972: 13). In April 1972 his successor Brian Faulkner and the rest of the Northern Ireland cabinet also resigned in protest at the Heath government's insistence that all security powers be brought under the control of London, effectively spelling the end of the Stormont era and the imposition of Direct Rule. Heath's view was that:

The transfer of security powers is an indispensable condition for progress in finding a practical solution in Northern Ireland. The Northern Ireland government's decision [to refuse the transfer] leaves us with no alternative to assuming full and direct responsibility for the administration of Northern Ireland. (Heath 1998: 78)

These tensions over the control of security policy went to the very heart of the character of the conflict. Both Labour and Conservative administrations had come to see the Unionist control over security as part of the problem in Northern Ireland rather than part of the solution (Rees 1985, Whitelaw 1989). While the British government may have disagreed with the Unionists about the tactical use of harsh security measures, they were willing to countenance such methods if they were convinced of the potential effectiveness of such methods to combat terrorism. The key difference for the British government was that they saw security policy as a means of containing political violence while a political solution was sought. To such a mindset the political character of the conflict was either axiomatic or irrelevant. For many in the Unionist government, on the other hand, security policy served as an insulator from accepting the political origins of the violence, security policy *was* the political solution.

Internment: Incapacitation of the Enemy

As in other jurisdictions wherein the authorities perceive themselves to be under threat by an enemy from within,[9] the tactic most favoured by those elements of Unionism and the British government who preferred a security solution to the violence in Northern Ireland was the

[9] See Nagata (1990), Saunders and Taylor (1988), Hiltermann (1990) regarding the use of internment in the USA and Australia during the Second World War and more recently in the Israeli–Palestinian conflict.

internment without trial of suspected terrorists. This power had been on the statutes in both the North and South since the partition of the island in 1921 (Campbell 1994). It had been introduced on three prior occasions in the North, 1931–4, 1938–45, and 1956–61 (McGuffin 1973). In each of those instances the Minister for Home Affairs in the Stormont government, in consultation with colleagues in the Northern Ireland cabinet, had exercised his powers to introduce internment under the existent Emergency legislation.[10] However, following the deployment of British troops in 1969, it became practically impossible for the Northern Ireland government to reintroduce internment without the support of the British army, and to do this they had to obtain the consent of the British government.[11]

On 9 August 1971, despite British army reluctance (Wilson 1989: 168) and the misgivings of the British government that it might not work, the Northern Ireland Prime Minister Brian Faulkner was given the go-ahead by London to reintroduce internment.[12] While the move was recognized as a political gamble, it was considered worth the risk if sufficient numbers of active paramilitaries could be taken out of action (Heath 1998).[13] The chief danger, ultimately realized, as perceived by both the army and the politicians, was that if the operation was badly conceived it would provoke yet more hostility amongst the

---

[10] The Civil Authorities (Special Powers) Acts (Northern Ireland) 1922–43, Regulation 12, gave the Minister for Home Affairs power to issue an Internment Order against a person 'who is suspected of acting or having acted or being about to act in a manner prejudicial to the preservation of the peace and the maintenance of order in Northern Ireland'.

[11] '[A] decision for internment is a decision taken by the Northern Ireland government after consultation with the government of the United Kingdom.' Mr Balniel, Minister of State for Defence, *Hansard*, HC (Series V) vol 823, col 212 (23 Sept. 1971).

[12] Spujt (1986: 714) argues that the Unionists were able to exercise a greater influence over security policy after the Conservative government replaced Labour in June 1970 as the Conservative Home Secretary Reginald Maudling was largely indifferent to Northern Irish affairs, unlike his predecessor Jim Callaghan. In the week previous to the introduction of internment Maudling had been at pains to stress to the House of Commons and the public that rumours that he had been blocking Faulkner's daily pressing for internment were false and that 'he would not shrink from introducing it if necessary' (Kelly 1972: 64).

[13] As Bowyer Bell has argued, for the Unionist leadership, internment had a number of directly positive implications. 'Faulkner wanted Internment. Internment had worked during the 1939–45 war and later during the IRA 1956–62 campaign. Whether it worked as a security measure in 1971, was one of the few remaining unplayed cards that would hush militant Unionist criticism, calm the majority with a symbolic triumph and so give him and the system time' (Bowyer Bell 1993: 208).

Catholics, increase support for the IRA, and actually miss many of the people at whom it was aimed.

Operation Demetrius, the army code-name for internment, went into operation on 9 August at 4.00 a.m. (Farrell 1976: 281). Of the 342 men arrested around the North, 116 were released within 48 hours. Amongst those who were taken from their beds were many retired Republicans, trade unionists, middle-class civil rights campaigners, a drunk man picked up at a bus stop, and several people held on mistaken identity.[14] Several of the people on the army's list turned out to be dead (Bishop and Mallie 1987: 186). The brutality of the arrest procedures had a deeply alienating effect not only on the individuals arrested but on the Catholic communities against which they were directed (Fields 1973). Between 9 August 1971 and 14 February 1972, 2,447 were detained with 934 later being released (Spujt 1986). It is now largely accepted by those who administered the internment system that many of those who were interned were either completely innocent or on the margins of political violence. As William Whitelaw, then Secretary of State for Northern Ireland put it:

> Now if you say that I put some in who shouldn't have been in, yes I would think that is certainly right . . . I have the greatest doubts looking back whether internment was ever right. I question whether internment is right unless you have really good intelligence and I think that was the mistake that was made initially. It was that internment was used as a weapon before intelligence was good enough to use it effectively. (quoted in Spujt 1986: 729)

Internees were held at Crumlin Road prison Belfast, in camps at Long Kesh and Magilligan, and for a time aboard the *Maidstone* prison ship moored in Belfast Lough, simply because the space was not available within the existing prison system (McGuffin 1973). Once arrested, individuals were interrogated using a variety of techniques derived from British army operations in other colonial contexts. As one former Republican internee told the author:

> I was arrested and taken to Girdwood Barracks and beaten by British soldiers and the RUC. I was forced to run a sort of obstacle course while I was beaten with batons and bit by army dogs. Then they took me into a room, placed a heavy bag over my head which went down as far as my chest so I could hardly breathe. I was then handcuffed, beaten and dragged into a helicopter where they

[14] As the Diplock Report subsequently acknowledged in somewhat tactful terms, 'the scale of the operation led to the arrest and detention of a number of persons against whom suspicion was founded on inadequate information' (Diplock 1972, para. 32).

Interrogation

beat me some more and then took off and kept dangling me out of the copter
... I didn't realise that they were hovering only a few feet from the ground, it
was a truly horrendous experience.[15]

Internment was activated almost exclusively against suspected Republicans and thus de facto against the Catholic community. In September
1971 the British Home Secretary stated quite candidly that the aim of
the internment policy was:

to hold in safety, where they can do no further harm, active members of the
IRA and, secondly, to obtain more information about their activities, their conspiracy and their organisation to help the security forces in their job of protecting the public as a whole.[16]

Throughout internment the authorities largely ignored Maudling's
'mild advice to add a few Protestants to the list' (Bowyer Bell 1993:
216). Despite the military's acknowledgement that 'certainly not every
Protestant hand was free from terrorism' (Hamill 1985: 62), detention
of Loyalists barely reached 70, and this was at the height of the Ulster
Workers Council Strike in May 1974 otherwise it stabilized around
50.[17] The number of detained Republican suspects reached nearly 640
in December 1973 and remained above 550 until the government began
its policy of phased release in July 1974 (Spujt 1986: 735). In total 2,060
suspected Republicans and 109 suspected Loyalists were interned
between 1971 and 1975 (Hogan and Walker 1989: 94). Such a clearly
partisan approach to political violence created outrage in the
Catholic/Nationalist community, much of it led by a number of prominent Catholic clerics and directed against the British government for
their capitulation to Unionist pressure (Faul and Murray 1973, Faul

---

[15] Interview with former Republican internee, 12 May 1998. Other internees were subjected to the so-called 'five techniques' of sensory deprivation discussed previously
including wall standing, hooding, continuous noise, deprivation of food, and deprivation of sleep (Hadden, Boyle, and Campbell 1990: 6).

[16] Hansard, HC (Series V) vol 823, col 8 (22 Sept. 1971). In the debate the following
day Prime Minister Edward Heath reiterated the exclusive focus on Republicans when
he argued that Faulkner's criteria for internment was such that no one was to be
interned without his 'being satisfied on evidence placed before him that the person concerned was and still is an active member of the Official or the Provisional wing of the
IRA, or has been closely implicated in the recent IRA campaign'. Hansard, HC (Series V)
vol 823, col 322 (23 Sept. 1971).

[17] The Council Strike was a general strike organized by the United Ulster Unionist
Council in 1974 in protest at the Sunningdale Agreement which had been signed that year
giving the Republic's government a largely symbolic say in the affairs of Northern
Ireland. Through industrial action and paramilitary intimidation the strikers brought
Northern Ireland to a virtual standstill and the agreement collapsed (Anderson 1994).

1975). It also led to an increased politicization and recruitment to the paramilitaries within the prisons by individuals angered at their incarceration.[18]

The explanation offered by the British government before both the European Commission and Court of Human Rights for the disparity was that Loyalist paramilitaries were smaller and more amorphous and that Republicans were better organized and thus responsible for more death and destruction.[19] Whilst statistics for these years are hard to compile, those published as an appendix to the New Ireland Forum Report suggest that between 1971 and 1975 Republicans killed 126, 255, 128, 98, and 102 for those years whilst Loyalist killed 21, 103, 80, 104, and 115 people (Dillon and Lehane: 1984). Although body counts are a fairly distasteful measure for levels of violence, the point is none the less important because the visible even-handed distribution of justice becomes a key tenet of the later criminalisation and managerialism models of dealing with political violence.

The legal mechanics for carrying out the procedure of incapacitating the Republican enemy were similarly rudimentary. Under the provisions of the old Stormont Special Powers Act the Minister for Home Affairs issued internment orders and while he could refer it to an Advisory Committee he was free to reject or accept that Committee's advice.[20] After the introduction of Direct Rule the British government modified this legislation to include a 'quasi-judicial element',[21] with the introduction of the Detention of Terrorists Order 1972. Under Article 4 of that order the Secretary of State could order the 'interim custody' of a 'suspected terrorist' for up to 28 days.[22] That detention was then examined by a 'Commissioner', who was in theory at least 'a person of legal experience'.

However, the defendant could be excluded from the hearing, evidence inadmissible in a criminal trial could be heard, and witnesses

---

[18] 'When they were initially selected it was clear that many of the men had no political commitment or partisan preferences within the loosely labelled "nationalist spectrum". The intense crowding and competition, the arousal of hatred and physical aggression, resulted in the polarisation of the internees into two groups, those sympathetic with and committed to the Official IRA and those committed to the Provisionals' (Fields 1973: 47).

[19] *Ireland v UK* 1978 Application No. 5310/71, para. 66.

[20] Civil Authorities (Special Powers) Act (NI) 1922–43, Reg. 12(3).

[21] *Hansard*, HC (Series V) vol 855, col 280 (17 Apr. 1973).

[22] The Detention of Terrorists (Northern Ireland) Order 1972, Article 4.

testifying to the involvement of the individual in terrorism (usually RUC officers) gave their evidence from behind screens. If the Commissioner was satisfied not only of concern in terrorism but also that 'detention was necessary for the protection of the public' then the detention order could be issued against him to be reviewed in one year. The burden of proof was a very high degree of probability although, since there was no necessity for reasonableness, 'bad faith' was the only effective grounds for challenge.[23] As the Gardiner Report later acknowledged, 'the procedures are unsatisfactory, or even farcical. If considered as judicial . . .The quasi-judicial procedures are a veneer to an enquiry which, to be effective, inevitably has no relationship to common law procedures' (Gardiner 1975: 44).

Apart from the political fallout, in purely military terms internment was an unmitigated disaster. The degree and intensity of the violence in the aftermath of internment has not been matched either before or

---

[23] The following excerpt from the transcript of a Commission hearing of a Loyalist suspect offers an instructive insight into the conduct of the hearing of a detention commission.

The first witness called is Officer A of the Royal Ulster Constabulary to give evidence from behind a screen. He produces a copy of the Act. (The prosecutor is referred to in the transcript as counsel.)

Counsel. Is the remainder of what you have to say as a result of information?

Officer A. It is.

Counsel. Can that be disclosed in your view . . . without the risk to safety of a person or persons?

Officer A. There would be a risk I feel if it was disclosed openly.

Commissioner. Well Mr Boal, I'm afraid the usual routine would appear to apply.

Boal (defence counsel). I don't accept that routine and I formally protest.

Commissioner. I'll exclude the respondent and his representative under Paragraph 17 (This states that the Commissioner may exclude the respondent and his representative if he considers any part of the proceedings may harm public security or endanger anyone's safety).

The tribunal sits in camera with only the Commissioner, Counsel and Officer A present. Then Boal and the defendant are readmitted and the hearing resumes.

Commissioner. The substance of the matter dealt with in your absence doesn't relate at all to the grounds. It related to the source, and that's all I can tell you, the most I can disclose, is that there was one informer and that he was paid and that the witness found him to be reliable. I regret I can't allow any other questions about the source.

Boal. In that case there is no useful function I can perform by way of cross examination.

Commissioner. I fear so.

Extract from *Sunday Times* (21 Dec. 1973), 'Trial by Tittle Tattle'.

since (Fay, Morrissey, and Smyth 1999). The principal justification for internment had been to take the principal players out of action and then make further inroads on their operations by gaining intelligence through interrogations. In the seven months prior to internment, eleven soldiers and seventeen civilians died; in the five months following internment, thirty-two British soldiers, five members of the Ulster Defence Regiment (UDR), and ninety-seven civilians were either shot dead or blown up (O'Malley 1990: 17). The intended objectives of internment had clearly not been achieved.

The introduction of internment had another less obvious implication in prison management terms. The method of holding internees was to serve, in effect, as the model subsequently adopted for detaining both sentenced paramilitary prisoners and those on remand charged with specific offences. Internees were held in *de facto* prisoner of war conditions, in segregated compounds, operated paramilitary command structures (amongst those who were actually members), and were guarded by British troops. Such a model gave both sentenced and remand prisoners campaigning for political status something to aim at. It also provided the authorities with a tried and tested method of holding large groups of prisoners in segregated conditions.

The introduction of internment had reflected a definition of Republicans as the enemy, and a desire to incapacitate such enemy suspects both to reduce levels of violence and as a broader symbolic punishment of those who opposed the Unionist state (McGuffin 1973, Farrell 1976). The British government's acquiescence in the decision to introduce the measure, and the manner of their subsequent administration of the system after Direct Rule (e.g. with the introduction of the quasi-judicial proceedings),[24] was reflective of a desire to placate Unionist demands for ever tougher security measures,[25] without completely alienating the Nationalist community. Once it became clear

[24] One former Republican internee, who also served time as a sentenced prisoner, told the author: 'The difference between the way the Brits ran internment and the way the Unionists ran it was that the Brits were just a bit cleverer about it. The Brits renamed it detention, they introduced a farce of a hearing and they had a revolving door policy of releasing a few and picking some more up. The end result was the same. The Unionists were more stupid or more honest maybe, depending on your point of view.' Interview with former Republican internee, 9 Oct. 1998.

[25] Both William Whitelaw and later Merlyn Rees were continuously harangued by Unionist politicians with allegations that any internees they decided to release were becoming reinvolved in terrorism. In fact, of the 800 persons who were released during the year 1972–3, only seven were charged with terrorist-related offences. *Hansard*, HC (Series V) vol 853, col 254 (26 Mar. 1973).

that the policy was failing on all counts, Merlyn Rees set up the Gardiner Committee with the express hope that it would recommend its phasing out.[26]

The Gardiner Report of 1975 duly delivered. It criticized internment as having brought the law into contempt, causing deep resentment and increasing the proficiencies of detainees to perpetrate violence (Gardiner 1975: 38–49).[27] The Gardiner Report grudgingly acknowledged the political connotations of internment without trial and concluded by spelling out the limitations of the measure as a means of containing violence:

it creates a myth of oppression which is part of the terrorist legend. We are of the opinion that detention cannot remain as a long term policy. In the short term, it may be an effective means of containing violence, but the prolonged effects of the use of detention are ultimately inimical to community life, fan a widespread sense of grievance and injustice, and obstruct those elements in Northern Ireland society which could lead to reconciliation. (Gardiner 1975: 43)

Special Category Status: Political Status and Negotiation with the Enemy

Amongst sentenced and remand prisoners, the most explicit recognition of the political nature of the violence during this era was the Special Category Status granted to prisoners convicted of terrorist crimes between 1972 and 1975. Prior to the granting of Special Category Status, these prisoners were held in Crumlin Road jail in non-segregated accommodation, with no free association, and were subject to periodic attempts to force the wearing of prison uniforms.[28]

In early 1972, Billy McKee, formerly head of the Belfast Brigade of the IRA, led forty Republican prisoners on hunger strike demanding

---

[26] 'The analysis and conclusions of a respected outside body would carry more weight than a government investigation and I hoped that the Gardiner Report would lead to informed public discussions before we proceeded to legislation. . . . As I told my Cabinet colleagues in November 1974, overall I was looking to the report as a means of moving towards the end of detention' (Rees 1985: 211).

[27] In fact, for those internees who were active Republicans internment proved a useful training ground. They began to organize themselves into paramilitary command structures similar to the sentenced prisoners within the internment camps, conducted similar drilling and lecturing activities, and, as noted above, were joined by individuals who had not actually been members of the paramilitary groupings when originally arrested. Interview with former Republican internee, 12 May 1998.

[28] Interview with former IRA prisoner, 1 Dec. 1994.

political status (discussed in more detail in Chapter 4). William Whitelaw, Secretary of State for Northern Ireland, conceded Special Category Status as McKee neared death.

As was noted previously, there are a number of possible and overlapping explanations for Whitelaw's decision. Firstly, there were considerable fears in government and amongst the security forces about the inevitable reaction that would have followed McKee's death (Coogan 1980: 48). Secondly, from a prison management perspective, the problem of dramatic increases in the prison population with only limited cellular space meant that holding prisoners in shared compound facilities appeared an attractive short-term option (Crawford 1979). Thirdly, the IRA had insisted on such a move as a precondition for the ceasefire and talks held between the two sides in July 1972 (Adams 1996). Finally, the reason offered by Whitelaw himself, was that he was also having talks with the SDLP which he feared would collapse if the concessions were not granted.[29]

What Special Category Status actually entailed was that prisoners had *de facto* prisoner of war status and enjoyed conditions similar to those of the internees. They were held in segregated accommodation from ordinary prisoners and prisoners of opposing paramilitary factions. Most sentenced prisoners were held in Nissen huts at Long Kesh with usually three or four huts within each compound, and a separate shower and latrine, all surrounded by high wire security fences around each compound or 'cage'. Prisoners were allowed free association, their own clothes, to drill and hold lectures, and essentially to run their cages along military style lines. Each cage had their own officer in command (OC) and all negotiations with the prison authorities were done through him (Adams 1990). As one former Special Category prisoner described to the author:

If you have ever seen *Colditz* or one of those old world war two prisoner of war movies, it was exactly like that. We were held in compounds behind high barbed wire fences, we lived in huts with a stove in them, we marched and drilled, we were given military and historical lectures on Irish history,

---

[29] 'The SDLP were anxious to show some benefit from the talks [with the British government]. In the Crumlin Road prison a group of IRA prisoners had gone on hunger strike to demand special "political" privileges . . . Already riots had followed a rumour that one of the prisoners had died. The SDLP felt that they could not continue the talks unless a concession was made . . . Against that background I agreed to the limited concession of Special Category Status' (Whitelaw 1989: 94).

everybody reported upwards through the camp staff [paramilitary command structure] and we used to get visits from the International Red Cross.[30]

As is discussed in more detail in the previous chapters on resistance strategies, during the period of Special Category Status prisoners employed a range of tactics to secure various concessions relating to their detention. By 1974 such concessions included full recognition of paramilitary command structures (including on sporadic occasions addressing prisoners by their rank e.g. OC, Education Officer, Quarter Master, etc.[31]), the right of the camp OCs to visit all compounds under their command once per week, weekly consultations with other factional commanders, and the right to vet prison staff who came into direct contact with the prisoners in order to avoid flashpoints (Coogan 1980: 60–1).

While violence did flare between prisoners and staff, in particular during the time when IRA prisoners burnt down their compounds (see Chapter 5), prison managers sought as much as possible to achieve their objectives through negotiation with the various paramilitary command structures (Crawford 1979).[32] In fact as one former governor in Long Kesh told the author, contact between prison staff and prisoners was quite infrequent.

They were in Nissen Huts, surrounded by a fence with a self contained community inside. The only time that community had contact with the prison service or the outside world was when a prisoner had to leave the compound to go for a visit, or go to the hospital and that was it. So they were self governed communities as such, . . . a very regulated community, supported by your community on the outside and by your community on the inside.[33]

Despite the fact that many prison officers were routinely accompanied on their duties by armed British troops, the prisoners' *de facto* control of space within the compounds meant that management could not impose their will without considerable application of resources and

---

[30] Interview with former IRA prisoner, 5 Aug. 1998.

[31] 'Republican prisoners would largely ignore you if you tried to talk to them and would just say talk to the OC. Some of OCs, Loyalist and Republican, would insist that you addressed them using their rank.' Interview with former prison officer, 12 Sept. 1996.

[32] Coogan (1980: 63) argues that, such was the level of co-operation between the prisoners and the prison authorities that, in Mar. 1976, the IRA prisoners demanded and were granted an advanced copy of a House of Commons speech by Merlyn Rees on the prisons and indeed amended some of the more vituperative language contained therein.

[33] Interview with former governor at Long Kesh, 20 Apr. 1999.

the potential for serious disorder.[34] The acceptance of this state of affairs was viewed by some in the army as analogous to the unacceptable challenge to the authorities posed by the no-go areas controlled by the IRA in Republican areas,[35] which were ultimately smashed by the army in July 1972 at the insistence of the Secretary of State.[36]

The prisoners' *de facto* control over large areas in the compounds undoubtedly represented a challenge to the power of the prison authorities. However, such discomfiture was mitigated by the fact that Special Category Status had been lawfully granted by the government, that the prison estate imposed limitations on the ways in which prisoners could be kept, and that, in managerial terms, the camps ran much more smoothly through open negotiation with paramilitary leaders than they would otherwise have done with a more confrontational approach.

It is important to stress that what was going on within the prisons was in effect a microcosm of what was happening outside the prison walls. Despite the high levels of violence in the period between 1971 and 1976, similar negotiations occurred between senior government figures and the Republican movement (in particular) on the outside.

On 7 July 1972, after an IRA truce had been called,[37] Secretary of State William Whitelaw, Minister of State Paul Shannon, and a number of officials met with the leaders of the IRA at Shannon's house in

[34] 'In reality the compounds were quite easy to manage. Prison staff relied upon the discipline of the paramilitaries to make sure that everything ran smoothly. Our job, along with the army, was to make sure that they didn't escape. There was no question of doing anything constructive about rehabilitation or anything like that with individual prisoners, but actually it wasn't a bad place to work.' Interview with prison officer with a number of years experience of working in the compounds, 19 Sept. 1996.

[35] 'I remember one of the camp officers [British army] saying to me during the compound era that we should just go into the compounds and show them who was boss like the army did when they smashed their way into the IRA no-go areas. I said that was all very well and good but what were we going to do with the prisoners afterwards, there was nowhere else to put them before the Maze was built.' Interview with former prison officer, 12 Sept. 1996.

[36] 'I had to act quickly and decisively on the security front. In particular, the Army had to regain control of the no-go areas in the Bogside and the Creggan in Londonderry. They were not only, rightly, a target of Protestant anger but also a symbol of weakness and failure in British rule. They were areas in the United Kingdom of Great Britain and Northern Ireland which the British government did not control' (Whitelaw 1989: 102).

[37] The terms of the truce were as follows: 'Operations were to cease on either side; the IRA were to enjoy freedom of movement on the streets as were the British; the IRA were given the right to bear arms; An end was agreed to searches of houses or cars and in particular to "P" searches [personal searches by army patrols carried out randomly of civilians]' (Coogan 1980: 49).

London (Mac Stiofain 1975). Gerry Adams, now president of Sinn Fein, was released from prison to be part of the delegation which were flown by the RAF from Belfast (Adams 1996). These talks ultimately came to no conclusion and hostilities were resumed within days.

Similarly, in 1975 the IRA Christmas truce (which had been set up after a group of Protestant Churchmen had met the IRA) was extended from 2 January until 10 February in order to facilitate negotiations with the British. Merlyn Rees, by then Secretary of State for Northern Ireland, had established fairly intricate means of monitoring the truce by setting up Incident Centres manned by civil servants 24 hours per day with direct links to an operations room in Stormont Castle. Rees had already met with the IRA when in opposition in July 1972 when he and Labour leader Harold Wilson met with Republican leaders in Dublin to try to get them to restore their abandoned ceasefire (Rees 1985: 27). In 1975, the arrangements were that IRA and Sinn Fein officials would bring allegations of abuses of the truce by the British army and these were duly processed. A steadily growing number of incidents led to the Centres being closed in November. The ceasefire was officially ended on 23 January 1976 with a raid by the British army on Sinn Fein offices.

The deployment of the army on the streets and in support of the prison service was indicative of a hard line government security policy allied with a pragmatic approach to the necessity for dialogue with the enemy. As in the prisons, the government talked and acted tough but not in many ways out of a principled abhorrence with the methods of their adversaries, but rather in order to strengthen their hand at the negotiation table.

The Diplock Courts and Emergency Legislation: Processing the Terrorists

The final element of the model which I have termed reactive containment was the process by which terrorist suspects were arrested, tried, and thus became prisoners. Although it does not relate directly to the way in which paramilitaries were dealt with in the prison system, the establishment by Emergency legislation of juryless Diplock trials of terrorist suspects using amended rules of evidence is important in understanding this model for at least two reasons. Firstly, as is discussed in some detail in Chapter 6, the courtroom became an important site of ideological and practical struggle between the authorities and the prisoners. For prisoners who were processed by the Diplock system, the abnormal methods used in their interrogation and trial remained a powerful symbolic reference point throughout the conflict in their assertion of the political nature of the process which incarcerated them.[38] Secondly, the introduction of the Diplock system confirmed the principle that the ordinary criminal justice system was not capable of dealing with the consequences of intense levels of political violence. The legal separation of paramilitary offences from ordinary offences was given clear institutional expression through the system of scheduling of terrorist offences discussed below.[39]

In October 1972 William Whitelaw appointed a review committee headed by Lord Diplock to consider 'what arrangements for the administration of justice in Northern Ireland could be made in order to deal more effectively with terrorist organisations . . . otherwise than by internment by the Executive' (Diplock 1972, para. 1). The Report, which was published in December 1972, proposed a range of measures

[38]   DIPLOCK COURT
There was no jury, none at all,
    The pig-in-wig was right,
    And only fools sought fit to stand
    And challenge him with fight,
    For this court is a farce, my friends,
    And Justice knows no light

    .   .   .   .   .   .

    They walked me through the Door of Doom
    Like pig to slaughter pen
    But pigs are treated better
    Than prisoners are my friend.
    And I in lonely fetters
    Of captured Irishmen
    And men ask why men rise to fight,
    To violence do resort,
    And why the days are filled with death
    And struggles' black report
    But see they not these blinded fools
    Lord Diplock's dirty court.

(Sands 1998: 127–34)

[39] The definition of terrorism which was outlined in the legislation establishing the Diplock Courts was repeated in all subsequent Emergency legislation in Northern Ireland. Terrorism was defined in the Emergency Provisions Act 1973 as 'the use of violence for political ends and includes any use of violence for the purpose of putting the public or any section of the public in fear.' As is discussed below, the denial of the political element of terrorist violence became a key strategy from 1976 onwards.

which were intended to overhaul the criminal justice system to enable the conviction of those suspected of involvement in paramilitary activities to be obtained more easily, thereby reducing reliance upon internment.

Recommendations were made concerning an extension of army and police powers to stop and question, search and seize, and arrest and detain. Stricter limitations on the availability of bail were introduced. The law governing the admissibility of confessions was relaxed in order to enable convictions based upon confession alone. Finally a system was recommended to suspend jury trial for a list of offences usually associated with the activities of paramilitary organizations (Hogan and Walker 1989). These were to be known as 'scheduled offences'[40] since they were listed in a schedule to the enabling legislation. The Commission concluded that jury trial was 'not practicable in the case of terrorist crimes in Northern Ireland because of the threat of intimidation of witnesses' (Diplock 1972, para. 17) and the risk that Loyalist defendants would be perversely acquitted by predominantly Protestant juries (Diplock 1972, paras. 35–7).[41]

The bulk of the Diplock Commission's proposals were enacted by Parliament soon after in the Northern Ireland (Emergency Provisions) Act 1973. Section 2 (1) of the Act provided that 'a trial on indictment of a scheduled offence shall be conducted by the court without a jury'. Viewing the introduction of the juryless courts as part of the broader package of Emergency legislation heralded by Diplock, Dickson (1992) underlines the increased significance of successfully obtaining confessions from terrorist suspects. As Jackson and Doran point out (1995: 31), some studies suggest that up to 80 per cent of all Diplock prosecutions were primarily based upon confessional evidence. The purpose of the measures as a whole was to remove impediments to the

---

[40] Scheduled offences (those listed in a schedule, i.e. an appendix, to the Emergency Provisions Act) included murder, manslaughter, serious offences against the person, arson, malicious damage, riot, offences under the Firearms Act (NI) 1969 and the Explosive Substances Act 1883, robbery and aggravated burglary, intimidation, membership of proscribed organizations, and collecting information likely to be of use to terrorists. The Act also empowered the Attorney-General to certify that particular cases of murder, manslaughter, and offences against the person should not be treated as scheduled offences and should, therefore, be tried by jury (i.e. ordinary crimes). Since 1973 juries have continued to function in Northern Ireland in civil cases, in coroners' courts, and in courts trying non-scheduled indictable offences. For a critical review of the process of scheduling see Walsh (1983), Jackson and Doran (1992).

[41] For a critique of the rationale for the abolition of juries in terrorist trials see Greer and White (1990).

securing of confessions, relaxing the rules on witness evidence, and thus secure more convictions (Cunningham 1991: 70).

Interestingly, however, Diplock did not recommend the abolition of internment. The Diplock Report argued instead that 'detention offered a temporary substitute for the rule of law' (Diplock 1972: 27–9). In the subsequent debate on the enabling legislation, the Conservative government cited approvingly Diplock's view that 'it was hoped that the "strengthened" courts alone would be able to deal with violence but that that time had not yet come'.[42] The critical view from Labour backbenchers, as expressed by Kevin McNamara, was that Diplock and the government in essence wanted it both ways, that is, that those who were acquitted could subsequently be interned and those who were interned could subsequently be tried if sufficient evidence was gained.[43] In fact, however, both Conservative and Labour front benches were reluctant to phase out internment unless they could be assured that it would not result in a further deterioration of the security situation (Spujt 1986).

Although originally envisaged as a temporary phenomenon, the Diplock system has become an 'institution with a sense of permanence' in the Northern Ireland criminal justice system, trying well in access of 10,000 defendants in the period between 1973 and the 1994 ceasefires (Jackson and Doran 1995: 16–19). While not spelling the end to internment, it represented a partial break from the notion of simply incapacitating Republicans as the primary enemy.

Instead Diplock is characteristic of a series of technocratic discourses and practices, perhaps crystallized more clearly after the ending of internment, wherein terrorism could be more effectively managed by the ordinary if somewhat altered criminal justice and prison systems. Part of the rationale of the Diplock system was as a corrective to the potential perverse acquittals of Loyalist suspects under the old jury system (Greer and White 1990: 58–65). While the Diplock system has not been immune to allegations of bias against Republicans and in favour of Loyalists (e.g. Walsh 1983: 102–4), as Jackson and Doran suggest these have been hard to substantiate (Jackson and Doran 1995: 30).

More importantly for current purposes, the system of juryless

---

[42] NIO Minister of State Van Straubenzee, *Hansard*, HC (Series V) vol 859, col 841 (5 July 1973).

[43] Kevin McNamara MP, *Hansard*, HC (Series V) vol 859, col 823 (5 July 1973).

courts supported by amended pre-trial and evidential procedures had at least two practical and symbolic implications for the management of paramilitary offenders in the prisons.

Firstly, as the number of internees was gradually reduced in 1974 and 1975, there was a steady increase in the number of prisoners either remanded or sentenced to be managed under the new system (NIPS 1977: 6). The increase in the remand and sentenced prison population in 1974 and 1975 occurred in the context of similar rates of violence as in 1973 (McKittrick *et al.* 1999) suggesting perhaps that many prisoners brought before the courts to be tried in the wake of Diplock might indeed (as Kevin McNamara had argued) have been interned in the pre-Diplock era.[44]

Secondly, at an ideological level, the Diplock system was indicative of a mindset which was soon to dominate official policy on the management of paramilitaries in general. The Diplock Report highlighted that paramilitaries could be dealt with using the ordinary albeit modified criminal justice process. It placed the emphasis of security policy on targeted arrests and interrogation carried out largely by the RUC rather than the more generalist sweeps effected by the army in internment-related operations. While the aberrations of Special Category Status and internment remained part of the state system it is possible to argue that the Diplock system could not properly come into its own as a technocratic response to political violence. However, once those measures were removed in the wake of the Gardiner Report in 1975, and the primacy of the police responsibility for dealing with terrorism was established, the state infrastructure (including the prison system) required for the criminalisation of political violence was complete.[45]

---

[44] In 1973 internees made up 26% of the total prison population, in 1974 23%, and in 1975 10%. Over the same period the prison population rose from 1,980 in 1973, to 2,517 in 1974, to 2,687 in 1975 (NIPS 1977: 24–6).

[45] An alternative argument would be that the Diplock Courts have proved sufficiently flexible to have been a constant feature of all three models for the management of political violence. In the period of containment, their special nature facilitated the granting of Special Category Status to those convicted by them. In the criminalisation phase, they were reinterpreted as standard criminal courts so that those sentenced by them could be deemed common criminals. Finally during the managerialism era, they have become a permanent, specialized feature of the criminal justice system dealing with one amongst a variety of different offender types.

Conclusion

Up until the Gardiner Report in 1975, the management of paramilitary prisoners in Northern Ireland was underpinned by the *de facto* recognition of the political character of the inmates. The deployment of British troops and their role in the administration of prisons; the internment of suspected paramilitaries; the granting of Special Category Status and simultaneous negotiations with the prisoners' comrades still at large; and the use of an amended criminal justice and judicial system; these all served to highlight the unusual nature of the prison inmates. Prisons were seen as sites for the containment of violent protagonists while a political solution was sought rather than as mechanisms for the defeat or rehabilitation of paramilitaries. Relations with prisoners were characteristic of the broader ideological acceptance of the political causes of the conflict.

The interaction of prison managers and staff with prisoners was also dictated to an extent by the limitations of the prison system itself. A prison system which was built to house just 600 prisoners managed by 292 staff in 1969 was forced to accommodate 2,687 prisoners by 1975 managed by 2,184 staff (NIPS 1977: 8). In such circumstances, the physical realities of the prison estate as well as staff shortages severely limited the authorities' ability to do other than contain paramilitary prisoners.[46] Until the opening of the H Blocks at the Maze (formerly Long Kesh) alongside the Special Category compounds in 1976, prison managers had little alternative to collective imprisonment at that site. However, the building of the eight H Blocks completed in 1977 was explicitly designed to 'enable high risk prisoners to be held in secure and high standard cellular conditions as part of the implementation of the policy of phasing out Special Category Status' (NIPS 1978: 8).

For many of the prisoners, and indeed some of the staff, the period of reactive containment assumed something of a golden era in Northern Ireland's prison history. For those prisoners sentenced after March 1976 and imprisoned in the H Blocks at Long Kesh, their goal was to achieve the status of their comrades still held in the compounds only a few hundred yards away (Campbell, McKeown, and O'Hagan

---

[46] One possibly instructive insight into the strain under which the prison service operated in the early 1970s was that between 1972 and 1976 no prison service *Annual Reports* were produced, in breach of Section 5 the Prison Act (Northern Ireland) 1953. The prison service report produced in 1977 covers the years 1972–6.

1994). For prison officers who worked in the cellular accommodation, particularly those who worked on the wings during the protests between 1976 and 1981, the period where contact with prisoners was limited largely to the compound perimeter fence became a running conversation of somewhat legendary proportions.[47] The new policy, which provoked such wistfulness and nostalgia amongst both prisoners and prison staff for earlier times, became known as criminalisation.

[47] Interview with former prison officer, 19 Sept. 1996.

9

Criminalisation, 1976–1981

Introduction

The policy which became known as criminalisation was really a fusion of political and military thought which combined a continuing military conflict with the terrorists with a concerted attempt to delegitimize and criminalise that which had been hitherto accepted as explicitly political violence.

Of the phases discussed in this book, the period 1976–81 probably comes closest to a coherent state philosophy and set of practices for handling paramilitary prisoners and the political conflict. As Bowyer Bell (1993: 429) argues, during 1974 there were signs of the beginning of an 'unarticulated strategy . . . a typical British response; no theory, only practice, unarticulated values, personal experience and self interest shaped by an Irish exposure'.

The Diplock Report (1972) had showed some elements of a criminalisation policy with its emphasis on using the ordinary if amended policing, criminal justice, and judicial system to process those convicted of political violence. As the Diplock Committee recognized, however, such a drive towards normalizing the response to violence was difficult to reconcile with a prison system which retained both internees and Special Category Status prisoners. The Gardiner Committee, which reported in January 1975, provided a clear template for a change of strategy in the prisons.

The Gardiner Committee appeared to argue that the ending of internment was a matter of timing rather than principle (Gardiner 1975, para. 148–9) and, as Secretary of State Merlyn Rees had hoped,[1]

---

[1] 'The issue of Special Category Status had been high on our agenda since first taking office and it was not for lack of consideration that I had not ended it earlier . . . We were simply unable to act without having prison cell accommodation and it was only when I decided to take the short cut of building the H Blocks at the Maze [as opposed to the green field site at Maghaberry] that we could begin to plan the ending of Special Category Status in earnest' (Rees 1985: 275).

made clear its view that Special Category Status should be phased out.[2] The language of the report provided the framework for a clear articulation of the criminalisation strategy to follow. While conscious of the likely results within the prisons and the physical limitations of the prison estate, the Gardiner Committee was forthright that its recommendations should be implemented as quickly as possible.[3] Thus once the appropriate accommodation was ready,[4] the prison system was ready to move to the forefront of a struggle designed to deny the political motivation of the paramilitary protagonists to the conflict.

Criminalisation and Ulsterisation

The Gardiner Report's recommendations pertaining to the prisons should be viewed in the broader context of shifts within security policy in general. Early in the Labour administration, Merlyn Rees had indicated the likely direction of Labour's broad security policy.[5] The White Paper of July 1974 indicated a desire for increased community co-operation with the police which would 'enable the army to make a planned orderly and progressive reduction in its present commitment and subsequently there would be no need for the army to become involved in a policing role'.[6] Following on from the recommendations

[2] 'Although recognising the pressures on those responsible at the time, we have come to the conclusion that the introduction of Special Category Status was a serious mistake ... We can see no justification for granting privileges to a large number of criminals convicted of very serious crimes, in many cases murder, merely because they claim political motivation. It supports their own view, which society must reject, that their political motivation in some way justifies their crimes. Finally, it is unfair to ordinary criminals, often guilty of far less serious crimes, who are subject to normal discipline' (Gardiner 1975, para. 107).

[3] 'We recognise to remove the privileges from existing special category prisoners would cause trouble within the prisons . . . On present plans it does not seem that it would be feasible to begin to phase out special category status on any scale until the new temporary cellular prison accommodation, recently announced by the Secretary of State, is ready in early 1976 . . . Nevertheless we recommend that the earliest practicable opportunity should be taken to end the special category. The first priority should be to stop admitting new prisoners to the special category' (Gardiner 1975, para. 104).

[4] Merlyn Rees, Hansard, HC (Series V) vol 894, cols 903–5 (22 June 1975).

[5] 'I believe the cornerstone of security policy should be a progressive increase in the role of the civilian law enforcement agencies in Northern Ireland. Sufficient members of the Army would remain in Northern Ireland to assist in maintaining law and order. But the government believe that in the long term it must be the community itself and normal police activities, not military operations alone, which would finally defeat the terrorists' (Merlyn Rees, Hansard, HC (Series V) vol 871, col 1466 (4 Apr. 1974)).

[6] The Northern Ireland Constitution, 1974, Cmnd. 5675 (cited in Cunningham 1991: 109).

contained in the Diplock and Gardiner Reports which had expanded police powers of arrest and interrogation, in the spring of 1976 a working party drawn from senior NIO, army, and RUC personnel appointed by Rees produced a secret document entitled 'The Way Ahead' (Ryder 1991: 84). It confirmed that security would be dominated by a policy of Ulsterisation.

Under such a policy RUC primacy over policing and public order was confirmed. RUC Regional Crime Squads were established to mirror the Active Service Unit structure of the IRA (Taylor 1980: 63). The RUC Reserve were to be expanded to take over many army functions, and the RUC were to be retrained and re-equipped. Finally, the police would be supported by the locally recruited regiment of the British army, the Ulster Defence Regiment (Ryder 1989).

The theoretical element to the strategy was quite simple but essential if the hitherto political connotations of the conflict were to be denied. The obvious guerrilla undertones to the ongoing conflict between the IRA and the British army could, to a degree, be contained and internalized if it was members of the RUC and locally based UDR who were on the front line. Rather than be seen as one side in the ongoing struggle, the British government felt that they could portray themselves, at least to an international audience (Gearty 1991a: 142), as neutral, trying to keep the peace in the ongoing factional fighting between two communities divided on religious and historical grounds. The British state could thus portray itself as *above* the Northern Ireland problem rather than an integral part of it (O'Dowd, Rolston, and Tomlinson 1980: 208).

A big recruitment drive was instituted within the RUC and accompanied by a commitment to reduce the number of British army regiments committed to Northern Ireland (Hamill 1985). In the spring of 1976, an Englishman, Kenneth Newman, was appointed as Chief Constable of the RUC with a brief to professionalize the force so that they could lose their historical tag of sectarianism amongst the Catholic community (Ellison and Smyth 2000). In January 1977, for the first time since 1969, the policy of police primacy was formalized by an agreement between the army GOC (General Officer Commanding troops in Northern Ireland) and the RUC, putting the Chief Constable in charge of overall security (Ryder 1989: 159).

This trend was not, however, paralleled by a softening of the interrogation and security policies of the police. Between 1976 and 1979 3,000 people were charged with terrorist offences, most of them on evidence obtained by confessions (Bishop and Mallie 1987: 321). The

RUC were under intense pressure to secure convictions and they responded by resorting frequently to physical beatings, threats, verbal abuse, intimidation, and generally oppressive treatment in an effort to extract confessions in the holding centres (Taylor 1980, Hogan and Walker 1989: 116). One individual, Brian Maguire, died as a result of injuries received during interrogation.

The techniques used in police holding centres like Castlereagh in Belfast led Amnesty International to conclude that 'maltreatment of suspected terrorists by the RUC has taken place with sufficient frequency to warrant the establishment of a public inquiry to investigate it' (Amnesty International 1978: 56). The government refused to accede to Amnesty's demand for a wide-ranging inquiry and established a more narrowly focused committee under Lord Justice Bennett. Even this committee refused to accept that all of those injured while in police custody had injured themselves as the police had claimed (Bennett 1979, paras. 19, 63).

While simultaneously withdrawing a number of British army regiments, the British government also chose to admit that the Special Air Services Regiment (an élite highly trained group specializing in covert guerrilla activity) was being deployed on 1 January 1976. While there is much evidence to suggest that the SAS had been deployed since the early 1970s (Dillon 1990, Murray 1990), 1976 saw a very public announcement of their presence and the deployment of more SAS personnel. This controversial regiment have been involved in some of the most contentious shootings by the security forces in Northern Ireland (Urban 1992). Thus while the police were to be given primary responsibility for anti-terrorist policing, and use of general army regiments was being reduced, specialist forces were to be given a higher profile in dealing with the very sharpest end of security policy.

The Gardiner Report had linked the changing nature of security policy with recommendations regarding political and social measures designed to marginalize the terrorists from their own communities.[7] This policy was to be energized under the direction of Roy Mason, who had

---

[7] 'A solution to the problems of Northern Ireland should be worked out in political terms, and must include further measures to promote social justice between classes and communities . . . Though these matters, strictly speaking, lie outside our terms of reference, we should like to see a number of developments: the implementation of the recommendations of the Van Straubenzee Report on Discrimination . . . further improvements in housing; and a new and more positive approach to community relations. Consideration should be given to a Bill of Rights' (Gardiner 1976: 7–8). A version of the Van Straubenzee Report was implemented in 1976 with the Fair Employment Act 1976 outlawing discrimination on the grounds of religion.

replaced Merlyn Rees as Secretary of State for Northern Ireland in 1976. Mason argued that the twin evils of Northern Ireland were terrorism and unemployment and vowed to attack both with vigour. He also made clear that, unlike his predecessors, he would 'never parley with terrorists' (Tomlinson 1980: 194). A keen advocate of 'untying the hands of the security forces' (Bowyer Bell 1993: 530), Mason continuously asserted that the 'IRA was on the run' during his tenure as Secretary of State.[8]

This tough military posture was allied on the other hand with 'relatively generous social policies', a stance mirrored by successive Conservative administrations in the 1980s (Gaffikin and Morrissey 1990: 206). From the mid-1970s onwards, considerable resources were deployed in areas such as West Belfast from which the Republican movement derives much of its support, albeit channelled through the more conservative elements within those communities such as the Catholic Church (Tomlinson 1998: 98). Mason argued that investment and jobs in such communities, such as the £78 million invested in the failed De Lorean car plant, was directly linked to undermining support for the IRA.[9]

In sum, therefore, the elements of what became known as criminalisation included a fusion of processing terrorists through the amended normal criminal justice system of Diplock Courts and Emergency legislation; an attempt to Ulsterise responsibility for security which married more professional policing methods with fairly harsh interrogation techniques designed to secure confessions; the passing of the sharper edge of the military conflict to specialist covert élite regiments rather than the more open conflict of the earlier period; the attempts to utilize investment and social policies in order to undermine support for paramilitarism in working-class communities in particular; and finally denying political motivation by continuous reference to the criminality of terrorism and the upholding of law and order.[10]

---

[8] 'We are squeezing the terrorists like rolling up a toothpaste tube. We are squeezing them out of their safe havens. We are squeezing them away from their money supplies. We are squeezing them out of society and into prison.' Interview with Roy Mason, *Daily Express* (Dec. 1977) (cited in Hamill 1985: 221).

[9] 'It is of the utmost political, social and psychological importance that the project should go ahead. This would be a hammer blow to the IRA.' Roy Mason, British Cabinet minutes produced in a legal action as a result of the De Lorean crash (cited in Tomlinson 1998: 121).

[10] 'The terrorist will continue to exist as long as he has enough public support to provide him a safe haven. But the terrorist can no longer be sure of this in Northern Ireland. The reason is clear. Increasingly people know the terrorist for what he is in Northern Ireland. Experience has taught again and again that the rule of law is the rule of a stable society' (Merlyn Rees, *Hansard*, HC (Series V) vol 908, cols 641–2 (25 Mar. 1976)).

As previously discussed, there are always tendencies when reviewing Northern Ireland history to overestimate the conspiratorial nature of various measures as a centralized, meticulously constructed and rigorously executed counter-insurgency strategy. Such a view is vigorously contested by some of the key actors such as Merlyn Rees who has argued, 'there wasn't a master plan. I'm not a master plan chap. I don't believe in that sort of thing' (cited in Taylor 1997: 202). However, in this instance, even if these various initiatives in fact emerged from disparate elements of the state infrastructure and the political instincts of a British government gradually moving beyond simply containing violence, the sum total of the various parts amounted to a dramatic change in conflict management policies. As the Gardiner Report had correctly identified, the key test of the success or failure of the new approach would be in the management of the Northern Ireland prison system.

Implementing Criminalisation: The Characteristics within the Prisons

Given that much of the preparatory work for the introduction of criminalisation had been ongoing while an IRA ceasefire was in place and while dialogue was taking place between the government and Republicans both in the prisons and in the community through the Incident Centres (see Chapter 8), few prisoners appeared to have considered the consequences of the ending of Special Category Status.[11] While the British government increased the rate of remission from 33 per cent to 50 per cent for all sentenced paramilitaries in order to make the change in policy more palatable to the prisoners, their instinctive opposition to the measure appeared undaunted.[12]

---

[11] 'When a British government Commission recommended in January 1975 the phasing out of political status (officially termed special category status), few realised the full significance of the recommendations . . . The British government had been engaged in talks with the Republican movement, and a truce agreed between the IRA and British forces was to last into the latter part of that year. As months passed, however, it became clear that the British were not interested in peace. They had exploited the truce while preparing counter insurgency measures whose objective was to isolate those engaged in the resistance struggle and to normalise life in the Six County state. A major part of British policy was the criminalisation of Republican prisoners' (Campbell, McKeown, and O'Hagan 1994: 1).

[12] 'It would appear now that there is no intention to reverse the decision [to remove Special Category Status] and the British government are determined to push this new scheme through regardless of the consequences . . . Already volunteers of Oglaigh na

Similarly with regard to the prison staff who were to be required to implement the new policy, they appear to have been equally unclear as to its likely consequences. As one former prison officer told the author, 'I don't suppose any of us really knew what to expect when the H Blocks were opened. We knew that the Provos were hardly going to take it lying down but as to what they would actually do, none of us knew.'[13]

Under the changes introduced by Merlyn Rees, any person convicted of a scheduled offence after 1 March 1976 was to be treated as an ordinary criminal with all special privileges removed. Male prisoners were sent to a newly constructed prison (quickly dubbed the H Blocks, since they were built in the shape of the letter H) erected alongside the compounds in Long Kesh. The legs of each H comprised of wings of twenty-five centrally heated eight-by-twelve-foot cells, a toilet area, and dining, recreation, and handicraft rooms; the central bar of the H was used for medical and administration quarters (NIPS 1977: 8).

With the abolition of Special Category Status Long Kesh thus became two prisons. The compounds, with their Nissen huts, continued to hold the declining number of Special Category prisoners. Anyone convicted of a political offence before 1 March 1976 continued to hold this status. Prisoners convicted of such offences after that date were confined to cells in the H Blocks. In order to signify the new policy direction Long Kesh was renamed the Maze prison although most prisoners and relatives persist to this day in referring to it as Long Kesh.

In the new changed physical conditions of the cellular Maze prison, the implementation of the policy of criminalisation began to take shape. On 14 September IRA prisoner Ciaran Nugent was the first prisoner sentenced under the new regime.[14] Nugent refused to wear a

---

hEireann [IRA] have been instructed that they are not to engage in any institutional schemes under the control of the prison administration. They are further instructed that they are not to wear any clothing provided by the prison administration, even if such clothes are of a civilian type. They will respond only to the commands and directives of their superior officers, regardless of the consequences. They are political prisoners and any other imagined label tagged on to them by the British government will not make the slightest difference to that very basic fact . . . We are prepared to die for the right to retain political status. Those who try to take it away must be fully prepared to pay the same price.' Statement issued by IRA prisoners, 27 Mar. 1976 (reproduced in Coogan 1980: 65–6).

[13] Interview with former prison officer, 12 Sept. 1996.

[14] The period of the blanket, dirty protest, and hunger strike is outlined in more detail in Chapter 4. Only sufficient narrative details are provided in this chapter in order to understand the events in so far as they related to prison management.

prison uniform and was therefore placed in a cell with only a blanket. The blanketmen were initially few in number and considerably isolated in their cells with only their blankets and a Bible (Taylor 1997: 204). However, over the next months and years Nugent's example was followed by several hundred other Republican prisoners—at any given moment between one-third and one-half of the men arriving at the Maze/Long Kesh—who also went 'on the blanket' (Republican Fact File 1991: 4).[15] As is discussed elsewhere, these protests were to be followed by the no wash, dirty protest, and ultimately hunger strike, by Republican prisoners resisting the criminalisation project.

Over the same period, I believe that the implementation of the policy of criminalisation in the prisons came to be characterized by a range of features. Although a number of these characteristics have been constants throughout the history of political imprisonment in Northern Ireland (and are considered elsewhere in this book), it is arguable that some reached their zenith during this era. It is also clear that a number of these features overlap and indeed, in some instances, appear somewhat contradictory. None the less by conceptualizing each as distinct influences in a thematic rather than chronological fashion, it may be possible to understand better the implementation of the criminalisation policy as a whole. The features which characterized criminalisation included: (i) rule enforcement and the assertion of power; (ii) the internalization of propagandist positions; (iii) brutality, violence, and dehumanization; (iv) hothouse management and political interference. Each is considered in turn below.

Rules Enforcement and the Assertion of Power

The application of prison rules and regulations is clearly one of the key elements of the successful management of a prison system (Loucks 1995). In particular it has been linked to the bureaucratic-lawful notion of prison management, wherein prison life becomes increasingly bureaucratized and codified through the diffusion of power and the atomization of the inmate community (Ditchfield 1990: 9). As was discussed above, Ditchfield (adapting the earlier US-based work of Barak Glanz) argues that this post-Second World War style of management saw an increasing curtailment of the power of both governors and staff

[15] By the end of 1977, 250 prisoners were taking part in the blanket protest (NIPS 1977: 5).

in favour of increasingly centralized and bureaucratic direction. In practice, even in a context where the discretion of staff and management has been formally limited, the actual implementation of rules and orders from above usually involves 'occasional tradeoffs, rule bending, creative application of regulations' (Vagg 1994: 150). As Liebling argues, staff normally understand that 'the decent thing' to do is selectively to underenforce the law, in order that the smooth flow of prison can continue (Liebling 2000: 345).

As is discussed in Chapter 6, British and American prisons were until relatively recently largely free from judicial oversight. The space between the formal legal framework of prisons and actual practices has led some commentators to describe prisons as sites characterized by arbitrariness, unfairness, and discretion (Fitzgerald and Sim 1982: 82). This may involve the application of vaguely formulated rules such as prosecuting a prisoner for 'in any way offending against good order and discipline' (Sparks, Bottoms, and Hay 1996: 182). It may also entail the over-enthusiastic use of prison rules, for example by unnecessarily searching prisoners, an action often viewed as a wind up to the prisoners on the receiving end (McDermott and King 1988). As Livingstone and Owen (1999: 450) have argued, while prisons are extensively rule bound institutions, the authorities can almost always point to a rule at some level in the hierarchy to justify any action taken.[16]

The removal of Special Category Status after March 1976 meant that paramilitary prisoners were subject to a set of prison rules applicable to all prisoners regardless of motivation (NIPS 1977: 5). Under Special Category Status prisoners had been exempt from such rules as the obligation to wear uniforms or conduct prison work, regulations which would in any case have been unenforceable in a context where the prison authorities had to negotiate access to the compounds via the prisoners' leadership. However, in the context of cellular

---

[16] Such justificatory discourses are analogous to examples within the policing literature wherein police forces have relied upon ostensibly objective policing techniques to mask potentially authoritarian or discriminatory policing practices. In such a scenario law and order or rule enforcement obfuscates the quintessentially political nature of the application of power. In the same way as 'hard policing' in Brixton (Scarman 1982: 110), public order policing of the miners' strike in Britain (Uglow 1988), or more recently, 'zero tolerance' policing in the USA and Britain (Hopkins-Burke 1998, Innes 1999) can in no sense be divorced from their political context, similarly the rigid application of prison disciplinary regulations in Northern Ireland post-Mar. 1976 formed an integral part of broader changes in government policy. For a critical analysis of the Northern Ireland conflict as a 'law and order' problem see McEvoy and Gormally (1997).

accommodation, enforcement of prison rules became a key element in the reassertion of prison officer power and in the determination to ensure that the Maze was run as a normal prison where the same rules were applied as to ordinary prisoners in the system.

Respondent. They were refusing to wear the prison uniform and that was a breach of prison discipline and that was all there was to it.

Interviewer. Did you regard this as an opportunity to break the IRA prisoners?

Respondent. I didn't see it that way. The policy had changed and it was our job to implement the changed policy. Obviously things were very different from working in the compounds.

Interviewer. Better or worse?

Respondent. I felt a lot better actually. I know some people preferred the compounds but actually I preferred to deal with a guy as an individual than as a group. You had a better chance of getting to know prisoners, although to be honest that was difficult, but you also didn't have to take any crap . . . it was more like working a normal prison, or at least it would have been if the provies [IRA] hadn't been protesting.[17]

At the Maze, disciplinary proceedings against prisoners rose from 245 offences and 336 punishments in 1975 to 774 offences and 708 punishments awarded in 1976 (NIPS 1977: 41–2). This represented an increase of 216 per cent and 111 per cent respectively. The largest increase in any disciplinary category of offences was insubordination, which rose from 109 in 1975 to 496 in 1976 (NIPS 1977: 41–2) an increase of 355 per cent. In 1977 the number of offences at the Maze rose even more dramatically to 3,548, and the number of punishments rose to 13,038 (NIPS 1978: 42). In 1978 the number of offences was 9,477 (with refusal to work or wear prison uniforms constituting 8,039 offences) and the number of punishments totalling 20,340 (NIPS 1978: 44). While the limitations of recorded disciplinary figures have been highlighted elsewhere (King and McDermott 1995: 98, Sparks, Bottoms, and Hay 1996: 237), and acknowledging that such figures occurred within the context of the prisoners' protests and a steady growth in the population,[18] none the less such huge increases do offer

---

[17] Interview with former prison officer, 12 Sept. 1996.

[18] The prison population at the Maze (amalgamating both the compound and cellular prison) rose from a highest number of 1,241 in 1975, to a highest number of 1,296 in 1976, an increase of 4% (NIPS 1978: 26–7). The figures for 1977 and 1978 are not broken down by individual prison. The overall male population figures for the period were

instructive insights into the changed nature of rule enforcement with the introduction of the criminalization policy.

As was noted in Chapter 6, the scale of rule enforcement and disciplinary breaches led to a slightly surreal cycle of charging and repeat offending. During the blanket and dirty protests, prisoners were charged in their cell every 14 or 28 days. An officer would go to the cell of the protesting prisoners, order him to put on a prison uniform and go to work, and upon refusal prepare two charge sheets which were then passed to adjudicating governors. The subsequent adjudications were normally carried out in the corridor in a context of prisoners banging, shouting, and using objects such as furniture, chamber pots, and mugs to create as much disturbance and noise as possible. Protesting prisoners invariably refused to answer the charges and were found guilty. This process was then repeated for each prisoner in 14 or 28 days, with prison staff eventually putting cell mates on the same charging and finding guilty cycle in order to speed the process up.[19]

As noted above, the prisoners' refusal to wear a uniform and to do prison work were two of the key elements of their protest. While presented within the objective framework of the management of prisons,[20] in effect the enforcement of regulations regarding uniforms and work became the epicentre of the political and ideological struggle between the prison authorities and the prisoners.[21] As it was an offence under the prison rules to leave one's cell improperly dressed, protesting

(1975) 2,438; (1976) 2,584; (1977) 2,739; (1978) 2861, suggesting that the overall increase in population was insufficient to account for the huge increase in disciplinary offences and punishments.

[19] Description from affidavit by Governor Terence Jackson, HMP Maze, reproduced in *Re Hughes' Application* 1986, NILR 9, 59–61.

[20] 'The successful operation of any prison system depends not only on the good management and the disciplined performance of their duties by members of the prison staff but also on the recognition by prisoners of the framework of regulation governing the operation of the prison. Such regulations are designed not only to preserve discipline and good order in the interests of the authorities but also to make sure as far as possible that prisoners serve their sentences in reasonable and humane conditions free from abuse either at the hands of staff or inmates . . . The offences listed [in the *Annual Report*] reflect the numbers engaged in the protest actions related to claims for special treatment for certain sentenced prisoners because of the alleged political motive for their crime' (NIPS 1980: 15).

[21] 'I suppose you could say it came down to who was in charge of the prison. The rules were clear and they were there to be enforced . . . it would have been hard to say that these prisoners were being treated like other prisoners if they had been allowed simply to ignore some of the basic prison rules.' Interview with former prison officer, 19 Sept. 1996.

prisoners were confined to their cells for 24 hours per day. Their non-co-operation meant the removal of the three privileged visits per month and the refusal to wear a uniform to the visiting area cost prisoners the fourth visit. Their contact with the outside world was thus limited to one censored letter per week in the first year of the protest (Beresford 1987: 27).[22] After some confrontations with prison officers where furniture was smashed, privileges such as beds and footlockers were removed leaving them with two men per cell, with a mattress, three blankets, and a Bible each.

Such unbending adherence to regulations amongst prison officers during the criminalisation era may be viewed in a number of lights. On the one hand, it may be seen (and is cogently articulated as such by some critical commentators and former prisoners) as the expression of a desire at ministerial and senior management level to crush the political will of Republican prisoners in particular (Campbell, McKeown, and O'Hagan 1994, Tomlinson 1995, McKeown 1998). Prison staff thus became the instrument of the criminalisation agenda.

On the other hand, some staff have argued to the author that strict rule enforcement came about because staff were often forced to operate without clear guidance from above, particularly in the early days of the criminalisation era. Clearly ministers and prison service senior managers became increasingly preoccupied with the protests in the latter part of the dirty protest and hunger strike era. However, some prison staff have spoken of a 'management vacuum' in the response to the protests and have challenged the notion of top down policy implementation during the criminalisation era.[23] One prison officer argued that they were merely implementing the rules and that 'it wasn't up to us to negotiate a settlement, all we could do was to enforce the rules until the politicians or the NIO made up their mind what to do'.[24] In the context of perceived indecision and a lack of direction in the early days of the protest, it is certainly tenable to argue that individuals from

---

[22] As discussed in Chapter 4, the prisoners ultimately relented and began receiving statutory visits again.

[23] *Interviewer.* During the criminalisation era, did you ever come under pressure to desist from recognizing the command structure?

Respondent. No, absolutely not, never . . . I do not recall ever being told by a minister, look we know what you normally do but now you can't, no never.

Interviewer. Did you ever instruct your staff to that effect?

Respondent. No, Never.   (Interview with former governor HMP Maze, 20 Apr. 1999.)

[24] Interview with former prison officer, 12 Sept. 1996.

a militaristic and hierarchical institution would resort to rule enforcement as an underpinning philosophy.

Whichever view is closer to the truth, the result remains that rigid rule enforcement during the protests rendered prison disciplinary procedures farcical. Such attitudes and practices exacerbated the protests and placed considerable obstacles in the way of resolving the dispute.[25] By framing the dispute within a maintenance of order paradigm prison staff and management contributed to a context in which pragmatism was seen as weakness, compromise as capitulation, and where the determination of the prisoners to resist was met by an equal determination that they would be defeated.

The Internalization of Propagandist Positions

The distinction between the dissemination of genuinely held beliefs and propagandist positions is often a blurred one. One widely cited definition of propaganda contends that the term propaganda can be used in a non-pejorative or neutral sense (Jowett and O'Donnell 1994). They define propaganda as 'the deliberate and systematic attempt to shape perceptions, manipulate cognitions, and direct behaviour to achieve a response that furthers the desired intent of the propagandist' (Jowett and O'Donnell 1994: 4). However, as Miller (1994: 71) argues, the identification of a propagandist in the real world is a matter of political argument which is linked to specific interests or ideologies. While clearly some commentators from both left and right define propaganda by reference to the source of the information (Wright 1991, Curtis 1984), this does not necessarily mean that such accounts are untruthful (Walton 1997). Rather, propaganda may be seen as the reconfiguration or the repackaging of particular truths, half-truths, or clear lies in order to support a predetermined ideological, political, or organizational position.

While some prison staff and governors suggested that at least in the early days of the criminalisation era ground level staff operated in something of a policy vacuum, others have argued that some staff appeared to internalize and believe in the criminalisation project:

I would say that there were definitely some of our staff, particularly those recruited in 1976 or 1977 or those who had never worked with paramilitaries

---

[25] One of the Republican prisoners' five demands became the restoration of remission lost as a result of disciplinary hearings arising from the earlier protests.

in the compounds, who really believed that these people were criminals . . . I mean they also came into work every day and saw the conditions these people were living in, the shit and piss and the filth and all, conditions entirely created by themselves [the prisoners], and they just thought these are a bunch of animals.[26]

As is discussed in Chapter 4, the prisoners' dirty protest in particular resonated with a series of long-standing racist and sectarian discourses linking filthiness and immorality to Irish Catholics.[27] For some of those prison staff recruited from Northern Ireland who came almost exclusively from the Protestant community, such sectarian views may already have existed. At an institutional level, however, the internalization of the criminalisation project by some staff may be linked to the relationship between the self-image of institutions and their occupational culture and working practices.

There is a considerable business and management literature which charts the symbiotic nature of such a relationship (Hampden-Turner 1990, Elwood 1995, Shenkar and Yuchtman-Yaar 1997). Staff may internalize, adapt, or reshape the public perception of what it is they are meant to be doing, even when the origins of that perception is a product of the public relations department (Hatch and Schultz 1997) or was originally envisaged as straight forwardly propagandist. Similarly within criminal justice agencies, some scholars have explored the ways in which organizational self-image based upon discourses of professionalism, impartiality, and upholding law and order are internalized and become *believed* by staff in agencies such as the RUC (Ellison 1997, Mulcahy 1997, 1999). Once insulated from unfavourable discourses by such a self-image, any criticisms may be met with genuine outrage.[28]

The internalization of the criminalisation project by at least some elements of the headquarters and management of the prison service

---

[26] Interview with prison governor, 12 Feb. 1996.

[27] See McVeigh (1995) for a discussion of anti-Irish racism and racism in Ireland. See also Brewer and Higgins (1998) for an in-depth discussion on anti-Catholicism in Northern Ireland.

[28] 'By seeking to establish a coherent, plausible and bounded frame of understanding, the RUC, like other organisations, seeks to present itself as legitimate, both by confounding alternative and subversive narratives and by asserting the adequacy—if not the supremacy—of its own account of itself. This involves the performance of a social and organisational reality which is deemed likely to attract support and thwart criticism. What is performed here is a narrative, a story, an account' (Mulcahy 1997: 3).

can be seen from their reaction to critical comments at various junctures during the protests. For example, the critical press conference
held by the Catholic Primate of Ireland Cardinal Thomas O'Fiaich in
July 1978 in which he described the conditions in the Maze as akin to
the sewers of Calcutta (Collins 1986: 324), produced the 'furious ill-
tempered response' from the Northern Ireland Office referred to in
Chapter 4 (O'Malley 1990: 173).[29] Such a reaction was indicative of an
institution which had indeed begun to *believe* in its public position.

Similarly at the level of the staff, the public comments in the media
at the time and other outlets often displayed a considerable sympathy
to the strategy of criminalising paramilitary prisoners. The public
position of the Prison Officers Association appeared to fluctuate
between criticisms of the government placing their members 'on the
front line' and an acceptance that the government could not 'give in to
terrorist prisoners'.[30]

Apart from asserting the criminal status of paramilitary prisoners,
much of the material produced by the prison service during this era
focused upon the preferability of the physical conditions of the new
cellular prison when compared to either the compounds or other prisons in Europe.[31] The theme of a modernizing prison system, with
excellent facilities being misused and damaged by unreasonable and
recalcitrant prisoners, was a basic tenet of the public statements issued
during the dirty protest and hunger strikes.[32] The unreasonableness of

[29] 'These criminals are totally responsible for the situation in which they find themselves. It is they who have been smearing excreta on the walls and pouring urine through
cell doors. It is they who by their actions are denying themselves the excellent modern
facilities of the prison. It is they alone who are creating bad conditions out of very good
conditions. Each and every prisoner has been tried under the judicial system established
in Northern Ireland by Parliament. Those found guilty, after the due process of law, if they
are sent to prison by the courts, serve their sentence for what they are, convicted criminals'
(NIO statement in response to Cardinal O'Fiaich, cited in Beresford 1987: 185–6).

[30] Interview with Prison Officers Association spokesperson, 17 Sept. 1996.

[31] 'The Cellular Maze Prison [is] one of the most modern in Western Europe . . . one
of the most comprehensive in the facilities it provides and is administered in a humanitarian fashion' (NIO 1980*a*: 1).

[32] 'The prisoners intensified their action in March 1978 by refusing to clean their cells,
wash, or use the toilets: they damaged the furniture and fittings of the cells with the
result that everything apart from the mattresses and blankets had to be removed. In spite
of the provocation from the prisoners taking part in this extremely distasteful form of
action, prison officers have sought to deal humanely with the prisoners concerned . . .
The publicity given to the protesting prisoners at Maze . . . tends to draw attention away
from notable progress which has been made in recent years in establishing a modern
prison system with first class facilities for work, vocational training, education and
recreation' (NIPS 1979: 5).

the prisoners' behaviour was constantly juxtaposed to the reasonable-ness and professionalism of prison staff and management.[33] For some of the prison officers working on the wings, who were sustained on such institutional discourses, the critical press coverage of the prison service engendered a sense of anger and frustration.

It used to really annoy me—you would pick up a morning newspaper and read all this Provo propaganda about what was going on in the Maze and about how terrible we all were. We were doing our jobs in terrible conditions, and we were getting murdered in our homes and you still got all this guff about prison offi-cer brutality and all, it was very frustrating.[34]

At least part of the reason for the frustration of prison staff and man-agers about their apparent failure to get their story across, was the ineptitude of the prison service's public relations strategy during the protests. The Northern Ireland Office dramatically increased its public relations expenditure during this era.[35] However, much of that increase was spent in the production of relatively crude propaganda leaflets designed for international consumption, including the selective clip-ping and assembling of montages of supportive journalistic comments (e.g. NIO 1980a, 1980b, 1981a, 1981b). One former prison service pub-lic relations manager described the quality of public relations during the protests as 'crude and ineffective, particularly to an international audience'.[36]

The improvement in Sinn Fein's public relations skills, albeit with considerably more limited resources (Curtis 1984: 273), the election of Bobby Sands as MP for Fermanagh South Tyrone, and the widespread international criticism of perceived British intransigence (Beresford

---

[33] 'The cell cleaning operation was stepped up so that fouled cells were cleaned almost weekly, and during the year it was decided to repaint the cells after every fourth clean-ing. Bed linen was offered to the prisoners in an attempt to make life more comfortable, but this was rejected. A further effort to introduce an item of normal everyday living took place on November 30th when the Governor issued one chair to each protestor without any pre-conditions. Later that evening the prisoners acted in concert to destroy the chairs . . . the provocation to staff both inside and outside the prison is unique both in its nature and its extent; once again we pay tribute to the restraint, calmness and devo-tion to duty displayed by the Governor and his staff who must carry out their work in such conditions and against a background of black propaganda and murderous attacks' (NIPS 1980: 16–17).

[34] Interview with former prison officer, 12 Sept. 1996.

[35] In 1976/7 the public relations budget for the Northern Ireland Office (which includes the prison service) was £584,665. By 1979 it had risen to £1,431,237 plus £344,181 for advertising (Miller 1994: 306).

[36] Briefing by prison service public relations officer attended by author, 30 June 1993.

1987: 132) has led most commentators to conclude that the prison service lost the propaganda war on the hunger strikes (Miller 1994: 84). Such a feeling amongst some prison staff appeared to add impetus to the sense of isolation and beleaguerment, and reinforced their belief in the criminalisation project.[37]

Brutality, Violence, and Dehumanization

There are a myriad of reasons offered in the literature to explain why prison officers may resort to violence in the execution of their duties. Some researchers have referred to a 'canteen culture of violence' amongst prison officers where an alarm bell signifying a potentially violent incident leads to 'a frisson of excitement that rushes around the prison like adrenaline' (King and McDermott 1995: 128). Staff violence has also been described as a response to a breakdown in order in a prison (Cavadino and Dignan 1997); a deterrent to, or revenge for, inmate violence (Kauffman 1988: 141); an expression of staff power over the inmates (Abbott 1981); an indication that prison officers may feel undervalued (Fitzgerald and Sim 1982: 123); evidence that prison staff may enjoy de facto impunity from prosecution or accountability (Scraton, Sim, and Skidmore 1991) or due to the personality or psychological make-up of individual officers.

As discussed above, while Northern Ireland prison staff and management tended to discount allegations of staff violence during the criminalisation protests as 'black propaganda' (NIPS 1980: 17), the truth is that prisoners were indeed subject to harsh beatings, scaldings, and humiliations. The written accounts of the prisoners themselves (Campbell, McKeown, and O'Hagan 1994), the descriptions told to other writers (Beresford 1987, O'Malley 1990, Taylor 1997) and international human rights bodies (Amnesty International 1980) as well as to the current author are fairly consistent. It appears unlikely that many prison officers were held accountable for such actions during that period.[38]

---

[37] *Interviewer*. What impact did all the negative publicity have on you and your colleagues?

Respondent. None at all as far as I was concerned. It just made me more determined to get the job done, more determined that the paramilitaries would not be victorious. (Interview with former prison officer, 12 Sept. 1996).

[38] The author was unable to access archival material relating to disciplinary proceedings taken against prison staff during the criminalisation era. However, in the interviews conducted with prison staff and managers who worked at the Maze at the time, no one

The potential for violent interchanges between staff and prisoners was clearly linked to the protest tactics of the prisoners. For example, when in 1978 the prisoners began their dirty protest, the exchanges over the contents of the prisoners' chamber pots often led to violent clashes (Clarke 1987: 72). The forced washing of prisoners could only be achieved by excessive use of force.[39] In the latter part of 1978 the prison administration introduced wing shifts wherein all men in one wing were moved to an empty wing, the walls and floors of the fouled cells were cleaned, and a pattern of forced moves every 6–7 days was established (Campbell, McKeown, and O'Hagan 1994: 49). The constant rotation of prisoners and an awareness that the prisoners were maintaining communications with the IRA on the outside through comms, provided the rationale for increased use of mirror searches where a number of prison officers would forcibly make a prisoner squat over a mirror while his anus, mouth, scrotum, and other areas were probed.[40]

The brutality and violence of some prison staff during this era may be understood on a number of levels.

At a strategic level, the objective of prison staff was to make the conditions for protesting prisoners so unbearable that they would be forced to come off the protest and join the conforming prisoners. Violence became a tactic designed to defeat the prisoners. Of a total of approximately 700 Republican prisoners held in cellular accommodation at the Maze, the number of protesting prisoners fluctuated from

could remember any such proceedings against staff. As the interview below suggests, staff appeared to enjoy considerable immunity for such activities.

Interviewer. Do you remember any staff being disciplined or sacked as a result of the beatings of prisoners?

Respondent. To be honest I don't remember many disciplinary proceedings against staff. I don't think the Provos [IRA] would have used the complaints mechanisms much in those days and given the working conditions and the fact that their colleagues were being murdered on the outside, I don't think staff would have been forthcoming. . . . Besides admitting to any illicit activity would have been seen as bad for morale, playing into the hands of the IRA propaganda of which there was a lot. (Interview with prison governor, 14 July 1997)

[39] 'It was a frightening experience. You're sitting in your cell and you have a long beard, long hair, you're filthy, and six big men come in, trail you up the wing by the feet, throw you into the bath and scrub you, shave you. They're wearing rubber gloves and all the rest. Every hair on your body they shave off, and then they throw you back in the cell' (Brendan Hughes, IRA OC during the dirty protest, cited in Stevenson 1996: 97–8).

[40] 'The wing shifts really marked a downward turn. More contact with screws meant more beatings, mirror searches, de-lousings and scalding baths, it was terrifying.' Interview with former IRA blanketman, 1 Dec. 1997.

around 300 in 1978 to almost 500 in 1980 (NIPS 1978: 5, Campbell, McKeown, and O'Hagan 1994: 107). As one former prison officer told the author, 'the clear objective was to whittle down the number of protesting prisoners, and increase the numbers on the conforming wings, it was that simple'.[41] Violence and humiliation were entirely consistent with that objective.

There were also a number of possible organizational explanations for the violent conduct of staff. The prison authorities had considerable difficulties in recruiting and maintaining staff members. The dropout rate for prison officers rose dramatically with the introduction of criminalization from one in five in 1975 to one in three in 1976.[42] Given such difficulties, the staff shortages during the 1970s in the prison service (exacerbated by the construction of the labour intensive cellular Maze) led to only the most peripheral screening of recruits (Taylor 1997: 220).[43] Given the poor calibre of some recruits, often placed in the most difficult of working conditions with only minimal training,[44] and an ongoing campaign of assassinations against them and their colleagues, considerable staff violence against prisoners was predictable.

At a more personal level, however, clearly staff brutality was linked to a process wherein the prisoners became dehumanized in the eyes of the prison officers. As discussed above, the dirty protest in particular resonated with sectarian anti-Catholic discourses concerning dirtiness and immorality. Such prejudice dovetailed with the mechanisms used to carry out the cleaning operations, wing shift, and mirror searches, all of which encouraged a depersonalized attitude to the prisoners. In the unreal scatological environment of the protesting wings, prison officers hosed cells and sometimes prisoners at pressures of 160 lbs per square inch (Clarke 1987: 75). As discussed previously, when these were replaced by industrial steam cleaners following an infestation of white maggots, lice, and scabies, the prison officers wore aluminium astronaut-like suits to carry out their tasks. As the photographs and accounts of the time highlight, the protesting prisoners, with their long hair and beards, naked, pale, and smelling of excrement, appeared less than human to those officers who were already predisposed to view and treat them as such.

---

[41] Interview with former prison officer, 19 Sept. 1996.

[42] *Irish Times* (7 Dec. 1977), 'Hard Times for Her Majesty's Prison Service'.

[43] Interview with former governor, HMP Maze, 20 Apr. 1999.

[44] 'In the 1970s it was bums on seats even before you had finished your basic training.' Interview with former governor, HMP Maze, 13 Aug. 1997.

Hothouse Management and Political and Security Interference

The phenomenon I am interested in is the people who have been around for twenty years, and I know most of them, people who made decisions that today we would think that was stupid. But they were all able, well intentioned, rational people who sat down with no particular agenda, well OK their agenda may have been set at some times by ministers, but they came to what they thought were rational decisions.[45]

The fourth element which characterized the management of paramilitary prisoners during the criminalisation era was a fusion of hothouse management with more direct input from ministers in the day to day running of the prisons. This was a scenario in which the already highly pressurized context of staff/inmate relations in the prisons was further complicated by increased interference from political and security sources which obscured the ability to make effective judgements on prison management. 'Hothouse management' was a phrase used by one prominent prison governor to describe decision-making processes wherein managers and policy-makers became so immersed in institutional dynamics, political pressures, and competing security configurations that they appeared to lose sight of broader political realities:

Decisions during the hunger strikes and dirty protests became so pressurized that looking back on it some of our people took their eye off the ball. As various people such as the Cardinal and the Irish Commission for Justice and Peace tried to make interventions around issues like civilian type clothing, we had lengthy discussions about what this meant, what would be the consequences in terms of the proliferation of laundry, how would the washing get done and so on, it was crazy but that is how it was. Hothouse management I called it, people under pressure who were not able to see the consequences of their decisions because they couldn't see the wood for the trees.[46]

At least part of the reason for the pressure on prison managers was the extension of ministerial influence deep into operational matters such as the wearing of prison uniforms. The relationship between what constitutes policy (and therefore legitimately falls within ministerial interest) and operational matters is often deliberately obfuscated in the management of prisons (Lewis 1997). Similar tensions have been observed elsewhere between headquarters-based managers and

---

[45] Interview with former governor, HMP Maze, 20 Apr. 1999.
[46] Interview with prison governor, 12 Feb. 1996.

managers within the prisons (Sparks, Bottoms, and Hay 1996: 134–9). However, the argument with regard to the era of criminalisation in Northern Ireland, in particular during the hunger strikes, is that in effect the running of one prison (the Maze) became of such central political significance that it became a political virility test at cabinet and prime ministerial level.[47] Even for those who were predisposed to find a resolution to the stand-off, the direct involvement of Mrs Thatcher in the dispute arguably lessened the room for pragmatic manoeuvrability.[48]

Policy formulation during this period was further complicated by the involvement of the British foreign office, the British foreign intelligence service MI6, and the domestic intelligence service MI5. Given their focus on the international damage to Britain's reputation, the Foreign Office have been widely reputed as having had a generally more conciliatory approach to the resolution of the hunger strike issue. Former Foreign Office Under-Secretary Ian Gilmour has acknowledged a 'difference of emphasis' from their colleagues at the NIO (O'Malley 1990: 197).

MI6, apparently with the agreement of the Foreign Office, had opened a direct line of secret negotiations with IRA representatives during the first and second hunger strikes, taking an apparently less confrontational line than the stated government position (Taylor 1997: 234, 247).[49] Operationally both MI5 and MI6 came under the direct control of the Ulster Security Liaison Committee (comprising

[47] 'It was perfectly clear to me and the prime minister and the rest of the cabinet that there was no way in which we were going to give in to the demands of the hunger strikers. It is said, and quite rightly, that she [Mrs Thatcher] was quite determined that we were not going to give in to the prisoners' demands. But I was no less determined. If I had been overruled in the cabinet and they said no, we'll have to give in to this, I would have resigned, I felt that strongly about it. She has a reputation in all sorts of fields for being fairly tough; in this particular case I was just as tough as she was and so was everybody else' (Humphrey Atkins, NI Secretary of State, cited in O'Malley 1990: 195).

[48] Garrett Fitzgerald, Irish Prime Minister at the time, recounts an interesting tale in his autobiography. At a particular juncture of the hunger strike, just after a visit by the Irish Commission for Justice and Peace had drawn up a document which Fitzgerald had hoped would contain a compromise acceptable to the prisoners, he met with the then NIO Minister of State Michael Allison. 'He [Michael Allison] gave the impression that he wanted to be more conciliatory but referred to "the lady behind the veil", namely the British Prime Minister' (Fitzgerald 1991: 368).

[49] This channel of communication between the British government and the IRA had existed since the 1975 ceasefire. It was reactivated in 1990 when the British government authorized secret discussions with senior Republicans Martin McGuinness and Gerry Kelly (Mallie and McKittrick 1996: 104).

representatives of MI6, MI5, the SAS, and RUC Special Branch (Greer 1995: 47–8). In practice, however, relations were strained and MI5 were considered the more hawkish in their approach to the hunger strikes as with other security-related issues (Block and Fitzgerald 1983). The result of these competing institutional priorities from the security services, and increased cabinet input into policy formulation from a Conservative administration less mindful to compromise, was further to narrow any opportunity for pragmatism amongst prison managers which might have existed.[50]

It would be wrong, however, to view such security and political influence as illiberal impositions from above on an otherwise rational and progressive tier of senior prison managers. At least some prison managers operated within a belief system which did not make them mindful to compromise with the terrorists.[51] Rather, what is being suggested here is that in a hierarchical institution such as the prison service, the impact of such a myriad of influences was to compress policy options, obscure more enlightened alternatives, and internalize a set of discourses which viewed compromise as analogous to surrender.

Conclusion

As is discussed in greater detail in Chapter 4, the hunger strikes ended on Saturday, 3 October 1981, following sustained interventions by the prisoners' families. The view of the prisoners was that they had failed to achieve their demands, in essence that they had lost. However, the pyrrhic nature of the government's victory was highlighted by the widespread international criticism of British intransigence, the emergence of Sinn Fein as a political force, and the granting of at least some of the prisoners' demands within a short period of the end of the protest. Secretary of State Jim Prior announced at a press conference a few days later that prisoners could wear their own clothes, 50 per cent

---

[50] 'We used to have meetings attended by the senior people from Maze management, the prisons minister, NIO and various spooks. Sometimes they argued amongst each other and sometimes they just condescended to those of us who actually worked in the prison service . . . it is no wonder it was such a balls up.' Interview with former prison governor, 12 Feb. 1996.

[51] Indeed some commentators have suggested that the individual personality of the governor at the Maze during this era was itself an impediment to the resolution of protests (Taylor 1997: 247). For a discussion on the influence of the modern prison governor on the ethos or culture of their prisons see Sparks, Hay, and Bottoms (1996: 137–9).

remission was returned, limited free association was granted, and prison work was narrowly defined to include only a small number of activities which prisoners could refuse to do without significant loss of privilege (O'Malley 1990). While the concessions which followed the end of the hunger strikes by no means heralded the reacceptance of political motivation, they did signify that the continued commitment to criminalisation would be tempered by considerably greater flexibility and pragmatism.

The increasingly rigid adherence to the principles of criminalisation as the prisoners stepped up their protest in the late 1970s obscured the origins of the policy as a means of managing political violence. At some stage in the deteriorating spiral of relations a management strategy became transmogrified into a series of ill-defined political principles which inevitably presented obstacles to effective management within the prisons. Unflinching rule enforcement, the internalization of propagandist positions, the dehumanization and brutalization of prisoners, and a lack of clarity in policy formulation interacted with a series of other ebbing and flowing influences on prison management over the period to produce an inflexible and unwielding policy which ultimately failed in its stated objective.

10

Managerialism, 1981–2000

Introduction

The period in the running of Northern Ireland's prisons between 1981 and 2000 is one that I have characterized in the chapter that follows as dominated by notions of managerialism.[1] In the wake of the political and managerial disaster of the hunger strike period, prison managers throughout the 1980s adopted increasingly pragmatic attitudes in their relations with prisoners. Such an approach did not signal the end to the objective of criminalising political motivation. The denial, undermining, and delimitation of political motivation remained as a key element of government prison policy in Northern Ireland, at least until the latter stages of the peace process in the mid-1990s. It was not, however, the only element of government policy. Managerialism arguably facilitated a more subtle pursuit of a broader range of responses to paramilitarism in the prisons. These responses were less ideologically rigid than criminalisation, increasingly technocratic, and varied widely from the most flexible and pragmatic to the most determined and impractical. Viewed as a whole over the period in question these may accurately be considered as a very different model of management for dealing with paramilitary prisoners.

Managerialism in the context of Northern Ireland prisons was characterized by a number of features during this period, not all of which were entirely consistent or wholly compatible.

Firstly, managerialism represented an increased acceptance that the prison system could not serve as a mechanism that would defeat political violence. As is discussed in the previous chapter, the experience of the hunger strikes with its associated levels of violence, negative

---

[1] With colleagues, the author has previously written of this period as one of normalization of relations between prison managers and paramilitary prisoners in Northern Ireland (see Gormally, McEvoy, and Wall 1993). The weaknesses in that explanatory construct are detailed below as well as the particular variant on the notion of 'managerialism' which I argue developed in the Northern Ireland prison system over the period.

international publicity, and the prison-related mobilization of Sinn Fein had clearly underlined the destabilizing consequences of making the prisons the key battleground with paramilitarism. The subsequent managerialist approach to dealing with such prisoners was under-pinned by an increased recognition of the limitations of the prisons in broader conflict management terms. Prisons became (at least until the period of the ceasefires) a place for managing the consequences of the conflict while the military or political solution was sought elsewhere. As in the period up until 1976, managerialism saw the prisons become the sites for holding the captured combatants rather than the battle-ground upon which their struggle could be beaten.

Secondly, managerialism within the prisons mirrored the develop-ment of policies and practices in other aspects of political and public life in Northern Ireland which increasingly came to see conflict and sectarian division as a feature which required management rather than resolution. The management of political violence required the sharp-ening of a number of strategies and techniques such as Emergency leg-islation, more specialized anti-terrorist policing strategies including a centralization of intelligence gathering, and shoot to kill operations against suspected terrorists (Ní Aoláin 2000). Crucially, however, as noted above, these were no longer presented as the means by which ter-rorism would be defeated but rather as techniques designed to curtail its impact or effectiveness while normal state management and policy-making continued. Within the prisons, the Northern Ireland prison service was to present and increasingly understand the management of paramilitary prisoners as one special client group amongst others such as young offenders, sex offenders, remandees, and so forth rather than the central relationship which defined its activities.

While managerial good practice in dealing with such prisoners required, to some extent, understanding and engaging with the reality of the political motivation of the various factions, this was presented and indeed understood as a technical rather than ideological question. Pragmatic engagement with paramilitary prisoners could be viewed within a paradigm of good management. It became sensible, narrow dialogue focused upon the minutiae of prison life rather than grand questions of political status.

Thirdly, as with the prison service in Britain, the Northern Ireland prison service became increasingly influenced by wider changes in pub-lic policy in Britain under the Thatcher government. These changes sought to transform the public sector bureaucracies into more efficient, effective, and value for money endeavours by inculcating private sector management and planning techniques in the delivery of services. Such changes were neither apolitical nor ideology free, but they were not primarily concerned with the struggle over political motivation with Northern Ireland paramilitaries. While these initiatives did not have a direct impact on prison management until the late 1980s, they did, however, provide a legitimating framework for a set of scientific and instrumentalist discourses to justify practices that had emerged in any case in the prisons after the hunger strike era. Relations with paramilitary prisoners became framed within strategic and business plans, key performance indicators, and the avoidance of unnecessary confrontation which was disruptive, expensive, and inefficient.

Fourthly, managerialism was characterized by ongoing attempts to demarcate and limit the power of paramilitaries within the prisons. Managerialism was not surrender, rather it involved a more careful choice of battlegrounds and more subtle ways of undermining paramilitary influence. Such strategies included the opening of Maghaberry prison in 1987,[2] a prison where excellent physical conditions and the hinted prospect of earlier release (particularly for life sentenced prisoners) was an implicit inducement for paramilitary prisoners to leave the segregated conditions at the Maze and serve their sentence in a normal integrated setting. Quarantining paramilitarism meant a series of gestures by prison management where a line was drawn in the sand, (e.g. on issues such as inter-wing association or the segregation of remand prisoners); this line was defended vigorously, and when positions became untenable or were overrun, this was followed by partial concessions and then a collective regrouping for the next battle.

Fifthly, managerialism saw the emergence of relative autonomy amongst prison managers in the formulation of policy and the delivery of services in the prisons. The changes in the style of interaction with paramilitary prisoners were not necessarily the result of a centrally determined and promulgated policy at ministerial level. As with reactive containment and criminalisation, while the personalities of various Secretaries of State and Prime Ministers were important during the period of managerialism (e.g. Jim Prior at the end of the hunger strike), the general absence of direct interference from Downing Street and the growth in the independence of prison managers encouraged greater

---

[2] The female part of Maghaberry prison opened the previous year in early 1986 and the old female prison at Armagh was closed (NIPS 1987: 1).

sensitivity in relations with prisoners in certain instances. Increased influence by prison managers at both institution and headquarters level was neither universal nor necessarily progressive. None the less, it did permit a greater flexibility for such managers in responding to prisoners' demands in comparison to, for example, the hothouse management which had effectively frozen any potential for pragmatic accommodation in the most demanding days of the hunger strikes.

Sixthly, the final defining characteristic of managerialism is its continued adherence to the formal policy of criminalisation and refusal to internalize the reality of political motivation. As is argued above, managerialism did permit, in some instances, a more flexible and arguably more subtle criminalisation agenda than that which had gone before. For example, processes designed to wean paramilitaries away from the Maze, to Maghaberry were handled sensitively, and focused primarily upon prisoners' personal decisions to give up violence to achieve political objectives rather than forcing such prisoners to accept the status of a criminal rather than that of a political prisoner.[3] However, the tenacity with which prison management and their ministerial overseers clung to the remnants of the criminalisation agenda and their failure to accept the clear logic of their increased recognition of political motivation became a key structural impediment in the wake of the first IRA and Loyalist ceasefires in 1994.

These features may be understood as components of the heuristic model of managerialism that I will argue characterized the management of paramilitary prisoners from 1981 onwards in Northern Ireland.

Before considering that period in more detail, two further points should be made at this juncture. Firstly, as with any attempt to examine historical trends over such a period, the managerial model inevitably involves some moulding and shaping of propositions and events in order to illuminate better the arguments being made. This means that, for example, the issues discussed are not necessarily arranged chronologically but rather developed in a thematic fashion.

---

[3] 'When I decided to leave the Wings at the Kesh [Maze] no screw or governor ever tried to suggest to me that this meant that I was accepting being a criminal. That would have been totally counter-productive from their perspective if the move had any tinge of shame or apology about it. All that was ever said was look, [name], nobody is saying this means that you are not a Republican, it just means that you don't think that the armed struggle is the way forward.' Interview with former INLA prisoner who left the Maze and moved to the integrated wings at Maghaberry, 5 Dec. 1993.

Secondly, as with the other models in this book, managerialism is a model drawn from particular historical events rather than an attempt to describe all of the events of note that occurred in Northern Ireland's prisons over this period. With such licence acknowledged, I will contest that these characteristics collectively represent a different style of prison management from that which had gone before.

What is Managerialism?

While the term managerialism is used throughout this chapter to explicate the changes in the style of prison management in Northern Ireland between 1981 and 1999, the term has a specific meaning in the literature of public administration and political science. It is often used to describe the process by which the public sector in Britain was radically transformed from the early 1980s onwards under the Conservative government. As is discussed below, the influence of such changes in Britain arguably did not impact upon the Northern Ireland prison service in a direct structural fashion until the late 1980s. However, given that some of the characteristics of what is now widely understood as managerialism (such as increased autonomy for managers) were at least part of Northern Ireland prison service *culture* from the very early 1980s, and the significance of the term throughout this chapter, it is important to be clear at this early juncture as to what is traditionally understood by managerialism.

Managerialism and the Public Sector in Britain

Managerialism emerged from the early 1980s as a key paradigm for operating and understanding the public sector in Britain and the USA (Hood 1991, Pollitt 1993, Clarke, Cochrane, and McLaughlin 1994, Kickert 1997). Its meaning and influence have been well described as 'a cultural formation and a distinctive set of ideologies and practices which form one of the underpinnings of an emergent political settlement . . . Managerialism . . . is shaping the remaking of the British state—its institutions and practices as well as its culture and ideology' (Clarke and Newman 1997: p.ix). Quite apart from its influence at the cultural and ideological level, managerialism changed the key public services which directly impact upon the lives of almost every citizen in Britain.

In essence, and with considerable variations across different government departments, managerialism was based on the premise that the introduction of private sector principles and practices into the management of the public sector could improve efficiency and effectiveness as well as reduce costs. As the then Secretary of State for the Environment Michael Heseltine argued in 1980, 'Efficient management is the key to the [national] revival . . . And the management ethos must run through our national life—private and public companies, civil service, nationalised industries, local government, the National Health Service' (Heseltine quoted in Pollitt 1993: p.vi). While the origins of managerialism may be partially traced to the political philosophy of new right politicians, it has also to be attributed to a series of broader global and international megatrends in governance (Hood 1991).[4] Initially managerialism was concerned primarily with overcoming the deficits of the bureaucratic ways of the machinery of government (Clarke and Newman 1997: 20). However, from the mid-1980s onwards other features such as market mechanisms, business techniques, and the creation of a culture of 'public entrepreneurship' in the state sector began to be pressed more vigorously (Osborne and Gaebler 1992).

Dunleavy and Hood (1994: 9) have simplified managerialism-inspired changes as follows:

- Reconfiguring budgets to be more transparent, with greater emphasis on outputs, not inputs, the former being measured by quantitative performance indicators.
- A view of organizations as a chain of low cost principal–agent relationships connected by a network of contracts linking incentives to performance.
- Disaggregating distinct functions within organizations into quasi-contractual or market forms, with a purchaser/provider distinction replacing previously unified planning and provision structures.
- Opening up provider functions to competition between agencies or between public agencies, firms, or not-for-profit organizations.
- Deconcentrating provider roles to the minimum feasible sized agency.

Managerialism was implemented through a series of government programmes throughout the 1980s. These included the Financial

---

[4] Hood (1991) argues that 'New Public Management' or managerialism is one of five megatrends in public administration together with 'less government', 'internationalisation', 'privatisation', and 'automation'.

Management Initiatives scheme, the creation of Next Steps Agencies, and the division of the provider/consumer functions in areas such as the National Health Service, central government agencies of the welfare state, and the education system (Pollitt 1993, Cutler and Waine 1994).

The Financial Management Initiatives, which began in 1982, were designed to inject the principles of budgeting and best practice of the commercial sphere into public bodies with an emphasis upon the three Es of Economy, Efficiency, and Effectiveness to be achieved and monitored through the introduction of performance indicators. Next Steps took this process one stage further as former government departments became Agencies with devolved budgets, greater managerial autonomy, and targets against which progress could be measured. The purchaser/provider divide was designed to separate formally the elements of various parts of institutions such as the National Health system between those who required and paid for particular services and those who were contracted to deliver them. Such a bifurcation was intended to create internal markets, encourage competition, dismantle monopolistic service provision arrangements, and thus improve efficiency (Salter 1993).

Initially the encroachment of managerialism into the criminal justice system was slower than in other parts of public administration in Britain. This was in part a result of the high political priority afforded to law and order and consequent willingness of the Conservatives to increase public spending on institutions such as the police. It was also associated with the peculiarities of elements of the criminal justice system (e.g. the independence of the courts system) which left them somewhat 'culturally segregated' from events in other parts of the public administration (Raine and Wilson 1997: 82). However, with crime rates rising despite increased expenditure the Conservative government became increasingly frustrated at the criminal justice system's failure to deliver, and it too became vulnerable to a range of managerialist strategies designed to encourage the various agencies to 'get their house in order' (McLaughlin and Muncie 1994: 117).

The criminal justice system as a whole was encouraged to act in a more *systemic* fashion (Bottoms 1995) with varying changes introduced across the probation service, the Home Office and the court service, the police, and the prison service. The strategies applied to the criminal justice system included the application of the Financial Management Initiative scheme, the construction of performance indicators, the use of management information systems, and, from the late

1980s onwards, scrutiny by the Audit Commission and the National Audit Office (Newburn 1995: 175). Such moves had far-reaching consequences.[5]

Within the English and Welsh prison systems, the principal managerialist focus were the Fresh Start package which dramatically altered management and working practices (King and McDermott 1991), and the encouragement of both fully privatized prisons and the contracting out of certain aspects of prison service delivery, and the granting of agency status to the prison service.

Fresh Start followed a critical report from a joint investigation between the Prison Department and a group of management consultants into the operation of the shift systems worked by prison officers (England and Wales Prison Service 1986). The report found that prisons could run safely and efficiently if prison officers worked an average of eight hours a week less in overtime. The then Home Secretary Douglas Hurd claimed that the report represented 'a telling indictment of . . . [existing] . . . working practices and made recommendations for a new system which would release large amounts of now unproductive capacity which ought to be used for other purposes.' (King and McDermott 1995: 29). Restrictive working practices such as the supervision of areas where there were no prisoners to supervise and lucrative overtime shifts were to be ended and governors' autonomy was to be limited by making them answerable to area managers within a new framework designed to 'make everyone accountable to someone' (Newburn 1995: 174).

While initially reluctant to countenance prison privatization,[6] a number of pro-privatization reports from the Home Affairs Select Committee and the Adam Smith Institute and intensive lobbying by

[5] For example, the application of the Financial Management Initiative to the probation service led to the production of the Statement of National Objectives and Priorities (SNOP) in 1984, and increasingly centralized control over activities and planning of all local probation services (Mair 1997). The court service was restructured to process cases more quickly and efficiently with greater powers delegated to magistrates' clerks and stipendiary magistrates, a range of system-flow-improving initiatives introduced and increased use of 'paper courts' in which guilty pleas were accepted in writing (Raine and Wilson 1997: 83). Similarly the police were increasingly asked to demonstrate their managerial effectiveness, value for money, and so forth with a revamped HM Inspectorate of Police and intense scrutiny by the Audit Commission in the late 1980s (McLaughlin and Muncie 1994: 128–32).

[6] 'I do not think there is a case, and I do not believe that the House would accept a case for auctioning or privatising the prisons or handing over the business of keeping prisoners safe to anyone other than government services.' Home Secretary Douglas Hurd, *Hansard*, HC (Series VI) vol 119, cols 1299 (16 July 1987).

backbench Conservatives saw a change of policy with the government recommending the contracting out of court and escort duties in the Green Paper of 1988 (Home Office 1988). In effect the advocates of privatization drew a distinction between the allocation and delivery of punishment (Sparks 1994: 23). By the time of the passage of the Criminal Justice Act in 1991 the potential for contracting out had been expanded beyond ancillary services to include any type of prison. In 1992 the Wolds remand prison under the management of Group Four became the first private prison in Britain for over a century (Morgan 1997). Wolds was followed by the opening of a number of further private prisons and further provisions for the contracting out of ancillary services such as education and catering. As Cavadino and Dignan conclude 'In a remarkably short period of time, therefore, prison privatisation in England & Wales has progressed from being a seemingly outlandish proposal to a fiercely competitive multi-million pound market' (Cavadino and Dignan 1997: 159).

The third significant element of the managerialist agenda for prisons was the establishment of the English and Welsh prison service as a Next Steps Agency in 1993. In the foreword to the *Annual Report* of 1993–4, chief executive Derek Lewis wrote that the 'move to Agency status signaled the beginning of fundamental changes designed to make the Prison Service a more effective, better performing organisation' (England and Wales Prison Service 1995, foreword). The Lygo Report into the management of the prison service which had recommended the introduction of agency status in 1991 concluded that the key factor in the success or failure of the new arrangement would be the ability of ministers to allow the prison service to operate in an almost autonomous mode while retaining the responsibility to parliament for overall policy (Livingstone and Owen 1999: 25). However, the constant political interference in operational matters by Home Secretary Michael Howard (Lewis 1997) and two official reports which have been highly critical of prison service management[7] have ensured that the exact nature of the relationship between the Home Secretary and the prison service agency has remained a controversial one.

Managerialism and the Northern Ireland Public Sector

Throughout the 1980s Northern Ireland was generally spared some of the more dramatic changes to economic and social policies which

---

[7] The reports were the Woodcock and Learmount investigations into high profile escapes from Whitemoor Special Unit and Parkhurst prison respectively.

affected the rest of the United Kingdom under the Thatcher government (Gaffikin and Morrissey 1990). While the electricity service was privatized, trust status was initiated for hospitals and social services, and compulsory competitive tendering was introduced for a number of local council services, changes to the public sector were less marked than in Britain and overall public spending remained comparatively high.[8] As Morison (1998: 114) notes, managerialism in the public sector in Northern Ireland arrived relatively late and without some of the initial enthusiasm that marked its introduction in Britain.

The slow read across may be accounted for by a number of factors. One factor was the rather different role of senior civil servants in Northern Ireland. Many senior civil servants assumed considerably enhanced power and policy-making influence under direct rule when British ministers often only spent a couple of days per week in the jurisdiction (Loughlin 1992, Morison and Livingstone 1995: 154). In addition, the extreme over-reliance of the Northern Ireland economy on the public sector for employment[9] created fears, even amongst the most Thatcherite of Conservative Ministers, that radical downsizing might be politically destabilizing in the jurisdiction (Gaffikin and Morrisey 1990). Finally, the very distinct structure of public administration in Northern Ireland in areas such as housing and local government encouraged a view that it should be treated differently (Connolly and Loughlin 1990). That said, while Northern Ireland was by and large spared the zeal of such drives as privatization, increased emphasis upon greater efficiency, target setting, performance indicators, agency, and the other aspects of managerialism, they have gradually become an integral part of public sector ideology and practices.

Managerialism and the Northern Ireland Prison Service

In 1988 the six departments of the Northern Ireland civil service were split into ten responsibility centres and requested to develop a strategic plan for the coming year under an initiative known as MIS (Management Information Systems). The prison service was one of the responsibility centres. After consultation with the senior policy

---

[8] Hewitt (1990) notes that in 1987 public expenditure in Northern Ireland per head of the population was 50% higher than in the rest of the United Kingdom.

[9] Over 40% of the workforce in Northern Ireland is directly employed in the public sector in Northern Ireland. However, as the agricultural and construction elements of the economy rely heavily upon public expenditure it is likely that well over half of all employment in the region is funded directly or indirectly by the state (Coopers and Lybrand 1996).

group,[10] strategic objectives were agreed with the prison minister and given to prison governors to implement. The NIPS *Annual Report* for that year noted that 'Along with all the areas of the public sector, the Prison Service has become increasingly conscious of the resources it consumes and the need to use them efficiently and economically. The public purse is not bottomless and resources spent on prisons cannot be spent elsewhere' (NIPS 1989: 2). That *Annual Report* also outlined for the first time the NIPS aims and objectives. These had been developed by the 'senior management' of the service (NIPS 1989: 4).[11] In addition a range of performance indicators were developed, although not published in the *Annual Report* (NIPS 1989: 29).

The reasons identified for the need for such a planning system were to develop and respond to changes in the prison population and over-provision of staff and accommodation; to produce efficiency savings and establish priorities for funding;[12] to develop proactive manage-

---

[10] The senior policy group is made up of the governors of the various prisons, the Controller (or Chief Executive) of prisons, and the senior headquarters-based officials of the Northern Ireland prison service.

[11] Aim and Objectives of the Northern Ireland Prison Service

The aim of the Northern Ireland Prison Service is to hold in secure and humane confinement persons who have been given into custody by the courts and to reduce the risk of re-offending by encouraging them to take full advantage of the opportunities offered during their confinement.

Within that aim specific objectives are:

(a) To keep in custody, with the degree of security and control by staff appropriate to each individual, persons committed to custody by the courts: and to produce or release them as required.

(b) To provide for all prisoners the necessities of life, including accommodation, food, exercise, health care and freedom to practise religion; and to provide the opportunity to engage in constructive activities, such as work, education, training, hobbies and sport, to fill at least the working day.

(c) To enable all prisoners to retain links with their families and to assist sentenced prisoners in their preparation for release into the community.

(d) To treat prisoners as individuals regardless of their religious beliefs or political opinions; and, as far as possible, to offer them the opportunity to serve their sentences free from paramilitary influence.

(e) To manage the resources allocated to the Prison Service economically and efficiently and, in particular, to enhance the morale and abilities of staff by providing the appropriate conditions of service, management structures and training. (NIPS 1989: 4)

[12] Northern Ireland has long been the most expensive place in the United Kingdom to incarcerate prisoners. For example, in 1998 the average cost per prisoner in Northern Ireland was £76,252 compared to an average cost of £24,473 for England and Wales (NI Affairs Committee 1998: p. vi). This actually represented a reduction in the Northern Ireland prison service by 15% over the past four years. The average cost per prisoner in 1988 was £56,255 (NIPS 1989).

ment; to develop a common approach to decision-making across all prisons and to improve performance and develop a corporate identity leading to a commitment to a common goal.[13] This exercise has been accurately described as 'an internal top down kind of process'[14] and criticized for the lack of ownership it engendered at the lower ranks in the service.[15]

Despite those weaknesses, the 1988/9 process may rightly be regarded as a watershed in the development of prison management in Northern Ireland. Since then, the process of planning has become infinitely more sophisticated and embedded in prison service culture and working practices,[16] the service became an agency in 1995, and 'key performance indicators' have become increasingly refined and specific. The year 1988 is not, however, a watershed simply because it marked the beginning of these various processes. It is true that the aim and objectives of the Northern Ireland prison service as outlined in 1989 have remained largely unchanged since then (NIPS 1999: 6). However, I believe that the real significance of that process was that it represented an attempt by the prison service senior management not only to articulate what exactly the prison service was meant to do but also to acknowledge and begin to promote the ways in which the prison

---

[13] Interview with prison governor, 9 Apr. 1998. This governor was one of those tasked with drawing up the strategic plan.

[14] Evidence of the chief executive of Northern Ireland Prison Agency Alan Shannon to the Northern Ireland Affairs Committee, 29 Apr. 1998, 10.

[15] Interview with prison governor, 9 Apr. 1998.

[16] The MIS initiative in 1989 has been followed by a range of managerial initiatives similar to those introduced in England and Wales. By way of illustration, the first of these followed a considerably more sophisticated strategic planning process in 1990 which produced a strategic plan entitled 'Serving the Community' published in 1991. This process involved greater consultation with staff and, as is discussed below, a range of stakeholder organizations outside the prison service. The prison service established a Management Support Unit as an in-house consultancy service to assist headquarters and governors in staffing, target setting, measuring effectiveness, and assessing value for money (NIPS 1992: 36). In 1993 the service drew up and published business plans and work was begun on a series of establishment contracts and plans for increased civilianization were announced under the Manpower Reforms Initiative (NIPS 1994: 1). In 1995 the prison service key targets and performance were published (NIPS 1996: 4–5) and in 1996/7 the prison service launched its Prison Service Review designed 'to improve organisational effectiveness' as well as a number of 'Prior Options Studies' on a range of services to prisoners such as the works department, pharmacy, and catering to consider their viability for contracting out (NIPS 1997: 18). In 1998/9 the prison service conducted an assessment to determine its readiness for the Investors in People accreditation, as well as a major staff reduction programme in light of the early release of paramilitary prisoners (NIPS 1999: 3–4).

service had actually changed during the 1980s, to say what they were actually doing.

Managerialism as the Articulation of Existing Ideology and Working Practices

As is detailed below, my argument is that the development of the aim and objectives by the prison service senior management team in 1987/8, subsequently elaborated upon in the 1991 Strategic Plan, were an articulation of what was already happening in the prison service. The aim and objectives were descriptive rather than aspirational. They represented an acknowledgement that the goalposts had in effect been both moved and narrowed. The purpose of prison management was no longer framed in macro conflict management objectives (such as the imposition of criminalisation or the defeat of the terrorists in the prisons) but rather presented as a more limited and technical set of institutional objectives. As Garland (1996: 459) has argued, managerialism encourages criminal justice agencies to be evaluated by internal goals 'rather than by reference to social goals such as reducing crime, catching criminal or reforming inmates, all of which involve too many contingencies and uncertainties'.

This is precisely what happened regarding the management of paramilitaries in Northern Ireland. Prison managers drew up the criteria by which they should be judged, as Garland puts it, on the basis of what the organization *does* rather than what it *achieves* (Garland 1996: 458). The emphasis in the 1988 *Annual Report* on security, amenability to the court, family links, facilities, and resource management could have been written for any prison service. As is detailed below, the commitment to 'as far as possible, offer' prisoners the opportunity to serve their sentences free from paramilitary influence was a candid acknowledgement of the changes which had occurred in the prison service throughout the 1980s.

In one sense, the process between 1987 and 1991 of defining what the prison service was meant to do may be viewed as a salutary one wherein managers made reluctant but realistic appraisals of what a prison system could hope to achieve when up to 50 per cent of its inmates were politically motivated. Another view, however, might suggest that the 1980s had produced a new confidence and assertiveness in the senior management of the prison service. Managers sought to highlight and celebrate their technical and managerial achievements with such a difficult prison population. As Clarke and Newman (1997: 66) argue, managerialism provides a rationalization for a non-partisan and depoliticized framework in which calculative technologies and scientific knowledge position managers as neutral and impersonal, above or outside the political fray. The language of managerialism provided the Northern Ireland prison service with a framework within which to make that assertion.

In the sections below, I will argue that the moral objection to paramilitarism, so prevalent during the era of criminalisation, became gradually subsumed in a scientific discourse on the effective and efficient management of paramilitaries during the 1980s. This involved moving away from cruder expressions of the criminalisation project to a more technical endeavour reminiscent of what Feeley and Simon have described as 'identifying and managing unruly groups' (Feeley and Simon 1992: 455). The management of paramilitaries became a series of actuarial techniques of risk management (Feeley and Simon 1992, Brownlee 1998). Like other such actuarial practices in the criminal justice system, while these changes in prison management were not ideology free (Simon 1988), they did encourage a largely instrumentalist approach to running the prisons.

To recap, I have argued that the period from 1981 onwards may be accurately reflected upon as a managerial model for the management of paramilitary prisoners. I have contested that this model contained a number of features or characteristics which were threaded through relations between management, staff, and prisoners during that period. I have contended that managerialism as it is traditionally understood in the public administration and political science literature had a direct impact on prison management from the late 1980s onwards. However, I have also claimed that in fact managerialist initiatives such as strategic planning, key performance indicators, efficiency drives, and so forth provided a set of discourses and working practices within which prison managers could frame the changed nature of their relationship with paramilitaries which had evolved in the 1980s in any case. The nature of those changes is outlined in the discussions below.

The Aftermath of the Hunger Strikes and the Demise of Defeating Terrorism through the Prisons

After his appointment as Secretary of State for Northern Ireland, Jim Prior had made it clear that he did not believe in talking of terms of 'defeating' the IRA prisoners. In his press conference held three days after the end of the hunger strikes, Prior indicated that 'now that the hunger strikes were over, improvements were possible but that there would be no question of a political or military system of prison administration or any return to Special Category Status' (cited NIPS 1982: 15). Such a view has remained the official government position. While prisoners remained on protest in the immediate wake of the hunger strikes with prison clothing the only obvious concession afforded to protesting prisoners, the gap between the official rhetoric and the reality of life in the H Blocks resulted in some Unionist commentators accusing the British government of having 'won the war and lost the peace' (O'Malley 1990: 211). As was discussed previously, by the end of 1981/beginning of 1982 the concessions granted in terms of prisoners' clothing, remission, inter-wing association, and narrow definitions of prison work had gone some way towards granting the prisoners' original demands. Such post-hunger strike pragmatism, or at least the absence of an organized desire for confrontation on the part of management, can be traced to a number of factors.

Firstly, as previously discussed, Jim Prior had demonstrated himself to be a considerably more flexible individual than his more Thatcherite predecessor Humphrey Atkins.[17] While the 1980s arguably saw greater autonomy in the management of prisons in Northern Ireland for its senior managers, as in Britain, clearly the individual personality of the Secretary of State or minister may have a direct bearing on prison policy at critical times (Lewis 1997). Prior's stated political desire to get the hunger strikes over as quickly as possible, and get things settled down while he pursued his political programme of rolling devolution for Northern Ireland (Prior 1986) clearly made him more amenable to policies which could reduce the potential for the prisons to remain a source of political instability.

Secondly, the changed tactics of the prisoners themselves influenced staff/inmate relations. As discussed previously, in the Maze prison the Republican leadership adopted a strategy of somewhat less confrontational tactics, clearly facilitating a reduction in strong-armed tactics by prison management and staff. While many of the prisoners were physically, emotionally, and psychologically drained in the aftermath of the dirty protest and hunger strike, the removal of the prison uniforms

---

[17] Prior had been dispatched by Mrs Thatcher to Northern Ireland as a form of punitive exile for one of her more 'wet' cabinet colleagues (Young 1991).

meant that prisoners were now out of their cells, washing and exercising and associating in groups with other Republican prisoners. The presence of large groups of prisoners on the wings affected the power balance within the prison.[18] Prisoners also decided to do limited prison work, nominating a number of prisoners to carry out work such as cleaning the wings. While initially resistant to the idea of permitting the prisoners to nominate who would carry out such tasks, in practice organized groups of prisoners often refused to do the work leaving only the organizational nominee to do the task. In such a context officers reasoned that it was better to have at least some of them working than none at all.[19]

A third and related reason for the apparent greater flexibility amongst prison staff and management was the attitude of the staff and management themselves. While some felt a sense of betrayal or frustration, the widespread feeling of exhaustion, the desire to get on with the job, and the lack of punitive direction from above perhaps eroded any will for organized confrontation with the prisoners. As one former officer then stationed in the Maze told the author :

We were all feeling pretty wrecked by it all. A lot of our people had been killed during all the protests, and we had put up with the most appalling working conditions, always under threat and worried about your family and so on, and then a couple of days after the hunger strikes Jim Prior says they can all wear their own uniform. A lot of guys seeing these Provos strutting about in their civilian clothes thought 'look the Provos have won and it was all for nothing'. They were right too but I don't think many of us really had the appetite for doing anything about it in 1981–1982, things had changed and what could we have done anyhow.[20]

The hunger strike era had infused a sense of resignation at both managerial and staff level in the Northern Ireland prison service that prisoners could not in effect be broken by forcing the symbols of criminal incarceration upon paramilitary prisoners. Quite apart from the disastrous political and security consequences in the community (Clarke

---

[18] 'I think some of the Loyalists and the screws were afraid of the men who had been on the blanket and in the hunger strikes. It was alright kicking the shit out of individuals in their cells but a different kettle of fish once they were out on the wings or in the canteen in numbers. Apart from that, they probably thought all these boys had been on the protest so long, living in their own shite and starving to death, they are all mad fuckers by now. They didn't really know how to handle us after the hunger strikes.' Interview with former IRA prisoner, 9 Oct. 1998.

[19] Interview with former prison officer, 19 Sept. 1996.

[20] Interview with former prison officer, 19 Sept. 1996.

1987), the constant conflict of the previous five years had sapped the will for confrontation and created a dynamic for exploring other ways in which the influence of paramilitaries could be curtailed and circumscribed while minimizing causes of unnecessary conflict. As one prison governor told the author:

I suppose there was a sense that just as the prisoners had to regroup, lick their wounds and think about the way forward after the hunger strikes, the Prison Service did the same thing. This did not mean capitulation or anything like it. What it did mean however is that people were perhaps more mindful of the disruptive consequences of confrontation and more willing to explore more subtle styles of management to get the desired result.[21]

The Disruption and Quarantining of Paramilitary Influence in the Prison System

As the governor above indicated, it would be wrong to view the actions of managers and staff as simple capitulation. A key element of the managerialism strategy has been the attempt to limit, quarantine, and marginalize paramilitary groupings. Prison managers and staff retained a clear recognition that they were engaged in an ongoing struggle to limit the influence of the paramilitaries despite the end of the hunger strikes. Inevitably the battlelines of that struggle would continuously focus on the attempts by Republicans and Loyalists to secure factional separation from each other. Managerialism celebrated the determination of managers in particular to face down the prisoners' resistance strategies.[22]

As has been noted previously, in a small prison system where so many of the prison population were politically motivated, prison managers did not have the option of dispersing dangerous prisoners to a wide number of distant prisons.[23] If prisoners could only be held

---

[21] Interview with prison governor, 13 Sept. 1997.

[22] 'In the summer these prisoners [paramilitaries at the Maze] insisted that they would not comply with the orders to move. Their insistence was matched by a determined response by Prison Service Headquarters and Local Management to not concede to an unacceptable demand. That decision was implemented by the prison Immediate Reaction Force. Their professionalism in removing those who had refused to do so voluntarily denied the paramilitaries the opportunity to mount an emotive propaganda campaign. By the end of the period under report Maze had returned to an uneasy calm . . .' (NIPS 1989: 9).

[23] For a discussion on the logic of dispersal in British and Spanish prisons respectively see Bottoms and Light (1987, esp. ch. 1) and Von Tangen Page (1998a).

securely in one or two prisons, the only option in trying to break up their cohesion and collective power was to employ tactics designed to disrupt the prisoners' organization within those prisons while simultaneously seeking to integrate paramilitaries with ordinary and oppositional prisoners. Both strategies became key planks of the managerial era in the 1980s.

The Red Book and the Disruption of the Paramilitary Leadership

The Hennessey Report which followed the mass breakout of IRA prisoners in 1983 recommended that 'one way in which the authorities may still be able to keep the initiative is by adopting such strategies as the rotation of individuals and groups between Blocks on a random but not infrequent basis, thus breaking up groups before they can create trouble' (Hennessey 1984: 56). In particular the Hennessey team were concerned that the leaders of the 1983 escape had been held in one place for a long period preceding the escape and therefore argued that such high risk prisoners should not be allowed to remain in the same cell or wing for too long (Hennessey 1984: 71). The implementation of these recommendations meant the devising of a system which became known as the Red Book for particularly dangerous paramilitary prisoners.

The system of wholesale wing shifts had been a feature of prison management throughout the dirty protest and hunger strike era in the Maze but had largely failed to obstruct the operation of the paramilitary command structure in the prison (Campbell, McKeown, and O'Hagan 1994). The Red Book classification system, however, was a more targeted attempt at disruption. Red Book prisoners were deemed 'top risk', they were moved frequently in the prison, checked on regularly by staff, accompanied on visits, and became ineligible for schemes such as compassionate home leave.[24]

The Red Book system became one of the key conditions issues on which Republican prisoners in particular began to campaign from 1987 onwards. As the 1988/9 *Annual Report* notes, 'The most serious challenge [from IRA prisoners] centred on a demand for the removal of an essential feature of the security measures associated with the management of the small numbers of prisoners in the highest security category' (NIPS 1989: 9). Prisoners argued, with some validity, that the

[24] Interview with prison governor, 13 Sept. 1997.

decisions as to who was or was not an extremely high risk prisoner appeared 'vague and capricious'.[25] While the Prison Service did give way to more frequent reviews of security classification in 1994 (NIPS 1995: 6), the system has formally continued to operate until the time of writing although with mixed results as to its effectiveness.

While the Red Book classification system clearly had a deleterious effect on some individual prisoners who were subjected to it,[26] the effect on the prisoners' ability to organize was less certain. The system had no discernible effect on preventing a number of major escape attempts (in Crumlin Road in 1989 and in the Maze in 1997), or on the one successful escape from the Maze in 1997. In fact, a number of prisoners and governors interviewed by the author have suggested that the principal impact of the constant rotation of prison leaders was counterproductive from a management perspective.[27] In effect, leadership responsibilities were shared more broadly so that greater numbers of prisoners acquired the necessary skills and experience. As one prisoner argued 'I think it actually gave us more strength in depth, it forced us to skill up larger numbers of prisoners in taking on camp staff responsibilities and it ensured that they could not leave any wing or block leaderless because there were always other people with the necessarily skills to take over.'[28]

Lines in the Sand: Segregation and the Quarantining of Paramilitary Influence

The other principal method which the prison authorities employed to delimit the influence of paramilitary organizations within the prisons was to resist the segregation of prisoners on factional lines. While the segregation of the Special Category prisoners still held in the compounds at the Maze was accepted as an irreversible reality, the prison service was determined throughout the 1980s and 1990s to resist further segregation in the system. Segregation by paramilitary faction meant facilitating the paramilitary command structure, the

[25] Letter from IRA prisoner to the Director of NIACRO, dated 10 Dec. 1991, responded to by the author.

[26] '[Name] was a client of ours and he was on the Red Book throughout the 1980s and I think it affected him. He became quite agitated easily, he said that the continuous movement made it difficult for him to form relationships with other prisoners, he couldn't get parole—yes I think it definitely damaged him.' Interview with solicitor, 12 May 1992.

[27] Interview with former IRA prisoner, 9 Oct. 1998

[28] Interview with former IRA prisoner, 11 June 1997.

opportunity to impose discipline, and the organizing and encouragement of collective resistance. In short, as Hennessey indicated, 'prisoners in segregated blocks are generally better able to plan and execute subversive activities of all kinds' (Hennessey 1984: 56).

Opposition to segregation was therefore one of the defining characteristics of managerialism. Where the prison authorities were periodically forced to retreat on the issue, battlelines were redrawn and management regrouped, squeezed the prisoners' room for manœuvre, and made them work hard for further concessions. While in reality this was a battle, or rather a number of battles which were ultimately lost by the prison authorities, the struggle was a keenly contested series of retreats over more than a decade rather than a decisive victory for the prisoners.

Segregation at the Maze

Securing factional segregation has been a key objective of both Republican and Loyalist prisoners since the beginning of the conflict in Northern Ireland. Obviously that objective had been secured during the period of Special Category Status in the compounds at Long Kesh (Maze). When Special Category Status was removed in 1976, the prison authorities made clear their intention to integrate Loyalists and Republicans after that date both in the new cellular accommodation at the Maze and amongst remand prisoners held at Crumlin Road prison (Coogan 1980).

The intention to quarantine the corrosive implications of paramilitary power through the resistance to segregation was, however, always circumscribed by political and operational realities. For example, with regard to those who had been sentenced before 1976, the Secretary of State reiterated in September 1982 that there would be no interference with the status of the remaining Special Category prisoners, and no attempt to move them from the compounds to the cellular Maze. This announcement was followed by a refurbishment of the existing accommodation in the compounds (NIPS 1983: 7). In effect, a decision was taken to accept the *status quo*, while simultaneously resisting further encroachments. The compound system remained largely unmolested by the authorities' desire to resist segregation, including when the final ninety were moved to cellular accommodation in June 1989 and retained all their Special Category privileges (NIPS 1989: 1).

In the cellular Maze, protesting Republican prisoners had been placed on to separate wings from the beginning of the dirty protest in the Maze in 1978 because of understandable Loyalist concerns about the deteriorating physical conditions. Those Republican prisoners who either came off the protest or who had never joined it in the first place were housed in integrated wings with the two Loyalist factions, sharing canteen, shower, and exercise facilities. When the protesting Republican prisoners decided formally to end their protest in 1982 and join their colleagues in the conforming wings, the key objective for prison management was to resist the inevitable attempts to achieve segregation in these hitherto integrated settings.

Once they [protesting Republican prisoners] came off the protest in late 1982 we thought that they would probably try to erode the integration which had been achieved in the conforming blocks and we thought that they would do it in collusion with the Loyalists. However knowing something is likely to happen and being able to stop it are two different things.[29]

When the protesting Republican prisoners ended their protest in November 1982, this meant that in effect they would outnumber Loyalist prisoners by approximately two to one.[30] IRA prisoners began a policy of deliberate violence and intimidation of the Loyalist prisoners causing them considerable concerns for their safety.[31] Loyalist prisoners claimed that bomb-making equipment and other evidence had been uncovered which suggested that a major attack by Republicans was imminent.[32]

Some Republicans interviewed by the author have suggested that in fact they had deliberately started rumours amongst the Loyalists exaggerating the nature of the threat.[33] None the less, concern for the safety

[29] Interview with former prison officer, 19 Sept. 1996.
[30] Interview with former IRA prisoner, 11 June 1997.
[31] *Irish News* (25 Sept. 1982), 'Loyalists in Maze Allege Death Threats'.
[32] 'For more than three months we have been asking for complete segregation from Republicans in the H Blocks and warning of what will happen, but these warnings of sectarian violence erupting have been dismissed as figments of our imagination . . . Our fears were vindicated when in a recent search of the prison workshops, items were found belonging to so called conforming Republican prisoners, such as primed incendiaries, batteries, watches, detonators, imitation firearms as well as petrol and a jelly-like substance capable of being used in napalm-type fire-bombs . . . The Loyalist prisoners find themselves in an increasingly perilous situation especially in the blocks where they are in a minority. With more justification than ever before, we demand complete segregation and we demand it now. Must we wait until someone is burned in his bed before the government acts? Nero fiddled while Rome burned.' Letter from a 'Loyalist Commander' to Democratic Unionist Party councillor William McCrea, reproduced *Irish News* (14 Sept. 1982) entitled 'McCrea warns Gowrie of Prison Death Threat'.
[33] Interview with former IRA prisoner, 9 Oct. 1998.

of Loyalist prisoners was sufficiently widespread to garner unusually broad political support from across the Unionist and Loyalist political landscape in favour of the campaign for segregation.[34] Loyalist prisoners also began a campaign of destruction as part of their protest,[35] followed by a dirty protest and threats to go on the offensive against Republican inmates.[36]

Once the Loyalist prisoners took the decision to begin their various protests, this meant that they were now classified as 'non-conforming' prisoners and separated on to their own wings, albeit with privileges such as non-statutory visits, remission, educational, and work facilities being removed.[37] The Republican prisoners, all of whom were now officially classified as 'conforming' prisoners, had also achieved de facto segregation but with full privileges having been restored. In effect, the position was completely reversed to that of the 1976–81 era.

The authorities expressed their opposition to the segregation issue in predictable operational and ideological terms.[38] At a political level, the response by the British government was an interesting departure from the hunger strike era wherein the centrality of political involvement in decision-making had been a key feature. Lord Gowrie, Conservative Prison Minister for Northern Ireland under Secretary of State James Prior, told a visiting delegation from the Democratic Unionist Party that 'the final decision on the allocation of accommodation and work [for paramilitary prisoners] must rest with the prison governors'.[39] While many Loyalists prisoners and their supporters saw

[34] Irish News (7 July 1983), 'Unionists Unite in Demand for Split Prisons'.

[35] Irish News (22 Oct. 1982), 'Rampage Damage Put at Thousands: Up to 170 Loyalists involved in a Five Day Spree of Vandalism'.

[36] 'Loyalist prisoners who have campaigned for security through segregation from Republicans are steadily becoming disillusioned with the democratic process in Ulster and democratic methods of protest . . . Prison governors and Republican prisoners are being held responsible for the hardship and suffering caused to Loyalist prisoners in recent months and both may experience the wrath of an enraged Loyalist prison population . . . We are here because we fought against absorption in a popish 32 county state and we have no plans to surrender to popery in prison.' Letter from 'Concerned Loyalist Prisoner', reproduced in Irish News (24 Jan. 1983), 'Death Threat to Republicans by Jailed Loyalist.'

[37] Interview with former UDA prisoner, 24 July 1998.

[38] 'There could be considerable problems for prison staff in operating in blocks and wings occupied entirely by prisoners with a single paramilitary affiliation. Paramilitary groups would almost certainly press for the prison authorities to act through the organisations command structure and spokesman.' Belfast Telegraph (28 Dec. 1982), 'Jail Segregation is Again Ruled Out by Lord Gowrie'.

[39] Newsletter (18 Nov. 1982), 'Prison Heads Must Decide, Says Gowrie'.

this, with some justification, as 'passing the buck',[40] none the less it does hint at the beginning of a loosening of political control over the management of the prisons.

The Loyalist campaign for segregation at the Maze continued throughout 1983. In April 1983 the government urged Loyalists to give up their protest, suggesting a compromise with which 'they would be reasonably pleased'.[41] A number of Loyalist prisoners responded by coming off the protest and were given a separate working area.[42] The dispute dragged on, however, throughout 1983 and into 1984 until the Loyalists ended their protest in February 1984, having as one Loyalist prisoner suggested to the author, 'not realized that they had achieved their objective a year before'.[43] The prison authorities continued to deny that segregation according to paramilitary faction had been granted in the Maze.[44]

In effect, once segregation at the Maze had been ceded by a combination of the Republican prisoners ending their protests and the Loyalist prisoners beginning theirs, any attempt to force integration would have been fraught with operational and political difficulties.

Attempts to force integration once prisoners had in effect gained significant control of the wings would undoubtedly have been met with fierce resistance and violence against both staff and oppositional inmates. On a political level, the Loyalist prisoners had demonstrated their ability to galvanize political support on this issue (perhaps uniquely) across a broad cross-section of Unionist and Loyal Orders' opinion.[45] Republicans had already demonstrated their skills in mobilizing popular support amongst Nationalists in support of prison protests during the hunger strike. Faced with a largely unified political

[40] *Newsletter* (18 Nov. 1982), 'Prison Heads Must Decide, Says Gowrie'.
[41] *Belfast Telegraph* (8 Apr. 1983), 'Gowrie urges Loyalist Inmates to End Protest'.
[42] *Newsletter* (29 Apr. 1983), 'Loyalists Claim Maze Victory but NIO Denies Segregation Move'.   [43] Interview with former UDA prisoner, 24 July 1998.
[44] 'On the contrary, Ministers have taken the view that an integrated prison system was desirable and made for more effective security and control. At present, a substantial number of paramilitary prisoners are segregated on a de facto basis, following the past protest action, which included the dirtying of cells. This arrangement is not regarded as satisfactory and is being kept under review.' *Belfast Telegraph* (5 July 1984), 'No Official Segregation in Maze Jail, Says NIO'.
[45] As well as the political support of Ian Paisley's Democratic Unionist Party, key individuals in the Official Unionist Party, and Independent Unionist and Loyalist politicians, the prisoners also received the support of a number of key Orange institutions including the Apprentice Boys and ultimately the Orange Order. *Belfast Telegraph* (3 Nov. 1983), 'Orangemen Back Jail Segregation'.

opposition amongst both Nationalists and Unionists to forced integration of prisoners,[46] the government and the prison authorities apparently decided to cede an unpleasant but difficult to oppose *de facto* segregation of prisoners at the Maze prison.

What is perhaps more interesting, however, is that within the framework of managerialism the authorities resisted the application of that operational and political logic in setting their face against further segregation elsewhere in the prison system. In effect, the Maze became the special case in the management of prisons in Northern Ireland. It became a large and prominent anomaly which had to be tolerated. However, it was an anomaly which needed to be managerially quarantined from the rest of the system lest it corrode the efforts at ordinary prison management which continued elsewhere despite the presence of paramilitaries.

Segregation at Magilligan and Crumlin Road

The other prisons in which the segregation issue continued as a major area of dispute were in Magilligan prison which held a combination of paramilitary and ordinary prisoners and Crumlin Road (Belfast) prison which served as the main remand prison for all male prisoners until the mid-1990s.

Following on from the *de facto* segregation of the Maze by 1984, those who had been supporting the campaign at the Maze shifted their attention to Magilligan where a similar campaign had been ongoing for some time.[47] Relations in the prison had been tense since the transfer of some paramilitary prisoners on shorter sentences to Magilligan from the Maze in 1981.[48] The campaign at Magilligan included a number of abortive hunger strikes by Loyalist prisoners,[49] a failed legal challenge under the European Convention of Human Rights,[50] and attacks by Loyalist and Republican inmates upon each other.[51] Republicans again considerably outnumbered Loyalists in Magilligan and Loyalist supporters claimed similar intimidatory tactics were

[46] The moderate Unionist Alliance Party have traditionally opposed the segregation of paramilitary prisoners.

[47] *Belfast Telegraph* (9 Aug. 1984), 'Segregation at Magilligan Plea is Turned Down'.

[48] These prisoners had been moved from the Maze to make way for groups of remand prisoners who had to be transferred from Crumlin Rd to the Maze after Loyalist prisoners wrecked A Wing in Crumlin Road (Colville 1992: 8).

[49] *Irish News* (5 June 1984), 'Prison Fast Ends'. See also Chapter 3.

[50] See also Chapter 6.

[51] *Derry Journal* (27 Apr. 1984), 'Tensions Rising in Magilligan'.

being used by the Republicans as had been employed in the Maze.[52] The prison authorities continued to refuse to accede to the demand of segregation. Their views remained that to do so would 'mean sacrificing part of the governor's control over affairs at the jail'.[53] The Northern Ireland Office also made it clear that 'an integrated system was the desirable way of operating in Northern Ireland in the best interests of all concerned and that the measures of segregation which had developed at the Maze (Cellular), mainly for historical reasons, would not be mirrored at Magilligan' (NIPS 1985: 1).

The prison population at Magilligan in the mid-1980s had a considerably different complexion from that at the Maze. It was designed to hold short-term prisoners and also prisoners of medium security risk who were serving fixed term sentences or coming to the end of such sentences (NIPS 1986: 4). This resulted in a prison population consisting of large numbers of ordinary prisoners, and groups of politically motivated prisoners who had been convicted of less serious offences.

While sporadic protests continued throughout the 1980s,[54] the opening of Maghaberry prison in 1987 (to which most long-term conforming paramilitary prisoners and long-term high security ordinaries were moved), the permanently high numbers of ordinary prisoners, and the relatively short-term sentences of most of the remaining politicals meant that the segregation campaign at Magilligan never assumed the same momentum as that at either Maze or Crumlin Road prison. By the early 1990s Magilligan prison had in effect become a prison for ordinary short-term prisoners. Prison managers apparently decided that it was better to limit the potential disruptive influence of 'nonconforming' paramilitary prisoners by ensuring that they were either kept at the Maze or in Crumlin Road.[55] With segregation achieved at the Maze prison, Crumlin Road emerged as the key battleground.

---

[52] 'Loyalist prisoners are being forced into cells adjacent to Republicans and the fear and tension suffered by these prisoners is being increased by instructions being shouted from one Republican cell to another. Many prisoners believe that the Republicans are plotting further acts of aggression . . .' Democratic Unionist Party Assemblyman Jack McKee, quoted in *Irish News* (4 Aug. 1984), 'Attack Raises Prison Fears'.

[53] Quoted in *Belfast Telegraph* (9 Aug. 1984), 'Segregation at Magilligan Plea is Turned Down'.

[54] In Apr. 1987 twenty-eight Loyalists prisoners attending a church service took an officer, the Minister, and a Catholic prisoner hostage and erected barricades in an apparently unplanned effort to secure segregation. The situation ended peacefully three days later without injuries, with the prison service claiming 'no concessions were made on the segregation issue' (NIPS 1988: 10).

[55] Interview with former prison officer, 19 Sept. 1996.

The interaction between politically motivated prisoners and the prison authorities at Crumlin Road prison during the era of managerialism became increasingly intense towards the late 1980s. As the main remand prison for all male prisoners, Crumlin Road always housed large numbers of paramilitary prisoners. Crumlin Road had been a key arena of struggle between the paramilitary prisoners and the authorities since the beginning of the conflict, having been the site of a number of high profile escapes and the hunger strike of the IRA commander Billy McKee and others which was widely viewed as having secured Special Category Status in 1976.[56] However, for prison staff who worked at Crumlin Road in the 1980s and 1990s, the prison was widely regarded as an institution wherein the authorities had managed to maintain their authority and control over the prisoners:

Once they [the Northern Ireland Office] caved in and granted segregation at the Maze, I preferred to stay where I was at Crumlin Road rather than work up there. The working conditions in the prison were poor, but it was a much more disciplinarian prison for both prisoners and staff and so you knew where you stood. That had its down side with senior staff always on your back but on the other hand no one wanted it to become another Maze where the paramilitaries were ruling the roost.[57]

While there were sporadic protests by prisoners throughout the 1980s in support of segregation, the period up until 1989 was characterized as 'comparatively peaceful' and operating 'without any great conflict' (Colville 1992: 9). Loyalist and Republican prisoners were formally integrated on the wings and landings throughout this period with prisoners from opposing factions occupying adjoining cells. As previously noted, in reality the prisoners operated a system of self-segregation in the prison. This meant that prisoners of opposing factions would make use of facilities such as the dining, recreational, and exercise yards on alternate days. While there were sporadic outbreaks of violence if opposing groups or individual prisoners met each other, the prison was viewed as less problematic than Magilligan by many staff.[58] Such a view was common, despite the fact that many of the prisoners were remandees and, as one former IRA prisoner told the author, 'often fresh from the military struggle and rarin' to get stuck in'.[59]

[56] See Chapter 3 and Chapter 5.
[57] Interview with former prison officer, 12 Sept. 1996.
[58] Interview with former prison officer, 19 Sept. 1996.
[59] Interview with former IRA Officer Commanding, 12 Sept. 1994.

Clearly such a working arrangement required the co-operation or at least acquiescence of both the prison management and the factional leaders, all of whom benefited from the accommodation. While continuing to press their claim for segregation, the paramilitary command structures operated largely unhindered. Similarly the prison authorities were able to stand by their opposition to segregation, emphasize their commitment to the individual treatment of prisoners, and maintain that Crumlin Road remained an integrated establishment.

By 1989 the strains upon the informal accommodation between prisoners and the prison service were becoming increasingly obvious. A number of factors appeared to contribute to the increased deterioration in relations. A major escape attempt by IRA prisoners led to the discovery of Semtex explosives and a pistol and was followed by a severe security clampdown. In addition a particular influx of younger and more militant paramilitaries, both from one particular rural IRA unit[60] and from the Loyalist paramilitaries who were by then matching Republican violence for the first time since the beginning of the conflict (Cusack and McDonald 1997), considerably increased the likelihood of more direct confrontation. Finally the fact that prisoners were increasingly spending an average of two years on remand at Crumlin Road (Colville 1992: 24), meant that prisoners were both able and willing to spend time in protest actions before being sentenced and moved to the segregated wings at the Maze.

Throughout 1989 and 1990 prisoners began to increase the level and frequency of attacks on each other and staff including scaldings, kickings, and attacks with bed ends as well as destruction of cells and other prison facilities.[61] Both Loyalists and Republican paramilitaries began to issue death threats against prison officers and Loyalists began to attack prison officers' homes, linking such actions directly to the segregation campaign.[62] Belfast City Council backed a call for segregation in the prison,[63] and a Republican pressure group, the Crumlin Road

---

[60] A number of prison staff and prison managers have argued to the author that the arrest and placing upon remand of a Tyrone-based unit of the IRA had a considerably destabilizing effect on the running of Crumlin Road prison.

[61] *Irish News* (17 Apr. 1990), 'Jail Rioters Unite to Stay Apart'.

[62] *Independent* (7 May 1990), 'Jail Segregation Campaign "Will Fail"'.

[63] *Belfast Telegraph* (12 May 1990), 'Belfast Council Narrowly Backs Jail Separation'. The DUP-sponsored motion would have gained much wider acceptance had they not added an amendment which also condemned the IRA after Sinn Fein had initially supported the motion. Sinn Fein withdrew their support but the motion was carried none the less.

Action Committee, carried out a high profile lobbying campaign designed to secure the same objective.[64]

The response from the Controller of Prisons John Steele appeared quite conciliatory, resistant to concessions on the substantive issue of segregation, but hinting at greater pragmatism if reciprocation was forthcoming from the prisoners.[65] Ministerial rhetoric, however, appeared to become increasingly firm in setting the government's face against movement on segregation.[66] In the 1989/90 *Annual Report* the prison service outlined their aims and objectives which included an aim to 'treat all prisoners as individuals regardless of their religious beliefs or political opinions and to offer them the opportunity to serve their sentences free from paramilitary influence' (NIPS 1990: 3). By 1991, however, this aim had been expanded upon to include a commitment to 'continuing to resist further segregation which acts against the best interest of prisoners, the efficiency of the Service and the long term stability of the wider community' (NIPS Strategic Plan 1991: 12). In effect prison management made clear their intention to resist further concessions on the issue in Crumlin Road.

As previously noted, the prisoners' campaign of violence and intimidation culminated in November 1991 when IRA prisoners placed a bomb in a canteen area behind a radiator which exploded when the Loyalists were using it, killing two Loyalist prisoners. While there has been some suggestion that the attack came about as a result of a Loyalist attack on a minibus carrying Republican prisoners' families (McEvoy *et al.* 1999), the deaths were immediately linked to the segregation campaign. Two weeks later the Loyalists retaliated with a joint UVF/UDA attack on the

[64] *Irish News* (14 Dec. 1990), 'Jail Segregation Call Renewed'.

[65] 'In Belfast prison, groups of remand prisoners have chosen to attack the prison fabric and its staff in their effort to achieve segregation. As in the past rival groups have striven to present the prison authorities as repressive in the face of what are presented as reasonable and justifiable demands. Ministers and the prison authorities have been very conscious that any major shifts in policy cannot be viewed in isolation, nor can the interests of individuals in the system be lightly set to one side merely for a quiet life . . . I am convinced that the major difficulties can be overcome. But our efforts to reduce confrontation must be reciprocated by a positive response from prisoners generally.' Controller of Prisons John Steele (NIPS 1990: 2).

[66] 'We will not countenance any further segregation in the system. We will not help the paramilitaries increase their power to threaten others outside the prison walls. We will help prisoners to break away from the paramilitary leaders. The paramilitaries want to use prisoners and their families as pawns to gain control over those linked to their organisations, to recruit new members and to plan more disruption and mayhem.' Northern Ireland Prisons Minister John Cope, quoted in the *Independent* (7 May 1990), 'Jail Segregation Campaign "Will Fail"'.

prison when an RPG 7 rocket attack was fired from the road at the window of a dining hall in which Republicans were eating (Cusack and McDonald 1997: 284). No one was injured. The murders of the Loyalist prisoners led to the appointment of Lord Colville to inquire into the 'operational policy in Belfast Prison for the management of paramilitary prisoners from oppositional factions' (Colville 1992).

The prison authorities argued that to permit further segregation would run contrary to their recently completed Mission statement and that 'segregation at Belfast prison would lead to more effective paramilitary domination of prisoners, a lessening of staff effectiveness and greater escape possibilities' (Colville 1992: 18). Colville agreed with the potential threat to security caused by segregation on either a landing or wing basis.[67] While he acceded to the demand for segregated visits, and called for reductions in the time spent on remand, in essence his report supported the maintenance of the self-segregation regime which he acknowledged produced 'a desolate sort of life' (Colville 1992: 29–30).

Vindication of the prison service position by an independent report did little to undermine the determination of the prisoners to continue their campaign. Prison staff were continuously attacked and intimidated, inmate on inmate violence at the prison continued, and eventually Loyalist prisoners secured their objective in September 1994 when they damaged the prison so badly that all remand paramilitary prisoners were transferred to segregated accommodation at the Maze.[68] Segregation did not, however, disappear as an issue. Even during the era of the peace process the issue remained of considerable political significance with dissident Loyalist and Republican groupings demanding either segregated accommodation in their current establishment (Maghaberry) or a move to their own segregated accommodation at the Maze.[69] The attempt at drawing a line in the sand on the segregation issue failed. As one prison officer told the author 'you might say

[67] 'I do not recommend to the Secretary of State that Republican and Loyalist paramilitary prisoners should be placed on separate landings or wings . . . What I cannot recommend is that a policy adopted in 1976 and co-ordinated now, with general public efforts to reduce sectarianism should be reversed as a result of a few ounces of semtex. I am aware that men died: but all the lessons from history suggest that segregation facilitates escapes and escapes will give freedom to paramilitary fanatics, of both factions, who will kill and maim outside the prison' (Colville 1992: 22).

[68] For a fuller discussion of these event see Chapter 5.

[69] As is discussed previously, the anti-peace process Loyalist Volunteer Force were in fact transferred from the integrated wings at Maghaberry to their own segregated accommodation at the Maze after their leader Billy Wright threatened to go on hunger

that history of segregation in the Northern Ireland prison system has been one long retreat, a case of trying to keep building dams and building ditches to contain their [paramilitary prisoners] influence. We tried but they just kept coming at us and they wore us down eventually.'[70]

Analysis of the Long Retreat on Segregation

In previously published work on this period, I have argued with colleagues that the determination of the prison authorities to resist segregation at Crumlin Road prison was an exception to an overall process of normalizing managerial relations with paramilitary prisoners (Gormally, McEvoy, and Wall 1993). While we were aware of prison managers' desire to restrict the influence of paramilitarism, in essence our argument was that prison managers had failed to internalize the logic of some of their more progressive activities in other parts of the prison system. Some years later, however, I believe it is perhaps appropriate to place a rather different emphasis on the prison service position regarding segregation.

Resistance to segregation in Crumlin Road and elsewhere was not an aberration but rather an entirely logical and rational attempt to quarantine paramilitary influence. It is indisputable that segregating prisoners by faction facilitated greater paramilitary control and influence over prisoners as well as making the planning and execution of escapes more easy. The acceptance by the prison service of the *de facto* reality of a system of self-segregation at Crumlin Road (wherein paramilitary command structures operated regardless) went hand in hand with a determination to resist further encroachments, and to expand integrated sections of the prison wherever possible.

The key difference between the era of managerialism and the period of criminalisation was the framework within which relations with paramilitary prisoners were understood and acted upon. In a system in which prisoners would automatically be transferred to segregated accommodation at the Maze once sentenced (if they wished), it would have been illogical to promote resistance to segregation solely on the basis of denying political status. During the criminalisation era issues

---

strike. At the time of writing, small numbers of the dissident Republican groupings the Real IRA and the Continuity IRA as well as the Loyalist Orange Volunteers are also pressing for segregated accommodation at Maghaberry, since the closure of the Maze prison following the last of the prisoner releases in the summer of 2000.

[70] Interview with former prison officer, 19 Sept. 1996.

such as segregation were explicitly laden with such political symbol-ism, intimately bound up with the broader political struggle, and thus restricted managerial decision-making. Managerialism, however, encouraged a technocratic, instrumentalist, and ostensibly depoliti-cized analysis by prison managers which facilitated the adoption of policies which were not entirely ideologically consistent.

Operational variances across different prisons became a series of distinct, technical managerial problems. Viewed in such a light, a diversity of regimes was not inconsistent. Rather, a prison system which included considerable paramilitary autonomy at the Maze, ordinary prisoners at Magilligan, integrated former paramilitaries at Maghaberry, and a self-segregating regime at Crumlin Road was an entirely rational reflection of the peculiar circumstances which the prison system was being asked to manage. Resisting segregation at Maze, Magilligan, and Crumlin Road during the 1980s and early 1990s became an expression of achieving operational aims (such as prevent-ing escapes or minimizing paramilitary control) not a strategy designed to defeat terrorism.

Of course on one level such a transmogrification into technicist dis-courses was somewhat fictitious. Strategic plans, aims, and objectives became expressions of the battlegrounds upon which the prison authorities chose either to resist or to engage constructively with the prisoners. As discussed above, the first articulation of strategic aims and objectives by the prison service in 1987/8 and the more developed strategic plan of 1991 afforded a new language within which to frame or claim legitimacy in the relations with prisoners, they did not remove the underlying struggles regarding issues such as segregation. At another level, however, such changes did herald a significant change in that prison managers increasingly allowed themselves to be circum-scribed by the managerialist paradigm. They arguably lost sight of the political and ideological dimensions of the work in which they were engaged. Such partiality was to become increasingly apparent in the period immediately after the first IRA and Loyalist ceasefires in 1994 and is discussed in the final chapter.

Treatment as Individuals and the Struggle Against Paramilitary Influence

In tandem with resistance to segregation the other key managerial struggle against paramilitarism was the commitment by the prison service to the treatment of prisoners as individuals. This too became a fundamental principle of prison management during this period, formally articulated after the senior management review of 1987/8 as a commitment to 'treat prisoners as individuals regardless of their religious beliefs or political opinions; and to offer them the opportunity to serve their sentences free from paramilitary influence' (NIPS 1989: 3). One interpretation of such a principle would be that prisoners were to receive equal treatment, regardless of their political views as either Loyalists or Republicans.[71] A less passive interpretation, and that shared by most paramilitary prisoners, was that the commitment to treatment as individuals was part of a rigorous and determined campaign to reduce the influence of the paramilitary groups.

Other than the resistance to segregation and the early reluctance to recognize command structures,[72] the most obvious expressions of the Northern Ireland prison service's commitment to treating prisoners as individuals were the provision of the integrated regime at Maghaberry prison and the willingness to extend concessions to all prisoners which were actually aimed at responding to the demands of the paramilitaries.

The Integrated Regime at Maghaberry

Maghaberry prison is a purpose built establishment on a green field site about 20 miles from Belfast. The prison was over fifteen years in the planning and took several years to construct. The original plan was to construct a new prison as a replacement for Crumlin Road following the escape from that prison in 1971 of thirteen Republican prisoners. The subsequent report by Sir Charles Cunningham and Gordon Chambers recommended that 'the ultimate solution seems to be the construction to modern designs of a secure prison for convicted persons in a different and more suitable site' (cited in Murray 1975: 13). A working party was established to find a suitable site and after a number of unsuccessful attempts and a lengthy public hearing chaired by

---

[71] It should be noted that the statutory protection against discrimination on the grounds of political opinion in Northern Ireland specifically excludes those who support the use of violence for political objectives. It was therefore perfectly legitimate under Fair Employment legislation to discriminate against active Loyalists or Republicans, at least while the armed conflict was ongoing. For a general discussion see McEvoy and White (1998).

[72] As is discussed in the section below, the reluctance to engage with the paramilitary command structure was largely abandoned in the Maze prison during the 1980s.

Lord Justice Murray, Maghaberry was chosen. The original plans to replace Crumlin Road as the main remand prison were altered, largely on the grounds of the proximity of Crumlin Road to the court,[73] and the plans were redesigned based upon HMP Frankland (NIPS 1983: 8).

The project had been recommended again by the Gardiner Committee in 1975 which clearly viewed the building of a new prison as a key part of the strategy designed to remove Special Category Status.[74] The site was acquired and regular updates on progress appear in the *Annual Reports* from 1978 onwards. However, as noted previously, it was not until March 1986 that the women's prison at Maghaberry opened (NIPS 1987: 2). The male prison initially held only a handful of supergrasses but gradually its population increased to over 100 by the end of 1988.

From its opening, the new prison was clearly seen as the flagship of a prison service determined to develop as normal a system as possible.[75] The prison authorities began shifting paramilitaries to Maghaberry who had previously disassociated at the Maze and who had until then been held in the conforming blocks there. These included the high profile former IRA prisoner Shane Paul O'Doherty who had been transferred from Britain after renouncing violence (O'Doherty 1993: 236, 238). The prison service posted flyers in the Maze prison highlighting the better physical conditions and facilities in Maghaberry but making it clear that prisoners would be expected to be fully integrated and fully conforming.[76] Between 1987 and 1989 the numbers on the wings at Maghaberry were expanded as a number of Republican and Loyalist

---

[73] Crumlin Road prison is opposite the principal courthouse for Belfast where most remand-related hearings and some paramilitary trials were heard, and is connected to the courthouse by a tunnel which runs underneath the road.

[74] 'The present situation of Northern Ireland's prisons is so serious that the provision of adequate prison accommodation demands that priority be given to it by the government in terms of money, materials and skilled labour such as has been afforded to no public project since the Second World War. Specifically we recommend that the government find suitable sites on which building can start immediately on both the proposed temporary cellular prison for 700 [which became Maze cellular] and the permanent prison for 400–500. . . .The failure of successive administrations to take earlier action has significantly reduced the effectiveness of the penal system. This situation must not be allowed to continue . . .' (Gardiner 1975, paras. 113 and 115).

[75] 'The way ahead was signaled by the opening of the male prison . . . with integral sanitation in every cell and extensive work and training facilities, it offers the best accommodation in the prison system. The intention is to make the most out of these excellent facilities by developing a regime which offers constructive opportunities to those prisoners who wish to take something worthwhile out of their sentences. A unit for selected life sentence prisoners is one possibility which is being explored' (NIPS 1988: 1).

[76] Interview with former IRA prisoner, 14 June 1996.

prisoners formally resigned from their respective organizations and were shifted from the Maze. Between 1988 and 1989 the number of prisoners at the Maze dropped from 817 to 585 and the number at Maghaberry rose from 104 to 275 (NIPS 1989: 8, 1990: 9). Despite these successes, prison officials remain coy that the prison was conceptualized as a means of eroding the influence of the paramilitaries:

Yes I know that the Republicans think Maghaberry was part of some grand counter-insurgency plan. It wasn't like that, in fact I think there might have been some reluctance initially about putting paramilitaries there in case they would try to destablise it in the way they had done to Maze. We had needed a new prison for years. We had a responsibility to provide accommodation to prisoners who wished to be free from paramilitary influence. The logic of getting some physical distance between such prisoners and their former colleagues dictated that we should put them in Maghaberry rather than on the integrated wings of the Maze. It was as straightforward as that.[77]

While the original plans for Maghaberry were not driven simply by the desire to wean prisoners away from the organized paramilitary wings at the Maze, it is clear that the prison's potential for such an effect was not lost on the prison authorities. Quite apart from the excellent physical conditions and facilities at the prison, hints were offered at the prospect of earlier release dates for indeterminate sentenced prisoners if they moved to Maghaberry.[78] The decision to site the Life Sentence Pre-Release Unit at Maghaberry, meant that both conforming and non-conforming paramilitary prisoners who had been given a release date were required to go through the pre-release scheme (discussed below) in integrated conditions. While the differential in terms of facilities between Maze and Maghaberry narrowed somewhat from the early 1990s,[79] the key difference remained a determination to retain the principle of treatment as an individual and the parallel will to resist attempts at segregation.[80]

[77] Interview with prison governor, 13 Sept. 1997.

[78] 'The moving of prisoners to integrated conditions . . . is certainly taken into account as a positive step, but that must be considered against all the other circumstances of each particular case.' Minister of State Ian Stuart, *Hansard*, HC (Series VI) vol 151, col 444 (20 Apr. 1989).

[79] In 1993 the Chief Inspector of Prisons suggested that, on the basis of his inspection of the Maze in June of that year, the Northern Ireland Office was deliberately allowing conditions to deteriorate in the prison in order to encourage prisoners to transfer to the integrated wings at Maghaberry (cited in Tomlinson 1995: 220).

[80] *Saoirse: Irish Freedom*, 143 (Mar. 1999), 'Republican Prisoners in Maghaberry: Political Status Denied'. This is the newsletter of Republican Sinn Fein, a splinter group opposed to the Good Friday Agreement and the political wing of the Continuity IRA, a number of whose members are imprisoned in Maghaberry.

Individualization of Treatment and the Impact on Ordinaries

One of the by-products of the prison service's public determination to treat all prisoners as individuals regardless of motivation has been to the direct benefit of ordinary non-politically motivated prisoners. Such benefits have been felt not only by the ordinaries at Maghaberry but throughout the system. Following protests by paramilitary prisoners, such prisoners have enjoyed the fruits of a number of management concessions to politicals in order to disguise the fact that movement on particular issues represented a concession to the terrorists.[81] So, for example, when the decision was made to remove the requirement to wear a prison uniform after the end of the second hunger strike, the change applied to all prisoners, both politically motivated and ordinary (NIPS 1982). Similarly the extensive home leave programme, the relaxation on the application of rules regarding prison work, the provisions relating to the release of life sentenced prisoners, were all enjoyed by ordinary prisoners even though their primary purpose was arguably aimed at the management of paramilitaries.[82]

At one level, such disparities may be accurately described as simply hypocritical expediency designed to obscure the *de facto* recognition of political motivation. On another, however, they are a reflection of a deep aversion to allowing the material reality of the treatment of politically motivated prisoners to be reflected in legislation, prison rules, or other public documents. As one prison officer suggested to the author: 'I suppose we would rather have lived with concessions to ordinaries than have the paramilitaries lauding it over us how they were winning.'[83]

---

[81] As one former non-political armed robber from a staunchly Loyalist background told the author: 'I was arrested and served time in England and when I got transferred back home I thought it was a holiday camp compared to over there. I used to say to all the lads from around home, well boys we have the Provos to thank for this. They used to go mad.' Interview with NIACRO client, 17 Apr. 1994.

[82] Similarly when the Conservative government decided to reintroduce 50% remission in 1995 in the wake of the first IRA ceasefire, this was presented not as a response to the cessation but on the grounds that this was 'bringing terrorist prisoners into line with the rest of the prison population in Northern Ireland'. In 1989, after a direct intervention from Mrs Thatcher requesting a fresh package of anti-terrorist measures after an IRA bomb had killed eight British soldiers at Ballygawley, remission rates for those convicted of terrorist offences had been reduced from 50% to 33%.

[83] Interview with former prison officer, 12 Sept. 1996.

Dialogue and Recognition: Managerialism and the Paramilitary Command Structures

It is a truism of most prison systems that managers require at least the acquiescence of the prisoners in order to make the system function effectively or efficiently. While some traditional prison management models have been run along more authoritarian lines, (as previously detailed by Barak-Glanz 1981 and Ditchfield 1990), the trend for the majority of modern prisons (with the notable exception of some US maximum security prisons, see Freeman 1999: 214–15) has been to try to maximize effective working relations between the prison staff and the prisoners. As the Control Review Committee remarked regarding the English system's treatment of long-term prisoners: 'Prisons cannot be run by coercion; they depend on the staff having a firm, confident and humane approach that enables them to maintain close contact with inmates without abrasive confrontation' (Control Review Committee 1984: 6, cited in Sparks, Bottoms, and Hay 1996: 9).

The key to the success of such an approach to prison management is a willingness by managers and staff to engage in dialogue with individual or groups of prisoners. Of course in the Northern Ireland context, where prisoners often insisted that dialogue should only take place through the paramilitary command structure, such discussions had the potential to become highly symbolic for all the protagonists. While dialogue did take place during the era of criminalisation, usually by referring to the prisoners' 'spokesman' rather than Officer Commanding, it was clearly ideologically problematic for staff to be open about such discussions and their implications.

Despite the service's formal commitment to individualization of treatment, throughout the 1980s prison managers became increasingly confident about their dialogue with paramilitary prison leaders. Such dialogue offered the opportunity to avoid unnecessary conflict, and defuse potentially destructive or damaging situations where minor issues had the potential to flare up into more serious incidents. That potential was considerably exacerbated when groups of inmates were sufficiently organized to utilize any grievances, injustices, or inflexibility as reasons for the mobilization of protest activities. In a context where the prisons were no longer viewed as the instrument for defeating terrorism, avoiding such protests or conflicts through dialogue was indeed eminently sensible management.

While such dialogue was a feature of prison relations in the early 1980s, particularly in the Maze prison, it went on largely surreptitiously in a fashion that was publicly deniable by the Northern Ireland Office. As one former prison officer suggested to the author, 'we would just act in a way that even if we were talking to Joe Bloggs and we wanted something to happen, we were still talking to an individual prisoner. We would just pretend that we were unaware that he was the paramilitaries' Officer Commanding or Education Officer or whatever.'[84] Increasingly, however, throughout the 1980s such discussions became routinized and prison governors would have regular discussions throughout the prison with the various leaders of the paramilitary factions, either as prearranged bilaterals or as they conducted their normal tours. One former Republican Officer Commanding interviewed pinpointed a sea change in attitudes towards formal recognition of the command structure in 1987 when the IRA prisoners presented a detailed document on conditions in the prison to prison management:

I think that was when attitudes on recognition changed in the formal sense. After a while during that conditions campaign they seemed to give up the pretence. We were being very sensible, very reasonable, arguing with them about inconsistencies in the rules, pointing out that we weren't asking for the world, issues like extending the shop, clothing, hi-fis and so on—eventually the governors were just talking to our camp staff [leadership] directly about it with no bullshit. We also got much of what we wanted from that campaign, small victories but important to build upon.[85]

By 1990 the prison authorities were so confident regarding dialogue with paramilitary leaders that they permitted a BBC television documentary crew to film IRA Officer Commanding Raymond McCartney in discussion with a prison governor. The segment of their interview which was broadcast focused on the size of the sausage rolls. Clearly, for the authorities concerned, such a discussion represented a question of culinary specification rather than an acknowledgement of the paramilitary command structure or the political status of the inmates.

During the 1990s the prison authorities became ever more frank about the nature of their discussions with the paramilitary leadership of the various factions. Of course such openness was encouraged by the peace process and the public dialogue between prison

---

[84] Interview with former prison officer, 19 Sept. 1996.
[85] Interview with former IRA Officer Commanding, 12 Sept. 1994.

commanders and various political leaders, including the Secretary of State for Northern Ireland (discussed in Chapter 11). The governor of the Maze prison became completely forthright in all television and press interviews about his regular structured meetings with each of the factional leaders in the prison. Even in circumstances where the prisoners have compromised the security of the prison, as in the case of the IRA tunnel discovered in 1996, the former Controller of Prisons candidly acknowledged that dialogue has become the favoured managerial response.[86]

At first blush, there might be a tendency to attribute the increased reliance upon discussions with prisoner groupings to a greater pragmatism on the part of the prison authorities during the era of managerialism. Without doubt, the potential for minimizing conflict through dialogue has been a major motivating factor for prison managers.[87] However, the engagement by the prisoners in dialogue upon a narrow range of topics, concerning the more mundane details of prison life, was itself viewed as significant by the prison authorities. Managerialism allowed the prison service to minimize the political or ideological significance of *their* participation in dialogue with paramilitary command structures by emphasizing the mundanity of the subject-matter and the organizational benefits in achieving a more stable prison system. Simultaneously it encouraged a set of internal institutional beliefs, which led managers to place broader significance on the prisoners' engagement in such dialogue, that they were in effect settling down to do their time and less concerned with the broader assertion of political status. As one senior prison official told the author:

[86] 'Now what is a governor to do in those circumstances [the failure to discover the tunnel through not carrying out headcounts] if he is not satisfied? Remember he is dealing with groups, organised groups, not individuals and that is what I think is unique to the Maze, and there are options. One option is to go in heavy handed with staff in riot gear and to achieve a particular result on a particular day. Now I think that there are many occasions where the governor of the Maze has had to consider that option, but he would often, most of the time in fact, reject that option in favour of discussion, negotiation or whatever. Now that would be true in any prison, I think that you would talk your way through a problem rather than resort to force, however minimum. In the Maze, I think there is the added dimension that if you do use force in the Maze to that degree, then there can be ramifications which go well beyond the prison, so those are the kind of balances which have to be weighed up both in the headquarters and in the senior management of the prison.' (Evidence of Alan Shannon, NI Select Affairs Committee 1998: 20).

[87] One prison governor described this strategy as 'the avoidance of exploitable issues'. Interview with prison governor, 20 Apr. 1999.

Once the Provos [IRA] are talking about the size of the sausage rolls, conditions and so on, they are just like ordinary prisoners anywhere. They are no
longer focused on the big issues like Special Category Status. It has to be considered a positive step in terms of trying to make this place something more
like a normal prison system.[88]

Such a view either failed to grasp or deliberately underplayed the significance of the interplay between material conditions and the prisoners' broader struggle for political status. It also fails to grasp the
one-way incrementalism at play in Northern Ireland. In a normal
prison setting (such as Whitemoor after the escape), if the authorities
fear that a prison has become too lax, they can try to put things back
in order. This is much more difficult in the Northern Ireland context.
From the simplistic demands for 'Political Status Now' in 1976, the
concrete meaning of political status had been successfully decon-
structed and redefined by Republican prisoners by 1979 into a number
of smaller, incremental, and obtainable objectives. Once an objective
was achieved, it was banked and the focus moved to another. While the
campaigns concerning segregation, conditions, and other matters by
Republican and Loyalist prisoners in the 1980s were of course concerned with issues such as prisoner safety, parcels, clothing, etc., all of
these occurred within a framework of the assertion for recognition of
political status. Within such a framework, televised negotiations with
the IRA Officer Commanding, albeit on the size of the sausage rolls,
were a considerable step forward towards that goal.

Life Sentenced Prisoners and the Pragmatic Assessment of Risk

The decision to release any life sentenced prisoner in Britain is normally
based on the twin criteria of assessing a tariff or retribution period for
the offence committed and an assessment of the risk to the public once
released. While there is a considerable debate as to the respective weight
to be placed on these elements (see generally Livingstone and Owen
1999: 366–415), the questions of deterrence and punishment are normally grouped as one strand of the criteria and separated from the consideration of risk.[89] In Northern Ireland, there are no fixed tariff periods

---

[88] Interview with prison governor, 13 Sept. 1999.
[89] Home Secretary Leon Brittan, *Hansard*, HC (Series VI) vol 49, cols 505–8 (30 Nov.
1983).

for life sentenced prisoners (NIO 1985, para. 8). Moreover, when in 1983 Home Secretary Leon Brittan announced that anyone who received a life sentence for terrorist offences in Britain would serve a minimum tariff of twenty years,[90] such a move was resisted in Northern Ireland on the grounds of what the Northern Ireland Secretary of State Jim Prior referred to as 'the special circumstances of the Province' (NIO 1985, para. 10, NIPS 1990: 28). The Secretary of State has a duty to consult but not be bound by the judiciary concerning the tariff period and thus a wide flexibility in assessing such tariff periods. In effect the decision to release indeterminate sentenced prisoners in Northern Ireland has been an Executive process guided by the fact that 'the overriding consideration is the need to protect the public from the risk of a repetition of the offence or some other crime of violence' (NIO 1985: 23).

Predicting the risk of reoffending in the release process has become one of the key areas in the management of long-term prisoners (Morris 1994). In the context of the unique prison population of Northern Ireland, where indeterminate sentenced prisoners[91] (the vast majority of whom had been convicted of murder) constituted up to 28 per cent of the sentenced population at one time (NIPS 1989: 6), the potential for the over-prediction of risk identified elsewhere (Bottoms 1977, Monahan 1981, Cavadino and Dignan 1997: 200) was clearly exacerbated. While the system for releasing lifers was originally infused with criteria designed to punish prisoners who maintained their paramilitary allegiance, and it has always been open to naked political manipulation,[92] none the less a pragmatic system evolved which saw the release of large numbers of paramilitary prisoners while the conflict was ongoing.

By the end of 1982 comparatively large numbers of prisoners who had been given such sentences at the beginning of the conflict were approaching or had reached the ten year stage. The prison service decided that 'the machinery for reviewing these cases on a regular basis, which had been operational since the 1970s, should be revised and upgraded' (NIPS 1985: 12).[93] A new review body, the Life Sentence

---

[90] Home Secretary Leon Brittan, *Hansard*, HC (Series VI) vol 49, col 506 (30 Nov. 1983).

[91] This includes both life sentenced prisoners and those sentenced to the Secretary of State's Pleasure (SOSPs) under the Children and Young Person Act, the latter being under 18 years of age at the time of the offence.

[92] In 1988 a British soldier Private Ian Thaine was released after serving three years of a life sentence and in 1995 Private Lee Clegg was released after four and a half years of his life sentence. Both had been convicted of murder.

[93] Between 1968 and 1983 only twenty life sentenced prisoners and two SOSPs were released in Northern Ireland, five of which were on medical grounds (NIPS 1983: 16).

Review Board, was created and met for the first time in March 1983. Chaired by the Permanent Under Secretary of the Northern Ireland Office, it is made up of senior NIO prison officials, a consultant forensic psychiatrist, a Principal Medical Officer from the Department of Health and Social Services, and the Chief Probation Officer. The Board makes recommendations to the Secretary of State who consults the trial judge (or Lord Chief Justice if the latter is dead) and determines whether the prisoner should be released on licence.[94]

Initially releases were very slow with four prisoners released in 1983 and two released in 1984 (NIPS 1985: 13). As in Britain (Padfield 1983), concerns regarding the closed nature of the hearings, the refusal to allow prison representation, and the apparently vague criteria employed in the decision-making process became the focus of considerable criticism in Northern Ireland (Rolston and Tomlinson 1988). In particular the issue of SOSPs, all of whom had been under 18 when convicted, became the focus of pressure from Unionist and Nationalist politicians, church groupings, and voluntary organizations. NIACRO (the Northern Ireland Association for the Care and Resettlement of Offenders) produced a document outlining their concerns which became the source for much of the subsequent campaigning (NIACRO 1984). Those concerns were picked up in the British government's annual review of Emergency legislation (Baker 1984). In January 1985, in response to this public pressure, the Northern Ireland Office produced an *Explanatory Memorandum* which outlined in detail the operation of the system for reviewing both life sentenced and SOSP prisoners (NIO 1985).

That document offers rich insights into the managerial mindset of those deciding on the release of indeterminate sentenced prisoners and is worth reproducing in some detail. It provided that such prisoners would be reviewed at three, six, and ten years by the Life Sentences Unit of Prison Regimes and that after ten each case would be referred to the full Life Sentence Review Board. Further reviews would subsequently be scheduled at the discretion of the Board (NIO 1985, para. 15). Prisoners would eventually be given a provisional release date about a year from their final review and ultimately released on licence by the Secretary of State subject to recall (NIO 1985, paras. 19, 20, 24, 25).

For current purposes, paragraphs 13 and 14 are probably of most interest. Both these sections are permeated by an ostensible

---

[94] *Hansard*, HL (Series V) vol 107, col 158 (7 July 1986).

commitment to treatment of prisoners as individuals simultaneously with a contradictory emphasis on the collective behaviour of paramilitary groupings.

Paragraph 13 of the Memorandum points to the need for reports compiled by staff in order to provide 'as comprehensive a picture of the prisoners as possible'. It goes on to state 'Clearly these reports depend largely on the prisoners being personally known to the reporting officers; they cannot be completed in any meaningful way where the prisoners refuses to co-operate in the reporting procedure, and will necessarily be fuller and generally more informative when a prisoner is taking part in a normal regime.' As is detailed below, the ways in which the reports themselves were framed is also of considerable interest.[95]

Paragraph 14 describes the extent to which paramilitary allegiance is taken into account in deciding on release. It suggests that problems of assessing the risk of an individual committing further acts of violence if released are 'specially difficult where the crime which led to the imposition of the life sentence was committed on behalf of a paramilitary organization, where the organization concerned is still perpetuating acts of violence and where there is no convincing evidence that the prisoner has entirely given up his affiliation to it' (NIPS 1985).

---

[95]   Class Officers Report

Prisoner's Number   Prisoner's Full Name

1. Record of Employment in Prison (with reasons for any change in work).
2. Particulars of Work Prisoner is engaged in.
3. Performance at Work and any aptitude shown.
4. How would you describe the prisoner's character. Delete as applicable.
   Pleasant/unpleasant; cunning/naive; deeply criminal/not so; truthful/deceitful; leader/easily led; easy to talk to/uncommunicative; independent/dependent on others; belligerent/ready to compromise;—other comments.
   How does he/she relate to staff—does relate well/does not relate well; does not approach staff/approaches staff only when necessary/approaches staff incessantly;—other comments.
5. Does he/she seek or avoid the company of hardline paramilitaries?
6. Is prison doing him/her any good. If so, in what way?
7. Detail any change of behaviour noticeable since last committal or last report.
8. Who visits? Are visits regular? What is prisoner's demeanour after visits?
9. With whom does he/she exchange letters?
10. How does he/she make use of his/her time?
11. Does he/she talk about his/her plans for release? What are they?
12. Do you think he/she would return to violence if released? If so, why?
13. Any other additional information or comments.
14. PO's remarks: Do you agree with the comments on the above?
    If not, please say where you disagree.
15. Any additional remarks.

Form AD 134B revised June 1987.

Understandably such criteria were denounced by the political parties affiliated to the paramilitary prisoners as in effect making the prisoners political hostages to the behaviour of the organization on the outside (Sinn Fein POW Dept. 1986: 7–8). Such suspicions appeared to be even more strongly confirmed by the statements issued by the then Prison Minister Nicholas Scott in a subsequent parliamentary debate on SOSPs.[96] Republican and Loyalist groupings were established to campaign against the review system (respectively the Campaign for Lifers and Justice for Lifers) and a further round of reports were produced from church and civil society groupings criticizing the operation of the review system (Campaign for Lifers n.d.; Justice for Lifers 1987, CAJ 1989, McGeorge 1990).[97]

One of the difficulties presented to the Republican leadership in particular was that while the organization had developed a line which was opposed to prisoners participating in the review process (as a criminalisation-type measure) many individual prisoners who had served lengthy sentences were in favour of participating. As one former life sentenced prisoner told the author:

The Movement were against taking part but a lot of men, particularly in the cages, started to take part in them so the line was changed. What we did was to agree certain formulations about questions of remorse, guilt and so forth, and to challenge the procedures and criteria at every turn. My own view was that it made no sense for us to take a position which facilitated the NIO in keeping Republican prisoners in jail.[98]

Paradoxically the effect of large numbers of indeterminate sentenced prisoners coming forward, particularly from the compounds (where prisoners had clearly maintained their paramilitary allegiance and where there had been no real possibility of staff making informed

[96] 'In coming to a conclusion as to whether a prisoner will or will not commit another offence outside, factors that must be taken into account are the organisations to which he or she has some allegiance and the level of violence outside the prison. . . . If the organisations that are committed to violence in the North of Ireland were to renounce violence as a way of achieving their political ends, that would obviously affect the judgement that I and my right hon. Friend the Secretary of State have to make about the release of prisoners.' Hansard, HC (Series VI) vol 107, cols 1331–2 (17 Dec. 1986).

[97] One of the dilemmas faced by NIACRO, CAJ, and similar groups with an interest in prisoners' rights was that in criticizing the extent of executive discretion in the process and thus inevitably inviting a more judicial process for overseeing such reviews, they were running the risk that prisoners might in fact serve longer sentences.

[98] Interview with former IRA prisoner, 14 June 1996.

assessments as to the prisoners' behaviour) was that in practice the more onerous aspects of the review process were very difficult to apply.

In February 1985 the prison authorities introduced a new pre-release home leave scheme for fixed term prisoners and towards the end of the year this was extended to include indeterminate sentenced prisoners whose cases had reached an advance stage in the process (NIPS 1986: 2). In 1986 this was extended so that such prisoners were given two-day periods of temporary release at six fortnightly intervals in the last three months of the sentence (NIPS 1987: 2). Such initiatives, designed to facilitate reintegration back into the community, were of considerable importance in reassuring the prison authorities about the risk presented by such prisoners upon release. As one prison governor told the author:

I think psychologically the pre-release programmes were very important for us. Here we were making judgements about these guys' behaviour, murderers and serious paramilitaries, and the LSRB was releasing them back into the community. The fact that they could behave on temporary releases developed our confidence in our judgements and probably made us sleep a little easier in our beds.[99]

(The increased reliance upon paramilitary discipline by the prison service is discussed in greater detail below).

The staged release of paramilitary prisoners at the end of an indeterminate sentence evolved into what became known as the working out scheme. This scheme was an interesting combination of coercion, incentive, and what has been described to the author as 'political cover'.[100]

The scheme was divided into three phases. In phase one, which was open ended, prisoners were given a provisional release date, offered a series of seminars (on issues such as housing, welfare rights, and re-establishing relationships), one 24-hour home leave per week, and one full weekend over the course of that phase. Prisoners were required to find work, either voluntary or paid (usually through one of the professional rehabilitation agencies such as probation or NIACRO) before moving on to phase two. In phase two, which lasted thirteen weeks, the

---

[99] Interview with prison governor, 13 Sept. 1999.

[100] 'The working out scheme provided ministers with a degree of political cover. At least if something went wrong during the release process, or even later on, ministers would have been able to say well we release these guys very gradually, very tentatively and we don't just let them loose on the public.' Interview with prison governor, 13 Sept. 1997.

prisoner went to work from the prison each day, returning again at night (Monday to Thursday) and spent the weekends at home. The third and final stage required the prisoner to live outside the prison, only reporting to the prison at regular intervals. At the end of this phase, the prisoner received his or her life licence and was released into the community with no further reporting requirement.[101]

This process was understandably regarded by prisoners as 'unnecessary and stressful, dragging it out, since the decision had been taken that we were ready for release'.[102] From the position of the authorities, however, this scheme provided prisoners with the opportunity for practical help with reintegration back into the community, a measured assessment of risk, and a system which was sufficiently politically robust to defend in the event of a major mishap.

Undoubtedly the overall life sentence release system has been one of the successes of the managerial era in Northern Ireland prison history. While quite correctly criticized for lack of procedural due process (CAJ 1989) and clear instances of political manipulation (as in the cases of British soldiers), it has none the less overseen a remarkably high number of releases of long-term prisoners. Between its inception and March 1995, some 374 indeterminate sentenced prisoners were released on licence, only eleven had their licences revoked for unreasonable behaviour, and only one was reconvicted of a terrorist offence.[103] As noted above, the vast majority of these prisoners had been convicted of murder and were released when levels of violence in the community remained high.

Managerialism encouraged the development of this unique system which was particularly tailored to the needs of Northern Ireland. Despite the potential of the framework outlined in the 1985 memorandum to favour disassociated paramilitary prisoners, the decision by non-conforming prisoners to engage in the review process saw large numbers of such prisoners being released.[104] That pragmatism resulted in prisoners serving considerably shorter life sentences in Northern Ireland than elsewhere. The average sentence served in the late 1980s was

---

[101] NIPS letter to the author, 10 Dec. 1992. The exact details of the scheme may have varied over the period of its operation but the basic structure has remained the same.

[102] Interview with former UVF life sentenced prisoner, 29 Sept. 1994.

[103] NIPS letter to the author, 12 Mar. 1995.

[104] The author has seen no reliable longitudinal data which would suggest a pattern of conforming prisoners being released earlier than their non-conforming counterparts, this despite the hints at such early release with the construction of Maghaberry.

twelve to thirteen years, rising to between fourteen and fifteen in the 1990s.[105] While prisoners were required to sign a form indicating that they had understood the terms of their licence prior to release, unlike some other jurisdictions, life sentenced prisoners were not required to sign any renunciation of unlawful activity or any undertaking to be of good behaviour.[106]

This release system, which retained its potential for arbitrariness, unfairness, and wide political discretion despite a number of judicial challenges, was a clear managerial success from the perspective of the authorities. Managerial objectives such as responding to public pressures concerning SOSPs were achieved by releasing almost all such prisoners in a fashion which minimized the apparent risks. No minister or senior prison official ever came under sustained political pressure to resign because of the activities of the life sentence review process.

For the most part, the achievements of the scheme were based on a clear eyed view by those involved in the process about the nature of paramilitary discipline and the usefulness of such prisoners in returning to paramilitary activity. As one governor told the author:

Our confidence in the LSRB process grew as we thought that they [paramilitary prisoners] were unlikely to mess it up for the ones coming behind them. We also knew that any ex-lifer was a spent force, they had done a long stretch for their cause and they were a 'red flag' in security terms, the RUC knew them and they could be whipped back in and have their licence revoked if there was a hint of reinvolvement in any terrorist stuff.[107]

Such judgements, which entailed an unclouded assessment of the nature of the discipline amongst paramilitary prisoners as well as the security reality of organized paramilitary violence, were to play a major role in a number of other prominent features of prisons in the managerial era.

The Reliance on Paramilitary Discipline

Other than the life sentence release schemes, there are a number of further examples which highlight to varying degrees the willingness of

---

[105] NIPS letter to the author, 12 Mar. 1995.

[106] For example, former ETA prisoners in Spain who accepted the government's *Reinsercion* package from the 1980s onwards were required to renounce the armed struggle (Gormally and McEvoy 1995).

[107] Interview with prison governor, 9 Apr. 1998.

prison managers to rely on paramilitary discipline in order to ensure the effective management of areas of the prison system. Until recently, in the context of the peace process and a number of extremely frank reports on the operation of the Maze (Narey 1998, Ramsbotham 1998), such credulity in the willingness and ability of paramilitary groupings to deliver was not expressed openly. None the less professional judgements by prison officials were undoubtedly influenced by such considerations and underpinned some of the most innovative developments of the managerial era.

Home Leave and Compassionate Leave

The rationale in most jurisdictions for the availability of home leave, compassionate parole, or prison furlough arrangements is that they provide prisoners with the opportunity to maintain better relationships with family and community and thus have an important role to play in the process of reintegration (see generally Whitehead, Turver, and Wheatley 1991). Such schemes have been dramatically reduced in the USA in the light of more conservative criminal justice policies generally, and the symbolism in particular of prison furlough programmes following the political capital made out of the Willie Horton case in the 1988 Presidential elections by the George Bush election team (Merlo and Benekos 1997).[108] In Britain, Lord Justice Woolf (1991) made explicit criticisms of the lack of availability of such schemes, although if anything their numbers have actually fallen since his report (Livingstone and Owen 1999: 237–8). While, significantly, progressive versions of such schemes remain operational in a number of European countries including Germany (Vogler 1989), the various Northern Ireland schemes remain amongst the most remarkable, given the serious nature of the offences committed by many of the prisoners.

The Northern Ireland prison service has always placed considerable emphasis on the importance of maintaining family relationships, having operated a Christmas home leave scheme since 1948. Until the early 1980s, however, prison managers were not by and large faced with the administrative decisions related to applications for home leave or compassionate home leave from large numbers of paramili-

---

[108] The campaign of the Democratic candidate Governor Michael Dukakis (Governor of Massachusetts) was damaged by the revelation that his state correctional policies had permitted Horton, a convicted murderer who had been sentenced to life imprisonment, to partake in a prison furlough scheme.

tary prisoners. While arguably more expansive than the English system, numbers receiving leave from prison were still comparatively small. For example, in 1983 131 prisoners were granted Christmas leave from a total sentenced population of 1,972 prisoners, a total of 6.6 per cent (NIPS 1984: 2). In 1993/4, the last year of home leave before the IRA and Loyalist ceasefires, 446 prisoners from a total sentenced population of 1,503 prisoners were given Christmas home leave, a rise to 29.7 per cent (NIPS 1995) or almost one in three of the sentenced population. Many of those prisoners released were long-term paramilitary prisoners.

The reason for such an enormous rise in the number of prisoners going on home leave was a progressive liberalization of the criteria for eligibility throughout the 1980s. In 1983 life sentenced prisoners, around 25–8 per cent of the sentenced population, were ineligible to apply for the Christmas leave scheme. For fixed term prisoners, that scheme was limited to star class (first time offenders) in the last six months of their sentence. In 1985, a new pre-release home leave scheme was introduced and for the first time Christmas home leave was extended to lifers who had reached an advanced stage in the review process (NIPS 1986: 2). The granting of compassionate home leave, in the case of death or serious illness of a close member of the family, for a period of between a few and 24 hours was extended to include lifers and SOSPs who had served at least six years (NIPS 1987: 2). Prisoners were not accompanied by a member of the prison service or the RUC on such leave. Prison managers viewed their extension of the various schemes as a measured response to the public pressure. As the prison service *Annual Report* for 1987 states:

Before any type of leave is granted, the most careful consideration is given to the risk that the prisoner might abscond or commit further offences. Such risk can never be eliminated altogether but the decision to release a prisoner temporarily is always taken seriously. Often representations pressing for home leave are received from MPs, parish priests or ministers, and chaplains. The benefits of home leave, particularly in compassionate circumstances, are shown in the letters and calls of appreciation (NIPS 1987: 22).

The expansion of the various schemes continued throughout the 1980s and 1990s as paramilitary prisoners invariably returned from these furloughs and the prisoners maintained relentless pressure both within the prison and outside for their extension.[109] In 1989 the Christmas home leave scheme was much enlarged and a summer home leave scheme was introduced, the latter being extended in 1990 to include lifers who had served thirteen years or who had a provisional release date (NIPS 1991: 22). In 1991 Christmas home leave was extended to include both first time offenders and prisoners who had served previous sentences, and prisoners were given the option of taking their five day summer leave either in July or August (NIPS 1991: 25). By September 1997, albeit in the context of a renewed IRA ceasefire, compassionate leave to attend funerals was extended from 48 to 72 hours, the periods of leave for prisoners who had served more than eleven years increased from 7 days to 10 and life sentenced prisoners who had been given a release date were entitled to fortnightly home leave (NIPS Press Release, Sept. 1997).

While the moves in 1997 were directly linked to the developing peace process, it is the progressive expansion of prison leave schemes while the conflict was ongoing that is of most interest for current purposes. By the early 1990s almost one in three sentenced prisoners left the prison at Christmas and summer and almost all paramilitary prisoners regularly returned on time.[110] This was all the more remarkable, when, as noted in Chapter 3, amongst the Republican prisoners at least, they regarded it as their duty as POWs to escape.[111]

---

[109] 'Each year monotonously produces the same old NIO practice of patting itself on the back. Statements are churned out by this body complimenting itself on its generosity in permitting some prisoners the luxury of spending the Christmas period at home in the company of loved ones. All self indulgent, all a façade which seeks to hide the cruel nature of British government policy in relation to prisoners in general . . . Although the NIO have given the appearance of softening its abrasive stance in relation to the treatment of prisoners by tinkering with the mechanisms pertaining to the issue of compassionate parole . . . No consideration has been given to the possibility of extending the period of compassionate parole to at least 72 hours considered essential by all prisoners aid groups. . . . This booklet is not concerned with scoring political points against the NIO. Its singular purpose is to address the existence of a very real deficiency in the present policy of the NIO towards the human rights and dignity of prisoners and their families.' Pat McGeown, Director Sinn Fein POW Dept. in *Issues on Compassionate Parole*, 1994: 2).

[110] While a small number of ordinary prisoners regularly absconded, very few paramilitary prisoners appeared to have done likewise. The author has been told a number of accounts by prison officers of rare delays or failures to return by paramilitary prisoners, including one account where staff claim an errant prisoner was physically returned to the prison by activists from his own organization, but the latter has proved impossible to verify.

[111] The author has been told of a number of individuals who have been engaged in the planning and execution of escape attempts, including the digging of the tunnel from the

Such a paradox can only be understood in the context of an awareness of the nature of paramilitary discipline. All prisoners were acutely
aware that their failure to return from a furlough or engagement in
unlawful activities while outside might place the entire scheme in jeop-
ardy. The steady expansion of the various schemes showed prison managers with increasing confidence in the predictability of the
paramilitary prisoners in this arena and the importance of such contacts with the families to all serving prisoners. As one experienced governor told the author: 'I think if any prisoner was foolhardy enough
not to come back [from home leave], he would be facing the wrath of
his organization on the outside, his fellow prisoners on the inside if he
got caught and the families, all of whom would be baying for his
blood. Anybody with any wit who was tempted would probably have
thought better of it.'[112]

As was discussed in Chapter 3, the significance of the boundaries to
such mutually beneficial accommodations are keenly appreciated by
all the protagonists. For example, the escape by IRA prisoner Liam
Averill from a Christmas party for prisoners' families in the Maze in
1994 was regarded by prison managers as 'a clear breach of faith'.[113] As
previously noted, Sinn Fein spokespeople on the other hand were at
pains in subsequent interviews to stress that the tacit understanding
regarding escapes only extended to Christmas home leave, and not to
parties happening within the confines of the prison.[114] Indeed, the
home leave scheme was unaffected by the Averill escape. However, in
order to avoid misunderstanding, the prison service increasingly
looked towards formalizing the informal relationships of trust which
have developed with organized paramilitary groupings.

Compacts and the Formal Encouragement of Responsibility

The period since the ceasefires in Northern Ireland saw an increased
openness in the prison service concerning the realities of life in the
Maze prison in particular. Increased access by the media, formal

Maze in 1997, who have gone on leave from the prison and then returned to resume their
escape activities. Interview with former IRA prisoner, 5 Aug. 1998. It should be noted,
however, that the former prisoner interviewed was not actually one of those involved in
the event in question.

[112] Interview with prison governor, 13 Sept. 1997.
[113] Interview with prison governor, 9 Apr. 1998.
[114] Interview with Mitchel McLaughlin, Sinn Fein chairperson, BBC Radio Ulster, 12
Dec. 1997.

meetings between the Secretary of State and the prison leadership, and ultimately the decision to release paramilitary prisoners under the Good Friday Agreement (discussed in detail in the next chapter) led the prison authorities to become much more frank about the way in which that prison is actually managed. That candour was most clearly reflected in the report by Her Majesty's Chief Inspector of Prisons Sir David Ramsbotham completed in November 1998.

Ramsbotham was asked by the then Secretary of State Mo Mowlam to carry out a full investigation into the Maze following the murder of two prisoners and the Averill escape. Ramsbotham noted a number of facts concerning the Maze. These included that many of the normal prison rules were not applied; that individual prisoners retained their political affiliations within prison and subordinated their individual needs to the needs of the collective body, such that all communication necessarily was done through the designated Officer Commanding; and that the level of self-determination and self-regulation could not be withdrawn without serious repercussions in the prison and the community (Ramsbotham 1998: 17.02). The implications of these facts for prisoners were that 'prisoners' hierarchies had been obliged to assume a high degree of responsibility for the welfare of prisoners they represented including their health, safety, welfare and development needs' (Ramsbotham 1998: 17.05).

While noting that on the whole his inspection team had been impressed by the extent to which these responsibilities were met, Ramsbotham suggested that there was scope for less mature and disciplined groups to abuse the privilege. He therefore recommended that:

protocols should be drawn up between the governor and each of the paramilitary groupings, specifying the responsibilities and obligations of each party, and to which both parties are signatories. These should cover the basics which were already subject to informal agreements such as the withdrawal of staff on the wings, 24 hour unlock and the submission to searching and twice daily headcounts, but should also specify the conduct to be expected of prisoners within visits and home leave . . . (Ramsbotham 1998: 17.07)

In effect Ramsbotham gave an official seal of approval to operating practices which had been occurring informally for a number of years. By legitimizing judgements based on the reliability of paramilitary discipline, and by specifying the consequences of non-compliance by either party, these compacts were designed to introduce a degree of accountability to both parties. Clearly such an open approach to the management of paramilitary prisoners has been facilitated by the context of the peace process and the imminent release of most of the prisoners. Its origins, however, lie in the series of professional judgements made by prison managers from the 1980s onwards, based upon a reliance on paramilitary discipline which could never have been openly acknowledged.

Partnership with Stakeholder Organizations and the Reduction of Conflict with Prisoners' Families

A further feature of the managerial era was an increased awareness of, and willingness on the part of, the prison service to work with a range of outside agencies in partnership towards the delivery of services. Partnerships and inter-agency co-operation have been identified elsewhere as key components of criminal justice and of managerialism in general (e.g. Bottoms 1995, Haines 1996). Such relationships have usually been seen as a component of less atomized and more systematized criminal justice process (Garland 1996: 455) in which co-ordination, information sharing, and goal settings between agencies are established and monitored. Such an approach is a recognition not only of the place of an institution as part of a larger system but also that a changed political climate, increased financial accountability, or more specific target setting may require putative ways of working, and methods of service delivery to be reformulated, delegated, or reassigned to partnership agencies.

In the context of Northern Ireland, this process involved the increased development of professional networks and relationships with a range of organizations throughout the 1980s. While relations had always existed between the prison service and the Probation Board who have staff assigned to each of the prisons, these networks became increasingly extended from the mid-1980s onwards to include voluntary organizations such as NIACRO (the Northern Ireland Association for the Care and Resettlement of Offenders), the Society of Friends (Quakers), Save the Children Fund, Extern, and other similar charitable associations. All of these groups offered a range of services to prisoners, ex-prisoners, or their families, including employment, training, advice, transport to the prisons, visiting centres, and child-minding facilities.

As discussed above, throughout the 1980s the Northern Ireland prison service went to considerable lengths to improve the quality of relationships between prisoners and their families through the extension of the various home leave schemes. For the families of politically motivated prisoners, however, much of the basic assistance such as transport to prison or babysitting was organized through the paramilitary prisoner welfare organizations. IRA prisoners' families were the responsibility of Sinn Fein Prisoners of War Department, and the Loyalist families fell under the Loyalist Prisoner Welfare Association (Ulster Volunteer Force and Red Hand Commando) and the Loyalist Welfare Association (Ulster Defence Association).

From the mid-1980s onwards a number of improvements were made by the prison service designed to improve conditions for prisoners' families, many of them made in consultation with various statutory and voluntary organizations working in the field. For example, purpose-built visitors centres were built outside each of the adult prisons, managed by the various voluntary organizations but paid for by statutory monies (SSI 1993). In September 1989, the Northern Ireland prison service introduced their interface policy which was designed to 'enhance the relationship between the public and the Prison Service, by improving the conditions and arrangements for visits to prisons' (NIO Unpublished Memorandum 1990). The production of this policy document meant a lengthy and detailed series of consultations with all of the organizations working in the area of prisoners' families, other than the paramilitary-associated prisoner welfare organizations.[115]

The cumulative effect of these changes was designed to add up to a qualitatively new experience for visitors and prisoners. Procedures at visitors' reception were simplified, removing the requirement for proof of identity, and prisoners were allowed to send out visiting permits direct to visitors. Waiting rooms and visit areas were improved to include televisions or piped music, toys for children, pictures on walls, and easy access to toilets. Special training for staff involved in visits was introduced, more information was offered to visitors, and governors regularly monitored the treatment of visitors. Visits could be extended beyond the standard thirty minutes where practicable, and a new visitors' centre was built at Magilligan prison. Finally, additional support was committed to voluntary organizations in providing transport to the prisons (NIO Unpublished Memorandum 1990).

---

[115] In a similar fashion, the process of drawing up the service's first strategic plan 'Serving the Community' in 1990 involved a number of planning sessions with similar 'stakeholder' agencies.

In effect the prison service sought to reduce the areas of conflict concerning relations with prisoners' families and to facilitate the professional agencies working in the area.

One instrumentalist view of these developments would be that they were part of a hearts and minds campaign designed to reduce paramilitary influence amongst the families. Certainly many families of politically motivated prisoners remained reluctant to avail themselves of the services of organizations such as NIACRO and probation and these agencies arguably failed to take sufficient account of the significance of political motivation in their working practices with prisoners' families (McEvoy et al. 1999).[116] The improvements in conditions for families and the increased co-operation with professional organizations could thus be viewed as a strategy to remove an important propaganda weapon from the paramilitaries and lessen the families' material reliance on the paramilitary welfare organizations.

While true in part, such a view underplays the fluid nature of the interaction between the various players and the managerial good sense of reducing conflict where possible. Statutory organizations such as the probation service and government-funded voluntaries such as NIACRO and Save the Children often adopted explicitly critical stances of government policies in the prisons on issues such as conditions, the transfer of prisoners, strip searching, and other matters. Working relationships developed between the prisoner welfare organizations and the professional agencies towards common goals which were not necessarily in the interests of the prison service.[117] Similarly, managerialism encouraged a mindset which saw improved relations with prisoners' families as a key strategic objective in

[116] One senior manager of a major voluntary organization involved in this area frankly acknowledged that she had 'little doubt that the comparatively generous funding of prisoners' families work was in part designed to reduce the influence of the prisoner welfare organizations'. Interview with NIACRO senior manager, 15 Apr. 1996.

[117] For example, the fieldwork for the research into paramilitary prisoners' families undertaken by NIACRO was carried out through the Loyalist and Republican prisoner welfare organizations (see McEvoy et al. 1999). Similarly, a long-running campaign of voluntary and trade union organizations of which the author was secretary 1990–5 involved NIACRO, the Committee on the Administration of Justice (CAJ), the National Association of Probation Officers (NAPO), and the Irish Commission of Prisoners Overseas (ICPO) in campaigning for the transfer of Irish prisoners from Britain to Ireland. This body worked throughout that period with the Republican grouping the Committee for the Transfer of Irish Prisoners. Although such relationships were often difficult and reflected the different foci of the various actors, none the less regular meetings, conferences, and liaison on individual prisoners and families was a constant feature of the campaign over a ten-year period.

producing a more humane prison system (e.g. NIPS 1995: 4). As one prison governor told the author, 'we improved the situation for visitors and children in the prisons because it was the right thing to do, not because we thought people could be weaned away from paramilitaries.'[118] The treatment of prisoners' families became a genuine indicator by which the professionalism of the service could be measured and not simply another weapon in the armoury against the paramilitaries.

Managerialism, Autonomy, and the Struggle for Organizational Power

The final feature of managerialism concerns organizational dynamics within the prison service itself rather than in terms of relations with paramilitary prisoners. Within such a paradigm, managerialism may also be seen as a struggle or a least a redistribution of organizational power within the prison service.

As was discussed earlier, the wake of the hunger strikes saw a decrease in ministerial interference as less interventionist ministers allowed greater autonomy for the prison service to get on with the job (Prior 1986). As Pollitt (1993: 9) has described, the idea that managers should be given the right to manage and the autonomy to make decisions to achieve agreed outcomes has become a central tenet in managerialism. Often organizations which have adopted a managerialist paradigm provide a juxtaposition of institutions which have ingested a set of managerial discourses, discourses which tend to vilify what went before and eulogize the new. Such organizations tend to see politicians as dogmatic, interfering, and unstable whereas managers are viewed as pragmatic, enabling, and strategic (Clarke and Newman 1997: 65). Such a juxtaposition fitted perfectly with the self-image of prison management which emerged in the 1980s.[119]

In practical terms, the disengagement by ministers is usually achieved through an increasing division between what are viewed as policy issues (which are ostensibly the preserve of ministers) and operational matters which are the concern of managers. As DuGay has argued, such a division is perhaps the ideal organizational innovation for ministers. Ministers still retain formal accountability to Parliament

---

[118] Interview with prison governor, 9 Apr. 1998.
[119] Interview with prison governor, 13 Aug. 1997.

for the conduct of policy and yet are simultaneously able to decide what is and is not a policy issue, in effect to have their cake and eat it (DuGay 1996). None the less for managers there are advantages too in nebulous formulations. So long as managerial innovations or accommodations do not result in clear political difficulties for ministers (such as those presented by escapes or murders in the prisons), non-interventionist ministers may leave them to their own devices. Even where events do take place which are more obviously of policy relevance, the vagueness of lines of accountability or responsibility have advantages for all concerned providing that none of the protagonists breaks rank and blames the other.[120] As one prison governor suggested to the author:

Most sensible people viewed the era of the hunger strike as the darkest days of the service. Decision-making was constantly being dictated from above without reference to the realities on the ground. I think by the mid to late 1980s a proper sense of balance had been reached wherein ministers were kept appropriately informed but people were not afraid to take decisions that needed to be taken.[121]

The increased autonomy enjoyed by prison service managers in Northern Ireland during the 1980s and 1990s is, as in any agency, both an ideological and a practical issue concerning organizational power (Clarke and Newman 1997: 56). The practical struggle to wield organizational power, against forces from above and below, ensures that managerialism remains a contested regime. If one considers the situation of the senior management of the Northern Ireland prison service based at headquarters, similar organizational dynamics are at play between competing forces which are not directly related to the prisoners and their ability to influence events.

Firstly in terms of relations with ministers, the relationship between the chief executive and the minister was only clarified with the

---

[120] Despite numerous escapes, a number of murders, and lengthy and sometimes critical inquiries, no prison minister or senior prison official in the Northern Ireland prison service has ever been fired or forced to resign because of prison-related events. Following the escape of Liam Averill in 1997, and the murder of Billy Wright and David Keyes in the Maze prison, the mutual support of ministers and senior prison service officials was viewed as crucial to the political survival of both. The way in which these events were handled has been favourably contrasted to the author by a number of senior prison service officials to the dispute and mutual recriminations between Derek Lewis and Michael Howard following the Woodcock and Learmount Reports.   [121] Interview with prison governor, 13 Aug. 1997.

granting of agency status in 1995.[122] Prior to that the exact interplay between individual ministers and prison service senior managers had not been clear.[123] As is discussed in the final chapter, their respective influences on policy formulation became an issue of some contention in the period following the ceasefires.

Secondly, from the senior management team downwards, until agency set out the responsibilities of the chief executive in April 1995, the position of the chief executive (formerly known as the Controller of Prisons) had no formal legal status in prisons. Headquarters had evolved as an entity in the early 1970s in a context where previously the governor of Crumlin Road prison was the *de facto* head of the prison service. In addition, the Prison Rules specify that 'the governor shall be in command of the prison' (Rule 116 [1], NI Prison Rules), an important legal nicety which even the most bullish of British ministers has been reluctant to challenge.[124] While the creation of the Senior Policy

---

[122] 'Ministers set the policy framework within which the Agency operates, allocates resources to the prison service and approves its Corporate and Business Plans, including its key targets. Ministers do not normally become involved in the day to day management of the Prison Service but expect to be consulted by the Chief Executive on the handling of operational matters which could give rise to significant public or Parliamentary concern. Ministers may also issue directions to the Chief Executive on the handling of any prisons matters which they consider give rise to such concerns.' Minutes of evidence from Alan Shannon, chief executive of the Northern Ireland prison service, given to the Northern Ireland Affairs Select Committee, Wednesday, 29 Apr. 1998 at 1. That constitutional position was formalized in the framework document published in Apr. 1995 when the prison service formally became a Next Steps Agency.

[123] One dynamic in this relationship which is difficult to detail with any accuracy is the impact of individual actors in the process. For example, as discussed above, the influence of Jim Prior as Secretary of State in the early 1980s is widely viewed as a key factor in facilitating a more pragmatic approach to the prisoners (e.g. Coogan 1995, Taylor 1997). Less well known, however, is the impact of the key individual officials involved. For example, studies by Rock (1995) and Rutherford (1996) have attributed much influence in criminal justice policy-making to key officials in the Home Office in Britain, the Solicitor-General's Office in Canada, and the Dutch Ministry of Justice. While the author was at one stage tempted to attribute a similar influence to the powerful personality of John Steele who was Controller of Prisons in Northern Ireland from the mid-1980s to the early 1990s (and Secretary to the Gardiner Committee in 1975), all of the governors and senior officials interviewed for this book have counselled against this. The commonly articulated view is that while Steele was clearly an influential figure in particular in establishing the strategic planning process in the late 1980s, many of the more pragmatic practices were already in place when he took over as head of the service.

[124] One governor interviewed by the author recounted an incident when former Prison Minister Michael Mates had requested to go down the wings of one of the prisons in Northern Ireland. The governor in question refused his permission on operational grounds. After some dispute, Mr Mates accepted that the governor's view should take precedence (interview with prison governor, 20 Apr. 1999).

Group was designed to ease the relations between headquarters and institutions, as discussed in the section on prison management, such tensions between what Giddens (1990) refers to as the 'place based and non-placed based structures' (cited in Sparks, Bottoms, and Hay 1996: 135) have remained a feature of Northern Ireland prisons.

Thirdly, if one then considers additional dynamics such as industrial relations between the Prison Officers Association, the disputed terrain of managerialism becomes all the more apparent. The Northern Ireland prison service's mixed record on industrial relations between staff and managers was referred to in Chapter 7. As was noted, throughout the 1970s and the 1980s the Northern Ireland POA has shown itself to be a fairly strong trade union which, as one POA official interviewed by the author suggested, 'was certainly not behind the door in protecting the rights of its members'.[125] The RUC were required to deal with prisoners on a number of occasions in the 1970s and 1980s during periods of prison officer industrial actions.[126] The *Annual Reports* for that period placed considerable emphasis upon the 'improvements in industrial relations', 'improvement of communication', and 'mutual appreciation of respective roles of staff in prisons and headquarters' (e.g. NIPS 1989: 34). The clear deficiencies in the RUC's ability to deal with prisoners considerably strengthened the bargaining position of the POA.

By 1989 the English and Welsh Prison Officers Association had eventually accepted the reductions of overtime which accompanied the Fresh Start initiative. However, the uniformed Northern Ireland prison

---

[125] Interview with spokesperson for the Northern Ireland Prison Officers Association, 17 Sept. 1999.

[126] In 1978, in line with their colleagues in Britain, prison officers began a series of industrial actions which led to the creation of a temporary prison staffed by police officers to receive newly sentenced prisoners (NIPS 1979: 8). Similar action occurred in 1980 and 1981 when another temporary prison was established under police control after prison officers began refusing to accept newly sentenced prisoners in support of a national claim for meal breaks. As the *Annual Report* for that year recounts with evident ire, 'this was not an issue in Northern Ireland but the POA in Northern Ireland engaged in the action in support of their colleagues in Great Britain' (NIPS 1981: 12). In 1982 an overtime ban by the POA regarding the payment of travel time again resulted in the authorities calling in the RUC to assist in the prisons (NIPS 1983: 6). During 1984 there was 'limited industrial action at the Maze' (NIPS 1985: 6) and in Dec. 1986 staff at the Maze took industrial action regarding the disciplining of a staff member (NIPS 1987: 6). In 1987 staff took industrial action on a number of occasions involving the application of the VIP protection scheme to officers, an attempt at reducing income tax concessions, the suspension of duty of an officer from the YOC, and, over several months at the Maze, regarding the supply of new wet weather clothing (NIPS 1988: 27).

staff, who earned considerably more money than their English and Welsh counterparts through a Northern Ireland danger allowance and an average of almost twice as much overtime (20 hours compared to 12 hours in Britain), rejected Fresh Start as an effective reduction in their pay.[127] Six months later the Northern Ireland Prison Officers Association accepted a revised and improved offer entitled the 'Way Forward' (NIPS 1989: 33) which continued their privileged position in comparison to their colleagues in Britain. The Way Forward allowed for an overall reduction in the Northern Ireland prison service's wage bill by committing to contracting hours which saw an increase in the basic pay of officers while removing the majority of overtime. However, in order to cover staffing shortfalls, the Way Forward allowed officers on a 46-hour week to be paid overtime once his/her 46 contract hours had been completed. The agreement contained a commitment to reduce the 46-hour contract over a period of five years to a basic 38.5 hour week. It was, as one POA spokesperson interviewed acknowledged, 'a pretty good deal for the officers'.[128]

It is clear that the general desire to reduce the power of trade unions which underpinned some of the thrust of managerialism in Britain met with a receptive audience amongst prison managers in Northern Ireland. Almost without exception prison managers and officials interviewed for this research have expressed frustration and a sense of exasperation at the perceived power of the POA to thwart management initiatives. The use of managerial initiatives to redress that perceived imbalance in power relations between the union and management was a key feature of the late 1980s and 1990s. In 1994/5 the introduction of the Framework Agreement in prison had the equivalent impact on overtime hours that the POA had been powerful enough to resist under the Fresh Start proposals in 1989. In 1995 the Crime and Disorder Act made it unlawful for prison officers to go on strike.

Less antagonistic relations with paramilitary prisoners arguably served to reduce the bargaining position of the POA. When officers were perceived to be in the front line in a strategy designed to defeat terrorism, their organizational power was considerably enhanced. However, as that strategy gave way to managerialism, it dissipated the

---

[127] While uniformed staff rejected Fresh Start, the governors and chief officers accepted it, thus amalgamating the former ranks of chief officers 1 and 2 into governors five and four respectively.

[128] Interview with spokesperson for the Northern Ireland Prison Officers Association, 17 Sept. 1999.

influence of the POA which remained a persistent critic of what they perceived as 'the surrender of control in the prisons to the paramilitaries'.[129]

From such a perspective, increasing centralism in headquarters-driven policies and practices, key performance indicators, staff reviews, and so forth can be seen as the outplaying of competing power relationships between the various actors. It is clear that some such developments have been informed, at least in part, by a headquarters view that local staff and management were not performing as effectively and efficiently as they might. Despite attempts to create greater ownership of strategic planning and development in the 1990s by a more bottom up approach, a them and us attitude between headquarters and the individual institutions and headquarters and main grade staff has remained a perennial problem.[130]

As was noted in Chapter 7, it is clear that managers failed to maintain the confidence and support of the main grade staff in changing the style of interaction with paramilitary prisoners during the era of managerialism. Staff's working lives were increasingly shaped by a context wherein political motivation was incrementally recognized but where that could not be publicly acknowledged until comparatively recently. Many prison officers saw what they regarded as an essentially weak management engaged in a process of continuously appeasing paramilitary prisoners without 'owning up to it'.[131] For some such officers, the increased *de facto* recognition of the paramilitaries and the gradual ceding of control of the prisoners had a corrosive impact upon their morale.

Conclusion

The prison management philosophy which I have characterized as managerialism was not an all-encompassing strategy but rather the coagulation of a number of disparate and sometimes contradictory policy and operational influences. As discussed earlier, the changes in the operation of the British public service generally, and criminal justice system in particular, played an increasingly significant influence in the way the prison service was managed in Northern Ireland from the

---

[129] Interview with spokesperson for the Northern Ireland Prison Officers Association, 17 Sept. 1999.   [130] Interview with prison governor, 9 Apr. 1998.
[131] Interview with former prison officer, 12 Sept. 1996.

late 1980s onwards. More significantly, perhaps, the managerial frame-work legitimized a series of existing working practices and ideologies which had already emerged after the hunger strikes.

Such changes were a reflection of the political and material realities of having to manage large numbers of disciplined and highly moti-vated paramilitary prisoners. The managerial endeavour emerged as a range of responses which were variously characterized by pragmatism, negotiation, and compromise as well as bullish determination, repres-sion, and a refusal to give way.

As in the era of reactive containment and criminalisation, the man-agement of prisons from 1981 onwards was shaped and contextualized by the ongoing dialectic with prisoners' strategies of resistance as well as broader political forces such as changes in government conflict man-agement strategies. Between 1969 and 1981 the styles of prison man-agement which evolved came about in a context where the prisons were at the forefront of the conflict. Managerialism, however, may be viewed as an attempt to steer the prisons away from the epicentre of the military and security conflict. Managerialism permitted the prison service to transmogrify their *raison d'être* from the defeat of terrorists in the prisons to a series of technical and professional discourses con-cerning the effective management of terrorist prisoners.

Such a view does not suggest that prison management became in any sense a value-free endeavour, untainted by the political and ideological influences which had characterized previous prison management styles. As is discussed above, the desire to resist paramilitary influence, the commitment to individualization of treatment, and the constant redrawing of battlelines with paramilitaries were all indicative of a mindset which retained a formal commitment to criminalisation at the very least. While such a commitment remained, it became increasingly curtailed, intersected with, and influenced by, a competing range of priorities. An open-eyed appreciation of the disaster of the hunger strikes, the desire to avoid conflict inside and outside the prisons, the determination to professionalize prison staff and management prac-tices and to deliver a value for money service, and the increasingly sophisticated tactics of the prisoners all served to limit considerably the potential for any crude application of the criminalisation agenda by prison managers.

While managerialism undoubtedly encouraged greater flexibility and pragmatism amongst prison managers and reduced conflict with prisoners, a number of potential criticisms should be pointed out.

Firstly, and perhaps most obviously from a prison management perspective, it facilitated a process over a two-decade period where prisoners took effective control over large sections of the prison estate and
operated within a considerably altered set of power relations with the
prison authorities. Such a process has been described to the author as
'the longest surrender in history'.[132] This is not a view that I accept. I
would argue that the maintenance of a regime for non-conforming
paramilitary prisoners other than that which pertained at the Maze
until July 2000 could not have been achieved without untenable levels
of repression. In that sense, managerialism is perhaps better viewed as
a reluctant acceptance of the reality of the prisoners' power base rather
than an unprincipled series of capitulations.

Secondly, while managerialism was to a degree characterized by the
avoidance of conflict, it certainly did not remove the potential for
repression or human rights abuses within the system.[133] While successive prison service strategic plans became increasingly specific concerning aims, objectives, and key target outputs and so forth, they have
consistently been criticized for their lack of detail on enforceable prisoners' rights (NIACRO 1992, CAJ 1998). As was discussed in Chapter
6, there was considerable resentment amongst staff and managers concerning increased judicial activism in the prisons and some staff have
expressed serious misgivings about the impact on prison management
of the incorporation of the European Convention on Human Rights.[134]
Managerialism is explicitly not a mindset through which the authorities seek to make themselves more accountable through external judicial scrutiny.

Thirdly, managerialism encouraged an understandable desire on the

---

[132] Interview with former prison officer, 12 Sept. 1996.

[133] For example, on 2 Mar. 1992 male prison officers entered the wings of Mourne
House, the female section of Maghaberry prison, allegedly singing, 'Happy Days are
Here Again'. All the thirty-two inmates, Republican, Loyalist, and ordinary, were
informed that they were to be strip searched. Twenty-two Republican prisoners refused
to co-operate and all, except one who was recovering from a hysterectomy, were forcibly
stripped and searched one by one in a process taking ten hours. Male warders were used
to break down cell doors and were apparently on the wings when the searches were carried out by female prison officers. Several prisoners and prison officers received injuries
and five women were charged with assaulting prison officers in the course of resisting the
search. This was the first time ever that the whole female prison had been strip searched.
Nothing which could have constituted a security threat was found. (For a historical
account of the strip searching of female politically motivated prisoners see McCafferty
1981.)

[134] Interview with prison officer, 12 May 1999.

part of the prison service to promote and celebrate their technical and scientific ability to manage paramilitary prisoners. Following the public relations disaster of the hunger strikes, the prison service increasingly adopted a policy of facilitating media access to the prisons, redefined their corporate image,[135] and began a policy of 'selling their success story'.[136] While successful media management has always been a key element of government strategy in Northern Ireland (Curtis 1984, Miller 1994, Rolston and Miller 1996), it is debatable whether the strategy of acknowledging *de facto* political status for terrorist prisoners was a packageable endeavour. This is particularly the case given the government's clear policy of denying the political character of the conflict at every opportunity in other spheres (Miller 1998). As one very experienced local broadcast journalist told the author 'I always got the impression from the prison service that they were really frustrated at us [the media] for our inability to see how clever they were. You would get outraged phone calls after a story about "the Maze is a holiday camp", but that is what it was . . . They seemed to have lost the plot a bit.'[137] Managerialism's celebration of the scientific and instrumentalist aspects of prison policy encouraged a separation of the technical from the political, divorced it from broader contradictory government policy, and resulted in a confusing public relations strategy.[138]

Fourthly, and in a similar vein, managerialism's technocratic view of prison management also encouraged managers to fail to internalize the logic of their own adopted positions. The ostensibly depoliticized analysis of managerialism facilitated the adoption of policies which

---

[135] The redefinement of the corporate image in 1990/1 included a new logo of the prison service. The traditional crown emblem was replaced by a new managerial logo of a diamond within a diamond, each vertically divided into two shades of blue.

[136] Briefing by prison service public relations officer attended by the author, 30 June 1993.

[137] Interview with former BBC Northern journalist, 12 Mar. 1999.

[138] In one incident discussed in more detail below, the prison authorities enlisted the support of the prisoners themselves in allowing journalists on to the wing at the Maze to 'set the record straight'. Prisoners were adamant that the prison authorities remained in control of the prison. IRA OC Padraig Wilson told reporters, 'If we had control, I wouldn't be sitting here today. I'd be fulfilling my duty to escape.' *Irish Times* (9 Jan. 1998), 'Maze Prisoners Reject Charges of Holiday Camp Treatment'. One *Daily Mail* reporter remarked that the purpose of the visit was: 'According to both the governor, and in a strange alliance, the prisoners, to persuade me and a number of other journalists that it [Maze] is a properly ordered and well-run institution.' The same reporter went on to opine that 'I remain unconvinced—as I am sure will those who saw the television coverage of what effectively amounted to Open Day.' *Daily Mail* (9 Jan. 1998), 'Taking My Chance in the Lion's Den'.

were not entirely ideologically consistent. Therefore it became possible to resist segregation at Crumlin Road while operating a completely segregated regime at the Maze, to delay and prevaricate on prisoner transfers from Britain to be nearer their families while operating progressive family-related policies in Northern Ireland,[139] and to deny the inevitability of prisoner releases in the wake of the ceasefires despite the clear importance of the prisoner issue to the potential for peace. Managerialism encouraged selective myopia at a political and ideological level which (as is discussed in the next chapter) contributed significantly to the breakdown of the first ceasefire in 1996.

[139] As discussed previously, the issue of the transfer of Irish politically motivated prisoners from Britain had been the source of a number of protests and hunger strikes during the 1970s. Resistance to transfer had largely come from the British Home Office, not least because of differences in remission rates between Northern Ireland and Britain with regard to those convicted of terrorist offences. Following a lengthy campaign by prisoners, their families, and the range of non-governmental organizations referred to above, an interdepartmental working party was established made up of members of the Northern Ireland Office, Home Office, and Scottish Office. The resulting Ferrers Report published in 1992 recommended that prisoners should be transferred to be nearer their families where possible but on the basis of renewable 'extended temporary transfers' which meant that the prisoners' release would still be governed by the transferring jurisdiction. Prisoners returning to Northern Ireland were to be transferred to Maghaberry. However, despite the technical capacity to give effect to such transfers, continued interference by the Home Office and Home Secretary Michael Howard in such transfers (even after the IRA ceasefire of 1994) meant the issue remained a highly politically contentious one. The insistence by the Northern Ireland Office that the matter was a technical one rather than highly politically symbolic, particularly during the ceasefire era, was a source of considerable frustration to all involved in the transfer campaign.

11

Prisoner Release, the Peace Process, and the Political Character of the Conflict

> It doesn't make any of us feel comfortable or happy to talk
> about releasing prisoners. But we also have to recognize that
> unless there is some agreement on such things there can be no
> agreement at all in Northern Ireland.[1]

Introduction

The final chapter of this book concerns the period from the IRA and Loyalist ceasefires in 1994 to the end of 2000.[2] This period is perhaps the most dramatic in the thirty year history of paramilitary imprisonment in Northern Ireland. The seemingly unthinkable has happened. Other than a small number of dissidents opposed to the peace process, at the time of writing, almost all paramilitary prisoners have been released under the terms of the Good Friday Agreement. British politicians including the Secretary of State have negotiated directly with serving paramilitary prisoners. Prisoners have been released to attend negotiations and organizational rallies on the outside. Considerable sums of European Union and statutory monies have been dedicated to ensure the successful reintegration of paramilitary prisoners. In short the release and reintegration of paramilitary prisoners has moved to the very core of the efforts at resolving the political conflict in Ireland.

This chapter firstly explores the historical context of prisoner release in Ireland North and South and the relevance of that history to

---

[1] Conservative Leader William Hague in an interview with BBC Radio news reproduced *Irish News* (25 Apr. 1998), 'Hague Defends His Support for Deal'.

[2] Extracts from this chapter were previously published in the *Fordham International Law Journal* (McEvoy 1999). I am grateful to the journal for permission to reproduce some of those discussions here.

the recent process. Secondly, the role of prisoners in the process of conflict resolution in the 1990s is examined including the period before and after the breakdown of the first IRA ceasefire. The provisions within the Good Friday Agreement and subsequent legislation are then analysed in so far as they relate to prisoner release as an incentive for peace amongst organizations outside the peace process; the decommissioning of paramilitary weapons; the victims of violence; and prisoner reintegration. Finally I argue that movement on the prisoner issue has represented a crucial acknowledgement by the British government of the political character of the conflict, and suggest that such an acknowledgement is required in Northern Ireland generally as part of the ongoing efforts at conflict solution.

The Historical Context Of The Early Release of Politically Motivated Prisoners In Ireland

Although it is little explored in the literature on conflict resolution and peace studies (Von Tangen Page 1998a), the concept of the early release from prison of former combatants has a prominent role in the international experience of political conflict resolution (Gormally and McEvoy 1995). More recently, the notion of the release of former combatants after a period of inter state violence has become one of the mainstays of international humanitarian law (Fleck and Boethe 1995) and indeed has been discussed as extending to non-state combatants (Lopez 1994).

One of the points often repeated during the course of the discussions on prisoner release in Northern Ireland, particularly by those who were opposed to such a move, was that it represented an unprecedented interference with the operation of the criminal justice process. As former Ulster Unionist security spokesperson Ken Maginnis argued, 'early releases outside the judicial system have never been made before'.[3] In fact, however, there is a long British history of doing exactly that. In Anglo-Saxon legal tradition, the power of the sovereign both to dispense and mitigate punishments in the wake of battles or wars was viewed as appropriate to either individual offenders or classes of offenders from at least the seventh century.

The British Parliament has enacted 110 acts of general pardon or amnesty for various classes of offenders (Kirchheimer 1961) most of

[3] *Irish News* (11 Aug. 1997), 'Mowlam Jail Hint Brings Political Fury'.

whom were involved in political or civil conflicts of one form or another. In Ireland, politically motivated offenders have been released from prison after hostilities have ceased after every period of political violence since the fourteenth century (Mullan 1995). An analysis of the various prisoner releases which have occurred in the twentieth century in particular (both South and North of the border) offer crucial insights into the process ultimately agreed under the Good Friday Agreement.

Prisoner Releases in the South, 1916–1962

Following the Easter Rising of 1916 and the execution of many of the leaders of the Rising, the British government imprisoned and interned thousands of prisoners in Ireland, England, and Wales (O'Mahony 1987). As previously discussed, Republican prisoners began to organize themselves in the prisons, and protested their status as political prisoners using tactics such as hunger strikes, the destruction of prison property, and escapes from prison (Longford and O'Neill 1974: 52–60). From December 1916 onwards, after David Lloyd George had become British Prime Minister, the release of large numbers of prisoners was ordered positively to effect public opinion in Ireland. In June 1917 a cabinet decision recommended the exercise of the 'royal prerogative of mercy' to many prisoners, an amnesty in all but name (Dangerfield 1979: 258). Of the seventy-three Sinn Fein candidates returned in the 1918 election, half were sentenced or interned prisoners at the time. Faced with the decisive election result, the government began to release the remaining prisoners from the Rising and all were out by April 1919.

After the Anglo–Irish War, and the partition of the island in 1920–1, discussions between the governments of the Irish Free State and Northern Ireland included the question of prisoner releases. At a meeting between Michael Collins (chairman of the provisional government in the South) and Northern premier Sir James Craig in January 1922, Collins insisted on an amnesty for those Republicans who had been held in the North since before the treaty was signed (Coogan 1990: 340). The two leaders met again in February, and finally on 30 March signed an 'Agreement between the Provisional Government and the Government of Northern Ireland'. The agreement included a provision that:

The two Governments shall, in cases agreed upon between the Signatories, arrange for the release of political prisoners in prison for offences before the date hereof. No offences committed after the 31st March, 1922, shall be open to consideration. (Boyle 1977: 173–5)

In the event, no prisoners were freed a̲s̲ ̲ ̲ ̲ ̲ment, which became redundant with the ̲ ̲ ̲ ̲South between those Republicans opposed t̲ ̲ ̲Free State government who supported it. Be̲ ̲courts into operation, the provisional government̲on 3 October giving dissidents twelve days to lay̲(Coogan 1987). By March 1923, 12,000 Republican pris̲by Free State forces. By virtue of the Indemnity, (British ̲1923, 'No action or other legal proceedings whatsoever' we̲to be instituted against any person acting in the service of the̲from the eve of the Easter Rising on 23 April 1916 to date. Likewi̲the end of the civil war the Indemnity Act 1923 stopped proceedings̲respect of any act done on behalf of the Free State since 27 June 1922 'in the course of the suppression of the state of rebellion'. De Valera, the leader of the anti-treaty faction, resisted proposals by some IRA officers to arrange a surrender of arms in exchange for an amnesty (Longford and O'Neill 1974: 225). The Indemnity Act 1924 had a wider scope applying to all parties in the conflict and led to all anti-treaty IRA prisoners being released.

In 1938, as previously discussed, the IRA started a campaign of bombing of targets in Northern Ireland and in Britain (Bowyer Bell 1979). In 1939, to cope both with the IRA campaign and the outbreak of the Second World War, the Irish government declared a state of emergency and introduced internment once again (Lee 1989: 223). Around 2,000 people were interned during the war years under various provisions and hundreds were convicted by military courts. A Republican Prisoners' Release Committee was established at the end of 1945 to press for the release of remaining prisoners. The campaign developed strongly and, led by Sean MacBride, the newly formed Clann na Phoblachta used it as a vehicle in pursuing their electoral ambitions (Murphy 1975, Coogan 1980, esp. 26–7). Clann took ten Dáil seats in the general election of 1948 and formed a coalition with Fine Gael. Within weeks of the change of government, the last five IRA prisoners were released from Portlaoise by order of the new Minister for Justice (Bowyer Bell 1979: 249).

Again in December 1956 the IRA formally began a border campaign with attacks on Northern Ireland (Coogan 1980: 377). On 4 July 1957, the Irish government introduced internment and by March 1958, 131 people were held in the Curragh. All were released, however, by 11 March 1959, a total of 206 having passed through the gates. Sentenced

…ourts and the special …After a largely unsuc-
…n 26 February 1962.[4]
…time of the ceasefire;
…whom were uncondi-
…ral amnesty, granted
…n.

…offers several prece-
…the aftermath of a
…onflict. In its early
…on the process of
…nt provided by the
…st that successive
…nt of the opposi-
… question of prisoner release in
… way appears to coincide with political expediency.
Such a quintessentially pragmatic approach to prisoner release was
reflected by Irish governments of varying political persuasions during
the current peace process and is discussed below.

Prisoner Releases in the North, 1920–1962

After the formation of the Northern Ireland state in 1920, one of the
first actions by the newly created provisional government was to
introduce a state of emergency and intern those suspected of being
members of the IRA; 130 of these prisoners were ultimately released
as part of the post-treaty releases (Farrell 1976). As noted above, a
number of Craig/Collins meetings provided for the 'release of political

---

[4] 'The leadership of the Resistance Movement has ordered the termination of the
campaign of resistance to British occupation . . . all arms and other materials have been
dumped and all full-time active service volunteers have been withdrawn.' Statement
released by Irish Republican Publicity Bureau, 26 Feb. 1962, Dublin.

[5] This is not to suggest that the treatment of politically motivated prisoners in the
South should be understood as more soft than their Northern or British counterparts.
Rather the author would contend that the approach taken in the South towards the prisoner question *after* various cessations of hostilities has been informed by a more intuitive
understanding of the emotional and political significance of the prisoner issue and its
historic potential to become a destabilizing element of the political landscape. Such
awareness has also traditionally been tempered by political expediency. For example, the
Irish government has to date refused to release the IRA murders of Garda Gerry
McCabe, killed in an abortive robbery just after the first IRA ceasefire even though these
prisoners quite clearly fall within the terms of the release provisions of the Good Friday
Agreement.

prisoners' but these failed to materialize when high levels of political violence continued. Apart from those interned, the courts were busy trying and sentencing suspected IRA men and the number of sentenced prisoners rose from 470 to 870 between April and October 1922. With the civil war raging in the South, divisions in the ranks in the North, and widespread loyalist violence and government repression, IRA activity petered out in the North by the autumn of 1922. Internment was ended in 1924 and internees were released. Sentenced prisoners were ultimately freed as a result of the tripartite agreement between the British government and the governments of the North and South signed in December 1925, when decisions on prisoner release formed part of a package of concessions in return for increased recognition of partition by the Free State government (Phoenix 1994: 333–4).

The outbreak of the Second World War led to the reintroduction of internment by the government in the North, in line with their counterparts in the South (Lyons 1983). By 1942, 802 suspected IRA men had been interned (Fisk 1983). The IRA campaign of that era was seriously hampered by internments, jailing, and executions both North and South. The Northern government released all internees at the end of the war. As in the 1920s, the release of interned politically motivated prisoners at the end of the Second World War was conditional that they kept the peace (McGuffin 1973). However, some sentenced prisoners remained in prison for several years after the war ended (Farrell 1976: 168).

After the IRA border campaign (1956–62), eighty-nine internees were released after signing a pledge renouncing violence. Twenty-five sentenced prisoners, from a total of ninety-four sentenced for serious offences, were released under the royal prerogative of mercy. It appears that some prisoners gave a verbal undertaking, and in seven cases entered into a voluntary recognizance before a resident magistrate to keep the peace and be of good character for a number of years.[6] The attitudes of the Northern Ireland judiciary during this period are instructive. As then Lord Chief Justice MacDermott noted when sentencing a number of IRA prisoners for an arms raid in Omagh:

It may well be that when you have time for reflection you will wonder whether the sentences which I am about to pass can be reduced or abated. Whether that will ever come to pass is a matter for the executive government and not for me, but I will say this, and if you do not heed it now I hope you will later. It seems to me unlikely that your sentences will be curtailed unless at least two

---

[6] Confidential correspondence to the author from a Northern Ireland Office source.

conditions are present—the first is that you yourselves will have turned your backs on violence, and the second is that the campaign of which you are at once the participants and the victims comes to a stop.[7]

The response of the Unionist government to that IRA ceasefire was also of interest. Brian Faulkner, then Minister of Home Affairs and later Prime Minister of Northern Ireland, addressed the Stormont parliament on the day after the announcement. He began by repudiating 'the implication . . . that there are persons in my prisons serving sentences for political offence', but later in a reply suggested that 'persons who have been sentenced for their part in political activities' could seek to avail themselves of the royal prerogative of mercy, as a number (unspecified) had already done. He suggested that he had 'no intention of authorizing a general release' and that 'the abandonment of the means to wage war will be an earnest of good faith; the retention of such will be an indication of the intent to resume the campaign'.[8] Of the twenty-six IRA prisoners still in jail at the end of the campaign, all were released by December 1963 within one year of the cessation of hostilities, with undertakings neither sought nor given and no handover of IRA weapons.[9]

The experiences of prisoner release in the North since partition are instructive for a number of reasons. Firstly, although releases occurred more slowly in the North than in the South the fact that they took place at all is significant given Unionist misgivings that Republicans would resume attacks on the Northern state. Secondly, Unionist ministers appeared more concerned with the symbolism of recognizing the political character of the IRA than their Southern counterparts. Thirdly, as suggested by Faulkner's statement, prisoner release should be related in some fashion to the question of the decommissioning of paramilitary weapons. All of these factors were to feature heavily in Unionist discourses on prisoner release in the North during the 1990s peace process.

Prisoners and the 1994 Ceasefire Declarations

It is beyond the scope of this book to examine in any detail the origins of the peace process in Ireland.[10] With regard to the prisons, however, the period preceding the IRA and Loyalist ceasefires in 1994 was character-

---

[7] *Ulster Newsletter* (16 Dec. 1956) 'Omagh Arms Raid Trial Concludes'.
[8] Northern Ireland House of Commons Official Report (Hansard) vol. 50, col. 1951, 27 Feb. 1962.
[9] Confidential correspondence from a Northern Ireland Office source.
[10] For an overview see Coogan (1995), Mallie and McKittrick (1996) De Bréadún (2001).

ized by intense discussions and negotiations within the ranks of the respective movements including the prisoners. One former Republican prisoner has suggested to the author that an earlier version of the discussion document sometimes referred to as TUAS (Totally Un-armed Strategy), which laid out the potential for a non-violent Republican strategy, had actually circulated amongst Republican prisoners in the early 1990s.[11] Certainly in the period before the announcement of the ceasefire on 31 August 1994, the leadership of the IRA prisoners were confident of the shape of the political settlement to come. As the then IRA Officer Commanding Sean Lynch indicated six months before the ceasefire:

We are a product of the political conflict. Within a negotiated settlement prisoners are one of the issues which need to be addressed. If there's a solution all prisoners should be released immediately. John Major might say differently, but all the men on this wing know that once there's a solution we're out.[12]

The Loyalists worked perhaps even harder to ensure that their prisoners were involved in the discussions which led to the Loyalist ceasefire in October 1994. In the weeks preceding the ceasefire declaration, leading Loyalist politicians were permitted to visit their prisoners in the Maze. The Ulster Defence Association in particular indicated that any ceasefire was explicitly predicated upon the support of their prisoners and indeed suggested at one stage that the ceasefire announcement should take place at the Maze car park to underline the prisoners' importance (Cusack and McDonald 1997: 319).[13] Unlike their Republican counterparts, who had commended 'the

[11] Interview with former IRA life sentenced prisoner, 17 Jan. 1996. TUAS outlined the favourable national and international political configuration for progress on Republican goals in the absence of armed struggle. Such factors included a sympathetic Fianna Failled administration in Dublin, John Hume's leadership of the SDLP, the interest of the US Presidency and the Irish American Lobby, and the unpopularity of the then Conservative government with fellow members of the European Union. Some commentators critical of the peace process suggested in the wake of the breakdown of the first IRA ceasefire in 1996 that TUAS might in fact mean 'Tactical Use of Unarmed Struggle'. See e.g. E. Harris, *Irish Times*, (24 Dec. 1996), 'Sinn Fein Line a Recipe for Strife'. Another former IRA prisoner (who was not in prison at the time of the ceasefires) has suggested that discussions with the prisoners on the ceasefires were minimal, a fact which caused some resentment amongst prisoners who felt excluded from the organizational decision-making process. Interview with former IRA prisoner, 9 Oct. 1998.

[12] Interview with Sean Lynch, IRA Officer Commanding, HMP Maze, 'Inside the Maze', *Guardian* (21 Feb. 1994).

[13] A senior figure within the PUP, the political wing of the UVF (the other major Loyalist paramilitary faction), has suggested to the author that while UVF prisoners were a crucial constituency in the preparations for peace, they were regarded as another

political prisoners who had sustained the struggle against all the odds for the past 25 years',[14] the Loyalist ceasefire statement 'solemnly promised to leave no stone unturned to secure their [the prisoners] freedom'.[15]

This subtle difference in emphasis was to characterize the behaviour of both sets of protagonists in their attitudes to political engagement after the first ceasefire. The British government instigated preliminary discussions between civil servants and representatives from Sinn Fein and the fringe Loyalist parties in December 1994. According to one former government negotiator who attended those meetings:

All the Loyalists wanted to talk about was prisoners. I suppose they had come to the conclusion that the Union was safe, therefore the main issue on their agenda was the prisoners. The 'Shinners' [Sinn Fein] however seemed reluctant to be drawn on discussions regarding prisoners . . .[16]

While Republicans did establish a pressure group Saoirse to campaign for the release of politically motivated prisoners following the first IRA ceasefire, they appeared concerned to avoid a focus upon the prisoner issue that would dilute their negotiating position on other matters such as constitutional change. As one IRA prisoner interviewed by the author in 1996 argued, 'I did not go to prison to get out of prison, movement on prisoners will not suffice'.[17] None the less the Major government's failure to move on prisoner issues, even on humanitarian issues such as the transfer of prisoners back to Northern Ireland to be closer to their families, was seen as indicative of the general lack of good will by a Conservative administration apparently motivated by 'the negativity of mistrust' (Coogan 1995: 381).

---

battalion of the UVF and appear to have had less power over political direction than their UDA counterparts in the Maze. Interview, 2 Dec. 1994. The Loyalist ceasefire was ultimately announced in Fernhill House Estate, a training ground for the original Ulster Volunteer Force who had drilled there at the beginning of the century in preparation for their armed resistance to the introduction of Home Rule in Ireland.

[14] Statement issued by the IRA Army Council, 31 Aug. 1994, declaring a complete cessation of military operations (Dublin: Irish Republican Publicity Bureau).

[15] Statement issued by the Combined Loyalist Military Command declaring a cessation of operational hostilities. Website http://www.uhb.fr/Langues/Cei/cfloy94.htm

[16] Confidential source.

[17] Interview with former IRA prisoner, 11 Dec. 1995.

The British Government Response to the 1994 Ceasefires: 'Minimalist and Begrudging'

The Irish government was quick to recognize the political importance of the prisoner issue, and began freeing prisoners within months of the 1994 ceasefire, releasing a total of thirty-six of the seventy IRA held in the Republic's jails by February 1996 in order to 'consolidate the peace process'.[18] While releases were halted as a result of the breakdown of the IRA ceasefire in February 1996, they began again within weeks of the announcement of the restoration of that ceasefire in July 1997,[19] and continued before and after the signing of the Good Friday Agreement (discussed below).

The response by the then British government, however, to the 1994 ceasefires in general and with regard to the prisoner issue in particular has been widely criticized. The British government began by insisting that the IRA should use the word 'permanent' regarding the ceasefire, refusing to countenance a reduction in security arrangements, and essentially adopted a position of demanding ever greater evidence of the Republicans' bona fides.[20] In retrospective justification of his

---

[18] *Irish Times* (10 June 1998), 'Freed IRA members Against Renewed Cease-fire'. The significance of the interplay between pragmatism and political symbolism was highlighted in Jan. 1995 when the Irish government announced their intention to use the provisions of the Criminal Justice Act 1960 in order to release IRA prisoners. That Act had originally been intended to facilitate the temporary release of 'ordinary prisoners'. A number of the nine IRA prisoners scheduled for release argued that such a mechanism undermined their status as political prisoners and argued that they would not leave unless release was granted under Section 33 of the Offences Against the State Act, the Emergency legislation under which they were tried. The government relinquished and the prisoners were given permanent release under the Emergency legislation on the condition that they did not 'through publicity or otherwise, do anything which might cause annoyance to, or distress to any person or to the family or friends of any person who may have been affected by the offences which led to their imprisonment'.

[19] *Irish News* (14 Aug. 1997), 'More Releases of Republican Prisoners May be on the Way'.

[20] One senior source in the Dublin government suggested prophetically just after the 1994 ceasefires, 'There are a lot of worries that our British friends don't seem to quite understand what is happening. The thing of making a fetish of the word permanent when the whole tenor of the thing was plain to see seems quite odd. This gratuitous stuff from the British doesn't actually reassure the Unionists. There is a growing concern at the inability of the British to actually read the potential of the present situation, and their capacity for getting impaled on the ritualistic side of things. We can't for the life of us see the need to inject all these negative notes that nothing can be done until something is somehow proven. I don't know where British pragmatism has gone to' (cited in Mallie and McKittrick 1996: 339).

government's caution, John Major argued in the wake of the break-down of the first IRA ceasefire that:

No-one, no-one took more risks for peace over the past two years, but we never lost sight of the fact that the IRA commitment had not been made for good. No responsible government could have done otherwise. This is why we and many others saw the decommissioning of illegal arms as a way of creating confidence . . . the IRA was continuing to train and plan for terrorist attacks . . . It remained ready to resume full scale terrorism at any time. The IRA peace was not true peace. Our caution about the IRA was only too justified (cited in Bew and Gillespie 1996: 166).

At one level, John Major's defence of the British government's position after the IRA bomb in Canary Wharf in London, 9 February 1996, may seem to be a reasonable vindication of a cautious security policy. The IRA ceasefire did come to an end after all. However, just over one year previously the then Chief Constable of the RUC Sir Hugh Annesley had stated, 'there is very little doubt in my mind that the leadership of the Republican movement were determined to go for the peaceful route when they announced the cease-fire, and I don't think the leadership has wavered in that in the intervening months and the cease-fire on their side has held very strongly'.[21] It would appear that, in the intervening year, policy was directed by overwhelming security concerns rather than in seeking to secure the peace, despite the initial view of the RUC.

Troop levels in Northern Ireland remained high, there was little suggestion of concrete reform of the RUC, no commitment to the removal of Emergency legislation, and the Diplock system remained active (CAJ 1995). Furthermore, MI5, who had been searching for a clear role since the end of the cold war (O'Hara 1994) and who had recently won a battle amongst the security services for primacy in combating Irish terrorism in Britain, consistently planted anti-peace process stories in the press (Urban 1996).[22] The latter had devoted over half of their 2,000 staff and £150 million budget to Irish terrorism in the run up to the IRA ceasefire.[23] As Albert Reynolds, former Taoiseach of the Irish Republic and a key architect of the peace process argued, it appeared that British policy was still being directed by elements of the political

[21] *Irish News* (26 Jan. 1995) 'IRA has not Wavered from Peace Path says Annesley'.
[22] Urban describes the *Sunday Times* reporting of that period as the 'inhouse journal of those elements of MI5 who were opposed to the peace process'. (Urban 1996).
[23] *Guardian* (28 Aug. 1995), 'Cease-fire cost MI5 its Biggest Contract'.

and military establishment who saw the cessation of violence as a sign of weakness,[24] and the peace process as a way of achieving the military defeat of the IRA.[25]

It is difficult to discern the exact degree to which those directing British government policy simply believed the more hawkish advice of MI5[26] over the RUC, used all-encompassing security concerns as an excuse for political inactivity, or were acting in accordance with deeply embedded ideological assumptions about how to respond to terrorism. The Conservative government had of course been engaged in secret dialogue with the Republican movement (represented by Martin McGuinness and Gerry Kelly) between 1990 and February 1993, which somewhat undermined any principled objection to negotiations with terrorism. No doubt policy formulation on the response to the ceasefires was further complicated by the fact that the Major government had only a slim majority in Parliament and was reliant on the votes of Unionists who opposed any dilution of the security stance. In any event, the lack of any substantive commitment to standing down the apparatus of state coercion was perceived, at least by Republicans and Nationalists, as a failure to respond to the cessation of violence (Mallie and McKittrick 1996).

Within the prisons, the most obvious example of the technocratic response which pervaded government reaction to the first ceasefires was the response of the prison service to the pressure for movement on prisoner release. While progressive measures such as home leave, life sentence releases, and improved arrangement for visitors continued and were developed, the service largely failed to grasp the key issue in

---

[24] Despite the high levels of violence previous to the ceasefire, an insightful glimpse of the views within parts of the security infrastructure regarding the peace process emerged in the biography of a former member of the security services, who had been killed in a major helicopter crash: 'Police and Army counter-terror operations so constrained the IRA that it was forced seriously to consider abandoning violence as a way of achieving its political goals . . . It could not mask the fact that its use of violence . . . had been thwarted thanks to the bravery and resourcefulness of officers like Ian Phoenix' (Holland and Phoenix 1996: 269).

[25] *Irish News* (27 Mar. 1995), 'British Still Aim to Beat the IRA, Claims ex Taoiseach'.

[26] The role of MI5 does not appear to have been consistent over the period of the ceasefires. They came under considerable criticism for their failure accurately to predict either the nature of the declaration of the IRA ceasefire or the breakdown of the cessation (Mallie and McKittrick 1996: 328). However, it is interesting to note that by June 1995 MI5 officers were making it clear that 'they accept the significance of the IRA's agreement to a cease-fire and do not believe it will collapse easily.' (*Guardian*. 9 June 1995, 'Security Services Say Cease-fire Will Hold').

the changed environment. It is my contention that the instrumentalist view which had come to dominate prison management during the period of managerialism was, for a considerable period, incapable of dealing with the reality that the prisons had returned to the centre of the political stage. Without clear political direction from above, scientific and technical discourses dominated a self-limiting paradigm within which senior prison officials either could not or would not grasp the political significance of the prisoner issue.

In response to the campaign for prisoner release, the prison service maintained the standard view that there were 'no political prisoners in British prisons', that distinction could not be made between prisoners on the grounds of alleged motivation and that individuals should not be 'rewarded' for committing acts of 'terrorism'.[27] The reluctance to formalize any of the practical distinctions between paramilitary and ordinary offenders in legislation or prison rules which had been a characteristic of managerialism, was threaded through the prison services response to the issue. Later in 1995, as the debate became more specific on the various modalities of release, the prison service raised a series of questionable legal arguments as to why paramilitary prisoners could not be afforded different release arrangements from those of ordinary prisoners.[28] Any criticism that such obduracy was eroding confidence in the cessations within the Republican and Loyalist communities was met with an ahistorical and circuitous logic that prisoners could not be distinguished on the basis of their motivation.[29]

For almost a year after the IRA ceasefire, there was no official statement from the British government on the matter. In August 1995 Secretary of State Sir Patrick Mayhew announced that there would be changes in remission rates allowing some prisoners to be released earlier. To the huge disappointment of prisoners, their organizations, and other campaigners, when the bill was introduced at the end of

---

[27] Meeting with senior NIO officials attended by the author, 12 Oct. 1994.

[28] For a detailed critique of those obstacles see Livingstone (1995c), 'Legal Options Regarding Early Release', copy on file at NIACRO Information Bank.

[29] At a conference organized by NIACRO in June 1995 on the prisoner release issue, in a heated private discussion with a senior prison service official, the author indicated that such was NIACRO's sense of exasperation, that the organization intended to release a press statement to the effect that the government's legal objections to early release were untruthful. The official responded that any such move would be discriminatory against ordinaries and might undermine the peace process!

October, it simply restored the remission rate of 50 per cent which had applied up until 1989.[30]

In presenting the bill, the government appeared uncertain as to whether it should be viewed as a simple housekeeping measure which brought paramilitary prisoners into line with ordinaries or whether it should be seen as a very cautious response to the ceasefires.[31] In addition, those coming under the new provision were to be released on licence and subject to recall by the Secretary of State, in effect leaving them in a worse position than paramilitaries sentenced before 1989 (when violence had been ongoing) and ordinary prisoners who had always benefited from 50 per cent remission.[32] The fact that the measure was unopposed by the Ulster Unionist Party[33] and the anti-peace process DUP and UK Unionist Party's Robert McCartney[34] ensured that it was widely perceived by prisoners' groupings as 'minimalist and begrudging'.[35] This was confirmed by the government's apparent ruling out of further movement on the prisoner issue.[36] The key potential of

[30] As noted above, in 1989 the government had reduced the rate of remission for those convicted of paramilitary offences from 50% to 33%. Ordinary prisoners, and those paramilitaries sentenced before 1989 had continued to benefit from 50% remission.

[31] 'The Bill has a simple purpose. It is to restore the practice which existed in Northern Ireland until 1989 and which had obtained since 1976, that all prisoners serving fixed terms of imprisonment, regardless of the nature of their offence, became eligible for release at the halfway stage of their sentence . . . The Bill is not an amnesty. It makes no concession to those who falsely claim that those who are convicted of terrorist offences somehow become political prisoners. It makes no concession to terrorism at all. On the contrary it will enable the penal system in Northern Ireland to make a positive, but proportionate and prudent response to the cease-fires, and to the welcome reduction of risk that has been brought about over the past year.' Hansard, HC (Series VI) vol 265, cols 21, 26 (30 Oct. 1995).

[32] 'I welcome the return to 50% remission in the Bill—but let me put it this way—it is no big deal. It is actually less than that which was operated by the Conservative and Unionist Government led by Baroness Thatcher between 1979 and 1989. One can pose this question. If a Tory government, during the war situation between 1979 and 1989 could live with 50% remission, cannot the present Tory government live with it during peace? . . . There are and should be no bonuses for the government in introducing the Bill and for any of us for supporting it. There should be no Brownie points in supporting the Bill.' Seamus Mallon, Deputy Leader of the SDLP, Hansard, HC (Series VI) vol 265, col 45 (30 Oct. 1995).

[33] Hansard, HC (Series VI) vol 265, col 34 (30 Oct. 1995), speech by John Taylor, Deputy Leader of the Official Unionist Party.

[34] Hansard, HC (Series VI) vol 265, col 39 (30 Oct. 1995), speech by Robert McCartney, UK leader Unionist Party, and col. 53, speech by Reverend William McCrea, Democratic Unionist Party.

[35] Interview with former UVF prisoner, 5 Nov. 1995.

[36] In response to a question by Conservative MP David Wilshire, Northern Ireland Secretary of State Sir Patrick Mayhew replied 'He asked whether it [the bill] was paving the way to further relaxations. It is not. He correctly asserted that it was not an amnesty

the prisoner issue as a confidence building measure to support the impetus for peace had been lost by an overly complex and minimalist scientific approach to the question of releases.

To many prisoners and their supporters, the legislation appeared as a calculated reiteration of the old criminalisation agenda and a refusal to accept that politically motivated prisoners should be treated any differently from those imprisoned for ordinary crimes. At one level such a response may be viewed as a predictably cautious if somewhat hypocritical approach by a weak Tory government which was in political hock to the Ulster Unionists and holding back on a key negotiating card. At another, it represents a deep ideological resistance to the notion of political status which had been at least partially submerged during the era of managerialism. The mantra that 'there are no political prisoners in British prisons' remained undimmed while the Northern Ireland prison system released several hundred paramilitary prisoners.

Some blame for permitting this question to emerge again as a source of political instability must be attributed to the prison service. Senior officials appeared to have forgotten the political significance of paramilitary prisoners as their technical and managerial skills in handling them had improved. As one governor in the Northern Ireland prison service told the author: 'Looking back, perhaps the Conservatives were not told forthrightly enough of the political dangers of messing about with the prisoners . . . there was a tendency to be too clever by half with some of the senior NIO people.'[37] Truisms about the significance of prisoner managers in the overall peace process, which have become common parlance amongst prison officials in recent times,[38] were denied with considerable vehemence and passion between 1994 and 1996.

In the context of a failure to move on other key demands of Sinn Fein and the Loyalist parties, such as the beginning of all-party negotiations, and the continued insistence on the decommissioning

and that the motivation was not to allow further concessions. It is not.' *Hansard*, HC (Series VI) vol 265, col 66 (30 Oct. 1995).

[37] Interview with prison governor, 20 Apr. 1999.

[38] 'the role of prisoners in the political process has been of considerable significance and I think once the decision had been taken to go for an all-embracing settlement, it was inevitable that the position of prisoners was going to be high on the priority list of some of the parties who were seeking to achieve a settlement, and therefore, the Prison Service has had to play a role in its advice to Ministers about what is achievable and what is not achievable, what are the consequences of various courses of actions and so on.' Evidence of chief executive of the Northern Ireland prison service Alan Shannon to the Northern Ireland Affairs Committee, 29 Apr. 1998, 15, col. 19.

of paramilitary weapons, the mishandling of the prisoner issue by the then British government was seen as symbolic of a broader failure to accept the political character of the conflict. The IRA ceasefire ended on 9 February 1996. As one Republican activist told the author:

I wouldn't say the prisoner issue broke the first ceasefire because it didn't. However it was viewed as symptomatic, it [the prisoners' issue] was one matter over which the Brits had complete discretion and they blew it. It was hard to convince anyone they were serious when they wouldn't even transfer prisoners back to be near their families. When they did finally move on releases towards the end of 1995 it was far too little too late.[39]

As the 1999 prison service *Annual Report* makes clear (NIPS 1999: 17), senior officials were instrumental in preparing the government's position on effecting prisoner releases and the subsequent legislation which gave effect to the Agreement. These were the same officials who had advised on the 1995 legislation. As a number of these individuals have vigorously contested to the author and others who were critical of the service's role in the collapse of the first ceasefire, a change of government with a strong majority and a much more pragmatic approach to the question of prisoners was reflected in the changed stance of the service. In both instances civil servants merely reflected the will of ministers in the classic top down notion of policy implementation (Mazmanian and Sabatier 1983, Sabatier 1997).

While such an assertion has some merit, it is not the entire story. The change of government was clearly crucial to the renewal of the IRA ceasefire and the pragmatism of Mo Mowlam,[40] as in the case of her predecessor Jim Prior in the wake of the hunger strikes, had a direct bearing on the shaping of policy with regard to the prisons. Civil servants clearly adjusted their positions to reflect the changed political landscape. It is none the less arguable that it required such a radical political transformation to shake the prison service from the managerial paradigm which had informed and inhibited policy-making with regard to prisons in the period between 1994 and 1997. It was not perhaps the case that prison managers had grasped the political

---

[39] Interview with Sinn Fein activist, 21 Jan. 1999.

[40] In Mar. 1995 the author and a colleague attended a meeting with the then shadow Secretary of State Mo Mowlam to brief her on the NIACRO comparative research on prisoner release. At that meeting Dr Mowlam made clear her view that movement on the prisoner issue was essential to maintaining the momentum towards peace.

significance of the prisoners and were pressing for more movement from reluctant Tory ministers. Rather, it is arguable, the minimalism which characterized the Tory response to the peace process in some senses mirrored the mindsets of some of those charged with running the prison system.

Prisoners, the Renewed IRA Ceasefire, and Negotiating the Agreement

In the period following the breakdown of the first IRA ceasefire, and with the Loyalist ceasefire showing considerable strain evidenced by a number of attacks on Catholic civilians, backbench Conservative MP Andrew Hunter suggested that the Tory government should consider reducing Loyalist prisoners' sentences in order to encourage the maintenance of their ceasefire.[41] While the then Conservative government did not take up this suggestion, the lessons of the failures of the first IRA ceasefire appeared to have been internalized by the Labour government who replaced them with a large majority in May 1997.

When Tony Blair took office he resolved to give Sinn Fein one more opportunity to join the Northern Ireland peace talks which had begun in June 1996, and from which Sinn Fein had been excluded because of the lack of an IRA ceasefire.[42] Following intensive discussions between the two governments and SDLP leader John Hume, and preliminary meetings with Sinn Fein, the British government published an Aide-Memoire, in essence meeting Sinn Fein's previously articulated requirements for a restoration of the IRA ceasefire. In return for a restoration of the 1994 cessation, Sinn Fein would be guaranteed entrance to the talks within six weeks of a ceasefire, the talks would be concluded within an agreed time frame (by May 1998), and the decommissioning issue should be resolved as envisaged in the Mitchell Report rather than as a precondition to substantive negotiations.[43] That Aide-Memoire also recognized 'the particular sensitivities of prisoner issues on all sides'.[44] On 19 July the IRA restored their complete cessation of military operations.

---

[41] *Irish Times* (14 Oct. 1996), 'Move to Cut Loyalist Prison Sentences'.
[42] Speech by Tony Blair at the Royal Ulster Agricultural Show, Belfast, 16 May 1997.
[43] Aide-Memoire Setting Out British Government's Position on the Entry of Sinn Fein into Political Development Talks, 25 June 1997 (Belfast: Northern Ireland Information Service). [44] ibid.

The refreshing pragmatism of the new Labour government[45] quickly manifested itself in the area of prisoners. In August, less than a month after the IRA ceasefire, Secretary of State Dr Mo Mowlam indicated that while she was not yet ready to consider prisoner releases 'as the cease-fire holds, other options become possible'.[46] The reticence seen during the first ceasefire amongst Republicans with regard to allowing prisoners to be used as bargaining chips also appeared to have dissipated. Republicans appeared more willing to discuss prisoners in a changed context wherein the issue was to be discussed as part of the all-party peace negotiations rather than in bilaterals with civil servants. In September 1997, on a visit to the Maze and Maghaberry prisons, Sinn Fein Chief Negotiator Martin McGuinness assured IRA prisoners in the Maze and Maghaberry that 'their release and the transfer and release of prisoners from England was a priority for us and that there could be not be a peace settlement without the release of all political prisoners'.[47]

The British government's willingness to engage realistically on the prisoner issue was severely tested when UDA prisoners voted in January 1998 to withdraw their support for the peace process.[48] As noted above, UDA prisoners in particular appeared to exercise considerably greater influence over their political wing (the UDP) than their counterparts in the IRA and UVF wings of the Maze. With a number of killings carried out over the Christmas 1997 period, some of them subsequently admitted by the UDA, the then Secretary of State took the decision to go into the prison and speak directly to the leadership of the UDA prisoners. Despite the increased openness of the managerial era, formal recognition of the paramilitary command structure by the Secretary of State was still a remarkable event. A fourteen-point document was presented to the prisoners which included provisions on the question of early release.[49] In what was widely perceived to have

---

[45] In 1996 a similar formulation which led to the renewal of the IRA ceasefire had been offered to John Major's government and rejected as 'not properly fitting the government's position'. Government Statement on Northern Ireland, 28 Nov. 1998 (Belfast: Northern Ireland Information Service).

[46] *Irish News* (11 Aug. 1997), 'Mowlam Jail Hint Brings Political Fury'.

[47] *Irish News* (19 Sept. 1997), 'Sinn Fein Briefs IRA Prisoners'.

[48] *Irish News* (5 Jan. 1998), 'UDA prisoners Reject Peace'.

[49] 'We [the British government] recognise that prisoner issues are important to parties on both sides. They too need to be resolved, alongside progress on other issues, to the satisfaction of the participants in the process. We have responsibility to maintain community confidence in the criminal justice system and in the political process. We are

been a huge political gamble, Dr Mowlam was successful in persuading the UDA prisoners to reverse their decision and reinstate their support for the peace process, resulting in extremely favourable media coverage for the British government's stance.[50]

As indicated to the UDA prisoners, in February 1998 the British government submitted a paper to the Liaison Subcommittee on confidence building measures regarding prisoners. Having received position papers from a number of the political parties (UDP, PUP, SDLP, Sinn Fein, and the Irish government—the rest of the parties did not address the issue), the British government indicated a willingness to 'work out an account of what could happen in respect of prisoner releases in the context of a peaceful and lasting settlement being agreed'.[51] In effect the government's position had clearly moved from whether prisoner release would happen, to a view on the modalities of release and the role of prisoners in the overall settlement.

For those involved in negotiating the section of the agreement dealing with prisoners on behalf of Sinn Fein and the Loyalist parties, the first of their key objectives was to ensure that the process for release would be completed within an agreed time frame. As Progressive Unionist prisons spokesperson William Smith indicated in March 1998, 'The PUP will not entertain any agreement that does not include a comprehensive release scheme to begin at the point of the agreement and within a given time frame.'[52] In the final hours of negotiation, as a two-year time frame for completion of the releases emerged as the most likely outcome, a number of remarkable events occurred including an approach by senior Republican Gerry Kelly to the Loyalists for an agreed position on a one-year time scale.[53] The other key objective, also ultimately successful, was to ensure that prisoner release was not conditional upon prior decommissioning of paramilitary weapons.

prepared in the liaison committees on confidence building measures to discuss parties concerns and to work out an account of what would happen in respect of prisoner releases in the context of an overall political settlement being agreed' (reproduced in *Irish News* (10 Jan. 1998), 'Prisoners Fate Tied to Settlement'.

[50] *Ulster Newsletter* (9 Jan. 1998), 'She's Brave, She's Crazy'; *Irish Times* (10 Jan. 1998), 'The Gamble Pays Off: Loyalist Prisoners Reverse their Position after Talks with Mowlam'; *Irish News* (10 Dec. 1998) 'New Hope as Maze Gamble Pays Off'; *Guardian* (10 Jan. 1998*b*) 'Finding Hope in the Maze'.

[51] *Prison Issues*, paper by the British government, liaison sub-committee on confidence building measures meeting, 4 Feb. 1998 (confidential source).

[52] *Irish News* (20 Mar. 1998),'Prisoner Releases Crucial Says PUP'.

[53] Interview with Sinn Fein activist, 25 Jan. 1999. According to Sinn Fein the Loyalists rejected Kelly's approach.

For mainstream Unionists, the provisions relating to all qualifying prisoners being released within two years were clearly amongst the most unpalatable elements of the agreement. A number of senior figures such as Jeffrey Donaldson within the Ulster Unionist Party dissented from the leadership on the day the agreement was concluded on the specific issue of prisoner release and the failure to address decommissioning.[54] Frantic efforts were made by the British government to minimize the consequences of the releases including a much copied handwritten note from the Prime Minister's Chief of Staff, dated the day of the agreement, pointing out the high numbers of prisoners who would have been released in any case under existing remission arrangements.[55] The final draft of the prisoner section of the agreement provided for the establishment of an independent commission in both the North and South, excluded organizations not on ceasefire, contained a two-year time frame and a deadline for enabling legislation by June 1998, and made specific reference to the need for appropriate reintegration mechanisms for paramilitary prisoners.[56]

Prisoners and the Referenda Campaigns

In the weeks and months following the conclusion of the agreement, the referenda North and South to implement its provisions and the

[54] *Belfast Telegraph* (18 May 1998), 'Donaldson's Fears Centre on Weapons and Prisoners'.

[55] Handwritten note from Jonathan Powell, Prime Minister's Chief of Staff to Ken Maginnis MP, 10 Apr. 1998.

[56]   PRISONERS
1. Both Governments will put in place mechanisms to provide for an accelerated programme for the release of prisoners, including transferred prisoners, convicted of scheduled offences in Northern Ireland or, in the case of those sentenced outside Northern Ireland, similar offences (referred to hereafter as qualifying prisoners). Any such arrangements will protect the rights of individual prisoners under national and international law.
2. Prisoners affiliated to organisations which have not established or are not maintaining a complete and unequivocal cease-fire will not benefit from the arrangements. The situation in this regard will be kept under review.
3. Both Governments will complete a review process within a fixed time frame and set prospective release dates for all qualifying prisoners. The review process would provide for the advance of the release dates of qualifying prisoners while allowing account to be taken of the seriousness of the offences for which the person was convicted and the need to protect the community. In addition, the intention would be that should the circumstances allow it, any qualifying prisoners who remained in custody two years after the commencement of the scheme would be released at that point.
4. The Governments will seek to enact the appropriate legislation to give effect to these arrangements by the end of June 1998. (The Good Friday Agreement 1998).

subsequent elections to the Northern Ireland Assembly, prisoners were to remain at the top of the political agenda. As Sinn Fein prepared for their historic Ard Fheis (party conference) to consider the party's view of the agreement and the difficult question of moving away from their abstentionist past to take up seats in the Northern Assembly, Republicans requested the temporary release of a number of prisoners to address the conference. Both the British and Irish governments accepted the importance of a public endorsement from the prisoners to the Republican party faithful. In total twenty-seven IRA prisoners were given parole for the Ard Fheis, two from Maghaberry, eight from Portlaoise prison in the Republic, and the rest from the Maze.[57]

Amongst those prisoners present at the Sinn Fein rally were a number of prisoners (the Balcombe Street Gang) who had recently been transferred from Britain to the Irish Republic. These prisoners, amongst the longest serving IRA prisoners, were treated to an emotional and tumultuous welcome. Michael O'Brien, Officer Commanding of the IRA prisoners in Portlaoise, used the example of these prisoners in his speech in favour of taking up seats in the Northern Assembly.[58] With support also forthcoming from the IRA's Officer Commanding in the Maze and the female prisoners at Maghaberry, the Sinn Fein leadership secured an overwhelming majority for the agreement and their strategy to take up their seats.[59]

While the unequivocal backing of the prisoners undoubtedly eased the passage of dramatic changes in Republican policy, the television images of IRA bombers being cheered and lauded as heroes had a predictably negative effect amongst Unionists in the North. While those Unionists led by David Trimble campaigning for a Yes vote in the referendum had established an early poll lead, the images emanating from the Sinn Fein Ard Fheis have been well described as 'Christmas for the

[57] *Irish Times* (11 May 1998*a*), 'High Profile Prisoners at Ard Fheis'.
[58] 'You may ask what has this got to do with the proposed assembly. It is this: after 23 years in British prisons, these men are our own Mandelas. They are fit, they are strong, they are unbowed, humorous, politically astute and aware, and they are full of honest opinion and integrity. And all of that comes on the back of trust, belief and above all, unity during those 23 years in the belly of the beast . . . United we can do whatever we want, just as those united POW's who have returned from England have endured and ultimately defeated the most barbaric prison system and conditions.' Reported in 'High Profile Prisoners at Ard Fheis', *Irish Times* (11 May 1998*a*).
[59] 331 of the 350 eligible delegates at the Ard Fheis voted in favour of Sinn Fein taking up their seats in the Assembly. *Irish Times* (11 May 1998*b*), 'Huge Vote in Favour of Taking Seats in the Assembly'.

No Vote'.[60] Unionist sources claimed that the Unionist Yes vote dropped by 10 per cent in the immediate aftermath of the Dublin conference.[61] While Irish Premier Bertie Ahern defended his and the British government's decision to release the prisoners for the Ard Fheis, reminding the Dáil that prisoners 'had been a significant force for peace and the agreement', he criticized the triumphalist tone of the prisoners' welcome.[62] A UDP event held later in the week in Belfast, at which leading UDA prisoner Michael Stone (out on home leave) was treated to a similar hero's welcome did little to assuage Unionist concerns.[63] While the Unionist Yes vote did recover to some extent in the final days of the campaign, the prisoners question remained the most commonly identified reason for voting against the agreement by Unionist voters.[64]

Both events were illustrative of the complex balancing act required in the management of the prisoners issue within the peace process. The laudable pragmatism shown by both governments in using flexibility on prisoner issues to encourage Republicans and Loyalists away from their violent past were offset by the serious misgivings held by large sections of Unionism towards prisoner release. While Nationalists appeared by and large to accept prisoner release as necessary in the process, Unionists (beyond the small electorate of the PUP and UDP) did not.[65]

The Prisoner Release Legislation

The interaction between prisoner release and peacemaking is sometimes viewed in terms of a carrot and stick approach, wherein releases are viewed as one incentive towards ending violence and released

---

[60] *Irish Times* (12 May 1998), 'Prisoners at Ard Fheis—Christmas for the No Lobby: The Prisoners Issue Could Damage the Yes Vote in Northern Ireland'.

[61] *Irish Times* (15 May 1998a), 'Unionist Support for Agreement Drops Sharply'.

[62] *Irish News* (15 May 1998a), 'Ahern Hits Out at IRA Triumphalism'.

[63] *Belfast Telegraph* (15 May 1998), 'Crowd Hails Stone Hero'.

[64] The releases of paramilitary prisoners was cited by 50% of those Official Unionist voters intending to vote No in the Referendum in polling a week before the Referendum (*Irish Times* Mori Poll, reported in the *Irish Times* 11 May 1998). As one Northern Ireland Office pollster reported 'The prisoners issue is dominating [Protestant] views of the referendum. What does it mean? They think it means something more fundamental than just the moral outrage . . . The prisoner issue becomes a symbol in their minds of a fundamental flaw, a kind of real concern, a worry, a heartache, a deeply emotional issue which then dominates everything else' (reported in *Sunday Tribune*, 17 May 1998, 'Say Hello to Gunmen, Wave Goodbye to Peace?')

[65] The possible reasons for the differences in views between the two main communities is discussed below.

prisoners may become hostages to ensure the continuance of the cease-fires. Although the view of prisoners as hostages or negotiating cards has featured in some of the discussions on prisoner release, such views are not afforded much expression in the legislation which gave effect to commitments in the Good Friday Agreement. The carrot and stick metaphor is perhaps of more analytical use with regard to the notion of prisoner release as a means of encouraging recalcitrant organizations into the peace processes and as a lever to secure concessions from paramilitary organizations in the area of decommissioning. Together with these two key ideas (perhaps better understood within a frame-work of reconciliation and healing) the questions of prisoner release and victims and the reintegration of paramilitary prisoners make up the four key thematic areas considered in the remainder of this chapter.

Before examining those issues it might be useful to offer a brief overview of the way in which prisoner release was given effect under the Northern Ireland (Sentences) Act in the North and the Criminal Justice (Release of Prisoners) Act 1998 in the Republic.

Under the Northern Ireland (Sentences) Act 1998 an independent commission was established with the responsibility for overseeing the release of qualifying paramilitary prisoners. The membership of that commission included a number of prominent individuals who had long argued for the release of paramilitary prisoners.[66] Qualifying prisoners are defined in the Act as prisoners convicted of a scheduled or terrorist offence before 10 April 1998 when the agreement was signed; that he/she is not a supporter of an organization not on ceasefire; that if released a prisoner would not be likely to become a supporter of such an organization; and, for life sentenced prisoners, that if released immediately the prisoner would not be a danger to the public.[67] The

[66] In an appointment of considerable symbolic importance, Brian Curran, former chair of the Amnesty Commission in South Africa which had released politically moti-vated prisoners there after Mandela became President in 1994, was appointed co-chair with retired civil servant Sir John Blelloch. As well as his South African experience, Curran had been associated with a number of initiatives in Northern Ireland and Britain 1995–8 organized by NIACRO (the Northern Ireland Association for the Care and Resettlement of Offenders) as part of their campaign for the release of paramilitary pris-oners. With the appointment of the NIACRO chief executive, a member of the NIACRO executive committee, and a prominent Northern Ireland human rights lawyer, as well as a range of independent experts from outside Northern Ireland, the make-up of the com-mission appeared designed to ensure that a pragmatic approach to prisoner release would be ensured.

[67] Northern Ireland (Sentences) Act 1998, s 3(2–7).

power of the Secretary of State to specify organizations under section 3(8–10) provided for both a monitoring function in ensuring that organizations maintain their 'complete and unequivocal' ceasefires, as well as allowing sufficient flexibility to encourage organizations not on ceasefire to declare a cessation and thus ultimately ensure that their prisoners would benefit from the early release mechanisms.

The process for releasing prisoners was that prisoners were encouraged to make applications for release to the commission, 446 of which were received by the commission by 21 August 1998.[68] These applications were then passed to the Northern Ireland prison service for confirmation of the accuracy of the offences and sentence details and confirmation that the prisoner belonged to a group eligible for release. When these were returned to the commission the prisoners were given a preliminary indication of whether or not they were to be freed early, which was then followed by a substantive determination.[69] Prisoners serving fixed term sentences had their sentences reduced by two-thirds.[70] For life sentenced prisoners, the commission calculated how long they would have normally served and reduced it by one-third.[71] Any remaining qualifying prisoners were to be released by June 2000. Dissatisfied prisoners were permitted to appeal to a different constituted panel of commissioners for a judicial review of the decisions. The Secretary of State retained an overall power to suspend or later revive the scheme or prevent the release of a person adjudged to be failing to meet any of the criteria outlined above.[72] The scheme came to an

---

[68] *Irish News* (21 Aug. 1998), 'Prisoners Out in A Fortnight'.

[69] Northern Ireland (Sentences) Act (Sentence Review Commissioners) Rules 1998, SI 1988/1859, ss. 14–15.

[70] Northern Ireland (Sentences) Act 1998, s 4(1)a.

[71] Northern Ireland (Sentences) Act 1998, s 6(1)a.

[72] Northern Ireland (Sentences) Act 1998, s 16. The most high profile use of this power has concerned the senior UDA prisoner Johnny 'Mad Dog' Adair. In the original decision to release Mr Adair, the Secretary of State came under considerable pressure from the police to delay his release for fear that he would re-engage in terrorism and use his paramilitary infrastructure to engage in the illegal drugs trade. *Sunday Times* (3 Jan. 1999), 'RUC Plea to Keep "Mad Dog" in Jail'; *Irish News* (4 Jan. 1999), 'RUC Silent on Adair Claim'. Adair was ultimately released after the then Secretary of State withdrew her objections. *Belfast Telegraph* (14 Sept. 1999), 'Adair Freed'. However he was rearrested and had his licence revoked in Aug. 2000 after the Secretary of State took a decision that he had been implicated in the 'commission, preparation and instigation of acts of terrorism', some of which were related to a feud between the UDA and UVF in which a number of people were killed including leading Loyalists. That decision was ultimately upheld by the Sentence Review Commission. *Irish Times* (23 Aug. 2000), 'Adair to Launch Legal Challenge', *Irish Times* (10 Jan. 2001), 'Adair's Prison Release Application is Turned Down.'

end with a total of 433 eligible prisoners released (193 Loyalists, 229 Republicans, and 11 others) by the end of October 2000. At the time of writing (February 2001), two prisoners have had their licences revoked.

In the Irish Republic a similar scheme has been introduced, albeit with the commission made up largely from officials in the Department of Justice. Given the Irish government's previous willingness to release prisoners, fresh legislation was perhaps not technically required. However, the Irish government were apparently well aware of the political and symbolic significance of creating a specific post-agreement release process. As Minister for Justice John O'Donoghue explained:

While specific legislation is not necessary to allow effect to be given to the releases envisaged in the Agreement a broader political issue is at stake. There is agreement on all sides of the house that we should do nothing which might be open to the perception that we are not complying fully with all the terms of the Agreement and in those circumstances there will be general support for the Bill.[73]

Releases recommenced in the Irish Republic almost immediately after the new commission was established and have included the man convicted of the murder of Lord Louis Mountbatten in 1979.[74] As noted above, together with the equivalent legislation for the North, these provisions may be analysed within a framework of four key areas.

Prisoner Release as an Incentive to Peace for Dissident Paramilitary Groupings: The Carrot?

The provisions for the release of prisoners in both jurisdictions permitted for the exclusion of those groupings initially opposed to the peace process and those continuing to engage in armed actions. These groupings included the Loyalist Volunteer Force, the Orange Volunteers, the Irish National Liberation Army, the Continuity IRA, and the Real IRA. However, in the event of a ceasefire being declared by any of these organizations, the legislation contained sufficient flexibility to allow the respective governments to recognize such cessations and to include such groupings in the release provisions. This strategy, allied with the changed political landscape of the post-agreement era and the

---

[73] Irish Minister for Justice, Equality, and Law Reform John O'Donohue, Criminal Justice (Release of Prisoners) Bill 1998, Second Stage, Dáil Debates Official Report, 2 July 1998.

[74] *Irish Times* (1 Aug. 1998), 'New Law Sees Six Freed from Portlaoise'. *Irish Times* (7 Aug. 1998), 'Man Convicted of Murder of Mountbatten is Freed'.

technical limitations of these smaller organizations, has proved quite successful.

The first of these groupings in the post-agreement era to declare a ceasefire was the dissident Loyalist grouping the LVF who announced a cessation in May 1998 during the run-up to the Referenda.[75] As previously noted, the LVF, formed as a breakaway from the larger UVF and led by the former head of the Mid-Ulster UVF Billy Wright, had been bitterly opposed to the peace process and the political direction taken by the UVF's political wing, the Progressive Unionist Party (Cusack and McDonald 1997). When Billy Wright himself was murdered in the Maze prison by the INLA in December 1997, the LVF retaliated with a number of random attacks on Catholic civilians and continued their campaign of violence up until May 1998. The LVF initially denied that their ceasefire was called in order to benefit from the early release provisions. However, their Officer Commanding in the Maze subsequently demanded 'parity of esteem to prisoners from other organizations on ceasefire'[76] and their spokesperson Pastor Kenny McClinton indicated a willingness to engage on decommissioning in return for movement on 'prison conditions'.[77] Their ceasefire was ultimately accepted by the British government on 12 November 1998 and approximately twenty-five LVF prisoners became eligible to apply for release at that juncture.[78]

On the Republican side, the INLA were the first of the dissident groupings to declare a ceasefire in the wake of the agreement. The INLA announced their ceasefire on 24 August 1998. Speaking from the

[75] 'The soldiers of the LVF have fought against the Irish peace process and the sell out of our country. This has not been an easy task especially when you have all the different sides fighting against you. Northern Ireland has come to a crucial part of its history, on the 22 May people will vote for a United Ireland through a yes or vote no to remain British and hold onto everything Protestant people hold dear . . . The LVF are now calling an unequivocal cease-fire to create the proper climate in people's minds, so when they do go to vote they will make the proper decision for Ulster and that is to vote no.' Reproduced in *Irish News* (15 May 1998*b*), 'LVF Announces Unequivocal Cease-fire'.

[76] *Irish Times* (12 Aug.1998), 'LVF Chief in Maze Confirms Cease-fire'.

[77] *Belfast Telegraph* (15 June 1998), 'LVF Seeks Prison Deal'.

[78] *Belfast Telegraph* (12 Nov. 1998), 'Mo to Accept LVF Cease-fire: Prisoners Join the Release Plan.' The government had been strongly encouraged to accept the bona fides of the LVF ceasefire by Unionists including First Minister Designate David Trimble as the LVF had indicated a willingness (subsequently realized) to decommission a small amount of weaponry. The Unionists believed that such a move by a Loyalist paramilitary grouping would increase pressure on the IRA to reciprocate, although the significance of the LVF weapons handover was dismissed by the larger Loyalist paramilitary groupings and Republicans. *Irish News* (19 Dec. 1998*a*), 'LVF Guns Handover is a Stunt Says PUP'.

Maze prison, INLA Officer Commanding in the jail Christopher McWilliams (the man responsible for shooting Billy Wright in the prison the previous year) argued that 'securing releases has never been our primary concern. At the end of the day, throughout the world in every conflict political prisoners have been an issue. If anything does come about, we will be part of it, we are confident of that.'[79] However much it weighed in their decision-making process, there was clearly an expectation amongst INLA prisoners that they would benefit from the early release provisions. That expectation was duly realized in the Irish Republic with the announcement by the Irish government that 'the INLA are to be regarded as qualifying prisoners under the provisions of the Good Friday Agreement'.[80] The British government followed suit in March 1999 making the INLA prisoners eligible in the North also.[81]

The most recent Republican grouping to declare a ceasefire were the Real IRA. As previously noted, the Real IRA were formed from the ranks of the mainstream IRA following a split in 1997 about the ongoing peace process, and in particular the IRA's agreement that Sinn Fein should sign up to the Mitchell principles of non-violence.[82] Led by a number of key figures from the mainstream IRA, this small grouping was responsible for the Omagh bombing in August 1998 which killed twenty-nine civilians and injured scores more. They 'suspended operations' three days after the bombing. Politically isolated from the Republican community, and under considerable pressure from the security forces North and South (who had been given sweeping new Emergency powers), as well as the mainstream IRA, the Real IRA called a ceasefire on 8 September 1998.[83] Real IRA sources subsequently claimed to the media that if their ceasefire held there was an understanding with the Irish government that most of their prisoners would be freed by the millennium other than anyone convicted of the Omagh bombing.[84] However, their continued engagement in a range of bombings and other attacks (despite not having formally declared an end to their cessation), and similar attacks by the Continuity IRA, would suggest that it is highly unlikely that any prisoners from the

[79] Reported in 'INLA's War is Over', *Irish News* (24 Aug. 1998).
[80] *Irish News* (19 Dec. 1998*b*), 'INLA Prisoners to be Freed'.
[81] *Belfast Telegraph* (5 Mar. 1999), 'INLA Prisoners Set for Freedom'.
[82] *Magill* (July 1998), 'Staying Out in the Cold'.
[83] *Irish News* (9 Sept. 1998), 'Real IRA Cease-fire as Pressure Bites'.
[84] *Irish News* (8 Dec. 1998), 'Foiled Real IRA Gang to be Freed by 2000.'

remaining dissident Republican groupings will benefit from early releases in the immediate future.

It is difficult to assess with accuracy the role that prisoner release has played in the decisions by the smaller anti-peace process groupings to call cessations. Clearly their prisoners expect to benefit from the early release provisions. It could well be argued that in a changed political landscape, wherein community support for violence is considerably reduced and an alternative non-violent direction is on offer, the release of prisoners became a more significant incentive than it might otherwise have been.

Prisoner Release and Decommissioning: The Stick?

As noted above, the insistence upon the prior decommissioning of paramilitary weapons before all-party talks could commence is widely viewed as having led to the collapse of the first IRA ceasefire in 1996. This issue (which remains a key area of dispute at the time of writing) is imbued with symbolic importance to Unionists, Loyalists, and Republicans in particular (Von Tangen Page 1998*b*). For Unionists, it is portrayed as a litmus test of the good faith of those seeking to move out of political violence.[85] For Loyalist and Republican paramilitaries, it is an act imbued with notions of surrender and runs contrary to an ideology deep within both sets of paramilitary protagonists which views such weapons as the final guarantors for the defence of their communities against attack by their enemies.

Some commentators have suggested that the question of prisoner release is connected to the provisions regarding prisoner release in the agreement (Ruane and Todd 1998, Morgan 2000). Although no such linkages are in fact made in the Agreement, considerable energies were expended by both Unionist and Conservatives MPs in the passage of the bill on prisoner release to make such a connection explicit. During the referendum campaign British Prime Minister Tony Blair made a number of statements which went as close as he could to link the question of prisoner release to decommissioning, primarily in order to shore up the haemorrhaging Unionist Yes vote, without rewriting the agreement. On 6 May he argued: 'It is essential that organisations that want to benefit from the early release of prisoners should give up violence. Decommissioning is part of that.'[86] In a speech delivered at

---

[85] *Irish Times* (29 Dec. 1998), 'Trimble Remains in Ditch over Arms'.
[86] *Hansard*, HC (series VI) vol 311, col 711 (6 May 1998).

Balmoral showgrounds in Belfast on 14 May 1998, Blair argued that the provisions relating to prisoner release and the other elements of the agreement were underpinned by a number of safeguards.[87] That speech allowed pro-agreement Unionists such as David Trimble to claim that 'plain and direct linkage between prisoner release and office (in the assembly) to a permanent end to violence and decommissioning is confirmed by the Prime Minister'.[88] However, as Trimble himself pointed out in the legislation which came before the British Parliament, any such suggestions had been 'lost in translation'.[89]

Like the agreement, the relevant legislation contained no such requirement. As Tory spokesperson Andrew McKay acknowledged at the time:

the opposition pressed for substantial decommissioning to take place before the early release of prisoners and for this to be incorporated into the legislation that is before us ... The most serious omission is that it does not establish a clear legislative linkage between some actual decommissioning having taken place and the accelerated release of prisoners.[90]

The Labour government held firm that prisoner release is not linked to actual decommissioning. As Security Minister Adam Ingram told the House of Commons:

The early release of prisoners is an integral part of the Agreement, one which the government are honouring in full. The government will not depart from the Agreement by introducing a direct linkage between decommissioning and prisoner releases which is not in the Agreement nor in the Northern Ireland (Sentences) Act 1998.[91]

---

[87] 'Non-violent means must be established in an objective, meaningful and verifiable way . . . In clarifying whether the terms and spirit of the agreement are being met and whether violence has been given up for good, there are a range of factors to be taken into account; first and foremost . . . that the so-called war is finished, done with, gone, the cease-fires are indeed complete and unequivocal, an end to bombings, killings and beatings, claimed or unclaimed, an end to targeting and the procurement of weapons, progressive dismantling of paramilitary structures actively directing and promoting violence, full co-operation with the Independent Commission on Decommissioning and no other organisations being deliberately used as proxies for violence. These factors provide evidence upon which to base an overall judgement, a judgement which will necessarily become more rigorous over time' reported in 'Blair Says Accord Points to Better Future; Full Text of Blair Speech', *Irish Times* (15 May 1998b).

[88] *Irish News* (15 May 1998c), 'Blair Boost to Yes Camp'.

[89] *Hansard*, HC (series VI) vol 313, col 1099 (10 June 1998).

[90] *Hansard*, HC (series VI) vol 313, cols 1093–4 (10 June 1998).

[91] *Hansard*, HC (series VI) vol 323, cols 487–8 (20 Jan. 1999).

As increasing numbers of prisoners were released, the government came under sustained pressure to halt or slow down prisoner releases until actual decommissioning occurred or until an end to paramilitary punishment beatings and shootings was achieved. In an increasingly acrimonious debate, Conservatives and Unionists accused Labour of mishandling the potential of using the prisoners as hostages or bargaining chips in return for progress on other issues within the gift of the paramilitaries.[92]

While the logic of using prisoners as a stick with which to prise concessions from or defeat paramilitaries is beguilingly simple, it fails to understand the complex dialectic between the larger paramilitary organizations and their prisoners. As previously discussed, attempts at using prisoners in such a fashion during the criminalisation era of 1976–81 were an unmitigated disaster in security and political terms. Greater pragmatism in the management of prisons in the 1980s and 1990s, on the other hand, undoubtedly contributed to an environment in which paramilitaries began to consider strategies other than violence. The history of political imprisonment in Ireland would suggest handling of prisoners is an issue around which confidence can be *built* or *eroded* within the paramilitary constituency. It is not an issue which can be used to *force* concessions.

While the decommissioning of paramilitary weapons is arguably a desirable part of the overall process of conflict resolution, it is crucially a *voluntary* process on the part of the paramilitaries. It remains at the time of writing an issue with the potential to trip up the maintenance of the political institutions set up under the agreement. If this happens, the British government may well come under renewed pressure to recall prisoners who have been released on licence as a punishment of the paramilitary groups. Leaving aside whether such general recalls are legally possible, it is highly unlikely, however, that such a move would actually result in progress towards the encouragement of voluntary acts of decommissioning.

Linkages between prisoner releases, decommissioning, punishment attacks, and the political process conceptually group different parts of the conflict resolution process in ways which militate against their resolution.

For Republicans, the issue of decommissioning is clearly linked to the question of demilitarization, the withdrawal of British troops, the

[92] *Irish Times* (28 Jan. 1999), 'Bipartisanship under Mounting Strain'.

dismantling of security installations, the controls of legally held weapons by Unionists, a new police service, the desire to avoid the tinge of surrender, and so forth. For the mainstream Loyalists (the UDA and UVF), decommissioning is tied up with the actions and attitudes of Republicans and their capacity to attack the Loyalist community. None of the groups accepts a *de facto* or *de jure* relationship between prisoner release and decommissioning.

Similarly for Republicans, the ending of punishment beatings and shootings is linked to an agreed formal policing structure, the culture of dependency on paramilitaries which has grown up in working-class communities, and the ability of local communities to take greater responsibility for problem solving in their own areas (Auld *et al.* 1997). While the phenomenon is arguably even more complex in Loyalist areas (Winston 1997), it is equally unconnected to the release of paramilitary prisoners. As Tony Blair has argued, ending prisoner release to force an end to punishments 'would have immense consequences for the prospects of lasting peace . . . it may be an imperfect process but it is better than no process at all'.[93]

Such a pragmatic view is not to allow the paramilitaries to have their cake and eat it. Rather it is an acknowledgement that the peace process requires the careful management of a number of discreet areas which cannot be achieved by the collapsing of each into an unmanageable whole in which political progress is stymied by the demand for movement in all other areas.[94] In drafting the legislation which gave effect to the agreement, the British and Irish governments were careful to retain maximum executive flexibility in maintaining firewalls between progress on the political front and the most difficult areas of the conflict resolution process. Whether it remains tenable to maintain issues such as decommissioning in arenas which are removed from the political process remains to be seen.

---

[93] Reported in 'Bipartisanship under Mounting Strain'. *Irish Times* (28 Jan. 1999).

[94] The principal strategy employed by the British government (and agreed to by the signatories to the agreement) has been to employ external independent commissions to oversee the most difficult areas of peacemaking while the political parties have sought to establish the political institutions. These have included the Sentence Review Commission on prisoner release, the independent Patten Commission designed to provide the template for a new policing service, and the De Chastelain Commission tasked with overseeing the decommissioning of paramilitary weapons.

Prisoner Release and the Victims of Violence

One of the most difficult issues regarding early release in the process of conflict resolution is the impact of releases upon those who have been victims of the conflict. The experiences of the victims of political violence in Northern Ireland and Britain are well documented (Parry and Parry 1995, Fay, Morrissey, and Smyth 1999, McKittrick *et al.* 1999). As demonstrated in other jurisdictions, the social and psychological consequences for those who have been either the victims or the families of victims during a violent political conflict are severe (Foster and Skinner 1990, Straker 1993, Dawes 1994). The release of a prisoner who has served their full sentence can in itself be traumatic for the family of those killed or injured by the prisoner (Maguire 1991). However, where such releases occur earlier than laid down by the original sentence, such feelings may be exacerbated.

For this and previous research the author has interviewed the victims of politically motivated violence, their organizations, and spokespeople in Northern Ireland as well as in Italy, Spain, South Africa, and Israel (Gormally and McEvoy 1995). In outlining the broad themes which emerged from those interviews, it is important to bear a number of things in mind.

First, the status of who is a 'victim' in a violent political conflict is itself a contested issue, with some arguing that it should be broadened beyond simply those injured or bereaved by the actions of 'terrorist' organizations (Wilkinson 1995). Clearly the actions of security forces kill and injure innocent people as well as combatants. In Northern Ireland, over 360 people have been killed by the security forces, half of them unarmed and uninvolved civilians (Amnesty International 1994). Only four members of the security services have been imprisoned for such offences, and all four have been released early and returned to their regiments. As noted previously, two of these have been released after serving less than four years of their life sentences (Currie and MacLean 1995). While a government investigation into the needs of victims did include reference to those killed or injured by state forces (Bloomfield 1998), the decision by Adam Ingram as Minister of Victims for Northern Ireland to meet with the families of IRA men killed by an SAS ambush at Loughall caused considerable controversy.[95] None the less, such victims insist that they too have a right to have their voices heard in discussions regarding prisoner release.

---

[95] *Belfast Telegraph* (26 Jan. 1999), 'Ingram Set to be Told of Shameful Meeting'.

Secondly, international experience would suggest that the views of victims regarding early release of prisoners are not monolithic. For example, in South Africa while there has been some attention directed at those who were subject to human rights abuses carried out by the ANC (Skweyiya Commission 1992), the main concern has been focused upon those who had suffered at the hands of the Apartheid regime. Official government policy has been to put the notion of retribution aside and acknowledge the dilemma of offering amnesty to those convicted of human rights abuses (Boraine 1994). In Italy much of the work concerning victims has been directed by church-based organizations and appears closely bound up with the Catholic notions of penance and atonement including reconciliation between victims and individual prisoners.[96] In Spain, the diversity of victims' views are in effect represented through a variety of organizations. A large Madrid-based organization (the Association of the Victims of Terrorism) actively campaigns against the reinsertion of prisoners who have renounced violence.[97] Other victims' organizations, largely based in the Basque region, tend to be involved in the peace and reconciliation movements with both Gesto por la Paz and Denon Artean accepting and supporting early release so long as prisoners have rejected violence.[98]

In Northern Ireland, even those victims groupings who are viewed as most hostile to the paramilitaries have acknowledged the diversity of views amongst victims concerning prisoner release (FAIT 1998). Some victims have argued that they should have a veto over any early release of prisoners (McBride 1995). Others, often supported by anti-agreement Unionist politicians, have made representations to the Sentence Review Commission expressing their concerns regarding the releases.[99] Still others handcuffed themselves to the turnstiles at the Maze prison in protest at the extension of Christmas parole to several high profile prisoners including one IRA prisoner convicted of the murder of nine civilians in a bomb planted on the Shankill Road in 1993.[100] This latter victim, Ms Michelle Williamson, whose parents were killed in the above IRA bombing on the Shankill Road in which one of the

---

[96] Interview with Father Guiseppe Brunetta, 30 Jan. 1995.
[97] Interview with Juan Perez and Paulino Baena Diaz, 9 Mar. 1995.
[98] Interview with Inaki Garcia, 7 Mar. 1995, interviews with Jesus Herrero and Txema Urkijo, 8 Mar. 1995.
[99] *Belfast Telegraph* (12 Aug. 1998), 'Prison Body Told of Concerns'.
[100] *Belfast Telegraph* (23 Dec. 1998a), 'Freed Prisoners Storm'.

bombers was also killed, also lodged an unsuccessful legal challenge to the early release process in September 1999 (Morgan 2000: 522–3).

On the other spectrum of the debate, some high profile victims have declared themselves in favour of early releases as part of a broader process of healing, reconciliation, and forgiveness. Mrs Joan Wilson, wife of the deceased peace campaigner Senator Gordon Wilson and mother of Marie Wilson who was killed at the IRA Remembrance Day bomb, suggested prison releases should be contemplated in such a context.[101] Other prominent peace activists who have lost loved ones have spoken publicly of their support for prisoner release as a component of peace-building (NIACRO 1995). Still others have argued that while they felt too emotionally close to the question of early release to come to a view either in favour or against, they needed additional resources such as counselling, compensation, and other support to cope with the trauma of the early releases (Wilkinson 1995).

At a late stage in the passage of the Sentences Act (1998), the government agreed to insert a mechanism in order to ensure that victims would be informed when prisoners related to their loss were to be released in order that they might prepare themselves.[102] However, that notification system has been criticized for having been managed by the prison service rather than a professional agency working with victims.[103] Confidence in its operation has been further undermined by a number of hurtful errors that have occurred including the decision to release an IRA prisoner on the tenth anniversary of the death of an RUC officer for whose murder he had been convicted.[104] Clearly the process for the early release of prisoners remains difficult for many of those bereaved and injured as a result of the conflict.

The Reintegration of Paramilitary Prisoners

The Governments continue to recognise the importance of measures to facilitate the reintegration of prisoners into the community by providing support both prior to and after release, including assistance directed towards availing of employment opportunities, re-training and/or re-skilling, and further education (The Good Friday Agreement 1998).

---

[101] *Belfast Telegraph* (14 Oct. 1996), 'We must Understand Jail Releases'.
[102] *Hansard*, HC (Series VI) vol 313, col 1160 (10 June 1998).
[103] Interview with Oliver Wilkinson, Director Victim Support (Northern Ireland) BBC Radio Ulster, *Morning Extra* 9 Oct. 1998.
[104] *Belfast Telegraph* (23 Dec. 1998*b*), 'Bingham: Halt the Releases'.

The notion of reintegrating paramilitary prisoners has always been a problematic one for many politically motivated prisoners. As previously discussed, many politicals have traditionally been reluctant to use some of the services of professional reintegration agencies such as probation or NIACRO, lest they be seen to be acquiescing to the label of 'criminal' (McEvoy *et al*. 1999). During the conflict and in the period after the 1994 ceasefires, in asserting their status as political, many paramilitary prisoners and their supporters argued that they were not in need of reintegration. They argued that they were not stigmatized by their communities and that they would not have committed their 'crimes' were it not for the political circumstances in which they found themselves (Sinn Fein 1995). The professional agencies argued that such ideological struggles should be ignored in the provision of practical services to prisoners.[105]

As the peace process unfolded, prisoner groupings (and the professional agencies) adapted their positions to one wherein prisoners would take advantage of pre- and post-release facilities. The model for such reintegration was a self-help model, wherein the former prisoners themselves would take responsibility for the management and delivery of services (Ritchie 1998). The European Union Peace and Reconciliation Fund, established by the European Union to support the peace process, made available £1.25 million to support prisoner reintegration in 1998. These monies are distributed through the Belfast-based Northern Ireland Voluntary Trust, a vastly experienced grant giving agency in the non-profit sector (NIVT 1998).

Given that projects are established and run by and large according to paramilitary factions, there are now over twenty-six community-based ex-prisoner projects spread throughout Northern Ireland.[106] IRA-affiliated Republicans established an umbrella project (Coiste na n-Iarchimi) to manage a range of their projects, and appointed a manager from outside the ranks of former Republican prisoners to run it.[107] The work covered by reintegration projects includes education, job

---

[105] 'It is important to the peace process as a whole that the different ideological perspectives of government and of the prisoners about the reasons why they are in prison be left aside and that we see prisoner reintegration as an integral factor in rebuilding our communities. Further it will have to be recognised that progress cannot be achieved without the active participation of the prisoners themselves.' Dave Wall, Director of NIACRO, Submission to the Forum for Peace and Reconciliation, 20 Jan. 1995 (Dublin: Forum for Peace and Reconciliation).

[106] Data made available to the author by Northern Ireland Voluntary Trust.

[107] *Irish News* (20 Jan. 1999), 'Prisoners Group Launched'.

skills programmes, financial and welfare advice, housing and accommodation, and family-orientated counselling (McShane 1998). While there has been some criticism of the provision of European Union funding to such projects,[108] to date these groups have not availed themselves of substantial alternative funding.[109] Former prisoners have also lobbied successfully to have the issue of discrimination against former prisoners included in the strategic plan for the new Northern Ireland Human Rights Commission which is tasked under the agreement with producing a Bill of Rights for Northern Ireland.[110] However, the real test of the commitments made in the agreement regarding reintegration will come when the European Union funding is exhausted and prisoners' groupings seek mainstream statutory monies.

Prisoner Release and the Acknowledgement of Political Motivation

We are on the brink of securing the de facto recognition of the political character of the conflict, a fact represented by the release of political prisoners.[111]

In this important interview Padraig Wilson, IRA Officer Commanding in the Maze, underlined the symbolic importance of the prisoner issue. The Good Friday Agreement has been famously described by the Deputy First Minister Designate, Seamus Mallon of the SDLP as 'Sunningdale for slow learners'.[112] This reference is to the failed 1973 agreement which contained a number of features similar to the 1998 agreement including a power sharing executive, limited cross-border co-operation, and the establishment of some human rights and non-discrimination protections (Bloomfield 1994). However, such a description of the Good Friday Accord undersells its complexity.

The Sunningdale process, like much of government policy during the

---

[108] *Observer* (10 Jan. 1999), 'Fury at Euro-Cash for Ex-terrorists'.

[109] *Ireland on Sunday* (17 Aug. 1998), 'Peace Pays Paltry Dividend for Victims and Ex-prisoners'.

[110] 'They [ex-prisoners] face discrimination when seeking employment, travel documents, welfare benefits, financial assistance, access to compensation for criminal injuries, the adoption of children or general community acceptance . . . The Northern Ireland Human Rights Commission believes that protecting the rights of ex-prisoners can play a useful role in reintegrating ex-prisoners from all sections of the community in Northern Ireland into a new, trusting and pluralistic society' (NIHRC 1999: 24).

[111] *Financial Times* (17 June 1998), 'IRA Chief in the Maze is Ready to Seek a New Way Out'.   [112] *Irish Times* (20 Oct. 1998), 'A Favourite Curmudgeon'.

conflict, reflected a mindset which sought to 're-establish normal constitutional politics in Northern Ireland', build the centre ground, politically marginalize and then contain the paramilitaries via an effective security policy (Cunningham 1991). The Good Friday Agreement on the other hand is characterized by a desire to bring the bulk of extremist opinion inside the process, an endeavour admittedly made easier in 1998 by the presence of organized political parties representative of Republicanism and Loyalism. Such parties had no electoral mandate in 1973. It could be argued that it represents an acceptance of the political motivation of paramilitaries, an implicit acknowledgement of the state as a protagonist in the conflict and a preference for politics over security—all of which underscore and are informed by a recognition of the political nature of the conflict.

Von Tangen Page (1998a: 164) has suggested that the more pragmatic approach adopted by the Irish government to the question of prisoner release when compared to their British counterparts was because the Irish state had not been directly targeted by the IRA campaign. Quite apart from the numerous acts of violence which occurred in the Republic during the conflict, such an analysis fails to take account of the political and ideological insights into the respective states provided by prisoner releases. While the Republic utilized harsh anti-terrorist laws, banned Sinn Fein from the airwaves for almost two decades, and occasionally treated paramilitary prisoners in a severe and brutal manner, there appeared little doubt that the conflict was other than political amongst the key political actors in the South (Hogan and Walker 1989, Finlay 1998, Whelan and Masterson 1998). For the British state on the other hand, from at least 1976 onwards, the separation of the political and security arena into two distinct sets of discourses and practices meant that key state actors appeared to lose sight of the political character of the conflict. The mismanagement of the peace process by the Major government, notwithstanding their need for Unionist support at Westminster, represents at some level a state's failure to move beyond a conflict mode of security discourses to an acceptance of the political character of the conflict required for effective peace-building.

In a violent political struggle, the treatment of prisoners is a mirror to the state's view of the conflict. The internment of suspects without trial and the granting of Special Category Status to prisoners in the early 1970s, the removal of such status from 1976 and the attempts at criminalisation until the early 1980s, and the policies of managerialism in the 1980s—all of these offer insights into the British government's ideological and political approach to the conflict during those eras. While they too have maintained the fiction that 'there are no political prisoners in British prisons' the willingness of the Labour government to engage sensibly on the prisoner issue is indicative of a mindset that has made the necessary transformation for conflict resolution.

The apparent *de facto* acceptance of the political motivation of paramilitaries does not imply either approval or appeasement. Neither Republicans nor Loyalists have achieved the stated objectives of their respective campaigns of violence. What it does entail, however, is an ability to distinguish the securitocratic rhetoric of criminalisation, to understand that unpalatable measures such as prisoner release are necessary in a process of conflict resolution, and to recognize that reform of certain structural elements of the state (such as policing and the criminal justice system) are prerequisite foundations for a new society. The prisoner issue may also be used as a prism through which to view other elements of the body politic beyond the British state.

It is no accident that the greatest obstacle to the Unionist Yes campaign was the issue of prisoner release. At one level, one might attribute this to the horrors of the past thirty years and the atrocities carried out by the IRA and other Republican groupings. Such an explanation is inadequate, however, ignoring as it does the fact that Nationalists voted overwhelmingly for an agreement which saw Loyalist prisoners released, despite the indiscriminate nature of Loyalists attacks on Catholics throughout the conflict. Another explanation, equally unconvincing, is the respective influence of Catholicism and Protestantism within Nationalism and Unionism. Such a view might juxtapose the variant theological emphases within the two religious blocks, the former with its New Testament emphasis on forgiveness and redemption, the latter with its Old Testament focus upon punishment and retribution. As with most religious explanations of Northern Ireland, such views do not stand up to analysis beyond the crudest of generalizations.

The key difference between the two principal communities on the prisoner issue may be attributed to their very different understandings of the conflict.

For Nationalists, both Republicans and supporters of the non-violent SDLP, the political character of the conflict has never really been in question. The indiscriminate nature of the Loyalist campaigns against the Catholic community have not dimmed the perception that the violence was political in character, aimed at the achievement of political objectives, and therefore capable of political resolution. No shade of Nationalist opinion has ever suggested that a military or security victory might be possible over Loyalist paramilitarism. Painful though prisoner releases have been for many Nationalists, they have been viewed by a clear majority of that community as necessary in order to resolve the conflict *politically*.[113]

For many Unionists on the other hand, terrorism was an aberration on the body politic perpetuated by a few Irredentist 'men of violence' for whatever combination of criminal or psychopathic reasons (Robinson 1980*b*, Cochrane 1997). With little support or sympathy for Loyalist prisoners beyond the narrow electoral base of the fringe Loyalist parties, and no comparable historical experience of political imprisonment to that of the Nationalist community in Ireland, the mainstream Unionist view of terrorist violence was sustained and nurtured by the official discourses of the state. Pro-Unionist security force members were not protagonists to the conflict but rather upholding law and order in the face of a vicious attack on *their* democratic state.

The refusal to recognize political motivation insulated Unionism from any acknowledgement of moral culpability in the conflict. The British state's denial of political motivation went to the core of Unionist denial of the need for change. So long as such a position was maintained by the British state, notions of Unionist bigotry or supremacist ideology as contributory factors to the origins and endurance of the conflict could be successfully suppressed (Clayton 1996). However, once the British state's *de facto* position on the recognition of political motivation had so manifestly changed (through prisoner releases), this represented a fundamental betrayal of the fiction of blamelessness. Prisoner releases, together with the other dramatic structural changes to policing, the criminal justice system, and equality and human rights protections have cumulatively made the Unionist *denial* of the nature of the conflict increasingly untenable.[114]

It would be putting the epistemological cart before the horse to suggest that prisoner releases have only occurred within the context of a shared acknowledgement of the political character of Northern Ireland's violent struggle. We are some distance from any shared view

[113] *Belfast Telegraph* (30 Sept. 1996), 'Most Nationalists Willing to Accept Some Kind of Amnesty'.

[114] For an analysis of the notion of denial with regard to human rights abuses see Cohen (1993, 1995).

of history in this jurisdiction. That said, a slim majority of Unionists did in the end vote in favour of the Good Friday Agreement and its provisions relating to prisoner release. Together with the overwhelming number of Nationalists, this constituted a 71 per cent majority in favour of the Accord. While support for the process has waxed and waned, and the decommissioning issue remains as a perennial cloud, the potential for a working consensus on the governance of Northern Ireland appears possible. If that happens, it will be the first time in the lifetime of the author that politics is conducted without significant numbers of paramilitary prisoners as a feature of the political landscape.

Epilogue
Political Prisons and the
Construction of Memory

In writing this book, I have been conscious of the need to avoid suggesting that this work represents a comprehensive narrative of the past thirty years of prison history. Rather it is one account, one story amongst the many which will undoubtedly emerge in the years to follow as other researchers, former prisoners, and prison staff offer their versions. This has been an attempt to draw out some central themes concerning prisoners' resistance, prison management, and prisoner release. The golden thread which permeates all of the analysis has been the dispute concerning the political status of the prisoners. This is a dispute which has at various times impacted directly upon the lives of most of the citizens in the jurisdiction.

Throughout this book I have argued that the prisons were a key site in the overall conflict. The significance of prisons as icons of fiction, punitive artefacts which offer insights into social or economic order, or as heuristic models to analyse the application of power or the dispersal of discipline, is well established in criminological literature (e.g. Garland 1990, Duncan 1996, Mathiesen 1997). Such a view, of prisons as a microcosm of the society outside, has become something of a truism in penal scholarship. The position which I have been suggesting, however, is that prisons in a conflict are particularly politically and ideologically *charged* sites. They define elements of the symbolic landscape of struggle. Such a view is arguably all the more relevant in the context of a 'low intensity conflict' (Kitson 1991), where the absence of major military encounters and the hit and run tactics of both paramilitary and state protagonists render the battlelines harder to discern. In such a context, what Mathiesen referred to as the 'action function' (Mathiesen 1990: 138) of imprisonment becomes all the more important, a positive observable sign which stands out and reassures that something is being done.

However, prisons are also places; they are geographical and cultural spaces; they represent what Steve Pile (1997: 27) has referred to as 'key sites of lived space in a political landscape'. Cultural geographers have over the past decade spent considerable energies in exploring the relationship between culture, identity, memory, spatiality, and place (Keith and Pile 1993, Sibley 1995, Taylor 2000). For example, Taylor (2000: 30) has argued that the notion of 'place' may be understood as a palimpsest, a text or manuscript on which social memories are recorded, erased, and overwritten.[1] In conflicts concerning the meaning of particular places, whether in clashes between aboriginal and settler identities in jurisdictions such as Australia (Gelder and Jacobs 1998), in ethno-national conflicts such as the Balkans or India (Ignatieff 1993, Shaw 2000), or in other areas of political struggle, these places offer physical road maps to the contours of such conflicts. The stories of the conflict may be literally embedded in the fabric of particularly important sites.

The Maze prison in particular has come to occupy a particular space in Northern Ireland's collective consciousness, albeit a fiercely contested one. It is an imposingly ugly and unique place, a site of several hundred acres which dominates the skyline (particularly at night) on one of the main arterial routes out of Belfast city.[2] Arguably one of the world's best-known prisons, its characteristic H Blocks have become a symbol synonymous with the most violent days of the

---

[1] For example, Charlesworth (1994) argues that the site of Auschwitz has been the locus for an acute contest over 'memorial space' since 1947. The site was originally chosen as a commemorative site by the Moscow-led Polish Communist Party, whose principal task was to suppress Polish nationalism. The victory of fascism was therefore best commemorated at a site which both recalled the Nazi horror but also where the Soviets had liberated Poles as well as Jews. Charlesworth argues that the early commemoration of the site was marked by attempts to de-Judaize Auschwitz, referring to 'victims' or 'people' rather than the specificity of Jewish suffering. In the 1970s, he argues, the camp became Catholicized as the current pope (then Archbishop of Krakow) led the campaign for the beatification of the Catholic martyr Father Maximilian Koble who had been killed at Auschwitz and with the subsequent establishment of a Carmelite convent in 1984 just the other side of the inner perimeter fence. Since 1947, these struggles over memory, ownership and commemoration have all been framed in the particular 'space' of the camp.

[2] Unionist MP Jeffrey Donaldson responded with some pique to criticism of the prison's aesthetic merit in the Westminster debate on the Northern Ireland Affairs Committee Report on prisons in Northern Ireland. He opined: 'The honourable Member for Hemel Hempstead may have been somewhat uncharitable when he described the prison [Maze] as a moonscape. It is in my constituency and when I am there I travel past it almost daily. Its architectural design may not be pleasing to the eye, but one must understand that the function of a prison is not to be architecturally pleasing but to secure the incarceration of those placed there by the judicial system.' *Hansard*, HC (Series VI) vol 343, col 124 (27 Jan. 2000).

conflict. The prison has now closed following the release of the final prisoners in August 2000 and a debate is emerging as to what should happen to the prison site. There appears a desire on the part of the prison authorities to bulldoze the site and eradicate it from the land-scape. That view has been given enthusiastic support from some Unionist politicians, most notably Sir Reg Empey (Enterprise Minister in the new devolved Assembly) who argued that it should be turned into an industrial park so that 'the painful memories' of the past would best be forgotten 'if it had a real use'.[3] Others, however, mostly former Republican prisoners, have suggested that at least part of the complex should be maintained as some form of a commemorative site for the conflict.

Similar dilemmas have been faced by other jurisdictions undergoing political transformation. In South Africa, Robben Island has become a central reference point to symbolize the transition to democracy, a symbol of what Harriet Deacon has referred to as that country's new 'moral maturity' (1998: 173). Her eloquent summary of the island's significance is worth reproducing:

Robben Island is no longer simply a repository of all that was considered neg-ative in society ('communism and terrorism' on the one hand or 'apartheid repression' on the other) . . . This shift, and the physical transition from high security prison to a public and positive national monument, has only become possible after the release of political prisoners from the island and South Africa's transition to democracy . . . the island's story has to be related very concretely to South Africa's history, to ensure that visitors are encouraged to think deeply enough about their own parts in the dissonant symphony of apartheid and their country's future. The island's story should also permit diversity; if it is to be a living monument for the new South Africa, its great opportunity lies in its opening outwards to other accounts of our past and future. (Deacon 1998: 178–9)

The Maze is not Robben Island and Northern Ireland is not South Africa. None the less, as I have argued above, the Northern Ireland

---

[3] *Observer* (30 July 2000), 'Empey: Turn Maze into an Industrial Park'. Perhaps sur-prisingly this view of putting the prison to an alternative use without any commemora-tion has attracted some support from former Loyalist prisoners. One high profile former UVF Special Category prisoner suggested in the same article that preserving any of the H Blocks would 'glorify the Republican Struggle' and 'create a shrine to the Hungerstrikers'. He suggested instead that it should be turned into a 'community resource' in order to compensate the people who had lived beside it throughout the conflict.

peace process has entailed little opportunity to achieve a shared understanding or recognition of our often competing histories. There
appears little current political energy amongst the key protagonists for
a comprehensive truth and reconciliation process in Northern Ireland
(Boraine 1999). Rather Northern Ireland and the Irish Republic have
seen pressure for the establishment of a number of individual inquiries
into controversial killings carried out directly by state forces or, where
there appears considerable evidence of state sponsored acts of political
violence, carried out by Loyalist paramilitaries.[4] More recently, political pressure has been mounted by Unionist politicians calling for an
inquiry into collusion between the Irish police (the Garda) and the
IRA.[5] While the public hearings which accompanied the Patten Commission on policing have been widely described as 'mini truth commission hearings', little of the testimony recorded in those hearings is
actually recorded in the report.[6] In such a context, we cannot afford to
pass up the opportunity to explore sites where we are compelled to
consider those competing histories. The complete eradication of such
an important site as the Maze seems to me to be not only an act of historical vandalism but a missed opportunity to engage in real peace-

---

[4] A public inquiry ordered by British Prime Minister Tony Blair into the killings of
thirteen civilians in Derry in 1972 by British paratroopers is ongoing at the time of writing. The inquiry is chaired by Lord Saville after the findings of the original Widgery
Tribunal have been effectively discredited by a twenty-seven year campaign. A similar
request, concerning the bombings in Dublin and Monaghan carried out by the UVF in
which thirty-three people were killed in 1973, is currently under consideration by the
Dublin government. Campaigners allege that there is strong evidence that the bombs
were planted at the behest of British military intelligence. There is also considerable
international and local pressure for independent inquires into the murder by Loyalists of
the two prominent human rights lawyers Pat Finucane and Rosemary Nelson, with campaigners again alleging strong evidence of security force/paramilitary collusion in their
murders. With regard to murders committed by Republicans, the Irish and British governments recently introduced *de facto* impunity legislation with regard to a number of
people who were killed and 'disappeared' by the IRA in the 1970s in order to encourage
the return of the bodies to their families. High profile digging operations in the Irish
Republic have to date only resulted in the return of three bodies.

[5] *Irish Times* (7 Jan. 2001), 'Trimble Calls for An Inquiry into Kingsmill Massacre'.

[6] One member of the commission has described the process of the public hearings to
the author as 'two completely contradictory histories, both true and both valid. One, the
Unionist history, is a testimony of the bravery, sacrifice and suffering of RUC officers
who defended their community against terrorism. The other, the Nationalist/Republican
history, is a testimony of extra-judicial killings, sectarian harassment, collusion with
Loyalist paramilitaries and so on.' The commissioners apparently took the decision that
rather than seek to reconcile these competing accounts, they would keep the report 'neutral' in tone and recommend the required reforms of policing without directly addressing the competing claims of the respective accounts. Confidential source.

building through the construction of a collective memory, albeit a contested one.

The processes by which memory is constructed is complex and beyond the scope of this book.[7] As a basic point of departure, however, if one accepts the Durkheimian notion that memory is influenced by the social world (rather than exclusively based upon an individual's personal life and experience) then the ways in which that social world is framed, portrayed, or indeed forgotten will inevitably play some part in its construction. Osiel's definition of collective memory is perhaps the most useful for current purposes.[8]

In particular, *real* sites, places where history *happened*, are particularly potent. Feeling what it was like, what Hayden (1999: 144) refers to as 'body memory', is difficult to evoke in a museum context detached from the historical site (Davison 1998). However, being in a historical place, whether a trench, a fighter plane, or a prison, 'moves us directly into place', places us in sites 'whose very immobility contributes to its distinct potency in matters of memory' (Casey 1987: 186). In effect, by being *in* such places, we are encouraged to engage with a broader set of memory discourses beyond our own personal or even group memories.

One of the ways in which the conflict was sustained in Northern Ireland was the complementary processes of historical nurturing and historical obliteration. Each of the protagonists, Nationalists/ Republicans, Unionists/Loyalists, and the British state promulgated (with varying degrees of success) distinct historical rationales for their conduct while in turn negating the rationales of the other (see generally McGarry and O'Leary 1995, Ruane and Todd 1996, Brewer and Higgins 1998). What is required in the post-conflict era of transformation is neither obliteration, nor an anodyne history-lite version of what went on over the past thirty years, but rather an attempt to find common history by treating the various antagonistic relationships seriously

---

[7] For an overview of the processes of individual and collective memory construction see e.g. Fentress and Wickham (1992), Baddeley (1994), Winter (1995), Schudson (1995), Glassberg (1996).

[8] 'Collective memory consists of the stories a society tells about momentous events in its history, the events that most profoundly affect the lives of its members and most arouse their passions for long periods . . . These events are also distinguished by the tendency for recollection of them to "hover over" subsequent events, providing compelling analogies of the most diverse variety. When a society's members interpret such an event in common fashion, they derive common lessons from it for the future' (Osiel 1997: 38–9).

(Wright 1993). What is required is warts and all history of the conflict, accessible to a mass audience, to coincide with the structural changes to our society.

As Cruz has argued with regard to Costa Rica and Nicaragua, 'Improving the chances for pluralistic peace in conflict ridden societies requires more than changing the leadership, reforming formal institutions or developing schemes for co-existence, important as all of these can be. It requires making critical entrepreneurs of us all: discerning citizens capable of distinguishing between history and fate' (Cruz 2000: 312).

It is my contention that the Maze prison has a role to play in the creation of such citizens; citizens encouraged to engage in a public conversation about what happened and why. Of course there are dangers in a conflict heritage approach to the preservation of sites of conflict. Lowenthal's (1996) concern that the heritage industry can promote a zone of exaggeration and myth-making which is somewhat distinct from traditional understandings of history is well taken. That said, properly managed sites do present an opportunity for opposing narratives to be voiced rather than silenced. A new society cannot be forged without a variety of acknowledgements of the past. Political prisons like the Maze provide such a setting in which reflection, contested claims-making, and acknowledgement may occur. They may become what De Kok (1998: 62) has referred to as 'cracked heirlooms', a process in which the dismantling, understanding, and reassembling of our key historical artefacts highlights the follies of our past and the pathway of our future.

Appendix 1
A Selected Chronology of Prison Events, 1971–2000

1971

(August) Internment without trial was introduced. Internees were held in Crumlin Road, *Maidstone* prison ship, and Magilligan and Long Kesh ex-army camps.

(October) Nine IRA prisoners escaped from Crumlin Road prison by using a rope ladder to climb over the outside wall.

1972

(January) Seven Republican detainees escaped from the *Maidstone* prison ship moored in Belfast harbour by squeezing through a porthole and swimming to shore.

(May) IRA leader Billy McKee and a number of other Republican prisoners went on hunger strike in Crumlin Road prison demanding political status.

(June/July) The IRA agreed to a private meeting with British Secretary of State William Whitelaw and other officials. As Billy McKee neared death, the British government ceded Special Category Status to paramilitary prisoners and also agreed to the release of Republican internee Gerry Adams to be part of the delegation for the meeting which was held in London. The IRA delegation were flown by the Royal Air Force from Aldergrove.

(November) IRA Chief of Staff Sean Mac Stiofain went on hunger and thirst strike in the Irish Republic after he was arrested and charged with IRA membership. Following 57 days on hunger strike, he came off in January 1974. He never recovered his status in the Republican movement as a result of ending his fast.

(December) The Diplock Report proposed a range of measures which were intended to overhaul the criminal justice system to enable easier convictions of paramilitaries activities, thereby reducing reliance upon internment. Recommendations were made to extend army and police powers to stop and question, search and seize, and arrest and detain. Stricter limitations were proposed on the availability of bail, the law governing the admissibility of confessions was to be relaxed in order to enable convictions upon confession alone. The commission also recommended the suspension of jury trial for a list of offences usually associated with the activities of paramilitary organizations. The bulk of the Diplock Commission's proposals were enacted by Parliament soon after in the Northern Ireland (Emergency Provisions) Act 1973.

1973

(January) Two hundred sentenced politicals were moved to Long Kesh from Crumlin Road.

(October) An IRA unit hired a helicopter and forced the pilot to fly to Mountjoy prison in the Irish Republic, landing in the exercise yard of the prison. Three senior Republicans including Seamus Twomey climbed on board and escaped.

(November) A number of IRA prisoners who had carried out the bombing of the Old Bailey began refusing food, demanding to be treated as political prisoners and to be transferred to Northern Ireland. The prisoners included Marion and Dolours Price, Hugh Feeney, and Gerry Kelly. The prisoners were force fed over a considerable period of time. In June 1974, another IRA prisoner Michael Gaughan died on hunger strike having been force fed for a month and a half. Under intense public pressure, and with Kelly and Feeney very ill, the then Home Secretary announced that the prisoners would be transferred, denying that his decision had been influenced by the hunger strikes. The prisoners came off their hunger strike in June 1974, but were not transferred until the following year.

1974

(August) In the Irish Republic, nineteen IRA prisoners blew their way out of Portlaoise prison using tiny amounts of smuggled gelignite and escaped.

(September) The first prison officer killed in the conflict was assassinated by Republicans.

(October) Republicans burned Long Kesh compounds.

(November) Hugh Coney, Republican internee, was shot dead by the British army while trying to escape from Long Kesh.

1975

(January) The Gardiner Report opined that the introduction of Special Category Status had been 'a serious mistake' and that it should be ended as soon as practicable and that internment could not remain as a long-term policy. The building of H Blocks at Long Kesh began.

1976

(February) IRA prisoner Frank Stagg died on hunger strike in England. He had gone on hunger strike in support of political status and protest at the refusal to transfer him to Ireland. He died after 61 days of his second hunger strike.

(March) Special Category Status was abolished for those convicted after this date. In order to make the change more palatable, automatic 50 per cent remission was introduced to replace the previous remission rate of 33 per cent. Any prisoner convicted of a paramilitary offence after that date was automatically sent to the newly constructed H Blocks, now known as Maze cellular.

(September) Ciaran Nugent, the first Republican prisoner to refuse to wear a prison uniform, went on the blanket protest. His example was followed by hundreds of other non-conforming Republican prisoners and a number of Loyalists over the next four years.

(December) The last internee was released. The power to intern was no longer used, although it remained on the statutes for over two decades.

1977

(April) A mass hunger strike in Portlaoise prison in the Irish Republic (in support of political status) ended after 47 days with no concessions won by the striking prisoners.

1978

(March) IRA blanketmen began to refuse to leave their cells and began their dirty protest, throwing urine and faeces out the windows, under the door, and smearing it on the walls of their cells.

(November) Albert Miles, deputy governor of the Maze, was shot dead, bringing to eight the number of prison staff members shot in three years.

1979

Nine prison officers, including one assistant governor, were killed during this year.

1980

(October) The first Republican hunger strike began in support of political status. Thirty-seven men and three women became involved. Political status was refined as a concept to 'five demands'. As one of the initial prisoners Sean McKenna neared death, a further twenty-seven prisoners went on strike on 15 December, and a further seven on 16 December 1980. Meanwhile a number of Republican female prisoners had also gone on hunger strike and on 12 December six UDA prisoners also began a hunger strike, demanding segregation from Republicans. The Northern Ireland Secretary of State gave a 34-page document to the prisoners via a mediator which appeared to contain the basis of a settlement. The document, the text of a speech which Atkins proposed to read out in Westminster the following day, addressed the prisoners as Republicans (rather than criminals), and offered concessions on 'civilian style clothing', letters, food parcels visits, and association. The prisoners called off the hunger strike on 18 December 1980.

(December) Loyalist prisoners took a number of hostages and went on to the roof at Crumlin Road prison seeking segregation from Republicans.

1981

(January) Eight remand IRA prisoners, including Joe Doherty, escaped from Crumlin Road.

(March) Arguing that the British government had reneged on the previous deal, Republican prisoners embarked on a second hunger strike on 1 March 1981 led by Bobby Sands. The day after the hunger strike began, IRA Officer Commanding Bik MacFarlane called off the dirty protest.

(April) Bobby Sands was elected MP for Fermanagh/South Tyrone running as an H Block candidate.

(May) Bobby Sands died after 66 days on hunger strike. His seat was subsequently won by his election agent, Owen Carron.

(June) Two H Block candidates won seats in the general election in the Irish Republic.

(May–October) A further nine Republican hunger strikers died. After sustained family interventions to save prisoners once they had lapsed into unconsciousness, the hunger strikes were called off. On 6 October, the new Secretary of State Jim Prior announced that all prisoners would be allowed to wear their own clothes, there would be 50 per cent remission of time lost through the protests, greater freedom of association between adjacent wings in the H Blocks, more visits, and the definition of prison work would be reviewed.

1982

(November) Strip searching of all female prisoners entering and leaving prison was formally instituted by the prison service. Protesting Republican prisoners at the Maze formally ended their post-hunger strike protests and were moved on to integrated wings. They now outnumbered Loyalist prisoners by approximately two to one on such wings. Loyalist prisoners began protests seeking segregation from Republicans. Loyalists began to wreck cell fittings and some began a dirty protest. Protesting Loyalist prisoners were then moved on to separate wings, had their privileges removed, and continued with their protests until February 1984.

1983

(March) After international protests, the level of strip searching in the women's prison at Armagh was dramatically reduced. The Life Sentence Review Board held its first meeting and fourteen lifers were released on licence. A Memorandum explaining the operation of the Board was published in 1985 after a major public campaign.

(September) Thirty-eight IRA prisoners escaped from the Maze prison. The prisoners seized control of H Block 7, removing uniforms and keys from prison officers. The prisoners took control of a delivery truck and arrived at the main gates as a new shift was coming into work in the prison. After having imprisoned a number of prison officers, the alarm was raised and the prisoners scattered, stabbing one officer in a scuffle who later died of a heart attack. The escape was subsequently examined in the detailed report of the Chief Inspector of Prisons, Sir James Hennessey.

1984

(January) Following the recommendations of the Hennessey Report, a number of additional security measures were introduced at the Maze prison. These included the increased movement and close supervision of top security prisoners who were designated as Red Book prisoners.

(August) Loyalist prisoners went on hunger strike in Magilligan demanding segregation. The protest was called off after two months. An attempted escape by two UDA prisoners from the Maze ended in tragedy when one of them was accidentally killed as he hid in a refuse lorry.

(December) British solder Private Ian Thaine who had been convicted of the murder of a civilian served a two and one-half year sentence before being released, returning to his regiment.

1985

(January) The prison service publicly launched an explanation of the sentence release procedure in its Explanatory Memorandum about the system.

(February) The prison authorities introduced a new pre-release home leave scheme for fixed term prisoners. Towards the end of the year this was extended to include indeterminate sentenced prisoners whose cases had reached an advanced stage in the process. In 1986 this was again extended so that such prisoners were given two-day periods of temporary release at six fortnightly intervals in the last three months of their sentence.

1986

(March) The women's prison at Maghaberry took in its first female prisoners when all inmates were transferred from the old Victorian prison at Armagh. While the male prison initially only held a small number of supergrass prisoners, male numbers steadily increased so that by the end of 1988 over 100 prisoners had been moved there.

1988

(June) The last three Special Category compounds were closed

1989

The *Annual Report* for the prison service for 1988 (published in 1989) outlined for the first time the NIPS aims and objectives. These had been developed by the senior management of the service. The process also saw the development of a range of performance indicators although these were not published in the *Annual Report*. The campaign for segregation at Crumlin Road gathered significant momentum during this year.

(August) The Christmas home leave scheme was much enlarged and a summer home leave scheme was introduced, the latter being extended in 1990 to include lifers who had served thirteen years or who had a provisional release date. Summer home leave was introduced for lifers with 143 released for long weekends.

(October) An attempted major escape from Crumlin Road was thwarted and the interface policy on improving prison visits was introduced.

1990

(September) A policeman was shot dead but the two prison officers travelling with him were released when they were captured at an IRA checkpoint near the border in South Armagh.

1991

(June) The prison service launched its first strategic plan, 'Serving the Community'.

(November) The ongoing campaign for segregation at Crumlin Road prison culminated in an IRA bomb which killed two Loyalist prisoners. Two weeks later Loyalist paramilitaries retaliated by launching a rocket propelled grenade attack from the road outside the prison. The grenade missed its intended target and no one was injured. The subsequent inquiry headed by Viscount Colville (March 1992) refused to grant segregation to remand paramilitary prisoners although physical changes in the prison facilitated the process of self-segregation.

1992

(February) The entire female prison at Maghaberry was forcibly strip searched.

(March) Crumlin Road prison escaper Joe Doherty was finally deported from the USA after a lengthy extradition and deportation legal battle.

1994

(July) Following prolonged disturbances by Loyalist prisoners, a group of Loyalists succeeded in reaching the roof of Crumlin Road prison. These actions were followed two weeks later by Loyalist prisoners in A and B wing rioting. They destroyed over 100 cells in one night and ultimately did so much damage to the fabric of the prison that the authorities decided that the prison was uninhabitable. All remand prisoners were moved to segregated accommodation at the Maze.

(September) Nine days after the IRA declared their complete cessation of military operations on 31 August 1994, five IRA prisoners and one British ordinary attempted to escape from the recently built Whitemoor prison in Cambridgeshire. One prison officer was shot by a prisoner sitting on top of the wall as he attempted to tackle the last two prisoners as they went up the rope ladder.

The Irish government began the first of a series of prisoner releases designed to 'support the peace process'.

1995

(January) The Irish government released nine more Republican prisoners.

(August) The NI Secretary of State Sir Patrick Mayhew announced that there would be changes in remission rates allowing some prisoners to be released earlier. The bill which was introduced at the end of October restored the remission rate of 50 per cent which had applied up until 1989.

1996

(April) Closure of Crumlin Road prison.

(October) Backbench Conservative MP Andrew Hunter suggested that the British government should consider reducing Loyalist prisoners' sentences in order to encourage the maintenance of their ceasefire.

1997

(March) A tunnel was discovered running from H7 in the Maze to within 30 metres of the perimeter fence.

(August) Labour Secretary of State Mo Mowlam indicated that while she was not yet ready to consider prisoner releases 'as the cease-fire holds, other options become possible'.

(December) LVF leader Billy Wright was killed by INLA prisoners in the Maze prisons. Wright was shot in a prison van as he was going to receive a prison visit.

(December) IRA prisoner Liam Averill escaped from the Maze having dressed up as a woman visitor. This escape, and the killing of Billy Wright, were subsequently examined in detail by the senior British prison official Martin Narey and his findings published in the Narey Report.

1998

(January) Secretary of State Mo Mowlam met with UDA prisoners in the Maze and persuaded them to reinstate their support for the peace process. She also presented the prisoners with a fourteen point document which included provisions on the question of early release.

(February) The British government submitted a paper to the Liaison Subcommittee on Confidence Building on measures in the multi-party talks regarding prisoners. Having received position papers from a number of the political parties (UDP, PUP, SDLP, Sinn Fein, and the Irish government—the rest of the parties did not address the issue), the British government indicated a willingness to 'work out an account of what could happen in respect of prisoner releases in the context of a peaceful and lasting settlement being agreed'.

(March) LVF prisoners tortured and murdered fellow LVF remand prisoner David Keyes in the Maze after he was suspected of becoming a police informer.

(April) The Good Friday Agreement was concluded. It included provisions for the release of all paramilitary prisoners belonging to organizations on cease-fire within two years.

(May) The British and Irish governments permitted a large number of Republican prisoners to attend the special Sinn Fein Ard Fheis. That meeting was required in order to change the party policy on entering a partitionist assembly and endorsing the agreement. The rapturous reception for some of the IRA's longest serving prisoners damaged the ongoing campaign for a Yes vote in the referendum amongst the Unionist electorate in the North. Michael Stone, a senior UDA prisoner, attended a similar Loyalist event organized by the UDP in the Ulster Hall.

(August) Following the passage of the Northern Ireland Sentences Act, the Sentence Review Commission began considering individual applications from prisoners seeking to qualify for the early release provisions: 446 applications were received by 21 August and prisoner releases began one month later. Similar legislation was introduced in the Irish Republic.

(November) The Secretary of State Mo Mowlam accepted the bona fides of the LVF ceasefire announced in May. This made LVF prisoners eligible to apply for early release. The Northern Ireland Affairs Committee published its report on prisons in Northern Ireland. Summaries of Sir David Ramsbotham's report into his inspection at the Maze were also made available.

1999

(March) The Secretary of State accepted the bona fides of the INLA ceasefire, thus making INLA prisoners eligible to apply for release.

(September) A legal challenge to the early release scheme was lodged by Ms Michelle Williamson whose parents were killed in an IRA bomb attack on the Shankill Road. The legal challenge ultimately failed.

2000

(August) The last of the politically motivated prisoners eligible for release under the Good Friday Agreement were released. In total 433 prisoners were released (193 Loyalists, 229 Republicans, 11 others). The Maze prison was closed.

(August) UDA leader Johnny Adair was recalled to prison after having his licence revoked by the Secretary of State. That decision was subsequently upheld by the Sentence Review Commission.

(September) Secretary of State Peter Mandelson announced that those who had escaped from custody during the conflict will no longer be sought under extradition proceedings and may return to Northern Ireland.

Appendix II
Notes on the Research Process

Introduction

This book began life as a part-time Ph.D. thesis in 1992/3. The original some-what vague hypothesis was constructed around the twin notions that (*a*) an exploration of the intersection of resistance and management strategies within the prisons in Northern Ireland was key to understanding both the conflict and any attempts at resolving it and (*b*) the dynamics at play in Northern Ireland prisons were of some interest to prison scholarship more generally. While those central contentions have been much tinkered with in the ensuing years, indeed abandoned and then gingerly resurrected on several occasions, they have none the less informed the methodology throughout.

That methodology entailed extensive literature and archival searches in a range of locations,[1] and a series of semi-structured interviews with key actors in the prison history. The fieldwork for the book has been carried out over the seven years of its writing. The first batch of interviews took place between 1993 and 1994, during the periods of extreme violence leading up to the IRA and Loyalist ceasefires. A second batch was carried out during the first IRA ceasefire (September 1994–February 1996) and a third in the aftermath of the second IRA ceasefire which included the period of the Stormont talks and the discussions regarding the implementation of the Good Friday Agreement.

Over fifty formal interviews were conducted for this research. A total of twenty-eight interviews were carried out with serving or former prisoners including twenty-one with serving or former Republican prisoners and seven with Loyalist prisoners. All interviews with prisoners took place either after they had been released, or (in a small number of cases) where prisoners were on Christmas or summer leave programmes. In addition, ten interviews were conducted with prison staff and governors, four with solicitors who conducted prison-related litigation cases, one with a voluntary sector senior manager, and a range of other miscellaneous individuals with an interest in prisons. All prison governors and staff had worked at either HMP Maze, Crumlin Road, or both.[2]

---

[1] These included the Northern Ireland Public Records Office, the Linen Hall Library, Belfast Central Library, the library of the University of Ulster, the Irish National Library in Dublin, the respective libraries of the *Irish News*, *Irish Times* (Dublin), *Belfast Telegraph*, *Ulster Newsletter*, and the library of the Queen's University of Belfast.

[2] Some data are also used in a few instances which were gleaned from interviews conducted by the author for other prison-related research e.g. the international experience of the release of politically motivated prisoners in other jurisdictions.

Interviews were either recorded, or, at the behest of the interviewee, contemporaneously written and rewritten after the interview. The data gleaned from these interviews were supplemented with hundreds of professional meetings, discussions, and informal conversations with a range of government officials, prison officers, former and serving prisoners, and Republican and Loyalist prison welfare representatives, victims of violence, and so forth over a seven year period.

In the first phase of the fieldwork, when the conflict was ongoing, assurances were given to all interviewees that they would remain anonymous in the book. Although this question of anonymity became less problematic for prisoners in the wake of the ceasefires, it remained a precondition for most of the prison staff interviewed. In the interests of uniformity all interviews are sourced by reference to the faction to which they belong, or their profession, and the date the interview occurred.

At an early stage in the research, it became clear that the possibility for conducting the fieldwork *inside* the prisons in Northern Ireland (and in particular inside the Maze and Belfast prisons) was remote. Such an approach would have involved (*a*) unfettered observational fieldwork within prisons (Jacobs 1977), what Dilulio (1987) referred to as 'soaking and poking', and (*b*) semi-structured interviews with serving prisoners and staff in the prison setting (e.g. Sparks, Bottoms, and Hay 1996). Northern Ireland has no tradition of such scholarship in its prisons. When I informally explored the potential of such a methodological approach with a sympathetic senior prison official in 1992, his frank response was 'not a mission'.

An initial letter to the prison service, which was sent in part as a tentative testing of the water and which sought access only to archival materials in HMP Belfast, was not answered. While significant co-operation was afforded to me by prison and NIO officials at all levels during the subsequent years of the research, and professional relationships have developed and been maintained, there was little realistic likelihood of conducting research of this nature inside the relevant prisons in Northern Ireland during the conflict.

Access and Recruitment

The problems of gaining access to other criminal justice organizations in Northern Ireland to carry out qualitative research have been detailed elsewhere (Brewer and Magee 1991, Ellison 1997). Similarly the difficulties of researching paramilitary or former paramilitaries have become a key focus in the methodological literature on dangerous or difficult fieldwork (Sluka 1990, Brewer 1993, Lee 1995). In the context of this research on paramilitary imprisonment in Northern Ireland, gaining access to prisoners, managers, and prison staff was directly related to the two professional posts which I have held since undertaking this book and a number of research projects and community-based activities in which I have been involved.

In September 1990 I was appointed as Information Officer at NIACRO and held that post until July 1995 when I took up an academic post at the newly established Institute of Criminology and Criminal Justice at Queen's University of Belfast. Both positions facilitated a considerable degree of access through professional networks.

NIACRO, the Northern Ireland Association for the Care and Resettlement of Offenders, is a major Northern Ireland charity which campaigns on behalf of prisoners, their families, ex-offenders, and young people at risk of offending in Northern Ireland. Having grown from a very small voluntary organization in the early 1970s, it now employs approximately eighty permanent staff and has an annual income of almost £2.5 million (NIACRO 1973, NIACRO 1999). While NIACRO receives substantial statutory funding, it has taken a persistently critical attitude to government policy on prisoners' rights issues and most notably on the question of the early release of politically motivated prisoners (Von Tangen Page 1998a). My responsibilities at NIACRO included drafting the organization policy on prison-related matters, serving as a public spokesperson in public and media engagements, and providing a legal advice service to individual prisoners and former prisoners (and their respective solicitors).

As with other practitioner researchers (Hammersley and Atkinson 1995), considerable advantages of access were doubtlessly gained where the outsider researcher may have had more difficulties. From the 1980s onwards, NIACRO had a long-standing structural relationship with the Northern Ireland prison service including regular formal meetings with the Controller and his senior staff, meetings which I attended. In addition, relationships were developed particularly from the late 1980s with the Republican and Loyalist prisoner welfare organizations, around the issue of prisoners' families and the campaign to transfer Irish prisoners from British prisons. In both instances, individuals from these various organizations were able to serve as gatekeepers (Lee 1993: 123–33, Hughes 1996), either agreeing to be interviewed, introducing me to other interview subjects, or authenticating my bona fides. The latter was particularly important with regard to interviewing the former paramilitary prisoners. As has been argued elsewhere, the role of gatekeepers is especially important where the research area is considered sensitive (Jupp 1989), and in particular where it concerns illegal organizations such as paramilitaries in Northern Ireland (Sluka 1990, Feldman 1991).

These professional affiliations did raise some methodological issues in relation to interviewing both prisoners and prison service staff.

For the prison service, while NIACRO had a professional relationship with the senior management, it was one where NIACRO was frequently critical of the policy and practice which the service was implementing. As both Brewer (1993) and Ellison (1997) found with regard to their research on the RUC, there is considerable sensitivity to criticism amongst criminal justice agencies in

Northern Ireland. With regard to the prison service, particularly in the early stages of the research, discussions with management and staff were sometimes couched in the same type of cautious and occasionally defensive discourse which characterized the interaction with NIACRO generally. Such difficulties are not uncommon with the practitioner researcher where interviewees may have difficulty in seeing the researcher out of role and may structure responses framed with what is expected within the familiar context (Bruce 1987).

With regard to former paramilitary prisoners, the NIACRO connection also had a number of implications. As is discussed at length in this book, paramilitary prisoners and their families have invested considerable energies in resisting attempts at various stages of the conflict to criminalise their activities and deny their political motivation. NIACRO, as an organization which worked with ordinaries, and which received considerable state funding, had always been treated with suspicion particularly by Republicans.[3] On the Loyalist side, similar suspicions with regard to a criminalising agenda were added to an apparent perception that NIACRO was a pro-Nationalist organization because of the location of the their headquarters in the Catholic area of Lower Ormeau Road and the religion of some of the key staff and their families.[4] These views were not static, they varied at different times of the research and between individuals, none the less they did form part of the context of gaining access.

After moving jobs to take up the position at Queen's, once again the professional context had a considerable impact upon access issues. While relationships with paramilitary prisoners and the senior officials in the prison service had been fairly well established by this stage (July 1995), I felt that I had insufficient data from the prison officers and governors who were actually staffing the prisons. I was fortunate that a number of officials, prison governors, and prison officers took up various courses at the Institute of Criminology and Criminal Justice and were willing to be interviewed and again to act as gatekeepers.

One possible impact of that structural relationship may be viewed in terms of the power relationship with such students. While I waited until these students had completed the relevant courses before interviewing them, none the less it could be argued that the power relationship which had been established was one of teacher student, where students may be expected to say things with which the tutor will agree. In the context of this book the implications of that relationship on the data is hard to gauge. These students were serving prison staff, with many years of experience and did not appear in the least intimi-

[3] At one stage during the hunger strikes in 1980/1 senior NIACRO staff met with Gerry Adams and other Republican leaders after an article appeared in the Republican newspaper *An Phoblacht* describing NIACRO as 'the soft end of the British War Machine'. Interview with NIACRO senior manager, 15 Apr. 1996.

[4] Interview with NIACRO senior manager, 15 Apr. 1996.

dated by my views and theories and indeed were more than willing (both during interviews and in class) to highlight areas where they disagreed with my conclusions.

A further factor of relevance to my methodology has been a number of research and community-based initiatives in which I became involved. In 1995, together with a NIACRO colleague, I undertook an international comparative research project on the early release of paramilitary prisoners (Gormally and McEvoy 1995). The results of that research were designed to contribute to the emerging debate on the issue in Northern Ireland. Being seen to campaign for the release of paramilitary prisoners, however much we attempted to frame our activities as 'informing the debate', brought me into contact with a considerably broader network of former prisoners and prison-related groupings whom I might not otherwise have reached. Similarly in 1997, again with colleagues, I became involved in a process designed to find alternatives to violent paramilitary punishment attacks through designing and implementing community-based restorative justice programmes (Auld *et al.* 1997). That process has resulted in the adoption by the Republican movement of a range of nonviolent programmes in local Nationalist communities, based upon the principle of restorative justice, as an alternative to the system of violent punishments which existed heretofore. In carrying out this work, I came into contact with a range of Republican ex-prisoners in particular, many of whom had been imprisoned or interned in the early years of the conflict, who once again were both willing to be interviewed and act as gatekeepers to others.

A final factor in conducting this research has been my own perceived religious affiliation. My name clearly denotes a Catholic background. As is extensively detailed in the literature on Northern Ireland, all citizens in the jurisdiction have a well developed system of informal antennae such as name, place of birth, and schools attended by which judgements on religion and related political viewpoints are invariably (and occasionally wrongly) determined (Brewer and Higgins 1998). As other researchers have demonstrated, being identified as either Catholic or Protestant in Northern Ireland in conducting sensitive research may facilitate access in interviewing subjects from one's own religious background (Jenkins 1984, Leonard 1993, McAuley 1994). The flip side to that dynamic is that it may impede access to members of the other religious community.

Despite strenuous efforts to achieve a balanced sample of Loyalist and Republican interviews amongst former paramilitary prisoners interviewed, this was not achieved. This may be due in part to my perceived religious affiliation, and, in part, to the practical difficulties of researching Loyalist paramilitarism identified elsewhere (Bruce 1992). With those limitations acknowledged, this book represents my best attempt to incorporate the views of Republicans, Loyalists, and prison staff/management in analysing the history of Northern Ireland's prisons over the past thirty years.

Bibliography

Abbot, J. H. (1981), *In the Belly of the Beast* (London: Arrow Books).

Abel, R. (1995), *Politics by Other Means: Law in the Struggle Against Apartheid 1980–1994* (London: Routledge).

Addameer (2000), *Reports From Behind the Bars* (Jerusalem: Addameer Prisoners Support and Human Rights Association).

Adams, G. (1986), *Free Ireland: Towards a Lasting Peace* (Kerry: Brandon).

—— (1990), *Cage Eleven* (Dingle: Brandon Books).

—— (1996), *Before the Dawn: An Autobiography* (London: Heinemann).

Adams, K. (1992), 'Adjusting to Prison Life', *Crime & Justice: A Review of Research*, 16, 275–359.

Adams, R. (1992), *Prison Riots in Britain and the USA* (Basingstoke: Macmillan).

Advisory Council on the Penal System (1968), *The Regime for Long Term Prisoners in Conditions of Maximum Security (Radzinowicz Report)* (London: HMSO).

Albertyn, C., and Davis, D. (1990), 'The Censure of Communism and the Political Trial in South Africa', in C. Sumner (ed.), *Censure, Politics and Criminal Justice* (Milton Keynes: Open University Press).

Alexander, N. (1992), 'Robben Island: A Site of Struggle', in N. Penn, H. Deacon, and N. Alexander (eds.), *Robben Island: The Politics of Rock & Sand* (Cape Town: Dept. of Adult Education and Extra Mural Studies), 68–84.

Alpert, G. (1979), 'Patterns of Change in Prisonization: A Longitudinal Analysis', *Criminal Justice & Behavior*, 6, 159–74.

Alspach, R. (ed.) (1979), *The Various Editions of the Plays of W. B. Yeats* (London: Macmillan).

Amnesty International (1978), *Report of an Amnesty Mission to Northern Ireland* (London: Amnesty International).

—— (1980), *Prisoners of Conscience in the USSR* (2nd edn., London: Amnesty International).

—— (1988), *Northern Ireland: Killings by the Security Forces and Supergrass Trials* (London: Amnesty International).

—— (1992), *Fair Trial Concerns in Northern Ireland: The Right of Silence* (London: Amnesty International).

—— (1994), *Political Killings in Northern Ireland* (London: Amnesty International).

Anderson, B. (1991), *Imagined Communities* (London: Verso).

Anderson, D. (1994), *14 May Days: The Inside Story of the Loyalist Strike of 1994* (Dublin: Gill & Macmillan).

Andrews, C. S. (1979), *Dublin Made Me* (Cork: Mercier Press).

Antonio, R. (1983), 'The Origin, Development and Contemporary Status of Critical Theory', *Sociological Quarterly*, 24 (Summer), 325–51.

Aretxaga, B. (1995), 'Dirty Protest: Symbolic Over-determination and Gender in Northern Ireland Ethnic Violence', *Ethos*, 23: 2, 123–49.

Arthur, M. (1987), *Northern Ireland's Soldiers Talking, 1969 to Today* (London: Sidgwick & Jackson).

Atlas, R. (1984), 'Violence in Prison: Environmental Influences', *Environment & Behavior*, 16: 3, 275–306.

Auld, J., Gormally, B., McEvoy, K., and Ritchie, M. (1997), *Designing a System of Restorative Justice in Northern Ireland* (Belfast: The Authors).

Baddeley, A. (1994), *Your Memory: A User's Guide* (2nd edn) Harmondsworth: Penguin).

Baker, Sir G. (1984), *Review of the Operation of the Northern Ireland (Emergency Provisions) Act 1978*, Cmnd. 9222 (London: HMSO).

Balbus, I. (1977), *The Dialectic of Legal Repression: Black Rebels Before the American Courts* (New Brunswick NJ: Transaction Books).

Bandura, A. (1990), 'Mechanisms of Moral Disengagement', in W. Reich (ed.) *Origins of Terrorism: Psychologies, Ideologies, Theologies, States of Mind* (Cambridge: Cambridge University Press).

Bankowski, Z., and Mungham G., (1976), *Images of Law* (London: Routledge & Kegan Paul).

Barak Glanz, I. (1981), 'Towards a Conceptual Schema of Prison Management Styles', *Prison Journal*, 61, 2.

Barker, A. (1998), 'Political Responsibility for UK Prison Security: Ministers Escape Again', *Public Administration*, 76: 1, 1–23.

Bean, J. (1994), *Over the Wall: True Stories of the Master Jailbreakers* (London: Headline).

Becker, J. (1989), *Hitler's Children: The Story of the Baader–Meinhof Terrorist Gang* (3rd edn., London: Pickwick).

Beetham, D. (1991), *The Legitimation of Power* (London: Macmillan).

Behan, B. (1958), *Borstal Boy* (London: Corgi).

Ben-David, S. (1992), 'Staff to Inmate Relations in a Total Institution: A Model of Five Models of Association', *International Journal of Offender Therapy and Comparative Criminology*, 36, 209–19.

—— Silfen, P., and Cohen, D. (1996), 'Fearful Custodial or Fearless Personal Relations: Prison Guards' Fear as a Factor Shaping Staff–Inmate Relation Prototype', *International Journal of Offender Therapy and Comparative Criminology*, 40: 2, 94–104.

Bennett, H. (1979), *A Report of the Committee of Inquiry into Police Interrogation Procedures in Northern Ireland*, Cmnd. 7397 (London: HMSO).

Bennett, L. (1974), 'The Application of Self Esteem Measures in a Correctional

Setting: Changes in Self Esteem During Incarceration', *Journal of Research in Crime & Delinquency*, 1, 9–15.

Bennett, W., and Feldman, M. (1981), *Reconstructing Reality in the Courtroom* (London: Tavistock).

Beresford, D. (1987), *Ten Men Dead* (London: Corgi).

Berkowitz, L. (1990), 'Biological Roots: Are Humans Inherently Violent?', in B. Glad (ed.) *Psychological Dimensions of War* (London: Sage).

—— (1993), *Aggression: Its Causes, Consequences, and Control* (New York and London: McGraw-Hill).

Berry, S. (1980), *To the Bitter Climax of Death if Necessary: The H-block Hunger Strike and the Struggle for Political Status* (London: Produced and Distributed for the SWP by Socialists Unlimited).

Bershad, L. (1977), 'Law and Corrections: A Management Perspective', *New England Journal of Prison Law*, 4, 49–82.

Best, J. (1987), 'Rhetoric in Claims-making: Constructing the Missing Children Problem', *Social Problems*, 34: 2, 101–21.

—— (1989), *Images of Issues* (New York: Aldine De Gruyer).

Bettelheim, B. (1986), *Surviving the Holocaust* (London: Flamingo).

Bew, P., and Patterson, H. (1985), *The British State and the Ulster Crisis: From Wilson to Thatcher* (London: Verso).

Bew, P. and Gillespie, G. (1993), *Northern Ireland: A Chronology of the Troubles* (Dublin: Gill & Macmillan).

—— and—— (1996), *The Northern Ireland Peace Process 1993–1996: A Chronology* (London: Serif, 1996).

—— Gibbon, P., and Patterson, H. (1996), *Northern Ireland 1921–1996: Political Forces and Social Classes* (London: Serif).

Bhabba, H. (1994), *The Location of Culture* (London: Routledge).

Bidna, H. (1975), 'Effects of Increased Security on Prison Violence', *Journal of Criminal Justice*, 3, 33–46.

Bishop, P., and Mallie, E. (1987), *The Provisional IRA* (London: Corgi).

Blair, A. (16 May 1997), Speech Delivered at the Royal Ulster Agricultural Show, Belfast. Reproduced by Northern Ireland Office (Belfast: Northern Ireland Information Service).

Block, J., and Fitzgerald, P. (1983), *British Intelligence and Covert Action: Africa, Middle East and Europe Since 1943* (Dingle: Brandon).

Bloomfield, K. (1994), *Stormont in Crisis: A Memoir* (Belfast: Blackstaff Press).

—— (1998), *We Will Remember Them: Report of the Northern Ireland Victims Commissioner* Cm (Belfast: HMSO).

Bockman, S. (1991), 'Interest, Ideology, and Claims-Making Activity', *Sociological Inquiry*, 61: 4, 452–70.

Bolton, G. (1991), 'The Strange Career of William De La Poer Beresford', in B. Reece (ed.) *Exiles from Erin: Convict Lives in Ireland and Australia* (Dublin: Gill & Macmillan).

Bolton, N., Smith, F., Heskin, K., and Banister, P. (1976), 'Psychological

Correlates of Long-term Imprisonment', *British Journal of Criminology*, 16, 38–47.

Boraine, A. (1994), *Truth And Reconciliation Commission* (Rondelbosch: Justice in Transmission).

—— (1999), *'All Truth is Bitter': A Report of the Visit of Dr Alex Boraine, Deputy Chairman of the South African Truth and Reconciliation Commission, to Northern Ireland* (Belfast: NIACRO).

Borland, J., King, R., and McDermott, K. (1995), 'The Irish in Prison: A Tighter Nick for the Micks', *British Journal of Sociology* 46: 3, 371–94.

Borneman, J. (1997), *Settling Accounts: Violence, Justice & Accountability in Post Socialist Europe* (Princeton: Princeton University Press).

Bottomley, A. K., Liebling, A., and Sparks, R. (1994), *Barlinnie Special Unit and Shotts Unit: An Assessment*, Scottish Prison Service Occasional Paper No. 7/1994 (Edinburgh: Scottish Prison Service).

Bottoms, A. (1977), 'Reflections on the Renaissance of Dangerousness', *Howard Journal of Criminal Justice*, 16, 70–96.

—— (1995), 'The Philosophy and Politics of Punishment and Sentencing', in C. Clarkson and R. Morgan (eds.), *The Politics of Sentencing Reform* (Oxford: Oxford University Press).

—— and Light, R. (1987), 'Introduction: Problems of Long Term Imprisonment', in A. Bottoms and R. Light (eds.) *Problems of Long Term Imprisonment* (Aldershot: Gower).

—— Hay, W., and Sparks, R. (1990), 'Situational and Social Approaches to the Prevention of Disorder in Long Term Prisons', *Prison Journal*, 80: 1, 83–95.

Boulton, D. (1973), *The UVF 1966–1973: An Anatomy of Loyalist Rebellion* (Dublin: Gill & Macmillan).

Bowker, L. (1980), *Prison Victimisation* (New York: Elsevier).

Bowyer Bell, J. (1979), *The Secret Army: The IRA* (Dublin: Poolbeg).

—— (1993), *The Irish Troubles: A Generation of Violence* (Dublin: Gill & Macmillan).

Boyle, J. (1977), *A Sense of Freedom* (London: Pan).

—— (1984), *The Pain of Confinement* (London: Pan).

Boyle, K. (1977), 'The Tallents Report on the Craig–Collins Pact of 30 March 1922', *The Irish Jurist*, NS 12:1, esp. 173–5.

—— Hadden, T., and Hillyard, P. (1975), *Law and State: The Case of Northern Ireland* (London: Martin Robertson).

—— —— and—— (1980), *Ten Years on in Northern Ireland: The Legal Control of Political Violence* (Belfast: Cobden Trust).

—— and,—— (1985), *Ireland: A Positive Proposal* (Harmondsworth: Penguin).

—— and Campbell, C. (1992), *Human Rights in Situations of Armed Conflict and Political Violence* (Santiago: Sinergos Consultores Ltda).

Braithwaite, R. (1992), *Violence: Understanding, Intervention and Prevention* (Oxford: Radcliffe Professional).

Brasswell, M., Montgomery, R., and Lombardo, L. (eds.) (1985), *Prison Violence in America* (2nd edn., Cincinatti: Anderson Publishing Co).

Brewer, J. (1993), 'Sensitivity as a Problem in Field Research: A Study of Routine Policing in Northern Ireland', in C. Rezetti and R. Lee (eds.), *Researching Sensitive Topics* (Newbury Park: Sage).

—— and Magee, K. (1991), *Inside the RUC: Routine Policing in a Divided Society* (Oxford : Clarendon Press).

—— and Higgins, G. (1998), *Anti-Catholicism in Northern Ireland 1600–1998: The Mote and the Beam* (London: Macmillan).

British & Irish Rights Watch (2000), 'Lethal Force: The Force Research Unit and State Involvement in Killings in Northern Ireland' (not published, author's copy).

Broderick, F., Colmand,G., Hegart, P., and Kilroy, J. (1995), *Where is Liberty? The Prosecution of Irish Republicans in the United States* (New York: Irish Northern Aid).

Brodsky, C. (1982), 'Work Stress in Correctional Institutions', *Journal of Prison Jail Health*, 2: 2, 74–102.

Bronstein, A. (1977), 'Reform without Change: The Future of Prisoners' Rights', *Civil Liberties Review*, 4, 27–45.

Brown, J. (1977), *Gandhi and Civil Disobedience: The Mahatma in Indian Politics* (Cambridge: Cambridge University Press).

Brown, N. (1959), *Life Against Death: The Psychoanalytical Meaning of History* (Middletown, Conn.: Wesleyan University Press).

Brownlee, I. (1998), 'New Labour—New Penology? Punitive Rhetoric and the Limits of Managerialism in Criminal Justice Policy', *Journal of Law and Society*, 25: 1, 313–35.

Bruce, S. (1987), 'Gulliver's Travels: The Native Sociologist', in N. McKeganey and S. Cunningham-Burley (eds.), *Enter the Sociologists: Reflections on the Practice of Sociology* (Aldershot: Avebury).

—— (1992), *The Red: Protestant Paramilitaries in Northern Ireland* (Oxford: Oxford University Press).

—— (1994), *The Edge of the Union* (Oxford: Oxford University Press).

—— (1995), 'Northern Ireland: Reappraising Loyalist Violence', in A. O'Day (ed.) *Terrorism's Laboratory* (Aldershot: Darmouth).

Brydensholt, H., Van der Goorbergh, M., Almeida, M., and Shapland, P. (1983), *Prison Management* (Strasbourg: Council of Europe).

Bukstel, L., and Kilman, P. (1980), 'Psychological Effects of Imprisonment on Confined Individuals', *Psychological Bulletin*, 88: 2, 469–93.

Buntman, F. (1996), 'The Politics of Conviction: Political Prisoner Resistance on Robben Island, 1962–1991, and its Implications for South African Politics and Resistance Theory', Ph.D. Thesis, University of Texas at Austin (made available by the author).

Burton, J. (1996), *Violence Explained: The Sources of Conflict, Violence and Crime and their Prevention* (Manchester: Manchester University Press).

Cairns, E. (1994), 'Understanding Conflict and Promoting Peace in Ireland: Psychology's Contribution', *Irish Journal of Psychology*, 15: 2, and 3, 480–93.

CAJ (1989), *Life Sentence and SOSP Prisoners in Northern Ireland*, CAJ pamphlet no. 12 (Belfast: Committee on the Administration of Justice).

—— (1995), *No Emergency, No Emergency Law: Emergency Legislation Related to Northern Ireland: The Case for Repeal* (Belfast: Committee on the Administration of Justice).

—— (1998), *A Guide to Prisoners' Rights in Northern Ireland* (Belfast: Committee on the Administration of Justice).

California, B. (1979), *Political Crime in Europe: A Comparative Study of France, Germany and England* (Berkeley: University of California Press).

Callaghan, J. (1973), *A House Divided: The Dilemma of Northern Ireland* (London: Collins).

Cameron, Lord (1969), *A Report into the Disturbance in Northern Ireland: Report of the Commission Appointed by the Governor of Northern Ireland*, Cmnd. 532 (Belfast: HMSO).

Campaign for Lifers (n.d. probably 1985/6), *Campaign for Lifers* (Belfast: Campaign for Lifers).

Campbell, B., McKeown L., and O'Hagan, P. (1994), *Nor Meekly Serve My Time: The H Block Struggle 1976–1981* (Belfast: Beyond the Pale Publications).

Campbell, C. (1989), 'Extradition to Northern Ireland: Prospects and Problems', *Modern Law Review*, 52: 5, 585–621.

—— (1994), *Emergency Law in Ireland, 1918–1925* (Oxford: Clarendon Press).

Canter, D., and Ambrose, I. (1980), *Prison Design and the Use Study: Final Report* (Guildford: University of Surrey).

Carbonneau, T. (1983), 'The Political Offence Exception as Applied in French Cases Dealing with the Extradition of Terrorists', *Michigan Yearbook of International Legal Studies*, 209, 223–4.

Cardozo, N. (1979), *Lucky Eyes and a High Heart* (London: Gollancz).

Carmichael, S. (1968), *Black Power: The Politics of Liberation in America* (London: Jonathan Cape)

Carter, K. (1995), 'The Occupational Socialisation of Prison Officers: An Ethnography', Ph.D. Thesis, University of Cardiff.

Casey, E. (1987), *Remembering: A Phenomenological Study* (Bloomington, Ind.: Indiana University Press).

Cavadino, M., and Dignan, J. (1997), *The Penal System: An Introduction* (2nd edn., London: Sage).

Challis, J. (1999), *The Northern Ireland Prison Service, 1920–1990: A History* (Belfast: Northern Ireland Prison Service).

Chambliss, W. (1975), *Criminal Law in Action* (Santa Barbara, Calif.: Hamilton).

Charlesworth, A. (1994), 'Contesting Places of Memory: The Case of Auschwitz', *Environment and Planning*, 12: 5, 579–97.

Cheek, F. (1984), *Stress Management for Correctional Officers and their Families* (College Park, MD.: American Correctional Association).

Chomsky, N. (1992), *Deterring Democracy* (London: Vintage Books).

Clarke, J., and Newman, J. (1997), *The Managerial State* (London: Sage).

—— Cochrane, E., and McLaughlin, E. (eds.), (1994), *Managing Social Policy* (London: Sage).

Clarke, L. (1987), *Broadening the Battlefield: The H Blocks and the Rise of Sinn Fein* (Dublin: Gill & Macmillan).

Clayton, P. (1996), *Enemies and Passing Friends: Settler Ideologies in Twentieth Century Ulster* (London: Pluto Press).

Clemmer, D. (1940), *The Prison Community* (New York: Rinehart & Winston, further edition 1958).

CLMC (1994), Statement issued by the Combined Loyalist Military Command Declaring a Cessation of Operational Hostilities. Website http://www.uhb.fr/Langues/Cei/cfloy94.htm

Cochrane, F. (1997), *Unionist Politics and the Politics of Unionism since the Anglo-Irish Agreement* (Cork: Cork University Press).

Cockburn, H. (1888), *An Examination of the Trials for Sedition Which Have Hitherto Occurred in Scotland,* (Edinburgh: David Douglas).

Cohen, A., Cole, G., and Bailey, R. (eds.), (1976), *Prison Violence* (Lexington, Mass.: Lexington Books).

Cohen, S. (1993), 'Human Rights and Crimes of the State: The Culture of Denial', *Australian and New Zealand Journal of Criminology*, 26: 2, 97–115.

—— (1995), 'Government Responses to Human Rights Reports: Claims, Denials and Counterclaims', *Human Rights Quarterly*, 18: 3, 517–43.

—— (1996), 'Crime and Politics: Spot the Difference', *British Journal of Sociology*, 47: 1, 1–21.

—— and Taylor, L. (1972), *Psychological Survival* (Harmondsworth: Penguin).

—— and—— (1976), *Escape Attempts: The Theory and Practice of Resistance to Everyday Life* (London: Allen Lane).

Cohn, A. (1998), 'The Failure of Correctional Management: Rhetoric Versus the Reality of Leadership', *Federal Probation*, 62: 1, 26–31.

Collins, T. (1986), *The Irish Hunger Strike* (Dublin: White Island Book Company).

Collins, W. (1995), 'The Eighth Amendment in Prisons: Does the Supreme Court Know Where it's Going?' in K. Haas and G. Alpert (eds.), *Dilemmas of Correction: Contemporary Readings* (3rd edn., Prospect Heights, Ill.: Waveland Press).

Colville, Viscount (1992), *A Report on the Operational Policy in Belfast Prison for the Management of Paramilitary Prisoners from Opposing Factions*, Cmnd. 1860 (London: HMSO).

Comaroff, J. (1985), *Body of Power, Spirit of Resistance: The Culture and History of a South African People* (Chicago: University of Chicago Press).

Concerned Relatives/Ex-prisoners Committee (1987), *Magilligan: A Cause for Concern* (Belfast: Concerned Relatives and Ex-prisoners Committee).

Connolly, A. (1982), 'Non-extradition for Political Offences: A Matter of Legal Obligation or Simply a Matter of Policy Choice?' *Irish Jurist*, 17, 59–82.

Connolly, J. (1987), *Collected Works*, (Dublin: New Books Publications).

Connolly, M., and Loughlin, S. (eds.), (1990), *Public Policy in Northern Ireland: Adoption or Adaption?* (Belfast: Policy Research Institute).

Coogan, T.P. (1980), *On the Blanket: The H Block Story* (Dublin: Ward River Press).

—— (1987), *The IRA* (London: Fontana).

—— (1990), *Michael Collins: A Biography* (London: Hutchinson).

—— (1993), De Valera: *Long Fellow, Long Shadow* (London: Hutchinson).

—— (1995), *The Troubles: Ireland's Ordeal 1966–1995 and the Search for Peace* (London: Hutchinson).

Cooke D. (1989), 'Containing Violent Prisoners: An Analysis of the Barlinnie Special Unit', *British Journal of Criminology*, 29, 129–43.

—— (1991), 'Violence in Prisons: The Influence of Regime Factors', *Howard Journal*, 30: 2, 95–109.

Coopers and Lybrand (1996), *Northern Ireland Economic Review* (Belfast: Coopers and Lybrand).

Coulter, C. (1991), *Web of Punishment: An Investigation* (Dublin: Attic Press).

Counterpoint UTV (22 Sept. 1993), *Unlocking the Maze*, Programme, unbroadcast extracts, and unused transcripts made available to the author by Chris Moore, producer (Belfast: Ulster Television Ltd).

Cover, R. (1975), *Justice Accused* (New Haven: Yale University Press).

Coyle, A. (1987), 'The Scottish Experience with Small Units', in A. Bottoms and R. Light (eds.), *Problems of Long Term Imprisonment* (Aldershot: Gower).

Crawford, C. (1979), 'Long Kesh: An Alternative Perspective', M.Sc. Thesis, Cranfield Institute of Technology.

—— (1999), *Defenders or Criminals?: Loyalist Prisoners and Criminalisation* (Belfast: Blackstaff Press).

Crelinsten, R. (1998), 'The Discourse and Practice of Counter Terrorism in Liberal Democracies', *Australian Journal of Politics and History*, 44: 3, 389–413.

Crenshaw, M. (1990), *Theories of Terrorism: Instrumental and Organizational Approaches* (University Park, Pa.: Pennsylvania State Press).

Cressey, D. (ed.), (1961) 'Introduction' in *The Prison: Studies in Institutional Organization and Change* (New York: Holt, Rinehart & Winston).

—— (1965), 'Prison Organizations', in C. March (ed.), *Handbook of Organizations* (Chicago: Rand McNally).

—— and Krassowski, W. (1958), 'Inmate Organisation and Anomie in American Prisons and Soviet Labor Camps', *Social Problems*, 5, 217–30.

Cripe, C. (1990), 'Courts, Corrections and the Constitution: A Practitioners View', in J. DiIulio (ed.), *Courts, Corrections and the Constitution* (Oxford: Oxford University Press).

Crossman, R. (1977), *The Diaries of a Cabinet Minister*, Vol. iii (London: Hamilton & Cape).

Crouch, B., and Alpert, G. (1982), 'Sex and Occupational Socialisation Among Prison Guards: A Longitudinal Study', *Criminology*, 18: 2, 227–36.

—— and Marquart, J. (1990), 'Resolving the Paradox of Reform: Litigation, Prisoner Violence and Perceptions of Risk', *Justice Quarterly*, 7: 103–22.

Cruz, C. (2000), 'Identity and Persuasion: How Nations Remember their Pasts and Make their Futures', *World Politics*, 52: 3, 275–312.

Culbertson, R. (1975), 'The Effects of Instutionalization on the Delinquent Inmate's Self-Concept', *Journal of Criminal Law and Criminology*, 66, 83–93.

Cullen, F., Link, B., Wolfe, N., and Frank, J. (1985), 'The Social Dimensions of Correctional Officers' Stress', *Justice Quarterly*, 2: 4, 505–33.

Cullen Owens, R. (1984), *Smashing Times: A History of the Irish Women's Suffragette Movement 1889–1922* (Dublin: Attic Press).

Cumaraswamy, P. (1998), *Report of the Special Rapporteur on the Independence of Judges and Lawyers, Report on the Mission of the Special Rapporteur to the United Kingdom of Great Britain and Northern Ireland* (Geneva: UN Commission on Human Rights).

Cummins, E. (1994), *The Rise and Fall of the California Radical Prison Movement* (Stanford, Calif.: Stanford University Press).

Cunningham, M. (1991), *British Government Policy in Northern Ireland 1968–1989: Its Nature and Execution* (Manchester: Manchester University Press).

Curran, P. (1988), 'Psychiatric Aspects of Terrorist Violence: Northern Ireland 1969–1987', *British Journal of Psychiatry*, 153, 470–5.

Currie, D., and MacLean, B. (1995), 'Critical Reflections on the Peace Process in Northern Ireland', *Humanity & Society*, 19: 3, 101–16.

Curtis, L. (1981), *The H Blocks: An Indictment of British Prison Policy in the North of Ireland* (London: Information on Ireland).

—— (1984), *Ireland: The Propaganda War* (London: Pluto).

Cusack, J., and McDonald, H. (1997), *UVF* (Dublin: Poolbeg).

Cutler, T. and Waine, B. (1994), *Managing the Welfare State* (London: Berg).

Dangerfield, G. (1979), *The Damnable Question: A Study in Anglo-Irish Relations* (London: Quartet).

Darby, J. (1993), *Dressed to Kill: Cartoonists and the Northern Ireland Conflict* (Belfast: Appletree).

Davidson, R. T. (1974), *Chicano Prisoners: The Key to San Quentin* (New York: Holt, Rinehart & Winston).

Davies, W. (1982), 'Violence in Prison', in M. Feldman (ed.), *Developments in the Study of Criminal Behaviour*, Vol. ii (Chichester: John Wiley).

—— and Burgess, P. (1988), 'Prison Officers' Experience as a Predictor of Risk of Attack: An Analysis within the British Prison System', *Medicine, Science and the Law*, 28, 135–8.

Davison, P. (1998), 'Museums and the Reshaping of Memory', in S. Nuttall and C. Coetzee (eds.), *Negotiating the Past: The Making of Memory in South Africa* (Oxford: Oxford University Press).

Dawes, A. (1994), 'The Emotional Impact of Political Violence', in A. Dawes, and P. Donald, *Childhood and Adversity* (Cape Town: David Philip).

Deacon, H. (1998), 'Remembering Tragedy, Constructing Modernity: Robben Island as a National Monument', in S. Nuttall and C. Coetzee (eds.), *Negotiating the Past: The Making of Memory in South Africa* (Oxford: Oxford University Press).

Dear, I. (1997), *Escape and Evasion: Prisoner of War Breakouts and the Routes to Safety in World War Two* (New York: Arms & Armour Press).

De Beaumont, G., and De Tocqueville, A. (1997), 'On the Penitentiary System in the United States and its Application to France: Historical Outline of Penitentiary System' (originally published 1833). Excerpts reproduced in J. Marquart and J. Sorensen (eds.), *Correctional Contexts: Contemporary & Classic Readings* (Los Angeles: Roxbury).

De Bréadún, D. (2001), *The Far Side of Revenge: Making Peace in Northern Ireland* (Dingle: Brandon).

De Certeau, M. (1984), *The Practice of Everyday Life* (Berkeley: University of California Press).

De Kok, I. (1998), 'Cracked Heirlooms: Memory on Exhibition', in S. Nuttall and C. Coetzee (eds.), *Negotiating the Past: The Making of Memory in South Africa* (Oxford: Oxford University Press).

Deleuze, G. (1977), 'Active and Reactive', in A. David (ed.), *The New Nietzsche: Contemporary Styles of Interpretation* (Cambridge: MIT Press).

Della Porta, D. (1995), *Social Movements, Political Violence and the State* (Cambridge: Cambridge University Press).

Desmond, C. (1983), *Persecution East and West: Human Rights, Political Prisoners, and Amnesty International* (Harmondsworth: Penguin).

Devlin, B. (1969), *The Price of My Soul* (London: Deutsch in Association with Pan Books Ltd.).

Dewar, M. (1985), *The British Army in Northern Ireland* (London: Arms & Armour Press).

Dews, P. (1987), *Logics of Disintegration: Post Structuralist Thought and the Chains of Critical Theory* (London: Verso).

Dickson, B. (1992), 'Northern Ireland's Emergency Legislation: The Wrong Medicine?', *Public Law*, 10, 592–624.

—— (1998), 'Judicial Review and Prisoners in Northern Ireland', *Public Law*, 16, 57–64.

Dillon, M. (1989), *The Shankill Butchers: A Case Study in Mass Murder* (London: Hutchinson).

—— (1990), *The Dirty War* (London: Arrow).

—— (1992), *Killer in Clowntown: Joe Doherty, the IRA and the Special Relationship* (London: Hutchinson).

—— and Lehane, P. (1984), *New Ireland Forum: The Cost of Violence Arising from the Northern Ireland Crisis since 1969* (Dublin: Republic of Ireland Stationary Office).

DiIulio J. (1987), *Governing Prisons: A Comparative Study of Correctional Management* (New York: Free Press).

Diplock, Lord (1972), *The Report of the Commission to Consider Legal Procedures to Deal With Terrorist Activities in Northern Ireland*, Cmnd. 5186 (Belfast: HMSO).

Ditchfield, J. (1990), *Control in Prisons: A Review of the Literature*, Home Office Research Study 118 (London: HMSO).

Douglas, G., and Jones, S. (1983), 'Prisoners and the European Convention of Human Rights', in M. Furmsto, R. Kerridge, and B. Sufrin (eds.), *The Effect on English Domestic Law of Membership of the European Communities and of Ratification of the European Convention of Human Rights* (London: Martinus Nijhoff).

Dreyfus, H., and Rabinow, P. (1982), *Michel Foucault: Beyond Structuralism and Hermeneutics* (Chicago: University of Chicago Press).

Dudley-Edwards, R. (1977), *Patrick Pearse: The Triumph of Failure* (Dublin: Poolbeg Press).

DuGay, P. (1996), *Consumption and Identity at Work* (London: Sage).

Duncan, M. (1996), *Romantic Outlaws, Beloved Prisons: The Unconscious Meanings of Crime and Punishment* (New York: New York University Press).

Dunleavy, P., and Hood, C. (1994), 'From Old Public Administration to New Public Management', *Public Money and Management* July–Sept. 9–16.

Dunne, D. (1988), *Out of the Maze: The True Story of the Biggest Jail Escape Since the War* (Dublin: Gill & Macmillan).

Dunne, T (1982), *Theobold Wolfe Tone, Colonial Outsider: An Analysis of his Political Philosophy* (Cork: Tower).

Durham, H., and McCormack, T. (1999), *The Changing Face of Conflict and the Efficacy of International Humanitarian Law* (Boston: Kluwer International).

Dyzenaus, D. (1991), *Hard Cases in Wicked Legal Systems: South African Law in the Perspective of Legal Philosophy* (Oxford: Clarendon Press).

Eckland Olson, S. (1986), 'Crowding, Social Control and Prison Violence: Evidence from the Post Ruiz Years in Texas', *Law and Society Review*, 20: 3, 389–421.

Edgar, K., and O'Donnell, I. (1998), 'Assault in Prison: The Victim's Contribution', *British Journal of Criminology*, 38: 4, 635–50.

Eichental, D., and Jacobs, J. (1991), 'Enforcing the Criminal Law in State Prisons', *Justice Quarterly*, 8, 283–303.

Elias, N. (1998), *On Civilization, Power, and Knowledge: Selected Writings* (Chicago: University of Chicago Press).

Elliot, M. (1989), *Wolfe Tone: Prophet of Irish Independence* (New Haven: Yale University Press).

Ellis, D. (1984), 'Crowding and Prison Violence—Integration of Research and Theory', *Criminal Justice and Behaviour*, 11: 3, 277–308.

Ellison, G. (1997), 'Professionalism in the RUC: An Examination of the Institutional Discourse', Ph.D. Thesis, University of Ulster.

—— and Martyn, G. (2000), 'Policing, Collective Action and Social Movement Theory: The Case of the Northern Ireland Civil Rights Campaign', *British Journal of Sociology*, 51, 681–99.

—— and Smyth, J. (2000), *The Crowned Harp: Policing Northern Ireland* (London: Pluto).

Ellman, M. (1993), *The Hunger Artists: Starving, Writing and Imprisonment* (London: Virago).

Elwood, W. (ed.), (1995), *Public Relations Inquiry as Rhetorical Criticism: Case Studies of Corporate Discourse and Social Influence* (Westport, Conn.: Praeger).

England and Wales Prison Service (1986), *HM Prison Service, Study of Prison Officers' Complementing and Shift Systems. Joint Study by Prison Department and PA Management Consultants* Vol. *i*. *Report* (London: HM Prison Service).

—— (1995), *Prison Service Annual Report* (London: HM Prison Service).

English, R., and Walker, G. (eds.), (1996) *Unionism in Modern Ireland: New Perspectives on Politics and Culture* (Dublin: Gill & Macmillan).

Epstein, J. (ed.), (1970), *The Great Conspiracy Trial* (New York: Random House).

Erickson, E. (1969), *Gandhi's Truth: On the Origins of Militant Non-violence* (New York: Norton).

FAIT (Families Against Intimidation and Terror) (1998), *The FAIT Submission to the NI Victims' Commission: 'Giving Victims a Fair Deal'* (Belfast: FAIT).

Fanon, F. (1959), *Studies in Dying Colonialism* (London: Earthscan; reprinted 1989).

Farrell, M. (1976), *The Orange State* (London: Pluto).

—— (1985), *Sheltering the Fugitive: The Extradition of Irish Political Offenders* (Cork: Mercier Press).

Faul, D. (1975), *The Shame of Merlyn Rees: 4th Year of Internment in Ireland, Long Kesh, 1974–1975* (Dungannon: Author).

—— and Murray, R. (1973), *Whitelaw's Tribunals: Long Kesh Internment Camp, November 1972, January 1973* (Dungannon: St Patrick's Academy).

Faulkner, B. (1978), *Memoirs of a Statesman* (London: Weidenfeld & Nicolson).

Fay, M. T., Morrissey M., and Smyth, M. (1999), *Northern Ireland's Troubles: The Human Costs* (London: Pluto Press).

Feehan, J. (1983), *Bobby Sands and the Tragedy of Northern Ireland* (Cork: Mercier Press).

Feeley, M., and Hanson, R. (1990), 'The Impact of Judicial Intervention on Prisons and Jails: A Framework for Analysis and a Review of the Literature', in J. DiIulio (ed.), *Courts, Corrections, and the Constitution* (Oxford: Oxford University Press).

—— and Simon, J. (1992), 'The New Penology: Notes on the Emerging Strategy of Corrections and its Implications', *Criminology*, 30: 4, 449–74.

—— and Rubin, E. (1998), *Judicial Policy Making and the Modern State: How the Courts Reformed America's Prisons* (Cambridge: Cambridge University Press).

Feldman, A. (1991), *Formations of Violence: The Narrative of the Body and Political Terror in Northern Ireland* (Chicago: University of Chicago Press).

Fentress, J., and Wickham, C. (1992), *Social Memory* (Oxford: Blackwell).

Fields, R. (1973), *A Society on the Run: A Psychology of Northern Ireland* (Harmondsworth: Penguin).

Ferrers Report (1992), 'The Report of the Interdepartmental Working Group's Review of the Provisions for the Transfer of Prisoners Between UK Jurisdictions', unpublished typescript copy available at House of Commons Library, Westminster.

Finlay, F. (1998), *Snakes and Ladders* (Dublin: New Island Books).

Fisk, R. (1983), *In Time of War: Ireland, Ulster and the Price of Neutrality, 1939–45* (London: Deutsch).

Fitzgerald, G. (1991), *All in a Life: An Autobiography* (Dublin: Gill & Macmillan).

Fitzgerald, M. (1977), *Prisoners in Revolt* (Harmondsworth: Penguin).

—— and Sim, J. (1982), *British Prisons* (2nd edn., Oxford: Blackwell Press).

Flanaghan, T. (1995), 'Adapting and Adjustment Among Long-Term Prisoners', in T. Flanaghan (ed.), *Long-Term Imprisonment: Policy Science and Correctional Practice* (London: Sage).

Fleck, D., and Boethe, M. (1995), *The Handbook of Humanitarian Law in Armed Conflicts* (New York: Oxford University Press).

Fleischer, M. (1989), *Warehousing Violence* (London: Sage).

Forgacs, D. (1988), *A Gramsci Reader: Selected Readings 1916–1935* (London: Lawrence & Wishart).

Foster, D., and Skinner D. (1990), 'Detention and Violence: Beyond Victimology', in N.C. Manganyi and A. du Toit (eds.), *Political Violence and the Struggle in South Africa* (London: Macmillan).

Foster, R. (1988), *Modern Ireland 1600–1972* (London: Penguin).

Foucault, M. (1978), *The History of Sexuality An Introduction,* Vol. i (London: Penguin).

Foucault, M. (1979), *Discipline & Punish: The Birth of the Prison* (London: Penguin).

—— (1980), 'The Question of Geography', in C. Gordon (ed.), *Power/Knowledge* (New York: Pantheon Books).

—— (1983), 'The Subject & Power', in H. Dreyfus and P. Rabinow (eds.), *Michel Foucault: Beyond Structuralism & Hermeneutics* (Chicago: University of Chicago Press).

—— (1986), 'Disciplinary Power and Subjection', in S. Lukes (ed.), *Power* (New York: New York University Press).

Frank, A. (1991), 'For a Sociology of the Body: An Analytical Review', in M. Featherstone, M. Hepworth and B. Turner (eds.) *The Body: Social Process and Cultural Theory* (London: Sage), 36–103.

Freeman, R. (1999), *Correctional Organization and Management: Public Policies, Challenges, Behavior and Structure* (Boston: Butterworth Heinemann).

French, J., and Raven, B. (1968), 'The Bases of Social Power', in D. Cartwright and A. Zander (eds.), *Group Dynamics: Research and Theory* (London: Tavistock).

Fuller, L. (1958), 'Positivism and Fidelity to Law—A Reply to Professor Hart', *Harvard Law Review*, 71, 630–72.

Gaffiken, F., and Morrissey, M. (1990), *Northern Ireland: The Thatcher Years* (London: Red Books).

Gardiner, Lord (1975), *The Report of a Committee to Consider in the Context of Civil Liberties and Human Rights, Measures to Deal with Terrorism in Northern Ireland*. Cmnd. 5847 (Belfast: HMSO).

Garland, D. (1990), *Punishment and Modern Society* (Oxford: Oxford University Press).

—— (1996), 'The Limits of the Sovereign State', *British Journal of Criminology*, 36, 445–71.

Gearing, M. (1979), 'The MMPI as a Primary Differentiator and Predictor of Behavior in Prison: A Methodological Critique and Review of the Recent Literature', *Psychological Bulletin*, 86, 929–63.

Gearty, C. (1991a), 'The Prisons and the Courts', in J. Muncie and R. Sparks (eds.), *Imprisonment: European Perspectives* (London: Harvester Wheatsheaf).

—— (1991b), *Terror* (London: Faber & Faber).

—— (1996) (ed.), *Terrorism* (Aldershot: Dartmouth).

Gelder, K., and Jacobs, J. (1998), *Uncanny Australia: Sacredness and Identity in a Post-Colonial Nation* (Melbourne: University of Melbourne Press).

Gibbs, J. (1981), 'Violence in Prisons: Its Extent, Nature and Consequences', in R. Roberg and V. Webb (eds.), *Critical Issues in Corrections* (New York: West Publishing Co.).

—— (1991), 'Environmental Congruence and Symptoms of Psychopathology: A Further Exploration of the Effects of Exposure to the Jail Environment', *Criminal Justice & Behavior*, 18, 351–74.

Giddens, A. (1984), *The Constitution of Society* (Cambridge: Polity Press).

—— (1990), *The Consequences of Modernity* (Cambridge: Polity Press).

—— (1991), *Modernity and Self-Identity: Self and Society in the Late Modern Age* (Cambridge: Polity Press).

Ginnell, L. (1894), *The Brehon Laws: A Legal Handbook* (London: T. F. Unwin).

Glad, B. (ed.), (1990) *Psychological Dimensions of War* (London: Sage).

Glassberg, D. (1996), 'Public History and the Study of Memory', *Public Historian*, 18, 7–23.

Goffman, E. (1961*a*), *Asylums: Essays on the Social Situation of Mental Patients and Other Inmates* (Garden City, NJ: Anchor).

—— (1961*b*) 'On the Characteristics of Total Institutions: Staff Inmate Relations', in D. Cressey (ed.), *The Prison: Studies in Institutional Organization and Change* (New York: Holt, Rinehart & Winston).

Gormally, B., McEvoy, K., and Wall, D. (1993), 'Criminal Justice in a Divided Society: Northern Ireland Prisons', in *Crime & Justice: A Review of Research*, 17, 51–135.

—— and —— (1995), *Release and Reintegration of Politically Motivated Prisoners in Northern Ireland: A Comparative Study of South Africa, Israel/Palestine, Italy, Spain, the Republic of Ireland and Northern Ireland* (Belfast: NIACRO).

Gramsci, A. (1971), *Selections from Prison Notebooks*, transl. Q. Hoare and G. Nowell Smith (London: Lawrence & Wishart).

Greenberg, D., and Stender, F. (1972), 'The Prison as a Lawless Agency', *Buffalo Law Review*, 799–821.

The Green Book (1987), *Constitution of Oglaigh na hEireann (Irish Republican Army) General Headquarters, General Army Orders (as revised 1987)* (Dublin: Publisher Unnamed).

Greenwood, C. (1989), 'Terrorism and Humanitarian Law: The Debate Over Additional Protocol 1', *Israel Yearbook on Human Rights*, 19, 187–207.

Greer, S. (1995), *Supergrasses: A Study in Anti-Terrorist Law Enforcement in Northern Ireland* (Oxford: Clarendon Press).

—— and White, A. (1990), 'A Return to Trial by Jury', in A. Jennings (ed.) *Justice Under Fire: The Abuse of Civil Liberties in Northern Ireland* (London: Pluto Press).

Guibentif, P. (1994), 'Approaching the Production of Law Through Habermas' Concept of Communicative Action', *Philosophy & Social Criticism*, 20: 4, 45–71.

Habermas, J. (1975), *Legitimation Crisis,* trans. T. McCarthy (Boston: Beacon Press).

—— (1981), *The Theory of Communicative Action, Vol. i. Reason and the Rationalization of Society*, trans. T. McCarthy (Boston: Beacon Press).

—— (1986), 'Law as Medium and Law as Institution', in G. Teubner (ed.), *Dilemmas in Law in the Welfare State* (New York: De Gruyter), 203–20.

—— (1992), *Faktizatat und Geltung*, trans. William Rehg (Frankfurt-on-Main: Suhrkamp).

Hadden, T., Boyle, K., and Campbell, C. (1990), 'Emergency Law in Northern Ireland: The Context', in A. Jennings (ed.), *Justice Under Fire: The Abuse of Civil Liberties in Northern Ireland* (London: Pluto).

Hadfield, B., and Weaver, E. (1994), 'Trends in Judicial Review in Northern Ireland', *Public Law,* 12, 12–16.

—— and —— (1995), 'Judicial Review in Perspective: An Investigation of Trends in the Use and Operation of the Judicial Review Procedure in Northern Ireland', *Northern Ireland Legal Quarterly* (Summer), 46: 2, 113–45.

Hagan, F. (1997), *Political Crime: Ideology and Criminality* (Needham Heights, Mass.: Allyn & Bacon).

Hain, P. (1984), *Political Trials in Britain: From the Past to the Present Day* (Harmondsworth: Penguin).

Haines, K. (1996), 'The End of Civilization: The Sociological Context of Criminal Justice Managerialism', Paper presented at the Institute of Criminology and Criminal Justice, Oct. 1996.

Hamill, D. (1985), *Pig in the Middle: The Army in Northern Ireland 1969–1984* (London: Methuen).

Hammersley, M., and Atkinson, P. (1995), *Ethnography: Principles in Practice* (2nd edn., London: Routledge).

Hampden-Turner, C. (1990), *Corporate Culture for Competitive Edge* (London: Piatkus).

Handler, J. (1978), *Social Movements and the Legal System: A Theory of Law Reform and Social Change* (New York: Academic Press).

Harer, M., and Steffenmeier, D. (1996), 'Race & Prison Violence', *Criminology,* 34: 3, 323–55.

Harnden, T. (1999), *Bandit Country: The IRA & South Armagh* (London: Hodder & Stoughton).

Harrington, C. (1994), 'Outlining a Theory of Legal Practice', in M. Cain and C. Harrington (eds.), *Lawyers in a Postmodern World: Translation and Transgression* (Buckingham: Open University Press).

Hart, H. (1983), 'Positivism and the Separation of Law and Morals', reprinted in H. Hart, *Essays in Jurisprudence and Philosophy* (Oxford: Clarendon Press), 49–87.

Hart, P. (1998), *The IRA and its Enemies: Violence and Community in Cork 1916–23* (Oxford: Clarendon Press).

Harvey, C. (1999), 'The Politics of Legality', *Northern Ireland Legal Quarterly,* 50: 4, 528–67.

—— and Livingstone, S. (1999), 'Human Rights and the Northern Ireland Peace Process', *European Human Rights Law Review,* 2, 164–77.

Hatch, M.J., and Schultz, M. (1997), 'Relations between Organizational Culture, Identity and Image', *European Journal of Marketing,* 31: 5–6, 356–65.

Hay, W., and Sparks, R. (1992), 'Vulnerable Prisoners: Risk in Long Term Prisons', in A. K. Bottomley, A. J. Fowles, and R. Reiner (eds.) *Criminal Justice: Theory & Practice* (London: British Society of Criminology).

Hayden, D. (1999), 'Landscapes of Loss and Remembrance: The Case of Little Tokyo in Los Angeles', in J. Winter and E. Sivan (eds.), *War & Remembrance in the Twentieth Century* (Cambridge: Cambridge University Press).

Healy, J. (1981), 'Notes towards a Study of the Irish Hunger Strikes', *Milltown Studies*, 8 (Autumn), 43–57.

—— (1982), 'The Civil War Hunger Strikes—October 1923', *Studies 71*, 283 (Autumn), 213–26.

—— (1984), 'Hungerstrikes Around the World', *Social Studies*, 8: 1, 81–108.

Heath, E. (1998), *The Course Of My Life: My Autobiography* (London: Hodder & Stoughton).

Heather, N. (1977), 'Personal Illness in Lifers and the Effects of Long Term Indeterminate Sentences', *British Journal of Criminology*, 17, 378–86.

Hecht, D., and Simone, M. (1994), *Invisible Governance* (New York: Autonomedia).

Hennessey, J. (1984), *A Report of an Inquiry by HM Chief Inspector of Prisons into the Security Arrangement at HMP Maze*, Cmnd. 203 (London: HMSO).

Hepburn, J. (1985), 'The Exercise of Power in Coercive Organizations: A Study of Prison Guards', *Criminology*, 23: 1, 145–64.

—— and Stratton, J. (1977), 'Total Institutions and Inmate Self Esteem', *British Journal of Criminology*, 17, 237–50.

Heskin, K. (1984), 'The Psychology of Terrorism in Northern Ireland', in Y. Alexander and A. O'Day (eds.), *Terrorism in Ireland* (Beckenham: Croom Helm).

—— (1994), 'Terrorism in Ireland: The Past and the Future', *Irish Journal of Psychology*, 15: 2 and 3, 469–79.

Hewitt, V. (1990), 'The Public Sector', in R. Harris, C. Jefferson, and J. Spencer (eds.), *The Northern Ireland Economy: A Comparative Study in the Economic Development of a Peripheral Region* (London: Longman).

Hickey, T. (1996), 'National Prison Project', in M. McShane, and F. Williams III (eds.), *Encyclopaedia of American Prisons* (New York: Garland), 329–30.

Hillyard, P. (1978), 'Police and Penal Services', in J. Darby and A. Williamson (eds.), *Violence and the Social Services in Northern Ireland* (London: Heinemann).

—— (1987), 'The Normalisation of Special Powers', in P. Scraton (ed.), *Law, Order and the Authoritarian State* (Milton Keynes: Open University Press).

Hiltermann, J. (1990), 'Review of the Report on the Visit to the Internment Installation at Dhahriya', *Journal of Palestinian Studies*, 18: 4, 122–34.

Hobsbawm, E. (1969), *Bandits* (London: Weidenfeld & Nicolson).

Hogan, G., and Walker, C. (1989), *Political Violence and the Law in Ireland* (Manchester: Manchester University Press).

Holland, J. (1989), *The American Connection: U.S. Guns, Money, and Influence in Northern Ireland* (Dublin: Poolbeg).

Holland, J. and McDonald, H. (1994), *The INLA, Deadly Divisions: The Story of One of Ireland's Most Ruthless Terrorist Organisations* (Dublin: Torc).

—— and Phoenix, S. (1996), *Phoenix: Policing the Shadows* (London: Hodder & Stoughton).

Holton, S. (ed.), (1996), *Suffrage Days: Stories from the Women's Suffrage Movement* (London: Routledge).

Home Office (1966), *Report of an Inquiry into Prison Escapes and Security* (Mountbatten Report), Cmnd. 3175 (London: HMSO).

—— (1979), *Report of the Committee of Inquiry into the United Kingdom Prison Service* (May Report), Cmnd. 7573 (London: HMSO).

—— (1987), *Special Units for Long Term Prisoners: Regimes, Management and Research. A Report Written by the Research and Advisory Group on Long Term Imprisonment* Cm (London: HMSO).

—— (1988), *Private Sector Involvement in the Remand System* Cm (London: HMSO).

Hood, C. (1991), 'A Public Management for All Seasons?', *Public Administration*, 69: 1, 3–19.

Hooks, B. (1991), 'Homeplace: A Site of Resistance', in B. Hooks (ed.), *Yearning: Race, Gender & Cultural Politics* (Boston: South End Press).

Hopkins-Burke, R. (ed.), (1998) *Zero Tolerance Policing* (Leicester: Perpetuity Press).

Hopkinson, M. (1988), *Green against Green: The Irish Civil War* (Dublin: Gill & Macmillan).

Houston, J. (1995), *Correctional Management: Functions, Skills and Systems* (Chicago: Nelson Hall).

Howe, A. (1994), *Punish and Critique: Towards a Feminist Analysis of Penality* (London: Routledge).

Hughes, G. (1996), 'The Politics of Criminological Research', in R. Sapsford (ed.), *Researching Crime and Criminal Justice* (Milton Keynes: Open University Press).

Hunt, A. (1993), *Explorations in Law and Society: Towards a Constitutive Theory of Law* (London: Routledge).

Hunt, G., Riegel, S., Morales, T., and Waldorf, D. (1993), 'Changes in Prison Culture—Prison Gangs and the Case of the Pepsi Generation', *Social Problems,* 40: 3, 398–409.

Huntington, S. (1991), *The Third Wave: Democratization in the Late Twentieth Century* (Norman, Okla.: University of Oklahoma Press).

Ibarra, P., and Kitsuse, J. (1993), 'Vernacular Constituents of Moral Discourse', in J. Holstein and G. Miller (eds.), *Reconsidering Social Constructionism* (New York: Aldine de Gruyter).

Ignatieff, M. (1993), *Blood & Belonging: Journeys into New Nationalism* (London: BBC Books).

Innes, M. (1999), 'An Iron Fist in an Iron Glove? The Zero Tolerance Policing Debate', *Howard Journal*, 38: 4, 397–410.

IRA Army Council (1994), Statement issued by the IRA Army Council 31 August 1994 declaring a Complete Cessation of Military Operations (Dublin: Irish Republican Publicity Bureau).

Iris (1991), 'The H Block Hunger Strike', No 16. (May) (Belfast: Sinn Fein).

Irvin, C. (1999), *Militant Nationalism: Between Movement and Party in Ireland and the Basque Country* (Minnesota: University of Minnesota Press).

Irwin, J. (1980), *Prisons in Turmoil* (Boston: Little Brown).

Jackson, B. (1988), *Law, Fact, and Narrative Coherence*. (Roby Merseyside: Deborah Charles Publications).

Jackson, G. (1970), *Soledad Brother: The Prison Letters of George Jackson* (Harmondsworth: Penguin).

Jackson, J., and Doran, S. (1992), 'Diplock & the Presumption Against Jury Trial: A Critique', *Criminal Law Review*, 755–66.

—— and —— (1995), *Judge Without Jury: Diplock Trials in the Adversary System* (Oxford: Clarendon Press).

Jacobs, J. (1976), 'Stratification and Conflict Amongst Prison Inmates', *Journal of Criminal Law and Criminology*, 66, 476–82.

—— (1977), *Stateville: The Penitentiary in Mass Society* (Chicago: University of Chicago Press).

—— (1983a), *New Perspectives on Prisons and Imprisonment* (London: Cornell University Press).

—— (1983b), 'The Prisoners' Rights Movement and its Impact', in J. Jacobs, *New Perspectives on Prisons and Imprisonment* (London: Cornell University Press), 33–61.

—— (1983c), 'Race Relations and Prisoner Subculture', in J. Jacobs, *New Perspectives on Prisons and Imprisonment* (London: Cornell University Press), 61–80.

—— and Kraft, L. (1978), 'Integrating the Keepers: A Comparison of Black & White Prison Guards in Illinois', *Social Problems*, 25: 3, 304–19.

Jenkins, R. (1984), 'Bringing it all Back Home: An Anthropologist in Belfast', in C. Bell and H. Roberts (eds.), *Social Researching: Politics, Problems, Practice* (London: Routledge & Kegan Paul).

Jensen, G., and Jones, D. (1976), 'Perspectives in Inmate Culture: A Study of Women in Prison', *Social Forces*, 54, 590–603.

Johnson, R. (1987), *Hard Time: Understanding and Reforming the Prison* (Belmont, Calif.: Brooks Cole).

—— (1996), *Hard Time: Understanding and Reforming the Prison* (2nd edn., Belmont, Calif.: Wadsworth).

—— and Toch, H. (eds.), (1982) *The Pains of Imprisonment* (Beverly Hills, Calif.: Sage).

Jowett, G., and O'Donnell, V. (1992), *Propaganda and Persuasion* (2nd edn., Beverly Hills, Calif.: Sage).

Jupp, V. (1989), *Methods of Criminological Research* (London: Allen & Unwin).

Jurik, N. (1985), 'Individual and Organizational Determinants of Correctional Officer Attitudes toward Inmates', *Criminology*, 23: 3, 523–39.

Justice for Lifers (1987), *Justice for Lifers* (Belfast: Justice for Lifers Group).

Kauffman, K. (1988), *Prison Officers and their World* (Cambridge MA: Harvard University Press).

Keane, J. (1996), *Reflections on Violence* (London: Verso).

Kee, R. (1976), *The Most Distressful Country: The Bold Fenian Men, Vol.* i. *The Green Flag* (London: Quartet Books).

Keightley, R. (1993), 'Political Offences and Indemnity in South Africa', *South African Journal of Human Rights*, 9: 3, 334–57.

Keith, M., and Pile, S. (eds.), (1993) *Place and the Politics of Identity* (London: Routledge).

Kelly, H. (1972), *How Stormont Fell* (Dublin: Gill & Macmillan).

Kelly, J. (1992), 'The Empire Strikes Back: The Taking of Joe Doherty', *Fordham Law Review*, 61: 2, 317–19.

Kelly, K. (1982), *The Longest War: Northern Ireland and the IRA* (Kerry: Brandon Books).

Kickert, W. (1997), 'Public Governance in the Netherlands: An Alternative to Anglo-American Managerialism', *Public Administration*, 75, 731–52.

King, R. (1987), 'New Generation Prisons: The Prison Building Programme and the Future of the Dispersal System', in A. Bottoms and R. Light (eds.), *Problems of Long Term Imprisonment* (Aldershot: Gower).

—— and Elliot, K. (1977), *Albany: Birth of a Prison—End of An Era* (London: Routledge & Kegan Paul).

—— and Morgan, R. (1980), *The Future of the Prison System* (Farnborough: Gower).

—— and McDermott, K. (1990), 'My Geranium is Subversive: Notes on the Management of Trouble in Prisons', *British Journal of Sociology*, 41: 4, 445–71.

—— and —— (1991), 'A Fresh Start: Managing the Prison Service', in R. Reiner and M. Cross (eds.), *Beyond Law & Order: Criminal Justice Policy & Politics into the 1990s* (London: Macmillan).

—— and —— (1995), *The State of Our Prisons* (Oxford: Clarendon Press).

Kinsell, L., and Shelden, R. (1981), 'A Survey of Correctional Officers at a Medium Security Prison', *Corrections Today*, 43: 1, 40–51.

Kirchheimer, O. (1961), *Political Justice: The Use of Legal Procedure for Political Ends* (Princeton: Princeton University Press).

Kitschelt, H. (1986), 'Political Opportunity Structures and Political Protest: Anti-Nuclear Movements in Four Countries', *British Journal of Political Science*, 16, 57–85.

Kitson, F. (1991), *Directing Operations* (London: Faber & Faber).

Klofas, J., and Toch, H. (1982), 'The Guard-Subculture Myth', *Journal of Research in Crime and Delinquency*, 19: 2, 238–54.

Kotsonournis, M. (1994), *Retreat from Revolution: The Dail Courts 1920–1924* (Dublin: Irish Academic Press).

Lane, A. (1979), *Nuremberg: A Nation on Trial* (London: Penguin).

Lawyers Committee for Human Rights (1993), *Human Rights and Legal Defence in Northern Ireland* (New York: Lawyers Committee for Human Rights).

—— (1996), *At the Crossroads: Human Rights and the Northern Ireland Peace Process* (New York: Lawyers Committee for Human Rights).

Lazarus, R., and Folkman, S. (1983), *Stress, Appraisal and Coping* (New York: Springer).

Learmont, J. (1995), *Review of the Prison Service Security in England and Wales and the Escape from Parkhurst Prison on Tuesday 3rd January 1995* Cmnd. 3020 (London: HMSO).

Lee, J. (1989), *Ireland 1912–1985: Politics and Society* (Cambridge: Cambridge University Press).

Lee, R. (1993), *Doing Research on Sensitive Topics* (London: Sage).

—— (1995), *Dangerous Fieldwork* (London: Sage).

Lenin, V. (1962), 'Partisan Warfare', in F. Osanka (ed.), *Modern Guerrilla Warfare* (Glencoe, Ill.: Free Press).

Leonard, M. (1993), 'Informal Work and Employment in Belfast: Researching a Sensitive Topic in a Politically Sensitive Locality', Paper presented at the Annual Conference of the British Sociological Association, University of Essex.

Lewis, D. (1997), *Hidden Agendas: Politics, Law and Disorder* (London: Hamish Hamilton).

Liebling, A. (2000), 'Prison Officers, Policing and the Use of Discretion', *Theoretical Criminology*, 4: 3, 333–57.

—— and Bosworth, M. (1995), 'Incentives in Prison Regimes', *Prison Service Journal*, 98, 57–64.

Light, S. (1985), 'Assaults on Prison Officers: Interaction Themes', in M. Craswell, R. Montgomery Jr, and L. Lombardo (eds.), *Prison Violence in America* (2nd edn., Cincinnati: Anderson Publishing).

—— (1991), 'Assaults on Prison Officers: Interactional Themes', *Justice Quarterly*, 8, 243–61.

Lindquist, C., and Whitehead, J. (1986), 'Burnout, Job Stress, and Job Satisfaction Amongst Southern Correctional Officers: Perceptions and Causal Factors', *Journal of Criminal Science*, 10: 4, 5–26.

Livingston, J. (1997), *Pragmatism and the Political Economy of Cultural Revolution* (Chapel Hill, NC: University of North Carolina Press).

Livingstone, S. (1994), 'The House of Lords and the Northern Ireland Conflict', *Modern Law Review*, 57: 3, 333–60.

—— (1995a), 'The Impact of Judicial Review on Prisons', in B. Hadfield (ed.), *Judicial Review: A Thematic Approach* (Dublin: Gill & Macmillan).

Livingstone, S. (1995*b*), 'Reviewing Northern Ireland in Strasbourg 1969–1994', in G. Quinn (ed.), *Irish Human Rights Handbook* (Dublin: Sweet & Maxwell).

—— (1995*c*), 'Legal Options Regarding Early Release', copy on file at NIACRO Information Bank, Belfast.

—— and Owen, T. (1999), *Prison Law: Texts and Materials* (2nd edn., Oxford: Oxford University Press).

Loftus, B. (1980), 'Images for Sale: Government and Security Force Advertising in Northern Ireland 1968–1978', *Oxford Art Journal*, 3: 2, 70–81.

Lombardo, L. (1989), *Guards Imprisoned: Correctional Officers at Work* (2nd edn., New York: Anderson).

Lombroso, C. (1968), *Crime: Its Causes and Remedies* (Montclair, NJ: Patterson Smith).

Longford, Earl of, and O'Neill, T. (1974), *Eamon De Valera* (London: Arrow).

Lopez, L. (1994), 'Uncivil Wars—The Challenge Of Applying International Humanitarian Law to Internal Armed-Conflicts', *New York University Law Review*, 69: 4–5, 916–62

Loucks, N. (1995), *Anything Goes: The Use of the 'Catch-all' Disciplinary Rule in Prison Service Establishments* (London: Prison Reform Trust).

Loughlin, J. (1992), 'Administering Policy in Northern Ireland', in B. Hadfield (ed.), *Northern Ireland: Politics and the Constitution* (Buckingham: Open University Press).

Loughlin, M. (1993), 'The Underside of the Law: Judicial Review and the Prison Disciplinary System', *Current Legal Problems*, 46: 2, 23–51.

Lowenthal, D. (1996), *Possessed by the Past: The Heritage Crusade and the Spoils of History* (New York: The Free Press).

Lynch, S. (1997), 'Jail Struggle: A Universal Struggle', *An Glor Gafa*, 8: 2, 15–18.

Lyons, F. (1983), *Ireland Since the Famine* (2nd edn., London: Fontana).

Lyons, H., and Harbinson, H. (1986), 'A Comparison of Political and Non-Political Murders in Northern Ireland, 1974–1984', *Medical Science Law*, 26: 3, 193–8.

McAuley, J. (1994), *The Politics of Identity: A Loyalist Community in Belfast* (Aldershot: Avebury).

—— (1995), 'Not a Game of Cowboys and Indians: The Ulster Defence Association in the 1990s', in A. O'Day (ed.), *Terrorism's Laboratory* (Aldershot: Dartmouth).

McBarnet, D. (1984), 'Law & Capital: The Role of Legal Form and Legal Actors', *International Journal of the Sociology of Law*, 12: 3, 231–8.

—— (1994), 'Legal Creativity: Law, Capital and Legal Avoidance', in M. Cain and C. Harrington (eds.), *Lawyers in a Postmodern World: Translation and Transgression* (Buckingham: Open University Press).

McBride, A. (1995), 'A Victim's Perspective', in *Perspectives on the Release of Politically Motivated Prisoners in Northern Ireland: A Conference Report* (Belfast: Protestant and Catholics Encounter.

McCafferty, N. (1981), *The Armagh Women* (Dublin: Co-op Books).

McCann, E. (1974), *War and an Irish Town* (Harmondsworth: Penguin).

—— Shiels, M., and Hannigan, B. (1992), *Bloody Sunday in Derry: What Really Happened* (Dingle: Brandon).

McCorckle, R., Miethe, T., and Drass, K. (1995), 'The Roots of Prison Violence: A Test of the Deprivation, Management and "Not so Total" Institutional Model', *Crime & Delinquency*, 41, 317–31.

McCorkle, L., and Korn, R. (1954), 'Resocialization Within Walls', *The Anals*, 293 (May) 88.

McDaniel, D. (1997), *Enniskillen: The Remembrance Sunday Bombing* (Dublin: Wolfhound Press).

McDermott, K., and King, R. (1988), 'Mind Games: Where the Action is in Prisons', *British Journal of Criminology*, 28: 3, 357–77.

McElrath, K. (1997), 'If You've Come a' Seeking Justice, No Irish Need Apply: Irish Republicans, Political Asylum and United States Foreign Policy', *Critical Criminology: An International Journal*, 8: 1, 93–109.

—— (2000), *Unsafe Haven: The United States, the IRA and Political Prisoners* (London: Pluto).

MacEoin, U. (1980), *Survivors* (Dublin: Argenta Publications).

McEvoy, K. (1999), 'The Agreement, Prisoner Release and the Political Character of the Conflict', *Fordham International Law Journal*, 26: 1, 145–81.

—— (2000), 'Law, Struggle and Political Transformation in Northern Ireland', *Journal of Law and Society*, 27: 4, 542–71.

—— and Gormally, B. (1997), 'Seeing is Believing: Positivist Terrorology, Peacemaking Criminology, and the Northern Ireland Peace Process', *Critical Criminology: An International Journal*, 8: 1, 9–31.

—— and White, C. (1998), 'Security Vetting in Northern Ireland: Loyalty Redress and Citizenship', *Modern Law Review*, 61: 3, 341–61.

—— O'Mahony, D., Horner C., and Lyner, O. (1999), 'The Home Front: The Families of Politically Motivated Prisoners in Northern Ireland', *British Journal of Criminology*, 39: 2, 175–97.

McGarry, J., and O'Leary, B. (eds.), (1990) *The Future of Northern Ireland* (Oxford: Clarendon Press).

—— and —— (eds.), (1993) *The Politics of Ethnic Conflict Regulation: Case Studies of Protracted Ethnic Conflicts.* (London: Routledge).

—— and —— (1995), *Explaining Northern Ireland Broken Images* (Oxford: Blackwell).

—— and —— (1999), *Policing Northern Ireland Proposals for a New Start* (Belfast: Blackstaff).

McGeorge, N. (1990), *A Fair Deal for Lifers* (Belfast: Northern Ireland Committee of Quaker, Peace & Service and Quaker Council for European Affairs).

McGuffin, J. (1973), *Internment* (Tralee: Anvil Books).

MacIntyre, A. (1995), 'Modern Irish Republicanism: The Product of British State Strategies', *Irish Political Studies*, 10, 97–122.

Mackenzie, D., and Golstein, L. (1985), 'Long-term Incarceration Impacts and Characteristics of Long-term Offenders: An Empirical Analysis', *Criminal Justice and Behavior*, 12, 395–414.

McKeown, L. (1998), *Unrepentant Fenian Bastards: The Social Construction of an Irish Republican Prisoner Community* (Belfast: Queen's University Belfast) (forthcoming in book form, published by Beyond the Pale).

McKittrick, D., Kelters, S., Feeney, B., and Thorton, C. (1999), *Lost Lives: The Stories of the Men, Women and Children who died as a Result of the Northern Ireland Troubles* (London: Mainstream Publishing).

McLaughlin, E., and Muncie, J. (1994), 'Managing the Criminal Justice System', in J. Clarke, A. Cochrane, and E. McLaughlin (eds.), *Managing Social Policy* (London: Sage).

MacManus, M. (1933), *Eamon De Valera* (Dublin: Talbot Press).

McNay, L. (1992), *Foucault & Feminism: Power, Gender and the Self* (Cambridge: Polity Press).

—— (1994), *Foucault: A Critical Introduction* (New York: Continuum).

McPhilemy, S. (1998), *The Committee: Political Assassination in Northern Ireland* (Niwot, Colo.: Roberts Rinehart Publishers).

McShane, L. (1998), *Politically Motivated Ex-Prisoners' Self Help Projects: Interim Report* (Belfast: Northern Ireland Voluntary Trust).

MacStiofain, S. (1975), *Revolutionary in Ireland* (Edinburgh: Gordon Cremonesi).

MacUileagoid, M. (1996), *From Fetters to Freedom: The Inside Story of Irish Jailbreaks* (Belfast: SASTA).

McVeigh, R. (1995), *The Racialisation of Irishness* (Belfast: Centre for Research and Documentation).

Mageean, P., and O'Brien, M. (1999), 'From the Margins to the Mainstream: Human Rights and the Good Friday Peace Agreement', *Fordham International Law Journal*, 22: 4, 1499–539.

Maguire, M. (1991), 'The Needs and Rights of Victims', *Crime & Justice: A Review of Research*, 14, 363–433.

Maguire, P. (1995), 'Judicial Review and Local Government', in B. Hadfield (ed.), *Judicial Review: A Thematic Approach* (Dublin: Gill & Macmillan).

Mair, G. (1997), 'Community Penalties and the Probation Service', in M. Maguire, R. Morgan, and R. Reiner (eds.), *The Oxford Handbook of Criminology* (2nd edn., Oxford: Clarendon Press).

Mallie, E., and McKittrick, D. (1996), *The Fight for Peace: The Secret Story Behind the Irish Peace Process* (London: Heinemann).

Mandela, N. (1994), *Long Walk to Freedom: The Autobiography of Nelson Mandela* (London: Abacus).

Martin, J. (1982), 'The Conflict in Northern Ireland: Marxist Interpretations', *Capitial & Class*, 18, 45–71.

Martin, S., and Eckland-Olson, S. (1987), *Texas Prisons: The Walls Came Tumbling Down* (Austin, Tex.: Texas Monthly Press).

Mathiesen, T. (1965), *Defences of the Weak* (London: Tavistock).

—— (1974), *The Politics of Abolition* (London: Martin Robertson).

—— (1980), *Law, Society and Political Action: Towards a Strategy Under Late Capitalism* (London: Academic Press).

—— (1990), *Prison On Trial: A Critical Assessment* (London: Sage).

—— (1997), 'The Viewer Society: Michel Foucault's Panopticon Revisited', *Theoretical Criminology*, 1: 2, 215–35.

Matthews, R. (1999), *Doing Time: An Introduction to the Sociology of Imprisonment* (Basingstoke: Macmillan).

Mazmanian, D., and Sabatier, P. (1983), *Implementation and Public Policy* (Chicago: Scott Foresman & Co.).

Mbeki, G. (1991), *Learning from Robben Island: The Prison Writings of Govan Mbeki* (Cape Town: David Philip).

Melucci, A.. (1996), *Challenging Codes: Collective Action in the Information Age* (Cambridge: Cambridge University Press).

Melville, S. (1972), *Letters From Attica* (New York: William Morrow & Co.).

Melvin, K., Gramling, L., and Gardner, W. (1985), 'A Scale to Measure Attitudes Towards Prisoners', *Criminal Justice and Behavior*, 12: 2, 241–53.

Merlo, A., and Benekos, P. (1997), 'Three Strikes and You're Out: The Political Sentencing Game', in J. Marquart and J. Sorensen (eds.), *Correctional Contexts: Contemporary & Classical Readings* (Los Angeles: Roxbury).

Metress, S. (1983), *The Hunger Strike and the Final Struggle* (Toledo, Oh.: Centre for Irish American Studies).

Mika, H., and Thomas, J. (1988), 'The Dialectics of Prisoner Litigation: Reformist Idealism or Social Praxis?', *Social Justice*, 15, 48–71.

Miller, D. (1994), *Northern Ireland: Propaganda and the Media* (London: Pluto).

—— (1996), 'The Northern Ireland Information Service and the Media', in D. Miller and B. Rolston (eds.), *War & Words: The Northern Ireland Media Reader* (Belfast: Beyond the Pale Publications).

—— (ed.), (1998), *Rethinking Northern Ireland: Culture, Ideology and Colonialism* (London: Longman).

Milovanovic, D. (1981), 'The Commodity-Exchange Theory of Law: In Search of a Perspective', *Crime and Social Justice*, 16 (Winter), 41–9.

—— (1988), 'Jailhouse Lawyers and Jailhouse Lawyering', *International Journal of Sociology of Law*, 16, 455–75.

—— and Thomas, J. (1989), 'Overcoming the Absurd: Prisoner Litigation as Primitive Rebellion', *Social Problems*, 36: 1, 48–61.

Mitchel, J. (1918), *Jail Journal* (Dublin: M. H. Gill & Son).

Moloney, E., and Pollak, A. (1986), *Paisley* (Swords: Poolbeg Press).

Monahan, J. (1981), *Predicting Violent Behaviour: An Assessment of Clinical Techniques* (London: Sage).

Morgan, A. (1988), *James Connolly: A Political Biography* (Manchester: Manchester University Press).

—— (2000), *The Belfast Agreement: A Practical Legal Analysis* (London: The Belfast Press Limited).

Morgan, R. (1997), 'Imprisonment: Current Concerns and a Brief History since 1945', in M. Maguire, R. Morgan and R. Reiner (eds.), *The Oxford Handbook of Criminology* (Oxford: Oxford University Press).

Morison, J. (1990), 'How to Change Things with Rules', in J. Morison and S. Livingstone (eds.), *Law, Society & Change* (Aldershot: Dartmouth).

—— (1998), 'The Public Sector in a Divided Society', in *People and Government Questions for Northern Ireland* (Belfast: Joseph Rowntree Foundation), 109–26.

—— (1999), 'Constitutionalism and Change: Representation, Governance, and Participation in the New Northern Ireland', *Fordham International Law Journal*, 22: 4, 1608–28.

—— and Leith, P. (1992), *The Barrister's World and the Nature of Law* (Milton Keynes: Open University Press).

—— and Livingstone, S. (1995), *Reshaping Public Power: Northern Ireland and the British Constitutional Crisis* (London: Sweet & Maxwell).

Morris N. (1994), 'Dangerousness & Incapacitation', in A. Duff and D. Garland (eds.), *A Reader in Punishment* (Oxford: Oxford University Press).

Morris, T., and Morris, P. (1963), *Pentonville: A Sociological Study of an English Prison* (London: Routledge).

Morrison, D. (1999), *Then The Walls Came Down: A Prison Journal* (Cork: Mercier Press).

Moss, D. (1989), *The Politics of Left-Wing Violence in Italy, 1969–85* (London: Macmillan).

Mulcahy, A. (1995), 'Claims-making and the Construction of Legitimacy: Press Coverage of the 1981 Northern Irish Hunger Strike', *Social Problems*, 42: 4, 449–67.

—— (1997), 'I'm Not Here to Look Back: I'm Here to Look Forward: The Role of Memory in Debates on the Legitimacy of the RUC', Paper presented at the British Criminology Conference, Queen's University of Belfast, 15–18 July 1997.

—— (1999), 'Visions of Normality: Peace and the Reconstruction of Policing in Northern Ireland', *Social & Legal Studies*, 8: 2, 277–95.

Mullan, D., and Scally, J. (1997), *Bloody Sunday: Massacre in Northern Ireland, the Eyewitness Accounts* (Niwot, Colo.: Roberts Rinehart).

Mullan, M. (1995), 'Pardon and Amnesty in Ireland to 1937', Unpublished Report (Belfast: NIACRO).

Munger, F. (1988), 'Law, Change & Litigation: A Critical Examination of An Empirical Research Tradition', *Law and Society Review*, 22: 1, 57–101.

Murphy, J. A. (1975), *Ireland in the Twentieth Century* (Dublin: Gill & Macmillan).

Murray, G. (1998), *John Hume and the SDLP: Impact and Survival in Northern Ireland* (Dublin: Irish Academic Press).

Murray, Justice D. (1975), *Report Of The Honourable Mr. Justice Murray To The Department Of Finance For Northern Ireland On A Local Inquiry Held To Consider A Proposal By That Department To Acquire Compulsorily Under The Above Order Certain Land At Maghaberry County Antrim For The Purpose Of Providing Prison Accommodation And Facilities On That Land* Cmnd. (Belfast: HMSO).

Murray, R. (1990), *The SAS in Ireland* (Cork: Mercier Press).

—— (1998), *State Violence in Northern Ireland, 1969–1997* (Cork: Mercier).

Nagata, D. (1990), 'The Japanese–American Internment: Perceptions of Moral Community, Fairness and Redress', *Journal of Social Issues*, 46: 1, 133–46.

Narey, M. (1998), *Report of an Inquiry into the Escape of a Prisoner from HMP Maze on 10th December 1997 and the Shooting of a Prisoner on 27th December 1997* Cmnd. 658 (London: HMSO).

Neir, A. (1995), 'Confining Dissent: The Political Prison', in N. Morris and D. Rothman (eds.), *The Oxford History of the Prison: The Practice of Punishment in Western Society* (Oxford: Oxford University Press).

Nelson, S. (1984), *Ulster's Uncertain Defenders: Loyalists and the Northern Ireland Conflict* (Belfast: Appletree Press).

Newburn, T. (1995), *Crime & Criminal Justice Policy* (London: Longman).

NIACRO (1973), *Annual Report of the Northern Ireland Association for the Care and Resettlement of Offenders* (Belfast: NIACRO).

—— (1984), *Detained at the Secretary of State's Pleasure* (Belfast: NIACRO).

—— (1992), *Justice, Safety and Openness: NIACRO Response to the Prison Service Strategic Plan* (Belfast: NIACRO).

—— (1994), *The Transfer of Irish Prisoners From Britain* (Belfast: NIACRO).

—— (1995), *Conference Report of the International Conference on the Early Release and Reintegration of Politically Motivated Prisoners* (Belfast: NIACRO).

—— (1999), *Annual Report of the Northern Ireland Association for the Care and Resettlement of Offenders* (Belfast: NIACRO).

Ní Aoláin, F. (2000), *The Politics of Force: Conflict Management and State Violence in Northern Ireland* (Belfast: Blackstaff Press).

Nietzsche, F. (1968), *The Will to Power* (New York: Vintage Books).

NIHRC (1999), *Draft Strategic Plan of the Northern Ireland Human Rights Commission* (Belfast: Northern Ireland Human Rights Commission).

Niming, F. (1990), 'Petitioners, Popperians and Hunger Strikers: The Uncoordinated Efforts of the 1989 Chinese Democratic Movement', in T. Saich (ed.), *The Chinese People's Movement: Perspectives on Spring 1989* (Armonk, NY: M.E. Sharpe).

NIPS (1971–99), *Annual Report of the Northern Ireland Prison Service* Cm (Belfast: HMSO).

—— (1990), *The Code of Conduct of the Northern Ireland Prison Service* Cm (Belfast: HMSO).

—— (1991), *Serving the Community: The Northern Ireland Prison Service in the 1990s* Cm (Belfast: HMSO).

—— (1997), 'Further Changes in Prison Regimes', Northern Ireland Office Press Release, 12 Sept. 1997 (Belfast: Northern Ireland Prison Service).

NIVT (1998), *Annual Report of the Northern Ireland Voluntary Trust* (Belfast: NIVT).

Northern Ireland Affairs Committee (1998), *Prison Service in Northern Ireland: Report and Proceedings of the Committee* Cm (London: HMSO).

Northern Ireland Election Website (1998), Election Results in Northern Ireland Since 1973, http://explorers.whyte.com/allsum.htm.

Northern Ireland Information Service (1997*a*), *Speech by Tony Blair At The Royal Ulster Agricultural Show Belfast*, 16 May 1997 (Belfast: Northern Ireland Information Service).

—— (1997*b*) Aide-Memoire Setting Out British Government's Position on the Entry of Sinn Fein into Political Development Talks (Belfast: Northern Ireland Information Service).

Northern Ireland Office (1980*a*), *H Blocks: The Facts* (Oct.) (Belfast: Northern Ireland Office).

—— (1980*b*), *H Blocks: The Reality* (Nov.) (Belfast: Northern Ireland Office).

—— (1981*a*), *Day to Day Life in Northern Ireland Prisons* (Mar.) (Belfast: Northern Ireland Office).

—— (1981*b*), *H Blocks: What the Papers Say* (July) (Belfast: Northern Ireland Office).

—— (1985), *Life Sentenced Prisoners In Northern Ireland: An Explanatory Memorandum* (Belfast: Northern Ireland Office).

—— (1990), Unpublished Memorandum on the Interface Initiative for the Improvement of Visiting Arrangements in Northern Ireland (Belfast: Northern Ireland Office).

Obafemi, Olu (1990), *Committed Theatre and Nationalist Struggle in Colonial Nigeria: Hubert Ogunde's Strike and Hunger* (Ibadan: Bookman Educational and Communication Services).

O'Bradaigh, R. (1998), Presidential Address at Republican Sinn Fein Ard Fheis, Drogheda, Co. Louth Nov 7th–8th 1998, Republican Sinn Fein Home Page.

O'Connor, U. (1970), *Brendan Behan* (London: Black Swan).

O'Dochartaigh, N. (1997), *From Civil Rights to Armalites: Derry and the Birth of the Irish Troubles* (Cork: Cork University Press).

O'Doherty, M. (1998), *The Trouble with Guns: Republican Strategy and the Provisional IRA* (Belfast: Blackstaff).

O'Doherty, S. P. (1993), *The Volunteer: A Former IRA Man's True Story* (London: Fount).

O'Donnell, P. (1966), *The Gates Flew Open* (Cork: Mercier Press).

O'Donoghue, F. (1971), *Sworn to be Free: The Complete Book of IRA Jailbreaks 1918–1921* (Tralee: Anvil Books).

O'Dowd, L., Rolston, B., and Tomlinson, M. (1980), *Northern Ireland: Between the Civil Rights and Civil War* (London: CSE Books).

O'Faolain, S. (1939), *Constance Marckievicz* (London: Cape).

O'Gorman, K. (1993), 'The Morality of Hunger Striking to Death', *Irish Theological Quarterly*, 59: 1, 55–69.

O'Hara L. (1994), *Turning Up the Heat: MI5 After the Cold War* (London: Phoenix Press).

O'Leary, B. (1997), 'The Conservative Stewardship of Northern Ireland, 1979–1997: Sound-bottomed Contradictions or Slow Learning?' *Political Studies*, 45, 663–76.

O'Mahony, S. (1987), *Frongoch: University of Revolution* (Dublin: FDR Teoranta).

O'Malley, P. (1983), *The Uncivil Wars* (Belfast: Blackstaff Press).

—— (1990), *Biting at the Grave: The Irish Hunger Strikes and the Politics of Despair* (Belfast: Blackstaff Press).

O'Muilleoir, M. (1999), *Belfast's Dome of Delight: City Hall Politics 1981–2000* (Belfast: Beyond the Pale Publications).

O'Neill, T. (1972), *The Autobiography of Terence O'Neill* (London: Hart-Davis).

O'Rawe, M., and Moore, L. (1997), *Human Rights on Duty: Principles for Better Policing, International Lessons for Northern Ireland* (Belfast: CAJ).

Orbach, S. (1986), *Hunger Strike: The Anorectic's Struggle as a Metaphor for Our Age* (New York: W.W. Norton & Co.).

Ortner, S. (1995), 'Resistances and the Problem of Ethnographic Refusal', *Society & History*, 37: 1, 173–93.

Osborne, D., and Gaebler, T. (1992), *Reinventing Government: How the Entrepreneurial Spirit is Transforming the Public Sector* (Reading, Mass.: Addison Wesley).

Osiel, M. (1997), *Mass Atrocity, Collective Memory and the Law* (New Brunswick, NJ: Transaction Publishers).

Owen, B. (1988), *The Reproduction of Social Control: A Study of Prison Workers at San Quentin* (New York: Praeger).

Padfield, N. (1983), 'Parole and the Life Sentence Prisoner', *Howard Journal*, 32, 87–98.

Paige, R. (1997), 'From Self-Preservation to Organized Crime: The Evolution of Inmate Gangs', in J. Marquart and J. Sorensen (eds.), *Correctional Contexts: Contemporary and Classical Readings* (Los Angeles: Roxbury).

Paisley, I. (1986), *Why No True Ulster Protestant Would Swallow the Ecumenical Pill*, sound recording (Belfast: Martyrs Memorial Recordings, cassette), (available QUB Library Special Collection).

Paisley, R. (1988), *Ian Paisley, My Father* (Basingstoke: Marshall Pickering).

Parker, C. (1994), 'The Logic of Professionalism: Stages of Domination in Legal Service Delivered to the Disadvantaged', *International Journal of Sociology of Law*, 22, 145–68.

Parry, C., and Parry, W. (1995), *Tim: An Ordinary Boy* (London: Coronet).

Patterson, N. (1989), 'Brehon Law in Late Medieval Ireland: Antiquarian and Obsolete or Traditional and Functional', *Cambridge Medieval Celtic Studies*, 17, 43–63.

Petrasek, D. (2000), *Ends and Means: Human Rights Approaches to Armed Groups* (Geneva: International Council on Human Rights Policy).

Philips, W. A. (1923), *The Revolution in Ireland* (London: Longmans).

Philliber, S. (1987), 'Thy Brother's Keeper: A Review of the Literature on Correctional Officers', *Justice Quarterly*, 4: 1, 9–37.

Phoenix, E. (1994), *Northern Nationalism: Nationalism, Politics and the Catholic Minority in Northern Ireland 1890–1940* (Belfast: Ulster Historical Foundation).

Pickett, B. (1996), 'Foucault and the Politics of Resistance', *Polity*, 28: 4, 445–66.

Piggot, R. (1883), *Personal Recollections of an Irish Nationalist Journalist* (London: Hodges Figgis).

Pile, S. (1997), 'Introduction: Opposition, Political Identities and Spaces of Resistance', in S. Pile and M. Keith (eds.), *Geographies of Resistance* (London: Routledge).

Pollitt, C. (1993), *Managerialism and the Public Services: Cuts, or Cultural Change in the 1990s?* (2nd edn., 1st edn. published 1990, Oxford: Blackwell).

Pollock, J. (1997), 'The Social World of the Prisoner', in J. Pollock (ed.), *Prisons: Today & Tomorrow* (Gaithersburg, Md.: Aspen).

Poole, E., and Pogrebin, M. (1987), 'Judicial Intervention and Work Alienation: A Study of Jails Guards', *Howard Journal*, 26, 217–31.

Porporino, F., and Zamble, E. (1984), 'Coping with Imprisonment', *Canadian Journal of Criminology*, 26, 403–21.

Powell, J. (1998), Letter from Prime Minister's Chief of Staff to Ken Maginnis MP, 10 Apr. 1998. Copy obtained by the author.

Primoratz I. (1990), 'What is Terrorism?', *Journal of Applied Philosophy*, 7, 129–38.

Prior, J. (1986), *A Balance of Power* (London: Hamilton).

Prison Issues, (1998) Paper submitted by the British Government, Liaison Subcommittee on Confidence Building Measures Meeting, 4th Feb. 1998 (confidential source).

Proal, L. (1973), *Political Crime* (Monclair, NJ: Patterson Smith originally published 1898).

Prungh, G. (1955), 'Prisoners at War: The POW Background', *Dickinson Law Review*, 60, 125–40.

Purdey, B. (1990), *Politics in the Street: The Origins of the Civil Rights Movement in Northern Ireland* (Belfast: Blackstaff Press).

Quinney, R. (1970), *The Social Reality of Crime*, (Boston: Little Brown and Co.).

—— (1977), *Class, State & Crime* (New York: David McKay & Co.).

Radzinowicz, L., and Hood, R. (1979), 'The Status of Political Prisoner in England: The Struggle for Recognition', *Virginia Law Review*, 65, 1421–81.

Raine, J., and Wilson, M. (1997), 'Beyond Managerialism in Criminal Justice', *Howard Journal*, 36: 1, 80–95.

Ramsay, I. (1993), 'What do Lawyers Do? Reflections on the Market for Lawyers', *International Journal of the Sociology of Law*, 23, 355–99.

Ramsbotham, D. (1998), *Report of an Inspection by Her Majesty's Chief Inspector of Prisons of HMP Maze* (Belfast: Northern Ireland Office).

Rasch, W. (1977), 'The Development of the Mental and Physical State of Persons Sentenced to Life Imprisonment', in R. Rizkalla, R. Levy, and R. Zauberman (eds.), *Long Term Imprisonment: An International Seminar* (Montreal: Centre International de Criminologie Comparée, University of Montreal).

Ray, L. (1993), *Rethinking Critical Theory: Emancipation in the Age of Global Social Movements* (London: Sage).

Rees, M. (1985), *Northern Ireland: A Personal Perspective* (London: Methuen).

Relatives Action Committee (n.d. approx. 1993), *End Forced Integration* (Belfast: Relatives Action Committee).

Renwick, A. (1978), *British Soldiers Speak Out on Ireland* (London: Information on Ireland).

Republican Fact File (1991), 'Republican Prisoners and the Prison Struggle in Ireland—Criminalisation Defeated by Prison Resistance', (Belfast: Sinn Fein Foreign Affairs Bureau).

Republican Press Centre (1977), *Prison Struggle: The Story of Continuing Resistance behind the Wire* (Belfast: Republican Press Centre).

Richardson, G. (1993), *Law, Process and Custody: Prisoners and Patients* (London: Weidenfield & Nicolson).

Ritchie, M. (1998), *Tus Nua: The Cost of Imprisonment* (Belfast: Upper Springfield Development Trust).

Robinson, P. (1980a), *Self Inflicted: An Exposure of the H Blocks Issue* (Belfast: Democratic Unionist Party).

—— (1980b), *Savagery and Suffering: A Glimpse at the Butchery and Brutality of the I.R.A* (Belfast: Democratic Unionist Party).

Rock, P. (1995), 'The Opening Stages Of Criminal Justice Policy-Making', *British Journal of Criminology*, 35: 1, 1–16.

Rojas, F. (1988), 'A Comparison of Change-oriented Legal Services in Latin America with Legal Services in North America and Europe', *International Journal of the Sociology of Law*, 16, 203–56.

Rolston, B. (1986), 'Review of Bew and Patterson 1985 and Boyle and Hadden 1985', *Journal of Law and Society*, 13: 2, 257–62.

—— (1991), *Politics and Painting: Murals and Conflict in Northern Ireland* (London: Associated University Press).

—— and Tomlinson, M. (1986), 'Long Term Imprisonment in Northern Ireland: Psychological or Political Survival?', in B. Rolston and M. Tomlinson (eds.), *The Expansion of European Prison Systems: Working Papers in European Criminology* (Belfast: European Group for the Study of Deviance and Social Control).

—— and —— (1988), 'The Challenge Within: Prisons & Propaganda in Northern Ireland', in M. Tomlinson, T. Varley and C. McCullagh (eds.), *Whose Law and Order* (Belfast: Queen's University Bookshop).

—— and Miller, D. (eds.), (1996) *War & Words: The Northern Ireland Media Reader* (Belfast: Beyond the Pale).

Routledge, P. (1997*a*), 'A Spatiality of Resistances: Theory and Practice in Nepal's Revolution of 1990', in S. Pile and M. Keith (eds.), *Geographies of Resistance* (London: Routledge).

—— (1997*b*), *John Hume: A Biography* (London: HarperCollins).

Ruane, J., and Todd, J. (1996), *The Dynamics of Conflict in Northern Ireland: Power, Conflict and Emancipation* (Cambridge: Cambridge University Press).

—— and —— (1998), 'Peace Processes and Communalism in Northern Ireland', in W. Grotty and D. Schmidt (eds.), *Ireland and the Politics of Change* (Harlow: Addison Wesley Longman).

Rutherford, A. (1996), *Transforming Criminal Policy: Spheres of Influence in the United States, the Netherlands and England & Wales During the 1980s* (Winchester: Waterside Press).

Ryan, M. (1978), *The Acceptable Pressure Group: Inequality in the Penal Lobby: A Case Study of the Howard League and RAP* (Farnborough: Saxon House).

—— (1994), *War & Peace in Ireland: Britain & Ireland and the New World Order* (London: Pluto Press).

Ryder, C. (1989), *The RUC: A Force Under Fire* (London: Methuen).

—— (1991), *The Ulster Defence Regiment: An Instrument of Peace?* (London: Methuen).

—— (2000), *Inside the Maze: The Untold Story of the Northern Ireland Prison Service* (London: Methuen).

Sabatier, P. (1997), 'Top Down and Bottom Up Approaches to Implementation Research', in M. Hill (ed.), *The Policy Process* (Hemel Hempstead: Prentice Hall).

Salter, B. (1993), 'The Politics of Purchasing in the National Health Service', *Policy & Politics*, 21: 3, 171–84.

Sands, B. (1998), *Bobby Sands: Writings From Prison* (Cork: Mercier Press).

Sappington, A. (1996), 'Relationship Among Prison Adjustment, Beliefs and Cognitive Coping Style', *International Journal of Offender Therapy and Comparative Criminology*, 40: 1, 54–62.

Sarat, A., and Scheingold, S. (eds.), (1998) *Cause Lawyering: Political Commitments and Professional Responsibilities* (New York: Oxford University Press).

Saunders, K., and Taylor, H. (1988), 'The Enemy Within: The Process of Internment of Enemy Aliens in Queensland 1939–45', *Australian Journal of Politics and History* 34: 1, 16–27.

Scarman, Lord (1982), *The Brixton Disorder 10th–12th April 1981*, Cmnd. 8427 (London: HMSO).

Schafer, S. (1974), *The Political Criminal: The Problem of Morality and Crime* (New York: The Free Press).

Scharf, M. (1988), 'Foreign Courts on Trial: Why U.S. Courts Should Avoid Applying the Inquiry Provision of the Supplementary U.S.–U.K. Extradition Treaty', *Stanford Journal of International Law*, 25: 1, 257–88.

Scheingold, S. (1974), *The Politics of Rights* (New Haven: Yale University Press).

Schlanger, M. (1999), 'Beyond the Hero Judge: Institutional Reform Litigation as Litigation', *Michigan Law Review*, 97: 6, 1994–2036.

Schmid, A. (ed.), (1982) *Violence as Communication: Insurgent Terrorism and the Western Media* (London: Sage).

—— Jongman, A., and Stohl, M. (1990), *Political Terrorism: A New Guide to Actors, Authors, Concepts, Databases, Theorists, and Literature* (Amsterdam: North Holland Publishing Company).

Schubert, M. (1986), 'Political Prisoners in West Germany: Their Situation and Some Consequences Concerning their Rights in Respect of the Treatment of Political Prisoners in International Law', in Rolston, B. and Tomlinson M. (eds.), *The Expansion of European Prison Systems*, Working Papers in European Criminology No. 7 (Belfast: The European Group for the Study of Deviance and Control).

Schudson, M. (ed.), (1995) *Memory Distortion: How Minds, Brains and Societies Reconstruct the Past* (Cambridge Mass.: Harvard University Press).

Scott, J. (1985), *Weapons of the Weak: Everyday Forms of Peasant Resistance* (New Haven: Yale University Press).

—— (1990), *Domination and the Arts of Resistance* (New Haven: Yale University Press).

Scraton, P., Sim, J. and Skidmore, P. (1991), *Prisons Under Protest* (Milton Keynes: Open University Press).

Sebok, A. (1999), 'Legal Positivism and American Slave Law: The Case of Chief Justice Shaw', in D. Dyzenhaus (ed.), *Recrafting the Rule of Law: The Limits of Legal Order* (Oxford: Hart Publishing).

Seymour, J. (1977), 'Niches in Prisons', in H. Toch (ed.), *Living in Prison: The Ecology of Survival* (New York: Free Press), 179–205.

Shaw, J. (2000), 'Ayodhya's Sacred Landscape: Ritual, Memory, Politics and Archaeological Fact', *Antiquity*, 74, 693–700.

Shelton, D. (1999), *Remedies in International Law* (New York: Oxford University Press).

Shenkar, O., and Yuchtman-Yaar, E. (1997), 'Reputation, Image, Prestige, and Goodwill: An Interdisciplinary Approach to Organizational Standing', *Human Relations*, 50: 11, 1361–81.

Shorer, C. (1965), 'The Gansers' Syndrome', *British Journal of Criminology*, 5, 120–31.

Sibley, D. (1995), *Geographies of Exclusion: Society and Difference in the West* (London: Routledge).

Silberman, M. (1995), *A World of Violence: Corrections in America* (Belmont, Calif.: Wadsworth).

Simon, J. (1988), 'The Ideological Effects of Actuarial Practices', *Law & Society Review*, 22: 4, 771–800.

Sinn Fein (1995), Submission to the Forum for Peace and Reconciliation, 20th January 1995 (Dublin: Forum for Peace and Reconciliation).

Sinn Fein POW Dept. (1986), *Lifers* (Belfast: Republican Publications).

—— (1994), *Issues on Compassionate Parole* (Belfast: Sinn Fein Prisoner of War Department).

Skweyiya Commission (1992), *African National Congress, Report of the Commission of Enquiry into Complaints by Former African National Congress Prisoners and Detainees* (Cape Town: ANC).

Sluka, J. (1990), 'Participant Observation in Violent Social Contexts', *Human Oganization*, 49, 114–26.

—— (1995), 'Domination, Resistance and Political-Culture in Northern-Ireland Catholic-Nationalist Ghettos', *Critique Of Anthropology*, 1, 71–102.

Smyth, C, (1987), *Ian Paisley: Voice of Protestant Ulster* (Edinburgh: Scottish Academic Press).

Smyth, J. (1987), 'Unintentional Mobilization: The Effects of the 1980–1981 Hunger-Strikes In Ireland', *Political Communication and Persuasion*, 4, 179–90.

Solzhenitsyn, A. (1963), *One Day in the Life of Ivan Denisovich* (New York: E. P. Dutton & Co.).

Sparks, R. (1994), 'Can Prisons be Legitimate? Penal Politics, Privatization and the Timeliness of an Old Idea', *British Journal of Criminology*, 34, 14–28.

—— and Bottoms, A. (1995), 'Legitimacy and Order in Prisons', *British Journal of Sociology*, 46, 45–62.

—— —— and Hay, W. (1996), *Prisons and the Problem of Order* (Oxford: Clarendon Press).

Spujt, R. (1986), 'Internment and Detention without Trial in Northern Ireland (1971–1975)', *Modern Law Review*, 49, 712–39.

SSI (1993), 'Prisoners' Families: An Inspection of Services Provided or Secured by the Probation Board for Prisoners' Families', Social Services Inspectorate Report (Belfast: Department of Social Services).

Steadman, H., Morrissey, J., and Robbins, P. (1985), 'Reevaluating the Custody-therapy Conflict Paradigm in Correctional Mental Health Settings', *Criminology*, 23, 165–79.

Steiner, H., and Alston, P. (1996), *International Human Rights in Context: Law, Politics, Morals, Text and Materials* (Oxford: Clarendon Press).

Stevens, D. (1994), 'The Depth of Imprisonment and Prisonization: Levels of Security and Prisoners' Anticipation of Future Violence', *Howard Journal*, 33: 2, 137–57.

Stevenson, J. (1996), *We Wrecked the Place: Contemplating an End to the Northern Ireland Troubles* (New York: The Free Press).

Stohr, M., Lovrich, N., and Wilson, G. (1994), 'Staff Stress in Contemporary Jails: Assessing Problem Severity and the Payoff of Progressive Personnel Practices', *Journal of Criminal Justice*, 22: 4, 313–27.

Stojkovic, S. (1984), 'Social Bases of Power & Control Mechanisms Amongst Prisoners in a Prison Organization', *Justice Quarterly*, 1: 4, 511–28.

—— (1995), 'Correctional Administrators' Accounts of their Work Worlds', *Howard Journal*, 34: 1, 64–80.

Straker, G. (1993), 'Exploring the Effects of Interacting with Survivors of Trauma', *Journal of Social Development in Africa*, 8: 2, 33–47.

Suchliki, J., Jorge, A., and Fernandez, D. (1985), *Cuba: Continuity and Change* (Coral Gable, Fla.: Institute of Inter-American Studies).

Sumners, R. (1997), 'How Law is Formal and Why it Matters', *Cornell Law Review*, 82: 5, 1165–229.

Swedberg, C. (1997), *In Enemy Hands: Personal Accounts of those Taken Prisoner in World War II* (Mechanicsburg, Pa.: Stackpole Books).

Sweeney, G. (1993), 'Irish Hunger Strikes and the Cult of Self Sacrifice', *Journal of Contemporary History*, 28, 421–37.

Swift, J. (1967), *Gulliver's Travels* (London: Penguin; originally publ. 1726).

Sykes, G. (1958), *The Society of Captives* (Princeton: Princeton University Press).

—— and Messinger, S. (1960), 'The Inmate Social System', in R. Cloward *et al.* (eds.), *Theoretical Studies in the Social Organisation of the Prison* (New York: Social Science Research Council).

Szász, B. (1972), *Volunteers for the Gallows: Anatomy of a Show-trial* (New York: Norton).

Szasz, T. (1971), *The Manufacture of Madness* (London: Routledge and Kegan Paul).

Tachiki, S. (1995), 'Indeterminate Sentences In Supermax Prisons Based Upon Alleged Gang Affiliations: A Re-examination of Procedural Protection and a Proposal for Greater Procedural Requirements', *California Law Review*, 83: 4, 1115–49.

Taylor, A. (2000), 'The Sun Always Shines on Perth: A Post Colonial

Geography of Identity, Memory & Place', *Australian Geographical Studies*, 38: 1, 27–35.

Taylor, P. (1980), *Beating the Terrorists? Interrogations in Omagh, Gough & Castlereagh* (Harmondsworth: Penguin).

—— (1997), *Provos: The IRA and Sinn Fein: The Book of the BBC TV Series* (London: Bloomsbury).

—— (1999), *Loyalists: The Book of the BBC Television Series* (London: Bloomsbury).

Teichman J. (1996), 'How to Define Terrorism', in C. Gearty (ed.), *Terrorism* (Aldershot: Dartmouth).

Thomas, C. (1977), 'Theoretical Perspectives on Prisonization: A Comparison of the Importation and Deprivation Models', *Journal of Criminal Law and Criminology*, 68, 135–45.

Thomas, J. (1984), 'Law and Social Praxis: Prisoner Civil Rights Litigation and Structural Mediations', in Spitzer, S. and Scull A., *Research in Law, Deviance and Social Control—A Research Annual*, 6, 141–69.

—— Harris, K., and Keeler, D. (1986), 'Issues and Misconceptions in Prisoner Litigation', *Criminology*, 24: 4, 901–19.

Thompson, E. P. (1977), *Whigs and Hunters: The Origins of the Black Act* (London: Penguin).

Toch, H. (1969), *An Inquiry into the Psychology of Violence* (Chicago: Aldine).

—— (1976), 'A Psychological View of Prison Violence', in A. Cohen, G. Cole, and R. Bailey (eds.), *Prison Violence*: (London: Lexington Books).

—— (ed.), (1977), *Living in Prison: The Ecology of Survival*)(New York: Macmillan).

Toch, H. (1978), 'Is a Correctional Officer by any Other Name a Screw?', *Criminal Justice Review*, 3: 2, 19–35.

—— (1992), *Living in Prison* (Washington: American Psychological Association).

Toller, W., and Tsagaris, B. (1996), 'Managing Institutional Gangs: A Practical Approach Combining Security and Human Services', *Corrections Today*, 58: 6, 110–15.

Tomlinson, M. (1980), 'Reforming Repression', in L. O'Dowd, B. Rolston, and M. Tomlinson, *Northern Ireland: Between the Civil Rights and Civil War* (London: CSE Books).

—— (1995), 'Imprisoned Ireland', in V. Ruggiero, M. Ryan and J. Sim (eds.), *Western European Penal Systems: A Critical Anatomy* (London: Sage).

—— (1998), 'Walking Backwards into the Sunset: British Policy and the Insecurity of Northern Ireland', in D. Miller (ed.), *Rethinking Northern Ireland: Culture, Ideology and Colonialism* (London: Longman).

Toolis, K. (1995), *Rebel Hearts: Journey within the IRA's Soul* (London: Picador).

Trew, K. (1992), 'Social Psychological Research on the Conflict', *The Psychologist*, 15, 342–4.

Tunnell, K. (ed.), (1993) *Political Crime in Contemporary America: A Critical Approach* (New York: Garland Publishing).

Turner, B. (1984), *The Body & Society: Explorations in Social Theory* (New York: Basil Blackwell).

Tushnet, M. (1984), 'An Essay on Rights', *Texas Law Review*, 62, 1363–403.

Uglow, S. (1988), *Policing Liberal Society* (Oxford: Oxford University Press).

Urban, M. (1992), *Big Boy's Rules: The Secret Struggle Against the IRA* (London: Faber & Faber).

—— (1996), *UK Eyes Alpha: Inside British Intelligence* (London: Faber & Faber).

Vagg, J. (1994), *Prison Systems: A Comparative Study of Accountability in England, France, Germany, and the Netherlands* (Oxford: Clarendon Press).

Vance, J. (1993), 'The War behind the Wire: The Battle to Escape from a German Prison Camp', in *Journal of Contemporary History*, 28, 675–93.

Van Den Wijngaert, C. (1980), *The Political Offence Exception to Extradition: The Delicate Problem of Balancing the Rights of the Individual and the International Public Order* (Boston: Kluwer).

Van Zyl Smit, D. (1987), 'Normal Prisons in an Abnormal Society', *Criminal Justice Ethics*, 6, 237–52.

Vogler, R. (1989), *Germany: A Guide to the Criminal Justice System* (London: Prisoners Abroad).

Von Tangen Page, M. (1996), 'The Inter-relationship of the Press and the Politicians During the 1981 Hungerstrike at the Maze Prison', in P. Catterall and S. McDougall (eds.), *The Northern Ireland Question in British Politics* (London: Macmillan).

—— (1998a), *Prisons, Peace & Terrorism* (London: Macmillan).

—— (1998b), 'Arms Decommissioning and the Northern Ireland Peace Agreement', *Security Dialogue*, 29: 4, 409–20.

Walker, C. (1984), 'Irish Republican Prisoners: Political Detainees, Prisoners of War or Common Criminals?', *The Irish Jurist*, 19, 189–225.

Wall, D. (1995), *Submission to the Forum for Peace and Reconciliation*, 20th Jan. 1995 (Dublin: Forum for Peace and Reconciliation).

Wallace, D. (1997), 'Prisoners' Rights: Historical Views', in J. Marquart, and J. Sorensen (eds.), *Correctional Contexts: Contemporary and Classic Readings* (Los Angeles: Roxbury Publishing Company).

Walsh, D. (1983), *The Use and Abuse of Emergency Regulations in Northern Ireland* (Nottingham: Russell).

Walton, D. (1997), 'What is Propaganda and What Exactly is Wrong With it?', *Public Affairs Quarterly*, 11: 4, 383–414.

Walzer, M. (1969), 'Prisoners of War: Does the Fight Continue After the Battle?', *American Political Science Review* , 63, 783–5.

Weber, M. (1966), *Max Weber on Law in Economy and Society* (Cambridge, Mass.: Harvard University Press).

Weinrib, E. (1993), 'The Jurisprudence of Legal Formalism', *Harvard Journal of Law & Public Policy*, 16: 3, 583–95.

Weitzer, R. (1995), *Policing under Fire: Ethnic Conflict and Police–Community Relations in Northern Ireland* (Albany, NY: State University of New York Press).

Whelan, K., and Masterson, E. (1998), *Bertie Ahern: Taoiseach & Peacemaker* (Dublin: Blackwater Press).

White, B. (1984), *John Hume: Statesman of the Troubles* (Belfast: Blackstaff Press).

White, S. (1988), *The Recent Work of Jürgen Habermas: Reason, Justice and Modernity* (Cambridge: Cambridge University Press).

Whitehead, P., Turver, N.,and Wheatley, J. (1991), *Probation, Temporary Release Schemes, and Reconviction: Theory and Practice* (Aldershot: Avebury).

Whitelaw, W. (1989), *The Whitelaw Memoirs* (London: Aurum Press).

Whyte, J. (1991), *Interpreting Northern Ireland* (Oxford: Oxford University Press).

Wilkinson, O. (1995), 'Victim Support in Northern Ireland', in NIACRO, *The Early Release of Politically Motivated Prisoners: Learning from the International Experience*, a Conference Report (Belfast: NIACRO).

Wilkinson, P. (1982), 'The Provisional IRA: An Assessment in the Wake of the 1981 Hunger Strike', *Government and Opposition*, 17: 2, 140–57.

—— (1986), *Terrorism and the Liberal State* (2nd edn., London: Macmillan).

Willet, T. (1983), 'Prison Guards in Private', *Canadian Journal of Criminology*, 25, 1–17.

Wilson, C. (1993), 'Going to Europe: Prisoners' Rights and the Effectiveness of European Standards', *International Journal of Sociology of Law*, 21: 245–64.

Wilson, T. (1989), *Ulster: Conflict & Consent* (Oxford: Blackwell).

Winston, T. (1997), 'Alternatives to Punishment Beatings and Shootings in a Loyalist Community in Belfast', *Critical Criminology*, 8: 1, 122–8.

Winter, J. (1995), *Sites of Memory: Sites of Mourning* (Cambridge: Cambridge University Press).

Wood, R. (ed.), (1990) *Remedial Law: When Courts Become Administrators* (Amherst, Mass.: University of Massachusetts Press).

Woodcock, J. (1994), *Report of the Enquiry into the Escape of Six Prisoners from the Special Security Unit at Whitemoor Prison, Cambridgeshire, on 9th September 1994*, Cmnd. 2471 (London: HMSO).

Woolf, Lord Justice (1991), *Prison Disturbances, April 1990* Cm (London: HMSO).

Wormith, J. (1984), 'Attitudes and Behaviour Change of Correctional Clientele: A Three Year Follow-up', *Criminology*, 22, 595–618.

Wright, F. (1993), 'Integrated Education and Political Identity', in C. Moffat (ed.), *Education Together for a Change: Integrated Education and Community Relations in Northern Ireland* (Belfast: Fortnight Education Trust).

Wright, J. (1991), *Terrorist Propaganda: The Red Army Faction and the Provisional IRA 1968–1986* (New York: St Martin Press).

Wright, K., and Goldstein, L. (1989), 'Correctional Environments', in L. Goldstein and D. MacKenzie (eds.), *The American Prison System: Issues in Research & Policy* (New York: Plenum).

Yackle, L. (1989), *Reform & Regret: The Story of Judicial Involvement in the Alabama Prison System* (New York: Oxford University Press).

Yeats, W. B. (1922), *The King's Threshold*, in *Collected Plays* (London: Macmillan).

Young, A. (1990), 'Strategies of Censure and the Suffragette Movement', in C. Sumner (ed.), *Censure, Politics and Criminal Justice* (Buckingham: Open University Press).

Young, H. (1991), *One of Us: A Biography of Margaret Thatcher* (London: Macmillan).

Younger, C. (1970), *Ireland's Civil War* (London: Fontana).

Zamble, E., and Porporino, F. (1988), *Coping, Behaviour and Adaptation in Prison Inmates* (New York: Springer-Verlag).

Zingraff, M. (1980), 'Inmate Assimilation: A Comparison of Male and Female Delinquents', *Criminal Justice and Behavior*, 7, 275–92.

Newspapers and Magazines Cited

An Glor Gafa (1997), 'Operation Tollan: In This Article Five of our Comrades tell the Story of An Tollan (the Tunnel) in Their own Words', *An Glor Gafa* (*The Captive Voice*), 8: 3 (Summer) (Dublin: An Phoblacht).

An Phoblacht/Republican News

Republican News (16 Nov. 1974), 'The Long Kesh Escape —As Told In Exclusive Statements By Some Of The Republican Prisoners Who Were Involved', Special Supplement to *Republican News* , 44 (Dublin: Republican News).
—— (8 Jan. 1998), 'How the Audacious Escape was Done: First Interview with Liam Averill' (Belfast: Republican News).
—— (18 May 1998), 'Reflections on the H Block/Armagh Prison Struggle' (Dublin: An Phoblacht).

Belfast Community Telegraph

Belfast Community Telegraph (29 Dec. 2000), 'Queen Lets Jail Break IRA Men Go Home' (Belfast: Belfast Telegraph Ltd.).

Belfast Telegraph

Belfast Telegraph (28 Dec. 1982), 'Jail Segregation is Again Ruled Out by Lord Gowrie' (Belfast: Belfast Telegraph Ltd.).
—— (8 Apr. 1983), 'Gowrie Urges Loyalist Inmates to End Protest' (Belfast: Belfast Telegraph Ltd.).
—— (3 Nov. 1983), 'Orangemen Back Jail Segregation' (Belfast: Belfast Telegraph Ltd.).
—— (5 July 1984), 'No Official Segregation in Maze Jail, Says NIO' (Belfast: Belfast Telegraph Ltd.).
—— (9 Aug. 1984), 'Segregation at Magilligan Plea is Turned Down' (Belfast: Belfast Telegraph Ltd.).
—— (12 May 1990), 'Belfast Council Narrowly Backs Jail Separation' (Belfast: Belfast Telegraph Ltd.).
—— (2 Sept. 1993), 'UVF Murder Fuels Fears of Warders' (Belfast: Belfast Telegraph Ltd.).
—— (4 Sept. 1993), 'Bereaved Loyalist: Prison Service Clarifies' (Belfast: Belfast Telegraph).
—— (19 July 1994), 'NIO Denies Surrender Over Rioting Loyalists: Cells

Uninhabitable as Inmates are Switched to the H Blocks' (Belfast: Belfast Telegraph Ltd.).

—— (30 Sept. 1996), 'Most Nationalists Willing to Accept Some Kind of Amnesty' (Belfast: Belfast Telegraph Ltd.).

—— (14 Oct. 1996), 'We must Understand Jail Releases' (Belfast: Belfast Telegraph Ltd.).

—— (15 May 1998), 'Crowd Hails Stone Hero' (Belfast: Belfast Telegraph Ltd.).

—— (18 May 1998) 'Donaldson's Fears Centre on Weapons and Prisoners' (Belfast: Belfast Telegraph Ltd.).

—— (15 June 1998), 'LVF Seeks Prison Deal' (Belfast: Belfast Telegraph Ltd.).

—— (12 Aug. 1998), 'Prison Body Told of Concerns' (Belfast: Belfast Telegraph Ltd.).

—— (12 Nov. 1998), 'Mo to Accept LVF Cease-fire: Prisoners Join the Release Plan' (Belfast: Belfast Telegraph Ltd.).

—— (23 Dec. 1998*a*),. 'Freed Prisoners Storm' (Belfast: Belfast Telegraph Ltd.).

—— (23 Dec. 1998*b*), 'Bingham: Halt the Releases' (Belfast: Belfast Telegraph Ltd.).

—— (26 Jan. 1999), 'Ingram Set to be Told of Shameful Meeting' (Belfast: Belfast Telegraph Ltd.).

—— (5 Mar. 1999), 'INLA Prisoners Set for Freedom' (Belfast: Belfast Telegraph Ltd.).

—— (14 Sept. 1999), 'Adair Freed' (Belfast: Belfast Telegraph Ltd.).

Daily Mail

Daily Mail (9 Jan. 1998), 'Taking My Chance in the Lion's Den' (London: Daily Mail Ltd.).

Derry Journal

Derry Journal (27 Apr. 1984), 'Tensions Rising in Magilligan' (Derry: Derry Journal Ltd.).

Financial Times

Financial Times (17 June 1998), 'IRA Chief in the Maze is Ready to Seek a New Way Out' (London: Financial Times Ltd.).

Guardian

Guardian (21 Feb. 1994), 'Inside the Maze' (London: Guardian Newspapers Ltd.).

—— (9 June 1995), 'Security Services Say Cease-fire Will Hold' (London: Guardian/Observer Newspapers Ltd.).

Guardian (28 Aug. 1995), 'Cease-fire cost MI5 its Biggest Contract' (London: Guardian/Observer Newspapers Ltd.).

—— (25 Mar. 1997), 'Who Runs the Maze?' (London: Guardian/Observer Newspapers Ltd.).

—— (10 Jan. 1998*a*), 'The Gamble Pays Off: Loyalist Prisoners Reverse their Position after Talks with Mowlam' (London: Guardian/Observer Newspapers Ltd.).

—— (10 Jan. 1998*b*), 'Finding Hope in the Maze' (London: Guardian/Observer Newspaper Ltd.).

Independent

Independent (7 May 1990), 'Jail Segregation Campaign "Will Fail"' (London: Independent Newspapers Ltd.).

Ireland on Sunday

Ireland on Sunday (14 Dec. 1997), 'Another Great Escape: Greg Harkin on how IRA Prisoner Liam Averill Walked Out the Maze "Holiday Camp"' (Dublin: Ireland on Sunday Newspaper Ltd.).

—— (17 Aug. 1998), 'Peace Pays Paltry Dividend for Victims and Ex-prisoners' (Dublin: Ireland on Sunday Newspapers Ltd.).

Irish News

Irish News (30 Mar. 1974),. 'Letter from IRA Prisoner Hugh Feeney Re Force-feeding in An English Prison' (Belfast: Irish News Ltd.).

—— (14 Sept. 1982), 'McCrea Warns Gowrie of Prison Death Threat' (Belfast: Irish News Ltd.).

—— (25 Sept. 1982), 'Loyalists in Maze Allege Death Threats' (Belfast: Irish News Ltd.).

—— (22 Oct. 1982), 'Rampage Damage Put at Thousands: Up to 170 Loyalists involved in a Five Day Spree of Vandalism' (Belfast: Irish News Ltd.).

—— (24 Jan. 1983), 'Death Threat to Republicans by Jailed Loyalist' (Belfast: Irish News Ltd.).

—— (7 July 1983), 'Unionists Unite in Demand for Split Prisons' (Belfast: Irish News Ltd.).

—— (5 June 1984), 'Prison Fast Ends' (Belfast: Irish News Ltd.).

—— (4 Aug. 1984), 'Attack Raises Prison Fears' (Belfast: Irish News Ltd.).

—— (17 Apr. 1990), 'Jail Rioters Unite to Stay Apart' (Belfast: Irish News Ltd.).

—— (14 Dec. 1990), 'Jail Segregation Call Renewed' (Belfast: Irish News Ltd.).

—— (23 Sept. 1993), 'The Key to Freedom' (Belfast: Irish News Ltd.).

—— (26 Jan. 1995), 'IRA has not Wavered from Peace Path says Annesley' (Belfast: Irish News Ltd.).

—— (27 Mar. 1995), 'British Still Aim to Beat the IRA, Claims ex Taoiseach' (Belfast: Irish News Ltd.).

—— (25 Mar. 1997), 'Escape Attempt is Latest in History of Break-outs' (Belfast: Irish News Ltd.).

—— (11 Aug. 1997), 'Mowlam Jail Hint Brings Political Fury' (Belfast: Irish News Ltd.).

—— (14 Aug. 1997), 'More Releases of Republican Prisoners May be on the Way' (Belfast: Irish News Ltd.).

—— (19 Sept. 1997), 'Sinn Fein Briefs IRA Prisoners' (Belfast: Irish News Ltd.).

—— (12 Dec. 1997) 'Mother Defends her Maze Escaper Son' (Belfast: Irish News Ltd.).

—— (29 Dec. 1997a), 'King Rat Was a Thorn in the Flesh of the UVF Leadership' (Belfast: Irish News Ltd.).

—— (29 Dec. 1997b), 'No Stranger to Violent Death' (Belfast: Irish News Ltd.).

—— (5 Jan. 1998), 'UDA prisoners Reject Peace' (Belfast: Irish News Ltd.).

—— (10 Jan. 1998), 'Prisoners Fate Tied to Settlement' (Belfast: Irish News Ltd.).

—— (3 Mar. 1998), 'LVF Threatens Maze Guards: Direct Action will Follow if Loyalists are Mistreated' (Belfast: Irish News Ltd.).

—— (17 Mar. 1998), 'Dead LVF Man Was Tortured' (Belfast: Irish News Ltd.).

—— (20 Mar. 1998), 'Prisoner Releases Crucial Says PUP' (Belfast: Irish News Ltd.).

—— (25 Apr. 1998), 'Hague Defends His Support for Deal' (Belfast: Irish News Ltd.).

—— (15 May 1998a), 'Ahern Hits Out at IRA Triumphalism' (Belfast: Irish News Ltd.).

—— (15 May 1998b), 'LVF Announces Unequivocal Cease-fire' (Belfast: Irish News Ltd.).

—— (15 May 1998c), 'Blair Boost to Yes Camp' (Belfast: Irish News Ltd.).

—— (21 Aug. 1998), 'Prisoners Out in A Fortnight' (Belfast: Irish News Ltd.).

—— (24 Aug. 1998), 'INLA's War is Over' (Belfast: Irish News Ltd.).

—— (9 Sept. 1998), 'Real IRA Cease-fire as Pressure Bites' (Belfast: Irish News Ltd.).

—— (8 Dec. 1998), 'Foiled Real IRA Gang to be Freed by 2000' (Belfast: Irish News Ltd.).

—— (10 Dec. 1998), 'New Hope as Maze Gamble Pays Off' (Belfast: Irish News Ltd.).

—— (19 Dec. 1998a), 'LVF Guns Handover is a Stunt Says PUP' (Belfast: Irish News Ltd.).

—— (19 Dec. 1998b), 'INLA Prisoners to be Freed' (Belfast: Irish News Ltd.).

—— (4 Jan. 1999), 'RUC Silent on Adair Claim' (Belfast: Irish News Ltd.).

—— (20 Jan. 1999), 'Prisoners Group Launched' (Belfast: Irish News Ltd.).

Irish Times

Irish Times (7 Dec. 1977), 'Hard Times for Her Majesty's Prison Service' (Dublin: Irish Times Ltd.).

—— (3 Sept. 1993), 'Loyalist Threat to Kill More Warders: UVF Demand Talks on Prison Conditions' (Dublin: Irish Times Ltd.).

—— (14 Oct. 1996), 'Move to Cut Loyalist Prison Sentences' (Dublin: Irish Times Ltd.).

—— (24 Dec. 1996) 'Sinn Fein Line a Recipe for Strife' (Dublin: Irish Times Ltd.).

—— (25 Mar. 1997*a*), 'Maze Governor's Resignation Sought After Tunnel Found' (Dublin: Irish Times Ltd.).

—— (25 Mar. 1997*b*), 'Rubble Noticed in Maze Cells After Tunnel Find' (Dublin: Irish Times Ltd.).

—— (25 Mar. 1997*c*), 'Republican Prisoners See Escape as Their Duty' (Dublin: Irish Times Ltd.).

—— (12 Dec. 1997), 'IRA Man's Escape from the Maze is a Hiccup, Says Hume' (Dublin: Irish Times Ltd.).

—— (10 Jan. 1998), 'The Gamble Pays Off: Loyalist Prisoners Reverse Their Position after talks with Mowlam' (Dublin: Irish Times Ltd.).

—— (17 Feb. 1998), 'McGuinness Says Sinn Fein Not Accountable for the IRA' (Dublin: Irish Times Ltd.).

—— (20 Feb. 1998), 'Law May Feel "Political Question" Marks No-Go Area' (Dublin: Irish Times Ltd.).

—— (17 Mar. 1998), 'Authorities Must Have Known Keys was at Risk' (Dublin: Irish Times Ltd.).

—— (11 May 1998*a*), 'High Profile Prisoners at Ard Fheis' (Dublin: Irish Times Ltd.).

—— (11 May 1998*b*), 'Huge Vote in Favour of Taking Seats in the Assembly' (Dublin: Irish Times Ltd.).

—— (12 May 1998), 'Prisoners at Ard Fheis—Christmas for the No Lobby: The Prisoners Issue Could Damage the Yes Vote in Northern Ireland' (Dublin: Irish Times Ltd.).

—— (15 May 1998*a*), Unionist Support for Agreement Drops Sharply' (Dublin: Irish Times Ltd.).

—— (15 May 1998*b*), 'Blair Says Accord Points to Better Future; Full Text of Blair Speech' (Dublin: Irish Times Ltd.).

—— (10 June 1998), 'Freed IRA members Against Renewed Cease-fire' (Dublin: Irish Times Ltd.).

—— (1 Aug. 1998), 'New Law Sees Six Freed from Portlaoise' (Dublin: Irish Times Ltd.).

—— (7 Aug. 1998), 'Man Convicted of Murder of Mountbatten is Freed' (Dublin: Irish Times Ltd.).

—— (12 Aug. 1998), 'LVF Chief in Maze Confirms Cease-fire' (Dublin: Irish Times Ltd.).

—— (20 Oct. 1998), 'A Favourite Curmudgeon' (Dublin: Irish Times Ltd.).

—— (29 Dec. 1998), 'Trimble Remains in Ditch over Arms' (Dublin: Irish Times Ltd.).

—— (28 Jan. 1999), 'Bipartisanship under Mounting Strain' (Dublin: Irish Times Ltd.).

—— (23 Aug. 2000), 'Adair to Launch Legal Challenge' (Dublin: Irish Times Ltd.).

—— (7 Jan. 2001), 'Trimble Calls for An Inquiry into Kingsmill Massacre' (Dublin: Irish Times Ltd.).

—— (10 Jan. 2001), 'Adair's Prison Release Application is Turned Down' (Dublin: Irish Times Ltd.).

—— (31 Jan. 2001), 'Trimble Acted Unlawfully in Sinn Fein Ban' (Dublin: Irish Times Ltd.).

Magill

Magill (July 1998), 'Staying Out in the Cold' (Dublin: Magill Ltd.).

New Ulster Defender

New Ulster Defender (June 1992), 'The War Goes On' 2: 2.

Newsletter

Ulster Newsletter (16 Dec. 1954), 'Omagh Arms Raid Trial Concludes' (Belfast: Ulster Newsletter Ltd.).

Newsletter (18 Nov. 1982), 'Prison Heads Must Decide, Says Gowrie' (Belfast: Ulster Newsletter Ltd.).

—— (29 Apr. 1983), 'Loyalists Claim Maze Victory but NIO Denies Segregation Move' (Belfast: Ulster Newsletter Ltd.).

—— (2 Sept. 1993), 'Terror Gang Kills Warder' (Belfast: Ulster Newsletter Ltd.).

—— (3 Sept. 1993), 'New Threat to Prison Staff' (Belfast: Ulster Newsletter Ltd.).

—— (8 July 1994), 'Inmates on the Rampage' (Belfast: Ulster Newsletter Ltd.).

—— (9 Jan. 1998), 'She's Brave, She's Crazy' (Belfast: Ulster Newsletter Ltd.).

Observer

Observer (25 Mar. 1998), 'Loyalist Smeared Blood on Maze Inmates to Shield Killer' (London: Guardian/Observer Newspapers).

—— (10 Jan. 1999), 'Fury at Euro-Cash for Ex-terrorists' (London: Guardian/Observer Newspapers).

—— (30 July 2000), 'Empey: Turn Maze into an Industrial Park' (London: Guardian/Observer Newspapers).

Saoirse

Saoirse: Irish Freedom, 143 (Mar. 1999), 'Republican Prisoners in Maghaberry: Political Status Denied' (Dublin: Republican Sinn Fein).

Sunday Times

Sunday Times (21 Dec. 1973), 'Trial by Tittle Tattle' (London: Sunday Times Ltd.).
—— (3 Jan. 1999), 'RUC Plea to Keep "Mad Dog" in Jail' (London: Sunday Times Ltd.).

Sunday Tribune

Sunday Tribune (26 Sept. 1993), 'Escape from H Block Seven' (Dublin: Sunday Tribune Ltd.).
—— (17 May 1998), 'Say Hello to Gunmen, Wave Goodbye to Peace?' (Dublin: Sunday Tribune Ltd.).

Table of Cases

Table of Statutes

Westminster Debates

Hansard

HC Debates (Series V) vol 823, col 8 (22 Sept. 1971).   212
HC Debates (Series V) vol 823, col 212 (23 Sept. 1971).   210
HC Debates (Series V) vol 823, col 322 (23 Sept. 1971).   212
HC Debates (Series V) vol 853, col 254 (26 Mar. 1973).   215
HC Debates (Series V) vol 855, col 280 (17 Apr. 1973).   213
HC Debates (Series V) vol 859, col 823 (5 July 1973).   223
HC Debates (Series V) vol 859, col 841 (5 July 1973).   223
HC Debates (Series V) vol 871, col 1466 (4 Apr. 1974).   228
HC Debate (Series V) vol 894, cols 903–5 (27 June 1975).   228
HC Debates (Series V) vol 908, col 641–2 (25 Mar. 1976).   231
HC Debates (Series VI) vol 49, cols 505–8 (30 Nov. 1983).   288, 289
House of Lords Official Report (Series V) vol 478, col 158 (7 July 1986). 290
HC Debates (Series VI) vol 107, cols 1331–2 (17 Dec 1986).   292
HC Debates (Series VI) vol 119, col 1229 (16 July 1987).   257
HC Debates (Series VI) vol 151, col 444 (20 Apr. 1989).   283
HC Debates (Series VI) vol 265, col 21, 26 (30 Oct. 1995).   327
HC Debates (Series VI) vol 265, col 34 (30 Oct. 1995).   327
HC Debates (Series VI) vol 265, col 45 (30 Oct. 1995).   327
HC Debates (Series VI) vol 265, col 49 (30 Oct. 1995).   327
HC Debates (Series VI) vol 265, col 66 (30 Oct. 1995).   327
HC Debates (Series VI) vol 311, col 711 (6 May 1998).   341
HC Debate (Series VI) vol 313, cols 1093–4 (10 June 1998).   342
HC Debates (Series VI) vol 313, col 1099 (10 June 1998).   342
HC Debates (Series VI) vol 313, col 1160 (10 June 1998).   347
HC Debates (Series VI) vol 323, cols 487–8 (20 Jan. 1999).   342
HC Debates (Series VI) vol 343, col 124 (27 Jan. 2000).   355

Dáil Debates

Dáil Debates, 19 Nov. 1939, No. 77, 831.   77
Dáil Debates, (Release of Prisoners Bill, 1998, second reading
    Dáil Debates, Official Report), 2 July 1998, vol 493, 5.   338

Index